McGraw-Hill's
ARIS Online Registration Code

to accompany

McGraw-Hill's ARIS (Assessment, Review, and Instruction System) is a web-based supplement that allows you to access homework, quizzing, tutorials and self-study material. You will use ARIS to view and complete assignments. Once you submit your assignments, your results are saved online so you can review your progress. ARIS also provides tools for self-assessment and self-study to help you succeed in this course. Don't wait; use the enclosed online registration code to get started with ARIS.

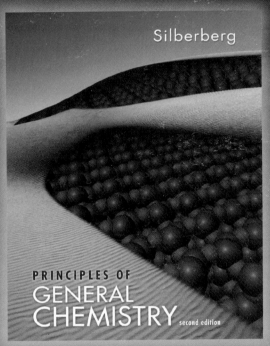

Silberberg

PRINCIPLES OF
GENERAL
CHEMISTRY second edition

STUDENTS: DO NOT THROW AWAY!

This is you personalized registration card for online access to textbook and assignment material.

The registration code on the back of this card allows you to access assignments and other material that your instructor requires for this course. The code is unique and for one specific McGraw-Hill product; it is not related to any other registration number or ID you may have. Once it is used, it cannot be re-used. Your student registration code protects valuable content. Your course materials contain much more than a textbook. You may be viewing animations, taking automatically graded assignments, or using the self-assessments to check your own understanding of the course content. The 20-character student registration code is the only way to safely and legally protect your access to this valuable content.

 **REGISTRATION PROCEDURES**

To register and activate your ARIS account, simply follow these easy steps...

- Go to http://www.mharis.com and click on "Need to Register/I'm a student"
- If your instructor has provided you with a student section code, enter it under the "Join a Course" section and click "Next".
- When prompted, enter the registration code listed below.
- Complete the brief online registration form.
- Suggestion: Bookmark your instructor's ARIS course URL for fast, easy access.
- If your instructor has not provided you with a section code, click "Next" under "Register for Self-Study Resources"
- Suggestion: before "Registering for Self-Study" click on "Plug-In Checker
- Follow Steps 1 and 2 by selecting your book by author. Click on "Silberberg Principles of Chemistry, 2e."
- When prompted, enter the registration code listed below.
- Complete the brief online registration form.
- Suggestion: Bookmark the URL for fast, easy access.

REGISTRATION CODE	XCFV-7KM6-KKHD-WPET-NKTW

Record your information below:

Instructor URL:	
USERNAME:	
PASSWORD:	

If you have trouble with registration, please contact Customer Support at

www.mhhe.com/support

Telephone Support for instructors and students: **(800) 331-5094**
Monday through Thursday: 8 am–11 pm; Friday: 8 am–6 pm; Sunday: 6 pm–11 pm.
All hours are Central Standard Time (CST).

 Learning Solutions   *The McGraw-Hill Companies*   ISBN-13: 978-0-07-747019-7   ISBN-10: 0-07-74701

Principles of
GENERAL
CHEMISTRY

Volume III

Second Edition

MARTIN S. SILBERBERG

UC SAN DIEGO

Learning Solutions

Boston   Burr Ridge, IL   Dubuque, IA   New York   San Francisco   St. Louis
Bangkok   Bogotá   Caracas   Lisbon   London   Madrid
Mexico City   Milan   New Delhi   Seoul   Singapore   Sydney   Taipei   Toronto

PRINCIPLES OF GENERAL CHEMISTRY, Second Edition
VOLUME III
UC SAN DIEGO

This book is a McGraw-Hill Learning Solutions textbook and contains select material from *Principles of General Chemistry*, Second Edition by Martin S. Silberberg. Copyright © 2010 by The McGraw-Hill Companies, Inc. Reprinted with permission of the publisher. Many custom published texts are modified versions or adaptations of our best-selling textbooks. Some adaptations are printed in black and white to keep prices at a minimum, while others are in color.

1 2 3 4 5 6 7 8 9 0 WDD WDD 12 11 10

ISBN-13: 978-0-07-747015-9
ISBN-10: 0-07-747015-X

Learning Solutions Manager: Danielle Meier
Production Editor: Jennifer Pickel
Cover Design: Fairfax Hutter
Printer/Binder: Quad/Graphics

22 CHAPTER

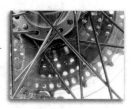

The Transition Elements and Their Coordination Compounds 756

23 CHAPTER

Nuclear Reactions and Their Applications 784

Kinetics: Rates and Mechanisms of Chemical Reactions

16

Key Principles
to focus on while studying this chapter

- The *rate of a reaction* is the *change* in the concentration of reactant (or product) per unit of time. Reaction rates vary over a wide range, but each reaction has a specific rate under a given set of conditions *(Introduction)*.

- The rate depends on *concentration* and *physical state* because reactants must collide to react. It depends even more on *temperature* because reactants must collide with enough kinetic energy *(Section 16.1)*.

- The rate changes as the reaction proceeds: it is fastest at the beginning of the reaction, when reactant concentration is highest, and slowest at the end. *Average rate* is the concentration change over a period of time and *instantaneous rate* is the change at any instant. Kinetic studies typically measure the *initial rate*, the rate at the instant the reactants are mixed; because products are not yet present, only the forward reaction is taking place *(Section 16.2)*.

- The rate of a reaction is expressed mathematically in a *rate law* (or *rate equation*). It consists of a temperature-dependent *rate constant* and one or more concentration terms raised to an exponent, called a *reaction order,* that defines how the concentration of that reactant affects the rate. The rate law must be determined by experiment, *not* from the balanced equation *(Section 16.3)*.

- An *integrated rate law* includes concentration *and* time as variables. It allows determination of the reaction order, as well as the *half-life,* the time required for half of a reactant to be used up. The half-life of a first-order reaction does *not* depend on reactant concentration *(Section 16.4)*.

- Temperature affects the rate of a reaction by influencing the rate constant. Molecules must have a minimum energy, the *energy of activation* (E_a), in order to react. The *Arrhenius equation* shows that rate increases with temperature and decreases with E_a *(Section 16.5)*.

- *Collision theory* proposes that, for a reaction to occur, reactant molecules must collide and the energy of the collision must exceed E_a. Higher temperature increases the frequency of collisions and, more importantly, the *fraction* of collisions with energy greater than E_a. A collision must also be *effective,* in that the atoms in the colliding molecules must be oriented correctly for a bond to form between them *(Section 16.6)*.

- *Transition state theory* explains that the E_a is the energy needed to form a high-energy species, which exists only momentarily, that includes partially broken reactant bonds and partially formed product bonds. Every step in a reaction has such a *transition state (activated complex) (Section 16.6)*.

- Chemists explain the rate law for an overall reaction by proposing a *reaction mechanism* that consists of several *elementary steps,* each with its own rate law. To be a valid mechanism, the sum of the elementary steps must give the balanced equation, the steps must be physically reasonable, and the mechanism must correlate with the rate law. The rate law of the slowest step (the *rate-determining step*) must give the overall rate law *(Section 16.7)*.

- A *catalyst* speeds a reaction in both directions but is not consumed. It functions by *lowering the E_a* of the rate-determining step of an alternative mechanism for the same overall reaction. Catalysts can function in the same *(homogeneous)* or a different *(heterogeneous)* phase from the reactants and products. They are essential components of many industrial and nearly all biological reactions *(Section 16.8)*.

Getting Things Moving *The metabolic processes of cold-blooded animals like these Nile crocodiles speed up as the temperatures rise toward midday. In this chapter, you'll see how temperature, as well as several other factors, influences the speed of a reaction.*

Outline

Concepts & Skills to Review
before studying this chapter

• influence of temperature on molecular
  speed (Section 5.6)

Until now we've taken a rather simple approach to chemical change: reactants mix and products form. A balanced equation is essential for calculating product yields from reactant amounts, but it tells us nothing about three dynamic aspects of a reaction: how fast the reaction proceeds, how far it proceeds toward products, and whether it proceeds by itself or needs some energy input to occur. We discuss the first of these aspects here and examine the others in upcoming chapters. **Chemical kinetics** is the study of *reaction rates,* the changes in concentrations of reactants (or products) as a function of time (Figure 16.1).

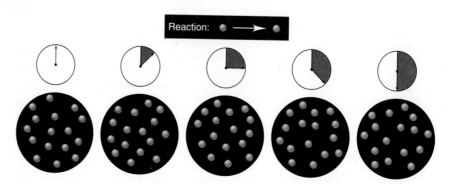

FIGURE 16.1 Reaction rate: the central focus of chemical kinetics. The rate at which reactant becomes product is the underlying theme of chemical kinetics. As time elapses, reactant *(purple)* decreases and product *(green)* increases.

Reactions occur at a wide range of rates. Some, like a neutralization, a precipitation, or an explosive redox process, seem to be over as soon as the reactants make contact—in a fraction of a second. Others, such as the reactions involved in cooking or rusting, take a moderate length of time, from minutes to months. Still others take much longer: the reactions that make up the human aging process continue for decades, and those involved in the formation of coal from dead plants take hundreds of millions of years.

Knowing how fast a chemical change occurs can be essential. How quickly a medicine acts or blood clots can make the difference between life and death. How long it takes for cement to harden or polyethylene to form can make the difference between profit and loss. In general, the rates of these diverse processes depend on the same variables, most of which chemists can manipulate to maximize yields within a given time or to slow down an unwanted reaction.

In this chapter, we first discuss reaction rate and then focus on the *reaction mechanism,* the steps a reaction goes through as reactant bonds are breaking and product bonds are forming.

16.1 FACTORS THAT INFLUENCE REACTION RATE

Let's begin our study of kinetics with a qualitative look at the key factors that affect how fast a reaction proceeds. Under any given set of conditions, *each reaction has its own characteristic rate,* which is determined by the chemical nature of the reactants. At room temperature, for example, hydrogen reacts explosively with fluorine but extremely slowly with nitrogen:

$$H_2(g) + F_2(g) \longrightarrow 2HF(g) \qquad \text{[very fast]}$$
$$3H_2(g) + N_2(g) \longrightarrow 2NH_3(g) \qquad \text{[very slow]}$$

We can control four factors that affect the rate of a given reaction: the concentrations of the reactants, the physical state of the reactants, the temperature at which the reaction occurs, and the use of a catalyst. We consider the first three factors here and discuss the fourth in Section 16.8.

1. *Concentration: molecules must collide to react.* A major factor influencing the rate of a given reaction is reactant concentration. A reaction can occur only when the reactant molecules collide. The more molecules present in the

container, the more frequently they collide, and the more often a reaction between them occurs. Thus, *reaction rate is proportional to the concentration of reactants:*

Rate ∝ collision frequency ∝ concentration

2. *Physical state: molecules must mix to collide.* The frequency of collisions between molecules also depends on the physical states of the reactants. When the reactants are in the same phase, as in an aqueous solution, random thermal motion brings them into contact. When they are in different phases, contact occurs only at the interface, so vigorous stirring and grinding may be needed. In these cases, *the more finely divided a solid or liquid reactant, the greater its surface area per unit volume, the more contact it makes with the other reactant, and the faster the reaction occurs.* Thus, a thick steel nail heated in oxygen glows feebly, but the same mass of fine steel wool bursts into flame. For the same reason, you start a campfire with wood chips and thin branches, not logs.

3. *Temperature: molecules must collide with enough energy to react.* Temperature usually has a major effect on the speed of a reaction. Recall that molecules in a sample of gas have a range of speeds, with the most probable speed dependent on the temperature (see Figure 5.12, p. 168). Thus, *at a higher temperature, more collisions occur in a given time.* Even more important, however, is the fact that temperature affects the kinetic energy of the molecules, and thus the *energy* of the collisions. Most collisions result in the molecules simply recoiling, with no reaction taking place. However, some collisions occur with sufficient energy for the molecules to react. Figure 16.2 shows the outcomes of a few collisions in the reaction between nitric oxide (NO) and ozone (O_3). At higher temperatures, more of the sufficiently energetic collisions occur. Thus, *raising the temperature increases the reaction rate by increasing the number and, especially, the energy of the collisions:*

Rate ∝ collision energy ∝ temperature

The *qualitative* idea that reaction rate is influenced by the frequency and energy of reactant collisions leads to several *quantitative* questions: How can we describe the dependence of rate on reactant concentration mathematically? Do all changes in concentration affect the rate to the same extent? Do all rates increase to the same extent with a given rise in temperature? How do reactant molecules use the collision energy to form product molecules, and is there a way to determine this energy? What do the reactants look like as they are turning into products? We address these questions in the following sections.

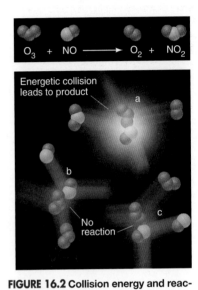

FIGURE 16.2 Collision energy and reaction rate. The reaction equation is shown in the panel. Although many collisions between NO and O_3 molecules occur, relatively few have enough energy to cause reaction. At this temperature, only collision *a* is energetic enough to lead to product; the reactant molecules in collisions *b* and *c* just bounce off each other.

SECTION 16.1 SUMMARY

Chemical kinetics deals with reaction rates and the stepwise molecular events by which a reaction occurs. • Under a given set of conditions, each reaction has its own rate. • Concentration affects rate by influencing the frequency of collisions between reactant molecules. • Physical state affects rate by determining the surface area per unit volume of reactant(s). • Temperature affects rate by influencing the frequency and, even more importantly, the energy of the reactant collisions.

16.2 EXPRESSING THE REACTION RATE

A *rate* is a change in some variable per unit of time. The most common examples relate to the rate of motion (speed) of an object, which is the change in its position (that is, the distance it travels) divided by the change in time. Suppose, for instance, we measure a runner's starting position, x_1, at time t_1 and final position, x_2, at time t_2. The runner's average speed is

$$\text{Rate of motion} = \frac{\text{change in position}}{\text{change in time}} = \frac{x_2 - x_1}{t_2 - t_1} = \frac{\Delta x}{\Delta t}$$

In the case of a chemical change, we are concerned with the **reaction rate,** the changes in concentrations of reactants or products per unit time: *reactant concentrations decrease while product concentrations increase.* Consider a general reaction, $A \longrightarrow B$. We quickly measure the starting reactant concentration (conc A_1) at t_1, allow the reaction to proceed, and then quickly measure the reactant concentration again (conc A_2) at t_2. The change in concentration divided by the change in time gives the *average* rate:

$$\text{Rate of reaction} = -\frac{\text{change in concentration of A}}{\text{change in time}} = -\frac{\text{conc } A_2 - \text{conc } A_1}{t_2 - t_1} = -\frac{\Delta(\text{conc A})}{\Delta t}$$

Note the minus sign. By convention, reaction rate is a *positive* number, but conc A_2 will always be *lower* than conc A_1, so the *change in (final − initial) concentration of reactant A is always negative.* We use the minus sign simply to convert the negative change in reactant concentration to a positive value for the rate. Suppose the concentration of A changes from 1.2 mol/L (conc A_1) to 0.75 mol/L (conc A_2) over a 125-s period. The average rate is

$$\text{Rate} = -\frac{0.75 \text{ mol/L} - 1.2 \text{ mol/L}}{125 \text{ s} - 0 \text{ s}} = 3.6 \times 10^{-3} \text{ mol/L·s}$$

We use *square brackets,* [ ], *to express concentration in moles per liter.* That is, [A] is the concentration of A in mol/L, so the rate expressed in terms of A is

$$\text{Rate} = -\frac{\Delta[A]}{\Delta t} \tag{16.1}$$

The rate has units of moles per liter per second (mol L^{-1} s^{-1}, or mol/L·s), or any time unit convenient for the particular reaction (minutes, years, and so on).

If instead we measure the *product* to determine the reaction rate, we find its concentration *increasing* over time. That is, conc B_2 is always *higher* than conc B_1. Thus, the *change* in product concentration, $\Delta[B]$, is *positive,* and the reaction rate for $A \longrightarrow B$ expressed in terms of B is

$$\text{Rate} = \frac{\Delta[B]}{\Delta t}$$

Average, Instantaneous, and Initial Reaction Rates

Examining the rate of a real reaction reveals an important point: not only the concentration, but *the rate itself varies with time as the reaction proceeds.* Consider the reversible gas-phase reaction between ethylene and ozone, one of many reactions that can be involved in the formation of photochemical smog:

$$C_2H_4(g) + O_3(g) \rightleftharpoons C_2H_4O(g) + O_2(g)$$

For now, we consider only reactant concentrations. You can see from the equation coefficients that for every molecule of C_2H_4 that reacts, a molecule of O_3 reacts with it. In other words, the concentrations of both reactants decrease at the same rate in this particular reaction:

$$\text{Rate} = -\frac{\Delta[C_2H_4]}{\Delta t} = -\frac{\Delta[O_3]}{\Delta t}$$

By measuring the concentration of either reactant, we can follow the reaction rate.

Suppose we have a known concentration of O_3 in a closed reaction vessel kept at 30°C (303 K). Table 16.1 shows the concentration of O_3 at various times during the first minute after we introduce C_2H_4 gas. The rate over the entire 60.0 s is the total change in concentration divided by the change in time:

$$\text{Rate} = -\frac{\Delta[O_3]}{\Delta t} = -\frac{(1.10 \times 10^{-5} \text{ mol/L}) - (3.20 \times 10^{-5} \text{ mol/L})}{60.0 \text{ s} - 0.0 \text{ s}} = 3.50 \times 10^{-7} \text{ mol/L·s}$$

Table 16.1 Concentration of O_3 at Various Times in Its Reaction with C_2H_4 at 303 K

Time (s)	Concentration of O_3 (mol/L)
0.0	3.20×10^{-5}
10.0	2.42×10^{-5}
20.0	1.95×10^{-5}
30.0	1.63×10^{-5}
40.0	1.40×10^{-5}
50.0	1.23×10^{-5}
60.0	1.10×10^{-5}

This calculation gives us the **average rate** over that period; that is, during the first 60.0 s of the reaction, ozone concentration decreases an *average* of 3.50×10^{-7} mol/L each second. However, the average rate does not show that the rate is changing, and it tells us nothing about how fast the ozone concentration is decreasing *at any given instant*.

We can see the rate change during the reaction by calculating the average rate over two shorter periods—one earlier and one later. Between the starting time 0.0 s and 10.0 s, the average rate is

$$\text{Rate} = -\frac{\Delta[O_3]}{\Delta t} = -\frac{(2.42 \times 10^{-5}\ \text{mol/L}) - (3.20 \times 10^{-5}\ \text{mol/L})}{10.0\ \text{s} - 0.0\ \text{s}} = 7.80 \times 10^{-7}\ \text{mol/L·s}$$

During the last 10.0 s, between 50.0 s and 60.0 s, the average rate is

$$\text{Rate} = -\frac{\Delta[O_3]}{\Delta t} = -\frac{(1.10 \times 10^{-5}\ \text{mol/L}) - (1.23 \times 10^{-5}\ \text{mol/L})}{60.0\ \text{s} - 50.0\ \text{s}} = 1.30 \times 10^{-7}\ \text{mol/L·s}$$

The earlier rate is six times as fast as the later rate. Thus, *the rate decreases during the course of the reaction*. This makes sense from a molecular point of view: as O_3 molecules are used up, fewer of them are present to collide with C_2H_4 molecules, so the rate, the change in their concentration over time, decreases.

The change in rate can also be seen by plotting the concentrations vs. the times at which they were measured (Figure 16.3). A curve is obtained, which means that the rate changes. *The slope of the straight line ($\Delta y / \Delta x$, that is, $\Delta[O_3]/\Delta t$) joining any two points gives the average rate over that period.*

The shorter the time period we choose, the closer we come to the **instantaneous rate,** the rate at a particular instant during the reaction. *The slope of a line tangent to the curve at a particular point gives the instantaneous rate at that time.* For example, the rate of the reaction of C_2H_4 and O_3 at 35.0 s after it began is 2.50×10^{-7} mol/L·s, the slope of the line drawn tangent to the curve through the point at which $t = 35.0$ s (line *d* in Figure 16.3). In general, we use the term *reaction rate* to mean the *instantaneous* reaction rate.

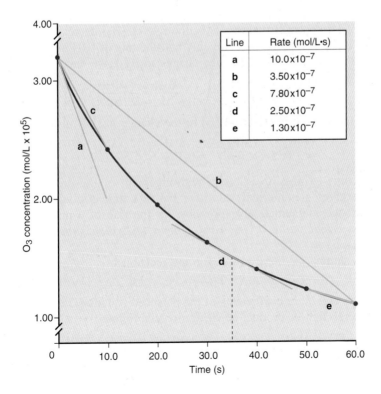

Line	Rate (mol/L·s)
a	10.0×10^{-7}
b	3.50×10^{-7}
c	7.80×10^{-7}
d	2.50×10^{-7}
e	1.30×10^{-7}

FIGURE 16.3 The concentration of O_3 vs. time during its reaction with C_2H_4. Plotting the data in Table 16.1 gives a curve because the rate changes during the reaction. The *average* rate over a given period is the slope of a line joining two points along the curve. The slope of line *b* is the average rate over the first 60.0 s of the reaction. The slopes of lines *c* and *e* give the average rate over the first and last 10.0-s intervals, respectively. Line *c* is steeper than line *e* because the average rate over the earlier period is higher. The *instantaneous* rate at 35.0 s is the slope of line *d*, the tangent to the curve at $t = 35.0$ s. The *initial* rate is the slope of line *a*, the tangent to the curve at $t = 0$ s.

As a reaction continues, the product concentrations increase, and so the reverse reaction (reactants ⟵ products) speeds up. To find the overall (net) rate, we would have to take both forward and reverse reactions into account and calculate the difference between their rates. A common way to avoid this complication for many reactions is to measure the **initial rate,** the instantaneous rate at the moment the reactants are mixed. Under these conditions, the product concentrations are negligible, so the reverse rate is negligible. The initial rate is measured by determining the slope of the line tangent to the curve at $t = 0$ s. In Figure 16.3, the initial rate is 10.0×10^{-7} mol/L·s (line a). Unless stated otherwise, we will use initial rate data to determine other kinetic parameters.

Expressing Rate in Terms of Reactant and Product Concentrations

So far, in our discussion of the reaction of C_2H_4 and O_3, we've expressed the rate in terms of the decreasing concentration of O_3. The rate is the same in terms of C_2H_4, but it is exactly the opposite in terms of the products because their concentrations are *increasing*. From the balanced equation, we see that one molecule of C_2H_4O and one of O_2 appear for every molecule of C_2H_4 and of O_3 that disappear. We can express the rate in terms of any of the four substances involved:

$$\text{Rate} = -\frac{\Delta[C_2H_4]}{\Delta t} = -\frac{\Delta[O_3]}{\Delta t} = +\frac{\Delta[C_2H_4O]}{\Delta t} = +\frac{\Delta[O_2]}{\Delta t}$$

Again, note the negative values for the reactants and the positive values for the products (usually written without the plus sign). Figure 16.4 shows a plot of the simultaneous monitoring of one reactant and one product. Because, in this case, product concentration increases at the same rate that reactant concentration decreases, the curves have the same shapes but are inverted.

In many other cases, though, the reactants disappear and the products appear at different rates. Consider the reaction between hydrogen and iodine to form hydrogen iodide:

$$H_2(g) + I_2(g) \longrightarrow 2HI(g)$$

For every molecule of H_2 that disappears, one molecule of I_2 disappears and *two* molecules of HI appear. In other words, the rate of $[H_2]$ decrease is the same as the rate of $[I_2]$ decrease, but both are only half the rate of [HI] increase. By referring the change in $[I_2]$ and [HI] to the change in $[H_2]$, we have

$$\text{Rate} = -\frac{\Delta[H_2]}{\Delta t} = -\frac{\Delta[I_2]}{\Delta t} = \frac{1}{2}\frac{\Delta[HI]}{\Delta t}$$

If we refer the change in $[H_2]$ and $[I_2]$ to the change in [HI] instead, we obtain

$$\text{Rate} = \frac{\Delta[HI]}{\Delta t} = -2\frac{\Delta[H_2]}{\Delta t} = -2\frac{\Delta[I_2]}{\Delta t}$$

Notice that this expression is just a rearrangement of the previous one; also note that it gives a numerical value for the rate that is double the previous value. Thus, the mathematical expression for the rate of a particular reaction and *the numerical value of the rate depend on which substance serves as the reference.*

We can summarize these results for any reaction,

$$a\text{A} + b\text{B} \longrightarrow c\text{C} + d\text{D}$$

where a, b, c, and d are coefficients of the balanced equation. In general, the rate is related to reactant or product concentrations as follows:

$$\text{Rate} = -\frac{1}{a}\frac{\Delta[A]}{\Delta t} = -\frac{1}{b}\frac{\Delta[B]}{\Delta t} = \frac{1}{c}\frac{\Delta[C]}{\Delta t} = \frac{1}{d}\frac{\Delta[D]}{\Delta t} \tag{16.2}$$

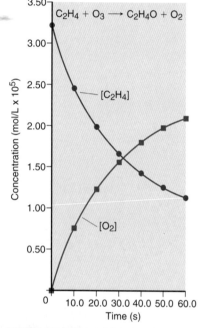

FIGURE 16.4 Plots of [C$_2$H$_4$] and [O$_2$] vs. time. Measuring reactant concentration, [C$_2$H$_4$], and product concentration, [O$_2$], gives curves of identical shapes but changing in opposite directions. The steep upward (positive) slope of [O$_2$] early in the reaction mirrors the steep downward (negative) slope of [C$_2$H$_4$] because the faster C$_2$H$_4$ is used up, the faster O$_2$ is formed. The curve shapes are identical in this case because the equation coefficients are identical.

| SAMPLE PROBLEM 16.1 | Expressing Rate in Terms of Changes in Concentration with Time |

Problem Because it has a nonpolluting combustion product (water vapor), hydrogen gas is used for fuel aboard the space shuttle and in prototype cars with Earth-bound engines:

$$2H_2(g) + O_2(g) \longrightarrow 2H_2O(g)$$

(a) Express the rate in terms of changes in $[H_2]$, $[O_2]$, and $[H_2O]$ with time.
(b) When $[O_2]$ is decreasing at 0.23 mol/L·s, at what rate is $[H_2O]$ increasing?
Plan (a) Of the three substances in the equation, let's choose O_2 as the reference because its coefficient is 1. For every molecule of O_2 that disappears, two molecules of H_2 disappear, so the rate of $[O_2]$ decrease is one-half the rate of $[H_2]$ decrease. By similar reasoning, we see that the rate of $[O_2]$ decrease is one-half the rate of $[H_2O]$ increase. **(b)** Because $[O_2]$ is decreasing, the change in its concentration must be negative. We substitute the negative value into the expression and solve for $\Delta[H_2O]/\Delta t$.
Solution (a) Expressing the rate in terms of each component:

$$\text{Rate} = -\frac{1}{2}\frac{\Delta[H_2]}{\Delta t} = -\frac{\Delta[O_2]}{\Delta t} = \frac{1}{2}\frac{\Delta[H_2O]}{\Delta t}$$

(b) Calculating the rate of change of $[H_2O]$:

$$\frac{1}{2}\frac{\Delta[H_2O]}{\Delta t} = -\frac{\Delta[O_2]}{\Delta t} = -(-0.23 \text{ mol/L·s})$$

$$\frac{\Delta[H_2O]}{\Delta t} = 2(0.23 \text{ mol/L·s}) = 0.46 \text{ mol/L·s}$$

Check (a) A good check is to use the rate expression to obtain the balanced equation: $[H_2]$ changes twice as fast as $[O_2]$, so two H_2 molecules react for each O_2. $[H_2O]$ changes twice as fast as $[O_2]$, so two H_2O molecules form from each O_2. From this reasoning, we get $2H_2 + O_2 \longrightarrow 2H_2O$. The $[H_2]$ and $[O_2]$ decrease, so they take minus signs; $[H_2O]$ increases, so it takes a plus sign. Another check is to use Equation 16.2, with $A = H_2$, $a = 2$; $B = O_2$, $b = 1$; $C = H_2O$, $c = 2$. Thus,

$$\text{Rate} = -\frac{1}{a}\frac{\Delta[A]}{\Delta t} = -\frac{1}{b}\frac{\Delta[B]}{\Delta t} = \frac{1}{c}\frac{\Delta[C]}{\Delta t}$$

or

$$\text{Rate} = -\frac{1}{2}\frac{\Delta[H_2]}{\Delta t} = -\frac{\Delta[O_2]}{\Delta t} = \frac{1}{2}\frac{\Delta[H_2O]}{\Delta t}$$

(b) Given the rate expression, it makes sense that the numerical value of the rate of $[H_2O]$ increase is twice that of $[O_2]$ decrease.
Comment Thinking through this type of problem at the molecular level is the best approach, but use Equation 16.2 to confirm your answer.

FOLLOW-UP PROBLEM 16.1 (a) Balance the following equation and express the rate in terms of the change in concentration with time for each substance:

$$NO(g) + O_2(g) \longrightarrow N_2O_3(g)$$

(b) How fast is $[O_2]$ decreasing when $[NO]$ is decreasing at a rate of 1.60×10^{-4} mol/L·s?

SECTION 16.2 SUMMARY

The average reaction rate is the change in reactant (or product) concentration over a change in time, Δt. The rate slows as reactants are used up. • The instantaneous rate at time t is obtained from the slope of the tangent to a concentration vs. time curve at time t. • The initial rate, the instantaneous rate at $t = 0$, occurs when reactants are just mixed and before any product accumulates. • The expression for a reaction rate, as well as its numerical value, depend on which reaction component is being monitored.

16.3 THE RATE LAW AND ITS COMPONENTS

The centerpiece of any kinetic study is the **rate law** (or **rate equation**) for the reaction in question. The rate law expresses the rate as a function of reactant concentrations, product concentrations, and temperature. Any hypothesis we make about how the reaction occurs on the molecular level must conform to the rate law because it is based on experimental fact.

In this discussion, we generally consider reactions for which the products do not appear in the rate law. In these cases, *the reaction rate depends only on reactant concentrations and temperature.* First, we look at the effect of concentration on rate for reactions occurring at a fixed temperature. For a general reaction,

$$a\text{A} + b\text{B} + \cdots \longrightarrow c\text{C} + d\text{D} + \cdots$$

the rate law has the form

$$\text{Rate} = k[\text{A}]^m[\text{B}]^n \cdots \tag{16.3}$$

Aside from the concentration terms, [A] and [B], the other parameters in Equation 16.3 require some definition. The proportionality constant k, called the **rate constant,** is specific for a given reaction at a given temperature; it does *not* change as the reaction proceeds. (As you'll see in Section 16.5, k *does* change with temperature and therefore determines how temperature affects the rate.) The exponents m and n, called the **reaction orders,** define how the rate is affected by reactant concentration. Thus, if the rate doubles when [A] doubles, the rate depends on [A] raised to the first power, $[\text{A}]^1$, so $m = 1$. Similarly, if the rate quadruples when [B] doubles, the rate depends on [B] raised to the second power, $[\text{B}]^2$, so $n = 2$. In another reaction, the rate may not change at all when [A] doubles; in that case, the rate does *not* depend on [A], or, to put it another way, the rate depends on [A] raised to the zero power, $[\text{A}]^0$, so $m = 0$. Keep in mind that the coefficients a and b in the general balanced equation are *not* necessarily related in any way to these reaction orders m and n.

A key point to remember is that *the components of the rate law—rate, reaction orders, and rate constant—must be found by experiment;* they cannot be deduced from the reaction stoichiometry. Chemists take an experimental approach to finding these components by

1. Using concentration measurements to find the *initial rate*
2. Using initial rates from several experiments to find the *reaction orders*
3. Using these values to calculate the *rate constant*

Many experimental techniques have been developed to accomplish the first of these steps, the measurement of concentrations in order to find initial rates; here are three common approaches. For reactions that involve a colored substance, *spectroscopic methods* can be used. For example, in the oxidation of nitrogen monoxide, only the product, nitrogen dioxide, is colored:

$$2\text{NO}(g) + \text{O}_2(g) \longrightarrow 2\text{NO}_2(g; \text{ brown})$$

As time proceeds, the brown color of the reaction mixture deepens.

For reactions that involve a change in number of moles of gas, the *change in pressure* can be monitored. Note that the above reaction could also be studied this way because 3 mol of gas becomes 2 mol of gas. As a result, the pressure in the reaction container decreases with time.

A third technique monitors a *change in conductivity.* In the reaction between an organic halide (2-bromo-2-methylpropane) and water,

$$(\text{CH}_3)_3\text{C}-\text{Br}(l) + \text{H}_2\text{O}(l) \longrightarrow (\text{CH}_3)_3\text{C}-\text{OH}(l) + \text{H}^+(aq) + \text{Br}^-(aq)$$

the HBr that forms is a strong acid and dissociates completely into ions; thus, the conductivity of the reaction mixture increases as time proceeds.

Once chemists have used initial rates to find reaction orders and have calculated the rate constant, they know the rate law and can then use it to predict the rate for any initial reactant concentrations. Let's proceed with finding the reaction orders and the rate constant.

Reaction Order Terminology

Before we see how reaction orders are determined from initial rate data, let's discuss the meaning of reaction order and some important terminology. We speak of a reaction as having an *individual* order "with respect to" or "in" each reactant as well as an *overall* order, which is simply the sum of the individual orders.

In the simplest case, a reaction with a single reactant A, the reaction is *first order* overall if the rate is directly proportional to [A]:

$$\text{Rate} = k[A]$$

It is *second order* overall if the rate is directly proportional to the square of [A]:

$$\text{Rate} = k[A]^2$$

And it is *zero order* overall if the rate is *not* dependent on [A] at all, a situation that is common in metal-catalyzed and biochemical processes, as you'll see later:

$$\text{Rate} = k[A]^0 = k(1) = k$$

Here are some real examples. For the reaction between nitrogen monoxide and ozone,

$$NO(g) + O_3(g) \longrightarrow NO_2(g) + O_2(g)$$

the rate law has been experimentally determined to be

$$\text{Rate} = k[NO][O_3]$$

This reaction is first order with respect to NO (or first order in NO), which means that the rate depends on NO concentration raised to the first power, that is, $[NO]^1$ (an exponent of 1 is generally omitted). It is also first order with respect to O_3, or $[O_3]^1$. This reaction is second order overall ($1 + 1 = 2$).

Now consider a different gas-phase reaction:

$$2NO(g) + 2H_2(g) \longrightarrow N_2(g) + 2H_2O(g)$$

The rate law for this reaction has been determined to be

$$\text{Rate} = k[NO]^2[H_2]$$

The reaction is second order in NO and first order in H_2, so it is third order overall.

Finally, for the reaction of 2-bromo-2-methylpropane and water that we considered earlier, the rate law has been found to be

$$\text{Rate} = k[(CH_3)_3CBr]$$

This reaction is first order in 2-bromo-2-methylpropane. Note that the concentration of H_2O does not even appear in the rate law. Thus, the reaction is zero order with respect to H_2O ($[H_2O]^0$). This means that the rate does not depend on the concentration of H_2O. We can also write the rate law as

$$\text{Rate} = k[(CH_3)_3CBr][H_2O]^0$$

Overall, this is a first-order reaction.

These examples demonstrate a major point: *reaction orders **cannot be** deduced from the balanced equation.* For the reaction between NO and H_2 and for the hydrolysis of 2-bromo-2-methylpropane, the reaction orders in the rate laws do *not* correspond to the coefficients of the balanced equations. Reaction orders *must* be determined from rate data.

Reaction orders are usually positive integers or zero, but they can also be fractional or negative. For the reaction

$$CHCl_3(g) + Cl_2(g) \longrightarrow CCl_4(g) + HCl(g)$$

a fractional order appears in the rate law:

$$\text{Rate} = k[CHCl_3][Cl_2]^{1/2}$$

This reaction order means that the rate depends on the square root of the Cl_2 concentration. For example, if the initial Cl_2 concentration is increased by a factor of 4, while the initial $CHCl_3$ concentration is kept the same, the rate increases by a factor of 2, the square root of the change in $[Cl_2]$. A negative exponent means that the rate *decreases* when the concentration of that component increases. Negative orders are often seen for reactions whose rate laws include products. For example, for the atmospheric reaction

$$2O_3(g) \rightleftharpoons 3O_2(g)$$

the rate law has been shown to be

$$\text{Rate} = k[O_3]^2[O_2]^{-1} = k\frac{[O_3]^2}{[O_2]}$$

If the O_2 concentration doubles, the reaction proceeds half as fast.

SAMPLE PROBLEM 16.2   Determining Reaction Order from Rate Laws

Problem For each of the following reactions, use the given rate law to determine the reaction order with respect to each reactant and the overall order:
(a) $2NO(g) + O_2(g) \longrightarrow 2NO_2(g)$; rate = $k[NO]^2[O_2]$
(b) $CH_3CHO(g) \longrightarrow CH_4(g) + CO(g)$; rate = $k[CH_3CHO]^{3/2}$
(c) $H_2O_2(aq) + 3I^-(aq) + 2H^+(aq) \longrightarrow I_3^-(aq) + 2H_2O(l)$; rate = $k[H_2O_2][I^-]$
Plan We inspect the exponents in the rate law, *not* the coefficients of the balanced equation, to find the individual orders, and then take their sum to find the overall reaction order.
Solution **(a)** The exponent of [NO] is 2, so the reaction is second order with respect to
NO,   first order with respect to O_2,   and   third order overall.

(b) The reaction is $\frac{3}{2}$ order in CH_3CHO and $\frac{3}{2}$ order overall.

(c) The reaction is first order in H_2O_2, first order in I^-,   and   second order overall.

The reactant H^+ does not appear in the rate law, so the reaction is zero order in H^+.
Check Be sure that each reactant has an order and that the sum of the individual orders gives the overall order.

FOLLOW-UP PROBLEM 16.2 Experiment shows that the reaction

$$5Br^-(aq) + BrO_3^-(aq) + 6H^+(aq) \longrightarrow 3Br_2(l) + 3H_2O(l)$$

obeys this rate law: rate = $k[Br^-][BrO_3^-][H^+]^2$. What are the reaction orders in each reactant and the overall reaction order?

Determining Reaction Orders Experimentally

Sample Problem 16.2 shows how to find the reaction orders from a known rate law. Now let's see how they are found from data *before* the rate law is known. Consider the reaction between oxygen and nitrogen monoxide, a key step in the formation of acid rain and in the industrial production of nitric acid:

$$O_2(g) + 2NO(g) \longrightarrow 2NO_2(g)$$

The rate law, expressed in general form, is

$$\text{Rate} = k[O_2]^m[NO]^n$$

To find the reaction orders, *we run a series of experiments, starting each one with a different set of reactant concentrations and obtaining an initial rate in each case.*

Table 16.2	Initial Rates for a Series of Experiments with the Reaction Between O_2 and NO		
	Initial Reactant Concentrations (mol/L)		**Initial Rate (mol/L·s)**
Experiment	**O_2**	**NO**	
1	1.10×10^{-2}	1.30×10^{-2}	3.21×10^{-3}
2	2.20×10^{-2}	1.30×10^{-2}	6.40×10^{-3}
3	1.10×10^{-2}	2.60×10^{-2}	12.8×10^{-3}
4	3.30×10^{-2}	1.30×10^{-2}	9.60×10^{-3}
5	1.10×10^{-2}	3.90×10^{-2}	28.8×10^{-3}

Table 16.2 shows experiments that change one reactant concentration while keeping the other constant. If we compare experiments 1 and 2, we see the effect of doubling $[O_2]$ on the rate. First, we take the ratio of their rate laws:

$$\frac{\text{Rate 2}}{\text{Rate 1}} = \frac{k[O_2]_2^m [NO]_2^n}{k[O_2]_1^m [NO]_1^n}$$

where $[O_2]_2$ is the O_2 concentration for experiment 2, $[NO]_1$ is the NO concentration for experiment 1, and so forth. Because k is a constant and $[NO]$ does not change between these two experiments, these quantities cancel:

$$\frac{\text{Rate 2}}{\text{Rate 1}} = \frac{[O_2]_2^m}{[O_2]_1^m} = \left(\frac{[O_2]_2}{[O_2]_1}\right)^m$$

Substituting the values from Table 16.2, we obtain

$$\frac{6.40 \times 10^{-3} \text{ mol/L·s}}{3.21 \times 10^{-3} \text{ mol/L·s}} = \left(\frac{2.20 \times 10^{-2} \text{ mol/L}}{1.10 \times 10^{-2} \text{ mol/L}}\right)^m$$

Dividing, we obtain

$$1.99 = (2.00)^m$$

Rounding to one significant figure gives

$$2 = 2^m; \quad \text{therefore,} \quad m = 1$$

The reaction is first order in O_2: when $[O_2]$ doubles, the rate doubles.

When an exponent is not this easy to determine by inspection, you can solve for it as follows: $a = b^x$, so $x = \log a / \log b$. Thus, we have $m = \log 1.99 / \log 2.00 = 0.993$, which rounds to 1.

To find the order with respect to NO, we compare experiments 3 and 1, in which $[O_2]$ is held constant and $[NO]$ is doubled:

$$\frac{\text{Rate 3}}{\text{Rate 1}} = \frac{k[O_2]_3^m [NO]_3^n}{k[O_2]_1^m [NO]_1^n}$$

As before, k is constant, and in this pair of experiments $[O_2]$ does not change, so these quantities cancel:

$$\frac{\text{Rate 3}}{\text{Rate 1}} = \left(\frac{[NO]_3}{[NO]_1}\right)^n$$

The actual values give

$$\frac{12.8 \times 10^{-3} \text{ mol/L·s}}{3.21 \times 10^{-3} \text{ mol/L·s}} = \left(\frac{2.60 \times 10^{-2} \text{ mol/L}}{1.30 \times 10^{-2} \text{ mol/L}}\right)^n$$

Dividing, we obtain

$$3.99 = (2.00)^n$$

Solving for n:

$$n = \log 3.99 / \log 2.00 = 2.00; \quad \text{therefore,} \quad n = 2$$

The reaction is second order in NO: when [NO] doubles, the rate quadruples. Thus, the rate law is

$$\text{Rate} = k[O_2][NO]^2$$

You may want to use experiment 1 in combination with experiments 4 and 5 to check this result.

SAMPLE PROBLEM 16.3 Determining Reaction Orders from Initial Rate Data

Problem Many gaseous reactions occur in car engines and exhaust systems. One of these is

$$NO_2(g) + CO(g) \longrightarrow NO(g) + CO_2(g) \qquad \text{rate} = k[NO_2]^m[CO]^n$$

Use the following data to determine the individual and overall reaction orders:

Experiment	Initial Rate (mol/L·s)	Initial [NO₂] (mol/L)	Initial [CO] (mol/L)
1	0.0050	0.10	0.10
2	0.080	0.40	0.10
3	0.0050	0.10	0.20

Plan We need to solve the general rate law for the reaction orders m and n. To solve for each exponent, we proceed as in the text, taking the ratio of the rate laws for two experiments in which only the reactant in question changes.

Solution Calculating m in $[NO_2]^m$: We take the ratio of the rate laws for experiments 1 and 2, in which $[NO_2]$ varies but [CO] is constant:

$$\frac{\text{Rate 2}}{\text{Rate 1}} = \frac{k[NO_2]_2^m[CO]_2^n}{k[NO_2]_1^m[CO]_1^n} = \left(\frac{[NO_2]_2}{[NO_2]_1}\right)^m \quad \text{or} \quad \frac{0.080 \text{ mol/L·s}}{0.0050 \text{ mol/L·s}} = \left(\frac{0.40 \text{ mol/L}}{0.10 \text{ mol/L}}\right)^m$$

Thus, $16 = 4.0^m$, so $m = \log 16/\log 4.0 = 2.0$. The reaction is second order in NO_2. Calculating n in $[CO]^n$: We take the ratio of the rate laws for experiments 1 and 3, in which [CO] varies but $[NO_2]$ is constant:

$$\frac{\text{Rate 3}}{\text{Rate 1}} = \frac{k[NO_2]_3^2[CO]_3^n}{k[NO_2]_1^2[CO]_1^n} = \left(\frac{[CO]_3}{[CO]_1}\right)^n \quad \text{or} \quad \frac{0.0050 \text{ mol/L·s}}{0.0050 \text{ mol/L·s}} = \left(\frac{0.20 \text{ mol/L}}{0.10 \text{ mol/L}}\right)^n$$

We have $1.0 = (2.0)^n$, so $n = 0$. The rate does not change when [CO] varies, so the reaction is zero order in CO.

Therefore, the rate law is

$$\text{Rate} = k[NO_2]^2[CO]^0 = k[NO_2]^2(1) = k[NO_2]^2$$

The reaction is second order overall.

Check A good check is to reason through the orders. If $m = 1$, quadrupling $[NO_2]$ would quadruple the rate; but the rate *more* than quadruples, so $m > 1$. If $m = 2$, quadrupling $[NO_2]$ would increase the rate by a factor of 16 (4^2). The ratio of rates is $0.080/0.005 = 16$, so $m = 2$. In contrast, increasing [CO] has no effect on the rate, which can happen only if $[CO]^n = 1$, so $n = 0$.

FOLLOW-UP PROBLEM 16.3 Find the rate law and the overall reaction order for the reaction $H_2 + I_2 \longrightarrow 2HI$ from the following data at 450°C:

Experiment	Initial Rate (mol/L·s)	Initial [H₂] (mol/L)	Initial [I₂] (mol/L)
1	1.9×10^{-23}	0.0113	0.0011
2	1.1×10^{-22}	0.0220	0.0033
3	9.3×10^{-23}	0.0550	0.0011
4	1.9×10^{-22}	0.0220	0.0056

To provide a thorough review of this idea, let's work one more sample problem, this time using molecular scenes to determine reaction orders.

SAMPLE PROBLEM 16.4 Determining Reaction Orders from a Series of Molecular Scenes

Problem At a particular temperature, two gases, A (red) and B (blue), react to form products. The following molecular scenes represent starting mixtures for four experiments run at the same volume, labeled 1 through 4, with their initial rates (in mol/L·s):

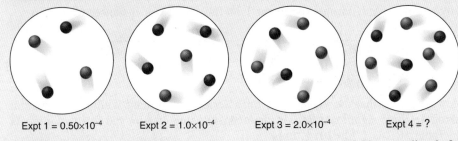

| Expt 1 = 0.50×10⁻⁴ | Expt 2 = 1.0×10⁻⁴ | Expt 3 = 2.0×10⁻⁴ | Expt 4 = ? |

Handwritten notes in right margin:
$$-\frac{1}{4}\frac{[NH_3]}{\Delta t} = +\frac{1}{6}$$
$$-\frac{1}{4}$$
$$-0.000875 = \frac{1}{6}x$$
$$\frac{3}{2}(0.25)$$

(a) What is the reaction order with respect to A? With respect to B? The overall order?
(b) Write the rate law for the reaction.
(c) Predict the initial rate of experiment 4.

Plan (a) As in previous situations, we find the individual reaction orders by seeing how a change in each reactant changes the rate. The difference here is that, instead of using concentration data, we count numbers of spheres. As before, if an increase in one reactant has no effect on the rate, the order with respect to that reactant is 0. Similarly, if the increase causes an increase in the rate by the same factor, the order is 1. And, if the increase in a reactant causes a square of that increase in the rate, the order is 2. The sum of the individual orders is the overall order. **(b)** To write the rate law, we use the orders from part (a) as exponents in the general rate law. **(c)** Using the results from Expts 1 through 3 and the rate law from part (b), we find the initial rate of Expt 4.

Solution (a) Finding the individual and overall orders: For reactant A (red), from Expts 1 and 2, the number of A doubles (from 2 to 4), while B is constant (at 2), and the rate doubles (from $0.5×10^{-4}$ mol/L·s to $1.0×10^{-4}$ mol/L·s), so the order with respect to A is 1. For reactant B (blue), from Expts 1 and 3, the number of B doubles (from 2 to 4), while the number of A is constant (at 2), and the rate quadruples (from $0.5×10^{-4}$ mol/L·s to $2.0×10^{-4}$ mol/L·s), so the order with respect to B is 2. The overall order is $1 + 2 = 3$.
(b) Writing the rate law: The general rate law is rate $= k[A]^m[B]^n$, so we have

$$\text{Rate} = k[A][B]^2$$

(c) Finding the initial rate of Expt 4: Comparing, for example, Expts 3 and 4, we see that the number of A doubles (from 2 to 4). Furthermore, the rate law shows that the reaction is first order in A. Therefore, the initial rate in Expt 4 should be $4.0×10^{-4}$ mol/L·s.

Check A good check is to compare other pairs of experiments. **(a)** Comparing Expts 2 and 3 shows that the number of B doubles, which causes the rate to quadruple, and A decreases by half, which causes the rate to halve; so the overall rate change should double (from $1.0×10^{-4}$ mol/L·s to $2.0×10^{-4}$ mol/L·s), which it does. **(c)** Comparing Expts 2 and 4, with A constant, shows that the number of B doubles, so the rate should quadruple, which means the initial rate of Expt 4 would be $4.0×10^{-4}$ mol/L·s, as we found.

FOLLOW-UP PROBLEM 16.4 The scenes below show three experiments at a given temperature involving reactants X (black) and Y (green), with their initial rates (in mol/L·s):

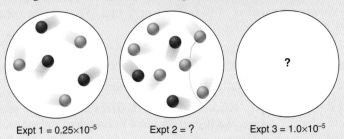

| Expt 1 = 0.25×10⁻⁵ | Expt 2 = ? | Expt 3 = 1.0×10⁻⁵ |

If the rate law for the reaction is rate $= k[X]^2$: **(a)** What is the initial rate of Expt 2?
(b) Draw a scene for Expt 3 that involves a single change of the scene for Expt 1.

Determining the Rate Constant

With the rate, reactant concentrations, and reaction orders known, the sole remaining unknown in the rate law is the rate constant, k. The rate constant is specific for a particular reaction *at a particular temperature*. The experiments with the reaction of O_2 and NO were run at the same temperature, so we can use data from any to solve for k. From experiment 1 in Table 16.2, for instance, we obtain

$$k = \frac{\text{rate 1}}{[O_2]_1[NO]_1^2} = \frac{3.21 \times 10^{-3} \text{ mol/L·s}}{(1.10 \times 10^{-2} \text{ mol/L})(1.30 \times 10^{-2} \text{ mol/L})^2}$$

$$= \frac{3.21 \times 10^{-3} \text{ mol/L·s}}{1.86 \times 10^{-6} \text{ mol}^3/L^3} = 1.73 \times 10^3 \text{ L}^2/\text{mol}^2\text{·s}$$

Always check that the values of k for a series are constant within experimental error. To three significant figures, the average value of k for the five experiments in Table 16.2 is 1.72×10^3 L^2/mol^2·s.

Note the units for the rate constant. With concentrations in mol/L and the reaction rate in units of mol/L·time, the units for k depend on the order of the reaction and, of course, the time unit. The units for k in our example, L^2/mol^2·s, are required to give a rate with units of mol/L·s:

$$\frac{\text{mol}}{\text{L·s}} = \frac{L^2}{\text{mol}^2\text{·s}} \times \frac{\text{mol}}{L} \times \left(\frac{\text{mol}}{L}\right)^2$$

The rate constant will *always* have these units for an overall third-order reaction with the time unit in seconds. Table 16.3 shows the units of k for some common overall reaction orders, but you can always determine the units mathematically.

Table 16.3 Units of the Rate Constant k for Several Overall Reaction Orders

Overall Reaction Order	Units of k (t in seconds)
0	mol/L·s (or mol L^{-1} s^{-1})
1	1/s (or s^{-1})
2	L/mol·s (or L mol^{-1} s^{-1})
3	L^2/mol^2·s (or L^2 mol^{-2} s^{-1})

General formula:

$$\text{Units of } k = \frac{\left(\dfrac{L}{\text{mol}}\right)^{\text{order}-1}}{\text{unit of } t}$$

SECTION 16.3 SUMMARY

An experimentally determined rate law shows how the rate of a reaction depends on concentration. If we consider only initial rates, the rate law often takes this form: rate = $k[A]^m[B]^n \cdots$. • With an accurate method for obtaining initial rates, reaction orders are determined experimentally by comparing rates for different initial concentrations, that is, by performing several experiments and varying the concentration of one reactant at a time to see its effect on the rate. • With rate, concentrations, and reaction orders known, only the rate constant remains to be calculated.

16.4 INTEGRATED RATE LAWS: CONCENTRATION CHANGES OVER TIME

Notice that the rate laws we've developed so far do not include time as a variable. They tell us the rate or concentration at a given instant, allowing us to answer a critical question, "How fast is the reaction proceeding at the moment when y moles per liter of A are reacting with z moles per liter of B?" However, by employing different forms of the rate laws, called **integrated rate laws,** we can consider the time factor and answer other questions, such as "How long will it take for x moles per liter of A to be used up?" and "What is the concentration of A after y minutes of reaction?"

Integrated Rate Laws for First-Order, Second-Order, and Zero-Order Reactions

Consider a simple first-order reaction, A $\longrightarrow$ B. (Because first- and second-order reactions are more common, we'll discuss them before zero-order reactions.) As we discussed previously, the rate can be expressed as the change in the concentration of A divided by the change in time:

$$\text{Rate} = -\frac{\Delta[A]}{\Delta t}$$

It can also be expressed in terms of the rate law:

$$\text{Rate} = k[\text{A}]$$

Setting these different expressions equal to each other gives

$$-\frac{\Delta[\text{A}]}{\Delta t} = k[\text{A}]$$

Using calculus, this expression is integrated over time to obtain the integrated rate law for a first-order reaction:

$$\ln \frac{[\text{A}]_0}{[\text{A}]_t} = kt \quad \text{(first-order reaction; rate} = k[\text{A}]) \quad \text{(16.4)}$$

where ln is the natural logarithm, $[\text{A}]_0$ is the concentration of A at $t = 0$, and $[\text{A}]_t$ is the concentration of A at any time t during an experiment. In mathematical terms, $\ln \frac{a}{b} = \ln a - \ln b$, so we have

$$\ln [\text{A}]_0 - \ln [\text{A}]_t = kt$$

For a general second-order reaction, the expression including time is quite complex, so let's consider the case in which the rate law contains only one reactant. Setting the rate expressions equal to each other gives

$$\text{Rate} = -\frac{\Delta[\text{A}]}{\Delta t} = k[\text{A}]^2$$

Integrating over time gives the integrated rate law for a second-order reaction involving one reactant:

$$\frac{1}{[\text{A}]_t} - \frac{1}{[\text{A}]_0} = kt \quad \text{(second-order reaction; rate} = k[\text{A}]^2) \quad \text{(16.5)}$$

For a zero-order reaction, we have

$$\text{Rate} = -\frac{\Delta[\text{A}]}{\Delta t} = k[\text{A}]^0$$

Integrating over time gives the integrated rate law for a zero-order reaction:

$$[\text{A}]_t - [\text{A}]_0 = -kt \quad \text{(zero-order reaction; rate} = k[\text{A}]^0 = k) \quad \text{(16.6)}$$

Sample Problem 16.5 shows one way integrated rate laws are applied.

SAMPLE PROBLEM 16.5 Determining the Reactant Concentration at a Given Time

Problem At 1000°C, cyclobutane (C_4H_8) decomposes in a first-order reaction, with the very high rate constant of 87 s^{-1}, to two molecules of ethylene (C_2H_4).
(a) If the initial C_4H_8 concentration is 2.00 M, what is the concentration after 0.010 s?
(b) What fraction of C_4H_8 has decomposed in this time?
Plan (a) We must find the concentration of cyclobutane at time t, $[C_4H_8]_t$. The problem tells us this is a first-order reaction, so we use the integrated first-order rate law:

$$\ln \frac{[C_4H_8]_0}{[C_4H_8]_t} = kt$$

We know k (87 s^{-1}), t (0.010 s), and $[C_4H_8]_0$ (2.00 M), so we can solve for $[C_4H_8]_t$.
(b) The fraction decomposed is the concentration that has decomposed divided by the initial concentration:

$$\text{Fraction decomposed} = \frac{[C_4H_8]_0 - [C_4H_8]_t}{[C_4H_8]_0}$$

Solution (a) Substituting the data into the integrated rate law:

$$\ln \frac{2.00 \text{ mol/L}}{[C_4H_8]_t} = (87 \text{ s}^{-1})(0.010 \text{ s}) = 0.87$$

Taking the antilog of both sides:

$$\frac{2.00 \text{ mol/L}}{[C_4H_8]_t} = e^{0.87} = 2.4$$

Solving for $[C_4H_8]_t$:

$$[C_4H_8]_t = \frac{2.00 \text{ mol/L}}{2.4} = 0.83 \text{ mol/L}$$

(b) Finding the fraction that has decomposed after 0.010 s:

$$\frac{[C_4H_8]_0 - [C_4H_8]_t}{[C_4H_8]_0} = \frac{2.00 \text{ mol/L} - 0.83 \text{ mol/L}}{2.00 \text{ mol/L}} = 0.58$$

Check The concentration remaining after 0.010 s (0.83 mol/L) is less than the starting concentration (2.00 mol/L), which makes sense. Raising e to an exponent slightly less than 1 should give a number (2.4) slightly less than the value of e (2.718). Moreover, the final result makes sense: a high rate constant indicates a fast reaction, so it's not surprising that so much decomposes in such a short time.

Comment Integrated rate laws are also used to solve for the time it takes to reach a certain reactant concentration, as in the follow-up problem.

FOLLOW-UP PROBLEM 16.5 At 25°C, hydrogen iodide breaks down very slowly to hydrogen and iodine: rate $= k[HI]^2$. The rate constant at 25°C is 2.4×10^{-21} L/mol·s. If 0.0100 mol of $HI(g)$ is placed in a 1.0-L container, how long will it take for the concentration of HI to reach 0.00900 mol/L (10.0% reacted)?

Determining the Reaction Order from the Integrated Rate Law

Suppose you don't know the rate law for a reaction and don't have the initial rate data needed to determine the reaction orders (which we did have in Sample Problem 16.3). Another method for finding reaction orders is a graphical technique that uses concentration and time data directly.

An integrated rate law can be rearranged into the form of an equation for a straight line, $y = mx + b$, where m is the slope and b is the y-axis intercept. For a first-order reaction, we have

$$\ln [A]_0 - \ln [A]_t = kt$$

Rearranging and changing signs gives

$$\ln [A]_t = -kt + \ln [A]_0$$
$$y \quad = \quad mx \; + \quad b$$

Therefore, a plot of $\ln [A]_t$ vs. time gives a straight line with slope $= -k$ and y intercept $= \ln [A]_0$ (Figure 16.5A).

For a simple second-order reaction, we have

$$\frac{1}{[A]_t} - \frac{1}{[A]_0} = kt$$

Rearranging gives

$$\frac{1}{[A]_t} = kt + \frac{1}{[A]_0}$$
$$y \quad = \quad mx \; + \quad b$$

In this case, a plot of $1/[A]_t$ vs. time gives a straight line with slope $= k$ and y intercept $= 1/[A]_0$ (Figure 16.5B).

For a zero-order reaction, we have

$$[A]_t - [A]_0 = -kt$$

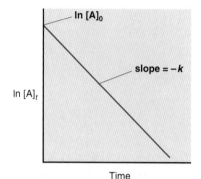

A First order

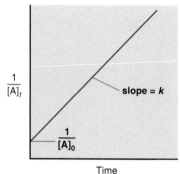

B Second order

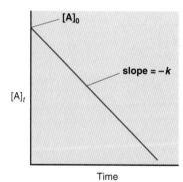

C Zero order

FIGURE 16.5 Integrated rate laws and reaction orders. A, Plot of $\ln [A]_t$ vs. time gives a straight line for a reaction that is first order in A. **B,** Plot of $1/[A]_t$ vs. time gives a straight line for a reaction that is second order in A. **C,** Plot of $[A]_t$ vs. time gives a straight line for a reaction that is zero order in A.

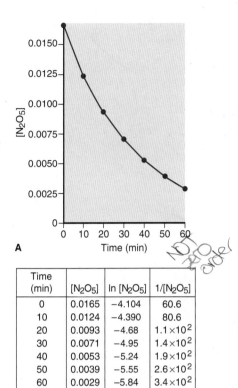

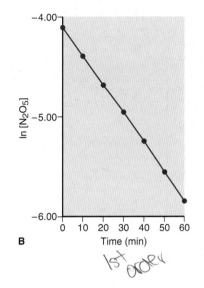

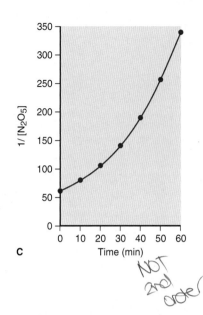

Time (min)	$[N_2O_5]$	$\ln [N_2O_5]$	$1/[N_2O_5]$
0	0.0165	−4.104	60.6
10	0.0124	−4.390	80.6
20	0.0093	−4.68	1.1×10^2
30	0.0071	−4.95	1.4×10^2
40	0.0053	−5.24	1.9×10^2
50	0.0039	−5.55	2.6×10^2
60	0.0029	−5.84	3.4×10^2

FIGURE 16.6 **Graphical determination of the reaction order for the decomposition of N_2O_5.** A table of time and concentration data for determining reaction order appears below the graphs. **A,** A plot of $[N_2O_5]$ vs. time is curved, indicating that the reaction is *not* zero order in N_2O_5. **B,** A plot of $\ln [N_2O_5]$ vs. time gives a straight line, indicating that the reaction *is* first order in N_2O_5. **C,** A plot of $1/[N_2O_5]$ vs. time is curved, indicating that the reaction is *not* second order in N_2O_5. Plots A and C support the conclusion from plot B.

Rearranging gives

$$[A]_t = -kt + [A]_0$$
$$y = mx + b$$

Thus, a plot of $[A]_t$ vs. time gives a straight line with slope $= -k$ and y intercept $= [A]_0$ (Figure 16.5C).

Therefore, some trial-and-error graphical plotting is required to find the reaction order from the concentration and time data:

- If you obtain a straight line when you plot $\ln$ [reactant] vs. time, the reaction is *first order* with respect to that reactant.
- If you obtain a straight line when you plot $1/$[reactant] vs. time, the reaction is *second order* with respect to that reactant.
- If you obtain a straight line when you plot [reactant] vs. time, the reaction is *zero order* with respect to that reactant.

Figure 16.6 shows how this approach is used to determine the order for the decomposition of N_2O_5. Because the plot of $\ln [N_2O_5]$ *is* linear and the plot of $1/[N_2O_5]$ *is not,* the decomposition of N_2O_5 must be first order in N_2O_5.

Reaction Half-Life

The **half-life ($t_{1/2}$)** of a reaction is the time required for the reactant concentration to reach half its initial value. A half-life is expressed in time units appropriate for a given reaction and is characteristic of that reaction at a given temperature.

At fixed conditions, *the half-life of a first-order reaction is a constant, independent of reactant concentration.* For example, the half-life for the first-order decomposition of N_2O_5 at 45°C is 24.0 min. The meaning of this value is that if we start with, say, 0.0600 mol/L of N_2O_5 at 45°C, after 24 min (one half-life),

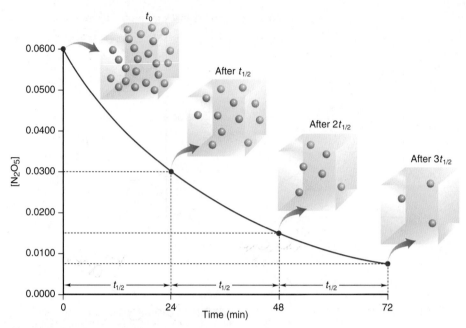

FIGURE 16.7 A plot of [N₂O₅] vs. time for three half-lives. During each half-life, the concentration is halved ($T = 45°C$ and $[N_2O_5]_0 = 0.0600$ mol/L). The blow-up volumes, with N_2O_5 molecules as colored spheres, show that after three half-lives, $\frac{1}{2} \times \frac{1}{2} \times \frac{1}{2} = \frac{1}{8}$ of the original concentration remains.

0.0300 mol/L has been consumed and 0.0300 mol/L remains; after 48 min (two half-lives), 0.0150 mol/L remains; after 72 min (three half-lives), 0.0075 mol/L remains, and so forth (Figure 16.7).

We can see from the integrated rate law why the half-life of a first-order reaction is independent of concentration:

$$\ln \frac{[A]_0}{[A]_t} = kt$$

After one half-life, $t = t_{1/2}$, and $[A]_t = \frac{1}{2}[A]_0$. Substituting, we obtain

$$\ln \frac{[A]_0}{\frac{1}{2}[A]_0} = kt_{1/2} \quad \text{or} \quad \ln 2 = kt_{1/2}$$

Then, solving for $t_{1/2}$, we have

$$t_{1/2} = \frac{\ln 2}{k} = \frac{0.693}{k} \quad \text{(first-order process; rate} = k[A]) \tag{16.7}$$

As you can see, *the time to reach one-half the starting concentration in a first-order reaction does not depend on what that starting concentration is.*

Radioactive decay of an unstable nucleus is another example of a first-order process. For example, the half-life for the decay of uranium-235 is 7.1×10^8 yr. This means that after 710 million years, a 1-kg sample of uranium-235 will contain 0.5 kg of uranium-235, and a 1-mg sample of uranium-235 will contain 0.5 mg. (We discuss the kinetics of radioactive decay thoroughly in Chapter 23.) Whether we consider a molecule or a radioactive nucleus, the *decomposition of each particle in a first-order process is independent of the number of other particles present.*

We'll work two sample problems to clarify this idea: the first generalizes it with molecular scenes, and the second applies it to real substances.

SAMPLE PROBLEM 16.6   Using Molecular Scenes to Determine Half-Life

Problem Compound A (red) converts to compound B (black) in a first-order process, as represented by the scenes below:

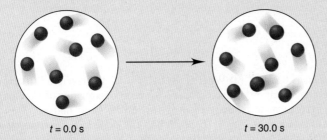

$$t = 0.0\ s \qquad\qquad t = 30.0\ s$$

(a) Find the half-life, $t_{1/2}$, of the reaction.
(b) Calculate the rate constant, k.
(c) Draw a scene that represents the reaction mixture after 2.00 min.

Plan (a) Given that the reaction is first order, we know the half-life is a constant. Counting the numbers of red and black spheres at the start and at the later time tells us how fast the reaction is proceeding. When half of the red spheres have become black, the elapsed time is the half-life. **(b)** We substitute the value of $t_{1/2}$ from part (a) into Equation 16.7 and solve for k. **(c)** Once we know how long it takes half of A to become B, we can calculate how many red and black spheres would be in the mixture at 2.00 min (120. s).

Solution (a) Examining the scenes to find $t_{1/2}$: At $t = 0.0$ s, there are 8 molecules of A (red) and no B (black). At $t = 30.0$ s, 6 of A and 2 of B are present, so one-quarter of A has reacted. Therefore, it takes twice as long (2 × 30.0 s) for half of the original 8 molecules of A to react: $t_{1/2} = 60.0$ s

(b) Finding the rate constant:

$$t_{1/2} = 0.693/k$$

therefore, $$k = 0.693/t_{1/2} = 0.693/60.0 \text{ s} = \boxed{1.16 \times 10^{-2}\, s^{-1}}$$

(c) If half of the original number of molecules react in 60.0 s, half of the remaining number react in two half-lives, or 120. s. The scene representing the mixture after 120. s is

Check For (b), rounding gives $0.7/60$ s^{-1}, which is slightly greater than 1×10^{-2} s^{-1}, so the answer seems correct.

FOLLOW-UP PROBLEM 16.6 Compound X (blue) undergoes a slow first-order transformation to Y (orange), as represented by the scenes below:

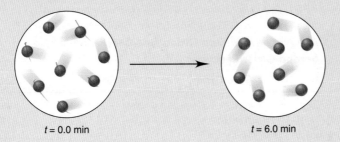

$$t = 0.0\ min \qquad\qquad t = 6.0\ min$$

Determine $t_{1/2}$ and k of the reaction.

SAMPLE PROBLEM 16.7   Determining the Half-Life of a First-Order Reaction

Problem Cyclopropane is the smallest cyclic hydrocarbon. Because its 60° bond angles reduce orbital overlap, its bonds are weak. As a result, it is thermally unstable and rearranges to propene at 1000°C via the following first-order reaction:

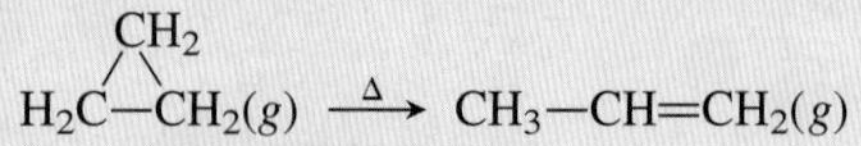

$$CH_2$$
$$H_2C-CH_2(g) \xrightarrow{\Delta} CH_3-CH=CH_2(g)$$

The rate constant is 9.2 s^{-1}. **(a)** What is the half-life of the reaction? **(b)** How long does it take for the concentration of cyclopropane to reach one-quarter of the initial value?
Plan (a) The cyclopropane rearrangement is first order, so to find $t_{1/2}$ we use Equation 16.7 and substitute for k (9.2 s^{-1}). **(b)** Each half-life decreases the concentration to one-half of its initial value, so two half-lives decrease it to one-quarter.
Solution (a) Solving for $t_{1/2}$:

$$t_{1/2} = \frac{\ln 2}{k} = \frac{0.693}{9.2 \text{ s}^{-1}} = 0.075 \text{ s}$$

It takes 0.075 s for half the cyclopropane to form propene at this temperature.
(b) Finding the time to reach one-quarter of the initial concentration:

$$\text{Time} = 2(t_{1/2}) = 2(0.075 \text{ s}) = 0.15 \text{ s}$$

Check For (a), rounding gives 0.7/9 s^{-1} = 0.08 s, so the answer seems correct.

FOLLOW-UP PROBLEM 16.7 Iodine-123 is used to study thyroid gland function. This radioactive isotope breaks down in a first-order process with a half-life of 13.1 h. What is the rate constant for the process?

In contrast to the half-life of a first-order reaction, the half-life of a second-order reaction *does* depend on reactant concentration:

$$t_{1/2} = \frac{1}{k[A]_0} \quad \text{(second-order process; rate} = k[A]^2)$$

Note that here *the half-life is **inversely** proportional to the initial reactant concentration.* This relationship means that a second-order reaction with a high initial reactant concentration has a shorter half-life, and one with a low initial reactant concentration has a longer half-life. Therefore, *as a second-order reaction proceeds, the half-life increases.*

In contrast to the half-life of a second-order reaction, *the half-life of a zero-order reaction is **directly** proportional to the initial reactant concentration:*

$$t_{1/2} = \frac{[A]_0}{2k} \quad \text{(zero-order process; rate} = k)$$

Thus, if a zero-order reaction begins with a high reactant concentration, it has a longer half-life than if it begins with a low reactant concentration. Table 16.4 summarizes the essential features of zero-, first-, and second-order reactions.

Table 16.4 **An Overview of Zero-Order, First-Order, and Simple Second-Order Reactions**

	Zero Order	First Order	Second Order
Rate law	rate = k	rate = $k[A]$	rate = $k[A]^2$
Units for k	mol/L·s	1/s	L/mol·s
Integrated rate law in straight-line form	$[A]_t =$ $-kt + [A]_0$	$\ln [A]_t =$ $-kt + \ln [A]_0$	$1/[A]_t =$ $kt + 1/[A]_0$
Plot for straight line	$[A]_t$ vs. time	$\ln [A]_t$ vs. time	$1/[A]_t$ vs. time
Slope, y intercept	$-k$, $[A]_0$	$-k$, $\ln [A]_0$	k, $1/[A]_0$
Half-life	$[A]_0/2k$	$(\ln 2)/k$	$1/k[A]_0$

SECTION 16.4 SUMMARY

Integrated rate laws are used to find either the time needed to reach a certain concentration of reactant or the concentration present after a given time. Rearrangements of the integrated rate laws allow us to determine reaction orders and rate constants graphically. • The half-life is the time needed for the reaction to consume half the reactant; for first-order reactions, it is independent of concentration.

16.5 THE EFFECT OF TEMPERATURE ON REACTION RATE

Temperature often has a major effect on reaction rate. As Figure 16.8A shows for a common organic reaction—hydrolysis, or reaction with water, of an ester—when reactant concentrations are held constant, the rate nearly doubles with each rise in temperature of 10 K (or 10°C). In fact, for many reactions near room temperature, an increase of 10°C causes a doubling or tripling of the rate.

Expt	[Ester]	[H$_2$O]	T (K)	Rate (mol/L·s)	k (L/mol·s)
1	0.100	0.200	288	1.04×10^{-3}	0.0521
2	0.100	0.200	298	2.02×10^{-3}	0.101
3	0.100	0.200	308	3.68×10^{-3}	0.184
4	0.100	0.200	318	6.64×10^{-3}	0.332

A

How does the rate law express this effect of temperature? If we collect concentration and time data for the same reaction run at *different* temperatures (T), and then solve each rate expression for k, we find that k increases as T increases. In other words, *temperature affects the rate by affecting the rate constant.* A plot of k vs. T gives a curve that increases exponentially (Figure 16.8B).

These results are consistent with studies made in 1889 by the Swedish chemist Svante Arrhenius, who discovered a key relationship between T and k. In its modern form, the **Arrhenius equation** is

$$k = Ae^{-E_a/RT} \qquad (16.8)$$

where k is the rate constant, e is the base of natural logarithms, T is the absolute temperature, and R is the universal gas constant. We'll discuss the meaning of the constant A, which is related to the orientation of the colliding molecules, in the next section. The E_a term is the **activation energy** of the reaction, which Arrhenius considered the *minimum energy* the molecules must have to react; we'll explore its meaning in the next section as well. This negative exponential relationship between T and k means that *as T increases, the negative exponent becomes smaller, so the value of k becomes larger, which means that the rate increases:*

$$\text{Higher } T \Longrightarrow \text{larger } k \Longrightarrow \text{increased rate}$$

We can calculate E_a from the Arrhenius equation by taking the natural logarithm of both sides and recasting the equation into one for a straight line:

$$\ln k = \ln A - \frac{E_a}{R}\left(\frac{1}{T}\right)$$
$$y = b + mx$$

A plot of $\ln k$ vs. $1/T$ gives a straight line whose slope is $-E_a/R$ and whose y intercept is $\ln A$ (Figure 16.9). Therefore, with the constant R known, we can determine E_a graphically from a series of k values at different temperatures.

Because the relationship between $\ln k$ and $1/T$ is linear, we can use a simpler method to find E_a if we know the rate constants at two temperatures, T_2 and T_1:

$$\ln k_2 = \ln A - \frac{E_a}{R}\left(\frac{1}{T_2}\right) \qquad \ln k_1 = \ln A - \frac{E_a}{R}\left(\frac{1}{T_1}\right)$$

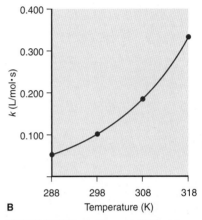

FIGURE 16.8 Dependence of the rate constant on temperature. A, In the hydrolysis of the ester ethyl acetate, $CH_3COOCH_2CH_3 + H_2O \rightleftharpoons$ $CH_3COOH + CH_3CH_2OH$ when reactant concentrations are held constant and temperature increases, the rate and rate constant increase. Note the near doubling of k with each rise of 10 K (10°C). **B,** A plot of rate constant vs. temperature for this reaction shows an exponentially increasing curve.

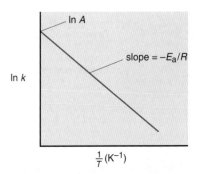

FIGURE 16.9 Graphical determination of the activation energy. A plot of $\ln k$ vs. $1/T$ gives a straight line with slope = $-E_a/R$.

When we subtract $\ln k_1$ from $\ln k_2$, the term $\ln A$ drops out and the other terms can be rearranged to give

$$\ln \frac{k_2}{k_1} = -\frac{E_a}{R}\left(\frac{1}{T_2} - \frac{1}{T_1}\right)$$

(16.9)

From this, we can solve for E_a.

SAMPLE PROBLEM 16.8 Determining the Energy of Activation

Problem The decomposition of hydrogen iodide,

$$2HI(g) \longrightarrow H_2(g) + I_2(g)$$

has rate constants of 9.51×10^{-9} L/mol·s at 500. K and 1.10×10^{-5} L/mol·s at 600. K. Find E_a.

Plan We are given the rate constants, k_1 and k_2, at two temperatures, T_1 and T_2, so we substitute into Equation 16.9 and solve for E_a.

Solution Rearranging Equation 16.9 to solve for E_a:

$$\ln \frac{k_2}{k_1} = -\frac{E_a}{R}\left(\frac{1}{T_2} - \frac{1}{T_1}\right)$$

$$E_a = -R\left(\ln \frac{k_2}{k_1}\right)\left(\frac{1}{T_2} - \frac{1}{T_1}\right)^{-1}$$

$$= -(8.314 \text{ J/mol·K})\left(\ln \frac{1.10 \times 10^{-5} \text{ L/mol·s}}{9.51 \times 10^{-9} \text{ L/mol·s}}\right)\left(\frac{1}{600. \text{ K}} - \frac{1}{500. \text{ K}}\right)^{-1}$$

$$= 1.76 \times 10^5 \text{ J/mol} = 1.76 \times 10^2 \text{ kJ/mol}$$

Comment Be sure to retain the same number of significant figures in $1/T$ as you have in T, or a significant error could be introduced. Round to the correct number of significant figures only at the final answer. On most pocket calculators, the expression $(1/T_2 - 1/T_1)$ is entered as follows: $(T_2)(1/x) - (T_1)(1/x) =$

FOLLOW-UP PROBLEM 16.8 The reaction $2NOCl(g) \longrightarrow 2NO(g) + Cl_2(g)$ has an E_a of 1.00×10^2 kJ/mol and a rate constant of 0.286 L/mol·s at 500. K. What is the rate constant at 490. K?

In this section and the previous two, we discussed a series of experimental and mathematical methods for the study of reaction kinetics. Figure 16.10 is a useful summary of this information. Note that the integrated rate law provides an alternative method for obtaining reaction orders and the rate constant.

SECTION 16.5 SUMMARY

As the Arrhenius equation shows, rate increases with temperature because a temperature rise increases the rate constant. • The activation energy, E_a, the minimum energy needed for a reaction to occur, can be determined graphically from k values at different T values.

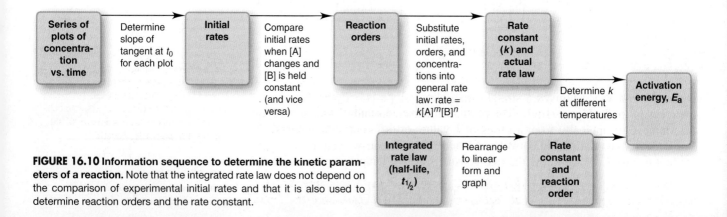

FIGURE 16.10 Information sequence to determine the kinetic parameters of a reaction. Note that the integrated rate law does not depend on the comparison of experimental initial rates and that it is also used to determine reaction orders and the rate constant.

16.6 EXPLAINING THE EFFECTS OF CONCENTRATION AND TEMPERATURE

The Arrhenius equation was developed empirically from the observations of many reactions. The two major models that explain the observed effects of concentration and temperature on reaction rate highlight different aspects of the reaction process but are completely compatible. *Collision theory* views the reaction rate as the result of particles colliding with a certain frequency and minimum energy. *Transition state theory* offers a close-up view of how the energy of a collision converts reactant to product.

Collision Theory: Basis of the Rate Law

The basic tenet of **collision theory** is that reactant particles—atoms, molecules, and ions—must collide with each other to react. Therefore, the number of collisions per unit time provides an upper limit on how fast a reaction can take place. The model restricts itself to simple one-step reactions in which two particles collide and form products: A + B $\longrightarrow$ products. With its emphasis on collisions between three-dimensional particles, this model explains why reactant concentrations are multiplied together in the rate law, how temperature affects the rate, and what influence molecular structure has on rate.

Why Concentrations Are Multiplied in the Rate Law If particles must collide to react, the laws of probability tell us why the rate depends on the *product* of the reactant concentrations, not their sum. Imagine that you have only two particles of A and two of B confined in a reaction vessel. Figure 16.11 shows that four A-B collisions are possible. If you add another particle of A, there can be six A-B collisions (3 × 2), not just five (3 + 2); add another particle of B, and there can be nine A-B collisions (3 × 3), not just six (3 + 3). Thus, collision theory is consistent with the observation that concentrations are *multiplied* in the rate law.

How Temperature Affects Rate: The Importance of Activation Energy Increasing the temperature of a reaction increases the average speed of particles and therefore their collision frequency. But collision frequency cannot be the only factor affecting rate. In fact, *in the vast majority of collisions, the molecules rebound without reacting.*

Arrhenius proposed that every reaction has an *energy threshold* that the colliding molecules must exceed in order to react. (An analogy might be an athlete who must exceed the height of the bar to accomplish a high jump.) This minimum collision energy is the *activation energy (E_a)*, the energy required to activate the molecules into a state from which reactant bonds can change into product bonds. Recall that at any given temperature, molecules have a range of kinetic energies; thus, their collisions have a range of energies as well. According to collision theory, *only those collisions with enough energy to exceed E_a can lead to reaction.*

We noted earlier that many reactions near room temperature approximately double or triple their rates with a 10°C rise in temperature. Is the rate increase due to a higher number of collisions? Actually, this has only a minor effect. Calculations show that a 10°C rise increases the average molecular speed by only 2%. If an increase in speed is the only effect of temperature and if the speed of each colliding molecule increases by 2%, we should observe at most a 4% increase in rate. Far more important is that *the temperature rise enlarges the fraction of collisions with enough energy to exceed the activation energy.* This key point is shown in Figure 16.12 (next page).

At a given temperature, the fraction f of molecular collisions with energy greater than or equal to the activation energy E_a is given by

$$f = e^{-E_a/RT}$$

where e is the base of natural logarithms, T is the absolute temperature, and R is the universal gas constant. [Notice that the right side of this equation is the central

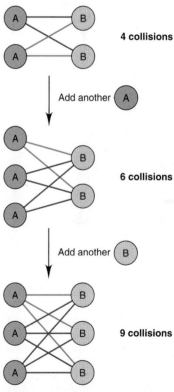

4 collisions

Add another (A)

6 collisions

Add another (B)

9 collisions

FIGURE 16.11 The dependence of number of possible collisions on the product of reactant concentrations. Concentrations are multiplied, not added, in the rate law because the number of possible collisions is the *product*, not the sum, of the numbers of particles present.

Table 16.5 The Effect of E_a and T on the Fraction (f) of Collisions with Sufficient Energy to Allow Reaction	
E_a (kJ/mol)	f (at T = 298 K)
50	1.70×10^{-9}
75	7.03×10^{-14}
100	2.90×10^{-18}
T	f (at E_a = 50 kJ/mol)
25°C (298 K)	1.70×10^{-9}
35°C (308 K)	3.29×10^{-9}
45°C (318 K)	6.12×10^{-9}

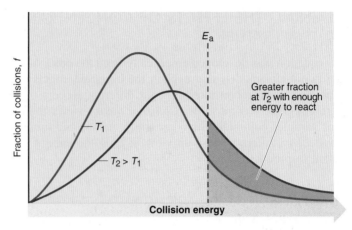

FIGURE 16.12 The effect of temperature on the distribution of collision energies. At the higher temperature, T_2, a larger fraction of collisions occur with enough energy to exceed E_a.

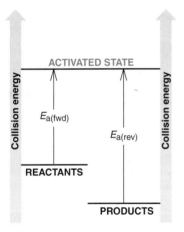

FIGURE 16.13 Energy-level diagram for a reaction. For molecules to react, they must collide with enough energy to reach an activated state. This minimum collision energy is the energy of activation, E_a. A reaction can occur in either direction, so the diagram shows two activation energies. Here, the forward reaction is exothermic and $E_{a(fwd)} < E_{a(rev)}$.

component in the Arrhenius equation (Equation 16.8).] *The magnitudes of both E_a and T affect the fraction of sufficiently energetic collisions.* In the top portion of Table 16.5, you can see the effect on this fraction of increasing E_a at a fixed temperature. Note how much the fraction shrinks with a 25-kJ/mol increase in activation energy. (As the height of the bar is raised, fewer athletes can accomplish the jump.) In the bottom portion of the table, you can see the effect on the fraction of increasing T at a fixed E_a of 50 kJ/mol, a typical value for many reactions. Note that the fraction nearly doubles for a 10°C increase. Doubling the fraction doubles the rate constant, which doubles the reaction rate.

A reversible reaction has two activation energies (Figure 16.13). The activation energy for the forward reaction, $E_{a(fwd)}$, is the energy difference between the activated state and the reactants; the activation energy for the reverse reaction, $E_{a(rev)}$, is the energy difference between the activated state and the products. The figure shows an energy-level diagram for an exothermic reaction, so the products are at a lower energy than the reactants, and $E_{a(fwd)}$ is less than $E_{a(rev)}$.

These observations are consistent with the Arrhenius equation; that is, *the smaller the E_a (or the higher the temperature), the larger the value of k, and the faster the reaction:*

$$\text{Smaller } E_a \text{ (or higher } T) \Longrightarrow \text{larger } k \Longrightarrow \text{increased rate}$$

Conversely, *the larger the E_a (or the lower the temperature), the smaller the value of k, and the slower the reaction:*

$$\text{Larger } E_a \text{ (or lower } T) \Longrightarrow \text{smaller } k \Longrightarrow \text{decreased rate}$$

How Molecular Structure Affects Rate The enormous number of molecular collisions per second is greatly reduced when we count only those with enough energy to react. However, even this tiny fraction of the total collisions does not reveal the true number of **effective collisions,** those that actually lead to product. In addition to colliding with enough energy, *the molecules must collide so that the reacting atoms make contact.* In other words, to be effective, a collision must have enough energy *and* a particular *molecular orientation*.

In the Arrhenius equation, the effect of molecular orientation is contained in the term A:

$$k = Ae^{-E_a/RT}$$

This term is called the **frequency factor,** the product of the collision frequency Z and an *orientation probability factor, p,* which is specific for each reaction: $A = pZ$. The factor p is related to the structural complexity of the colliding particles. You can think of it as the ratio of effectively oriented collisions to all possible collisions. For example, Figure 16.14 shows a few of the possible collision orientations for the following simple gaseous reaction:

$$NO(g) + NO_3(g) \longrightarrow 2NO_2(g)$$

Of the five collisions shown, only one has an orientation in which the N of NO makes contact with an O of NO_3. Actually, the orientation probability factor (*p* value) for this reaction is 0.006: only 6 collisions in every 1000 (1 in 167) have an orientation that can lead to reaction.

Collisions between individual atoms have *p* values near 1: almost no matter how they hit, as long as the collision has enough energy, the particles react. In such cases, the rate constant depends only on the frequency and energy of the collisions. At the other extreme are biochemical reactions, in which the reactants are often two small molecules that can react only when they collide with a specific tiny region of a giant molecule—a protein or nucleic acid. The orientation probability factor for these reactions is often less than 10^{-6}: fewer than one in a million sufficiently energetic collisions leads to product. The fact that countless such biochemical reactions are occurring right now, as you read this sentence, helps make the point that the number of collisions per second is truly astounding.

Transition State Theory: Molecular Nature of the Activated Complex

Collision theory is a simple, easy-to-visualize model, but it provides no insight about why the activation energy is needed and how the activated molecules look. To understand these aspects of the process, we turn to **transition state theory,** which focuses on the high-energy species that forms through an effective collision.

Visualizing the Transition State Recall from our discussion of energy changes (Chapter 6) that the internal energy of a system is the sum of its kinetic and potential energies. When two molecules approach one another, some kinetic energy is converted to potential energy as the electron clouds repel each other. At the moment of a head-on collision, the molecules stop, and their kinetic energy is converted to the potential energy of the collision. *If this potential energy is less than the activation energy, the molecules recoil,* bouncing off each other, somewhat like billiard balls; the molecules zoom apart without reacting.

The tiny fraction of molecules that are oriented effectively *and* moving at the highest speed behave differently. *Their kinetic energy pushes them together with enough force to overcome repulsions and react.* Nuclei in one atom attract electrons in another; atomic orbitals overlap and electron densities shift; some bonds lengthen and weaken while others start to form. At some point during this smooth transformation, what exists is *neither reactant nor product but a transitional species with partial bonds.* This extremely unstable species, which is called the **transition state,** or **activated complex,** exists only at the instant when the reacting system is highest in potential energy. Thus, *the activation energy is the quantity needed to stretch and deform bonds in order to reach the transition state.*

Consider the reaction between methyl bromide and hydroxide ion:

$$CH_3Br + OH^- \longrightarrow CH_3OH + Br^-$$

The electronegative bromine makes the carbon of methyl bromide partially positive. If the reactants are moving toward each other fast enough and are oriented effectively when they collide, the negatively charged oxygen in OH^- approaches the carbon with enough energy to begin forming a C—O bond, which causes the C—Br bond to weaken. In the transition state (Figure 16.15), C is surrounded by five atoms (trigonal bipyramidal), which never occurs in its stable compounds. This high-energy species has three normal C—H bonds and two partial bonds, one from C to O and the other from C to Br. Reaching this transition state is no guarantee that the reaction will proceed to products. A transition state can change

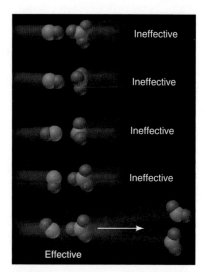

FIGURE 16.14 The importance of molecular orientation to an effective collision. Only one of the five orientations shown for the collision between NO and NO_3 has the correct orientation to lead to product. In the effective orientation, contact occurs between the atoms that will become bonded in the product.

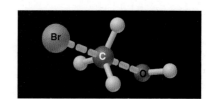

FIGURE 16.15 Nature of the transition state in the reaction between CH_3Br and OH^-. Note the partial (elongated) C—O and C—Br bonds and the trigonal bipyramidal shape of the transition state of this reaction.

in either direction: if the C—O bond continues to shorten and strengthen, products form; however, if the C—Br bond becomes shorter and stronger again, the transition state reverts to reactants.

Depicting the Change with Reaction Energy Diagrams A useful way to depict the events we just described is with a **reaction energy diagram,** which shows the potential energy of the system during the reaction as a smooth curve. Figure 16.16 shows the reaction energy diagram for the reaction of CH_3Br and OH^-, and also includes electron density relief maps, structural formulas, and molecular-scale views at various points during the change.

The horizontal axis, labeled "Reaction progress," indicates that reactants change to products from left to right. This reaction is exothermic, so reactants are higher in energy than products. The diagram also shows activation energies for the forward and reverse reactions; in this case, $E_{a(fwd)}$ is less than $E_{a(rev)}$. This difference, which reflects the change in bond energies, equals the heat of reaction, ΔH_{rxn}:

$$\Delta H_{rxn} = E_{a(fwd)} - E_{a(rev)} \qquad (16.10)$$

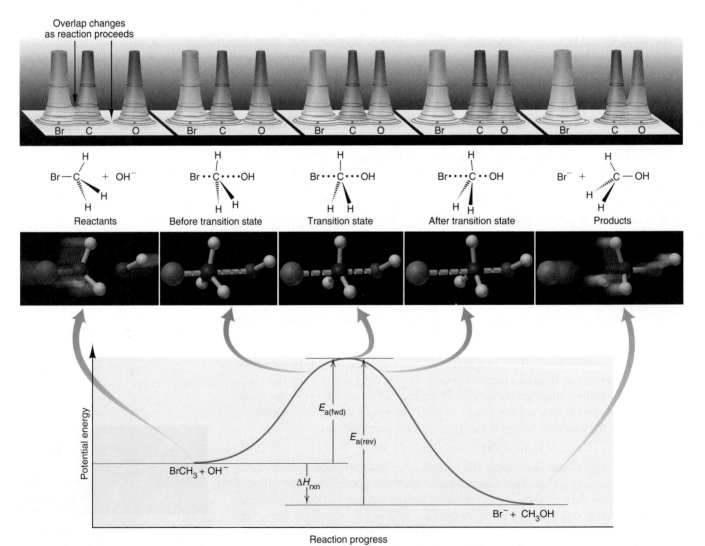

FIGURE 16.16 Reaction energy diagram for the reaction between CH_3Br and OH^-. A plot of potential energy vs. reaction progress shows the relative energy levels of reactants, products, and transition state joined by a curved line, as well as the activation energies of the forward and reverse steps and the heat of reaction. The electron density relief maps, structural formulas, and molecular-scale views depict the change at five points. Note the gradual bond forming and bond breaking as the system goes through the transition state.

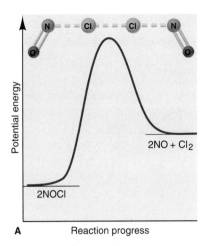

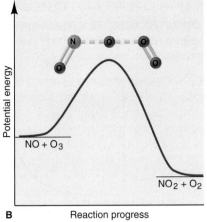

FIGURE 16.17 Reaction energy diagrams and possible transition states for two reactions.
A, 2NOCl(g) $\longrightarrow$ 2NO(g) + Cl$_2$(g) (Despite the formula NOCl, the atom sequence is ClNO.)
B, NO(g) + O$_3$(g) $\longrightarrow$ NO$_2$(g) + O$_2$(g)
Note that reaction A is endothermic and B is exothermic.

Transition state theory proposes that *every reaction (and every step in an overall reaction) goes through its own transition state,* from which it can continue in either direction. We imagine how a transition state might look by examining the reactant and product bonds that change. Figure 16.17 depicts reaction energy diagrams for two simple reactions. Note that the shape of the postulated transition state in each case is based on a specific collision orientation between the atoms that become bonded to form the product.

SAMPLE PROBLEM 16.9 Drawing Reaction Energy Diagrams and Transition States

Problem A key reaction in the upper atmosphere is

$$O_3(g) + O(g) \longrightarrow 2O_2(g)$$

The $E_{a(fwd)}$ is 19 kJ, and the ΔH_{rxn} for the reaction as written is −392 kJ. Draw a reaction energy diagram for this reaction, postulate a transition state, and calculate $E_{a(rev)}$.

Plan The reaction is highly exothermic (ΔH_{rxn} = −392 kJ), so the products are much lower in energy than the reactants. The small $E_{a(fwd)}$ (19 kJ) means the energy of the reactants lies slightly below that of the transition state. We use Equation 16.10 to calculate $E_{a(rev)}$. To postulate the transition state, we sketch the species and note that one of the bonds in O$_3$ weakens, and this partially bonded O begins forming a bond to the separate O atom.

Solution Solving for $E_{a(rev)}$:

$$\Delta H_{rxn} = E_{a(fwd)} - E_{a(rev)}$$

So, $\qquad E_{a(rev)} = E_{a(fwd)} - \Delta H_{rxn} = 19 \text{ kJ} - (-392 \text{ kJ}) = \boxed{411 \text{ kJ}}$

The reaction energy diagram (not drawn to scale), with transition state, is

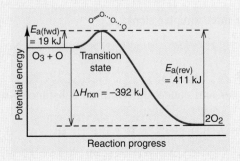

Check Rounding to find $E_{a(\text{rev})}$ gives $\sim\!20 + 390 = 410$.

FOLLOW-UP PROBLEM 16.9 The following reaction energy diagram depicts another key atmospheric reaction. Label the axes, identify $E_{a(\text{fwd})}$, $E_{a(\text{rev})}$, and ΔH_{rxn}, draw and label the transition state, and calculate $E_{a(\text{rev})}$ for the reaction.

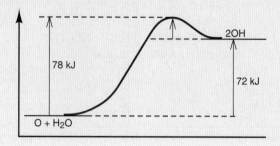

SECTION 16.6 SUMMARY

According to collision theory, reactant particles must collide to react, and the number of collisions depends on the product of the reactant concentrations. • At higher temperatures, more collisions have enough energy to exceed the activation energy (E_a). • The relative E_a values for the forward and the reverse reactions depend on whether the overall reaction is exothermic or endothermic. • Molecules must collide with an effective orientation in order to react, so structural complexity decreases rate. • Transition state theory pictures the kinetic energy of the particles changing to potential energy during a collision. • Given a sufficiently energetic collision and an effective molecular orientation, the reactant species become an unstable transition state, which either forms product(s) or reverts to reactant(s). • A reaction energy diagram depicts the changing energy of the chemical system as it progresses from reactants through transition state(s) to products.

16.7 REACTION MECHANISMS: STEPS IN THE OVERALL REACTION

Imagine trying to figure out how a car works just by examining the body, wheels, and dashboard. It can't be done—you need to look under the hood and inside the engine to see how the parts fit together and function. Similarly, because our main purpose is to know how a reaction works *at the molecular level*, examining the overall balanced equation is not much help—we must "look under the yield arrow and inside the reaction" to see how reactants change into products.

When we do so, we find that most reactions occur through a **reaction mechanism,** a sequence of single reaction steps that sum to the overall reaction. For example, a possible mechanism for the overall reaction

$$2A + B \longrightarrow E + F$$

might involve these three simpler steps:

(1) $A + B \longrightarrow C$
(2) $C + A \longrightarrow D$
(3) $D \longrightarrow E + F$

Adding them together and canceling common substances, we obtain the overall equation:

$$A + B + \cancel{C} + A + \cancel{D} \longrightarrow \cancel{C} + \cancel{D} + E + F \quad \text{or} \quad 2A + B \longrightarrow E + F$$

Note what happens to C and to D in this mechanism. C is a product in step 1 and a reactant in step 2, and D is a product in 2 and a reactant in 3. Each functions as a **reaction intermediate,** a substance that is formed and used up during the overall reaction. Reaction intermediates do not appear in the overall balanced equation but are absolutely essential for the reaction to occur. They are usually unstable relative to the reactants and products but are far more stable than transition states (activated complexes). Reaction intermediates are molecules with normal bonds and are sometimes stable enough to be isolated.

Chemists *propose* a reaction mechanism to explain how a particular reaction might occur, and then they *test* the mechanism. This section focuses on the nature of the individual steps and how they fit together to give a rate law consistent with experimental results.

Elementary Reactions and Molecularity

The individual steps, which together make up a proposed reaction mechanism, are called **elementary reactions** (or **elementary steps**). Each describes a *single molecular event,* such as one particle decomposing or two particles colliding and combining. *An elementary step is **not** made up of simpler steps.*

An elementary step is characterized by its **molecularity,** the number of *reactant* particles involved in the step. Consider the mechanism for the breakdown of ozone in the stratosphere. The overall reaction is

$$2O_3(g) \longrightarrow 3O_2(g)$$

A two-step mechanism has been proposed for this reaction. Notice that the two steps sum to the overall reaction. The first elementary step is a **unimolecular reaction,** one that involves the decomposition or rearrangement of a single particle:

(1) $O_3(g) \longrightarrow O_2(g) + O(g)$

The second step is a **bimolecular reaction,** one in which two particles react:

(2) $O_3(g) + O(g) \longrightarrow 2O_2(g)$

Some *termolecular* elementary steps occur, but they are extremely rare because the probability of three particles colliding simultaneously with enough energy and with an effective orientation is very small. Higher molecularities are not known. Unless evidence exists to the contrary, it makes good chemical sense to propose only unimolecular or bimolecular reactions as the elementary steps in a reaction mechanism.

The rate law for an elementary reaction, unlike that for an overall reaction, *can* be deduced from the reaction stoichiometry. An elementary reaction occurs in one step, so its rate must be proportional to the product of the reactant concentrations. Therefore, *we use the equation coefficients as the reaction orders in the rate law for an elementary step; that is, reaction order equals molecularity* (Table 16.6). Remember that this statement holds *only* when we know that the reaction is elementary; you've already seen that for an overall reaction, the reaction orders must be determined experimentally.

Table 16.6 **Rate Laws for General Elementary Steps**		
Elementary Step	**Molecularity**	**Rate Law**
A $\longrightarrow$ product	Unimolecular	Rate = $k[A]$
2A $\longrightarrow$ product	Bimolecular	Rate = $k[A]^2$
A + B $\longrightarrow$ product	Bimolecular	Rate = $k[A][B]$
2A + B $\longrightarrow$ product	Termolecular	Rate = $k[A]^2[B]$

SAMPLE PROBLEM 16.10   Determining Molecularity and Rate Laws
for Elementary Steps

Problem The following two reactions are proposed as elementary steps in the mechanism
for an overall reaction:
(1) $NO_2Cl(g) \longrightarrow NO_2(g) + Cl(g)$
(2) $NO_2Cl(g) + Cl(g) \longrightarrow NO_2(g) + Cl_2(g)$
(a) Write the overall balanced equation.
(b) Determine the molecularity of each step.
(c) Write the rate law for each step.
Plan We find the overall equation from the sum of the elementary steps. The molecularity of each step equals the total number of reactant particles. We write the rate law for
each step using the molecularities as reaction orders.
Solution (a) Writing the overall balanced equation:

$$NO_2Cl(g) \longrightarrow NO_2(g) + Cl(g)$$
$$\underline{NO_2Cl(g) + Cl(g) \longrightarrow NO_2(g) + Cl_2(g)}$$
$$NO_2Cl(g) + NO_2Cl(g) + \cancel{Cl(g)} \longrightarrow NO_2(g) + \cancel{Cl(g)} + NO_2(g) + Cl_2(g)$$
$$2NO_2Cl(g) \longrightarrow 2NO_2(g) + Cl_2(g)$$

(b) Determining the molecularity of each step: The first elementary step has only one reactant, NO_2Cl, so it is unimolecular. The second elementary step has two reactants, NO_2Cl
and Cl, so it is bimolecular.
(c) Writing rate laws for the elementary reactions:
(1) $Rate_1 = k_1[NO_2Cl]$
(2) $Rate_2 = k_2[NO_2Cl][Cl]$
Check In part (a), be sure the equation is balanced; in part (c), be sure the substances in
brackets are the reactants of each elementary step.

FOLLOW-UP PROBLEM 16.10 The following elementary steps constitute a proposed
mechanism for a reaction:
(1) $2NO(g) \longrightarrow N_2O_2(g)$
(2) $2H_2(g) \longrightarrow 4H(g)$
(3) $N_2O_2(g) + H(g) \longrightarrow N_2O(g) + HO(g)$
(4) $2HO(g) + 2H(g) \longrightarrow 2H_2O(g)$
(5) $H(g) + N_2O(g) \longrightarrow HO(g) + N_2(g)$
(a) Write the balanced equation for the overall reaction.
(b) Determine the molecularity of each step.
(c) Write the rate law for each step.

The Rate-Determining Step of a Reaction Mechanism

All the elementary steps in a mechanism do not have the same rate. Usually, one
step is so much slower than the others that it limits how fast the overall reaction
proceeds. This step is called the **rate-determining step** (or **rate-limiting step**).

THINK OF IT THIS WAY
A Rate-Determining Step
for Traffic Flow

As an analogy for the rate-determining step, imagine driving home on a six-lane
avenue that passes over a bridge. Traffic is flowing smoothly in your direction,
when an accident in the right lane slows everyone down just a bit. Then, the flow
picks up again, until the road narrows to one lane for the bridge's tollbooth. Traffic slows so much that it takes longer to get over the bridge than the rest of the
trip combined. The bottleneck over the bridge, rather than the time driving on the
street and even the accident delay, determines how long the overall trip home takes.

*Because the rate-determining step limits the rate of the overall reaction, its
rate law represents the rate law for the overall reaction.* Consider the reaction
between nitrogen dioxide and carbon monoxide:

$$NO_2(g) + CO(g) \longrightarrow NO(g) + CO_2(g)$$

If the overall reaction were an elementary reaction—that is, if the mechanism consisted of only one step—we could immediately write the overall rate law as

$$\text{Rate} = k[NO_2][CO]$$

However, as you saw in Sample Problem 16.3, experiment shows that the actual rate law is

$$\text{Rate} = k[NO_2]^2$$

Therefore, we know immediately that the reaction shown cannot be elementary.

A proposed two-step mechanism is

(1) $NO_2(g) + NO_2(g) \longrightarrow NO_3(g) + NO(g)$ [slow; rate determining]
(2) $NO_3(g) + CO(g) \longrightarrow NO_2(g) + CO_2(g)$ [fast]

Note that NO_3 functions as a reaction intermediate in the mechanism. Rate laws for these elementary steps are

(1) $\text{Rate}_1 = k_1[NO_2][NO_2] = k_1[NO_2]^2$
(2) $\text{Rate}_2 = k_2[NO_3][CO]$

Note that if $k_1 = k$, *the rate law for the rate-determining step (step 1) is identical to the experimental rate law.* Because the first step is slow, $[NO_3]$ is very low; thus, the fast second step cannot increase the overall rate, and the reaction takes essentially as long as the first step. Here you can see one reason a reactant (in this case, CO) has a reaction order of zero: it takes part in the reaction only *after* the rate-determining step.

Correlating the Mechanism with the Rate Law

Conjuring up a reasonable reaction mechanism can be a classic example of the use of the scientific method. We use observations and data from rate experiments to hypothesize what the individual steps might be and then test our hypothesis by gathering further evidence. If the evidence supports it, we continue to apply that mechanism; if not, we propose a new one. However, *we can never prove, just from data, that a particular mechanism represents the actual chemical change, only that it is consistent with it.*

Regardless of the elementary steps proposed for a mechanism, they must meet three criteria:

1. *The elementary steps must add up to the overall balanced equation.* We cannot wind up with more (or fewer) reactants or products than are present in the balanced equation.
2. *The elementary steps must be physically reasonable.* As we noted, most steps should involve one reactant particle (unimolecular) or two (bimolecular). Steps with three reactant particles (termolecular) are very unlikely.
3. *The mechanism must correlate with the rate law.* Most importantly, a mechanism must support the experimental facts shown by the rate law, not the other way around.

Let's see how the mechanisms of several reactions conform to these criteria and how the elementary steps fit together.

Mechanisms with a Slow Initial Step We've already seen one mechanism with a rate-determining first step—that for the reaction of NO_2 and CO. Another example is the reaction between nitrogen dioxide and fluorine gas:

$$2NO_2(g) + F_2(g) \longrightarrow 2NO_2F(g)$$

The experimental rate law is first order in NO_2 and in F_2:

$$\text{Rate} = k[NO_2][F_2]$$

The accepted mechanism for the reaction is

(1) $NO_2(g) + F_2(g) \longrightarrow NO_2F(g) + F(g)$ [slow; rate determining]
(2) $NO_2(g) + F(g) \longrightarrow NO_2F(g)$ [fast]

FIGURE 16.18 Reaction energy diagram for the two-step reaction of NO_2 and F_2. Each step in the mechanism has its own transition state. The proposed transition state is shown for step 1. Reactants for the second step are the F atom intermediate and the second molecule of NO_2. Note that the first step is slower (higher E_a). The overall reaction is exothermic ($\Delta H_{rxn} < 0$).

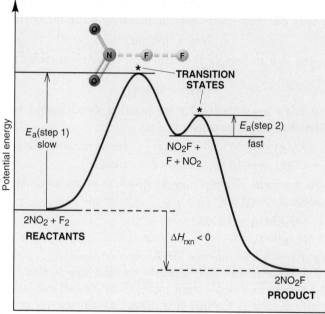

Molecules of reactant and product appear in both elementary steps. The free fluorine atom is a reaction intermediate.

Does this mechanism meet the three crucial criteria?

1. The elementary reactions sum to the balanced equation:

$$NO_2(g) + NO_2(g) + F_2(g) + \cancel{F(g)} \longrightarrow NO_2F(g) + NO_2F(g) + \cancel{F(g)}$$

or

$$2NO_2(g) + F_2(g) \longrightarrow 2NO_2F(g)$$

2. Both steps are bimolecular, so they are chemically reasonable.
3. The mechanism gives the rate law for the overall equation. To show this, we write the rate laws for the elementary steps:

    (1) $\text{Rate}_1 = k_1[NO_2][F_2]$
    (2) $\text{Rate}_2 = k_2[NO_2][F]$

Step 1 is the rate-determining step and therefore gives the overall rate law, with $k_1 = k$. Because the second molecule of NO_2 appears in the step that follows the rate-determining step, it does not appear in the overall rate law. Thus, we see that *the overall rate law includes only species active in the reaction up to and including those in the rate-determining step.* This point was also illustrated by the mechanism for NO_2 and CO shown earlier. Carbon monoxide was absent from the overall rate law because it appeared *after* the rate-determining step.

Figure 16.18 is a reaction energy diagram for the reaction of NO_2 and F_2. Note that

- *Each step in the mechanism has its own transition state.* (Note that only one molecule of NO_2 reacts in step 1, and only the first transition state is depicted.)
- The F atom intermediate is a reactive, unstable species (as you know from halogen chemistry), so it is higher in energy than the reactants or product.
- The first step is slower (rate limiting), so its activation energy is *larger* than that of the second step.
- The overall reaction is exothermic, so the product is lower in energy than the reactants.

Mechanisms with a Fast Initial Step If the rate-determining step in a mechanism is *not* the initial step, it acts as a bottleneck later in the reaction sequence. As a result, the product of a fast initial step builds up and starts reverting to reactant, while waiting for the slow step to remove it. With time, the product of the initial step is changing back to reactant as fast as it is forming. In other words, the *fast initial step reaches equilibrium*. As you'll see, this situation allows us to fit the mechanism to the overall rate law.

Consider once again the oxidation of nitrogen monoxide:

$$2NO(g) + O_2(g) \longrightarrow 2NO_2(g)$$

The experimentally determined rate law is

$$\text{Rate} = k[NO]^2[O_2]$$

and a proposed mechanism is

(1) $NO(g) + O_2(g) \rightleftharpoons NO_3(g)$ [fast, reversible]
(2) $NO_3(g) + NO(g) \longrightarrow 2NO_2(g)$ [slow; rate determining]

Note that, with cancellation of the reaction intermediate NO_3, the first criterion is met because the sum of the steps gives the overall equation. Also note that the second criterion is met because both steps are bimolecular.

To meet the third criterion (that the mechanism conforms to the overall rate law), we first write rate laws for the elementary steps:

(1) $\text{Rate}_{1(\text{fwd})} = k_1[NO][O_2]$
      $\text{Rate}_{1(\text{rev})} = k_{-1}[NO_3]$

where k_{-1} is the rate constant for the reverse reaction.

(2) $\text{Rate}_2 = k_2[NO_3][NO]$

Now we must show that the rate law for the rate-determining step (step 2) gives the overall rate law. As written, it does not, because it contains the intermediate NO_3, and *an overall rate law can include only reactants (and products)*. Therefore, we must eliminate $[NO_3]$ from the step 2 rate law. To do so, we express $[NO_3]$ in terms of reactants. Step 1 reaches equilibrium when the forward and reverse rates are equal:

$$\text{Rate}_{1(\text{fwd})} = \text{Rate}_{1(\text{rev})} \quad \text{or} \quad k_1[NO][O_2] = k_{-1}[NO_3]$$

To express $[NO_3]$ in terms of reactants, we isolate it algebraically:

$$[NO_3] = \frac{k_1}{k_{-1}}[NO][O_2]$$

Then, substituting for $[NO_3]$ in the rate law for step 2, we obtain

$$\text{Rate}_2 = k_2[NO_3][NO] = k_2\left(\frac{k_1}{k_{-1}}[NO][O_2]\right)[NO] = \frac{k_2 k_1}{k_{-1}}[NO]^2[O_2]$$

This rate law is identical to the overall rate law, with $k = \dfrac{k_2 k_1}{k_{-1}}$.

Thus, to test the validity of a mechanism with a fast initial, reversible step:

1. Write rate laws for both directions of the fast step and for the slow step.
2. Show the slow step's rate law is equivalent to the overall rate law, by *expressing [intermediate] in terms of [reactant]*: set the forward rate law of the fast, reversible step equal to the reverse rate law, and solve for [intermediate].
3. Substitute the expression for [intermediate] into the rate law for the slow step to obtain the overall rate law.

Several end-of-chapter problems, including 16.61 and 16.62, provide additional examples of this approach.

SECTION 16.7 SUMMARY

The mechanisms of most common reactions consist of two or more elementary steps, reactions that occur in one step and depict a single chemical change. • The molecularity of an elementary step equals the number of reactant particles and is the same as the reaction order of its rate law. Unimolecular and bimolecular steps are common. • The rate-determining, or rate-limiting (slowest), step determines how fast the overall reaction occurs, and its rate law represents the overall rate law. • Reaction intermediates are species that form in one step and react in a later one. • The steps in a proposed mechanism must add up to the overall reaction, be physically reasonable, and conform to the overall rate law. If a fast step precedes a slow step, the fast step reaches equilibrium, and the concentrations of intermediates in the rate law of the slow step must be expressed in terms of reactants.

16.8 CATALYSIS: SPEEDING UP A CHEMICAL REACTION

There are many situations in which the rate of a reaction must be increased for it to be useful. In an industrial process, for example, a higher rate often determines whether a new product can be made economically. Sometimes, we can speed up a reaction sufficiently with a higher temperature, but energy is costly and many substances are heat sensitive and easily decomposed. Alternatively, we can often employ a **catalyst,** a substance that increases the rate *without* being consumed in the reaction. Because catalysts are not consumed, only very small, nonstoichiometric quantities are generally required. Nevertheless, these substances are employed in so many important processes that several million tons of industrial catalysts are produced annually in the United States alone! Nature is the master designer and user of catalysts. Even the simplest bacterium employs thousands of biological catalysts, known as *enzymes,* to speed up its cellular reactions. Every organism relies on enzymes to sustain life.

Each catalyst has its own specific way of functioning, but in general, *a catalyst causes a lower activation energy, which in turn makes the rate constant larger and the rate higher.* Two important points stand out in Figure 16.19:

• A catalyst speeds up the forward *and* reverse reactions. A reaction with a catalyst *does not yield more product* than one without a catalyst, but it yields the product *more quickly*.
• A catalyst causes a *lower activation energy* by providing a *different mechanism* for the reaction, and thus a new, lower energy pathway.

FIGURE 16.19 Reaction energy diagram for a catalyzed and an uncatalyzed process. A catalyst speeds a reaction by providing a new, lower energy pathway, in this case by replacing the one-step mechanism with a two-step mechanism. Both forward and reverse rates are increased to the same extent, so *a catalyst does not affect the overall reaction yield.* (The only activation energy shown for the catalyzed reaction is the larger one for the forward direction.)

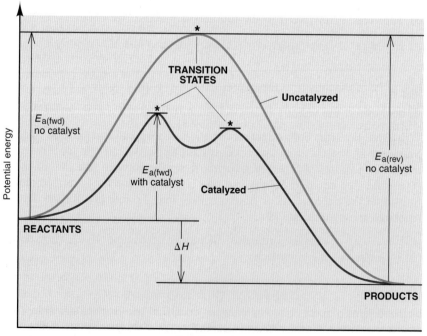

Consider a general *uncatalyzed* reaction that proceeds by a one-step mechanism involving a bimolecular collision:

$$A + B \longrightarrow product \qquad [slower]$$

In the *catalyzed* reaction, a reactant molecule interacts with the catalyst, so the mechanism might involve a two-step pathway:

$$A + catalyst \longrightarrow C \qquad [faster]$$
$$C + B \longrightarrow product + catalyst \qquad [faster]$$

Note that *the catalyst is not consumed,* as its definition requires. Rather, it is used and then regenerated, and the activation energies of both steps are lower than the activation energy of the uncatalyzed pathway.

Chemists recognize two general categories of catalyst—homogeneous and heterogeneous—based on whether the catalyst occurs in the same phase as the reactant and product.

Homogeneous Catalysis

A **homogeneous catalyst** exists in solution with the reaction mixture. All homogeneous catalysts are gases, liquids, or soluble solids.

A thoroughly studied example of homogeneous catalysis is the hydrolysis of an organic ester (RCOOR′), a reaction introduced in Section 15.4:

$$R-\overset{O}{\underset{\|}{C}}-O-R' + H_2O \rightleftharpoons R-\overset{O}{\underset{\|}{C}}-OH + R'-OH$$

Here R and R′ are hydrocarbon groups, $R-\overset{O}{\underset{\|}{C}}-OH$ is a carboxylic acid, and R′—OH is an alcohol. The reaction rate is low at room temperature but can be increased greatly by adding a small amount of strong acid, which provides H^+ ion, the catalyst in the reaction; strong bases, which supply OH^- ions, also speed ester hydrolysis, but by a slightly different mechanism.

In the first step of the acid-catalyzed reaction (Figure 16.20), the H^+ of a hydronium ion forms a bond to the double-bonded O atom. From the resonance forms, we see that the bonding of H^+ then makes the C atom more positive, which *increases its attraction* for the partially negative O atom of water. In effect, H^+ increases the likelihood that the bonding of water, which is the rate-determining step, will take place. Several steps later, a water molecule, acting as a base, removes the H^+ and returns it to solution. Thus, H^+ acts as a catalyst because it speeds up the reaction but is not itself consumed: it is used up in one step and re-formed in another.

Many digestive enzymes, which catalyze the hydrolysis of proteins, fats, and carbohydrates during the digestion of foods, employ very similar mechanisms. The difference is that the acids or bases that speed these reactions are not the strong inorganic reagents used in the lab, but rather specific amino-acid side chains of the enzymes that release or abstract H^+ ions.

Heterogeneous Catalysis

A **heterogeneous catalyst** speeds up a reaction that occurs in a separate phase. The catalyst is most often a solid interacting with gaseous or liquid reactants. Because reaction occurs on the solid's surface, heterogeneous catalysts usually have enormous surface areas for contact, between 1 and 500 m^2/g. Interestingly, many reactions that occur on a metal surface, such as the decomposition of HI on gold and the decomposition of N_2O on platinum, are zero order because the rate-determining step occurs on the surface itself. Thus, despite an enormous surface area, once the reactant gas covers the surface, increasing the reactant concentration cannot increase the rate.

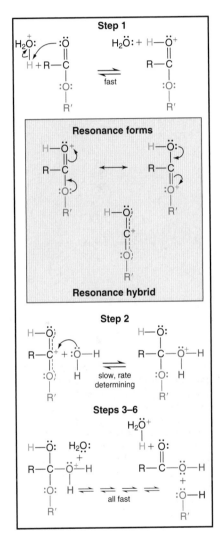

FIGURE 16.20 Mechanism for the catalyzed hydrolysis of an organic ester. In step 1, the catalytic H^+ ion binds to the electron-rich oxygen. The resonance hybrid of this product *(see gray panel)* shows the C atom is more positive than it would ordinarily be. The enhanced charge on C attracts the partially negative O of water more strongly, increasing the fraction of effective collisions and thus speeding up step 2, the rate-determining step. Loss of R′OH and removal of H^+ by water occur in a final series of fast steps.

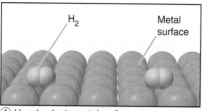

① H_2 adsorbs to metal surface

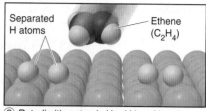

② Rate-limiting step is H—H bond breakage.

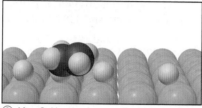

③ After C_2H_4 adsorbs, one C—H forms.

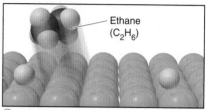

④ Another C—H bond forms; C_2H_6 leaves surface.

FIGURE 16.21 The metal-catalyzed hydrogenation of ethylene (ethene).

One of the most important examples of heterogeneous catalysis is the addition of H_2 to the C=C bonds of organic compounds to form C—C bonds. The petroleum, plastics, and food industries frequently use catalytic **hydrogenation.** The conversion of vegetable oil into margarine is one example.

The simplest hydrogenation converts ethylene (ethene) to ethane:

$$H_2C=CH_2(g) + H_2(g) \longrightarrow H_3C—CH_3(g)$$

In the absence of a catalyst, the reaction occurs very slowly. At high H_2 pressure in the presence of finely divided Ni, Pd, or Pt, the reaction becomes rapid even at ordinary temperatures. These Group 8B(10) metals catalyze by *chemically adsorbing the reactants onto their surface* (Figure 16.21). The H_2 lands and splits into separate H atoms chemically bound to the solid catalyst's metal atoms (catM):

$$H—H(g) + 2catM(s) \longrightarrow 2catM—H \text{ (H atoms bound to metal surface)}$$

Then, C_2H_4 adsorbs and reacts with two H atoms, one at a time, to form C_2H_6. The H—H bond breakage is the rate-determining step in the overall process, and interaction with the catalyst's surface provides the low-E_a step as part of an alternative reaction mechanism.

Catalysis in Nature

Besides the industrial examples we just discussed, many catalytic processes occur in natural settings as well, and a brief description of two important systems follows. The first concerns the remarkable abilities of catalysts inside you, and the second focuses on how catalysis operates in the stratosphere.

Cellular Catalysis: The Function of Enzymes Within every living cell, thousands of individual reactions occur in dilute solution at ordinary temperatures and pressures. The rates of these reactions respond smoothly to various factors, including concentration changes, signals from other cells, and environmental stresses. Virtually every cell reaction is catalyzed by its own specific **enzyme,** a protein whose complex three-dimensional shape (Section 15.6)—and thus its function—has been perfected through natural selection.

Every enzyme has an **active site,** a small region whose shape results from those of the side chains (R groups) of the amino acids that make it up. When reactant molecules, called the *substrates,* bind to an active site, usually through *intermolecular forces,* the chemical change begins. With molar masses ranging from 15,000 to 1,000,000 g/mol, most enzymes are enormous relative to their substrates, and they are often embedded within membranes. Thus, like a heterogeneous catalyst, an enzyme provides a surface on which a substrate is immobilized temporarily, waiting for another reactant to land nearby. Like a homogeneous catalyst, the active-site R groups interact directly with the substrates in multistep sequences.

Enzymes are incredibly *efficient* catalysts. Consider the hydrolysis of urea, a key component in amino-acid metabolism:

$$(NH_2)_2C{=}O(aq) + 2H_2O(l) + H^+(aq) \longrightarrow 2NH_4^+(aq) + HCO_3^-(aq)$$

In water at room temperature, the rate constant for the uncatalyzed reaction is $3{\times}10^{-10}$ s^{-1}. Under the same conditions in the presence of the enzyme urease (pronounced "*yur*-ee-ase"), the rate constant increases 10^{14}-fold, to $3{\times}10^4$ s^{-1}! Enzymes are also extremely *specific:* urease catalyzes *only* this hydrolysis reaction, and no other enzyme does so.

There are two main models of enzyme action. In the *lock-and-key model,* when the "key" (substrate) fits the "lock" (active site), the chemical change begins. However, experiments show that, in many cases, the enzyme changes shape when the substrate lands at its active site. Thus, rather than a rigidly shaped lock in which a particular key fits, the *induced-fit model* pictures a "hand" (substrate) entering a "glove" (active site), causing it to attain its functional shape.

Enzymes act through a variety of catalytic mechanisms. In some cases, the active-site R groups bring the reacting atoms of the substrates closer together. In other cases, the R groups stretch the substrate bond that is to be broken. Some R groups provide an H$^+$ ion that increases the speed of a rate-determining step; others remove an H$^+$ ion at a critical step. Regardless of their specific mode of action, *all enzymes function by binding to the reaction's transition state and thus stabilizing it.* In this way, the enzyme lowers the activation energy, which increases the reaction rate.

Atmospheric Catalysis: Depletion of the Ozone Layer Both homogeneous and heterogeneous catalysis play key roles in the depletion of ozone from the stratosphere. At Earth's surface, ozone is an air pollutant, contributing to smog and other problems. In the stratosphere, however, a natural layer of ozone absorbs UV radiation from the Sun. If this radiation reaches the surface, it can break bonds in DNA, promote skin cancer, and damage simple life forms at the base of the food chain.

Stratospheric ozone concentrations are maintained naturally by a simple sequence of reactions:

$$O_2 \xrightarrow{\text{UV}} 2O$$
$$O + O_2 \longrightarrow O_3 \qquad \text{[ozone formation]}$$
$$O + O_3 \longrightarrow 2O_2 \qquad \text{[ozone breakdown]}$$

In 1995, Paul J. Crutzen, Mario J. Molina, and F. Sherwood Rowland received the Nobel Prize in chemistry for showing that chlorofluorocarbons (CFCs), used as aerosol propellants and air-conditioning coolants, were disrupting this sequence by catalyzing the breakdown reaction. CFCs are unreactive in the lower atmosphere, but slowly rise to the stratosphere, where UV radiation cleaves them:

$$CF_2Cl_2 \xrightarrow{\text{UV}} CF_2Cl\cdot + Cl\cdot$$

(The dots are unpaired electrons resulting from bond cleavage.) Like many species with unpaired electrons (free radicals), atomic Cl is very reactive. It reacts with ozone to produce chlorine monoxide (ClO·), which then reacts to regenerate Cl atoms:

$$O_3 + Cl\cdot \longrightarrow ClO\cdot + O_2$$
$$ClO\cdot + O \longrightarrow \cdot Cl + O_2$$

The sum of these steps is the ozone breakdown reaction:

$$O_3 + \cdot Cl + \cdot ClO + O \longrightarrow \cdot ClO + O_2 + \cdot Cl + O_2$$

or

$$O_3 + O \longrightarrow 2O_2$$

Thus, the Cl atom is a homogeneous catalyst: it exists in the same phase as the reactants, speeds the reaction by allowing a different mechanism, and is regenerated. During its stratospheric half-life of about 2 years, each Cl atom speeds the breakdown of about 100,000 ozone molecules.

High levels of chlorine monoxide over Antarctica have given rise to an *ozone hole*, an area of the stratosphere showing a severe reduction of ozone. The hole enlarges by heterogeneous catalysis, as stratospheric clouds and dust from volcanic activity provide a surface that speeds formation of Cl atoms by other mechanisms. Despite international agreements that will phase out production of CFCs by 2010, and similar compounds by 2040, full recovery of the ozone layer is likely to take the rest of this century! The good news is that halogen levels in the lower atmosphere have already begun to fall.

SECTION 16.8 SUMMARY

A catalyst is a substance that increases the rate of a reaction without being consumed. It accomplishes this by providing an alternative mechanism with a lower activation energy. • Homogeneous catalysts function in the same phase as the reactants. Heterogeneous catalysts act in a different phase from the reactants. • The hydrogenation of carbon-carbon double bonds takes place on a solid catalyst, which speeds the breakage of the H—H bond in H_2. • Enzymes are biological catalysts with spectacular efficiency and specificity. • Chlorine atoms derived from CFC molecules catalyze the breakdown of stratospheric ozone.

CHAPTER REVIEW GUIDE

The following sections provide many aids to help you study this chapter. (Numbers in parentheses refer to pages, unless noted otherwise.)

● **LEARNING OBJECTIVES** *These are concepts and skills to know after studying this chapter.*

Related section (§), sample problem (SP), and end-of-chapter problem (EP) numbers are listed in parentheses.

1. Explain why reaction rate depends on concentration, physical state, and temperature (§ 16.1) (EPs 16.1–16.6)
2. Understand how reaction rate is expressed in terms of changing reactant and product concentrations over time, and distinguish among average, instantaneous, and initial rates (§ 16.2) (SP 16.1) (EPs 16.7–16.19)
3. Describe the information needed to determine the rate law, and explain how to calculate reaction orders and rate constant (§ 16.3) (SPs 16.2–16.4) (EPs 16.20–16.28)
4. Understand how to use integrated rate laws to find concentration at a given time (or vice versa) and reaction order, and explain the meaning of half-life (§ 16.4) (SPs 16.5–16.7) (EPs 16.29–16.34)

5. Explain the importance of activation energy and the effect of temperature on the rate constant (Arrhenius equation) (§ 16.5) (SP 16.8) (EPs 16.35–16.40)
6. Understand collision theory (why concentrations are multiplied, how temperature affects the fraction of collisions exceeding E_a, and how rate depends on the number of effective collisions) and transition state theory (how E_a is used to form the transition state and how a reaction energy diagram depicts the progress of a reaction) (§ 16.6) (SP 16.9) (EPs 16.41–16.52)
7. Understand elementary steps and molecularity, and be able to construct a valid reaction mechanism with either a slow or a fast initial step (§ 16.7) (SP 16.10) (EPs 16.53–16.64)
8. Explain how a catalyst speeds a reaction by lowering E_a, and distinguish between homogeneous and heterogeneous catalysis (§ 16.8) (EPs 16.65, 16.66)

● **KEY TERMS** *These important terms appear in boldface·in the chapter and are defined again in the Glossary.*

chemical kinetics (508)	**Section 16.3**	half-life ($t_{1/2}$) (523)	effective collision (530)
Section 16.2	rate law (rate equation) (514)	**Section 16.5**	frequency factor (530)
reaction rate (510)	rate constant (514)	Arrhenius equation (527)	transition state theory (531)
average rate (511)	reaction orders (514)	activation energy (E_a) (527)	transition state (activated
instantaneous rate (511)	**Section 16.4**	**Section 16.6**	complex) (531)
initial rate (512)	integrated rate law (520)	collision theory (529)	reaction energy diagram (532)

Section 16.7

reaction mechanism (534)
reaction intermediate (535)
elementary reaction
  (elementary step) (535)

molecularity (535)
unimolecular reaction (535)
bimolecular reaction (535)
rate-determining (rate-
  limiting) step (536)

Section 16.8

catalyst (540)
homogeneous catalyst (541)
heterogeneous catalyst (541)

hydrogenation (542)
enzyme (542)
active site (542)

• **KEY EQUATIONS AND RELATIONSHIPS** *Numbered and screened concepts are listed for you to refer to or memorize.*

16.1 Expressing reaction rate in terms of reactant A (510):

$$\text{Rate} = -\frac{\Delta[A]}{\Delta t}$$

16.2 Expressing the rate of a general reaction (512):

$$a\text{A} + b\text{B} \longrightarrow c\text{C} + d\text{D}$$

$$\text{Rate} = -\frac{1}{a}\frac{\Delta[A]}{\Delta t} = -\frac{1}{b}\frac{\Delta[B]}{\Delta t} = \frac{1}{c}\frac{\Delta[C]}{\Delta t} = \frac{1}{d}\frac{\Delta[D]}{\Delta t}$$

16.3 Writing a general rate law (for a case not involving products) (514):

$$\text{Rate} = k[A]^m[B]^n \cdots$$

16.4 Calculating the time to reach a given [A] in a first-order reaction (rate = k[A]) (521):

$$\ln\frac{[A]_0}{[A]_t} = kt$$

16.5 Calculating the time to reach a given [A] in a simple second-order reaction (rate = $k[A]^2$) (521):

$$\frac{1}{[A]_t} - \frac{1}{[A]_0} = kt$$

16.6 Calculating the time to reach a given [A] in a zero-order reaction (rate = k) (521):

$$[A]_t - [A]_0 = -kt$$

16.7 Finding the half-life of a first-order process (524):

$$t_{1/2} = \frac{\ln 2}{k} = \frac{0.693}{k}$$

16.8 Relating the rate constant to the temperature (Arrhenius equation) (527):

$$k = Ae^{-E_a/RT}$$

16.9 Calculating the activation energy (rearranged form of Arrhenius equation) (528):

$$\ln\frac{k_2}{k_1} = -\frac{E_a}{R}\left(\frac{1}{T_2} - \frac{1}{T_1}\right)$$

16.10 Relating the heat of reaction to the forward and reverse activation energies (532):

$$\Delta H_{rxn} = E_{a(fwd)} - E_{a(rev)}$$

• **BRIEF SOLUTIONS TO FOLLOW-UP PROBLEMS** *Compare your own solutions to these calculation steps and answers.*

16.1 (a) $4NO(g) + O_2(g) \longrightarrow 2N_2O_3(g)$;

$$\text{rate} = -\frac{\Delta[O_2]}{\Delta t} = -\frac{1}{4}\frac{\Delta[NO]}{\Delta t} = \frac{1}{2}\frac{\Delta[N_2O_3]}{\Delta t}$$

(b) $-\dfrac{\Delta[O_2]}{\Delta t} = -\dfrac{1}{4}\dfrac{\Delta[NO]}{\Delta t} = -\dfrac{1}{4}(-1.60\times10^{-4}\ \text{mol/L·s})$

$\qquad = 4.00\times10^{-5}\ \text{mol/L·s}$

16.2 First order in Br^-, first order in BrO_3^-, second order in H^+, fourth order overall.

16.3 Rate = $k[H_2]^m[I_2]^n$. From experiments 1 and 3, $m = 1$. From experiments 2 and 4, $n = 1$.
Therefore, rate = $k[H_2][I_2]$; second order overall.

16.4 (a) The rate law shows the reaction is zero order in Y, so the rate is not affected by doubling Y: rate of Expt 2 = $0.25\times10^{-5}\ \text{mol/L·s}$

(b) The rate of Expt 3 is four times that of Expt 1, so [X] doubles.

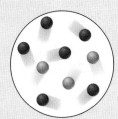

16.5 $1/[HI]_1 - 1/[HI]_0 = kt$;
$111\ \text{L/mol} - 100\ \text{L/mol} = (2.4\times10^{-21}\ \text{L/mol·s})(t)$
$t = 4.6\times10^{21}\ \text{s (or } 1.5\times10^{14}\ \text{yr)}$

16.6 By inspection, we see that one-quarter of the original number remain after 6.0 min, so one-half remain after 3.0 min:
$t_{1/2} = 3.0\ \text{min}$; $k = 0.693/3.0\ \text{min} = 0.23\ \text{min}^{-1}$

16.7 $t_{1/2} = (\ln 2)/k$; $k = 0.693/13.1\ \text{h} = 5.29\times10^{-2}\ \text{h}^{-1}$

16.8 $\ln\dfrac{0.286\ \text{L/mol·s}}{k_1} = -\dfrac{1.00\times10^5\ \text{J/mol}}{8.314\ \text{J/mol·K}}\times\left(\dfrac{1}{500.\ \text{K}} - \dfrac{1}{490.\ \text{K}}\right)$

$\qquad = 0.491$

$\qquad k_1 = 0.175\ \text{L/mol·s}$

16.9

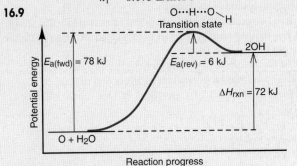

16.10 (a) Balanced equation:
$2NO(g) + 2H_2(g) \longrightarrow N_2(g) + 2H_2O(g)$
(b) Step 2 is unimolecular. All others are bimolecular.
(c) $\text{Rate}_1 = k_1[NO]^2$; $\text{rate}_2 = k_2[H_2]$; $\text{rate}_3 = k_3[N_2O_2][H]$;
$\text{rate}_4 = k_4[HO][H]$; $\text{rate}_5 = k_5[H][N_2O]$.

PROBLEMS

Problems with colored numbers are answered in Appendix E. Sections match the text and provide the numbers of relevant sample problems. Bracketed problems are grouped in pairs (indicated by a short rule) that cover the same concept. Comprehensive Problems are based on material from any section or previous chapter.

Factors That Influence Reaction Rate

16.1 What variable of a chemical reaction is measured over time to obtain the reaction rate?

16.2 How does an increase in pressure affect the rate of a gas-phase reaction? Explain.

16.3 A reaction is carried out with water as the solvent. How does the addition of more water to the reaction vessel affect the rate of the reaction? Explain.

16.4 A gas reacts with a solid that is present in large chunks. Then the reaction is run again with the solid pulverized. How does the increase in the surface area of the solid affect the rate of its reaction with the gas? Explain.

16.5 How does an increase in temperature affect the rate of a reaction? Explain the two factors involved.

16.6 In a kinetics experiment, a chemist places crystals of iodine in a closed reaction vessel, introduces a given quantity of hydrogen gas, and obtains data to calculate the rate of hydrogen iodide formation. In a second experiment, she uses the same amounts of iodine and hydrogen, but she first warms the flask to 130°C, a temperature above the sublimation point of iodine. In which of these two experiments does the reaction proceed at a higher rate? Explain.

Expressing the Reaction Rate
(Sample Problem 16.1)

16.7 Define *reaction rate*. Assuming constant temperature and a closed reaction vessel, why does the rate change with time?

16.8 (a) What is the difference between an average rate and an instantaneous rate? (b) What is the difference between an initial rate and an instantaneous rate?

16.9 Give two reasons to measure initial rates in a kinetics study.

16.10 For the reaction $A(g) \longrightarrow B(g)$, sketch two curves on the same set of axes that show
(a) The formation of product as a function of time
(b) The consumption of reactant as a function of time

16.11 For the reaction $C(g) \longrightarrow D(g)$, [C] vs. time is plotted:

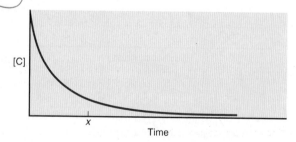

How do you determine each of the following?
(a) The average rate over the entire experiment

(b) The reaction rate at time x
(c) The initial reaction rate
(d) Would the values in parts (a), (b), and (c) be different if you plotted [D] vs. time? Explain.

16.12 The compound AX_2 decomposes according to the equation $2AX_2(g) \longrightarrow 2AX(g) + X_2(g)$. In one experiment, $[AX_2]$ was measured at various times and these data were obtained:

Time (s)	$[AX_2]$ (mol/L)
0.0	0.0500
2.0	0.0448
6.0	0.0300
8.0	0.0249
10.0	0.0209
20.0	0.0088

(a) Find the average rate over the entire experiment.
(b) Is the initial rate higher or lower than the rate in part (a)? Use graphical methods to estimate the initial rate.

16.13 (a) Use the data from Problem 16.12 to calculate the average rate from 8.0 to 20.0 s.
(b) Is the rate at exactly 5.0 s higher or lower than the rate in part (a)? Use graphical methods to estimate the rate at 5.0 s.

16.14 Express the rate of reaction in terms of the change in concentration of each of the reactants and products:
$$A(g) + 2B(g) \longrightarrow C(g)$$
When [B] is decreasing at 0.5 mol/L·s, how fast is [A] decreasing?

16.15 Express the rate of reaction in terms of the change in concentration of each of the reactants and products:
$$2D(g) + 3E(g) + F(g) \longrightarrow 2G(g) + H(g)$$
When [D] is decreasing at 0.1 mol/L·s, how fast is [H] increasing?

16.16 Reaction rate is expressed in terms of changes in concentration of reactants and products. Write a balanced equation for
$$\text{Rate} = -\frac{1}{2}\frac{\Delta[N_2O_5]}{\Delta t} = \frac{1}{4}\frac{\Delta[NO_2]}{\Delta t} = \frac{\Delta[O_2]}{\Delta t}$$

16.17 Reaction rate is expressed in terms of changes in concentration of reactants and products. Write a balanced equation for
$$\text{Rate} = -\frac{\Delta[CH_4]}{\Delta t} = -\frac{1}{2}\frac{\Delta[O_2]}{\Delta t} = \frac{1}{2}\frac{\Delta[H_2O]}{\Delta t} = \frac{\Delta[CO_2]}{\Delta t}$$

16.18 The decomposition of nitrosyl bromide is followed by measuring total pressure because the number of moles of gas changes; it cannot be followed colorimetrically because both NOBr and Br_2 are reddish brown:
$$2NOBr(g) \longrightarrow 2NO(g) + Br_2(g)$$
Use the data in the table to answer the following:
(a) Determine the average rate over the entire experiment.
(b) Determine the average rate between 2.00 and 4.00 s.
(c) Use graphical methods to estimate the initial reaction rate.
(d) Use graphical methods to estimate the rate at 7.00 s.
(e) At what time does the instantaneous rate equal the average rate over the entire experiment?

Time (s)	[NOBr] (mol/L)
0.00	0.0100
2.00	0.0071
4.00	0.0055
6.00	0.0045
8.00	0.0038
10.00	0.0033

16.19 Although the depletion of stratospheric ozone threatens life on Earth today, its accumulation was one of the crucial processes that allowed life to develop in prehistoric times:

$$3O_2(g) \longrightarrow 2O_3(g)$$

(a) Express the reaction rate in terms of $[O_2]$ and $[O_3]$.
(b) At a given instant, the reaction rate in terms of $[O_2]$ is 2.17×10^{-5} mol/L·s. What is it in terms of $[O_3]$?

The Rate Law and Its Components
(Sample Problems 16.2 to 16.4)

16.20 The rate law for the general reaction

$$aA + bB + \cdots \longrightarrow cC + dD + \cdots$$

is rate $= k[A]^m[B]^n \cdots$.
(a) Explain the meaning of k.
(b) Explain the meanings of m and n. Does $m = a$ and $n = b$? Explain.
• (c) If the reaction is first order in A and second order in B, and time is measured in minutes (min), what are the units for k?

16.21 By what factor does the rate change in each of the following cases (assuming constant temperature)?
(a) A reaction is first order in reactant A, and [A] is doubled.
(b) A reaction is second order in reactant B, and [B] is halved.
(c) A reaction is second order in reactant C, and [C] is tripled.

16.22 Give the individual reaction orders for all substances and the overall reaction order from the following rate law:

$$\text{Rate} = k[BrO_3^-][Br^-][H^+]^2$$

16.23 Give the individual reaction orders for all substances and the overall reaction order from the following rate law:

$$\text{Rate} = k\frac{[O_3]^2}{[O_2]}$$

16.24 By what factor does the rate in Problem 16.22 change if each of the following changes occurs: (a) $[BrO_3^-]$ is doubled; (b) $[Br^-]$ is halved; (c) $[H^+]$ is quadrupled?

16.25 By what factor does the rate in Problem 16.23 change if each of the following changes occurs: (a) $[O_3]$ is doubled; (b) $[O_2]$ is doubled; (c) $[O_2]$ is halved?

16.26 For the reaction

$$4A(g) + 3B(g) \longrightarrow 2C(g)$$

the following data were obtained at constant temperature:

Experiment	Initial [A] (mol/L)	Initial [B] (mol/L)	Initial Rate (mol/L·min)
1	0.100	0.100	5.00
2	0.300	0.100	45.0
3	0.100	0.200	10.0
4	0.300	0.200	90.0

(a) What is the order with respect to each reactant? (b) Write the rate law. (c) Calculate k (using the data from experiment 1).

16.27 For the reaction

$$A(g) + B(g) + C(g) \longrightarrow D(g)$$

the following data were obtained at constant temperature:

Expt	Initial [A] (mol/L)	Initial [B] (mol/L)	Initial [C] (mol/L)	Initial Rate (mol/L·s)
1	0.0500	0.0500	0.0100	6.25×10^{-3}
2	0.1000	0.0500	0.0100	1.25×10^{-2}
3	0.1000	0.1000	0.0100	5.00×10^{-2}
4	0.0500	0.0500	0.0200	6.25×10^{-3}

(a) What is the order with respect to each reactant? (b) Write the rate law. (c) Calculate k (using the data from experiment 1).

16.28 Phosgene is a toxic gas prepared by the reaction of carbon monoxide with chlorine:

$$CO(g) + Cl_2(g) \longrightarrow COCl_2(g)$$

These data were obtained in a kinetics study of its formation:

Experiment	Initial [CO] (mol/L)	Initial [Cl₂] (mol/L)	Initial Rate (mol/L·s)
1	1.00	0.100	1.29×10^{-29}
2	0.100	0.100	1.33×10^{-30}
3	0.100	1.00	1.30×10^{-29}
4	0.100	0.0100	1.32×10^{-31}

(a) Write the rate law for the formation of phosgene.
(b) Calculate the average value of the rate constant.

Integrated Rate Laws: Concentration Changes Over Time
(Sample Problems 16.5 to 16.7)

16.29 How are integrated rate laws used to determine reaction order? What is the order in reactant if a plot of
(a) The natural logarithm of [reactant] vs. time is linear?
(b) The inverse of [reactant] vs. time is linear?
(c) [Reactant] vs. time is linear?

16.30 Define the *half-life* of a reaction. Explain on the molecular level why the half-life of a first-order reaction is constant.

16.31 For the simple decomposition reaction

$$AB(g) \longrightarrow A(g) + B(g)$$

rate $= k[AB]^2$ and $k = 0.2$ L/mol·s. How long will it take for [AB] to reach $\frac{1}{3}$ of its initial concentration of 1.50 M?

16.32 For the reaction in Problem 16.31, what is [AB] after 10.0 s?

16.33 In a first-order decomposition reaction, 50.0% of a compound decomposes in 10.5 min. (a) What is the rate constant of the reaction? (b) How long does it take for 75.0% of the compound to decompose?

16.34 A decomposition reaction has a rate constant of 0.0012 yr⁻¹.
(a) What is the half-life of the reaction? (b) How long does it take for [reactant] to reach 12.5% of its original value?

The Effect of Temperature on Reaction Rate
(Sample Problem 16.8)

16.35 Use the exponential term in the Arrhenius equation to explain how temperature affects reaction rate.

16.36 How is the activation energy determined from the Arrhenius equation?

16.37 (a) Graph the relationship between k (y axis) and T (x axis). (b) Graph the relationship between $\ln k$ (y axis) and $1/T$ (x axis). How is the activation energy determined from this graph?

16.38 The rate constant of a reaction is 4.7×10^{-3} s^{-1} at 25°C, and the activation energy is 33.6 kJ/mol. What is k at 75°C?

16.39 The rate constant of a reaction is 4.50×10^{-5} L/mol·s at 195°C and 3.20×10^{-3} L/mol·s at 258°C. What is the activation energy of the reaction?

16.40 Understanding the high-temperature formation and breakdown of the nitrogen oxides is essential for controlling the pollutants generated from power plants and cars. The first-order breakdown of dinitrogen monoxide to its elements has rate constants of 0.76/s at 727°C and 0.87/s at 757°C. What is the activation energy of this reaction?

Explaining the Effects of Concentration and Temperature
(Sample Problem 16.9)

16.41 What is the central idea of collision theory? How does this idea explain the effect of concentration on reaction rate?

16.42 Is collision frequency the only factor affecting rate? Explain.

16.43 Arrhenius proposed that each reaction has an energy threshold that must be reached for the particles to react. The kinetic theory of gases proposes that the average kinetic energy of the particles is proportional to the absolute temperature. How do these concepts relate to the effect of temperature on rate?

16.44 (a) For a reaction with a given E_a, how does an increase in T affect the rate? (b) For a reaction at a given T, how does a decrease in E_a affect the rate?

16.45 Assuming the activation energies are equal, which of the following reactions will occur at a higher rate at 50°C? Explain:
$$NH_3(g) + HCl(g) \longrightarrow NH_4Cl(s)$$
$$N(CH_3)_3(g) + HCl(g) \longrightarrow (CH_3)_3NHCl(s)$$

16.46 For the reaction $A(g) + B(g) \longrightarrow AB(g)$, how many unique collisions between A and B are possible if there are four particles of A and three particles of B present in the vessel?

16.47 For the reaction $A(g) + B(g) \longrightarrow AB(g)$, how many unique collisions between A and B are possible if 1.01 mol of $A(g)$ and 2.12 mol of $B(g)$ are present in the vessel?

16.48 At 25°C, what is the fraction of collisions with energy equal to or greater than an activation energy of 100. kJ/mol?

16.49 If the temperature in Problem 16.48 is increased to 50.°C, by what factor does the fraction of collisions with energy equal to or greater than the activation energy change?

16.50 For the reaction $ABC + D \rightleftharpoons AB + CD$, $\Delta H^\circ_{rxn} = -55$ kJ/mol and $E_{a(fwd)} = 215$ kJ/mol. Assuming a one-step reaction, (a) draw a reaction energy diagram; (b) calculate $E_{a(rev)}$; and (c) sketch a possible transition state if ABC is V-shaped.

16.51 For the reaction $A_2 + B_2 \longrightarrow 2AB$, $E_{a(fwd)} = 125$ kJ/mol and $E_{a(rev)} = 85$ kJ/mol. Assuming the reaction occurs in one step, (a) draw a reaction energy diagram; (b) calculate ΔH°_{rxn}; and (c) sketch a possible transition state.

16.52 Aqua regia, a mixture of HCl and HNO_3, has been used since alchemical times to dissolve many metals, including

gold. Its orange color is due to the presence of nitrosyl chloride. Consider this one-step reaction for the formation of this compound:
$$NO(g) + Cl_2(g) \longrightarrow NOCl(g) + Cl(g) \qquad \Delta H^\circ = 83 \text{ kJ}$$
(a) Draw a reaction energy diagram, given $E_{a(fwd)}$ is 86 kJ/mol.
(b) Calculate $E_{a(rev)}$.
(c) Sketch a possible transition state for the reaction. (*Note:* The atom sequence of nitrosyl chloride is Cl—N—O.)

Reaction Mechanisms: Steps in the Overall Reaction
(Sample Problem 16.10)

16.53 Is the rate of an overall reaction lower, higher, or equal to the average rate of the individual steps? Explain.

16.54 Explain why the coefficients of an elementary step equal the reaction orders of its rate law but those of an overall reaction do not.

16.55 Is it possible for more than one mechanism to be consistent with the rate law of a given reaction? Explain.

16.56 What is the difference between a reaction intermediate and a transition state?

16.57 Why is a bimolecular step more reasonable physically than a termolecular step?

16.58 If a slow step precedes a fast step in a two-step mechanism, do the substances in the fast step appear in the rate law? Explain.

16.59 A proposed mechanism for the reaction of carbon dioxide with hydroxide ion in aqueous solution is
(1) $CO_2(aq) + OH^-(aq) \longrightarrow HCO_3^-(aq)$ [slow]
(2) $HCO_3^-(aq) + OH^-(aq) \longrightarrow CO_3^{2-}(aq) + H_2O(l)$ [fast]
(a) What is the overall reaction equation?
(b) Identify the intermediate(s), if any.
(c) What are the molecularity and the rate law for each step?
(d) Is the mechanism consistent with the actual rate law: rate $= k[CO_2][OH^-]$?

16.60 A proposed mechanism for the gas-phase reaction between chlorine and nitrogen dioxide is
(1) $Cl_2(g) + NO_2(g) \longrightarrow Cl(g) + NO_2Cl(g)$ [slow]
(2) $Cl(g) + NO_2(g) \longrightarrow NO_2Cl(g)$ [fast]
(a) What is the overall reaction equation?
(b) Identify the intermediate(s), if any.
(c) What are the molecularity and the rate law for each step?
(d) Is the mechanism consistent with the actual rate law: rate $= k[Cl_2][NO_2]$?

16.61 The proposed mechanism for a reaction is
(1) $A(g) + B(g) \rightleftharpoons X(g)$ [fast]
(2) $X(g) + C(g) \longrightarrow Y(g)$ [slow]
(3) $Y(g) \longrightarrow D(g)$ [fast]
(a) What is the overall equation?
(b) Identify the intermediate(s), if any.
(c) What are the molecularity and the rate law for each step?
(d) Is the mechanism consistent with the actual rate law: rate $= k[A][B][C]$?
(e) Is the following one-step mechanism equally valid: $A(g) + B(g) + C(g) \longrightarrow D(g)$?

16.62 Consider the following mechanism:
(1) $ClO^-(aq) + H_2O(l) \rightleftharpoons HClO(aq) + OH^-(aq)$ [fast]
(2) $I^-(aq) + HClO(aq) \longrightarrow HIO(aq) + Cl^-(aq)$ [slow]
(3) $OH^-(aq) + HIO(aq) \longrightarrow H_2O(l) + IO^-(aq)$ [fast]
(a) What is the overall equation?
(b) Identify the intermediate(s), if any.

(c) What are the molecularity and the rate law for each step?

(d) Is the mechanism consistent with the actual rate law: rate = $k[ClO^-][I^-]$?

16.63 In a study of nitrosyl halides, a chemist proposes the following mechanism for the synthesis of nitrosyl bromide:

$$NO(g) + Br_2(g) \rightleftharpoons NOBr_2(g) \quad \text{[fast]}$$
$$NOBr_2(g) + NO(g) \longrightarrow 2NOBr(g) \quad \text{[slow]}$$

If the rate law is rate = $k[NO]^2[Br_2]$, is the proposed mechanism valid? If so, show that it satisfies the three criteria for validity.

16.64 The rate law for $2NO(g) + O_2(g) \longrightarrow 2NO_2(g)$ is rate = $k[NO]^2[O_2]$. In addition to the mechanism in the text, the following ones have been proposed:

I $2NO(g) + O_2(g) \longrightarrow 2NO_2(g)$

II $2NO(g) \rightleftharpoons N_2O_2(g)$ [fast]
   $N_2O_2(g) + O_2(g) \longrightarrow 2NO_2(g)$ [slow]

III $2NO(g) \rightleftharpoons N_2(g) + O_2(g)$ [fast]
   $N_2(g) + 2O_2(g) \longrightarrow 2NO_2(g)$ [slow]

(a) Which of these mechanisms is consistent with the rate law?

(b) Which is most reasonable chemically? Why?

Catalysis: Speeding Up a Chemical Reaction

16.65 Consider the reaction $N_2O(g) \xrightarrow{Au} N_2(g) + \frac{1}{2}O_2(g)$.

(a) Is the gold a homogeneous or a heterogeneous catalyst?

(b) On the same set of axes, sketch the reaction energy diagrams for the catalyzed and the uncatalyzed reactions.

16.66 Does a catalyst increase reaction rate by the same means as a rise in temperature does? Explain.

Comprehensive Problems

Problems with an asterisk (*) are more challenging.

16.67 Consider the following reaction energy diagram:

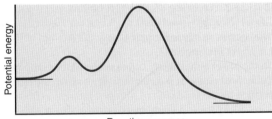

(a) How many elementary steps are in the reaction mechanism?

(b) Which step is rate limiting?

(c) Is the overall reaction exothermic or endothermic?

16.68 The catalytic destruction of ozone occurs via a two-step mechanism, where X can be any of several species:

(1) $X + O_3 \longrightarrow XO + O_2$ [slow]

(2) $XO + O \longrightarrow X + O_2$ [fast]

(a) Write the overall reaction.

(b) Write the rate law for each step.

(c) X acts as _____, and XO acts as _____.

(d) High-flying aircraft release NO, which catalyzes this process, into the stratosphere. When O_3 and NO concentrations are 5×10^{12} molecules/cm³ and 1.0×10^9 molecules/cm³, respectively, what is the rate of O_3 depletion (k for the rate-determining step is 6×10^{-15} cm³/molecule·s)?

16.69 A slightly bruised apple will rot extensively in about 4 days at room temperature (20°C). If it is kept in the refrigerator at 0°C, the same extent of rotting takes about 16 days. What is the activation energy for the rotting reaction?

16.70 Benzoyl peroxide, a substance widely used to treat acne, has a half-life of 9.8×10^3 days when refrigerated. How long will it take to lose 5% of its potency (95% remaining)?

16.71 The rate law for the reaction

$$NO_2(g) + CO(g) \longrightarrow NO(g) + CO_2(g)$$

is rate = $k[NO_2]^2$; one possible mechanism is shown on p. 537.

(a) Draw a reaction energy diagram for that mechanism, given that $\Delta H°_{overall} = -226$ kJ/mol.

(b) The following alternative mechanism has been proposed:

(1) $2NO_2(g) \longrightarrow N_2(g) + 2O_2(g)$ [slow]

(2) $2CO(g) + O_2(g) \longrightarrow 2CO_2(g)$ [fast]

(3) $N_2(g) + O_2(g) \longrightarrow 2NO(g)$ [fast]

Is the alternative mechanism consistent with the rate law? Is one mechanism more reasonable physically? Explain.

16.72 In acidic solution, the breakdown of sucrose into glucose and fructose has this rate law: rate = $k[H^+][\text{sucrose}]$. The initial rate of sucrose breakdown is measured in a solution that is 0.01 M H^+, 1.0 M sucrose, 0.1 M fructose, and 0.1 M glucose. How does the rate change if

(a) [Sucrose] is changed to 2.5 M?

(b) [Sucrose], [fructose], and [glucose] are all changed to 0.5 M?

(c) [H^+] is changed to 0.0001 M?

(d) [Sucrose] and [H^+] are both changed to 0.1 M?

16.73 The following molecular scenes represent starting mixtures I and II for the reaction of A (black) with B (orange):

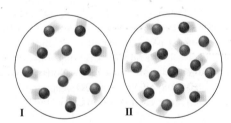

Each sphere counts as 0.010 mol, and the volume is 0.50 L. If the initial rate in I is 8.3×10^{-4} mol/L·min, what is the initial rate in II?

16.74 Biacetyl, the flavoring that makes margarine taste "just like butter," is extremely stable at room temperature, but at 200°C it undergoes a first-order breakdown with a half-life of 9.0 min. An industrial flavor-enhancing process requires that a biacetyl-flavored food be heated briefly at 200°C. How long can the food be heated and retain 85% of its buttery flavor?

16.75 At body temperature (37°C), k of an enzyme-catalyzed reaction is 2.3×10^{14} times greater than k of the uncatalyzed reaction. Assuming that the frequency factor A is the same for both reactions, by how much does the enzyme lower the E_a?

16.76 A biochemist studying breakdown of the insecticide DDT finds that it decomposes by a first-order reaction with a half-life of 12 yr. How long does it take DDT in a soil sample to decompose from 275 ppbm to 10. ppbm (parts per billion by mass)?

16.77 Proteins in the body undergo continual breakdown and synthesis. Insulin is a polypeptide hormone that stimulates fat and muscle to take up glucose. Once released from the pancreas, it has a first-order half-life in the blood of 8.0 min. To maintain an adequate blood concentration of insulin, it must be replenished in a time interval equal to $1/k$. How long is this interval?

16.78 The hydrolysis of sucrose occurs by this overall reaction:

$$C_{12}H_{22}O_{11}(s) + H_2O(l) \longrightarrow C_6H_{12}O_6(aq) + C_6H_{12}O_6(aq)$$

sucrose   glucose   fructose

A nutritional biochemist obtains the following kinetic data:

[Sucrose] (mol/L)	Time (h)
0.501	0.00
0.451	0.50
0.404	1.00
0.363	1.50
0.267	3.00

(a) Determine the rate constant and the half-life of the reaction.
(b) How long does it take to hydrolyze 75% of the sucrose?
(c) Other studies have shown that this reaction is actually second order overall but appears to follow first-order kinetics. (Such a reaction is called a *pseudo–first-order reaction*.) Suggest a reason for this apparent first-order behavior.

16.79 Is each of these statements true? If not, explain why.
(a) At a given T, all molecules have the same kinetic energy.
(b) Halving the P of a gaseous reaction doubles the rate.
(c) A higher activation energy gives a lower reaction rate.
(d) A temperature rise of 10°C doubles the rate of any reaction.
(e) If reactant molecules collide with greater energy than the activation energy, they change into product molecules.
(f) The activation energy of a reaction depends on temperature.
(g) The rate of a reaction increases as the reaction proceeds.
(h) Activation energy depends on collision frequency.
(i) A catalyst increases the rate by increasing collision frequency.
(j) Exothermic reactions are faster than endothermic reactions.
(k) Temperature has no effect on the frequency factor (A).
(l) The activation energy of a reaction is lowered by a catalyst.
(m) For most reactions, ΔH_{rxn} is lowered by a catalyst.
(n) The orientation probability factor (p) is near 1 for reactions between single atoms.
(o) The initial rate of a reaction is its maximum rate.
(p) A bimolecular reaction is generally twice as fast as a unimolecular reaction.
(q) The molecularity of an elementary reaction is proportional to the molecular complexity of the reactant(s).

16.80 The molecular scenes below represent the first-order reaction as cyclopropane (red) is converted to propene (green):

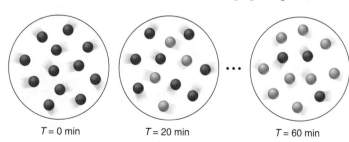

$T = 0$ min $T = 20$ min $T = 60$ min

Determine (a) the half-life and (b) the first-order rate constant.

16.81 Even when a mechanism is consistent with the rate law, later experimentation may show it to be incorrect or only one of several alternatives. As an example, the reaction between hydrogen and iodine has the following rate law: rate = $k[H_2][I_2]$. The long-accepted mechanism proposed a single bimolecular step; that is, the overall reaction was thought to be elementary:

$$H_2(g) + I_2(g) \longrightarrow 2HI(g)$$

In the 1960s, however, spectroscopic evidence showed the presence of free I atoms during the reaction. Kineticists have since proposed a three-step mechanism:
(1) $I_2(g) \rightleftharpoons 2I(g)$ [fast]
(2) $H_2(g) + I(g) \rightleftharpoons H_2I(g)$ [fast]
(3) $H_2I(g) + I(g) \longrightarrow 2HI(g)$ [slow]
Show that this mechanism is consistent with the rate law.

* 16.82 Many drugs decompose in blood by a first-order process.
(a) Two tablets of aspirin supply 0.60 g of the active compound. After 30 min, this compound reaches a maximum concentration of 2 mg/100 mL of blood. If the half-life for its breakdown is 90 min, what is its concentration (in mg/100 mL) 2.5 h after it reaches its maximum concentration?
(b) In 8.0 h, secobarbital sodium, a common sedative, reaches a blood level that is 18% of its maximum. What is $t_{1/2}$ of the decomposition of secobarbital sodium in blood?
(c) The blood level of the sedative phenobarbital sodium drops to 59% of its maximum after 20. h. What is $t_{1/2}$ for its breakdown in blood?
(d) For the decomposition of an antibiotic in a person with a normal temperature (98.6°F), $k = 3.1 \times 10^{-5}$ s^{-1}; for a person with a fever at 101.9°F, $k = 3.9 \times 10^{-5}$ s^{-1}. If the sick person must take another pill when $\frac{2}{3}$ of the first pill has decomposed, how many hours should she wait to take a second pill? A third pill?
(e) Calculate E_a for decomposition of the antibiotic in part (d).

16.83 In Houston (near sea level), water boils at 100.0°C. In Cripple Creek, Colorado (near 9500 ft), it boils at 90.0°C. If it takes 4.8 min to cook an egg in Cripple Creek and 4.5 min in Houston, what is E_a for this process?

16.84 In the lower atmosphere, ozone is one of the components of photochemical smog. It is generated in air when nitrogen dioxide, formed by the oxidation of nitrogen monoxide from car exhaust, reacts by the following mechanism:

(1) $NO_2(g) \xrightarrow{k_1}{h\nu} NO(g) + O(g)$
(2) $O(g) + O_2(g) \xrightarrow{k_2} O_3(g)$

Assuming the rate of formation of atomic oxygen in step 1 equals the rate of its consumption in step 2, use the data below to calculate (a) the concentration of atomic oxygen [O]; (b) the rate of ozone formation.

$k_1 = 6.0 \times 10^{-3}$ s^{-1}	$[NO_2] = 4.0 \times 10^{-9}$ M
$k_2 = 1.0 \times 10^6$ L/mol·s	$[O_2] = 1.0 \times 10^{-2}$ M

16.85 The scenes depict four initial reaction mixtures for the reaction of A (blue) and B (yellow), with and without a solid present (gray cubes). The initial rate, $-\Delta[A]/\Delta t$ (in mol/L·s), is shown for each sphere representing 0.010 mol and the container volume at 0.50 L.

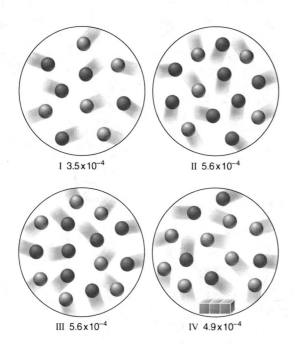

I 3.5×10⁻⁴

II 5.6×10⁻⁴

III 5.6×10⁻⁴

IV 4.9×10⁻⁴

(a) What is the rate law in the absence of a catalyst?
(b) What is the overall reaction order?
(c) Find the rate constant.
(d) Do the gray cubes have a catalytic effect? Explain.

16.86 Like any catalyst, palladium, platinum, and nickel catalyze both directions of a reaction: addition of hydrogen to (hydrogenation) and its elimination from (dehydrogenation) carbon double bonds.
(a) Which variable determines whether an alkene will be hydrogenated or dehydrogenated?
(b) Which reaction requires a higher temperature?
(c) How can all-*trans* fats arise during hydrogenation of fats that contain some *cis*- double bonds?

16.87 Chlorine is commonly used to disinfect drinking water, and inactivation of pathogens by chlorine follows first-order kinetics. The following data show *E. coli* inactivation:

Contact time (min)	Percent (%) inactivation
0.00	0.0
0.50	68.3
1.00	90.0
1.50	96.8
2.00	99.0
2.50	99.7
3.00	99.9

(a) Determine the first-order inactivation constant, k. [*Hint:* % inactivation = $100 \times (1 - [A]_t/[A]_0)$.]
(b) How much contact time is required for 95% inactivation?

16.88 The reaction and rate law for the gas-phase decomposition of dinitrogen pentaoxide are

$$2N_2O_5(g) \longrightarrow 4NO_2(g) + O_2(g) \qquad \text{rate} = k[N_2O_5]$$

Which of the following can be considered valid mechanisms for the reaction?

I   One-step collision

II $2N_2O_5(g) \longrightarrow 2NO_3(g) + 2NO_2(g)$ [slow]
    $2NO_3(g) \longrightarrow 2NO_2(g) + 2O(g)$ [fast]
    $2O(g) \longrightarrow O_2(g)$ [fast]

III $N_2O_5(g) \rightleftharpoons NO_3(g) + NO_2(g)$ [fast]
    $NO_2(g) + N_2O_5(g) \longrightarrow 3NO_2(g) + O(g)$ [slow]
    $NO_3(g) + O(g) \longrightarrow NO_2(g) + O_2(g)$ [fast]

IV $2N_2O_5(g) \rightleftharpoons 2NO_2(g) + N_2O_3(g) + 3O(g)$ [fast]
    $N_2O_3(g) + O(g) \longrightarrow 2NO_2(g)$ [slow]
    $2O(g) \longrightarrow O_2(g)$ [fast]

V $2N_2O_5(g) \longrightarrow N_4O_{10}(g)$ [slow]
    $N_4O_{10}(g) \longrightarrow 4NO_2(g) + O_2(g)$ [fast]

* **16.89** Consider the following organic reaction, in which one halogen replaces another in an alkyl halide:

$$CH_3CH_2Br + KI \longrightarrow CH_3CH_2I + KBr$$

In acetone, this particular reaction goes to completion because KI is soluble in acetone but KBr is not. In the mechanism, I^- approaches the carbon *opposite* to the Br (see Figure 16.16, p. 532, with I^- instead of OH^-). After Br^- has been replaced by I^- and precipitates as KBr, other I^- ions react with the ethyl iodide by the same mechanism.
(a) If we designate the carbon bonded to the halogen as C-1, what is the shape around C-1 and the hybridization of C-1 in ethyl iodide?
(b) In the transition state, one of the two lobes of the unhybridized 2p orbital of C-1 overlaps a p orbital of I, while the other lobe overlaps a p orbital of Br. What is the shape around C-1 and the hybridization of C-1 in the transition state?
(c) The deuterated reactant, CH_3CHDBr (where D is ^2H), has two optical isomers because C-1 is chiral. When the reaction is run with one of the isomers, the ethyl iodide is *not* optically active. Explain.

16.90 Figure 16.21 (p. 542) shows key steps in the metal-catalyzed (M) hydrogenation of ethylene:

$$C_2H_4(g) + H_2(g) \xrightarrow{\text{M}} C_2H_6(g)$$

Use the following symbols to write a mechanism that gives the overall equation:

H_2(ads)	adsorbed hydrogen molecules
M—H	hydrogen atoms bonded to metal atoms
C_2H_4(ads)	adsorbed ethylene molecules
C_2H_5(ads)	adsorbed ethyl radicals

16.91 A (green), B (blue), and C (red) are structural isomers. The molecular filmstrip depicts them undergoing a chemical change as time proceeds.

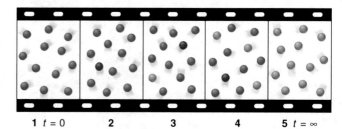

1 $t = 0$ 2   3   4   5 $t = \infty$

(a) Write a mechanism for the reaction.
(b) What role does C play?

Thermodynamics: Entropy, Free Energy, and the Direction of Chemical Reactions

20

Key Principles
to focus on while studying this chapter

- A process such as a rock falling or a fuel burning is called *spontaneous* because, once started, it continues by itself. Neither the first law of thermodynamics (law of conservation of energy) nor the sign of ΔH can predict which reactions are spontaneous. A *reaction proceeding toward equilibrium* is a spontaneous process *(Section 20.1)*.

- The total kinetic energy of a system consists of all the rotations, vibrations, and translations of its particles, each of which is *quantized*. A *microstate* of the system is any specific combination of these quantized energy states. The *entropy* (S) of a system is directly related to the *number of microstates* (W) throughout which the system *disperses its energy*, which is closely associated with the *freedom of motion* of the particles. A substance has more entropy in its gaseous state than in its liquid state and more entropy in its liquid state than in its solid state *(Section 20.1)*.

- The *second law of thermodynamics* states that a spontaneous process occurs in the direction that increases the entropy of the universe (system plus surroundings). In other words, a change occurs spontaneously if the energy of the universe becomes more dispersed *(Section 20.1)*.

- The *third law of thermodynamics*—the entropy of a perfect crystal is zero at 0 K—allows us to calculate *absolute* entropies. The *standard molar entropy* ($S°$) of a substance is influenced by temperature, physical state, dissolution, and atomic size or molecular complexity *(Section 20.1)*.

- Gases have such high entropy that if a reaction has a net increase in moles of gas, the standard entropy change of the reaction is positive ($\Delta S°_{rxn} > 0$); if a reaction has a net decrease in moles of gas, $\Delta S°_{rxn} < 0$ *(Section 20.2)*.

- For a spontaneous process, $\Delta S_{univ} > 0$, so the only way the entropy of the system can decrease is if the entropy of the surroundings increases even more. For a process at equilibrium, $\Delta S = 0$ *(Section 20.2)*.

- The *free energy change* (ΔG) of a process is a measure of its spontaneity. Because $\Delta G = \Delta H - T\Delta S$ and the temperature affects the size of $T\Delta S$, temperature influences reaction spontaneity. The free energy of a system decreases in a spontaneous process; that is, if $\Delta S_{univ} > 0$, $\Delta G_{sys} < 0$ *(Section 20.3)*.

- The portion of the total energy change available to do *work* is ΔG. In any real process, however, some of the free energy is always *lost as heat*. In a *coupling of reactions*, a spontaneous step with a larger negative ΔG drives a nonspontaneous step with a smaller positive ΔG *(Section 20.3)*.

- Reaction spontaneity ($\Delta G < 0$) depends on two factors: the free energy change at standard conditions, $\Delta G°$, and the size of the reaction quotient, Q. No matter what the starting conditions, any process is spontaneous until $Q = K$ ($\Delta G = 0$) *(Section 20.4)*.

Lifting the Load *In this chapter, we examine the relationship between the energy of a reaction, such as the combustion of fuel in the Space Shuttle, and the work it can do.*

Outline

In the last few chapters, we've posed and answered some essential questions about chemical and physical change: How fast does the change occur, and how is this rate affected by concentration and temperature? How much product will be present when the net change ceases, and how is this yield affected by concentration and temperature?

But why does a change occur in the first place? From everyday experience, it seems that some changes happen by themselves—that is, spontaneously—almost as if a force were driving them in one direction and not the other. Turn on a gas stove, for example, and the methane mixes with oxygen and burns immediately to yield carbon dioxide and water vapor. But those products will not remake methane and oxygen no matter how long they mix. A new steel shovel left outside slowly rusts, but put a rusty one outside and it won't become shiny. A cube of sugar dissolves in a cup of coffee after a few seconds of stirring, but stir for another century and the dissolved sugar won't reappear as a cube. In this chapter, we discuss the nature of such spontaneous changes. The principles of thermodynamics that we cover here apply, as far as we know, to every system in the universe!

20.1 THE SECOND LAW OF THERMODYNAMICS: PREDICTING SPONTANEOUS CHANGE

In a formal sense, a **spontaneous change** of a system, whether a chemical or physical change or just a change in location, is one that occurs by itself under specified conditions, without a continuous input of energy from outside the system. The freezing of water, for example, is spontaneous when the system is at 1 atm and $-5°C$. A spontaneous process such as burning or falling may need a little "push" to get started—a spark to ignite gasoline, a shove to knock a book off your desk—but once the process begins, it keeps going without the need for any continuous external input of energy.

In contrast, for a *nonspontaneous* change to occur, the surroundings must supply the system with a *continuous* input of energy. A book falls spontaneously, but it rises only if something else, such as a human hand (or a strong wind), supplies energy in the form of work. Under a given set of conditions, *if a change is spontaneous in one direction, it is **not** spontaneous in the other.*

The term *spontaneous* does not mean *instantaneous* or imply anything about how long a process takes to occur; it means that, given enough time, the process will happen by itself. Many processes are spontaneous but slow—ripening, rusting, and (happily!) aging.

A chemical reaction proceeding toward equilibrium is an example of a spontaneous change. As you learned in Chapter 17, we can predict the net direction of the reaction—its spontaneous direction—by comparing the reaction quotient (Q) with the equilibrium constant (K). But *why* is there a drive to attain equilibrium? And what determines the value of the equilibrium constant? Can we tell the *direction* of a spontaneous change in cases that are not as obvious as burning gasoline or falling books? Because energy changes seem to be involved, let's begin by reviewing the idea of conservation of energy to see whether it can help uncover the criterion for spontaneity.

Limitations of the First Law of Thermodynamics

In Chapter 6, we discussed the first law of thermodynamics (the law of conservation of energy) in relation to physical and chemical change. It states that the internal energy (E) of a system, the sum of the kinetic and potential energy of all its particles, changes when heat (q) and/or work (w) are gained or lost:

$$\Delta E = q + w$$

Whatever is not part of the system (sys) is part of the surroundings (surr), so the system and surroundings together constitute the universe (univ):

$$E_{univ} = E_{sys} + E_{surr}$$

Heat and/or work gained by the system is lost by the surroundings, and vice versa:

$$(q + w)_{sys} = -(q + w)_{surr}$$

It follows from these ideas that *the total energy of the universe is constant:*[*]

$$\Delta E_{sys} = -\Delta E_{surr} \quad \text{therefore} \quad \Delta E_{sys} + \Delta E_{surr} = 0 = \Delta E_{univ}$$

Is the first law sufficient to explain why a natural process takes place as it does? It certainly accounts for the energy involved. When gasoline burns in your car's engine, the first law states that the potential energy difference between the chemical bonds in the fuel mixture and those in the exhaust gases is converted to the kinetic energy of the moving car and its parts plus the heat released to the environment. If you could measure the work and heat involved, you would find that energy is conserved as it is converted from one form to another.

However, the first law does not help us make sense of the *direction* of the change. Why doesn't the heat released in the car engine convert exhaust fumes back into gasoline and oxygen? This change would not violate the first law—energy would still be conserved—but it would never happen. The first law by itself tells nothing about the direction of a spontaneous change, so we must look elsewhere for a way to predict that direction.

The Sign of ΔH Cannot Predict Spontaneous Change

In the mid-19th century, some scientists thought that the sign of the enthalpy change (ΔH), the heat gained or lost at constant pressure (q_P), was the criterion for spontaneity. They thought exothermic processes ($\Delta H < 0$) were spontaneous and endothermic ones ($\Delta H > 0$) were nonspontaneous. This hypothesis has a lot of support from observation: many spontaneous processes *are* exothermic. All combustion reactions, such as methane burning, are spontaneous and exothermic:

$$CH_4(g) + 2O_2(g) \longrightarrow CO_2(g) + 2H_2O(g) \quad \Delta H^\circ_{rxn} = -802 \text{ kJ}$$

Iron metal oxidizes spontaneously and exothermically:

$$2Fe(s) + \tfrac{3}{2}O_2(g) \longrightarrow Fe_2O_3(s) \quad \Delta H^\circ_{rxn} = -826 \text{ kJ}$$

Ionic compounds, such as NaCl, form spontaneously and exothermically from their elements:

$$Na(s) + \tfrac{1}{2}Cl_2(g) \longrightarrow NaCl(s) \quad \Delta H^\circ_{rxn} = -411 \text{ kJ}$$

However, in many other cases, the sign of ΔH is no help. An exothermic process occurs spontaneously under certain conditions, whereas the opposite, endothermic, process occurs spontaneously under other conditions. Consider the following examples of phase changes, dissolving salts, and chemical changes.

At ordinary pressure, water freezes below 0°C but melts above 0°C. Both changes are spontaneous, but the first is exothermic and the second endothermic:

$$H_2O(l) \longrightarrow H_2O(s) \quad \Delta H^\circ_{rxn} = -6.02 \text{ kJ } (\textit{exo}\text{thermic; spontaneous at } T < 0°C)$$
$$H_2O(s) \longrightarrow H_2O(l) \quad \Delta H^\circ_{rxn} = +6.02 \text{ kJ } (\textit{endo}\text{thermic; spontaneous at } T > 0°C)$$

At ordinary pressure and room temperature, liquid water vaporizes spontaneously in dry air, another endothermic change:

$$H_2O(l) \longrightarrow H_2O(g) \quad \Delta H^\circ_{rxn} = +44.0 \text{ kJ}$$

In fact, all melting and vaporizing are endothermic changes that are spontaneous under proper conditions.

---

[*]Any modern statement of conservation of energy must take into account mass-energy equivalence and the processes in stars, which convert enormous amounts of matter into energy. These can be included by stating that the total *mass-energy* of the universe is constant.

Recall from Chapter 13 that most water-soluble salts have a positive $\Delta H°_{soln}$ yet dissolve spontaneously:

$$NaCl(s) \xrightarrow{H_2O} Na^+(aq) + Cl^-(aq) \qquad \Delta H°_{soln} = +3.9 \text{ kJ}$$
$$NH_4NO_3(s) \xrightarrow{H_2O} NH_4^+(aq) + NO_3^-(aq) \qquad \Delta H°_{soln} = +25.7 \text{ kJ}$$

Some endothermic chemical changes are also spontaneous:

$$N_2O_5(s) \longrightarrow 2NO_2(g) + \tfrac{1}{2}O_2(g) \qquad \Delta H°_{rxn} = +109.5 \text{ kJ}$$
$$Ba(OH)_2 \cdot 8H_2O(s) + 2NH_4NO_3(s) \longrightarrow$$
$$Ba^{2+}(aq) + 2NO_3^-(aq) + 2NH_3(aq) + 10H_2O(l) \qquad \Delta H°_{rxn} = +62.3 \text{ kJ}$$

Freedom of Particle Motion and Dispersal of Particle Energy

What features common to the previous endothermic processes can help us see why they occur spontaneously? In each case, the particles that make up the matter have more freedom of motion after the change occurs. And this means that their energy of motion becomes more dispersed. As you'll see shortly, "dispersed" means spread over more quantized energy levels.

Phase changes lead from a solid, in which particle motion is restricted, to a liquid, in which the particles have more freedom to move around each other, to a gas, with its much greater freedom of particle motion. Along with this greater freedom of motion, the energy of the particles becomes dispersed over more levels. Dissolving a salt leads from a crystalline solid and pure liquid to ions and solvent molecules moving and interacting throughout the solution; their energy of motion, therefore, is much more dispersed. In the chemical reactions shown above, *fewer* moles of crystalline solids produce *more* moles of gases and/or solvated ions. In these cases, there is not only more freedom of motion, but more particles to disperse their energy over more levels.

Thus, in each process, the particles have more freedom of motion and, therefore, their energy of motion has more levels over which to be dispersed:

less freedom of particle motion $\longrightarrow$ more freedom of particle motion
localized energy of motion $\longrightarrow$ dispersed energy of motion

Phase change: solid $\longrightarrow$ liquid $\longrightarrow$ gas
Dissolving of salt: crystalline solid + liquid $\longrightarrow$ ions in solution
Chemical change: crystalline solids $\longrightarrow$ gases + ions in solution

In thermodynamic terms, a change in the freedom of motion of particles in a system, that is, in the dispersal of their energy of motion, is a key factor determining the direction of a spontaneous process.

Entropy and the Number of Microstates

Let's see how freedom of motion and dispersal of energy relate to spontaneous change. Picture a system of, say, 1 mol of N_2 gas and focus on one molecule. At any instant, it is moving through space (translating) at a specific speed, it is rotating at a specific frequency, and its atoms are vibrating at a specific frequency. In the next instant, the molecule collides with another or with the container, and these motional (kinetic) energy states change. In our brief discussion of IR spectroscopy (Section 9.3), we mentioned that, just as the electronic energy states of molecules are quantized, so are their vibrational, translational, and rotational energy states. The complete quantum state of the molecule at any instant is given by the specific electronic, translational, rotational, and vibrational states.

All the quantized states of the whole system of N_2 molecules is called a *microstate*. At any one instant, the total energy of the system is dispersed throughout one microstate; in the next instant, the energy of the system is dispersed throughout a different microstate. Many quantum states are possible for a single molecule, and the number of microstates possible for the system of 1 mol of molecules is staggering—on the order of $10^{10^{23}}$. For any given set of conditions, each microstate has the same total energy as any other. Therefore, each microstate is equally possible for the system, and the laws of probability say that, over time, all microstates are equally likely. If we focus only on microstates associated with thermal energy (that is, *not* electronic energy states), the number of microstates for a system is the number of ways it can disperse its thermal (kinetic) energy among the various modes of motion of all its molecules.

In 1877, the Austrian mathematician and physicist Ludwig Boltzmann related the number of microstates (W) to the **entropy (S)** of the system:

$$S = k \ln W \qquad (20.1)$$

where k, the *Boltzmann constant,* is the universal gas constant (R) divided by Avogadro's number (N_A), or R/N_A, and equals 1.38×10^{-23} J/K. The term W is just a number of microstates, so it has no units; therefore, S has units of joules/kelvin (J/K). Since the system's total energy is dispersed in only one microstate at any one instant, the total number of microstates possible determines the extent of energy dispersal and, thus, the entropy. Therefore,

- A system with fewer microstates (smaller W) has *lower entropy (lower S).*
- A system with more microstates (larger W) has *higher entropy (higher S).*

For our earlier examples,

lower entropy (fewer microstates) $\longrightarrow$ higher entropy (more microstates)

Phase change: solid $\longrightarrow$ liquid $\longrightarrow$ gas

Dissolving of salt: crystalline solid + liquid $\longrightarrow$ ions in solution

Chemical change: crystalline solids $\longrightarrow$ gases + ions in solution

(In Chapter 13, we used some of these ideas to explain solution behavior.)

Changes in Entropy If a physical or chemical change results in a greater number of microstates, there are more ways to disperse the energy of the system, and so the entropy increases:

$$S_{\text{more microstates}} > S_{\text{fewer microstates}}$$

If the change results in a lower number of microstates, the entropy decreases.

Like internal energy (E) and enthalpy (H), entropy is a state function and, thus, depends only on the present state of the system, not on the path it took to arrive at that state (Chapter 6). Therefore, the change in entropy of the system (ΔS_{sys}) depends only on the difference between its final and initial values:

$$\Delta S_{\text{sys}} = S_{\text{final}} - S_{\text{initial}}$$

Like any state function, $\Delta S_{\text{sys}} > 0$ when its value increases during a change. For example, when dry ice sublimes to gaseous carbon dioxide, we have

$$CO_2(s) \longrightarrow CO_2(g) \qquad \Delta S_{\text{sys}} = S_{\text{gaseous CO}_2} - S_{\text{solid CO}_2} > 0$$

Similarly, $\Delta S_{\text{sys}} < 0$ when the entropy decreases during a change, as when water vapor condenses:

$$H_2O(g) \longrightarrow H_2O(l) \qquad \Delta S_{\text{sys}} = S_{\text{liquid H}_2\text{O}} - S_{\text{gaseous H}_2\text{O}} < 0$$

Or consider the decomposition of dinitrogen tetraoxide (written as $O_2N—NO_2$):

$$O_2N—NO_2(g) \longrightarrow 2NO_2(g)$$

When the N—N bond in 1 mol of dinitrogen tetraoxide molecules breaks, the 2 mol of NO_2 molecules have many more available rotational, vibrational, and translational motions; thus, in any given instant, their energy is dispersed throughout any one of a greater number of microstates:

$$\Delta S_{\text{sys}} = \Delta S_{\text{rxn}} = S_{\text{final}} - S_{\text{initial}} = S_{\text{products}} - S_{\text{reactants}} = 2S_{\text{NO}_2} - S_{\text{N}_2\text{O}_4} > 0$$

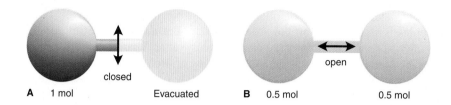

FIGURE 20.1 Spontaneous expansion of a gas. The container consists of two identical flasks connected by a stopcock. **A,** With the stopcock closed, 1 mol of neon gas occupies one flask, and the other is evacuated. **B,** Open the stopcock, and the gas expands spontaneously until each flask contains 0.5 mol.

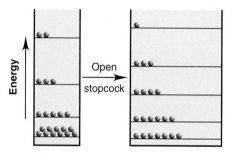

FIGURE 20.2 The entropy increase due to expansion of a gas. The energy levels available to a group of 21 gas particles are depicted as horizontal lines in a vertical box of narrow width. Each distribution of energies for the 21 particles represents one microstate. When the stopcock is opened, the volume increases, as indicated by the wider box on the right, and the particles have more freedom of motion and more energy levels available. At constant temperature, the total energy of the particles remains constant, but their energy has more ways to be distributed, so there are more microstates possible, and the entropy increases.

Quantitative Meaning of an Entropy Change Two different approaches for quantifying an entropy change give the same result. The first is a statistical approach based on the number of microstates possible for a system at any given instant. The second is based on the heat absorbed (or released) by the system. We'll explore both for a system of 1 mol of a gas expanding from 1 L to 2 L and behaving ideally, much as neon does at 298 K:

1 mol neon (initial: 1 L and 298 K) $\longrightarrow$ 1 mol neon (final: 2 L and 298 K)

1. *The approach based on number of microstates.* We use this approach to find ΔS_{sys} by applying Equation 20.1. Figure 20.1A shows a container consisting of two identical flasks connected by a stopcock, with 1 mol of neon in the left flask and an evacuated right flask. We know that when we open the stopcock (Figure 20.1B), the gas will expand to fill both flasks to 0.5 mol each—but *why?* Opening the stopcock increases the volume, which increases the number of translational energy levels available as it increases the number of particle locations. As a result, the particles will occupy more energy levels, so the number of possible microstates—and the entropy—increases.

Figure 20.2 presents this idea with particles on energy levels in a box of changeable volume. Note that when the stopcock opens, there are more energy levels, and they are closer together, so more distributions of particles are possible.

In Figure 20.3, we symbolically represent the number of microstates by the locations of particles in two attached flasks. Let's start with one neon atom and think through what happens as we add more atoms to the system, and open the stopcock. At a given instant, an atom in the left flask has its energy in one of some number (W) of possible microstates, and it has the same number possible in the right flask. Opening the stopcock increases the volume, which increases the number of possible locations and translational energy levels. As a result, the system has 2^1, or 2 *times* as many microstates available when the atom moves through both flasks (final state, W_{final}) as when it is confined to one (initial state, $W_{initial}$).

With more atoms, different sets of them can occupy various energy levels, and each distribution of occupied levels represents a microstate. Thus, as Figure 20.3 shows for two atoms, A and B, moving through both flasks, there are 2^2, or 4, times as many alternative microstates as when they are confined initially to one flask—some number of microstates with A and B in the left, the same number with A in the left and B in the right, that number with B in the left and A in the right, and that number with A and B in the right. Add another atom, and there are 2^3, or 8, times as many alternative microstates when the stopcock is open. With 10 Ne atoms, there are 2^{10}, or 1024, times as many microstates possible for the gas in both flasks. Finally, with 1 mol (N_A) of Ne, there are 2^{N_A} times as many microstates possible for the atoms in the larger volume (W_{final}) as in the smaller ($W_{initial}$). Thus, for 1 mol, we have

$$\frac{W_{final}}{W_{initial}} = 2^{N_A}$$

Now let's find ΔS_{sys} through the Boltzmann equation, $S = k \ln W$. From the properties of logarithms (Appendix A), we know that $\ln A - \ln B = \ln A/B$. Thus,

$$\Delta S_{sys} = S_{final} - S_{initial} = k \ln W_{final} - k \ln W_{initial} = k \ln \frac{W_{final}}{W_{initial}}$$

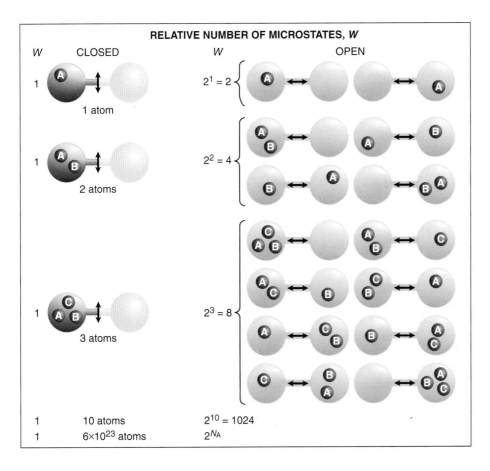

RELATIVE NUMBER OF MICROSTATES, W

FIGURE 20.3 Expansion of a gas and the increase in number of microstates. When a gas confined to one flask is allowed to spread through two flasks, the energy of the particles is dispersed over more microstates, and so the entropy is higher. Each combination of particles in the available volume represents a different microstate. The increase in the number of possible microstates that occurs when the volume increases is given by 2^n, where n is the number of particles.

Also, from Appendix A, $\ln A^y = y \ln A$; thus, with $k = R/N_A$, we have

$$\Delta S_{sys} = \frac{R}{N_A} \ln 2^{N_A} = \left(\frac{R}{N_A}\right) N_A \ln 2 = R \ln 2$$

$$= (8.314 \text{ J/mol·K})(0.693) = 5.76 \text{ J/mol·K}$$

2. *The approach based on heat changes.* As you know, when a sample of gas is heated, it expands. Let's compare the entropy change we found from the statistical approach—a gas expanding into a vacuum—to the entropy change that occurs when a gas is heated and does work on the surroundings. This approach for finding the entropy change uses the relationship

$$\Delta S_{sys} = \frac{q_{rev}}{T} \qquad (20.2)$$

where T is the temperature at which the heat change occurs and q is the heat absorbed. The subscript "rev" refers to a *reversible process*, one that occurs slowly enough for equilibrium to be maintained, so that the direction of the change can be reversed by an *infinitesimal* reversal of conditions.

We can approximate the reversible expansion of the same sample of neon gas by placing it in a piston-cylinder assembly surrounded by a heat reservoir to maintain constant temperature, and confining the gas by the "pressure" of a beaker of sand resting on the piston (Figure 20.4). We remove one grain of sand (an "infinitesimal" change in pressure) with a pair of tweezers, and the gas expands a tiny amount, raising the piston and doing work, $-w$. If the neon behaves ideally, it absorbs from the heat reservoir a tiny increment of heat q, equivalent to $-w$. We remove another grain of sand, and the gas expands a tiny bit more and absorbs another tiny increment of heat. This expansion is very close to being reversible

FIGURE 20.4 A "reversible" change. At constant temperature, changing the pressure by tiny increments approximates a reversible change in volume. Remove a grain of sand, and the gas does a tiny quantity of work, $-w$, to the surroundings and absorbs a tiny quantity of heat, q. The sum of all the quantities of heat divided by T is the change in entropy.

because we can reverse it at any point by putting a grain of sand back into the beaker, which causes a tiny quantity of work done by the surroundings compressing the gas and a tiny release of heat into the reservoir. If we continue this expansion process to 2 L and apply calculus through the process of integration, which adds together all the tiny increments of heat, we find q_{rev} is 1718 J. Thus, applying Equation 20.2, the entropy change is

$$\Delta S_{sys} = \frac{q_{rev}}{T} = \frac{1718 \text{ J}}{298 \text{ K}} = 5.76 \text{ J/K}$$

Notice that this is the same value we obtained previously. That first approach, which is often limited to simple systems like ideal gases, shows how a system's entropy changes when the volume occupied by the particles increases, and it allows us to visualize the changes in terms of energy dispersal. This second approach, which involves incremental heat changes, is not as easy to visualize, but is applicable to more complex systems.

Entropy and the Second Law of Thermodynamics

Now back to our earlier question: what criterion determines the direction of a spontaneous process? The change in entropy is the key, but to evaluate that change correctly, we must consider more than just the system. After all, some processes, such as ice melting or a crystal dissolving, occur spontaneously, and the system ends up with higher entropy; other processes, such as water freezing or a crystal forming, occur spontaneously, and the system ends up with lower entropy. But if we consider changes in *both* the system *and* its surroundings, we find that *all real processes occur spontaneously in the direction that increases the entropy of the universe (system plus surroundings).* This is one way to state the **second law of thermodynamics.**

The second law places no limitations on the entropy change of the system *or* the surroundings: either may be negative; that is, either system *or* surroundings may have lower entropy after the process. The law does state, however, that for a spontaneous process, the *sum* of the entropy changes must be positive. If the entropy of the system decreases, the entropy of the surroundings must increase even more to offset the system's decrease, so that the entropy of the universe (system *plus* surroundings) increases. A quantitative statement of the second law is, for any real spontaneous process,

$$\Delta S_{univ} = \Delta S_{sys} + \Delta S_{surr} > 0 \tag{20.3}$$

Standard Molar Entropies and the Third Law

Both entropy and enthalpy are state functions, but the nature of their values differs in a fundamental way. Recall that we cannot determine absolute *enthalpies* because we have no easily measurable starting point, no baseline value for the enthalpy of a substance. Therefore, we measure only enthalpy *changes*.

In contrast, we *can* determine the absolute *entropy* of a substance. To do so, we apply the **third law of thermodynamics,** which states that *a perfect crystal has zero entropy at a temperature of absolute zero:* $S_{sys} = 0$ at 0 K. "Perfect" means that all the particles are aligned flawlessly in the crystal structure, with no defects of any kind. At absolute zero, all particles in the crystal have the minimum energy, so there is only one microstate, only one way the energy can be dispersed: thus, in Equation 20.1, $W = 1$, so $S = k \ln 1 = 0$. When we warm the crystal, its total energy increases and thus can be dispersed into more than one microstate. Thus, $W > 1$, $\ln W > 0$, and $S > 0$.

To obtain a value for S at a given temperature, we first cool a crystalline sample of the substance as close to 0 K as possible. Then we heat it in small increments, dividing q by T to get the increase in S for each increment, and add up all the entropy increases to the temperature of interest, usually 298 K. The entropy of a substance at a given temperature is therefore an *absolute* value that is equal to the entropy increase obtained when the substance is heated from 0 K to that temperature.

As with other thermodynamic variables, we usually compare entropy values for substances in their *standard states* at the temperature of interest: *1 atm for gases, 1 M for solutions, and the pure substance in its most stable form for solids or liquids.* Because entropy is an *extensive* property, that is, one that depends on the amount of substance, we are interested in the **standard molar entropy (S°)** in units of J/mol·K (or Jmol^{-1}K^{-1}). The $S°$ values at 298 K for many elements, compounds, and ions appear, with other thermodynamic variables, in Appendix B.

Predicting Relative $S°$ Values of a System Based on an understanding of systems at the molecular level and the effects of heat absorbed, we can see how the entropy of a substance is affected by conditions. Let's consider the effects of temperature, the most fundamental condition, and also physical state, dissolution, and atomic size or molecular complexity. (All $S°$ values in the following discussion have units of J/mol·K and, unless stated otherwise, refer to the system at 298 K.)

1. *Temperature changes.* For a given substance, $S°$ *increases as the temperature rises.* Consider these typical values for copper metal:

T (K):	273	295	298
$S°$:	31.0	32.9	33.2

The temperature increases as heat is absorbed ($q > 0$), which represents an increase in the average kinetic energy of the particles. Recall from Figure 5.12 (p. 168) that the kinetic energies of gas particles are distributed over a range, which becomes wider as the temperature rises, and a similar behavior holds for liquids and solids. With more microstates available in which the energy can be dispersed at any instant, the entropy of the substance goes up. In other words, raising the temperature allows more possible microstates. Figure 20.5 provides three ways to view the effect of temperature on entropy.

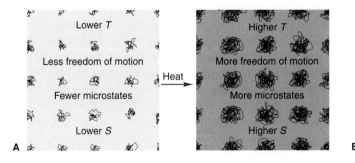

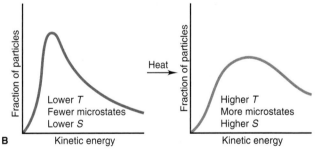

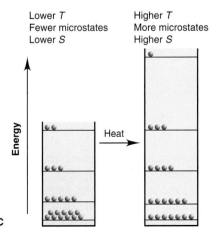

FIGURE 20.5 Visualizing the effect of temperature on entropy. A, These computer simulations show the paths of particle centers in a crystal. At any $T > 0$ K, each particle moves about its lattice position: the higher the temperature, the greater the movement. Adding heat increases the total energy. Therefore, the particles have greater freedom of motion, and their energy is more dispersed; thus, the entropy increases. **B,** At any T, there is a range of occupied energy levels and, thus, a certain number of available microstates. As heat is added, the total energy increases, and the range of occupied energy levels becomes greater: lower T means fewer microstates (lower S); higher T means more microstates (higher S). **C,** The energy levels available to a group of 21 gas particles are shown as horizontal lines in a vertical box of fixed width. The height of the box represents the total energy and number of energy levels available: at lower T, the box is short, and at higher T, it is tall. Thus, when heat is added, the total energy increases *and* becomes more dispersed, so entropy increases.

FIGURE 20.6 The increase in entropy from solid to liquid to gas. A plot of entropy vs. temperature for O_2 includes selected entropy values (in J/mol·K). Note the gradual increase in entropy within a phase and the abrupt increase at a phase change. The molecular-scale views depict the increase in freedom of motion as the solid melts and, even more so, as the liquid vaporizes.

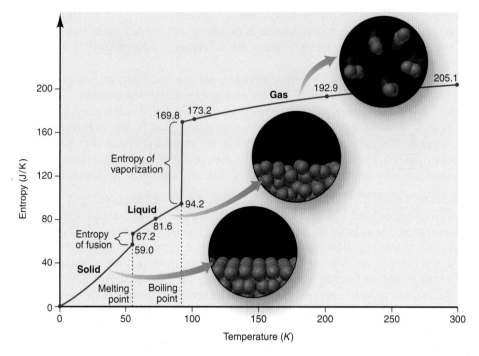

2. *Physical states and phase changes.* For a phase change such as melting or vaporizing, heat is absorbed ($q > 0$). The particles have more freedom of motion and their energy is more dispersed, so the entropy change is positive. Thus, $S°$ *increases for a substance as it changes from a solid to a liquid to a gas:*

	Na	H_2O	C(graphite)
$S°$ (s or l):	51.4(s)	69.9(l)	5.7(s)
$S°$(g):	153.6	188.7	158.0

Figure 20.6 shows how the entropy of molecular oxygen changes as it is heated from solid to liquid to gas, and the behavior of O_2 is typical of many other substances. Note the gradual increase within a phase as the temperature rises and the large, sudden increase at the phase change. Particles in the solid vibrate about their positions but, on average, remain fixed. The energy of the solid has the fewest microstates available and, thus, the least dispersed energy and the lowest entropy. As the temperature rises, the entropy gradually increases with the increase in the particles' kinetic energy. When the solid melts, the particles move much more freely between and around each other, so there is an abrupt increase in entropy. Further heating increases the speed of the particles in the liquid, and the entropy increases gradually. Finally, the particles undergo another, and much larger, abrupt entropy increase as a gas. That is, *the increase in entropy from liquid to gas is much larger than that from solid to liquid:* $\Delta S°_{vap} >> \Delta S°_{fus}$.

3. *Dissolving a solid or liquid.* The entropy of a dissolved molecular solid or liquid is *greater* than the entropy of the pure solute. For ionic solutes, however, the nature of solute *and* solvent affects the overall change:

	NaCl	$AlCl_3$	CH_3OH
$S°$ (s or l):	72.1(s)	167(s)	127(l)
$S°$(aq):	115.1	−148	132

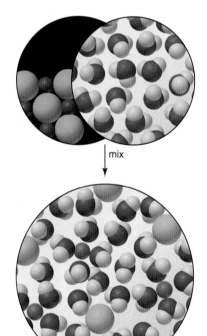

FIGURE 20.7 The entropy change accompanying the dissolution of a salt. When a crystalline salt and pure liquid water form a solution, the entropy change has two contributions: a positive contribution as the crystal separates into ions and the pure liquid disperses them, and a negative contribution as water molecules become organized around each ion. The relative magnitudes of these contributions determine the overall entropy change. The entropy of a salt solution is usually *greater* than that of the solid and water.

When an ionic solid dissolves in water, the crystal breaks down, and the ions experience a great increase in freedom of motion as they separate, with their energy dispersed into more possible microstates. We expect the entropy of the ions themselves to be greater in the solution than in the crystal. However, some of the water molecules become arranged around the ions (Figure 20.7), which

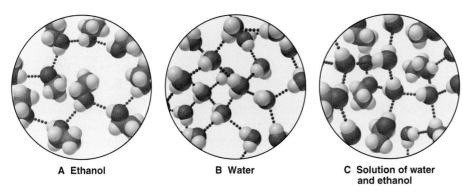

| A Ethanol | B Water | C Solution of water and ethanol |

FIGURE 20.8 The small increase in entropy when ethanol dissolves in water. Pure ethanol **(A)** and pure water **(B)** have many intermolecular H bonds. **C,** In a solution of these two substances, the molecules form H bonds to one another, so their freedom of motion does not change significantly. Thus, the entropy increase is relatively small and is due solely to random mixing.

limits their freedom of motion (see Figure 13.2, p. 400). In fact, for small, multiply charged ions, some solvent molecules become so organized around the ions that their energy of motion becomes less dispersed. This negative portion of the total entropy change can lead to *negative S°* values for the ions in solution. For example, in the case of $AlCl_3$ above, the $Al^{3+}(aq)$ ion has such a negative $S°$ value (-313 J/mol·K) that when $AlCl_3$ dissolves in water, even though $S°$ of $Cl^-(aq)$ is positive, the overall entropy of aqueous $AlCl_3$ is lower than that of solid $AlCl_3$.*

For molecular solutes, the increase in entropy upon dissolving is typically much smaller than for ionic solutes. After all, for a solid such as glucose, there is no separation into ions, and for a liquid such as methanol or ethanol (Figure 20.8), the breakdown of a crystal structure is absent as well. Furthermore, in these small alcohols and in pure water, the molecules form many H bonds, so there is relatively little change in their freedom of motion when they are mixed. The small increase in the entropy of dissolved methanol or ethanol arises from the separation of identical molecules from each other in the pure solute and in water when the molecules are mixed.

4. *Dissolving a gas.* The particles in a gas already have so much freedom of motion—and, thus, such highly dispersed energy—that they lose some when they dissolve in a liquid or solid. Therefore, the entropy of a solution of a gas in a liquid or in a solid is always *less* than the entropy of the gas itself. For instance, when gaseous O_2 [$S°(g) = 205.0$ J/mol·K] dissolves in water, its entropy decreases dramatically [$S°(aq) = 110.9$ J/mol·K] (Figure 20.9). When a gas dissolves in another gas, however, the entropy increases as a result of the separation and mixing of the molecules.

5. *Atomic size or molecular complexity.* In general, differences in entropy values for substances in the same phase are based on atomic size and molecular complexity. Within a periodic group, energy levels become closer together for heavier atoms, which means the number of possible microstates, and thus molar entropy, increases down the group:

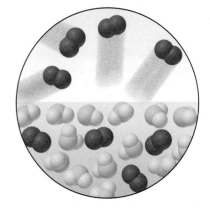

FIGURE 20.9 The large *decrease* in entropy of a gas when it dissolves in a liquid. The chaotic movement and high entropy of molecules of O_2 are reduced greatly when the gas dissolves in water.

	Li	Na	K	Rb	Cs
Atomic radius (pm):	152	186	227	248	265
Molar mass (g/mol):	6.941	22.99	39.10	85.47	132.9
$S°(s)$:	29.1	51.4	64.7	69.5	85.2

*An $S°$ value for a hydrated ion can be negative because it is relative to the $S°$ value for the hydrated proton, $H^+(aq)$, which is assigned a value of 0. In other words, $Al^{3+}(aq)$ has a lower entropy than $H^+(aq)$.

The same trend of increasing entropy down a group holds for similar compounds:

	HF	HCl	HBr	HI
Molar mass (g/mol):	20.01	36.46	80.91	127.9
$S°(g)$:	173.7	186.8	198.6	206.3

For an element that occurs in different forms (allotropes), the entropy is *higher* in the form that allows the atoms more freedom of motion, which disperses their energy because there are more microstates. For example, the $S°$ of graphite is 5.69 J/mol·K, whereas the $S°$ of diamond is 2.44 J/mol·K. In diamond, covalent bonds extend in three dimensions, allowing the atoms little movement; in graphite, covalent bonds extend only within a two-dimensional sheet, and motion of the sheets relative to each other is relatively easy.

For compounds, entropy increases with chemical complexity, that is, with the number of atoms in a formula unit or molecule of the compound. This trend holds for both ionic and covalent substances, as long as they are in the same phase:

	NaCl	$AlCl_3$	P_4O_{10}	NO	NO_2	N_2O_4
$S°(s)$:	72.1	167	229			
$S°(g)$:				211	240	304

The trend is based on the types of movement, and thus number of microstates, possible for the atoms (or ions) in each compound. For example, among the nitrogen oxides listed above, the two atoms of NO can vibrate only toward and away from each other. The three atoms of NO_2 have more vibrational motions, and the six atoms of N_2O_4 have even more (Figure 20.10).

For larger molecules, we also consider how one part of a molecule moves relative to other parts. A long hydrocarbon chain can rotate and vibrate in more ways than a short one, so entropy increases with chain length. A ring compound, such as cyclopentane (C_5H_{10}), has lower entropy than the corresponding chain compound, pentene (C_5H_{10}), because the ring structure restricts freedom of motion:

	$CH_4(g)$	$C_2H_6(g)$	$C_3H_8(g)$	$C_4H_{10}(g)$	$C_5H_{10}(g)$	$C_5H_{10}(cyclo, g)$	$C_2H_5OH(l)$
$S°$:	186	230	270	310	348	293	161

Remember, these trends hold only for *substances in the same physical state.* Gaseous methane (CH_4) has higher entropy than liquid ethanol (C_2H_5OH), even though ethanol molecules are more complex. When gases are compared with liquids, *the effect of physical state usually dominates that of molecular complexity.*

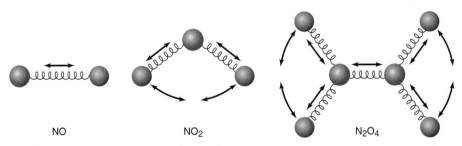

NO   NO₂   N₂O₄

FIGURE 20.10 Entropy and vibrational motion. A diatomic molecule, such as NO, can vibrate in only one way. NO_2 can vibrate in more ways, and N_2O_4 in even more. Thus, as the number of atoms increases, a molecule can disperse its vibrational energy over more microstates, and so has higher entropy.

SAMPLE PROBLEM 20.1	Predicting Relative Entropy Values

Problem Choose the member with the higher entropy in each of the following pairs, and justify your choice [assume constant temperature, except in part (e)]:
(a) 1 mol of $SO_2(g)$ or 1 mol of $SO_3(g)$
(b) 1 mol of $CO_2(s)$ or 1 mol of $CO_2(g)$
(c) 3 mol of $O_2(g)$ or 2 mol of $O_3(g)$
(d) 1 mol of KBr(s) or 1 mol of KBr(aq)
(e) Seawater at 2°C or at 23°C
(f) 1 mol of $CF_4(g)$ or 1 mol of $CCl_4(g)$

Plan In general, we know that particles with more freedom of motion have more microstates into which to disperse their kinetic energy, so they have higher entropy, and that raising the temperature increases entropy. We apply the general categories described in the text to choose the member with the higher entropy.

Solution (a) 1 mol of $SO_3(g)$. For equal numbers of moles of substances with the same types of atoms in the same physical state, the more atoms in the molecule, the more types of motion available, and thus the higher the entropy.

(b) 1 mol of $CO_2(g)$. For a given substance, entropy increases in the sequence $s < l < g$.

(c) 3 mol of $O_2(g)$. The two samples contain the same number of oxygen atoms but different numbers of molecules. Despite the greater complexity of O_3, the greater number of molecules dominates in this case because there are many more microstates possible for three moles of particles than for two moles.

(d) 1 mol of KBr(aq). The two samples have the same number of ions, but their motion is more limited and their energy less dispersed in the solid than in the solution.

(e) Seawater at 23°C. Entropy increases with rising temperature.

(f) 1 mol of $CCl_4(g)$. For similar compounds, entropy increases with molar mass.

FOLLOW-UP PROBLEM 20.1 For 1 mol of substance at a given temperature, select the member with the higher entropy in each of the following pairs, and give the reason for your choice:
(a) $PCl_3(g)$ or $PCl_5(g)$
(b) $CaF_2(s)$ or $BaCl_2(s)$
(c) $Br_2(g)$ or $Br_2(l)$

SECTION 20.1 SUMMARY

A change is spontaneous under specified conditions if it occurs in a given direction without a continuous input of energy. • Neither the first law of thermodynamics nor the sign of ΔH predicts the direction of a spontaneous change. • All spontaneous processes involve an increase in the dispersion of energy. • Entropy is a state function that measures the extent of energy dispersal into the number of microstates possible for a system, which is related to the freedom of motion of its particles. • The second law of thermodynamics states that, in a spontaneous process, the entropy of the universe (system plus surroundings) increases. • Absolute entropy values can be found because perfect crystals have zero entropy at 0 K (third law). • Standard molar entropy $S°$ (J/mol·K) is affected by temperature, phase changes, dissolution, and atomic size or molecular complexity.

20.2 CALCULATING THE CHANGE IN ENTROPY OF A REACTION

In addition to understanding trends in $S°$ values for different substances or for the same substance in different phases, chemists are especially interested in learning how to predict the sign *and* calculate the value of the change in entropy as a reaction occurs.

Entropy Changes in the System: Standard Entropy of Reaction (ΔS°_{rxn})

Based on the ideas we just discussed, we can often predict the sign of the **standard entropy of reaction, ΔS°_{rxn}**, the entropy change that occurs when all reactants and products are in their standard states. If a reaction involves one or more gases, a deciding event is usually a change in the number of moles of gas. Because gases have such great freedom of motion and thus high molar entropies, *if the number of moles of gas increases, ΔS°_{rxn} is usually positive; if the number decreases, ΔS°_{rxn} is usually negative.*

For example, when $H_2(g)$ and $I_2(s)$ form $HI(g)$, the total number of moles of *substance* stays the same, but we predict that the entropy increases because the number of moles of *gas* increases:

$$H_2(g) + I_2(s) \longrightarrow 2HI(g) \qquad \Delta S^\circ_{rxn} = S^\circ_{products} - S^\circ_{reactants} > 0$$

When ammonia forms from its elements, 4 mol of gas produces 2 mol of gas, so we predict that the entropy decreases:

$$N_2(g) + 3H_2(g) \rightleftharpoons 2NH_3(g) \qquad \Delta S^\circ_{rxn} = S^\circ_{products} - S^\circ_{reactants} < 0$$

In general *we cannot predict the sign of the entropy change unless the reaction involves a change in number of moles of gas.*

Recall that by applying Hess's law (Chapter 6), we can combine ΔH°_f values to find the standard heat of reaction, ΔH°_{rxn}. Similarly, we combine S° values to find the standard entropy of reaction, ΔS°_{rxn}:

$$\Delta S^\circ_{rxn} = \Sigma m S^\circ_{products} - \Sigma n S^\circ_{reactants} \qquad (20.4)$$

where m and n are the amounts (mol) of the individual species, given by their coefficients in the balanced equation. For the formation of ammonia, we have

$$\Delta S^\circ_{rxn} = [(2 \text{ mol } NH_3)(S^\circ \text{ of } NH_3)] - [(1 \text{ mol } N_2)(S^\circ \text{ of } N_2) + (3 \text{ mol } H_2)(S^\circ \text{ of } H_2)]$$

From Appendix B, we find the appropriate S° values:

$$\Delta S^\circ_{rxn} = [(2 \text{ mol})(193 \text{ J/mol·K})] - [(1 \text{ mol})(191.5 \text{ J/mol·K}) + (3 \text{ mol})(130.6 \text{ J/mol·K})]$$
$$= -197 \text{ J/K}$$

As we predicted from the decrease in number of moles of gas, $\Delta S^\circ_{rxn} < 0$.

SAMPLE PROBLEM 20.2   Calculating the Standard Entropy of Reaction, ΔS°_{rxn}

Problem Calculate ΔS°_{rxn} for the combustion of 1 mol of propane at 25°C:

$$C_3H_8(g) + 5O_2(g) \longrightarrow 3CO_2(g) + 4H_2O(l)$$

Plan To determine ΔS°_{rxn}, we apply Equation 20.4. We predict the sign of ΔS°_{rxn} from the change in the number of moles of gas: 6 mol of gas yields 3 mol of gas, so the entropy will probably decrease ($\Delta S^\circ_{rxn} < 0$).

Solution Calculating ΔS°_{rxn}. Using Appendix B values,

$$\Delta S^\circ_{rxn} = [(3 \text{ mol } CO_2)(S^\circ \text{ of } CO_2) + (4 \text{ mol } H_2O)(S^\circ \text{ of } H_2O)]$$
$$- [(1 \text{ mol } C_3H_8)(S^\circ \text{ of } C_3H_8) + (5 \text{ mol } O_2)(S^\circ \text{ of } O_2)]$$
$$= [(3 \text{ mol})(213.7 \text{ J/mol·K}) + (4 \text{ mol})(69.9 \text{ J/mol·K})]$$
$$- [(1 \text{ mol})(269.9 \text{ J/mol·K}) + (5 \text{ mol})(205.0 \text{ J/mol·K})]$$
$$= -374 \text{ J/K}$$

Check $\Delta S^\circ < 0$, so our prediction is correct. Rounding gives $[3(200) + 4(70)] - [270 + 5(200)] = 880 - 1270 = -390$, close to the calculated value.

Comment Remember that when there is no change in the amount (mol) of gas, you *cannot* confidently predict the sign of ΔS°_{rxn}.

FOLLOW-UP PROBLEM 20.2 Balance the following equations, predict the sign of ΔS°_{rxn} if possible, and calculate its value at 25°C:
(a) $NaOH(s) + CO_2(g) \longrightarrow Na_2CO_3(s) + H_2O(l)$
(b) $Fe(s) + H_2O(g) \longrightarrow Fe_2O_3(s) + H_2(g)$

Entropy Changes in the Surroundings: The Other Part of the Total

In many spontaneous reactions, such as the synthesis of ammonia and the combustion of propane, we see that the entropy of the reacting system decreases ($\Delta S^\circ_{rxn} < 0$). The second law dictates that, for a spontaneous process, *decreases in the entropy of the system can occur only if **increases** in the entropy of the surroundings outweigh them.* Let's examine the influence of the surroundings—in particular, the addition (or removal) of heat and the temperature at which this heat change occurs—on the *total* entropy change.

The essential role of the surroundings is to *either add heat to the system or remove heat from it.* In essence, the surroundings function as an enormous heat source or heat sink, one so large that its temperature remains constant, even though its entropy changes through the loss or gain of heat. The surroundings participate in the two possible types of enthalpy changes as follows:

1. *Exothermic change.* Heat lost by the system is gained by the surroundings. This heat gain increases the freedom of motion of particles, which allows their energy to be more dispersed, so the entropy of the surroundings increases:

   For an exothermic change: $q_{sys} < 0$, $q_{surr} > 0$,   and $\Delta S_{surr} > 0$

2. *Endothermic change.* Heat gained by the system is lost by the surroundings. This heat loss reduces the freedom of motion of particles, which makes their energy less dispersed, so the entropy of the surroundings decreases:

   For an endothermic change: $q_{sys} > 0$, $q_{surr} < 0$,   and $\Delta S_{surr} < 0$

The *temperature* of the surroundings when the heat is transferred also affects ΔS_{surr}. Consider the effect of an exothermic reaction at low or high temperature:

- At a lower temperature, such as 20 K, there is very little random motion in the surroundings and, thus, relatively little energy. This means there are fewer energy levels in each microstate, and fewer available microstates, in which to disperse the energy. Therefore, transferring heat to the surroundings has a large effect on how much the energy is dispersed.
- At a higher temperature, such as 298 K, the surroundings already have a relatively large quantity of energy dispersed. There are more energy levels in each microstate, and a greater number of available microstates. Thus, transferring the same amount of heat has a smaller effect on the total dispersal of energy.

THINK OF IT THIS WAY
Balancing Your Checkbook and Heating the Surroundings

A financial analogy may clarify the relative changes in entropy arising from heating the surroundings. If you have $10 in your checking account, a $10 deposit represents a 100% increase in your net worth. But if you have $1000 in the account, the same $10 deposit represents only a 1% increase. Thus, a given addition, whether of heat to the surroundings or money to your bank account, has a greater effect at a lower initial state than at a higher initial state.

Putting these ideas together, *the change in entropy of the surroundings is directly related to an opposite change in the heat of the system and inversely related to the temperature at which the heat is transferred.* Combining these relationships gives an equation that is closely related to Equation 20.2:

$$\Delta S_{surr} = -\frac{q_{sys}}{T}$$

Recall that for a process at *constant pressure,* the heat (q_P) is ΔH, so

$$\Delta S_{surr} = -\frac{\Delta H_{sys}}{T} \qquad (20.5)$$

This means that we can calculate ΔS_{surr} by measuring ΔH_{sys} and the temperature T at which the change takes place.

To restate the central point, if a spontaneous reaction has a negative ΔS_{sys} (energy dispersed throughout fewer microstates), ΔS_{surr} must be positive enough (energy dispersed throughout many more microstates) for ΔS_{univ} to be positive (energy dispersed throughout a net increase of microstates). Sample Problem 20.3 illustrates this situation for one of the reactions we considered earlier.

SAMPLE PROBLEM 20.3 Determining Reaction Spontaneity

Problem At 298 K, the formation of ammonia has a negative ΔS°_{sys}:

$$N_2(g) + 3H_2(g) \longrightarrow 2NH_3(g) \qquad \Delta S^{\circ}_{sys} = -197 \text{ J/K}$$

Calculate ΔS_{univ}, and state whether the reaction occurs spontaneously at this temperature.
Plan For the reaction to occur spontaneously, $\Delta S_{univ} > 0$, and so ΔS_{surr} must be greater than $+197$ J/K. To find ΔS_{surr}, we need ΔH°_{sys}, which is the same as ΔH°_{rxn}. We use ΔH°_{f} values from Appendix B to find ΔH°_{rxn}. Then, we use ΔH°_{rxn} and the given T (298 K) to find ΔS_{surr}. To find ΔS_{univ}, we add the calculated ΔS_{surr} to the given ΔS°_{sys} (-197 J/K).
Solution Calculating ΔH°_{sys}:

$$
\begin{aligned}
\Delta H^{\circ}_{sys} &= \Delta H^{\circ}_{rxn} \\
&= [(2 \text{ mol NH}_3)(-45.9 \text{ kJ/mol})] - [(3 \text{ mol H}_2)(0 \text{ kJ/mol}) + (1 \text{ mol N}_2)(0 \text{ kJ/mol})] \\
&= -91.8 \text{ kJ}
\end{aligned}
$$

Calculating ΔS_{surr}:

$$\Delta S_{surr} = -\frac{\Delta H^{\circ}_{sys}}{T} = -\frac{-91.8 \text{ kJ} \times \dfrac{1000 \text{ J}}{1 \text{ kJ}}}{298 \text{ K}} = 308 \text{ J/K}$$

Determining ΔS_{univ}:

$$\Delta S_{univ} = \Delta S^{\circ}_{sys} + \Delta S_{surr} = -197 \text{ J/K} + 308 \text{ J/K} = \boxed{111 \text{ J/K}}$$

$\Delta S_{univ} > 0$, so the reaction occurs spontaneously at 298 K (see figure in margin).
Check Rounding to check the math, we have

$$
\begin{aligned}
\Delta H^{\circ}_{rxn} &\approx 2(-45 \text{ kJ}) = -90 \text{ kJ} \\
\Delta S_{surr} &\approx -(-90{,}000 \text{ J})/300 \text{ K} = 300 \text{ J/K} \\
\Delta S_{univ} &\approx -200 \text{ J/K} + 300 \text{ J/K} = 100 \text{ J/K}
\end{aligned}
$$

Given the negative ΔH°_{rxn}, Le Châtelier's principle predicts that low temperature should favor NH_3 formation, and so the answer is reasonable.
Comments 1. Note that ΔH° has units of kJ, whereas ΔS has units of J/K. Don't forget to convert kJ to J, or you'll introduce a large error.
2. This example highlights the distinction between thermodynamic and kinetic considerations. Even though NH_3 forms spontaneously, it does so slowly; in the industrial production of ammonia by the Haber process (Section 17.6), a catalyst is used to form NH_3 at a practical rate.

FOLLOW-UP PROBLEM 20.3 Does the oxidation of FeO(s) to $Fe_2O_3(s)$ occur spontaneously at 298 K?

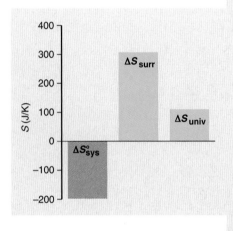

The Entropy Change and the Equilibrium State

For a process spontaneously approaching equilibrium, $\Delta S_{univ} > 0$. When the process reaches equilibrium, there is no longer any force driving it to proceed further and, thus, no net change in either direction; that is, $\Delta S_{univ} = 0$. At that point, any entropy change in the system is exactly balanced by an opposite entropy change in the surroundings:

At equilibrium: $\Delta S_{univ} = \Delta S_{sys} + \Delta S_{surr} = 0$ or $\Delta S_{sys} = -\Delta S_{surr}$

For example, let's calculate ΔS_{univ} for a phase change. For the vaporization-condensation of 1 mol of water at 100°C (373 K),

$$H_2O(l; 373 \text{ K}) \rightleftharpoons H_2O(g; 373 \text{ K})$$

First, we find ΔS_{univ} for the forward change (vaporization) by calculating ΔS°_{sys}:

$$\Delta S^{\circ}_{sys} = \Sigma m S^{\circ}_{products} - \Sigma n S^{\circ}_{reactants} = S^{\circ} \text{ of } H_2O(g; 373 \text{ K}) - S^{\circ} \text{ of } H_2O(l; 373 \text{ K})$$
$$= 195.9 \text{ J/K} - 86.8 \text{ J/K} = 109.1 \text{ J/K}$$

As we expect, the entropy of the system increases ($\Delta S^{\circ}_{sys} > 0$) as the liquid absorbs heat and changes to a gas.

For ΔS_{surr}, we have

$$\Delta S_{surr} = -\frac{\Delta H^{\circ}_{sys}}{T}$$

where $\Delta H^{\circ}_{sys} = \Delta H^{\circ}_{vap}$ at 373 K = 40.7 kJ/mol = 40.7×10^3 J/mol. For 1 mol of water, we have

$$\Delta S_{surr} = -\frac{\Delta H^{\circ}_{vap}}{T} = -\frac{40.7 \times 10^3 \text{ J}}{373 \text{ K}} = -109 \text{ J/K}$$

The surroundings lose heat, and the negative sign means that the entropy of the surroundings decreases. The two entropy changes have the same magnitude but opposite signs, so they cancel:

$$\Delta S_{univ} = 109 \text{ J/K} + (-109 \text{ J/K}) = 0$$

For the reverse change (condensation), ΔS_{univ} also equals zero, but ΔS°_{sys} and ΔS_{surr} have signs opposite those for vaporization. A similar treatment of a chemical change shows the same result: the entropy change of the forward reaction is *equal in magnitude but opposite in sign* to the entropy change of the reverse reaction. Thus, *when a system reaches equilibrium, neither the forward nor the reverse reaction is spontaneous,* and so there is no net reaction in either direction.

Spontaneous Exothermic and Endothermic Reactions: A Summary

We can now see why exothermic and endothermic spontaneous reactions occur. No matter what its *enthalpy* change, a reaction occurs because the total *entropy* of the reacting system *and* its surroundings increases. The two possibilities are

1. *For an exothermic reaction* ($\Delta H_{sys} < 0$), heat is released by the system, which increases the freedom of motion and energy dispersed and, thus, the entropy of the surroundings ($\Delta S_{surr} > 0$).

- If the reacting system yields products whose entropy is greater than that of the reactants ($\Delta S_{sys} > 0$), the total entropy change ($\Delta S_{sys} + \Delta S_{surr}$) will be positive (Figure 20.11A).
- If, on the other hand, the entropy of the system decreases as the reaction occurs ($\Delta S_{sys} < 0$), the entropy of the surroundings must increase even more ($\Delta S_{surr} >> 0$) to make the total ΔS positive (Figure 20.11B).

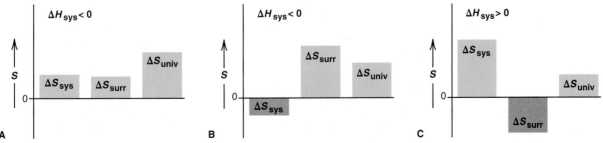

FIGURE 20.11 Components of ΔS_{univ} for spontaneous reactions. For a reaction to occur spontaneously, ΔS_{univ} must be positive. **A,** An exothermic reaction in which ΔS_{sys} increases; the size of ΔS_{surr} is not important. **B,** An exothermic reaction in which ΔS_{sys} decreases; ΔS_{surr} must be larger than ΔS_{sys}. **C,** An endothermic reaction in which ΔS_{sys} increases; ΔS_{surr} must be smaller than ΔS_{sys}.

2. *For an endothermic reaction* ($\Delta H_{sys} > 0$), the heat lost by the surroundings decreases molecular freedom of motion and dispersal of energy and, thus, decreases the entropy of the surroundings ($\Delta S_{surr} < 0$). Therefore, the only way an endothermic reaction can occur spontaneously is if ΔS_{sys} is positive and large enough ($\Delta S_{sys} \gg 0$) to outweigh the negative ΔS_{surr} (Figure 20.11C).

SECTION 20.2 SUMMARY

The standard entropy of reaction, ΔS_{rxn}°, is calculated from S° values. • When the amount (mol) of gas (Δn_{gas}) increases in a reaction, usually $\Delta S_{rxn}^{\circ} > 0$. • The value of ΔS_{surr} is related directly to ΔH_{sys}° and inversely to the T at which the change occurs. • In a spontaneous change, the entropy of the system can decrease only if the entropy of the surroundings increases even more. • For a system at equilibrium, $\Delta S_{univ} = 0$.

20.3 ENTROPY, FREE ENERGY, AND WORK

By making *two* separate measurements, ΔS_{sys} and ΔS_{surr}, we can predict whether a reaction will be spontaneous at a particular temperature. It would be useful, however, to have *one* criterion for spontaneity that we can find by examining the system only. The Gibbs free energy, or simply **free energy (G),** is a function that combines the system's enthalpy and entropy:

$$G = H - TS$$

Named for Josiah Willard Gibbs (1839–1903), the physicist who proposed it and laid much of the foundation for chemical thermodynamics, this function provides the criterion for spontaneity we've been seeking.

Free Energy Change and Reaction Spontaneity

The free energy change (ΔG) is a measure of the spontaneity of a process and of the useful energy available from it. Let's see how the free energy change is derived from the second law of thermodynamics. Recall that by definition, the entropy change of the universe is the sum of the entropy changes of the system and the surroundings:

$$\Delta S_{univ} = \Delta S_{sys} + \Delta S_{surr}$$

At constant pressure,

$$\Delta S_{surr} = -\frac{\Delta H_{sys}}{T}$$

Substituting for ΔS_{surr} gives a relationship that lets us focus solely on the system:

$$\Delta S_{univ} = \Delta S_{sys} - \frac{\Delta H_{sys}}{T}$$

Multiplying both sides by $-T$ gives

$$-T\Delta S_{univ} = \Delta H_{sys} - T\Delta S_{sys}$$

Now we can use the new free energy quantity to replace the enthalpy and entropy terms. From $G = H - TS$, the *Gibbs equation* shows the change in the free energy of the system (ΔG_{sys}) at constant temperature and pressure:

$$\Delta G_{sys} = \Delta H_{sys} - T\Delta S_{sys} \tag{20.6}$$

Combining this equation with the previous one shows that

$$-T\Delta S_{univ} = \Delta H_{sys} - T\Delta S_{sys} = \Delta G_{sys}$$

*The **sign** of ΔG tells if a reaction is spontaneous.* The second law dictates

- $\Delta S_{univ} > 0$ for a spontaneous process
- $\Delta S_{univ} < 0$ for a nonspontaneous process
- $\Delta S_{univ} = 0$ for a process at equilibrium

Of course, absolute temperature is always positive, so

$$T\Delta S_{univ} > 0 \quad \text{or} \quad -T\Delta S_{univ} < 0 \text{ for a spontaneous process}$$

Because $\Delta G = -T\Delta S_{univ}$, we know that

- $\Delta G < 0$ for a spontaneous process
- $\Delta G > 0$ for a nonspontaneous process
- $\Delta G = 0$ for a process at equilibrium

An important point to keep in mind is that if a process is *nonspontaneous* in one direction ($\Delta G > 0$), it is *spontaneous* in the opposite direction ($\Delta G < 0$). By using ΔG, we have not incorporated any new ideas, but we can predict reaction spontaneity from one variable (ΔG_{sys}) rather than two (ΔS_{sys} and ΔS_{surr}).

Calculating Standard Free Energy Changes

Because free energy (G) combines three state functions, H, S, and T, it is also a state function. As with enthalpy, we focus on the free energy *change* (ΔG).

The Standard Free Energy Change As we did with the other thermodynamic variables, to compare the free energy changes of different reactions we calculate the *standard* **free energy change ($\Delta G°$),** which occurs when all components of the system are in their standard states. Adapting the Gibbs equation (20.6), we have

$$\Delta G°_{sys} = \Delta H°_{sys} - T\Delta S°_{sys} \qquad (20.7)$$

This important relationship is used frequently to find any one of these three central thermodynamic variables, given the other two, as in Sample Problem 20.4.

SAMPLE PROBLEM 20.4 Calculating $\Delta G°_{rxn}$ from Enthalpy and Entropy Values

Problem Potassium chlorate, a common oxidizing agent in fireworks and matchheads, undergoes a solid-state disproportionation reaction when heated:

$$4KClO_3(s) \xrightarrow{\Delta} 3KClO_4(s) + KCl(s)$$

Use $\Delta H°_f$ and $S°$ values to calculate $\Delta G°_{sys}$ ($\Delta G°_{rxn}$) at 25°C for this reaction.

Plan To solve for $\Delta G°$, we need values from Appendix B. We use $\Delta H°_f$ values to calculate $\Delta H°_{rxn}$ ($\Delta H°_{sys}$), use $S°$ values to calculate $\Delta S°_{rxn}$ ($\Delta S°_{sys}$), and then apply Equation 20.7.

Solution Calculating $\Delta H°_{sys}$ from $\Delta H°_f$ values (with Equation 6.8):

$$\begin{aligned}
\Delta H°_{sys} = \Delta H°_{rxn} &= \Sigma m\Delta H°_{f(products)} - \Sigma n\Delta H°_{f(reactants)} \\
&= [(3 \text{ mol } KClO_4)(\Delta H°_f \text{ of } KClO_4) + (1 \text{ mol } KCl)(\Delta H°_f \text{ of } KCl)] \\
&\quad - [(4 \text{ mol } KClO_3)(\Delta H°_f \text{ of } KClO_3)] \\
&= [(3 \text{ mol})(-432.8 \text{ kJ/mol}) + (1 \text{ mol})(-436.7 \text{ kJ/mol})] \\
&\quad - [(4 \text{ mol})(-397.7 \text{ kJ/mol})] \\
&= -144 \text{ kJ}
\end{aligned}$$

Calculating $\Delta S°_{sys}$ from $S°$ values (with Equation 20.4):

$$\begin{aligned}
\Delta S°_{sys} = \Delta S°_{rxn} &= [(3 \text{ mol } KClO_4)(S° \text{ of } KClO_4) + (1 \text{ mol } KCl)(S° \text{ of } KCl)] \\
&\quad - [(4 \text{ mol } KClO_3)(S° \text{ of } KClO_3)] \\
&= [(3 \text{ mol})(151.0 \text{ J/mol·K}) + (1 \text{ mol})(82.6 \text{ J/mol·K})] \\
&\quad - [(4 \text{ mol})(143.1 \text{ J/mol·K})] \\
&= -36.8 \text{ J/K}
\end{aligned}$$

Calculating $\Delta G°_{sys}$ at 298 K:

$$\Delta G°_{sys} = \Delta H°_{sys} - T\Delta S°_{sys} = -144 \text{ kJ} - \left[(298 \text{ K})(-36.8 \text{ J/K})\left(\frac{1 \text{ kJ}}{1000 \text{ J}}\right)\right] = -133 \text{ kJ}$$

Check Rounding to check the math:

$\Delta H° \approx [3(-433 \text{ kJ}) + (-440 \text{ kJ})] - [4(-400 \text{ kJ})] = -1740 \text{ kJ} + 1600 \text{ kJ} = -140 \text{ kJ}$

$\Delta S° \approx [3(150 \text{ J/K}) + 85 \text{ J/K}] - [4(145 \text{ J/K})] = 535 \text{ J/K} - 580 \text{ J/K} = -45 \text{ J/K}$

$\Delta G° \approx -140 \text{ kJ} - 300 \text{ K}(-0.04 \text{ kJ/K}) = -140 \text{ kJ} + 12 \text{ kJ} = -128 \text{ kJ}$

All values are close to the calculated ones.

Comments 1. For a spontaneous reaction under *any* conditions, the free energy change, ΔG, is negative. Under standard-state conditions, a spontaneous reaction has a negative *standard* free energy change; that is, $\Delta G° < 0$.

2. This reaction is spontaneous, but the rate is very low in the solid. When $KClO_3$ is heated slightly above its melting point, the ions are free to move and the reaction occurs readily.

FOLLOW-UP PROBLEM 20.4 Determine the standard free energy change at 298 K for the reaction $2NO(g) + O_2(g) \longrightarrow 2NO_2(g)$.

The Standard Free Energy of Formation Another way to calculate $\Delta G°_{rxn}$ is with values for the **standard free energy of formation ($\Delta G°_f$)** of the components; $\Delta G°_f$ is the free energy change that occurs when 1 mol of compound is made *from its elements,* with all components in their standard states. Because free energy is a state function, we can combine $\Delta G°_f$ values of reactants and products to calculate $\Delta G°_{rxn}$ no matter how the reaction takes place:

$$\Delta G°_{rxn} = \Sigma m \Delta G°_{f(products)} - \Sigma n \Delta G°_{f(reactants)} \tag{20.8}$$

$\Delta G°_f$ values have properties similar to $\Delta H°_f$ values:

- $\Delta G°_f$ of an element in its standard state is zero.
- An equation coefficient (*m* or *n* above) multiplies $\Delta G°_f$ by that number.
- Reversing a reaction changes the sign of $\Delta G°_f$.

Many $\Delta G°_f$ values appear along with those for $\Delta H°_f$ and $S°$ in Appendix B.

SAMPLE PROBLEM 20.5 Calculating $\Delta G°_{rxn}$ from $\Delta G°_f$ Values

Problem Use $\Delta G°_f$ values to calculate $\Delta G°_{rxn}$ for the reaction in Sample Problem 20.4:

$$4KClO_3(s) \longrightarrow 3KClO_4(s) + KCl(s)$$

Plan We apply Equation 20.8 to calculate $\Delta G°_{rxn}$.

Solution $\Delta G°_{rxn} = \Sigma m \Delta G°_{f(products)} - \Sigma n \Delta G°_{f(reactants)}$

$= [(3 \text{ mol } KClO_4)(\Delta G°_f \text{ of } KClO_4) + (1 \text{ mol } KCl)(\Delta G°_f \text{ of } KCl)]$

$- [(4 \text{ mol } KClO_3)(\Delta G°_f \text{ of } KClO_3)]$

$= [(3 \text{ mol})(-303.2 \text{ kJ/mol}) + (1 \text{ mol})(-409.2 \text{ kJ/mol})]$

$- [(4 \text{ mol})(-296.3 \text{ kJ/mol})]$

$= -134 \text{ kJ}$

Check Rounding to check the math:

$\Delta G°_{rxn} \approx [3(-300 \text{ kJ}) + 1(-400 \text{ kJ})] - 4(-300 \text{ kJ})$

$= -1300 \text{ kJ} + 1200 \text{ kJ} = -100 \text{ kJ}$

Comment The slight discrepancy between this answer and that obtained in Sample Problem 20.4 is within experimental error. As you can see, when $\Delta G°_f$ values are available for a reaction taking place at 25°C, this method is simpler than that in Sample Problem 20.4.

FOLLOW-UP PROBLEM 20.5 Use $\Delta G°_f$ values to calculate the free energy change at 25°C for each of the following reactions:

(a) $2NO(g) + O_2(g) \longrightarrow 2NO_2(g)$ (from Follow-up Problem 20.4)

(b) $2C(graphite) + O_2(g) \longrightarrow 2CO(g)$

ΔG and the Work a System Can Do

The science of thermodynamics was born soon after the invention of the steam engine, and one of its most practical ideas relates the free energy change and the work a system can do:

- For a spontaneous process ($\Delta G < 0$) at constant T and P, ΔG is the *maximum useful work obtainable **from** the system as the process takes place:*

$$\Delta G = w_{max} \qquad (20.9)$$

- For a nonspontaneous process ($\Delta G > 0$) at constant T and P, ΔG is the *minimum work that must be done **to** the system to make the process take place.*

The free energy change is the maximum work a system can *possibly* do. But the work the system *actually* does depends on how the free energy is released. Suppose an expanding gas does work by lifting an object. The gas can do nearly the maximum work if the weight of the object can be adjusted in tiny increments and lifted in many small steps (see Figure 20.4). In this way, the gas lifts the object in a very high number of steps. The maximum work could be done only in an infinite number of steps; that is, *the maximum work is done by a spontaneous process only if it is carried out reversibly.* In any *real* process, work is done irreversibly—in a finite number of steps—so *we can never obtain the maximum work.* The free energy not used for work is lost as heat.

Consider the work done by a *battery,* a packaged spontaneous redox reaction that releases free energy to the surroundings (flashlight, radio, motor, or other device). If we connect the battery terminals to each other through a short piece of wire, ΔG_{sys} is released all at once but does no work—it just heats the wire and battery and outside air, which increases the freedom of motion of the particles in the universe. If we connect the battery terminals to a motor, ΔG_{sys} is released more slowly, and much of it runs the motor; however, some is still lost as heat. Only if a battery could discharge infinitely slowly could we obtain the maximum work. This is the compromise that all engineers must face—*no real process uses all the available free energy to do work because some is always changed to heat.*

The Effect of Temperature on Reaction Spontaneity

In most cases, the enthalpy contribution (ΔH) to the free energy change (ΔG) is much *larger* than the entropy contribution ($T\Delta S$). For this reason, most exothermic reactions are spontaneous: the negative ΔH helps make ΔG negative. However, the *temperature of a reaction influences the magnitude of the $T\Delta S$ term,* so, for many reactions, the overall spontaneity depends on the temperature.

By scrutinizing the signs of ΔH and ΔS, we can predict the effect of temperature on the sign of ΔG. The values for the thermodynamic variables in this discussion are based on standard state values from Appendix B, but we show them without the degree sign to emphasize that the relationships among ΔG, ΔH, and ΔS are valid at any conditions. Also, we assume that ΔH and ΔS change little with temperature, which is true as long as no phase changes occur.

Let's examine the four combinations of positive and negative ΔH and ΔS, two that are independent of T and two that are dependent on T:

- *Temperature-independent cases.* When ΔH and ΔS have *opposite* signs, the reaction occurs spontaneously either at all temperatures or at none.
  1. *Reaction is spontaneous at all temperatures:* $\Delta H < 0$, $\Delta S > 0$. Both contributions favor the spontaneity of the reaction. ΔH is negative and ΔS is positive, so $-T\Delta S$ is negative; thus, ΔG is always negative. Most combustion reactions are in this category. The decomposition of hydrogen peroxide, a common disinfectant, is also spontaneous at all temperatures:

$$2H_2O_2(l) \longrightarrow 2H_2O(l) + O_2(g) \qquad \Delta H = -196 \text{ kJ and } \Delta S = 125 \text{ J/K}$$

$\Delta G = \Delta H - T\Delta S$

2. *Reaction is nonspontaneous at all temperatures:* $\Delta H > 0$, $\Delta S < 0$. Both contributions oppose the spontaneity of the reaction. ΔH is positive and ΔS is negative, so $-T\Delta S$ is positive; thus, ΔG is always positive. The formation of ozone from oxygen is not spontaneous at any temperature:

$$3O_2(g) \longrightarrow 2O_3(g) \qquad \Delta H = 286 \text{ kJ and } \Delta S = -137 \text{ J/K}$$

- *Temperature-dependent cases.* When ΔH and ΔS have the *same* sign, the relative magnitudes of the $-T\Delta S$ and ΔH terms determine the sign of ΔG. In these cases, the magnitude of T is crucial to reaction spontaneity.

3. *Reaction is spontaneous at higher temperatures:* $\Delta H > 0$ *and* $\Delta S > 0$. Here, ΔS favors spontaneity ($-T\Delta S < 0$), but ΔH does not. For example,

$$2N_2O(g) + O_2(g) \longrightarrow 4NO(g) \qquad \Delta H = 197.1 \text{ kJ and } \Delta S = 198.2 \text{ J/K}$$

With a positive ΔH, the reaction will occur spontaneously only when $-T\Delta S$ is large enough to make ΔG negative, which will happen at higher temperatures. The oxidation of N_2O occurs spontaneously at $T > 994$ K.

4. *Reaction is spontaneous at lower temperatures:* $\Delta H < 0$ *and* $\Delta S < 0$. Now, ΔH favors spontaneity, but ΔS does not ($-T\Delta S > 0$). For example,

$$4Fe(s) + 3O_2(g) \longrightarrow 2Fe_2O_3(s) \qquad \Delta H = -1651 \text{ kJ and } \Delta S = -549.4 \text{ J/K}$$

With a negative ΔH, the reaction will occur spontaneously only if the $-T\Delta S$ term is smaller than the ΔH term, and this happens at lower temperatures. The production of iron(III) oxide occurs spontaneously at any $T < 3005$ K.

Table 20.1 summarizes these four possible combinations of ΔH and ΔS, and Sample Problem 20.6 applies them, using molecular scenes.

Table 20.1	Reaction Spontaneity and the Signs of ΔH, ΔS, and ΔG			
ΔH	ΔS	$-T\Delta S$	ΔG	**Description**
−	+	−	−	Spontaneous at all T
+	−	+	+	Nonspontaneous at all T
+	+	−	+ or −	Spontaneous at higher T; nonspontaneous at lower T
−	−	+	+ or −	Spontaneous at lower T; nonspontaneous at higher T

SAMPLE PROBLEM 20.6 Using Molecular Scenes to Determine the Signs of ΔH, ΔS, and ΔG

Problem The following scenes represent a familiar phase change for water (blue spheres):

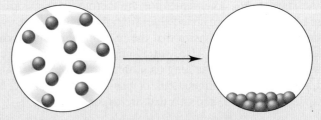

(a) What are the signs of ΔH and ΔS for this process? Explain.
(b) Is the process spontaneous at all T, no T, low T, or high T? Explain.
Plan The scenes depict water vapor on the left and liquid water on the right. **(a)** From the scenes, we determine any change in amount of gas, which indicates the sign of ΔS, and any change in the freedom of motion of the particles, which indicates whether heat is absorbed or released, and thus the sign of ΔH. **(b)** The question refers to the sign of ΔG (+ or −) at the different temperature possibilities, so we apply Equation 20.6 and refer to the previous text discussion and Table 20.1.

Solution (a) The scenes represent the condensation of water vapor, so the amount of gas decreases dramatically, and the separated molecules give up energy as they come closer together. Therefore, $\Delta S < 0$ and $\Delta H < 0$. (b) According to Equation 20.6, with ΔS negative, the $-T\Delta S$ term is positive. In order for $\Delta G < 0$, the magnitude of T must be small. Therefore, the process is spontaneous at low T.

Check The answer in part (b) seems reasonable based on our analysis in part (a). The answer makes sense because we know from everyday experience that water condenses spontaneously, and it does so at low temperatures.

FOLLOW-UP PROBLEM 20.6 The following molecular scenes represent the gas-phase decomposition of X_2Y_2 to X_2 (red) and Y_2 (blue):

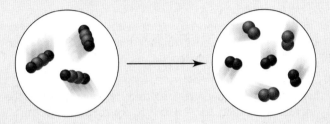

(a) What is the sign of ΔS for the reaction?
(b) If the reaction is spontaneous only above 325°C, what is the sign of ΔH? Explain.

As you saw in Sample Problem 20.4, one way to calculate ΔG is from enthalpy and entropy changes. Because ΔH and ΔS usually change little with temperature if no phase changes occur, we use their values at 298 K to examine the effect of temperature on ΔG and, thus, on reaction spontaneity.

SAMPLE PROBLEM 20.7 Determining the Effect of Temperature on ΔG

Problem A key step in the production of sulfuric acid is the oxidation of $SO_2(g)$ to $SO_3(g)$:
$$2SO_2(g) + O_2(g) \longrightarrow 2SO_3(g)$$
At 298 K, $\Delta G = -141.6$ kJ; $\Delta H = -198.4$ kJ; and $\Delta S = -187.9$ J/K.
(a) Use the data to decide if this reaction is spontaneous at 25°C, and predict how ΔG will change with increasing T.
(b) Assuming that ΔH and ΔS are constant with T, is the reaction spontaneous at 900.°C?
Plan (a) We note the sign of ΔG to see if the reaction is spontaneous and the signs of ΔH and ΔS to see the effect of T. (b) We use Equation 20.6 to calculate ΔG from the given ΔH and ΔS at the higher T (in K).
Solution (a) $\Delta G < 0$, so the reaction is spontaneous at 298 K: SO_2 and O_2 will form SO_3 spontaneously. With $\Delta S < 0$, the term $-T\Delta S > 0$, and this term will become more positive at higher T. Therefore,
ΔG will become less negative, and the reaction less spontaneous, with increasing T.
(b) Calculating ΔG at 900.°C ($T = 273 + 900. = 1173$ K):
$$\Delta G = \Delta H - T\Delta S = -198.4 \text{ kJ} - [(1173 \text{ K})(-187.9 \text{ J/K})(1 \text{ kJ}/1000 \text{ J})] = 22.0 \text{ kJ}$$
$\Delta G > 0$, so the reaction is nonspontaneous at the higher T.
Check The answer in part (b) seems reasonable based on our prediction in part (a). The arithmetic seems correct, given considerable rounding:
$$\Delta G \approx -200 \text{ kJ} - [(1200 \text{ K})(-200 \text{ J/K})/1000 \text{ J}] = +40 \text{ kJ}$$

FOLLOW-UP PROBLEM 20.7 A reaction is nonspontaneous at room temperature but *is* spontaneous at −40°C. What can you say about the signs and relative magnitudes of ΔH, ΔS, and $-T\Delta S$?

The Temperature at Which a Reaction Becomes Spontaneous As you have just seen, when the signs of ΔH and ΔS are the same, some reactions that are nonspontaneous at one temperature become spontaneous at another, and vice versa. It would certainly be useful to know the temperature at which a reaction becomes spontaneous. This is the temperature at which a positive ΔG switches to a negative ΔG because of the changing magnitude of the $-T\Delta S$ term. We find this crossover temperature by setting ΔG equal to zero and solving for T:

$$\Delta G = \Delta H - T\Delta S = 0$$

Therefore, $$\Delta H = T\Delta S \quad \text{and} \quad T = \frac{\Delta H}{\Delta S} \qquad (20.10)$$

Consider the reaction of copper(I) oxide with carbon, which does *not* occur at lower temperatures but is used at higher temperatures in a step during the extraction of copper metal from chalcocite, its principal ore:

$$Cu_2O(s) + C(s) \longrightarrow 2Cu(s) + CO(g)$$

We predict this reaction has a positive entropy change because the number of moles of gas increases; in fact, $\Delta S = 165$ J/K. Furthermore, because the reaction is *non*spontaneous at lower temperatures, it must have a positive ΔH (58.1 kJ). As the $-T\Delta S$ term becomes more negative at higher temperatures, it will eventually outweigh the positive ΔH term, and the reaction will occur spontaneously.

Let's calculate ΔG for this reaction at 25°C and then find the temperature above which the reaction is spontaneous. At 25°C (298 K),

$$\Delta G = \Delta H - T\Delta S = 58.1 \text{ kJ} - \left(298 \text{ K} \times 165 \text{ J/K} \times \frac{1 \text{ kJ}}{1000 \text{ J}}\right) = 8.9 \text{ kJ}$$

Because ΔG is positive, the reaction will not proceed on its own at 25°C. At the crossover temperature, $\Delta G = 0$, so

$$T = \frac{\Delta H}{\Delta S} = \frac{58.1 \text{ kJ} \times \dfrac{1000 \text{ J}}{1 \text{ kJ}}}{165 \text{ J/K}} = 352 \text{ K}$$

At any temperature above 352 K (79°C), a moderate one for recovering a metal from its ore, the reaction occurs spontaneously. Figure 20.12 depicts this result. The line for $T\Delta S$ rises steadily (and thus the $-T\Delta S$ term becomes more negative) with rising temperature. This line crosses the relatively constant ΔH line at 352 K. At any higher temperature, the $-T\Delta S$ term is greater than the ΔH term, so ΔG is negative.

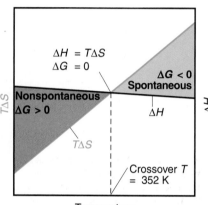

FIGURE 20.12 The effect of temperature on reaction spontaneity. The two terms that make up ΔG are plotted against T. The figure shows a relatively constant ΔH and a steadily increasing $T\Delta S$ (and thus more negative $-T\Delta S$) for the reaction between Cu_2O and C. At low T, the reaction is nonspontaneous ($\Delta G > 0$) because the positive ΔH term has a greater magnitude than the negative $T\Delta S$ term. At 352 K, $\Delta H = T\Delta S$, so $\Delta G = 0$. At any higher T, the reaction becomes spontaneous ($\Delta G < 0$) because the $-T\Delta S$ term dominates.

Coupling of Reactions to Drive a Nonspontaneous Change

When studying a multistep reaction, chemists often find that a nonspontaneous step is driven by a spontaneous step in a **coupling of reactions.** *One step supplies enough free energy for the other to occur,* as when the combustion of gasoline (spontaneous) supplies enough free energy to move a car (nonspontaneous).

Look again at the reaction of copper(I) oxide with carbon. Previously, we found that the *overall* reaction becomes spontaneous above 352 K. Dividing the reaction into two steps, we find that, even at the slightly higher temperature of 375 K, decomposition of copper(I) oxide to its elements is not spontaneous:

$$Cu_2O(s) \longrightarrow 2Cu(s) + \tfrac{1}{2}O_2(g) \qquad \Delta G_{375} = 140.0 \text{ kJ}$$

But the oxidation of carbon to CO is:

$$C(s) + \tfrac{1}{2}O_2(g) \longrightarrow CO(g) \qquad \Delta G_{375} = -143.8 \text{ kJ}$$

Coupling these reactions allows the reaction with the larger negative ΔG to "drive" the one with the smaller positive ΔG. Adding the reactions together gives

$$Cu_2O(s) + C(s) \longrightarrow 2Cu(s) + CO(g) \qquad \Delta G_{375} = -3.8 \text{ kJ}$$

Many biochemical processes—including the syntheses of proteins, nucleic acids, and fatty acids, the maintenance of ion balance, and the breakdown of nutrients—have nonspontaneous steps. Coupling these steps to spontaneous ones is a life-sustaining strategy that is common to *all organisms*. A key spontaneous biochemical reaction is the hydrolysis of a high-energy molecule called **adenosine triphosphate (ATP)** to adenosine diphosphate (ADP):

$$\text{ATP}^{4-} + \text{H}_2\text{O} \rightleftharpoons \text{ADP}^{3-} + \text{HPO}_4^{2-} + \text{H}^+ \qquad \Delta G^{\circ\prime} = -30.5 \text{ kJ}$$

(For biochemical systems, the standard-state concentration of H^+ is $10^{-7}\,M$, not the usual $1\,M$, and the standard free energy change has the symbol $\Delta G^{\circ\prime}$.) In the metabolic breakdown of glucose, for example, the initial step, which is nonspontaneous, is the addition of a phosphate group to a glucose molecule:

$$\text{Glucose} + \text{HPO}_4^{2-} + \text{H}^+ \rightleftharpoons [\text{glucose phosphate}]^- + \text{H}_2\text{O} \qquad \Delta G^{\circ\prime} = 13.8 \text{ kJ}$$

Coupling this reaction to ATP hydrolysis makes the overall process spontaneous. If we add the two reactions, HPO_4^{2-}, H^+, and H_2O cancel, and we obtain

$$\text{Glucose} + \text{ATP}^{4-} \rightleftharpoons [\text{glucose phosphate}]^- + \text{ADP}^{3-} \qquad \Delta G^{\circ\prime} = -16.7 \text{ kJ}$$

Coupling of the two reactions is accomplished through an enzyme (Section 16.8) that simultaneously binds glucose and ATP and catalyzes the transfer of the phosphate group. The ADP is combined with phosphate to regenerate ATP in reactions catalyzed by other enzymes. Thus, there is a continuous cycling of ATP to ADP and back to ATP again to supply energy to cells (Figure 20.13).

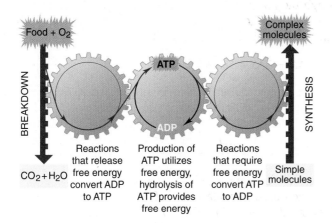

FIGURE 20.13 The cycling of metabolic free energy through ATP. Processes that release free energy are coupled to the formation of ATP from ADP, whereas those that require free energy are coupled to the hydrolysis of ATP to ADP.

SECTION 20.3 SUMMARY

The sign of the free energy change, $\Delta G = \Delta H - T\Delta S$, is directly related to reaction spontaneity: a negative ΔG corresponds to a positive ΔS_{univ}. • We use the standard free energy of formation (ΔG_f°) to calculate $\Delta G_{\text{rxn}}^{\circ}$ at 25°C. • The maximum work a system can do is never obtained from a real (irreversible) process because some free energy is always converted to heat. • The magnitude of T influences the spontaneity of temperature-dependent reactions (same signs of ΔH and ΔS) by affecting the size of $T\Delta S$. For such reactions, the T at which the reaction becomes spontaneous can be estimated by setting $\Delta G = 0$. • A nonspontaneous reaction ($\Delta G > 0$) can be coupled to a more spontaneous one ($\Delta G \ll 0$) to make it occur. For example, in organisms, the hydrolysis of ATP drives many reactions with a positive ΔG.

20.4 FREE ENERGY, EQUILIBRIUM, AND REACTION DIRECTION

The sign of ΔG allows us to predict reaction direction, but it is not the only way to do so. In Chapter 17, we predicted direction by comparing the values of the reaction quotient (Q) and the equilibrium constant (K). Recall that

- If $Q < K$ ($Q/K < 1$), the reaction as written proceeds to the right.
- If $Q > K$ ($Q/K > 1$), the reaction as written proceeds to the left.
- If $Q = K$ ($Q/K = 1$), the reaction has reached equilibrium, and there is no net reaction in either direction.

As you might expect, these two ways of predicting reaction spontaneity—the sign of ΔG and the magnitude of Q/K—are related. Their relationship emerges when we compare the signs of $\ln Q/K$ with ΔG:

- If $Q/K < 1$, then $\ln Q/K < 0$: reaction proceeds to the right ($\Delta G < 0$).
- If $Q/K > 1$, then $\ln Q/K > 0$: reaction proceeds to the left ($\Delta G > 0$).
- If $Q/K = 1$, then $\ln Q/K = 0$: reaction is at equilibrium ($\Delta G = 0$).

Note that the signs of ΔG and $\ln Q/K$ are identical for a given reaction direction. In fact, ΔG and $\ln Q/K$ are proportional to each other and made equal through the constant RT:

$$\Delta G = RT \ln \frac{Q}{K} = RT \ln Q - RT \ln K \qquad (20.11)$$

What does this central relationship mean? As you know, Q represents the concentrations (or pressures) of a system's components at any time during the reaction, whereas K represents them when the reaction has reached equilibrium. Therefore, Equation 20.11 says that ΔG depends on how different the ratio of concentrations, Q, is from the equilibrium ratio, K.

The last term in Equation 20.11 is very important. By choosing standard-state values for Q, we obtain the standard free energy change ($\Delta G°$). When all concentrations are 1 M (or all pressures 1 atm), ΔG equals $\Delta G°$ and Q equals 1:

$$\Delta G° = RT \ln 1 - RT \ln K$$

We know that $\ln 1 = 0$, so the $RT \ln Q$ term drops out, and we have

$$\Delta G° = -RT \ln K \qquad (20.12)$$

This relationship allows us to calculate the standard free energy change of a reaction ($\Delta G°$) from its equilibrium constant, or vice versa. Because $\Delta G°$ is related logarithmically to K, even a small change in the value of $\Delta G°$ has a large effect on the value of K. Table 20.2 shows the K values that correspond to a range of $\Delta G°$ values. Note that as $\Delta G°$ becomes more positive, K becomes smaller, which means the reaction reaches equilibrium with less product and more reactant. Similarly, as $\Delta G°$ becomes more negative, K becomes larger. For example, if $\Delta G° = +10$ kJ, $K \approx 0.02$, which means that the product terms are about $\frac{1}{50}$ those of the reactant terms; whereas, if $\Delta G° = -10$ kJ, they are 50 times larger.

Table 20.2 **The Relationship Between $\Delta G°$ and K at 298 K**

$\Delta G°$ (kJ)	K	Significance	
200	9×10^{-36}	Essentially no forward reaction; reverse reaction goes to completion	
100	3×10^{-18}		
50	2×10^{-9}		FORWARD REACTION / REVERSE REACTION
10	2×10^{-2}		
1	7×10^{-1}		
0	1	Forward and reverse reactions proceed to same extent	
−1	1.5		
−10	5×10^{1}		
−50	6×10^{8}		
−100	3×10^{17}	Forward reaction goes to completion; essentially no reverse reaction	
−200	1×10^{35}		

Of course, reactions do not usually begin with all components in their standard states. By substituting the relationship between $\Delta G°$ and K (Equation 20.12) into the expression for ΔG (Equation 20.11), we obtain a relationship that applies to any starting concentrations:

$$\Delta G = \Delta G° + RT \ln Q \qquad (20.13)$$

Sample Problems 20.8 and 20.9 illustrate some ways to apply Equations 20.12 and 20.13; the first sample problem employs molecular scenes to examine these ideas, while the second highlights an industrial reaction.

SAMPLE PROBLEM 20.8 Using Molecular Scenes to Find ΔG for a Reaction at Nonstandard Conditions

Problem The molecular scenes below represent three mixtures of A_2 (black) and B_2 (green) forming AB. Each molecule represents 0.10 mol, and the volume is 1 L. The equation is

$$A_2(g) + B_2(g) \rightleftharpoons 2AB(g) \qquad \Delta G° = -3.4 \text{ kJ/mol}$$

(a) If mixture 1 is at equilibrium, calculate K.
(b) Which reaction mixture has the lowest (most negative) ΔG, and which has the highest (most positive)?
(c) Is the reaction spontaneous when $[A_2] = [B_2] = [AB] = 1.0\ M$?
Plan (a) Mixture 1 is at equilibrium, so we first write the expression for Q and then find the molarity of each substance from the numbers of molecules to calculate K. **(b)** To find ΔG, we apply Equation 20.13. We are given $\Delta G°$ (-3.4 kJ/mol), and we know R (8.314 J/mol·K). We calculate T from Equation 20.12 with the value of K that we found in part (a), and substitute the molarity of each substance to get Q. **(c)** The concentration 1.0 M represents the standard state, and we substitute that concentration into Q in Equation 20.13 and solve for ΔG, which in this case equals $\Delta G°$.
Solution (a) Writing the expression for Q and calculating K:

$$A_2(g) + B_2(g) \rightleftharpoons 2AB(g) \qquad Q = \frac{[AB]^2}{[A_2][B_2]} \qquad K = \frac{(0.40)^2}{(0.20)(0.20)} = 4.0$$

(b) Calculating T from Equation 20.12 for use in Equation 20.13:

$$\Delta G° = -RT \ln K = -\frac{3.4 \text{ kJ}}{\text{mol}} = -\left(\frac{8.314 \text{ J}}{\text{mol·K}}\right) T \ln 4.0$$

$$T = \frac{\dfrac{-3.4 \text{ kJ}}{\text{mol}}\left(\dfrac{1000 \text{ J}}{1 \text{ kJ}}\right)}{-\left(\dfrac{8.314 \text{ J}}{\text{mol·K}}\right)\ln 4.0} = 295 \text{ K}$$

Calculating the value of ΔG for each mixture from Equation 20.13:
For mixture 1:

$$\Delta G = \Delta G° + RT \ln Q = -3.4 \text{ kJ} + RT \ln 4.0$$

$$= -3.4 \text{ kJ}\left(\frac{1000 \text{ J}}{1 \text{ kJ}}\right) + \left(\frac{8.314 \text{ J}}{\text{mol·K}}\right)(295 \text{ K}) \ln 4.0$$

$$= -3400 \text{ J} + 3400 \text{ J} = 0.0 \text{ J}$$

For mixture 2:

$$\Delta G = -3.4 \text{ kJ} + RT \ln \frac{(0.20)^2}{(0.30)(0.30)}$$

$$= -3.4 \text{ kJ}\left(\frac{1000 \text{ J}}{1 \text{ kJ}}\right) + \left(\frac{8.314 \text{ J}}{\text{mol·K}}\right)(295 \text{ K}) \ln 0.44 = -5.4 \times 10^3 \text{ J}$$

For mixture 3:

$$\Delta G = -3.4 \text{ kJ/mol} + RT \ln \frac{(0.60)^2}{(0.10)(0.10)}$$

$$= -3.4 \text{ kJ/mol}\left(\frac{1000 \text{ J}}{1 \text{ kJ}}\right) + \left(\frac{8.314 \text{ J}}{\text{mol·K}}\right)(295 \text{ K}) \ln 36 = 5.4 \times 10^3 \text{ J}$$

Mixture 2 has the most negative ΔG, and mixture 3 has the most positive ΔG.

(c) Finding ΔG when $[A_2] = [B_2] = [AB] = 1.0\ M$:

$$\Delta G = \Delta G^\circ + RT\ln Q = -3.4\ \text{kJ/mol} + RT\ln\frac{(1.0)^2}{(1.0)(1.0)}$$

$$= -3.4\ \text{kJ/mol} + RT\ln 1.0 = -3.4\ \text{kJ/mol}$$

Yes, the reaction is spontaneous when the components are in their standard states.
Check In (b), round to check the arithmetic; for example, for mixture 3,

$$\Delta G \approx -3000\ \text{J} + (8\ \text{J/mol·K})(300\ \text{K})4 \approx 7000\ \text{J}$$

which is in the correct ballpark.
Comment 1. By using the properties of logarithms, we didn't have to calculate T and ΔG in (b). In mixture 2, $Q < 1$, so $\ln Q$ is negative, which makes ΔG more negative. Also, note that $Q(0.44) < K(4.0)$, so $\Delta G < 0$. In mixture 3, $Q > 1$ (and is greater than it is in mixture 1), so $\ln Q$ is positive, which makes ΔG positive. Also, $Q(36) > K(4.0)$, so $\Delta G > 0$.
2. In (b), the value of zero for ΔG of the equilibrium mixture (mixture 1) makes sense, because a system at equilibrium has released all of its free energy.

FOLLOW-UP PROBLEM 20.8 The scenes below depict mixtures of X_2 (tan) and Y_2 (blue) forming XY_2. Each molecule represents 0.10 mol, and the volume is 1 L. The equation is $X_2(g) + 2Y_2(g) \rightleftharpoons 2XY_2(g);\ \Delta G^\circ = -1.3\ \text{kJ/mol}$.

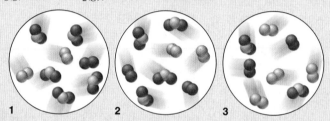

1   2   3

(a) If $K = 2$, which mixture is at equilibrium? **(b)** Rank the three mixtures from the lowest (most negative) ΔG to highest (most positive) ΔG. **(c)** What is the sign of ΔG for the change that occurs as each nonequilibrium mixture approaches equilibrium?

SAMPLE PROBLEM 20.9   Calculating ΔG at Nonstandard Conditions

Problem The oxidation of SO_2, which we considered in Sample Problem 20.7,

$$2SO_2(g) + O_2(g) \longrightarrow 2SO_3(g)$$

is too slow at 298 K to be useful in the manufacture of sulfuric acid. To overcome this low rate, the process is conducted at an elevated temperature.
(a) Calculate K at 298 K and at 973 K. ($\Delta G^\circ_{298} = -141.6\ \text{kJ/mol}$ for reaction as written; using ΔH° and ΔS° values at 973 K, $\Delta G^\circ_{973} = -12.12\ \text{kJ/mol}$ for reaction as written.)
(b) In experiments to determine the effect of temperature on reaction spontaneity, two sealed containers are filled with 0.500 atm of SO_2, 0.0100 atm of O_2, and 0.100 atm of SO_3 and kept at 25°C and at 700.°C. In which direction, if any, will the reaction proceed to reach equilibrium at each temperature?
(c) Calculate ΔG for the system in part (b) at each temperature.
Plan (a) We know ΔG°, T, and R, so we can calculate the K's from Equation 20.12.
(b) To determine if a net reaction will occur at the given pressures, we calculate Q with the given partial pressures and compare it with each K from part (a). **(c)** Because these are not standard-state pressures, we calculate ΔG at each T from Equation 20.13 with the values of ΔG° (given) and Q [found in part (b)].
Solution (a) Calculating K at the two temperatures:

$$\Delta G^\circ = -RT\ln K \qquad \text{so} \qquad K = e^{-(\Delta G^\circ/RT)}$$

At 298 K, the exponent is

$$-(\Delta G^\circ/RT) = -\left(\frac{-141.6\ \text{kJ/mol} \times \dfrac{1000\ \text{J}}{1\ \text{kJ}}}{8.314\ \text{J/mol·K} \times 298\ \text{K}}\right) = 57.2$$

So
$$K = e^{-(\Delta G^\circ/RT)} = e^{57.2} = 7\times10^{24}$$

At 973 K, the exponent is

$$-(\Delta G°/RT) = -\left(\frac{-12.12 \text{ kJ/mol} \times \frac{1000 \text{ J}}{1 \text{ kJ}}}{8.314 \text{ J/mol·K} \times 973 \text{ K}}\right) = 1.50$$

So

$$K = e^{-(\Delta G°/RT)} = e^{1.50} = 4.5$$

(b) Calculating the value of Q:

$$Q = \frac{P_{SO_3}^2}{P_{SO_2}^2 \times P_{O_2}} = \frac{0.100^2}{0.500^2 \times 0.0100} = 4.00$$

Because $Q < K$ at both temperatures, the denominator will decrease and the numerator increase—more SO_3 will form—until Q equals K. However, the reaction will go far to the right at 298 K   while approaching equilibrium, whereas it will move only slightly to the right at 973 K.

(c) Calculating ΔG, the nonstandard free energy change, at 298 K:

$$\Delta G_{298} = \Delta G° + RT \ln Q$$

$$= -141.6 \text{ kJ/mol} + \left(8.314 \text{ J/mol·K} \times \frac{1 \text{ kJ}}{1000 \text{ J}} \times 298 \text{ K} \times \ln 4.00\right)$$

$$= -138.2 \text{ kJ/mol}$$

Calculating ΔG at 973 K:

$$\Delta G_{973} = \Delta G° + RT \ln Q$$

$$= -12.12 \text{ kJ/mol} + \left(8.314 \text{ J/mol·K} \times \frac{1 \text{ kJ}}{1000 \text{ J}} \times 973 \text{ K} \times \ln 4.00\right)$$

$$= -0.9 \text{ kJ/mol}$$

Check Note that in parts (a) and (c) we made the energy units in free energy changes (kJ) consistent with those in R (J). Based on the rules for significant figures in addition and subtraction, we retain one digit to the right of the decimal place in part (c).

Comment For these starting gas pressures at 973 K, the process is barely spontaneous ($\Delta G = -0.9$ kJ/mol), so why use a higher temperature? Like the synthesis of NH_3 (Section 17.6), this process is carried out at a higher temperature *with a catalyst* to attain a higher *rate*, even though the *yield* is greater at a lower temperature.

FOLLOW-UP PROBLEM 20.9 At 298 K, hypobromous acid (HBrO) dissociates in water with a K_a of 2.3×10^{-9}.
(a) Calculate $\Delta G°$ for the dissociation of HBrO.
(b) Calculate ΔG if $[H_3O^+] = 6.0 \times 10^{-4}$ M, $[BrO^-] = 0.10$ M, and $[HBrO] = 0.20$ M.

Another Look at the Meaning of Spontaneity At this point, let's discuss some terminology related to, but distinct from, the terms *spontaneous* and *nonspontaneous*. Consider the general reaction A ⇌ B, for which $K = [B]/[A] > 1$; therefore, the reaction proceeds largely from left to right (Figure 20.14A). From pure A to the equilibrium point, $Q < K$ and the curved *green* arrow indicates that the reaction is spontaneous ($\Delta G < 0$). From there on, the curved *red* arrow shows that the reaction is nonspontaneous ($\Delta G > 0$). From pure B to the equilibrium point, $Q > K$ and the reaction is also spontaneous ($\Delta G < 0$), but not thereafter. In either case, *the free energy decreases as the reaction proceeds, until it reaches a minimum at the equilibrium mixture: $Q = K$ and $\Delta G = 0$*. For the overall reaction A ⇌ B (starting with all components in their standard states), $G_B°$ is smaller than $G_A°$, so $\Delta G°$ is negative, which corresponds to $K > 1$. We call this a *product-favored* reaction because the final state of the system contains mostly product.

Now consider the opposite situation, a general reaction C ⇌ D, for which $K = [D]/[C] < 1$: the reaction proceeds only slightly from left to right (Figure 20.14B). Here, too, whether we start with pure C or pure D, the reaction is spontaneous ($\Delta G < 0$) until the equilibrium point. But here, the equilibrium mixture contains mostly C (the reactant), so we say the reaction is *reactant favored*. In this case, $G_D°$ is *larger* than $G_C°$, so $\Delta G°$ is *positive*, which corresponds to $K < 1$.

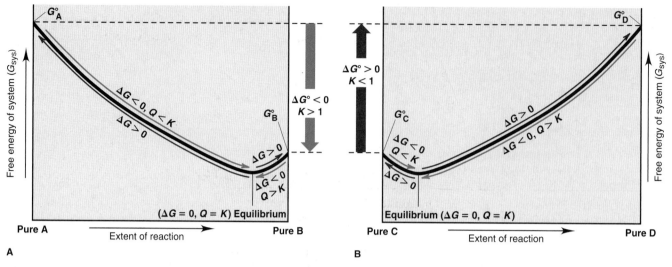

FIGURE 20.14 The relation between free energy and the extent of reaction. The free energy of the system is plotted against the extent of reaction. Each reaction proceeds spontaneously ($Q \neq K$ and $\Delta G < 0$; *curved green arrows*) from either pure reactants (A or C) or pure products (B or D) *to* the equilibrium mixture, at which point $\Delta G = 0$. The reaction *from* the equilibrium mixture to either pure reactants or products is nonspontaneous ($\Delta G > 0$; *curved red arrows*). **A,** For the product-favored reaction A $\rightleftharpoons$ B, $G_A^\circ > G_B^\circ$, so $\Delta G^\circ < 0$ and $K > 1$. **B,** For the reactant-favored reaction C $\rightleftharpoons$ D, $G_D^\circ > G_C^\circ$, so $\Delta G^\circ > 0$ and $K < 1$.

The point is that *spontaneous* refers to that portion of a reaction in which the free energy is decreasing, that is, from some starting mixture to the equilibrium mixture, whereas *product-favored* refers to a reaction that goes predominantly, but not necessarily completely, to product (see Table 20.2).

SECTION 20.4 SUMMARY

Two ways of predicting reaction direction are from the value of ΔG and from the relation of Q to K. These variables represent different aspects of the same phenomenon and are related to each other by $\Delta G = RT \ln Q/K$. When $Q = K$, the system can release no more free energy. • Beginning with Q at the standard state, the free energy change is ΔG°, and it is related to the equilibrium constant by $\Delta G^\circ = -RT \ln K$. For nonstandard conditions, ΔG has two components: ΔG° and $RT \ln Q$. • Any nonequilibrium mixture of reactants and products moves spontaneously ($\Delta G < 0$) toward the equilibrium mixture. A product-favored reaction goes predominantly toward product and, thus, has $K > 1$ and $\Delta G^\circ < 0$.

CHAPTER REVIEW GUIDE

The following sections provide many aids to help you study this chapter. (Numbers in parentheses refer to pages, unless noted otherwise.)

• LEARNING OBJECTIVES *These are concepts and skills to review after studying this chapter.*

Related section (§), sample problem (SP), and end-of-chapter problem (EP) numbers are listed in parentheses.

1. Discuss the meaning of a spontaneous change, and explain why the first law or the sign of ΔH° cannot predict its direction (§ 20.1) (EPs 20.1–20.3, 20.8, 20.9)

2. Understand the meaning of entropy (S) in terms of the number of microstates through which a system's energy is dispersed; describe how the second law provides the criterion for spontaneity, how the third law allows us to find absolute values of standard molar entropies (S°), and how conditions and properties of substances influence S° (§ 20.1) (SP 20.1) (EPs 20.4–20.7, 20.10–20.23)

3. Calculate ΔS_{rxn}° from S° of reactants and products, understand the influence of ΔS_{surr}° on ΔS_{rxn}°, and describe the relationships be-

tween ΔS_{surr} and ΔH_{sys} and between ΔS_{univ} and K (§ 20.2) (SPs 20.2, 20.3) (EPs 20.24–20.35)

4. Derive the free energy change (ΔG) from the second law, and explain how ΔG is related to work; explain why temperature (T) affects the spontaneity of some reactions but not others; describe how a spontaneous change drives a nonspontaneous one; calculate ΔG_{rxn}° from ΔH_f° and S° values or from ΔG_f° values and quantify the effect of T on ΔG°; obtain the T at which a reaction becomes spontaneous (§ 20.3) (SPs 20.4–20.7) (EPs 20.36–20.51)

5. Know the relationships of ΔG to Q/K, ΔG° to K, and ΔG to ΔG° and Q, and understand why ΔG decreases as a reaction moves toward equilibrium (§ 20.4) (SPs 20.8, 20.9) (EPs 20.52–20.67)

- ## KEY TERMS *These important terms appear in boldface in the chapter and are defined again in the Glossary.*

Section 20.1
spontaneous change (670)
entropy (S) (673)
second law of
  thermodynamics (676)
third law of
  thermodynamics (676)

standard molar entropy
  ($S°$) (677)
Section 20.2
standard entropy of reaction
  ($\Delta S°_{rxn}$) (682)

Section 20.3
free energy (G) (686)
standard free energy change
  ($\Delta G°$) (687)
standard free energy of
  formation ($\Delta G°_f$) (688)

coupling of reactions (692)
adenosine triphosphate
  (ATP) (693)

- ## KEY EQUATIONS AND RELATIONSHIPS *Numbered and screened concepts are listed for you to refer to or memorize.*

20.1 Defining entropy in terms of the number of microstates (W) in which the energy of a system can be distributed (673):
$$S = k \ln W$$

20.2 Quantifying the entropy change in terms of heat absorbed (or released) in a reversible process (675):
$$\Delta S_{sys} = \frac{q_{rev}}{T}$$

20.3 Stating the second law of thermodynamics, for a spontaneous process (676):
$$\Delta S_{univ} = \Delta S_{sys} + \Delta S_{surr} > 0$$

20.4 Calculating the standard entropy of reaction from the standard molar entropies of reactants and products (682):
$$\Delta S°_{rxn} = \Sigma m S°_{products} - \Sigma n S°_{reactants}$$

20.5 Relating the entropy change in the surroundings to the enthalpy change of the system and the temperature (683):
$$\Delta S_{surr} = -\frac{\Delta H_{sys}}{T}$$

20.6 Expressing the free energy change of the system in terms of its component enthalpy and entropy changes (Gibbs equation) (686):
$$\Delta G_{sys} = \Delta H_{sys} - T\Delta S_{sys}$$

20.7 Calculating the standard free energy change from standard enthalpy and entropy changes (687):
$$\Delta G°_{sys} = \Delta H°_{sys} - T\Delta S°_{sys}$$

20.8 Calculating the standard free energy change from the standard free energies of formation (688):
$$\Delta G°_{rxn} = \Sigma m\Delta G°_{f(products)} - \Sigma n\Delta G°_{f(reactants)}$$

20.9 Relating the free energy change to the maximum work a process can perform (689):
$$\Delta G = w_{max}$$

20.10 Finding the temperature at which a reaction becomes spontaneous (692):
$$T = \frac{\Delta H}{\Delta S}$$

20.11 Expressing the free energy change in terms of Q and K (694):
$$\Delta G = RT \ln \frac{Q}{K} = RT \ln Q - RT \ln K$$

20.12 Expressing the free energy change when Q is evaluated at the standard state (694):
$$\Delta G° = -RT \ln K$$

20.13 Expressing the free energy change for nonstandard initial conditions (694):
$$\Delta G = \Delta G° + RT \ln Q$$

- ## BRIEF SOLUTIONS TO *FOLLOW-UP PROBLEMS* *Compare your own solutions to these calculation steps and answers.*

20.1 (a) $PCl_5(g)$: higher molar mass and more complex molecule; (b) $BaCl_2(s)$: higher molar mass; (c) $Br_2(g)$: gases have more freedom of motion and dispersal of energy than liquids.

20.2 (a) $2NaOH(s) + CO_2(g) \longrightarrow Na_2CO_3(s) + H_2O(l)$
$\Delta n_{gas} = -1$, so $\Delta S°_{rxn} < 0$
$\Delta S°_{rxn} = [(1 \text{ mol } H_2O)(69.9 \text{ J/mol·K})$
$\quad + (1 \text{ mol } Na_2CO_3)(139 \text{ J/mol·K})]$
$\quad - [(1 \text{ mol } CO_2)(213.7 \text{ J/mol·K})$
$\quad + (2 \text{ mol } NaOH)(64.5 \text{ J/mol·K})]$
$\quad = -134 \text{ J/K}$
(b) $2Fe(s) + 3H_2O(g) \longrightarrow Fe_2O_3(s) + 3H_2(g)$
$\Delta n_{gas} = 0$, so cannot predict sign of $\Delta S°_{rxn}$
$\Delta S°_{rxn} = [(1 \text{ mol } Fe_2O_3)(87.4 \text{ J/mol·K})$
$\quad + (3 \text{ mol } H_2)(130.6 \text{ J/mol·K})]$
$\quad - [(2 \text{ mol } Fe)(27.3 \text{ J/mol·K})$
$\quad + (3 \text{ mol } H_2O)(188.7 \text{ J/mol·K})]$
$\quad = -141.5 \text{ J/K}$

20.3 $2FeO(s) + \frac{1}{2}O_2(g) \longrightarrow Fe_2O_3(s)$
$\Delta S°_{sys} = (1 \text{ mol } Fe_2O_3)(87.4 \text{ J/mol·K})$
$\quad - [(2 \text{ mol } FeO)(60.75 \text{ J/mol·K})$
$\quad + (\frac{1}{2} \text{ mol } O_2)(205.0 \text{ J/mol·K})]$
$\quad = -136.6 \text{ J/K}$
$\Delta H°_{sys} = (1 \text{ mol } Fe_2O_3)(-825.5 \text{ kJ/mol})$
$\quad - [(2 \text{ mol } FeO)(-272.0 \text{ kJ/mol})$
$\quad + (\frac{1}{2} \text{ mol } O_2)(0 \text{ kJ/mol})]$
$\quad = -281.5 \text{ kJ}$
$\Delta S_{surr} = -\frac{\Delta H°_{sys}}{T} = -\frac{(-281.5 \text{ kJ} \times 1000 \text{ J/kJ})}{298 \text{ K}} = +945 \text{ J/K}$
$\Delta S_{univ} = \Delta S°_{sys} + \Delta S_{surr} = -136.6 \text{ J/K} + 945 \text{ J/K}$
$\quad = 808 \text{ J/K}$; reaction is spontaneous at 298 K.

20.4 Using $\Delta H°_f$ and $S°$ values from Appendix B,
$\Delta H°_{rxn} = -114.2 \text{ kJ}$ and $\Delta S°_{rxn} = -146.5 \text{ J/K}$
$\Delta G°_{rxn} = \Delta H°_{rxn} - T\Delta S°_{rxn} = -114.2 \text{ kJ}$
$\quad - [(298 \text{ K})(-146.5 \text{ J/K})(1 \text{ kJ}/1000 \text{ J})]$
$\quad = -70.5 \text{ kJ}$

20.5 (a) ΔG°_{rxn} = (2 mol NO_2)(51 kJ/mol)
    $-$ [(2 mol NO)(86.60 kJ/mol)
    $+$ (1 mol O_2)(0 kJ/mol)]
    = -71 kJ
(b) ΔG°_{rxn} = (2 mol CO)(-137.2 kJ/mol) $-$ [(2 mol C)(0 kJ/mol)
    $+$ (1 mol O_2)(0 kJ/mol)]
    = -274.4 kJ

20.6 (a) More moles of gas are present after the reaction, so $\Delta S > 0$.
(b) The problem says the reaction is spontaneous ($\Delta G < 0$) only above 325°C, which implies high T. If $\Delta S > 0$, $-T\Delta S < 0$, so ΔG will become negative at higher T only if $\Delta H > 0$.

20.7 ΔG becomes negative at lower T, so $\Delta H < 0$, $\Delta S < 0$, and $-T\Delta S > 0$. At lower T, the negative ΔH value becomes larger than the positive $-T\Delta S$ value.

20.8 (a) Mixture 2 is at equilibrium. (b) 3 (most negative) $< 2 < 1$ (most positive). (c) Any reaction mixture moves spontaneously toward equilibrium, so both changes have a negative ΔG.

20.9 (a) $\Delta G^{\circ} = -RT \ln K = -8.314$ J/mol·K $\times \dfrac{1\ kJ}{1000\ J} \times 298$ K
    $\times \ln (2.3 \times 10^{-9})$
    = 49 kJ/mol
(b) $Q = \dfrac{[H_3O^+][BrO^-]}{[HBrO]} = \dfrac{(6.0 \times 10^{-4})(0.10)}{0.20} = 3.0 \times 10^{-4}$
$\Delta G = \Delta G^{\circ} + RT \ln Q$
    = 49 kJ/mol
    $+ \left[8.314\ \text{J/mol·K} \times \dfrac{1\ kJ}{1000\ J} \times 298\ \text{K} \times \ln (3.0 \times 10^{-4}) \right]$
    = 29 kJ/mol

PROBLEMS

Problems with **colored** *numbers are answered in Appendix E. Sections match the text and provide the numbers of relevant sample problems. Bracketed problems are grouped in pairs (indicated by a short rule) that cover the same concept. Comprehensive Problems are based on material from any section or previous chapter.*

Note: Unless stated otherwise, problems refer to systems at 298 K (25°C). Solving these problems may require values from Appendix B.

The Second Law of Thermodynamics: Predicting Spontaneous Change
(Sample Problem 20.1)

20.1 Distinguish between the terms *spontaneous* and *instantaneous*. Give an example of a process that is spontaneous but very slow, and one that is very fast but not spontaneous.

20.2 Distinguish between the terms *spontaneous* and *nonspontaneous*. Can a nonspontaneous process occur? Explain.

20.3 State the first law of thermodynamics in terms of (a) the energy of the universe; (b) the creation or destruction of energy; (c) the energy change of system and surroundings. Does the first law reveal the direction of spontaneous change? Explain.

20.4 State qualitatively the relationship between entropy and freedom of particle motion. Use this idea to explain why you will probably never (a) be suffocated because all the air near you has moved to the other side of the room; (b) see half the water in your cup of tea freeze while the other half boils.

20.5 Why is ΔS_{vap} of a substance always larger than ΔS_{fus}?

20.6 How does the entropy of the surroundings change during an exothermic reaction? An endothermic reaction? Other than the examples cited in text, describe a spontaneous endothermic process.

20.7 (a) What is the entropy of a perfect crystal at 0 K?
(b) Does entropy increase or decrease as the temperature rises?
(c) Why is $\Delta H^{\circ}_f = 0$ but $S^{\circ} > 0$ for an element?
(d) Why does Appendix B list ΔH°_f values but not ΔS°_f values?

20.8 Which of these processes are spontaneous: (a) water evaporating from a puddle in summer; (b) a lion chasing an antelope; (c) an unstable isotope undergoing radioactive disintegration?

20.9 Which of these processes are nonspontaneous: (a) methane burning in air; (b) a teaspoonful of sugar dissolving in a cup of hot coffee; (c) a soft-boiled egg becoming raw?

20.10 Predict the sign of ΔS_{sys} for each process: (a) a piece of wax melting; (b) silver chloride precipitating from solution; (c) dew forming.

20.11 Predict the sign of ΔS_{sys} for each process: (a) alcohol evaporating; (b) a solid explosive converting to a gas; (c) perfume vapors diffusing through a room.

20.12 Without using Appendix B, predict the sign of ΔS° for
(a) $2K(s) + F_2(g) \longrightarrow 2KF(s)$
(b) $NH_3(g) + HBr(g) \longrightarrow NH_4Br(s)$
(c) $NaClO_3(s) \longrightarrow Na^+(aq) + ClO_3^-(aq)$

20.13 Without using Appendix B, predict the sign of ΔS° for
(a) $H_2S(g) + \frac{1}{2}O_2(g) \longrightarrow \frac{1}{8}S_8(s) + H_2O(g)$
(b) $HCl(aq) + NaOH(aq) \longrightarrow NaCl(aq) + H_2O(l)$
(c) $2NO_2(g) \longrightarrow N_2O_4(g)$

20.14 Without using Appendix B, predict the sign of ΔS° for
(a) $CaCO_3(s) + 2HCl(aq) \longrightarrow CaCl_2(aq) + H_2O(l) + CO_2(g)$
(b) $2NO(g) + O_2(g) \longrightarrow 2NO_2(g)$
(c) $2KClO_3(s) \longrightarrow 2KCl(s) + 3O_2(g)$

20.15 Without using Appendix B, predict the sign of ΔS° for
(a) $Ag^+(aq) + Cl^-(aq) \longrightarrow AgCl(s)$
(b) $KBr(s) \longrightarrow KBr(aq)$

(c) $CH_3CH{=}CH_2(g) \longrightarrow$ $\overset{\displaystyle CH_2}{\underset{\displaystyle H_2C-CH_2(g)}{\diagup\,\diagdown}}$

20.16 Predict the sign of ΔS for each process:
(a) $C_2H_5OH(g)$ (350 K and 500 torr) $\longrightarrow$
            $C_2H_5OH(g)$ (350 K and 250 torr)
(b) $N_2(g)$ (298 K and 1 atm) $\longrightarrow N_2(aq)$ (298 K and 1 atm)
(c) $O_2(aq)$ (303 K and 1 atm) $\longrightarrow O_2(g)$ (303 K and 1 atm)

20.17 Predict the sign of ΔS for each process:
(a) $O_2(g)$ (1.0 L at 1 atm) $\longrightarrow O_2(g)$ (0.10 L at 10 atm)
(b) $Cu(s)$ (350°C and 2.5 atm) $\longrightarrow$ $Cu(s)$ (450°C and 2.5 atm)
(c) $Cl_2(g)$ (100°C and 1 atm) $\longrightarrow Cl_2(g)$ (10°C and 1 atm)

20.18 Predict which substance has greater molar entropy. Explain.
(a) Butane $CH_3CH_2CH_2CH_3(g)$ or 2-butene $CH_3CH{=}CHCH_3(g)$
(b) Ne(g) or Xe(g)   (c) $CH_4(g)$ or $CCl_4(l)$

20.19 Predict which substance has greater molar entropy. Explain.
(a) $CH_3OH(l)$ or $C_2H_5OH(l)$ (b) $KClO_3(s)$ or $KClO_3(aq)$
(c) $Na(s)$ or $K(s)$

20.20 Without consulting Appendix B, arrange each group in order of *increasing* standard molar entropy ($S°$). Explain.
(a) Graphite, diamond, charcoal
(b) Ice, water vapor, liquid water   (c) O_2, O_3, O atoms

20.21 Without consulting Appendix B, arrange each group in order of *increasing* standard molar entropy ($S°$). Explain.
(a) Glucose ($C_6H_{12}O_6$), sucrose ($C_{12}H_{22}O_{11}$), ribose ($C_5H_{10}O_5$)
(b) $CaCO_3$, $Ca + C + \frac{3}{2}O_2$, $CaO + CO_2$
(c) $SF_6(g)$, $SF_4(g)$, $S_2F_{10}(g)$

20.22 Without consulting Appendix B, arrange each group in order of *decreasing* standard molar entropy ($S°$). Explain.
(a) $ClO_4^-(aq)$, $ClO_2^-(aq)$, $ClO_3^-(aq)$
(b) $NO_2(g)$, $NO(g)$, $N_2(g)$ (c) $Fe_2O_3(s)$, $Al_2O_3(s)$, $Fe_3O_4(s)$

20.23 Without consulting Appendix B, arrange each group in order of *decreasing* standard molar entropy ($S°$). Explain.
(a) Mg metal, Ca metal, Ba metal
(b) Hexane (C_6H_{14}), benzene (C_6H_6), cyclohexane (C_6H_{12})
(c) $PF_2Cl_3(g)$, $PF_5(g)$, $PF_3(g)$

Calculating the Change in Entropy of a Reaction
(Sample Problems 20.2 and 20.3)

20.24 For the reaction depicted in the molecular scenes, X is red and Y is green.

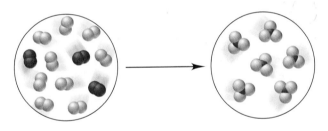

(a) Write a balanced equation.
(b) Determine the sign of ΔS.
(c) Which species has the highest molar entropy?

20.25 What property of entropy allows Hess's law to be used in the calculation of entropy changes?

20.26 Describe the equilibrium condition in terms of the entropy changes of a system and its surroundings. What does this description mean about the entropy change of the universe?

20.27 For the reaction $H_2O(g) + Cl_2O(g) \longrightarrow 2HClO(g)$, you know $\Delta S°_{rxn}$ and $S°$ of $HClO(g)$ and of $H_2O(g)$. Write an expression to determine $S°$ of $Cl_2O(g)$.

20.28 For each reaction, predict the sign and find the value of $\Delta S°$:
(a) $3NO(g) \longrightarrow N_2O(g) + NO_2(g)$
(b) $3H_2(g) + Fe_2O_3(s) \longrightarrow 2Fe(s) + 3H_2O(g)$
(c) $P_4(s) + 5O_2(g) \longrightarrow P_4O_{10}(s)$

20.29 For each reaction, predict the sign and find the value of $\Delta S°$:
(a) $3NO_2(g) + H_2O(l) \longrightarrow 2HNO_3(l) + NO(g)$
(b) $N_2(g) + 3F_2(g) \longrightarrow 2NF_3(g)$
(c) $C_6H_{12}O_6(s) + 6O_2(g) \longrightarrow 6CO_2(g) + 6H_2O(g)$

20.30 Find $\Delta S°$ for the combustion of ethane (C_2H_6) to carbon dioxide and gaseous water. Is the sign of $\Delta S°$ as expected?

20.31 Find $\Delta S°$ for the reaction of nitric oxide with hydrogen to form ammonia and water vapor. Is the sign of $\Delta S°$ as expected?

20.32 Find $\Delta S°$ for the formation of $Cu_2O(s)$ from its elements.

20.33 Find $\Delta S°$ for the formation of $CH_3OH(l)$ from its elements.

20.34 Sulfur dioxide is released in the combustion of coal. Scrubbers use aqueous slurries of calcium hydroxide to remove the SO_2 from flue gases. Write a balanced equation for this reaction and calculate $\Delta S°$ at 298 K [$S°$ of $CaSO_3(s)$ = 101.4 J/mol·K].

20.35 Oxyacetylene welding is used to repair metal structures, including bridges, buildings, and even the Statue of Liberty. Calculate $\Delta S°$ for the combustion of 1 mol of acetylene (C_2H_2).

Entropy, Free Energy, and Work
(Sample Problems 20.4 to 20.7)

20.36 What is the advantage of calculating free energy changes rather than entropy changes to determine reaction spontaneity?

20.37 Given that $\Delta G_{sys} = -T\Delta S_{univ}$, explain how the sign of ΔG_{sys} correlates with reaction spontaneity.

20.38 (a) Is an endothermic reaction more likely to be spontaneous at higher temperatures or lower temperatures? Explain.
(b) The change depicted below occurs at constant pressure. Explain your answers to each of the following: (1) What is the sign of ΔH? (2) What is the sign of ΔS? (3) What is the sign of ΔS_{surr}? (4) How does the sign of ΔG vary with temperature?

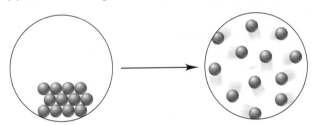

20.39 With its components in their standard states, a certain reaction is spontaneous only at high T. What do you know about the signs of $\Delta H°$ and $\Delta S°$? Describe a process for which this is true.

20.40 Calculate $\Delta G°$ for each reaction using $\Delta G°_f$ values:
(a) $2Mg(s) + O_2(g) \longrightarrow 2MgO(s)$
(b) $2CH_3OH(g) + 3O_2(g) \longrightarrow 2CO_2(g) + 4H_2O(g)$
(c) $BaO(s) + CO_2(g) \longrightarrow BaCO_3(s)$

20.41 Calculate $\Delta G°$ for each reaction using $\Delta G°_f$ values:
(a) $H_2(g) + I_2(s) \longrightarrow 2HI(g)$
(b) $MnO_2(s) + 2CO(g) \longrightarrow Mn(s) + 2CO_2(g)$
(c) $NH_4Cl(s) \longrightarrow NH_3(g) + HCl(g)$

20.42 Find $\Delta G°$ for the reactions in Problem 20.40 using $\Delta H°_f$ and $S°$ values.

20.43 Find $\Delta G°$ for the reactions in Problem 20.41 using $\Delta H°_f$ and $S°$ values.

20.44 Consider the oxidation of carbon monoxide:
$$CO(g) + \tfrac{1}{2}O_2(g) \longrightarrow CO_2(g)$$
(a) Predict the signs of $\Delta S°$ and $\Delta H°$. Explain.
(b) Calculate $\Delta G°$ by two different methods.

20.45 Consider the combustion of butane gas:
$$C_4H_{10}(g) + \tfrac{13}{2}O_2(g) \longrightarrow 4CO_2(g) + 5H_2O(g)$$
(a) Predict the signs of $\Delta S°$ and $\Delta H°$. Explain.
(b) Calculate $\Delta G°$ by two different methods.

20.46 One reaction used to produce small quantities of pure H_2 is

$$CH_3OH(g) \rightleftharpoons CO(g) + 2H_2(g)$$

(a) Determine $\Delta H°$ and $\Delta S°$ for the reaction at 298 K.
(b) Assuming that these values are relatively independent of temperature, calculate $\Delta G°$ at 28°C, 128°C, and 228°C.
(c) What is the significance of the different values of $\Delta G°$?

20.47 A reaction that occurs in the internal combustion engine is

$$N_2(g) + O_2(g) \rightleftharpoons 2NO(g)$$

(a) Determine $\Delta H°$ and $\Delta S°$ for the reaction at 298 K.
(b) Assuming that these values are relatively independent of temperature, calculate $\Delta G°$ at 100.°C, 2560.°C, and 3540.°C.
(c) What is the significance of the different values of $\Delta G°$?

20.48 Use $\Delta H°$ and $\Delta S°$ values for the following process at 1 atm to find the normal boiling point of Br_2: $Br_2(l) \rightleftharpoons Br_2(g)$

20.49 Use $\Delta H°$ and $\Delta S°$ values to find the temperature at which these sulfur allotropes reach equilibrium at 1 atm:

$$S(\text{rhombic}) \rightleftharpoons S(\text{monoclinic})$$

20.50 As a fuel, $H_2(g)$ produces only nonpolluting $H_2O(g)$ when it burns. Moreover, it combines with $O_2(g)$ in a fuel cell (Chapter 21) to provide electrical energy.
(a) Calculate $\Delta H°$, $\Delta S°$, and $\Delta G°$ per mol of H_2 at 298 K.
(b) Is the spontaneity of this reaction dependent on T? Explain.
(c) At what temperature does the reaction become spontaneous?

20.51 The United States requires a renewable component in automobile fuels. The fermentation of glucose from corn produces ethanol, which is added to gasoline to fulfill this requirement:

$$C_6H_{12}O_6(s) \longrightarrow 2C_2H_5OH(l) + 2CO_2(g)$$

Calculate $\Delta H°$, $\Delta S°$, and $\Delta G°$ for the reaction at 25°C. Is the spontaneity of this reaction dependent on T? Explain.

Free Energy, Equilibrium, and Reaction Direction
(Sample Problems 20.8 and 20.9)

20.52 (a) If $K \ll 1$ for a reaction, what do you know about the sign and magnitude of $\Delta G°$? (b) If $\Delta G° \ll 0$ for a reaction, what do you know about the magnitude of K? Of Q?

20.53 The scenes and the graph relate to the reaction of $X_2(g)$ (black) with $Y_2(g)$ (orange) to form $XY(g)$.
(a) If reactants and products are in their standard states, what quantity is represented on the graph by x?
(b) Which scene represents point 1? Explain. (c) Which scene represents point 2? Explain.

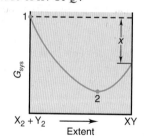

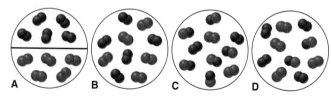

20.54 How is the free energy change of a process related to the work that can be obtained from the process? Is this quantity of work obtainable in practice? Explain.

20.55 What is the difference between $\Delta G°$ and ΔG? Under what circumstances does $\Delta G = \Delta G°$?

20.56 Calculate K at 298 K for each reaction:
(a) $NO(g) + \frac{1}{2}O_2(g) \rightleftharpoons NO_2(g)$

(b) $2HCl(g) \rightleftharpoons H_2(g) + Cl_2(g)$
(c) $2C(\text{graphite}) + O_2(g) \rightleftharpoons 2CO(g)$

20.57 Calculate K at 298 K for each reaction:
(a) $2H_2S(g) + 3O_2(g) \rightleftharpoons 2H_2O(g) + 2SO_2(g)$
(b) $H_2SO_4(l) \rightleftharpoons H_2O(l) + SO_3(g)$
(c) $HCN(aq) + NaOH(aq) \rightleftharpoons NaCN(aq) + H_2O(l)$

20.58 Use Appendix B to determine the K_{sp} of Ag_2S.
20.59 Use Appendix B to determine the K_{sp} of CaF_2.

20.60 For the reaction $I_2(g) + Cl_2(g) \rightleftharpoons 2ICl(g)$, calculate K_p at 25°C [$\Delta G_f°$ of $ICl(g) = -6.075$ kJ/mol].

20.61 For the reaction $CaCO_3(s) \rightleftharpoons CaO(s) + CO_2(g)$, calculate the equilibrium P_{CO_2} at 25°C.

20.62 The K_{sp} of $PbCl_2$ is 1.7×10^{-5} at 25°C. What is $\Delta G°$? Is it possible to prepare a solution that contains $Pb^{2+}(aq)$ and $Cl^-(aq)$, at their standard-state concentrations?

20.63 The K_{sp} of ZnF_2 is 3.0×10^{-2} at 25°C. What is $\Delta G°$? Is it possible to prepare a solution that contains $Zn^{2+}(aq)$ and $F^-(aq)$ at their standard-state concentrations?

20.64 The equilibrium constant for the reaction

$$2Fe^{3+}(aq) + Hg_2^{2+}(aq) \rightleftharpoons 2Fe^{2+}(aq) + 2Hg^{2+}(aq)$$

is $K_c = 9.1 \times 10^{-6}$ at 298 K.
(a) What is $\Delta G°$ at this temperature?
(b) If standard-state concentrations of the reactants and products are mixed, in which direction does the reaction proceed?
(c) Calculate ΔG when $[Fe^{3+}] = 0.20$ M, $[Hg_2^{2+}] = 0.010$ M, $[Fe^{2+}] = 0.010$ M, and $[Hg^{2+}] = 0.025$ M. In which direction will the reaction proceed to achieve equilibrium?

20.65 The formation constant for the reaction

$$Ni^{2+}(aq) + 6NH_3(aq) \rightleftharpoons Ni(NH_3)_6^{2+}(aq)$$

is $K_f = 5.6 \times 10^8$ at 25°C.
(a) What is $\Delta G°$ at this temperature?
(b) If standard-state concentrations of the reactants and products are mixed, in which direction does the reaction proceed?
(c) Determine ΔG when $[Ni(NH_3)_6^{2+}] = 0.010$ M, $[Ni^{2+}] = 0.0010$ M, and $[NH_3] = 0.0050$ M. In which direction will the reaction proceed to achieve equilibrium?

20.66 High levels of ozone (O_3) cause rubber to deteriorate, green plants to turn brown, and many people to have difficulty breathing.
(a) Is the formation of O_3 from O_2 favored at all T, no T, high T, or low T?
(b) Calculate $\Delta G°$ for this reaction at 298 K.
(c) Calculate ΔG at 298 K for this reaction in urban smog where $[O_2] = 0.21$ atm and $[O_3] = 5 \times 10^{-7}$ atm.

20.67 A $BaSO_4$ slurry is ingested before the gastrointestinal tract is x-rayed because it is opaque to x-rays and defines the contours of the tract. Ba^{2+} ion is toxic, but the compound is nearly insoluble. If $\Delta G°$ at 37°C (body temperature) is 59.1 kJ/mol for the process

$$BaSO_4(s) \rightleftharpoons Ba^{2+}(aq) + SO_4^{2-}(aq)$$

what is $[Ba^{2+}]$ in the intestinal tract? (Assume that the only source of SO_4^{2-} is the ingested slurry.)

Comprehensive Problems
Problems with an asterisk (*) are more challenging.

20.68 According to the advertisement, "a diamond is forever."
(a) Calculate $\Delta H°$, $\Delta S°$, and $\Delta G°$ at 298 K for the phase change

$$\text{Diamond} \longrightarrow \text{graphite}$$

(b) Given the conditions under which diamond jewelry is normally kept, argue for and against the statement in the ad.

(c) Given the answers in part (a), what would need to be done to make synthetic diamonds from graphite?

(d) Assuming $\Delta H°$ and $\Delta S°$ do not change with temperature, can graphite be converted to diamond spontaneously at 1 atm?

20.69 Replace each question mark with the correct information:

	ΔS_{rxn}	ΔH_{rxn}	ΔG_{rxn}	Comment
(a)	+	−	−	?
(b)	?	0	−	Spontaneous
(c)	−	+	?	Not spontaneous
(d)	0	?	−	Spontaneous
(e)	?	0	+	?
(f)	+	+	?	$T\Delta S > \Delta H$

20.70 What is the change in entropy when 0.200 mol of potassium freezes at 63.7°C ($\Delta H_{fus} = 2.39$ kJ/mol)?

* 20.71 Hemoglobin carries O_2 from the lungs to tissue cells, where the O_2 is released. The protein is represented as Hb in its unoxygenated form and as Hb·O_2 in its oxygenated form. One reason CO is toxic is that it competes with O_2 in binding to Hb:

$$Hb·O_2(aq) + CO(g) \rightleftharpoons Hb·CO(aq) + O_2(g)$$

(a) If $\Delta G° \approx -14$ kJ at 37°C (body temperature), what is the ratio of [Hb·CO] to [Hb·O_2] at 37°C with [O_2] = [CO]?

(b) How is Le Châtelier's principle used to treat CO poisoning?

20.72 Magnesia (MgO) is used for fire brick, crucibles, and furnace linings because of its high melting point. It is produced by decomposing magnesite ($MgCO_3$) at around 1200°C.

(a) Write a balanced equation for magnesite decomposition.

(b) Use $\Delta H°$ and $S°$ values to find $\Delta G°$ at 298 K.

(c) Assuming $\Delta H°$ and $S°$ do not change with temperature, find the minimum temperature at which the reaction is spontaneous.

(d) Calculate the equilibrium P_{CO_2} above $MgCO_3$ at 298 K.

(e) Calculate the equilibrium P_{CO_2} above $MgCO_3$ at 1200 K.

20.73 The molecular scene depicts a gaseous equilibrium mixture at 460°C for the reaction of H_2 (blue) and I_2 (purple) to form HI. Each molecule represents 0.010 mol and the container volume is 1.0 L. (a) Is $K_c >$, =, or < 1? (b) Is $K_p >$, =, or < K_c? (c) Calculate $\Delta G°_{rxn}$. (d) How would the value of $\Delta G°_{rxn}$ change if the purple molecules represented H_2 and the blue I_2? Explain.

20.74 Methanol, a major industrial feedstock, is made by several catalyzed reactions, such as $CO(g) + 2H_2(g) \longrightarrow CH_3OH(l)$.

(a) Show that this reaction is thermodynamically feasible.

(b) Is it favored at low or at high temperatures?

(c) One concern about using CH_3OH as an auto fuel is its oxidation in air to yield formaldehyde, $CH_2O(g)$, which poses a health hazard. Calculate $\Delta G°$ at 100.°C for this oxidation.

20.75 (a) Write a balanced equation for the gaseous reaction between N_2O_5 and F_2 to form NF_3 and O_2. (b) Determine $\Delta G°_{rxn}$.

(c) Find ΔG_{rxn} at 298 K if $P_{N_2O_5} = P_{F_2} = 0.20$ atm, $P_{NF_3} = 0.25$ atm, and $P_{O_2} = 0.50$ atm.

20.76 Consider the following reaction:

$$2NOBr(g) \rightleftharpoons 2NO(g) + Br_2(g) \qquad K = 0.42 \text{ at } 373 \text{ K}$$

Given that $S°$ of NOBr(g) = 272.6 J/mol·K and that $\Delta S°_{rxn}$ and $\Delta H°_{rxn}$ are constant with temperature, find

(a) $\Delta S°_{rxn}$ at 298 K   (b) $\Delta G°_{rxn}$ at 373 K

(c) $\Delta H°_{rxn}$ at 373 K   (d) $\Delta H°_f$ of NOBr at 298 K

(e) $\Delta G°_{rxn}$ at 298 K   (f) $\Delta G°_f$ of NOBr at 298 K

20.77 Calculate the equilibrium constants for decomposition of the hydrogen halides at 298 K: $2HX(g) \rightleftharpoons H_2(g) + X_2(g)$ What do these values indicate about the extent of decomposition of HX at 298 K? Suggest a reason for this trend.

20.78 The key process in a blast furnace during the production of iron is the reaction of Fe_2O_3 and carbon to yield Fe and CO_2.

(a) Calculate $\Delta H°$ and $\Delta S°$. [Assume C(graphite).]

(b) Is the reaction spontaneous at low or at high T? Explain.

(c) Is the reaction spontaneous at 298 K?

(d) At what temperature does the reaction become spontaneous?

20.79 Bromine monochloride is formed from the elements:

$$Cl_2(g) + Br_2(g) \longrightarrow 2BrCl(g)$$
$$\Delta H°_{rxn} = -1.35 \text{ kJ/mol} \qquad \Delta G°_f = -0.88 \text{ kJ/mol}$$

Calculate (a) $\Delta H°_f$ and (b) $S°$ of BrCl(g).

20.80 Solid N_2O_5 reacts with water to form liquid HNO_3. Consider the reaction with all substances in their standard states.

(a) Is the reaction spontaneous at 25°C?

(b) The solid decomposes to NO_2 and O_2 at 25°C. Is the decomposition spontaneous at 25°C? At what T is it spontaneous?

(c) At what T does *gaseous* N_2O_5 decompose spontaneously? Explain the difference between this T and that in part (b).

20.81 Find K for (a) the hydrolysis of ATP, (b) the reaction of glucose with HPO_4^{2-} to form glucose phosphate, and (c) the coupled reaction between ATP and glucose. (d) How does each K change when T changes from 25°C to 37°C?

* 20.82 Energy from ATP hydrolysis drives many nonspontaneous cell reactions:

$$ATP^{4-}(aq) + H_2O(l) \rightleftharpoons$$
$$ADP^{3-}(aq) + HPO_4^{2-}(aq) + H^+(aq) \qquad \Delta G°' = -30.5 \text{ kJ}$$

Energy for the reverse process comes ultimately from glucose metabolism:

$$C_6H_{12}O_6(s) + 6O_2(g) \longrightarrow 6CO_2(g) + 6H_2O(l)$$

(a) Find $\Delta G°_{rxn}$ for metabolism of 1 mol of glucose. (b) How many moles of ATP can be produced by metabolism of 1 mol of glucose? (c) If 36 mol of ATP is formed, what is the actual yield?

20.83 A chemical reaction, such as HI forming from its elements, can reach equilibrium at many temperatures. In contrast, a phase change, such as ice melting, is in equilibrium at a given pressure only at the melting point. (a) Which graph depicts how G_{sys} changes for the formation of HI? Explain. (b) Which graph depicts how G_{sys} changes as ice melts at 1°C and 1 atm? Explain.

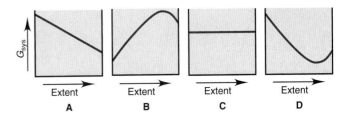

* 20.84 Consider the formation of ammonia:

$$N_2(g) + 3H_2(g) \rightleftharpoons 2NH_3(g)$$

(a) Assuming that $\Delta H°$ and $\Delta S°$ are constant with temperature, find the temperature at which $K_p = 1.00$. (b) Find K_p at 400.°C, a typical temperature for NH_3 production. (c) Given the lower K_p at the higher temperature, why are these conditions used industrially?

21

Electrochemistry: Chemical Change and Electrical Work

Plating It On *Electroplating gold onto the silver of the NBA championship trophy requires electrical energy. Batteries, on the other hand, supply electrical energy.*

Outline

Key Principles
to focus on while studying this chapter

- *Oxidation-reduction (redox) reactions* involve the movement of electrons from one species to another. The *half-reaction method* of balancing redox reactions separates the overall reaction into two half-reactions, which mimics the actual separation of an *electrochemical cell* into two *half-cells*. Two types of electrochemical cells are distinguished by whether they generate electrical energy or use it *(Section 21.1)*.

- In a *voltaic cell,* a spontaneous redox reaction ($\Delta G < 0$) is separated into an oxidation half-reaction (which occurs at the *anode*) and a reduction half-reaction (which occurs at the *cathode*). Electrons flow from anode to cathode through an external circuit, releasing electrical energy, and ions flow through a *salt bridge* to complete the circuit and balance the charge within the cell *(Section 21.2)*.

- The anode has a greater ability to give up electrons than the cathode, and the *cell potential,* or *voltage* (E_{cell}), is related to this difference. A negative ΔG (spontaneous reaction) correlates with a positive E_{cell}. Under standard-state conditions, each half-reaction is associated with a *standard electrode potential* ($E°_{half-cell}$). Pairs of half-reactions can be combined to determine unknown electrode potentials and to write spontaneous redox reactions *(Section 21.3)*.

- The standard free energy change ($\Delta G°$), the standard cell potential ($E°_{cell}$), and the equilibrium constant (K) are interrelated *(Section 21.4)*.

- Cell potential at nonstandard conditions (E_{cell}) changes during operation of a cell. The *Nernst equation* shows that E_{cell} depends on $E°_{cell}$ and a term that corrects for nonstandard concentrations. During the operation of a voltaic cell, the reactant concentration starts out higher than the product concentration and gradually lowers until $Q = K$ and the cell can do no more work *(Section 21.4)*.

- In a *concentration cell,* each half-cell houses the same half-reaction, but the solution concentrations are different. During operation, the solution in the anode half-cell spontaneously becomes more concentrated and that in the cathode half-cell becomes less concentrated until the concentrations are equal *(Section 21.4)*.

- A *battery* is a group of voltaic cells arranged in series. In a *primary battery,* reactants become products until equilibrium is reached, at which point the battery is discarded. A *secondary battery* can be recharged by using an external energy source to convert the products back into reactants. In a *fuel cell,* reactants enter and products leave continually *(Section 21.5)*.

- *Corrosion* is a spontaneous electrochemical process with similarities to the operation of a voltaic cell. It is a major economic problem because the anode is typically a metal tool or structure *(Section 21.6)*.

- In an *electrolytic cell,* an external energy source drives a *non*spontaneous redox reaction ($\Delta G > 0$). In the electrolysis of a molten binary salt, the cation is reduced to the metal and the anion is oxidized to the nonmetal. For an aqueous salt solution, the products depend on whether water or one of the ions requires less energy to be reduced or oxidized. Electrolysis is employed industrially to isolate elements from their ores. The amount of product formed is proportional to the quantity of charge flowing through the cell (Faraday's law) *(Section 21.7)*.

|f you think thermodynamics relates mostly to expanding gases inside steam engines and has few practical, everyday applications, just look around. Some applications are probably within your reach right now, in the form of battery-operated devices—laptop computer, palm organizer, DVD remote, and, of course, wristwatch—or in the form of metal-plated jewelry or silverware. The operation and creation of these objects, and the many similar ones you use daily, involve the principles we cover in this chapter.

Electrochemistry, certainly one of the most important areas of applied thermodynamics, is the study of the relationship between chemical change and electrical work. It is typically investigated through the use of **electrochemical cells,** systems that incorporate a redox reaction to produce or utilize electrical energy.

Concepts & Skills to Review
before studying this chapter

- redox terminology (Section 4.5)
- activity series of the metals (Section 4.6)
- free energy, work, and equilibrium (Sections 20.3 and 20.4)
- Q vs. K (Section 17.4) and ΔG vs. $\Delta G°$ (Section 20.4)

21.1 REDOX REACTIONS AND ELECTROCHEMICAL CELLS

Whether an electrochemical process releases or absorbs free energy, it always involves the *movement of electrons from one chemical species to another* through an oxidation-reduction (redox) reaction. In this section, we review the redox process and describe the half-reaction method of balancing redox reactions. Then we see how such reactions are used in the two types of electrochemical cells.

A Quick Review of Oxidation-Reduction Concepts

In electrochemical reactions, as in any redox process, *oxidation* is the loss of electrons, and *reduction* is the gain of electrons. An *oxidizing agent* is the species that does the oxidizing, taking electrons from the substance being oxidized. A *reducing agent* is the species that does the reducing, giving electrons to the substance being reduced. After the reaction, the oxidized substance has a higher (more positive or less negative) oxidation number (O.N.), and the reduced substance has a lower (less positive or more negative) one. Keep in mind three key points:

- Oxidation (electron loss) always accompanies reduction (electron gain).
- The oxidizing agent is reduced, and the reducing agent is oxidized.
- The total number of electrons gained by the atoms/ions of the oxidizing agent always equals the total number lost by the atoms/ions of the reducing agent.

Figure 21.1 presents these ideas for the aqueous reaction between zinc metal and a strong acid. Be sure you can identify the oxidation and reduction parts of a redox process. If you're having trouble, see the full discussion in Chapter 4.

PROCESS	$Zn(s) + 2H^+(aq) \longrightarrow Zn^{2+}(aq) + H_2(g)$	
OXIDATION • One reactant loses electrons. • Reducing agent is oxidized. • Oxidation number increases.	Zinc **loses** electrons. Zinc is the reducing agent and becomes **oxidized**. The oxidation number of Zn **increases** from 0 to +2.	
REDUCTION • Other reactant gains electrons. • Oxidizing agent is reduced. • Oxidation number decreases.	Hydrogen ion **gains** electrons. Hydrogen ion is the oxidizing agent and becomes **reduced**. The oxidation number of H **decreases** from +1 to 0.	

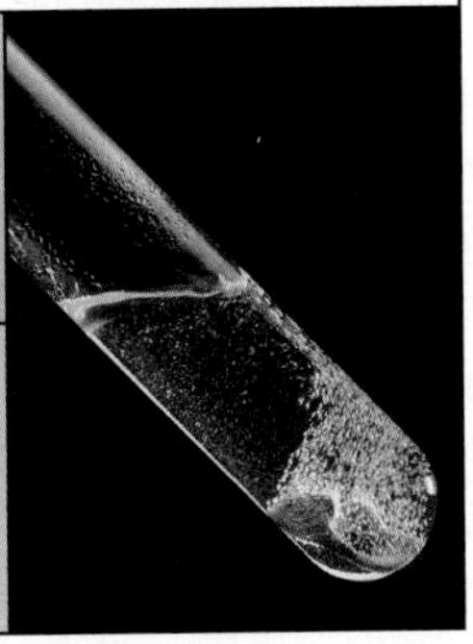

FIGURE 21.1 A summary of redox terminology. In the reaction between zinc and hydrogen ion, Zn is oxidized and H^+ is reduced.

Half-Reaction Method for Balancing Redox Reactions

The **half-reaction method** for balancing redox reactions *divides the overall redox reaction into oxidation and reduction half-reactions.* Each half-reaction is balanced for atoms and charge. Then, one or both are multiplied by some integer to make electrons gained equal electrons lost, and the half-reactions are recombined to give the balanced redox equation. The half-reaction method is commonly used for studying electrochemistry because

- It separates the oxidation and reduction steps, which reflects their actual physical separation in electrochemical cells.
- It is readily applied to redox reactions that take place in acidic or basic solution, which is common in these cells.
- It (usually) does *not* require assigning O.N.s. (In cases where the half-reactions are not obvious, we assign O.N.s to determine which atoms undergo a change and write half-reactions with the species that contain those atoms.)

In general, we begin with a "skeleton" ionic reaction, which shows only the species that are oxidized and reduced. *If the oxidized form of a species is on the left side of the skeleton reaction, the reduced form of that species must be on the right, and vice versa.* Unless H_2O, H^+, and OH^- are being oxidized or reduced, they do not appear in the skeleton reaction. The following steps are used in balancing a redox reaction by the half-reaction method:

Step 1. Divide the skeleton reaction into two half-reactions, each of which contains the oxidized and reduced forms of one of the species. (Which half-reaction is the oxidation and which is the reduction will become clear in the next step.)

Step 2. Balance the atoms and charges in each half-reaction.
- Atoms are balanced *in order:* atoms other than O and H, then O, and then H.
- Charge is balanced by *adding electrons* (e^-). They are added *to the left in the reduction half-reaction* because the reactant gains them; they are added *to the right in the oxidation half-reaction* because the reactant loses them.

Step 3. If necessary, multiply one or both half-reactions by an integer to make the number of e^- gained in the reduction equal the number lost in the oxidation.

Step 4. Add the balanced half-reactions, and include states of matter.

Step 5. Check that the atoms and charges are balanced.

We'll balance a redox reaction that occurs in acidic solution first and then go through Sample Problem 21.1 to balance one in basic solution.

FIGURE 21.2 The redox reaction between dichromate ion and iodide ion. When $Cr_2O_7^{2-}$ *(left)* and I^- *(center)* are mixed in acid solution, they react to form Cr^{3+} and I_2 *(right).*

Balancing Redox Reactions in Acidic Solution When a redox reaction occurs in acidic solution, H_2O molecules and H^+ ions are available for balancing. Even though we've usually used H_3O^+ to indicate the proton in water, we use H^+ in this chapter because it makes the balanced equations less complex.

Let's balance the redox reaction between dichromate ion and iodide ion to form chromium(III) ion and solid iodine, which occurs in acidic solution (Figure 21.2). The skeleton ionic reaction shows only the oxidized and reduced species:

$$Cr_2O_7^{2-}(aq) + I^-(aq) \longrightarrow Cr^{3+}(aq) + I_2(s) \quad \text{[acidic solution]}$$

Step 1. Divide the reaction into half-reactions, each of which contains the oxidized and reduced forms of one species. The two chromium species make up one half-reaction, and the two iodine species make up the other:

$$Cr_2O_7^{2-} \longrightarrow Cr^{3+}$$
$$I^- \longrightarrow I_2$$

Step 2. Balance atoms and charges in each half-reaction. We use H_2O to balance O atoms, H^+ to balance H atoms, and e^- to balance positive charges.

- For the $Cr_2O_7^{2-}/Cr^{3+}$ half-reaction:

a. *Balance atoms other than O and H.* We balance the two Cr on the left with a coefficient 2 on the right:

$$Cr_2O_7^{2-} \longrightarrow 2Cr^{3+}$$

b. *Balance O atoms by adding H_2O molecules.* Each H_2O has one O atom, so we add seven H_2O on the right to balance the seven O in $Cr_2O_7^{2-}$:

$$Cr_2O_7^{2-} \longrightarrow 2Cr^{3+} + 7H_2O$$

c. *Balance H atoms by adding H^+ ions.* Each H_2O contains two H, and we added seven H_2O, so we add 14 H^+ ions on the left:

$$+12 \quad 14H^+ + Cr_2O_7^{2-} \longrightarrow 2Cr^{3+} + 7H_2O \; +6$$

d. *Balance charge by adding electrons.* Each H^+ ion has a 1+ charge, and 14 H^+ plus $Cr_2O_7^{2-}$ gives 12+ on the left. Two Cr^{3+} give 6+ on the right. There is an excess of 6+ on the left, so we add six e^- on the left:

$$6e^- + 14H^+ + Cr_2O_7^{2-} \longrightarrow 2Cr^{3+} + 7H_2O$$

This half-reaction is balanced, and we see it is the *reduction* because electrons appear on the *left, as reactants:* the reactant $Cr_2O_7^{2-}$ gains electrons (is reduced), so $Cr_2O_7^{2-}$ is the *oxidizing agent.* (Note that the O.N. of Cr decreases from +6 on the left to +3 on the right.)

- For the I^-/I_2 half-reaction:

a. *Balance atoms other than O and H.* Two I atoms on the right require a coefficient 2 on the left:

$$2I^- \longrightarrow I_2$$

b. *Balance O atoms with H_2O.* Not needed; there are no O atoms.

c. *Balance H atoms with H^+.* Not needed; there are no H atoms.

d. *Balance charge with e^-.* To balance the 2− on the left, we add two e^- on the right:

$$2I^- \longrightarrow I_2 + 2e^-$$

This half-reaction is balanced, and it is the *oxidation* because electrons appear on the *right, as products:* the reactant I^- loses electrons (is oxidized), so I^- is the *reducing agent.* (Note that the O.N. of I increases from −1 to 0.)

Step 3. Multiply each half-reaction, if necessary, by an integer so that the number of e^- lost in the oxidation equals the number of e^- gained in the reduction. Two e^- are lost in the oxidation and six e^- are gained in the reduction, so we multiply the oxidation by 3:

$$3(2I^- \longrightarrow I_2 + 2e^-)$$
$$6I^- \longrightarrow 3I_2 + 6e^-$$

Step 4. Add the half-reactions together, canceling substances that appear on both sides, and include states of matter. In this example, only the electrons cancel:

$$\cancel{6e^-} + 14H^+ + Cr_2O_7^{2-} \longrightarrow 2Cr^{3+} + 7H_2O$$
$$\underline{6I^- \longrightarrow 3I_2 + \cancel{6e^-}}$$
$$6I^-(aq) + 14H^+(aq) + Cr_2O_7^{2-}(aq) \longrightarrow 3I_2(s) + 7H_2O(l) + 2Cr^{3+}(aq)$$

Step 5. Check that atoms and charges balance:

Reactants (6I, 14H, 2Cr, 7O; 6+) $\longrightarrow$ products (6I, 14H, 2Cr, 7O; 6+)

Balancing Redox Reactions in Basic Solution As you just saw, in acidic solution, H_2O molecules and H^+ ions are available for balancing. As Sample Problem 21.1 shows, in basic solution, H_2O molecules and OH^- ions are available.

Only one additional step is needed to balance a redox equation that takes place in basic solution. It appears after both half-reactions have first been balanced *as if they took place in acidic solution* (steps 1 and 2), the e⁻ lost have been made equal to the e⁻ gained (step 3), and the half-reactions have been combined (step 4). At this point, *we add one OH⁻ ion* **to both sides of the equation** *for every H⁺ ion present.* (We label this step "4 Basic.") The H⁺ ions on one side are combined with the added OH⁻ ions to form H_2O, and OH⁻ ions appear on the other side of the equation. Excess H_2O molecules are canceled, and states of matter are identified. Finally, we check that atoms and charges balance (step 5).

SAMPLE PROBLEM 21.1 Balancing Redox Reactions by the Half-Reaction Method

Problem Permanganate ion is a strong oxidizing agent, and its deep purple color makes it useful as an indicator in redox titrations. It reacts in basic solution with the oxalate ion to form carbonate ion and solid manganese dioxide. Balance the skeleton ionic equation for the reaction between $NaMnO_4$ and $Na_2C_2O_4$ in basic solution:

$$MnO_4^-(aq) + C_2O_4^{2-}(aq) \longrightarrow MnO_2(s) + CO_3^{2-}(aq) \qquad \text{[basic solution]}$$

Plan We proceed through step 4 as if this took place in acidic solution. Then, we add the appropriate number of OH⁻ ions and cancel excess H_2O molecules (step 4 Basic).

Solution

1. Divide into half-reactions.

$$MnO_4^- \longrightarrow MnO_2 \qquad\qquad\qquad C_2O_4^{2-} \longrightarrow CO_3^{2-}$$

2. Balance.

a. Atoms other than O and H,
   Not needed

a. Atoms other than O and H,
   $$C_2O_4^{2-} \longrightarrow 2CO_3^{2-}$$

b. O atoms with H_2O,
   $$MnO_4^- \longrightarrow MnO_2 + 2H_2O$$

b. O atoms with H_2O,
   $$2H_2O + C_2O_4^{2-} \longrightarrow 2CO_3^{2-}$$

c. H atoms with H⁺,
   $$4H^+ + MnO_4^- \longrightarrow MnO_2 + 2H_2O$$

c. H atoms with H⁺,
   $$2H_2O + C_2O_4^{2-} \longrightarrow 2CO_3^{2-} + 4H^+$$

d. Charge with e⁻,
   $$3e^- + 4H^+ + MnO_4^- \longrightarrow MnO_2 + 2H_2O$$
   [reduction]

d. Charge with e⁻,
   $$2H_2O + C_2O_4^{2-} \longrightarrow 2CO_3^{2-} + 4H^+ + 2e^-$$
   [oxidation]

3. Multiply each half-reaction, if necessary, by some integer to make e⁻ lost equal e⁻ gained.

$$2(3e^- + 4H^+ + MnO_4^- \longrightarrow MnO_2 + 2H_2O)$$
$$6e^- + 8H^+ + 2MnO_4^- \longrightarrow 2MnO_2 + 4H_2O$$

$$3(2H_2O + C_2O_4^{2-} \longrightarrow 2CO_3^{2-} + 4H^+ + 2e^-)$$
$$6H_2O + 3C_2O_4^{2-} \longrightarrow 6CO_3^{2-} + 12H^+ + 6e^-$$

4. Add half-reactions, and cancel substances appearing on both sides.
The six e⁻ cancel, eight H⁺ cancel to leave four H⁺ on the right, and four H_2O cancel to leave two H_2O on the left:

$$6e^- + 8H^+ + 2MnO_4^- \longrightarrow 2MnO_2 + 4H_2O$$
$$\underline{2\ 6H_2O + 3C_2O_4^{2-} \longrightarrow 6CO_3^{2-} + 4\ 12H^+ + 6e^-}$$
$$2MnO_4^- + 2H_2O + 3C_2O_4^{2-} \longrightarrow 2MnO_2 + 6CO_3^{2-} + 4H^+$$

4 Basic. Add OH⁻ to both sides to neutralize H⁺, and cancel H_2O.
Adding four OH⁻ to both sides forms four H_2O on the right, two of which cancel the two H_2O on the left, leaving two H_2O on the right:

$$2MnO_4^- + 2H_2O + 3C_2O_4^{2-} + 4OH^- \longrightarrow 2MnO_2 + 6CO_3^{2-} + [4H^+ + 4OH^-]$$
$$2MnO_4^- + 2H_2O + 3C_2O_4^{2-} + 4OH^- \longrightarrow 2MnO_2 + 6CO_3^{2-} + 2\ 4H_2O$$

Including states of matter gives the final balanced equation:

$$2MnO_4^-(aq) + 3C_2O_4^{2-}(aq) + 4OH^-(aq) \longrightarrow 2MnO_2(s) + 6CO_3^{2-}(aq) + 2H_2O(l)$$

5. Check that atoms and charges balance.

$$(2Mn, 24O, 6C, 4H; 12-) \longrightarrow (2Mn, 24O, 6C, 4H; 12-)$$

Comment As a final step, we can obtain the balanced *molecular* equation for this reaction by noting the number of moles of each anion in the balanced ionic equation and adding the correct number of moles of spectator ions (in this case, Na^+) to obtain neutral compounds. Thus, for instance, balancing the charge of 2 mol of MnO_4^- requires 2 mol of Na^+, so we have $2NaMnO_4$. The balanced molecular equation is

$$2NaMnO_4(aq) + 3Na_2C_2O_4(aq) + 4NaOH(aq) \longrightarrow$$
$$2MnO_2(s) + 6Na_2CO_3(aq) + 2H_2O(l)$$

FOLLOW-UP PROBLEM 21.1 Write a balanced molecular equation for the reaction between $KMnO_4$ and KI in basic solution. The skeleton ionic reaction is

$$MnO_4^-(aq) + I^-(aq) \longrightarrow MnO_4^{2-}(aq) + IO_3^-(aq) \qquad \text{[basic solution]}$$

The half-reaction method reveals a great deal about redox processes and is essential to understanding electrochemical cells. The major points are

- Any redox reaction can be treated as the sum of a reduction and an oxidation half-reaction.
- Atoms and charge are conserved in each half-reaction.
- Electrons lost in one half-reaction are gained in the other.
- Although the half-reactions are treated separately, electron loss and electron gain occur simultaneously.

An Overview of Electrochemical Cells

We distinguish two types of electrochemical cells based on the general thermo-dynamic nature of the reaction:

1. A **voltaic cell** (or **galvanic cell**) uses a spontaneous reaction ($\Delta G < 0$) to generate electrical energy. In the cell reaction, the difference in chemical potential energy between higher energy reactants and lower energy products is converted into electrical energy. This energy is used to operate the load—flashlight bulb, CD player, car starter motor, or other electrical device. In other words, *the system does work on the surroundings.* All batteries contain voltaic cells.
2. An **electrolytic cell** uses electrical energy to drive a nonspontaneous reaction ($\Delta G > 0$). In the cell reaction, electrical energy from an external power supply converts lower energy reactants into higher energy products. Thus, *the surroundings do work on the system.* Electroplating and recovering metals from ores involve electrolytic cells.

The two types of cell have certain design features in common, shown in Figure 21.3 on the next page. Two **electrodes,** which conduct the electricity between cell and surroundings, are dipped into an **electrolyte,** a mixture of ions (usually in aqueous solution) that are involved in the reaction or that carry the charge. An electrode is identified as either **anode** or **cathode** depending on the half-reaction that takes place there:

- *The oxidation half-reaction occurs at the anode.* Electrons are lost by the substance being oxidized (reducing agent) and *leave the cell* at the anode.
- *The reduction half-reaction occurs at the cathode.* Electrons are gained by the substance being reduced (oxidizing agent) and *enter the cell* at the cathode.

As shown in Figure 21.3, the relative charges of the electrodes are *opposite* in the two types of cell. As you'll see in the following sections, these opposite charges result from the different phenomena that cause the electrons to flow.

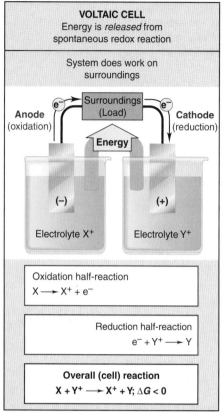

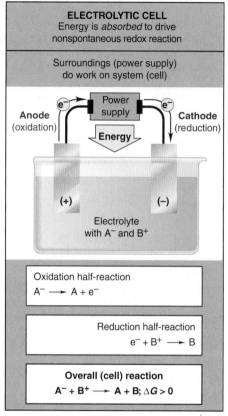

A   **B**

FIGURE 21.3 General characteristics of voltaic and electrolytic cells. A voltaic cell **(A)** generates energy from a spontaneous reaction ($\Delta G < 0$), whereas an electrolytic cell **(B)** requires energy to drive a nonspontaneous reaction ($\Delta G > 0$). In both types of cell, two electrodes dip into electrolyte solutions, and an external circuit provides the means for electrons to flow between them. Most important, notice that oxidation takes place at the anode and reduction takes place at the cathode, but the relative electrode charges are opposite in the two cells.

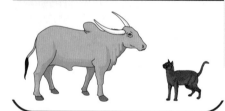

THINK OF IT THIS WAY
Which Half-Reaction Occurs at Which Electrode?

Here are some memory aids to help you connect the half-reaction with its electrode:
1. The words *anode* and *oxidation* start with vowels; the words *cathode* and *reduction* start with consonants.
2. Alphabetically, the *A* in anode comes before the *C* in cathode, and the *O* in oxidation comes before the *R* in reduction.
3. Look at the first syllables and use your imagination:

 ANode, OXidation; REDuction, CAThode ⇒ AN OX and a RED CAT

SECTION 21.1 SUMMARY

An oxidation-reduction (redox) reaction involves the transfer of electrons from a reducing agent to an oxidizing agent. • The half-reaction method of balancing divides the overall reaction into half-reactions that are balanced separately and then recombined. • The two types of electrochemical cells are based on redox reactions. In a voltaic cell, a spontaneous reaction generates electricity and does work on the surroundings; in an electrolytic cell, the surroundings supply electricity that does work to drive a nonspontaneous reaction. In both types, two electrodes dip into electrolyte solutions; oxidation occurs at the anode, and reduction occurs at the cathode.

21.2 VOLTAIC CELLS: USING SPONTANEOUS REACTIONS TO GENERATE ELECTRICAL ENERGY

If you put a strip of zinc metal in a solution of Cu^{2+} ion, the blue color of the solution fades as a brown-black crust of Cu metal forms on the Zn strip (Figure 21.4). Judging from what we see, the reaction involves the reduction of Cu^{2+} ion to Cu

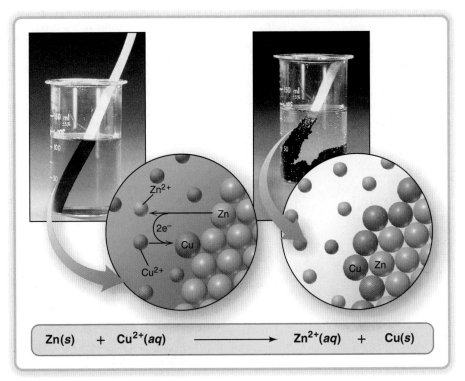

$$Zn(s) \ + \ Cu^{2+}(aq) \longrightarrow Zn^{2+}(aq) \ + \ Cu(s)$$

FIGURE 21.4 The spontaneous reaction between zinc and copper(II) ion. When a strip of zinc metal is placed in a solution of Cu^{2+} ion, a redox reaction begins *(left)*, in which the zinc is oxidized to Zn^{2+} and the Cu^{2+} is reduced to copper metal. As the reaction proceeds *(right)*, the deep blue color of the solution of hydrated Cu^{2+} ion lightens, and the Cu "plates out" on the Zn and falls off in chunks. (The Cu appears black because it is very finely divided.) At the atomic scale, each Zn atom loses two electrons, which are gained by a Cu^{2+} ion. The process is summarized with symbols in the balanced equation.

metal, which must be accompanied by the oxidation of Zn metal to Zn^{2+} ion. The overall reaction consists of two half-reactions:

$$Cu^{2+}(aq) \ + \ 2e^- \longrightarrow Cu(s) \qquad \text{[reduction]}$$
$$Zn(s) \longrightarrow Zn^{2+}(aq) \ + \ 2e^- \qquad \text{[oxidation]}$$
$$\overline{Zn(s) \ + \ Cu^{2+}(aq) \longrightarrow Zn^{2+}(aq) \ + \ Cu(s) \qquad \text{[overall reaction]}}$$

In the remainder of this section, we examine this spontaneous reaction as the basis of a voltaic (galvanic) cell.

Construction and Operation of a Voltaic Cell

Electrons are being transferred in the Zn/Cu^{2+} reaction (Figure 21.4), but the system does not generate electrical energy because the oxidizing agent (Cu^{2+}) and the reducing agent (Zn) are in the same beaker. If, however, the half-reactions are physically separated and connected by an external circuit, the electrons are transferred by traveling through the circuit and an electric current is produced.

This separation of half-reactions is the essential idea behind a voltaic cell (Figure 21.5A, next page). The components of each half-reaction are placed in a separate container, or **half-cell,** which consists of one electrode dipping into an electrolyte solution. The two half-cells are joined by the circuit, which consists of a wire and a salt bridge (the inverted U tube in the figure; we'll discuss its function shortly). In order to measure the voltage generated by the cell, a voltmeter is inserted in the path of the wire connecting the electrodes. A switch (not shown) closes (completes) or opens (breaks) the circuit. By convention, *the oxidation half-cell (anode compartment) is shown on the left and the reduction*

Animation: Operation of a Voltaic Cell

energy is released

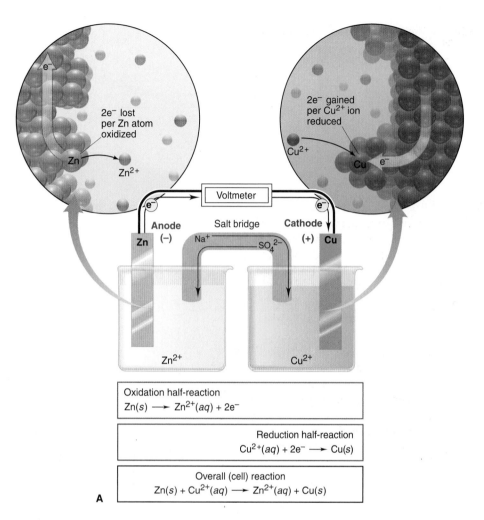

A

Oxidation half-reaction
$$Zn(s) \longrightarrow Zn^{2+}(aq) + 2e^-$$

Reduction half-reaction
$$Cu^{2+}(aq) + 2e^- \longrightarrow Cu(s)$$

Overall (cell) reaction
$$Zn(s) + Cu^{2+}(aq) \longrightarrow Zn^{2+}(aq) + Cu(s)$$

FIGURE 21.5 A voltaic cell based on the zinc-copper reaction. A, The anode half-cell (oxidation) consists of a Zn electrode dipping into a Zn^{2+} solution. The two electrons generated in the oxidation of each Zn atom move through the Zn bar and the wire, and into the Cu electrode, which dips into a Cu^{2+} solution in the cathode half-cell (reduction). There, the electrons reduce Cu^{2+} ions. Thus, electrons flow left to right through electrodes and wire. A salt bridge contains unreactive Na^+ and SO_4^{2-} ions that maintain neutral charge in the electrolyte solutions: anions in the salt bridge flow to the left, and cations flow to the right. The voltmeter registers the electrical output of the cell. **B,** After the cell runs for several hours, the Zn anode weighs less because Zn atoms have been oxidized to aqueous Zn^{2+} ions, and the Cu cathode weighs more because aqueous Cu^{2+} ions have been reduced to Cu metal.

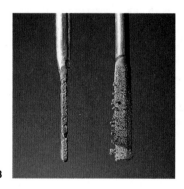

B

half-cell (cathode compartment) on the right. Here are the key points about the Zn/Cu^{2+} voltaic cell:

1. *The oxidation half-cell.* In this case, the anode compartment consists of a zinc bar (the anode) immersed in a Zn^{2+} electrolyte (such as a solution of zinc sulfate, $ZnSO_4$). The zinc bar is the reactant in the oxidation half-reaction, and it conducts the released electrons *out* of its half-cell.

2. *The reduction half-cell.* In this case, the cathode compartment consists of a copper bar (the cathode) immersed in a Cu^{2+} electrolyte [such as a solution of copper(II) sulfate, $CuSO_4$]. Copper metal is the product in the reduction half-reaction, and the bar conducts electrons *into* its half-cell.

3. *Relative charges on the electrodes.* The electrode charges are determined by the *source of electrons* and the *direction of electron flow* through the circuit. In this cell, zinc atoms are oxidized at the anode to Zn^{2+} ions and electrons. The Zn^{2+} ions enter the solution, while the electrons enter the bar and then the wire. *The electrons flow left to right* through the wire to the cathode, where Cu^{2+} ions in the solution accept them and are reduced to Cu atoms. As the cell operates, electrons are continuously generated at the anode and consumed at the cathode. Therefore, the anode has an excess of electrons and a negative charge *relative* to the cathode. *In any* **voltaic** *cell, the anode is negative and the cathode is positive.*

4. *The purpose of the salt bridge.* The cell cannot operate unless the circuit is complete. The oxidation half-cell originally contains a neutral solution of Zn^{2+}

and SO_4^{2-} ions, but as Zn atoms in the bar lose electrons, the solution would develop a net positive charge from the Zn^{2+} ions entering. Similarly, in the reduction half-cell, the neutral solution of Cu^{2+} and SO_4^{2-} ions would develop a net negative charge as Cu^{2+} ions leave the solution to form Cu atoms. If the half-cells did not remain neutral, the resulting charge imbalance would stop cell operation. To avoid this situation and enable the cell to operate, the two half-cells are joined by a **salt bridge**, which acts as a "liquid wire," allowing ions to flow through both compartments and complete the circuit. The salt bridge shown in Figure 21.5A is an inverted U tube containing a solution of the nonreacting ions Na^+ and SO_4^{2-} in a gel. The solution cannot pour out, but ions can diffuse through it into or out of the half-cells.

To maintain neutrality in the reduction half-cell (right; cathode compartment) as Cu^{2+} ions change to Cu atoms, Na^+ ions move from the salt bridge into the solution (and some SO_4^{2-} ions move from the solution into the salt bridge). Similarly, to maintain neutrality in the oxidation half-cell (left; anode compartment) as Zn atoms change to Zn^{2+} ions, SO_4^{2-} ions move from the salt bridge into that solution (and some Zn^{2+} ions move from the solution into the salt bridge). Thus, as Figure 21.5A shows, the circuit is completed *as electrons move left to right through the wire, while anions move right to left and cations move left to right through the salt bridge.*

5. *Active vs. inactive electrodes.* The electrodes in the Zn/Cu^{2+} cell are *active* because the metal bars themselves are components of the half-reactions. As the cell operates, the mass of the zinc electrode gradually decreases, and the $[Zn^{2+}]$ in the anode half-cell increases. At the same time, the mass of the copper electrode increases, and the $[Cu^{2+}]$ in the cathode half-cell decreases; we say that the Cu^{2+} "plates out" on the electrode. Look at Figure 21.5B to see how the electrodes look, removed from their half-cells, after several hours of operation.

For many redox reactions, there are no reactants or products capable of serving as electrodes, so *inactive* electrodes are used. Most commonly, inactive electrodes are rods of *graphite* or *platinum*: they conduct electrons into or out of the half-cells but cannot take part in the half-reactions. In a voltaic cell based on the following half-reactions, for instance, the reacting species cannot act as electrodes:

$$2I^-(aq) \longrightarrow I_2(s) + 2e^- \qquad \text{[anode; oxidation]}$$
$$MnO_4^-(aq) + 8H^+(aq) + 5e^- \longrightarrow Mn^{2+}(aq) + 4H_2O(l) \qquad \text{[cathode; reduction]}$$

Therefore, each half-cell consists of inactive electrodes immersed in an electrolyte solution that contains *all the reactant species involved in that half-reaction* (Figure 21.6). In the anode half-cell, I^- ions are oxidized to solid I_2. The electrons that are released flow into the graphite anode, through the wire, and into the graphite cathode. From there, the electrons are consumed by MnO_4^- ions, which are reduced to Mn^{2+} ions. (A KNO_3 salt bridge is used.)

As Figures 21.5A and 21.6 show, there are certain consistent features in the *diagram* of any voltaic cell. The physical arrangement includes the half-cell containers, electrodes, wire, and salt bridge, and the following details appear:

- Components of the half-cells: electrode materials, electrolyte ions, and other substances involved in the reaction
- Electrode name (anode or cathode) and charge. By convention, the anode compartment always appears *on the left.*
- Each half-reaction with its half-cell and the overall cell reaction
- Direction of electron flow in the external circuit
- Nature of ions and direction of ion flow in the salt bridge

You'll see how to specify these details and diagram a cell shortly.

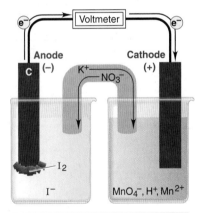

Oxidation half-reaction
$2I^-(aq) \longrightarrow I_2(s) + 2e^-$

Reduction half-reaction
$MnO_4^-(aq) + 8H^+(aq) + 5e^- \longrightarrow$ $Mn^{2+}(aq) + 4H_2O(l)$

Overall (cell) reaction
$2MnO_4^-(aq) + 16H^+(aq) + 10I^-(aq) \longrightarrow$ $2Mn^{2+}(aq) + 5I_2(s) + 8H_2O(l)$

FIGURE 21.6 A voltaic cell using inactive electrodes. The reaction between I^- and MnO_4^- in acidic solution does not have species that can be used as electrodes, so inactive graphite (C) electrodes are used.

Notation for a Voltaic Cell

A useful shorthand notation describes the components of a voltaic cell. For example, the notation for the Zn/Cu^{2+} cell is

$$Zn(s) \mid Zn^{2+}(aq) \parallel Cu^{2+}(aq) \mid Cu(s)$$

Key parts of the notation are

- The components of the anode compartment (oxidation half-cell) are written *to the left* of the components of the cathode compartment (reduction half-cell).
- A single vertical line represents a phase boundary. For example, $Zn(s) \mid Zn^{2+}(aq)$ indicates that the *solid* Zn is a *different* phase from the *aqueous* Zn^{2+}. A comma separates the half-cell components that are in the *same* phase. For example, the notation for the voltaic cell housing the reaction between I^- and MnO_4^- shown in Figure 21.6 is

$$\text{graphite} \mid I^-(aq) \mid I_2(s) \parallel H^+(aq), MnO_4^-(aq), Mn^{2+}(aq) \mid \text{graphite}$$

  That is, in the cathode compartment, H^+, MnO_4^-, and Mn^{2+} ions are all in aqueous solution with solid graphite immersed in it. Often, we specify the concentrations of dissolved components; for example, if the concentrations of Zn^{2+} and Cu^{2+} are 1 *M*, we write

$$Zn(s) \mid Zn^{2+}(1\ M) \parallel Cu^{2+}(1\ M) \mid Cu(s)$$

- Half-cell components usually appear in the same order as in the half-reaction, and electrodes appear at the far left and far right of the notation.
- A double vertical line indicates the separated half-cells and represents the phase boundary on either side of the salt bridge (the ions in the salt bridge are omitted because they are not part of the reaction).

SAMPLE PROBLEM 21.2   Describing a Voltaic Cell with Diagram and Notation

Problem Draw a diagram, show balanced equations, and write the notation for a voltaic cell that consists of one half-cell with a Cr bar in a $Cr(NO_3)_3$ solution, another half-cell with an Ag bar in an $AgNO_3$ solution, and a KNO_3 salt bridge. Measurement indicates that the Cr electrode is negative relative to the Ag electrode.

Plan From the given contents of the half-cells, we can write the half-reactions. We must determine which is the anode compartment (oxidation) and which is the cathode (reduction). To do so, we must find the direction of the spontaneous redox reaction, which is given by the relative electrode charges. Electrons are released into the anode during oxidation, so it has a negative charge. We are told that Cr is negative, so it must be the anode; and, therefore, Ag is the cathode.

Solution Writing the balanced half-reactions. The Ag electrode is positive, so the half-reaction consumes e^-:

$$Ag^+(aq) + e^- \longrightarrow Ag(s) \qquad \text{[reduction; cathode]}$$

The Cr electrode is negative, so the half-reaction releases e^-:

$$Cr(s) \longrightarrow Cr^{3+}(aq) + 3e^- \qquad \text{[oxidation; anode]}$$

Writing the balanced overall cell reaction. We triple the reduction half-reaction to balance e^- and then combine the half-reactions to obtain the overall reaction:

$$Cr(s) + 3Ag^+(aq) \longrightarrow Cr^{3+}(aq) + 3Ag(s)$$

Determining direction of electron and ion flow. The released e^- in the Cr electrode (negative) flow through the external circuit to the Ag electrode (positive). As Cr^{3+} ions enter the anode electrolyte, NO_3^- ions enter from the salt bridge to maintain neutrality. As Ag^+ ions leave the cathode electrolyte and plate out on the Ag electrode, K^+ ions enter from the salt bridge to maintain neutrality. The diagram of this cell is shown in the margin. Writing the cell notation:

$$Cr(s) \mid Cr^{3+}(aq) \parallel Ag^+(aq) \mid Ag(s)$$

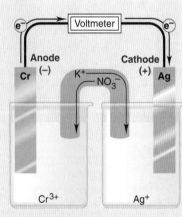

Oxidation half-reaction
$Cr(s) \longrightarrow Cr^{3+}(aq) + 3e^-$

Reduction half-reaction
$Ag^+(aq) + e^- \longrightarrow Ag(s)$

Overall (cell) reaction
$Cr(s) + 3Ag^+(aq) \longrightarrow Cr^{3+}(aq) + 3Ag(s)$

Check Always be sure that the half-reactions and cell reaction are balanced, the half-cells contain *all* components of the half-reactions, and the electron and ion flow are shown. You should be able to write the half-reactions from the cell notation as a check.
Comment To diagram a voltaic cell, use the direction of the spontaneous reaction to identify the oxidation (anode; negative) and reduction (cathode; positive) half-reactions.

FOLLOW-UP PROBLEM 21.2 In one compartment of a voltaic cell, a graphite rod dips into an acidic solution of $K_2Cr_2O_7$ and $Cr(NO_3)_3$; in the other, a tin bar dips into a $Sn(NO_3)_2$ solution. A KNO_3 salt bridge joins them. The tin electrode is negative relative to the graphite. Draw a diagram of the cell, show the balanced equations, and write the cell notation.

SECTION 21.2 SUMMARY

A voltaic cell consists of oxidation (anode) and reduction (cathode) half-cells, connected by a wire to conduct electrons and a salt bridge to maintain charge neutrality as the cell operates. • Electrons move from anode (left) to cathode (right), while cations move from the salt bridge into the cathode half-cell and anions from the salt bridge into the anode half-cell. • The cell notation shows the species and their phases in each half-cell, as well as the direction of current flow.

21.3 CELL POTENTIAL: OUTPUT OF A VOLTAIC CELL

The purpose of a voltaic cell is to convert the free energy change of a spontaneous reaction into the kinetic energy of electrons moving through an external circuit (electrical energy). This electrical energy is proportional to the *difference in electrical potential between the two electrodes,* which is called the **cell potential** (E_{cell}), also the **voltage** of the cell or the **electromotive force (emf).**

Electrons flow spontaneously from the negative to the positive electrode, that is, toward the electrode with the more positive electrical potential. Thus, when the cell operates *spontaneously,* there is a *positive* cell potential:

$$E_{cell} > 0 \text{ for a spontaneous process} \qquad (21.1)$$

The more positive E_{cell} is, the more work the cell can do, and the farther the reaction proceeds to the right as written. A *negative* cell potential, on the other hand, is associated with a *nonspontaneous* cell reaction. If $E_{cell} = 0$, the reaction has reached equilibrium and the cell can do no more work.

How are the units of cell potential related to those of energy available to do work? As you've seen, work is done when charge moves between electrode compartments that differ in electrical potential. The SI unit of electrical potential is the **volt (V),** and the SI unit of electrical charge is the **coulomb (C).** By definition, for two electrodes that differ by 1 volt of electrical potential, 1 joule of energy is released (that is, 1 joule of work can be done) for each coulomb of charge that moves between the electrodes. Thus,

$$1 \text{ V} = 1 \text{ J/C} \qquad (21.2)$$

Table 21.1 lists the voltages of some commercial and natural voltaic cells. Next, we'll see how to measure cell potential.

Table 21.1 Voltages of Some Voltaic Cells	
Voltaic Cell	**Voltage (V)**
Lithium-ion laptop battery	3.7
Lead-acid car battery (6 cells = 12 V)	2.1
Common alkaline flashlight battery	1.5
Calculator battery (mercury)	1.3
Electric eel (~5000 cells in 6-ft eel = 750 V)	0.15
Nerve of giant squid (across cell membrane)	0.070

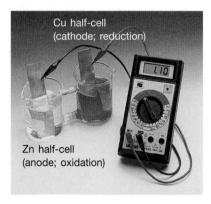

Cu half-cell
(cathode; reduction)

Zn half-cell
(anode; oxidation)

FIGURE 21.7 Measurement of a standard cell potential. The zinc-copper cell, operating at 298 K under standard-state conditions, produces a voltage of 1.10 V.

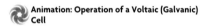

Animation: Operation of a Voltaic (Galvanic) Cell

Standard Cell Potentials

The measured potential of a voltaic cell is affected by changes in concentration as the reaction proceeds and by energy losses due to heating of the cell and the external circuit. Therefore, in order to compare the output of different cells, we obtain a **standard cell potential** ($E°_{cell}$), the potential measured at a specified temperature (usually 298 K) with no current flowing* and *all components in their standard states:* 1 atm for gases, 1 M for solutions, the pure solid for electrodes. When the zinc-copper cell that we diagrammed in Figure 21.5 begins operating under standard state conditions, that is, when $[Zn^{2+}] = [Cu^{2+}] = 1$ M, the cell produces 1.10 V at 298 K (Figure 21.7):

$$Zn(s) + Cu^{2+}(aq; 1\ M) \longrightarrow Zn^{2+}(aq; 1\ M) + Cu(s) \qquad E°_{cell} = 1.10\ V$$

Standard Electrode (Half-Cell) Potentials Just as each half-reaction makes up part of the overall reaction, the potential of each half-cell makes up a part of the overall cell potential. The **standard electrode potential** ($E°_{half-cell}$) is the potential associated with a given half-reaction (electrode compartment) when all the components are in their standard states.

By convention, *a standard electrode potential always refers to the half-reaction written as a* **reduction.** For the zinc-copper reaction, for example, the standard electrode potentials for the zinc half-reaction ($E°_{zinc}$, anode compartment) and for the copper half-reaction ($E°_{copper}$, cathode compartment) refer to the processes written as reductions:

$$Zn^{2+}(aq) + 2e^- \longrightarrow Zn(s) \qquad E°_{zinc}\ (E°_{anode}) \qquad \text{[reduction]}$$
$$Cu^{2+}(aq) + 2e^- \longrightarrow Cu(s) \qquad E°_{copper}\ (E°_{cathode}) \qquad \text{[reduction]}$$

The overall cell reaction involves the *oxidation* of zinc at the anode, not the *reduction* of Zn^{2+}, so we reverse the zinc half-reaction:

$$Zn(s) \longrightarrow Zn^{2+}(aq) + 2e^- \qquad \text{[oxidation]}$$
$$Cu^{2+}(aq) + 2e^- \longrightarrow Cu(s) \qquad \text{[reduction]}$$

The overall redox reaction is the sum of these half-reactions:

$$Zn(s) + Cu^{2+}(aq) \longrightarrow Zn^{2+}(aq) + Cu(s)$$

Because electrons flow spontaneously toward the copper electrode (cathode), it must have a more positive $E°_{half-cell}$ than the zinc electrode (anode). Therefore, to obtain a positive $E°_{cell}$, we subtract $E°_{zinc}$ from $E°_{copper}$:

$$E°_{cell} = E°_{copper} - E°_{zinc}$$

We can generalize this result for any voltaic cell: *the standard cell potential is the difference between the standard electrode potential of the cathode (reduction) half-cell and the standard electrode potential of the anode (oxidation) half-cell:*

$$E°_{cell} = E°_{cathode\ (reduction)} - E°_{anode\ (oxidation)} \qquad \text{(21.3)}$$

For a spontaneous reaction at standard conditions, $E°_{cell} > 0$.

Determining $E°_{half-cell}$: The Standard Hydrogen Electrode What portion of $E°_{cell}$ for the zinc-copper reaction is contributed by the anode half-cell (oxidation of Zn) and what portion by the cathode half-cell (reduction of Cu^{2+})? That is, how can we know half-cell potentials if we can only measure the potential of the complete cell? Half-cell potentials, such as $E°_{zinc}$ and $E°_{copper}$, are not absolute quantities, but rather are values *relative* to that of a standard. *This standard reference half-cell has its standard electrode potential defined as zero ($E°_{reference} \equiv 0.00\ V$).*

---

*The current required to operate modern digital voltmeters makes a negligible difference in the value of $E°_{cell}$.

The **standard reference half-cell** is a **standard hydrogen electrode,** which consists of a specially prepared platinum electrode immersed in a 1 M aqueous solution of a strong acid, $H^+(aq)$ [or $H_3O^+(aq)$], through which H_2 gas at 1 atm is bubbled. Thus, the reference half-reaction is

$$2H^+(aq; 1\ M) + 2e^- \rightleftharpoons H_2(g; 1\ atm) \qquad E^\circ_{reference} = 0.00\ V$$

Now we can construct a voltaic cell consisting of this reference half-cell and another half-cell whose potential we want to determine. With $E^\circ_{reference}$ defined as zero, the overall E°_{cell} allows us to find the unknown standard electrode potential, $E^\circ_{unknown}$. When H_2 is oxidized, the reference half-cell is the anode, and so reduction occurs at the unknown half-cell:

$$E^\circ_{cell} = E^\circ_{cathode} - E^\circ_{anode} = E^\circ_{unknown} - E^\circ_{reference} = E^\circ_{unknown} - 0.00\ V = E^\circ_{unknown}$$

When H^+ is reduced, the reference half-cell is the cathode, and so oxidation occurs at the unknown half-cell:

$$E^\circ_{cell} = E^\circ_{cathode} - E^\circ_{anode} = E^\circ_{reference} - E^\circ_{unknown} = 0.00\ V - E^\circ_{unknown} = -E^\circ_{unknown}$$

Figure 21.8 shows a voltaic cell that has the Zn/Zn^{2+} half-reaction in one compartment and the H^+/H_2 (or H_3O^+/H_2) half-reaction in the other. The zinc electrode is negative relative to the hydrogen electrode, so we know that the zinc is being oxidized and is the anode. The measured E°_{cell} is +0.76 V, and we use this value to find the unknown standard electrode potential, E°_{zinc}:

$$
\begin{array}{lll}
2H^+(aq) + 2e^- \longrightarrow H_2(g) & E^\circ_{reference} = 0.00\ V & \text{[cathode; reduction]} \\
Zn(s) \longrightarrow Zn^{2+}(aq) + 2e^- & E^\circ_{zinc} = ?\ V & \text{[anode; oxidation]} \\
\hline
Zn(s) + 2H^+(aq) \longrightarrow Zn^{2+}(aq) + H_2(g) & E^\circ_{cell} = 0.76\ V &
\end{array}
$$

$$E^\circ_{cell} = E^\circ_{cathode} - E^\circ_{anode} = E^\circ_{reference} - E^\circ_{zinc}$$

$$E^\circ_{zinc} = E^\circ_{reference} - E^\circ_{cell} = 0.00\ V - 0.76\ V = -0.76\ V$$

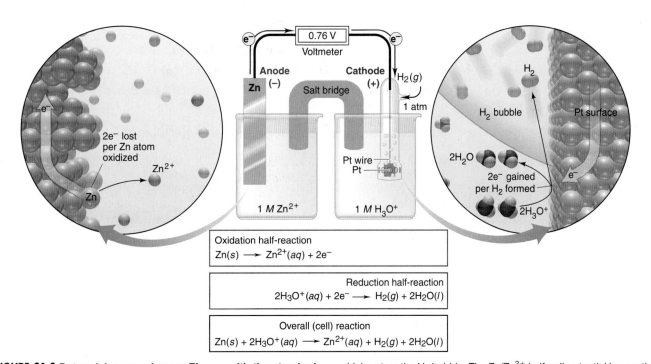

FIGURE 21.8 Determining an unknown $E^\circ_{half-cell}$ with the standard reference (hydrogen) electrode. A voltaic cell has the Zn half-reaction in one half-cell and the hydrogen reference half-reaction in the other. The magnified view of the hydrogen half-reaction shows two H_3O^+ ions being reduced to two H_2O molecules and an H_2 molecule, which enters the H_2 bubble. The Zn/Zn^{2+} half-cell potential is negative (anode), and the cell potential is 0.76 V. The potential of the standard reference electrode is defined as 0.00 V, so the cell potential equals the negative of the anode potential; that is,

$$0.76\ V = 0.00\ V - E^\circ_{zinc} \qquad \text{so} \qquad E^\circ_{zinc} = -0.76\ V$$

Now let's return to the zinc-copper cell and use the measured value of E_{cell}° (1.10 V) and the value we just found for E_{zinc}° to calculate E_{copper}°:

$$E_{cell}^{\circ} = E_{cathode}^{\circ} - E_{anode}^{\circ} = E_{copper}^{\circ} - E_{zinc}^{\circ}$$
$$E_{copper}^{\circ} = E_{cell}^{\circ} + E_{zinc}^{\circ} = 1.10 \text{ V} + (-0.76 \text{ V}) = 0.34 \text{ V}$$

By continuing this process of constructing cells with one known and one unknown electrode potential, we can find many other standard electrode potentials.

SAMPLE PROBLEM 21.3   Calculating an Unknown $E_{half\text{-}cell}^{\circ}$ from E_{cell}°

Problem A voltaic cell houses the reaction between aqueous bromine and zinc metal:

$$Br_2(aq) + Zn(s) \longrightarrow Zn^{2+}(aq) + 2Br^-(aq) \qquad E_{cell}^{\circ} = 1.83 \text{ V}$$

Calculate $E_{bromine}^{\circ}$, given $E_{zinc}^{\circ} = -0.76$ V.

Plan E_{cell}° is positive, so the reaction is spontaneous as written. By dividing the reaction into half-reactions, we see that Br_2 is reduced and Zn is oxidized; thus, the zinc half-cell contains the anode. We use Equation 21.3 to find $E_{unknown}^{\circ}$ ($E_{bromine}^{\circ}$).

Solution Dividing the reaction into half-reactions:

$$Br_2(aq) + 2e^- \longrightarrow 2Br^-(aq) \qquad E_{unknown}^{\circ} = E_{bromine}^{\circ} = ? \text{ V}$$
$$Zn(s) \longrightarrow Zn^{2+}(aq) + 2e^- \qquad E_{zinc}^{\circ} = -0.76 \text{ V}$$

Calculating $E_{bromine}^{\circ}$:

$$E_{cell}^{\circ} = E_{cathode}^{\circ} - E_{anode}^{\circ} = E_{bromine}^{\circ} - E_{zinc}^{\circ}$$
$$E_{bromine}^{\circ} = E_{cell}^{\circ} + E_{zinc}^{\circ} = 1.83 \text{ V} + (-0.76 \text{ V})$$
$$= 1.07 \text{ V}$$

Check A good check is to make sure that calculating $E_{bromine}^{\circ} - E_{zinc}^{\circ}$ gives E_{cell}°: 1.07 V $-$ (-0.76 V) = 1.83 V.

Comment Keep in mind that, whichever is the unknown half-cell, reduction is the cathode half-reaction and oxidation is the anode half-reaction. Always subtract E_{anode}° from $E_{cathode}^{\circ}$ to get E_{cell}°.

FOLLOW-UP PROBLEM 21.3 A voltaic cell based on the reaction between aqueous Br_2 and vanadium(III) ions has $E_{cell}^{\circ} = 1.39$ V:

$$Br_2(aq) + 2V^{3+}(aq) + 2H_2O(l) \longrightarrow 2VO^{2+}(aq) + 4H^+(aq) + 2Br^-(aq)$$

What is $E_{vanadium}^{\circ}$, the standard electrode potential for the reduction of VO^{2+} to V^{3+}?

Relative Strengths of Oxidizing and Reducing Agents

One of the things we can learn from measuring potentials of voltaic cells is the relative strengths of the oxidizing and reducing agents involved. Three oxidizing agents present in the voltaic cell just discussed are Cu^{2+}, H^+, and Zn^{2+}. We can rank their relative oxidizing strengths by writing each half-reaction as a gain of electrons (reduction), with its corresponding standard electrode potential:

$$Cu^{2+}(aq) + 2e^- \longrightarrow Cu(s) \qquad E^{\circ} = 0.34 \text{ V}$$
$$2H^+(aq) + 2e^- \longrightarrow H_2(g) \qquad E^{\circ} = 0.00 \text{ V}$$
$$Zn^{2+}(aq) + 2e^- \longrightarrow Zn(s) \qquad E^{\circ} = -0.76 \text{ V}$$

The more positive the E° value, the more readily the reaction (as written) occurs; thus, Cu^{2+} gains two electrons more readily than H^+, which gains them more readily than Zn^{2+}. In terms of strength as an oxidizing agent, therefore, $Cu^{2+} >$ $H^+ > Zn^{2+}$. Moreover, this listing also ranks the strengths of the reducing agents: $Zn > H_2 > Cu$. Notice that this list of half-reactions in order of *decreasing* half-cell potential shows, *from top to bottom,* the oxidizing agents (reactants) *decreasing* in strength and the reducing agents (products) *increasing* in strength; that is, Cu^{2+} (top left) is the strongest oxidizing agent, and Zn (bottom right) is the strongest reducing agent.

Table 21.2   Selected Standard Electrode Potentials (298 K)

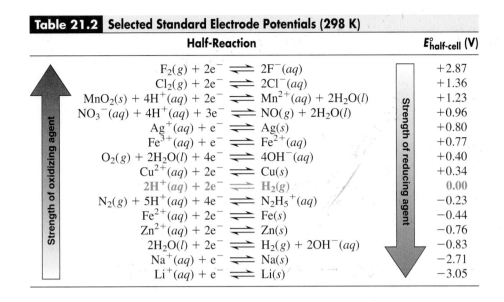

Half-Reaction	$E^\circ_{\text{half-cell}}$ (V)
$F_2(g) + 2e^- \rightleftharpoons 2F^-(aq)$	+2.87
$Cl_2(g) + 2e^- \rightleftharpoons 2Cl^-(aq)$	+1.36
$MnO_2(s) + 4H^+(aq) + 2e^- \rightleftharpoons Mn^{2+}(aq) + 2H_2O(l)$	+1.23
$NO_3^-(aq) + 4H^+(aq) + 3e^- \rightleftharpoons NO(g) + 2H_2O(l)$	+0.96
$Ag^+(aq) + e^- \rightleftharpoons Ag(s)$	+0.80
$Fe^{3+}(aq) + e^- \rightleftharpoons Fe^{2+}(aq)$	+0.77
$O_2(g) + 2H_2O(l) + 4e^- \rightleftharpoons 4OH^-(aq)$	+0.40
$Cu^{2+}(aq) + 2e^- \rightleftharpoons Cu(s)$	+0.34
$2H^+(aq) + 2e^- \rightleftharpoons H_2(g)$	0.00
$N_2(g) + 5H^+(aq) + 4e^- \rightleftharpoons N_2H_5^+(aq)$	−0.23
$Fe^{2+}(aq) + 2e^- \rightleftharpoons Fe(s)$	−0.44
$Zn^{2+}(aq) + 2e^- \rightleftharpoons Zn(s)$	−0.76
$2H_2O(l) + 2e^- \rightleftharpoons H_2(g) + 2OH^-(aq)$	−0.83
$Na^+(aq) + e^- \rightleftharpoons Na(s)$	−2.71
$Li^+(aq) + e^- \rightleftharpoons Li(s)$	−3.05

Strength of oxidizing agent (increases upward)   Strength of reducing agent (increases downward)

By combining many pairs of half-cells into voltaic cells, we can create a list of reduction half-reactions and arrange them in *decreasing* order of standard electrode potential (from most positive to most negative). Such a list, called an *emf series* or a *table of standard electrode potentials,* appears in Appendix D; a few examples are given in Table 21.2.

There are several key points to keep in mind:

- All values are relative to the standard hydrogen (reference) electrode:

$$2H^+(aq; 1\,M) + 2e^- \rightleftharpoons H_2(g; 1\text{ atm}) \qquad E^\circ_{\text{reference}} = 0.00 \text{ V}$$

- By convention, the half-reactions are written as *reductions,* which means that *only reactants are oxidizing agents and only products are reducing agents.*
- The more positive the $E^\circ_{\text{half-cell}}$, the more readily the half-reaction occurs.
- Half-reactions are shown with an equilibrium arrow because each can occur as a reduction or an oxidation (that is, take place at the cathode or anode, respectively), depending on the $E^\circ_{\text{half-cell}}$ of the other half-reaction.
- As Appendix D (and Table 21.2) is arranged, the strength of the oxidizing agent (reactant) *increases going up (bottom to top),* and the strength of the reducing agent (product) *increases going down (top to bottom).*

Thus, $F_2(g)$ is the strongest oxidizing agent (has the largest positive E°), which means $F^-(aq)$ is the weakest reducing agent. Similarly, $Li^+(aq)$ is the weakest oxidizing agent (has the most negative E°), which means $Li(s)$ is the strongest reducing agent.

Writing Spontaneous Redox Reactions Appendix D can be used to write spontaneous redox reactions, which is useful for constructing voltaic cells.

Every redox reaction is the sum of two half-reactions, so there is a reducing agent and an oxidizing agent on each side. In the zinc-copper reaction, for instance, Zn and Cu are the reducing agents, and Cu^{2+} and Zn^{2+} are the oxidizing agents. The stronger oxidizing and reducing agents react spontaneously to form the weaker oxidizing and reducing agents:

$$\underset{\substack{\text{stronger} \\ \text{reducing agent}}}{Zn(s)} + \underset{\substack{\text{stronger} \\ \text{oxidizing agent}}}{Cu^{2+}(aq)} \longrightarrow \underset{\substack{\text{weaker} \\ \text{oxidizing agent}}}{Zn^{2+}(aq)} + \underset{\substack{\text{weaker} \\ \text{reducing agent}}}{Cu(s)}$$

THINK OF IT THIS WAY
Redox Couples and Acid-Base Pairs

Notice the analogy between redox and acid-base reactions: Just as a stronger oxidizing agent forms a weaker reducing agent, a stronger acid forms a weaker conjugate base. Therefore, a stronger acid and base react spontaneously to form a weaker base and acid, just as stronger oxidizing and reducing agents react spontaneously to form weaker reducing and oxidizing agents. In one case, protons are transferred; in the other case, electrons are.

Based on the order of the $E°$ values in Appendix D, *the stronger oxidizing agent (species on the left) has a half-reaction with a larger (more positive or less negative) $E°$ value, and the stronger reducing agent (species on the right) has a half-reaction with a smaller (less positive or more negative) $E°$ value.* Therefore, a spontaneous reaction ($E°_{cell} > 0$) will occur between an oxidizing agent and any reducing agent that lies *below* it in the list. For instance, Zn (right) lies below Cu^{2+} (left), and Cu^{2+} and Zn react spontaneously. In other words, *for a spontaneous reaction to occur, the half-reaction higher in the list proceeds at the cathode as written, and the half-reaction lower in the list proceeds at the anode in reverse.* This pairing ensures that the stronger oxidizing agent (higher on the left) and stronger reducing agent (lower on the right) will be the reactants.

However, if we know the electrode potentials, we can write a spontaneous redox reaction even if Appendix D is not available. Let's choose a pair of half-reactions from the appendix and, without referring to their relative positions in the list, use them to write a spontaneous redox reaction:

$$Ag^+(aq) + e^- \longrightarrow Ag(s) \qquad E°_{silver} = 0.80 \text{ V}$$
$$Sn^{2+}(aq) + 2e^- \longrightarrow Sn(s) \qquad E°_{tin} = -0.14 \text{ V}$$

There are two steps involved:

1. Reverse one of the half-reactions into an oxidation step such that the difference of the electrode potentials (cathode *minus* anode) gives a *positive* $E°_{cell}$. Note that when we reverse the half-reaction, we need *not* reverse the sign of $E°_{half-cell}$ because the minus sign in Equation 21.3 ($E°_{cell} = E°_{cathode} - E°_{anode}$) will do that.
2. Add the rearranged half-reactions to obtain a balanced overall equation. Be sure to multiply by coefficients so that e^- lost equals e^- gained and to cancel species common to both sides.

(You may be tempted in this particular case to add the two half-reactions as written, because you obtain a positive $E°_{cell}$, but you would then have two oxidizing agents forming two reducing agents, which cannot occur.)

We want to pair the stronger oxidizing and reducing agents as reactants. The larger (more positive) $E°$ value for the silver half-reaction means that Ag^+ is a stronger oxidizing agent (gains electrons more readily) than Sn^{2+}, and the smaller (more negative) $E°$ value for the tin half-reaction means that Sn is a stronger reducing agent (loses electrons more readily) than Ag. Therefore, we reverse the tin half-reaction (but *not* the sign of $E°_{tin}$):

$$Sn(s) \longrightarrow Sn^{2+}(aq) + 2e^- \qquad E°_{tin} = -0.14 \text{ V}$$

Subtracting $E°_{half-cell}$ of the tin half-reaction (anode, oxidation) from $E°_{half-cell}$ of the silver half-reaction (cathode, reduction) gives a positive $E°_{cell}$; that is, 0.80 V − (−0.14 V) = 0.94 V.

With the half-reactions written in the correct direction, we must next make sure that the *number of electrons lost in the oxidation equals the number gained in the reduction.* In this case, we double the silver (reduction) half-reaction. Adding the half-reactions and applying Equation 21.3 gives the balanced equation and E_{cell}:

$$
\begin{aligned}
2Ag^+(aq) + 2e^- &\longrightarrow 2Ag(s) & E°_{silver} &= 0.80 \text{ V} & &\text{[reduction]} \\
Sn(s) &\longrightarrow Sn^{2+}(aq) + 2e^- & E°_{tin} &= -0.14 \text{ V} & &\text{[oxidation]} \\
\hline
Sn(s) + 2Ag^+(aq) &\longrightarrow Sn^{2+}(aq) + 2Ag(s) & E°_{cell} &= E°_{silver} - E°_{tin} = 0.94 \text{ V}
\end{aligned}
$$

With the reaction spontaneous as written, the stronger oxidizing and reducing agents are reactants, which confirms that Sn is a stronger reducing agent than Ag, and Ag^+ is a stronger oxidizing agent than Sn^{2+}.

A very important point to note is that, when we doubled the coefficients of the silver half-reaction to balance the number of electrons, we did *not* double its $E°$ value—it remained 0.80 V. That is, *changing the balancing coefficients of a half-reaction does **not** change the $E°$ value*. The reason is that a standard electrode potential is an *intensive* property, one that does *not* depend on the amount of substance present. The potential is the *ratio* of energy to charge. When we change the coefficients, thus changing the amount of substance, the energy *and* the charge change proportionately, so their ratio stays the same. (Recall that density, which is also an intensive property, does not change with the amount of substance because the mass *and* the volume change proportionately.)

SAMPLE PROBLEM 21.4   Writing Spontaneous Redox Reactions

Problem Combine the following three half-reactions into three balanced equations (A, B, and C) for spontaneous reactions, and calculate $E°_{cell}$ for each.

(1) $NO_3^-(aq) + 4H^+(aq) + 3e^- \longrightarrow NO(g) + 2H_2O(l)$	$E° = 0.96$ V
(2) $N_2(g) + 5H^+(aq) + 4e^- \longrightarrow N_2H_5^+(aq)$	$E° = -0.23$ V
(3) $MnO_2(s) + 4H^+(aq) + 2e^- \longrightarrow Mn^{2+}(aq) + 2H_2O(l)$	$E° = 1.23$ V

Plan To write the redox equations, we combine the possible pairs of half-reactions: (1) and (2), (1) and (3), and (2) and (3). They are all written as reductions, so the oxidizing agents appear as reactants and the reducing agents appear as products. In each pair, we reverse the reduction half-reaction that has the smaller (less positive or more negative) $E°$ value to an oxidation to obtain a positive $E°_{cell}$. We make e^- lost equal e^- gained, without changing the magnitude of the $E°$ value, add the half-reactions together, and then apply Equation 21.3 to find $E°_{cell}$.

Solution Combining half-reactions (1) and (2) gives equation (A). The $E°$ value for half-reaction (1) is larger (more positive) than that for (2), so we reverse (2) to obtain a positive $E°_{cell}$:

(1) $NO_3^-(aq) + 4H^+(aq) + 3e^- \longrightarrow NO(g) + 2H_2O(l)$	$E° = 0.96$ V
(rev 2) $N_2H_5^+(aq) \longrightarrow N_2(g) + 5H^+(aq) + 4e^-$	$E° = -0.23$ V

To make e^- lost equal e^- gained, we multiply (1) by four and the reversed (2) by three; then add half-reactions and cancel appropriate numbers of common species (H^+ and e^-):

$4NO_3^-(aq) + 16H^+(aq) + 12e^- \longrightarrow 4NO(g) + 8H_2O(l)$	$E° = 0.96$ V
$3N_2H_5^+(aq) \longrightarrow 3N_2(g) + 15H^+(aq) + 12e^-$	$E° = -0.23$ V

(A) $3N_2H_5^+(aq) + 4NO_3^-(aq) + H^+(aq) \longrightarrow 3N_2(g) + 4NO(g) + 8H_2O(l)$

$$E°_{cell} = 0.96 \text{ V} - (-0.23 \text{ V}) = 1.19 \text{ V}$$

Combining half-reactions (1) and (3) gives equation (B). Half-reaction (1) must be reversed:

(rev 1) $NO(g) + 2H_2O(l) \longrightarrow NO_3^-(aq) + 4H^+(aq) + 3e^-$	$E° = 0.96$ V
(3) $MnO_2(s) + 4H^+(aq) + 2e^- \longrightarrow Mn^{2+}(aq) + 2H_2O(l)$	$E° = 1.23$ V

We multiply reversed (1) by two and (3) by three, then add and cancel:

$2NO(g) + 4H_2O(l) \longrightarrow 2NO_3^-(aq) + 8H^+(aq) + 6e^-$	$E° = 0.96$ V
$3MnO_2(s) + 12H^+(aq) + 6e^- \longrightarrow 3Mn^{2+}(aq) + 6H_2O(l)$	$E° = 1.23$ V

(B) $3MnO_2(s) + 4H^+(aq) + 2NO(g) \longrightarrow 3Mn^{2+}(aq) + 2H_2O(l) + 2NO_3^-(aq)$

$$E°_{cell} = 1.23 \text{ V} - 0.96 \text{ V} = 0.27 \text{ V}$$

Combining half-reactions (2) and (3) gives equation (C). Half-reaction (2) must be reversed:

(rev 2) $N_2H_5^+(aq) \longrightarrow N_2(g) + 5H^+(aq) + 4e^-$	$E° = -0.23$ V
(3) $MnO_2(s) + 4H^+(aq) + 2e^- \longrightarrow Mn^{2+}(aq) + 2H_2O(l)$	$E° = 1.23$ V

We multiply reaction (3) by two, add the half-reactions, and cancel:

$$N_2H_5^+(aq) \longrightarrow N_2(g) + 5H^+(aq) + 4e^- \qquad E° = -0.23 \text{ V}$$

$$2MnO_2(s) + 8H^+(aq) + 4e^- \longrightarrow 2Mn^{2+}(aq) + 4H_2O(l) \qquad E° = 1.23 \text{ V}$$

(C) $N_2H_5^+(aq) + 2MnO_2(s) + 3H^+(aq) \longrightarrow N_2(g) + 2Mn^{2+}(aq) + 4H_2O(l)$

$$E°_{cell} = 1.23 \text{ V} - (-0.23 \text{ V}) = 1.46 \text{ V}$$

Check As always, check that atoms and charge balance on each side of the equation. A good way to check that the reactions are spontaneous is to list the given half-reactions in order of decreasing $E°$ value:

$$MnO_2(s) + 4H^+(aq) + 2e^- \longrightarrow Mn^{2+}(aq) + 2H_2O(l) \qquad E° = 1.23 \text{ V}$$

$$NO_3^-(aq) + 4H^+(aq) + 3e^- \longrightarrow NO(g) + 2H_2O(l) \qquad E° = 0.96 \text{ V}$$

$$N_2(g) + 5H^+(aq) + 4e^- \longrightarrow N_2H_5^+(aq) \qquad E° = -0.23 \text{ V}$$

Then the oxidizing agents (reactants) decrease in strength going down the list, so the reducing agents (products) decrease in strength going up. Each of the three spontaneous reactions (A, B, and C) should combine a reactant with a product that is lower down on this list.

FOLLOW-UP PROBLEM 21.4 Is the following reaction spontaneous as written?

$$3Fe^{2+}(aq) \longrightarrow Fe(s) + 2Fe^{3+}(aq)$$

If not, write the equation for the spontaneous reaction, calculate $E°_{cell}$, and rank the three species of iron in order of decreasing reducing strength.

Relative Reactivities of Metals In Chapter 4, we discussed the activity series of the metals (see Figure 4.14), which ranks metals by their ability to "displace" one another from aqueous solution. Now you'll see *why* this displacement occurs, as well as why many, but not all, metals react with acid to form H_2, and why a few metals form H_2 even in water.

1. *Metals that can displace H_2 from acid.* The standard hydrogen half-reaction represents the reduction of H^+ ions from an acid to H_2:

$$2H^+(aq) + 2e^- \longrightarrow H_2(g) \qquad E° = 0.00 \text{ V}$$

To see which metals reduce H^+ (referred to as "displacing H_2") from acids, choose a metal, write its half-reaction as an oxidation, combine this half-reaction with the hydrogen half-reaction, and see if $E°_{cell}$ is positive. What you find is that the metals Li through Pb, those that lie *below* the standard hydrogen (reference) half-reaction in Appendix D, give a positive $E°_{cell}$ when reducing H^+. Iron, for example, reduces H^+ from an acid to H_2:

$$Fe(s) \longrightarrow Fe^{2+}(aq) + 2e^- \qquad E° = -0.44 \text{ V} \quad \text{[anode; oxidation]}$$

$$2H^+(aq) + 2e^- \longrightarrow H_2(g) \qquad E° = 0.00 \text{ V} \quad \text{[cathode; reduction]}$$

$$Fe(s) + 2H^+(aq) \longrightarrow H_2(g) + Fe^{2+}(aq) \qquad E°_{cell} = 0.00 \text{ V} - (-0.44 \text{ V}) = 0.44 \text{ V}$$

The lower the metal in the list, the stronger it is as a reducing agent; therefore, the more positive its half-cell potential when the half-reaction is reversed, and the higher the $E°_{cell}$ for its reduction of H^+ to H_2. *If $E°_{cell}$ for the reduction of H^+ is more positive for metal A than it is for metal B, metal A is a stronger reducing agent than metal B and a more* **active** *metal.*

2. *Metals that cannot displace H_2 from acid.* Metals that are *above* the standard hydrogen (reference) half-reaction *cannot* reduce H^+ from acids. When we reverse the metal half-reaction, the $E°_{cell}$ is negative, so the reaction does not occur. For example, the coinage metals—copper, silver, and gold,

which are in Group 1B(11)—are not strong enough reducing agents to reduce H^+ from acids:

$$Ag(s) \longrightarrow Ag^+(aq) + e^- \qquad E° = 0.80 \text{ V} \quad \text{[anode; oxidation]}$$
$$\underline{2H^+(aq) + 2e^- \longrightarrow H_2(g) \qquad E° = 0.00 \text{ V} \quad \text{[cathode; reduction]}}$$
$$2Ag(s) + 2H^+(aq) \longrightarrow 2Ag^+(aq) + H_2(g) \qquad E°_{cell} = 0.00 \text{ V} - 0.80 \text{ V} = -0.80 \text{ V}$$

The higher the metal in the list, the more negative is its $E°_{cell}$ for the reduction of H^+ to H_2, the lower is its reducing strength, and the less active it is. Thus, gold is less active than silver, which is less active than copper.

3. *Metals that can displace H_2 from water.* Metals active enough to reduce H_2O lie *below that half-reaction:*

$$2H_2O(l) + 2e^- \longrightarrow H_2(g) + 2OH^-(aq) \qquad E = -0.42 \text{ V}$$

(The value shown here is the *nonstandard* electrode potential because, in pure water, $[OH^-]$ is 1.0×10^{-7} M, not the standard-state value of 1 M.) For example, when sodium reacts in water (with the Na half-reaction reversed and doubled):

$$2Na(s) \longrightarrow 2Na^+(aq) + 2e^- \qquad E° = -2.71 \text{ V} \quad \text{[anode; oxidation]}$$
$$\underline{2H_2O(l) + 2e^- \longrightarrow H_2(g) + 2OH^-(aq) \qquad E = -0.42 \text{ V} \quad \text{[cathode; reduction]}}$$
$$2Na(s) + 2H_2O(l) \longrightarrow 2Na^+(aq) + H_2(g) + 2OH^-(aq)$$
$$E_{cell} = -0.42 \text{ V} - (-2.71 \text{ V}) = 2.29 \text{ V}$$

The alkali metals [Group 1A(1)] and the larger alkaline earth metals [Group 2A(2)] can reduce water, or displace H_2 from H_2O (Figure 21.9).

4. *Metals that can displace other metals from solution.* We can predict whether one metal can reduce the aqueous ion of another metal. Any metal lower in the list in Appendix D can reduce the ion of a metal that is higher up, and thus displace that metal from solution. For example, zinc can displace iron from solution:

$$Zn(s) \longrightarrow Zn^{2+}(aq) + 2e^- \qquad E° = -0.76 \text{ V} \quad \text{[anode; oxidation]}$$
$$\underline{Fe^{2+}(aq) + 2e^- \longrightarrow Fe(s) \qquad E° = -0.44 \text{ V} \quad \text{[cathode; reduction]}}$$
$$Zn(s) + Fe^{2+}(aq) \longrightarrow Zn^{2+}(aq) + Fe(s) \qquad E°_{cell} = -0.44 \text{ V} - (-0.76 \text{ V}) = 0.32 \text{ V}$$

This particular reaction has tremendous economic importance in protecting iron from rusting, as you'll see later in this chapter.

Oxidation half-reaction
$Ca(s) \longrightarrow Ca^{2+}(aq) + 2e^-$

Reduction half-reaction
$2H_2O(l) + 2e^- \longrightarrow H_2(g) + 2OH^-(aq)$

Overall (cell) reaction
$Ca(s) + 2H_2O(l) \longrightarrow Ca(OH)_2(aq) + H_2(g)$

FIGURE 21.9 The reaction of calcium in water. Calcium is one of the metals active enough to displace H_2 from H_2O.

SECTION 21.3 SUMMARY

The output of a cell is called the cell potential (E_{cell}) and is measured in volts (1 V = 1 J/C). • When all substances are in their standard states, the output is the standard cell potential ($E°_{cell}$). $E°_{cell} > 0$ for a spontaneous reaction at standard-state conditions. • By convention, a standard electrode potential ($E°_{half-cell}$) refers to the *reduction* half-reaction. $E°_{cell}$ equals $E°_{half-cell}$ of the cathode *minus* $E°_{half-cell}$ of the anode. • Using a standard hydrogen (reference) electrode, other $E°_{half-cell}$ values can be measured and used to rank oxidizing (or reducing) agents (see Appendix D). • Spontaneous redox reactions combine stronger oxidizing and reducing agents to form weaker ones. • A metal can reduce another species (H^+, H_2O, or an ion of another metal) if $E°_{cell}$ for the reaction is positive.

21.4 FREE ENERGY AND ELECTRICAL WORK

In Chapter 20, we discussed the relationship of useful work, free energy, and the equilibrium constant. In this section, we examine this relationship in the context of electrochemical cells and see the effect of concentration on cell potential.

Standard Cell Potential and the Equilibrium Constant

As you know from Section 20.3, a spontaneous reaction has a *negative* free energy change ($\Delta G < 0$), and you've just seen that a spontaneous electrochemical reaction has a *positive* cell potential ($E_{cell} > 0$). Note that *the signs of ΔG and E_{cell}*

are opposite for a spontaneous reaction. These two indications of spontaneity are proportional to each other:

$$\Delta G \propto -E_{cell}$$

Let's determine this proportionality constant by focusing on the electrical work done (w, in joules), which is the product of the potential (E_{cell}, in volts) and the amount of charge that flows (in coulombs). The value used for E_{cell} is measured with no current flowing and, therefore, no energy lost to heating the cell. Thus, E_{cell} is the maximum voltage possible for the cell, and the work is the maximum work possible (w_{max}). For work done *by* the cell *on* the surroundings, this quantity is negative:*

$$w_{max} = -E_{cell} \times charge$$

Equation 20.9 (p. 689) shows that the maximum work done *on* the surroundings is ΔG:

$$w_{max} = -E_{cell} \times charge = \Delta G \quad \text{and so} \quad \Delta G = -E_{cell} \times charge$$

The charge that flows through the cell equals the number of moles of electrons (n) transferred times the charge of 1 mol of electrons (symbol F):

$$Charge = \text{moles of } e^- \times \frac{charge}{\text{mol } e^-} \quad \text{or} \quad charge = nF$$

The charge of 1 mol of electrons is the **Faraday constant (F),** named in honor of Michael Faraday, the 19th-century British scientist who pioneered the study of electrochemistry:

$$F = \frac{96{,}485 \text{ C}}{\text{mol } e^-}$$

Because 1 V = 1 J/C, we have 1 C = 1 J/V, and

$$F = 9.65 \times 10^4 \, \frac{J}{V \cdot \text{mol } e^-} \quad \text{(3 sf)} \tag{21.4}$$

Substituting for charge, the proportionality constant is nF:

$$\Delta G = -nFE_{cell} \tag{21.5}$$

When all of the components are in their standard states, we have

$$\Delta G^\circ = -nFE^\circ_{cell} \tag{21.6}$$

Using this relationship, we can relate the standard cell potential to the equilibrium constant of the redox reaction. Recall from Equation 20.12 that

$$\Delta G^\circ = -RT \ln K$$

Substituting for ΔG° from Equation 21.6 gives

$$-nFE^\circ_{cell} = -RT \ln K$$

Solving for E°_{cell} gives

$$E^\circ_{cell} = \frac{RT}{nF} \ln K \tag{21.7}$$

Figure 21.10 summarizes the interconnections among the standard free energy change, the equilibrium constant, and the standard cell potential. The procedures presented in Chapter 20 for determining K required that we know ΔG°, either from ΔH° and ΔS° values or from ΔG°_f values. For redox reactions, we now have a direct experimental method for determining K *and* ΔG°: measure E°_{cell}.

---

*Recall from Chapter 20 that only a reversible process can do maximum work. For no current to flow and the process to be reversible, E_{cell} must be opposed by an equal potential in the measuring circuit: if the opposing potential is infinitesimally smaller, the cell reaction goes forward; if it is infinitesimally larger, the reaction goes backward.

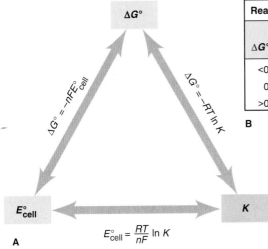

Reaction Parameters at the Standard State			
$\Delta G°$	K	$E°_{cell}$	Reaction at standard-state conditions
<0	>1	>0	Spontaneous
0	1	0	At equilibrium
>0	<1	<0	Nonspontaneous

B

FIGURE 21.10 The interrelationship of $\Delta G°$, $E°_{cell}$, and K. A, Any one of these three central thermodynamic parameters can be used to find the other two. **B,** The signs of $\Delta G°$ and $E°_{cell}$ determine the reaction direction at standard-state conditions.

It is common practice to simplify Equation 21.7 in calculations by

- Substituting the known value of 8.314 J/(mol rxn·K) for the constant R
- Substituting the known value of 9.65×10^4 J/(V·mol e⁻) for the constant F
- Substituting the standard temperature of 298.15 K for T, but keeping in mind that the cell can run at other temperatures.
- Multiplying by 2.303 to convert from natural to common (base-10) logarithms. This conversion shows that a *10-fold change in K makes $E°_{cell}$ change by 1.*

Thus, when n moles of e⁻ are transferred per mole of reaction in the balanced equation, this simplified relation between $E°_{cell}$ and K gives

$$E°_{cell} = \frac{RT}{nF} \ln K = 2.303 \frac{RT}{nF} \log K = 2.303 \times \frac{8.314 \frac{J}{\text{mol rxn·K}} \times 298.15 \text{ K}}{\frac{n \text{ mol e⁻}}{\text{mol rxn}} \left(9.65 \times 10^4 \frac{J}{\text{V·mol e⁻}}\right)} \log K$$

And, we have

$$E°_{cell} = \frac{0.0592 \text{ V}}{n} \log K \quad \text{or} \quad \log K = \frac{nE°_{cell}}{0.0592 \text{ V}} \quad \text{(at 298.15 K)} \quad \text{(21.8)}$$

SAMPLE PROBLEM 21.5 Calculating K and $\Delta G°$ from $E°_{cell}$

Problem Lead can displace silver from solution:

$$Pb(s) + 2Ag^+(aq) \longrightarrow Pb^{2+}(aq) + 2Ag(s)$$

As a consequence, silver is a valuable byproduct in the industrial extraction of lead from its ore. Calculate K and $\Delta G°$ at 298.15 K for this reaction.

Plan We divide the spontaneous redox equation into the half-reactions and use values from Appendix D to calculate $E°_{cell}$. Then, we substitute this result into Equation 21.8 to find K and into Equation 21.6 to find $\Delta G°$.

Solution Writing the half-reactions and their $E°$ values:

(1) $Ag^+(aq) + e^- \longrightarrow Ag(s)$ $E° = 0.80$ V
(2) $Pb^{2+}(aq) + 2e^- \longrightarrow Pb(s)$ $E° = -0.13$ V

Calculating $E°_{cell}$: We double (1), reverse (2), add the half-reactions, and subtract $E°_{lead}$ from $E°_{silver}$:

$2Ag^+(aq) + 2e^- \longrightarrow 2Ag(s)$	$E° = 0.80$ V
$Pb(s) \longrightarrow Pb^{2+}(aq) + 2e^-$	$E° = -0.13$ V
$Pb(s) + 2Ag^+(aq) \longrightarrow Pb^{2+}(aq) + 2Ag(s)$	$E°_{cell} = 0.80 \text{ V} - (-0.13 \text{ V}) = 0.93$ V

Calculating K with Equations 21.7 and 21.8:

$$E^{\circ}_{cell} = \frac{RT}{nF} \ln K = 2.303 \frac{RT}{nF} \log K$$

The adjusted half-reactions show that 2 mol of e^- are transferred per mole of reaction as written, so $n = 2$. Then, performing the substitutions for R and F that we just discussed with the cell running at 25°C (298.15 K), we have

$$E^{\circ}_{cell} = \frac{0.0592 \text{ V}}{2} \log K = 0.93 \text{ V}$$

So, $\log K = \dfrac{0.93 \text{ V} \times 2}{0.0592 \text{ V}} = 31.42$ and $K = 2.6 \times 10^{31}$

Calculating ΔG° (Equation 21.6):

$$\Delta G^{\circ} = -nFE^{\circ}_{cell} = -\frac{2 \text{ mol } e^-}{\text{mol rxn}} \times \frac{96.5 \text{ kJ}}{\text{V} \cdot \text{mol } e^-} \times 0.93 \text{ V} = -1.8 \times 10^2 \text{ kJ/mol rxn}$$

Check The three variables are consistent with the reaction being spontaneous at standard-state conditions: $E^{\circ}_{cell} > 0$, $\Delta G^{\circ} < 0$, and $K > 1$. Be sure to round and check the order of magnitude: in the ΔG° calculation, for instance, $\Delta G^{\circ} \approx -2 \times 100 \times 1 = -200$, so the overall math seems right. Another check would be to obtain ΔG° directly from its relation with K:

$$\Delta G^{\circ} = -RT \ln K = -8.314 \text{ J/mol rxn} \cdot \text{K} \times 298.15 \text{ K} \times \ln(2.6 \times 10^{31})$$
$$= -1.8 \times 10^5 \text{ J/mol rxn} = -1.8 \times 10^2 \text{ kJ/mol rxn}$$

FOLLOW-UP PROBLEM 21.5 When cadmium metal reduces Cu^{2+} in solution, Cd^{2+} forms in addition to copper metal. Given that $\Delta G^{\circ} = -143$ kJ, calculate K at 25°C. What is E°_{cell} of a voltaic cell that uses this reaction?

The Effect of Concentration on Cell Potential

So far, we've considered cells with all components in their standard states. But most cells don't start at those conditions, and even if they did, the concentrations change after a few moments of operation. Moreover, in all practical voltaic cells, such as batteries, reactant concentrations are far from standard-state values. Clearly, we must be able to determine E_{cell}, the cell potential under nonstandard conditions.

To do so, let's derive an expression for the relation between cell potential and concentration based on the relation between free energy and concentration. Recall from Chapter 20 (Equation 20.13) that ΔG equals ΔG° (the free energy change when the system moves from standard-state concentrations to equilibrium) *plus* $RT \ln Q$ (the free energy change when the system moves from nonstandard-state to standard-state concentrations):

$$\Delta G = \Delta G^{\circ} + RT \ln Q$$

ΔG is related to E_{cell} and ΔG° to E°_{cell} (Equations 21.5 and 21.6), so we substitute for them and get

$$-nFE_{cell} = -nFE^{\circ}_{cell} + RT \ln Q$$

Dividing both sides by $-nF$, we obtain the **Nernst equation,** developed by the German chemist Walther Hermann Nernst in 1889:

$$E_{cell} = E^{\circ}_{cell} - \frac{RT}{nF} \ln Q \tag{21.9}$$

The Nernst equation says that a cell potential under any conditions depends on the potential at standard-state concentrations *and* a term for the potential at nonstandard-state concentrations. How do changes in Q affect cell potential? From Equation 21.9, we see the following:

- When $Q < 1$ and thus [reactant] > [product], $\ln Q < 0$, so $E_{cell} > E^\circ_{cell}$.
- When $Q = 1$ and thus [reactant] = [product], $\ln Q = 0$, so $E_{cell} = E^\circ_{cell}$.
- When $Q > 1$ and thus [reactant] < [product], $\ln Q > 0$, so $E_{cell} < E^\circ_{cell}$.

As before, to obtain a simplified form of the Nernst equation for use in calculations, let's substitute known values of R and F, operate the cell at 298.15 K, and convert to common (base-10) logarithms:

$$E_{cell} = E^\circ_{cell} - \frac{RT}{nF} \ln Q = E^\circ_{cell} - 2.303 \frac{RT}{nF} \log Q$$

$$= E^\circ_{cell} - 2.303 \times \frac{8.314 \dfrac{\text{J}}{\text{mol rxn·K}} \times 298.15 \text{ K}}{\dfrac{n \text{ mol e}^-}{\text{mol rxn}} \left(9.65 \times 10^4 \dfrac{\text{J}}{\text{V·mol e}^-} \right)} \log Q$$

And we obtain:

$$E_{cell} = E^\circ_{cell} - \frac{0.0592 \text{ V}}{n} \log Q \quad \text{(at 298.15 K)} \qquad \textbf{(21.10)}$$

Remember that the expression for Q *contains only those species with concentrations (and/or pressures) that can vary;* thus, solids do not appear, even when they are the electrodes. For example, in the reaction between cadmium and silver ion, the Cd and Ag electrodes do not appear in the expression for Q:

$$\text{Cd}(s) + 2\text{Ag}^+(aq) \longrightarrow \text{Cd}^{2+}(aq) + 2\text{Ag}(s) \qquad Q = \frac{[\text{Cd}^{2+}]}{[\text{Ag}^+]^2}$$

SAMPLE PROBLEM 21.6 Using the Nernst Equation to Calculate E_{cell}

Problem In a test of a new reference electrode, a chemist constructs a voltaic cell consisting of a Zn/Zn^{2+} half-cell and an H_2/H^+ half-cell under the following conditions:

$$[\text{Zn}^{2+}] = 0.010 \, M \qquad [\text{H}^+] = 2.5 \, M \qquad P_{\text{H}_2} = 0.30 \text{ atm}$$

Calculate E_{cell} at 298.15 K.

Plan To apply the Nernst equation and determine E_{cell}, we must know E°_{cell} and Q. We write the spontaneous reaction, calculate E°_{cell} from standard electrode potentials (Appendix D), and use the given pressure and concentrations to find Q. (Recall that the ideal gas law allows us to use P at constant T as another way of writing concentration, n/V.) Then we substitute into Equation 21.10.

Solution Determining the cell reaction and E°_{cell}:

$2\text{H}^+(aq) + 2e^- \longrightarrow \text{H}_2(g)$	$E^\circ = 0.00$ V
$\text{Zn}(s) \longrightarrow \text{Zn}^{2+}(aq) + 2e^-$	$E^\circ = -0.76$ V
$2\text{H}^+(aq) + \text{Zn}(s) \longrightarrow \text{H}_2(g) + \text{Zn}^{2+}(aq)$	$E^\circ_{cell} = 0.00 \text{ V} - (-0.76 \text{ V}) = 0.76 \text{ V}$

Calculating Q:

$$Q = \frac{P_{\text{H}_2} \times [\text{Zn}^{2+}]}{[\text{H}^+]^2} = \frac{0.30 \times 0.010}{2.5^2} = 4.8 \times 10^{-4}$$

Solving for E_{cell} at 25°C (298.15 K), with $n = 2$:

$$E_{cell} = E^\circ_{cell} - \frac{0.0592 \text{ V}}{n} \log Q$$

$$= 0.76 \text{ V} - \left[\frac{0.0592 \text{ V}}{2} \log (4.8 \times 10^{-4}) \right] = 0.76 \text{ V} - (-0.0982 \text{ V}) = \boxed{0.86 \text{ V}}$$

Check After you check the arithmetic, reason through the answer: $E_{cell} > E^\circ_{cell}$ (0.86 > 0.76) because the $\log Q$ term was negative, which is consistent with $Q < 1$; that is, the amounts of products, P_{H_2} and $[\text{Zn}^{2+}]$, are smaller than the amount of reactant, $[\text{H}^+]$.

FOLLOW-UP PROBLEM 21.6 Consider a voltaic cell based on the following reaction: $\text{Fe}(s) + \text{Cu}^{2+}(aq) \rightleftharpoons \text{Fe}^{2+}(aq) + \text{Cu}(s)$. If $[\text{Cu}^{2+}] = 0.30 \, M$, what must $[\text{Fe}^{2+}]$ be to increase E_{cell} by 0.25 V above E°_{cell} at 25°C?

Changes in Potential During Cell Operation

The potential of the zinc-copper cell changes as concentrations change during cell operation. The only concentrations that change are [reactant] = $[Cu^{2+}]$ and [product] = $[Zn^{2+}]$:

$$Zn(s) + Cu^{2+}(aq) \rightleftharpoons Zn^{2+}(aq) + Cu(s) \qquad Q = \frac{[Zn^{2+}]}{[Cu^{2+}]}$$

The positive $E°_{cell}$ (1.10 V) means that this reaction proceeds *spontaneously* from the standard-state conditions, at which $[Zn^{2+}] = [Cu^{2+}] = 1\,M$ ($Q = 1$), to some point at which $[Zn^{2+}] > [Cu^{2+}]$ ($Q > 1$). Now, suppose that we start the cell when $[Zn^{2+}] < [Cu^{2+}]$ ($Q < 1$), for example, when $[Zn^{2+}] = 1.0 \times 10^{-4}\,M$ and $[Cu^{2+}] = 2.0\,M$. In this case, the cell potential is *higher* than the standard cell potential:

$$E_{cell} = E°_{cell} - \frac{0.0592\ V}{2} \log \frac{[Zn^{2+}]}{[Cu^{2+}]} = 1.10\ V - \left(\frac{0.0592\ V}{2} \log \frac{1.0 \times 10^{-4}}{2.0} \right)$$

$$= 1.10\ V - \left[\frac{0.0592\ V}{2}(-4.30) \right] = 1.10\ V + 0.127\ V = 1.23\ V$$

As the cell operates, $[Zn^{2+}]$ increases (as the Zn electrode deteriorates) and $[Cu^{2+}]$ decreases (as Cu plates out on the Cu electrode). Although the changes during this process occur smoothly, if we keep Equation 21.10 in mind, we can identify four general stages of operation. Figure 21.11A shows the first three. The main point to note is that *as the cell operates, its potential decreases:*

Stage 1. $E_{cell} > E°_{cell}$ when $Q < 1$: When the cell begins operation, $[Cu^{2+}] > [Zn^{2+}]$, so the $[(0.0592\ V/n) \log Q]$ term < 0 and $E_{cell} > E°_{cell}$.

As cell operation continues, $[Zn^{2+}]$ increases and $[Cu^{2+}]$ decreases; thus, Q becomes larger, the $[(0.0592\ V/n) \log Q]$ term becomes less negative (more positive), and E_{cell} decreases.

Stage 2. $E_{cell} = E°_{cell}$ when $Q = 1$: At the point when $[Cu^{2+}] = [Zn^{2+}]$, $Q = 1$, so the $[(0.0592\ V/n) \log Q]$ term $= 0$ and $E_{cell} = E°_{cell}$.

Stage 3. $E_{cell} < E°_{cell}$ when $Q > 1$: As the $[Zn^{2+}]/[Cu^{2+}]$ ratio continues to increase, the $[(0.0592\ V/n) \log Q]$ term > 0, so $E_{cell} < E°_{cell}$.

Stage 4. $E_{cell} = 0$ when $Q = K$: Eventually, the $[(0.0592\ V/n) \log Q]$ term becomes so large that it equals $E°_{cell}$, which means that E_{cell} is zero. This occurs *when the system reaches **equilibrium**: no more free energy is released, so the cell can do no more work.* At this point, we say that a battery is "dead."

Figure 21.11B summarizes these four key stages in the operation of a voltaic cell.

FIGURE 21.11 The relation between E_{cell} and log Q for the zinc-copper cell. **A,** A plot of E_{cell} vs. Q (on a logarithmic scale) for the zinc-copper cell shows a linear decrease. When $Q < 1$ *(left)*, [reactant] is relatively high, and the cell can do relatively more work. When $Q = 1$, $E_{cell} = E°_{cell}$. When $Q > 1$ *(right)*, [product] is relatively high, and the cell can do relatively less work. **B,** A summary of the changes in E_{cell} as the cell operates, including the changes in $[Zn^{2+}]$, denoted [P] for [product], and $[Cu^{2+}]$, denoted [R] for [reactant].

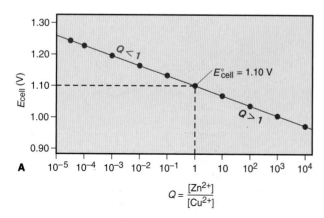

$$Q = \frac{[Zn^{2+}]}{[Cu^{2+}]}$$

A

Changes in E_{cell} and Concentration			
Stage in cell operation	Q	Relative [P] and [R]	$\dfrac{0.0592\ V}{n} \log Q$
1. $E > E°$	<1	[P] < [R]	<0
2. $E = E°$	=1	[P] = [R]	=0
3. $E < E°$	>1	[P] > [R]	>0
4. $E = 0$	=K	[P] ≫ [R]	=$E°$

B

Let's find K for the zinc-copper cell. At equilibrium, Equation 21.10 becomes

$$0 = E°_{cell} - \left(\frac{0.0592 \text{ V}}{n}\right) \log K, \text{ which rearranges to } E°_{cell} = \frac{0.0592 \text{ V}}{n} \log K$$

Note that this result is identical to Equation 21.8, which we obtained from $\Delta G°$. Solving for K of the zinc-copper cell ($E°_{cell} = 1.10$ V),

$$\log K = \frac{2 \times E°_{cell}}{0.0592 \text{ V}}, \quad \text{so} \quad K = 10^{(2 \times 1.10 \text{ V})/0.0592 \text{ V}} = 10^{37.16} = 1.4 \times 10^{37}$$

Thus, the zinc-copper cell does work until the $[Zn^{2+}]/[Cu^{2+}]$ ratio is *very* high.

Concentration Cells

If you mix a concentrated solution of a salt with a dilute solution of the salt, the final concentration equals some intermediate value. A **concentration cell** employs this phenomenon to generate electrical energy. The two solutions are in separate half-cells, so they do not mix; rather, their concentrations become equal as the cell operates.

How a Concentration Cell Works Suppose that both compartments of a voltaic cell house the Cu/Cu^{2+} half-reaction. The cell reaction is the sum of identical half-reactions, written in opposite directions, so the *standard* half-cell potentials cancel ($E°_{copper} - E°_{copper}$) and $E°_{cell}$ is zero. This occurs because standard electrode potentials are based on concentrations of 1 M. *In a concentration cell, however, the half-reactions are the same but the **concentrations** are different.* As a result, even though $E°_{cell}$ equals zero, the *nonstandard* cell potential, E_{cell}, does *not* equal zero because it depends on the *ratio of concentrations*.

In Figure 21.12A, a concentration cell has 0.10 M Cu^{2+} in the anode half-cell and 1.0 M Cu^{2+}, a 10-fold higher concentration, in the cathode half-cell:

$$Cu(s) \longrightarrow Cu^{2+}(aq; 0.10 \text{ } M) + 2e^- \quad \text{[anode; oxidation]}$$
$$Cu^{2+}(aq; 1.0 \text{ } M) + 2e^- \longrightarrow Cu(s) \quad \text{[cathode; reduction]}$$

The overall cell reaction is the sum of the half-reactions:

$$Cu^{2+}(aq; 1.0 \text{ } M) \longrightarrow Cu^{2+}(aq; 0.10 \text{ } M) \quad E_{cell} = ?$$

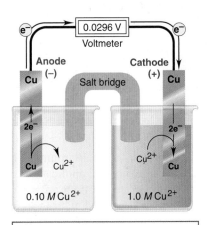

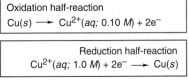

Oxidation half-reaction
$Cu(s) \longrightarrow Cu^{2+}(aq; 0.10 \text{ } M) + 2e^-$

Reduction half-reaction
$Cu^{2+}(aq; 1.0 \text{ } M) + 2e^- \longrightarrow Cu(s)$

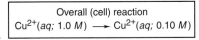

Overall (cell) reaction
$Cu^{2+}(aq; 1.0 \text{ } M) \longrightarrow Cu^{2+}(aq; 0.10 \text{ } M)$

A

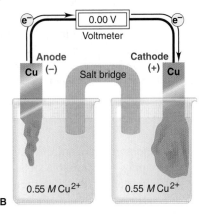

B

FIGURE 21.12 A concentration cell based on the Cu/Cu²⁺ half-reaction. A, The half-reactions are the same, so $E°_{cell} = 0$. The cell operates because the half-cell concentrations are different, which makes $E_{cell} > 0$ in this case. **B,** The cell operates until the half-cell concentrations are equal. Note the change in electrodes (exaggerated here for clarity) and the identical color of the solutions.

The cell potential at the initial concentrations of 0.10 M (dilute) and 1.0 M (concentrated), with $n = 2$, is obtained from the Nernst equation:

$$E_{cell} = E°_{cell} - \frac{0.0592\ V}{2} \log \frac{[Cu^{2+}]_{dil}}{[Cu^{2+}]_{conc}} = 0\ V - \left(\frac{0.0592\ V}{2} \log \frac{0.10\ M}{1.0\ M} \right)$$

$$= 0\ V - \left[\frac{0.0592\ V}{2} (-1.00) \right] = 0.0296\ V$$

As you can see, because $E°_{cell}$ for a concentration cell equals zero, E_{cell} for nonstandard conditions depends entirely on the $[(0.0592\ V/n) \log Q]$ term.

What is actually going on as this cell operates? In the half-cell with dilute electrolyte (anode), the Cu atoms in the electrode give up electrons and become Cu^{2+} ions, which enter the solution and make it *more* concentrated. The electrons released at the anode flow to the cathode compartment. There, Cu^{2+} ions in the concentrated solution pick up the electrons and become Cu atoms, which plate out on the electrode, so that solution becomes *less* concentrated. As in any voltaic cell, E_{cell} decreases until equilibrium is attained, which happens when $[Cu^{2+}]$ is the same in both half-cells (Figure 21.12B). The same final concentration would result if we mixed the two solutions, but no electrical work would be done.

SAMPLE PROBLEM 21.7 Calculating the Potential of a Concentration Cell

Problem A concentration cell consists of two Ag/Ag$^+$ half-cells. In half-cell A, electrode A dips into 0.010 M AgNO$_3$; in half-cell B, electrode B dips into 4.0×10^{-4} M AgNO$_3$. What is the cell potential at 298.15 K? Which electrode has a positive charge?

Plan The standard half-cell reactions are identical, so $E°_{cell}$ is zero, and we calculate E_{cell} from the Nernst equation. Because half-cell A has a higher [Ag$^+$], Ag$^+$ ions will be reduced and plate out on electrode A. In half-cell B, Ag will be oxidized and Ag$^+$ ions will enter the solution. As in all voltaic cells, reduction occurs at the cathode, which is positive.

Solution Writing the spontaneous reaction: The [Ag$^+$] decreases in half-cell A and increases in half-cell B, so the spontaneous reaction is

$$Ag^+(aq;\ 0.010\ M)\ [\text{half-cell A}] \longrightarrow Ag^+(aq;\ 4.0 \times 10^{-4}\ M)\ [\text{half-cell B}]$$

Calculating E_{cell}, with $n = 1$:

$$E_{cell} = E°_{cell} - \frac{0.0592\ V}{1} \log \frac{[Ag^+]_{dil}}{[Ag^+]_{conc}} = 0\ V - \left(0.0592\ V \log \frac{4.0 \times 10^{-4}}{0.010} \right)$$

$$= 0.0828\ V$$

Reduction occurs at the cathode, electrode A: $Ag^+(aq;\ 0.010\ M) + e^- \longrightarrow Ag(s)$. Thus, electrode A has a positive charge due to a relative electron deficiency.

FOLLOW-UP PROBLEM 21.7 A concentration cell is built using two Au/Au^{3+} half-cells. In half-cell A, [Au^{3+}] = 7.0×10^{-4} M, and in half-cell B, [Au^{3+}] = 2.5×10^{-2} M. What is E_{cell}, and which electrode is negative?

Applications of Concentration Cells Chemists, biologists, and environmental scientists apply the principle of a concentration cell in a host of applications. The most important is the measurement of unknown ion concentrations in materials from various sources, such as blood, soil, natural waters, and industrial waste water; recent advances allow such measurement in the picomolar to femtomolar (10^{-12}–10^{-15} M) range. The most common laboratory application is measurement of [H$^+$] to determine pH. Suppose we construct a concentration cell based on the H$_2$/H$^+$ half-reaction, in which the cathode compartment houses the standard hydrogen electrode and the anode compartment has the same apparatus dipping into an unknown [H$^+$] in solution. The half-reactions and overall reaction are

$$H_2(g;\ 1\ atm) \longrightarrow 2H^+(aq;\ \text{unknown}) + 2e^- \quad [\text{anode; oxidation}]$$

$$\underline{2H^+(aq;\ 1\ M) + 2e^- \longrightarrow H_2(g;\ 1\ atm)} \quad\quad [\text{cathode; reduction}]$$

$$2H^+(aq;\ 1\ M) \longrightarrow 2H^+(aq;\ \text{unknown}) \quad\quad E_{cell} = ?$$

As for the Cu/Cu^{2+} concentration cell, $E°_{cell}$ is zero; however, the half-cells differ in $[H^+]$, so E_{cell} is *not* zero. From the Nernst equation, with $n = 2$, we obtain

$$E_{cell} = E°_{cell} - \frac{0.0592 \text{ V}}{2} \log \frac{[H^+]^2_{unknown}}{[H^+]^2_{standard}}$$

Substituting 1 M for $[H^+]_{standard}$ and 0 V for $E°_{cell}$ gives

$$E_{cell} = 0 \text{ V} - \frac{0.0592 \text{ V}}{2} \log \frac{[H^+]^2_{unknown}}{1^2} = -\frac{0.0592 \text{ V}}{2} \log [H^+]^2_{unknown}$$

Because $\log x^2 = 2 \log x$ (see Appendix A), we obtain

$$E_{cell} = -\left[\frac{0.0592 \text{ V}}{2} (2 \log [H^+]_{unknown})\right] = -0.0592 \text{ V} \times \log [H^+]_{unknown}$$

Substituting $-\log [H^+] = pH$, we have

$$E_{cell} = 0.0592 \text{ V} \times pH$$

Thus, by measuring E_{cell}, we can find the pH.

In the routine measurement of pH, a concentration cell incorporating two hydrogen electrodes is too bulky and difficult to maintain. Instead, as was pointed out in Chapter 18, a pH meter is used. As shown in Figure 21.13A, two separate electrodes dip into the solution being tested. One of them is a *glass electrode*, which consists of an Ag/AgCl half-reaction immersed in an HCl solution of fixed concentration (usually 1.000 M) and enclosed by a thin ($\sim$0.05 mm) membrane made of a special glass that is highly sensitive to the presence of H^+ ions. The other electrode is a reference electrode, typically a *saturated calomel electrode*. It consists of a platinum wire immersed in a paste of Hg_2Cl_2 (calomel), liquid Hg, and saturated KCl solution. The glass electrode monitors the solution's $[H^+]$ relative to its own fixed internal $[H^+]$, and the instrument converts the potential difference between the glass and reference electrodes into a measure of pH. In modern instruments, a combination electrode is used, which houses both electrodes in one tube (Figure 21.13B).

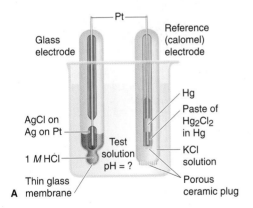

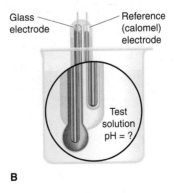

FIGURE 21.13 The laboratory measurement of pH. A, The glass electrode *(left)* is a self-contained Ag/AgCl half-cell immersed in an HCl solution of known concentration and enclosed by a thin glass membrane. It monitors the external $[H^+]$ in the solution relative to its fixed internal $[H^+]$. The saturated calomel electrode *(right)* acts as a reference. **B,** Most modern laboratories use a combination electrode, which houses both the glass and reference electrodes in one tube.

SECTION 21.4 SUMMARY

A spontaneous process is indicated by a negative ΔG or a positive E_{cell}, which are related: $\Delta G = -nFE_{cell}$. The ΔG of the cell reaction represents the maximum amount of electrical work the cell can do. • Because the standard free energy change, $\Delta G°$, is related to $E°_{cell}$ and to K, we can use $E°_{cell}$ to determine K. • At nonstandard conditions, the Nernst equation shows that E_{cell} depends on $E°_{cell}$ and a correction term based on Q. E_{cell} is high when Q is small (high [reactant]), and it decreases as the cell operates. At equilibrium, ΔG and E_{cell} are zero, which means that $Q = K$. • Concentration cells have identical half-reactions, but solutions of differing concentration; thus, they generate electrical energy as the concentrations become equal. Ion-specific electrodes, such as the pH electrode, measure the concentration of one species.

21.5 ELECTROCHEMICAL PROCESSES IN BATTERIES

Batteries are ingeniously engineered devices that house rather unusual half-reactions and half-cells, but they operate through the same electrochemical principles we've been discussing. Strictly speaking, a **battery** is a self-contained group of voltaic cells arranged in series (plus-to-minus-to-plus, and so on), so that their individual voltages are added together. In everyday speech, however, the term may also be applied to a single voltaic cell. In this section, we examine the three categories of batteries—primary, secondary, and fuel cells—and note important examples, including some newer designs, of each.

Primary (Nonrechargeable) Batteries

A *primary battery* cannot be recharged, so it is discarded when the components have reached their equilibrium concentrations, that is, when the cell is "dead." We'll discuss the alkaline battery and the mercury and silver "button" batteries.

Alkaline Battery The ubiquitous alkaline battery has a zinc anode case that houses a mixture of MnO_2 and an alkaline paste of KOH and water. The cathode is an inactive graphite rod (Figure 21.14). The half-reactions are

Anode (oxidation): $\qquad\qquad Zn(s) + 2OH^-(aq) \longrightarrow ZnO(s) + H_2O(l) + 2e^-$

Cathode (reduction): $\quad MnO_2(s) + 2H_2O(l) + 2e^- \longrightarrow Mn(OH)_2(s) + 2OH^-(aq)$

Overall (cell) reaction:

$$Zn(s) + MnO_2(s) + H_2O(l) \longrightarrow ZnO(s) + Mn(OH)_2(s) \qquad E_{cell} = 1.5 \text{ V}$$

The alkaline battery powers portable radios, toys, flashlights, and so on, is safe, has a long shelf life, and comes in many sizes.

FIGURE 21.14 Alkaline battery.

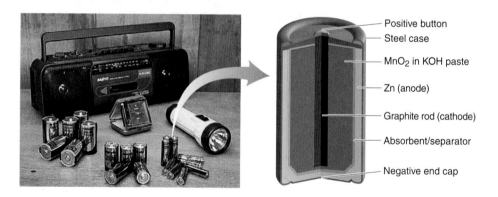

- Positive button
- Steel case
- MnO_2 in KOH paste
- Zn (anode)
- Graphite rod (cathode)
- Absorbent/separator
- Negative end cap

Mercury and Silver (Button) Batteries Mercury and silver batteries are quite similar. Both use a zinc container as the anode (reducing agent) in a basic medium. The mercury battery employs HgO as the oxidizing agent, the silver uses Ag_2O, and both use a steel can around the cathode. The solid reactants are compacted with KOH and separated with moist paper. The half-reactions are

Anode (oxidation): $\qquad\qquad\qquad Zn(s) + 2OH^-(aq) \longrightarrow ZnO(s) + H_2O(l) + 2e^-$

Cathode (reduction) (mercury): $\quad HgO(s) + H_2O(l) + 2e^- \longrightarrow Hg(l) + 2OH^-(aq)$

Cathode (reduction) (silver): $\quad Ag_2O(s) + H_2O(l) + 2e^- \longrightarrow 2Ag(s) + 2OH^-(aq)$

Overall (cell) reaction (mercury):

$$Zn(s) + HgO(s) \longrightarrow ZnO(s) + Hg(l) \qquad E_{cell} = 1.3 \text{ V}$$

Overall (cell) reaction (silver):

$$Zn(s) + Ag_2O(s) \longrightarrow ZnO(s) + 2Ag(s) \qquad E_{cell} = 1.6 \text{ V}$$

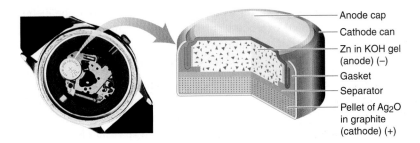

FIGURE 21.15 Silver button battery.

Both cells are manufactured as small button-sized batteries. The mercury cell is used in calculators. Because of its very steady output, the silver cell is used in watches, cameras, heart pacemakers, and hearing aids (Figure 21.15). Their major disadvantages are toxicity of discarded mercury and high cost of silver cells.

Secondary (Rechargeable) Batteries

In contrast to primary batteries, a *secondary, or rechargeable, battery* is recharged when it runs down *by supplying electrical energy to reverse the cell reaction* and re-form reactant. In other words, in this type of battery, the voltaic cells are periodically converted to electrolytic cells to restore *nonequilibrium* concentrations of the cell components. By far the most widely used secondary battery is the common car battery. Two newer types are the nickel–metal hydride battery and the lithium-ion battery.

Lead-Acid Battery A typical lead-acid car battery has six cells connected in series, each of which delivers about 2.1 V for a total of about 12 V. Each cell contains two lead grids loaded with the electrode materials: high-surface-area Pb in the anode and high-surface-area PbO_2 in the cathode. The grids are immersed in an electrolyte solution of $\sim$4.5 M H_2SO_4. Fiberglass sheets between the grids prevent shorting due to physical contact (Figure 21.16). When the cell discharges, it generates electrical energy as a voltaic cell:

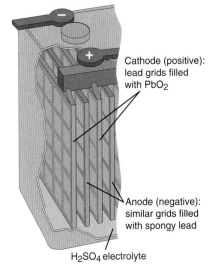

Cathode (positive): lead grids filled with PbO_2

Anode (negative): similar grids filled with spongy lead

H_2SO_4 electrolyte

FIGURE 21.16 Lead-acid battery.

Anode (oxidation): $\qquad Pb(s) + HSO_4^-(aq) \longrightarrow PbSO_4(s) + H^+(aq) + 2e^-$

Cathode (reduction):

$\qquad PbO_2(s) + 3H^+(aq) + HSO_4^-(aq) + 2e^- \longrightarrow PbSO_4(s) + 2H_2O(l)$

Notice that both half-reactions produce Pb^{2+} ions, one through the oxidation of Pb, the other through the reduction of PbO_2. The Pb^{2+} forms $PbSO_4(s)$ at both electrodes by reacting with HSO_4^-.

Overall (cell) reaction (discharge):

$\qquad PbO_2(s) + Pb(s) + 2H_2SO_4(aq) \longrightarrow 2PbSO_4(s) + 2H_2O(l) \qquad E_{cell} = 2.1$ V

When the cell is recharged, it uses electrical energy as an electrolytic cell, and the half-cell and overall reactions are reversed.

Overall (cell) reaction (recharge):

$\qquad 2PbSO_4(s) + 2H_2O(l) \longrightarrow PbO_2(s) + Pb(s) + 2H_2SO_4(aq)$

For more than a century, car and truck owners have relied on the lead-acid battery to provide the large burst of current to the starter motor needed to start the engine—and to do so for years in both hot and cold weather. Nevertheless, there are problems with the lead-acid battery, mainly loss of capacity and safety concerns. Loss of capacity arises from several factors, including corrosion of the positive (Pb) grid, detachment of active material as a result of normal mechanical bumping, and the formation of large crystals of $PbSO_4$, which make recharging more difficult.

Most of the safety concerns have been remedied in modern batteries. Older batteries had a cap on each cell for monitoring electrolyte density and replacing water lost on overcharging. During recharging, some water could be electrolyzed to H_2 and O_2, which could explode if sparked, and splatter H_2SO_4. Modern batteries are sealed, so they don't require addition of water during normal operation, and they use flame attenuators to reduce the explosion hazard.

Nickel–Metal Hydride (Ni-MH) Battery Concerns about the toxicity of the nickel-cadmium (nicad) battery are leading to its replacement by the nickel–metal hydride (Ni-MH) battery. The anode half-reaction oxidizes the hydrogen absorbed within a metal alloy (designated M; e.g., $LaNi_5$) in a basic (KOH) electrolyte, while nickel(III) in the form of NiO(OH) is reduced at the cathode (Figure 21.17):

Anode (oxidation): $\quad\quad\quad\quad MH(s) + OH^-(aq) \longrightarrow M(s) + H_2O(l) + e^-$

Cathode (reduction): $NiO(OH)(s) + H_2O(l) + e^- \longrightarrow Ni(OH)_2(s) + OH^-(aq)$

Overall (cell) reaction: $\quad MH(s) + NiO(OH)(s) \longrightarrow M(s) + Ni(OH)_2(s)$

$$E_{cell} = 1.4 \text{ V}$$

The cell reaction is reversed during recharging. The Ni-MH battery is common in cordless razors, camera flash units, and power tools. It is lightweight, has high power, and is nontoxic, but it may discharge excessively during long-term storage.

FIGURE 21.17 Nickel–metal hydride battery.

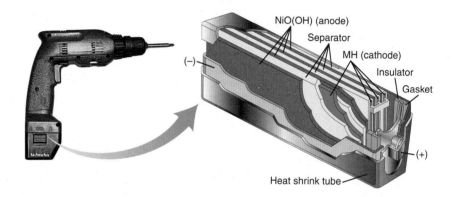

NiO(OH) (anode)
Separator
MH (cathode)
Insulator
Gasket
(−)
(+)
Heat shrink tube

Lithium-Ion Battery The secondary lithium-ion battery has an anode of Li atoms that lie between sheets of graphite (designated Li_xC_6). The cathode is a lithium metal oxide, such as $LiMn_2O_4$ or $LiCoO_2$, and a typical electrolyte is $1\ M$ $LiPF_6$ in an organic solvent, such as a mixture of dimethyl carbonate and methylethyl carbonate. Electrons flow through the circuit, while solvated Li^+ ions flow from anode to cathode within the cell (Figure 21.18). The cell reactions are

Anode (oxidation): $\quad\quad\quad\quad\quad\quad\quad\quad Li_xC_6 \longrightarrow xLi^+ + xe^- + C_6(s)$

Cathode (reduction): $Li_{1-x}Mn_2O_4(s) + xLi^+ + xe^- \longrightarrow LiMn_2O_4(s)$

Overall (cell) reaction: $\quad\quad Li_xC_6 + Li_{1-x}Mn_2O_4(s) \longrightarrow LiMn_2O_4(s) + C_6(s)$

$$E_{cell} = 3.7 \text{ V}$$

The cell reaction is reversed during recharging. The lithium-ion battery powers countless laptop computers, cell phones, and camcorders. Its key drawbacks are expense and the flammability of the organic solvent.

FIGURE 21.18 Lithium-ion battery.

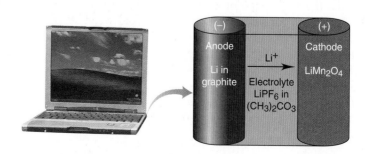

(−)
Anode
Li in graphite
Li^+
Electrolyte
$LiPF_6$ in
$(CH_3)_2CO_3$
(+)
Cathode
$LiMn_2O_4$

Fuel Cells

In contrast to primary and secondary batteries, a **fuel cell,** sometimes called a *flow battery,* is not self-contained. The reactants (usually a combustible fuel and oxygen) enter the cell, and the products leave, generating electricity through the controlled oxidation of the fuel. In other words, *fuel cells use combustion to produce electricity.* The fuel does not burn because, as in other batteries, the half-reactions are separated, and the electrons are transferred through an external circuit.

The most common fuel cell being developed for use in cars is the *proton exchange membrane (PEM) cell,* which uses H_2 as the fuel and has an operating temperature of around 80°C (Figure 21.19). The cell reactions are

Anode (oxidation): $\qquad\qquad\qquad\qquad 2H_2(g) \longrightarrow 4H^+(aq) + 4e^-$

Cathode (reduction): $\quad O_2(g) + 4H^+(aq) + 4e^- \longrightarrow 2H_2O(g)$

Overall (cell) reaction: $\qquad\quad 2H_2(g) + O_2(g) \longrightarrow 2H_2O(g) \qquad E_{cell} = 1.2\ V$

The reactions in fuel cells have much lower rates than those in other batteries, so they require an *electrocatalyst* to decrease the activation energy (Section 16.8). The PEM cell electrodes are composites consisting of nanoparticles of a Pt-based catalyst deposited on graphite. These are embedded in a polymer electrolyte membrane having a perfluoroethylene backbone ($-[F_2C-CF_2]_n-$) with attached sulfonic acid groups (RSO_3^-) that play a key role in ferrying protons from anode to cathode.

Hydrogen fuel cells have been used for years to provide electricity and pure water during space flights. In the very near future, similar ones will supply electric power for transportation, residential, and commercial needs. Already, every major car manufacturer has a fuel-cell prototype. By themselves, these cells produce no pollutants, and they convert about 75% of the fuel's bond energy into useable power, in contrast to 40% for a coal-fired power plant and 25% for a gasoline-powered car engine. Of course, their overall environmental impact will depend on how the H_2 is obtained; for example, electrolyzing water with solar power will have a negligible impact, whereas electrolyzing it with electricity from a coal-fired plant will have a sizeable one. Despite steady progress, current fuel-cell research remains focused on lowering costs by improving membrane conductivity and developing more efficient electrocatalysts.

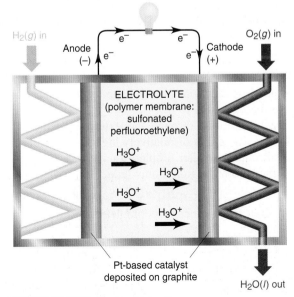

FIGURE 21.19 Hydrogen fuel cell.

Batteries contain several voltaic cells in series and are classified as primary (e.g., alkaline, mercury, and silver), secondary (e.g., lead-acid, nickel–metal hydride, and lithium-ion), or fuel cell. • Supplying electricity to a rechargeable (secondary) battery reverses the redox reaction, forming more reactant for further use. • Fuel cells generate a current through the controlled oxidation of a fuel such as H_2.

21.6 CORROSION: A CASE OF ENVIRONMENTAL ELECTROCHEMISTRY

By now, you may be thinking that spontaneous electrochemical processes are always beneficial, but consider the problem of **corrosion,** the natural redox process that oxidizes metals to their oxides and sulfides. In chemical terms, corrosion is the reverse of isolating a metal from its oxide or sulfide ore; in electrochemical terms, the process shares many similarities with the operation of a voltaic cell. Damage from corrosion to cars, ships, buildings, and bridges runs into tens of billions of dollars annually, so it is a major problem in much of the world. We focus here on the corrosion of iron, but many other metals, such as copper and silver, also corrode.

The Corrosion of Iron

The most common and economically destructive form of corrosion is the rusting of iron. About 25% of the steel produced in the United States is made just to replace steel already in use that has corroded. Contrary to the simplified equation shown earlier in the text, rust is *not* a direct product of the reaction between iron and oxygen but arises through a complex electrochemical process. Let's look at the facts of iron corrosion and then use the features of a voltaic cell to explain them:

1. Iron does not rust in dry air: moisture must be present.
2. Iron does not rust in air-free water: oxygen must be present.
3. The loss of iron and the depositing of rust often occur at *different* places on the *same* object.
4. Iron rusts more quickly at low pH (high $[H^+]$).
5. Iron rusts more quickly in contact with ionic solutions.
6. Iron rusts more quickly in contact with a less active metal (such as Cu) and more slowly in contact with a more active metal (such as Zn).

Picture the magnified surface of a piece of iron or steel (Figure 21.20). Strains, ridges, and dents in contact with water are typically the sites of iron loss (fact 1). These sites are called *anodic regions* because the following half-reaction occurs there:

$$Fe(s) \longrightarrow Fe^{2+}(aq) + 2e^- \qquad \text{[anodic region; oxidation]}$$

Once the iron atoms lose electrons, the damage to the object has been done, and a pit forms where the iron is lost.

The freed electrons move through the external circuit—the piece of iron itself—until they reach a region of relatively high O_2 concentration (fact 2), near the surface of a surrounding water droplet, for instance. At this *cathodic region,* the electrons released from the iron atoms reduce O_2 molecules:

$$O_2(g) + 4H^+(aq) + 4e^- \longrightarrow 2H_2O(l) \qquad \text{[cathodic region; reduction]}$$

Notice that this overall redox process is complete; thus, the iron loss has occurred without any rust forming:

$$2Fe(s) + O_2(g) + 4H^+(aq) \longrightarrow 2Fe^{2+}(aq) + 2H_2O(l)$$

Rust forms through another redox reaction in which the reactants make direct contact. The Fe^{2+} ions formed originally at the anodic region disperse through

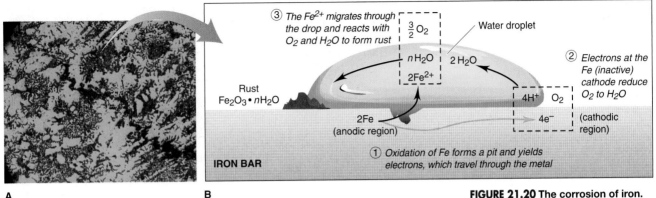

③ The Fe^{2+} migrates through the drop and reacts with O_2 and H_2O to form rust

$\frac{3}{2} O_2$

Water droplet

$n H_2O$ $2 H_2O$

$2Fe^{2+}$

② Electrons at the Fe (inactive) cathode reduce O_2 to H_2O

Rust
$Fe_2O_3 \cdot nH_2O$

$4H^+$ O_2

$4e^-$ (cathodic region)

2Fe
(anodic region)

IRON BAR

① Oxidation of Fe forms a pit and yields electrons, which travel through the metal

FIGURE 21.20 The corrosion of iron. **A,** A close-up view of an iron surface. Corrosion usually occurs at a surface irregularity. **B,** A schematic depiction of a small area of the surface, showing the steps in the corrosion process.

A   B

the surrounding water and react with O_2, often at some distance from the pit (fact 3). The overall reaction for this step is

$$2Fe^{2+}(aq) + \tfrac{1}{2}O_2(g) + (2 + n)H_2O(l) \longrightarrow Fe_2O_3 \cdot nH_2O(s) + 4H^+(aq)$$

[The inexact coefficient n for H_2O in the above equation appears because rust, $Fe_2O_3 \cdot nH_2O$, is a form of iron(III) oxide with a variable number of waters of hydration.] The rust deposit is really incidental to the damage caused by loss of iron—a chemical insult added to the original injury.

Adding the previous two equations together shows the overall equation for the rusting of iron:

$$2Fe(s) + \tfrac{3}{2}O_2(g) + nH_2O(l) + 4H^+(aq) \longrightarrow Fe_2O_3 \cdot nH_2O(s) + 4H^+(aq)$$

The canceled H^+ ions are shown to emphasize that they act as a catalyst; that is, they speed the process as they are used up in one step of the overall reaction and created in another. As a result of this action, rusting is faster at low pH (high $[H^+]$) (fact 4). Ionic solutions speed rusting by improving the conductivity of the aqueous medium near the anodic and cathodic regions (fact 5). The effect of ions is especially evident on ocean-going vessels and on the underbodies and around the wheel wells of cars driven in cold climates, where salts are used to melt ice on slippery roads.

In many ways, the corrosion process resembles that in a voltaic cell:

- Anodic and cathodic regions are separated in space.
- The regions are connected via an external circuit through which the electrons travel.
- In the anodic region, iron behaves like an active electrode, whereas in the cathodic region, it is inactive.
- The moisture surrounding the pit functions somewhat like a salt bridge, a means for ions to ferry back and forth and keep the solution neutral.

Protecting Against the Corrosion of Iron

A common approach to preventing or limiting corrosion is to eliminate contact with the corrosive factors. The simple act of washing off road salt removes the ionic solution from auto bodies. Iron objects are frequently painted to keep out O_2 and moisture, but if the paint layer chips, rusting proceeds. More permanent coatings include chromium plated on plumbing fixtures.

The only fact regarding corrosion that we have not yet addressed concerns the relative activity of other metals in contact with iron (fact 6), which leads to the most effective way to prevent corrosion. The essential idea is that *iron functions as both anode and cathode in the rusting process, but it is lost only at the anode.* Therefore, anything that makes iron behave more like the anode increases

FIGURE 21.21 The effect of metal-metal contact on the corrosion of iron. A, When iron is in contact with a less active metal, such as copper, the iron loses electrons more readily (is more anodic), so it corrodes faster. **B,** When iron is in contact with a more active metal, such as zinc, the zinc acts as the anode and loses electrons. Therefore, the iron is cathodic, so it does not corrode. The process is known as *cathodic protection.*

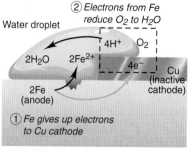
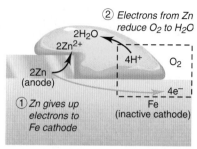

A Enhanced corrosion   **B** Cathodic protection

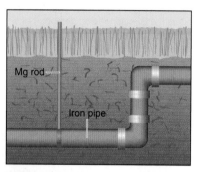

FIGURE 21.22 The use of sacrificial anodes to prevent iron corrosion. In cathodic protection, an active metal, such as magnesium or aluminum, is connected to underground iron pipes to prevent their corrosion. The active metal is sacrificed instead of the iron.

corrosion. As you can see in Figure 21.21A, when iron is in contact with a *less* active metal (weaker reducing agent), such as copper, its anodic function is enhanced. As a result, when iron plumbing is connected directly to copper plumbing, the iron pipe corrodes rapidly.

On the other hand, anything that makes iron behave more like the cathode prevents corrosion. In *cathodic protection,* iron makes contact with a *more* active metal (stronger reducing agent), such as zinc. The iron becomes cathodic and remains intact, while the zinc acts as the anode and loses electrons (Figure 21.21B). Coating steel with a "sacrificial" layer of zinc is the basis of the *galvanizing* process. In addition to blocking physical contact with H_2O and O_2, the zinc is "sacrificed" (oxidized) instead of the iron.

Sacrificial anodes are employed to protect iron and steel structures (pipes, tanks, oil rigs, and so on) in marine and moist underground environments. The metals most frequently used for this purpose are magnesium and aluminum because they are much more active than iron. As a result, they act as the anode while iron acts as the cathode (Figure 21.22). Another advantage of these metals is that they form adherent oxide coatings, which slows their own corrosion.

SECTION 21.6 SUMMARY

Corrosion damages metal structures through a natural electrochemical change. • Iron corrosion occurs in the presence of oxygen and moisture and is increased by high $[H^+]$, high [ion], or contact with a less active metal, such as Cu. Fe is oxidized and O_2 is reduced in one redox reaction, while rust (hydrated form of Fe_2O_3) is formed in another reaction that often takes place at a different location. • Because Fe functions as both anode and cathode in the process, an iron or steel object can be protected by physically covering its surface or joining it to a more active metal (such as Zn, Mg, or Al), which acts as the anode in place of the Fe.

21.7 ELECTROLYTIC CELLS: USING ELECTRICAL ENERGY TO DRIVE NONSPONTANEOUS REACTIONS

Up to now, we've been considering voltaic cells, those that generate electrical energy from a spontaneous redox reaction. The principle of an electrolytic cell is exactly the opposite: *electrical energy from an external source drives a non-spontaneous reaction.*

Construction and Operation of an Electrolytic Cell

Let's examine the operation of an electrolytic cell by constructing one from a voltaic cell. Consider the tin-copper voltaic cell in Figure 21.23A. The Sn anode will gradually become oxidized to Sn^{2+} ions, and the Cu^{2+} ions will gradually

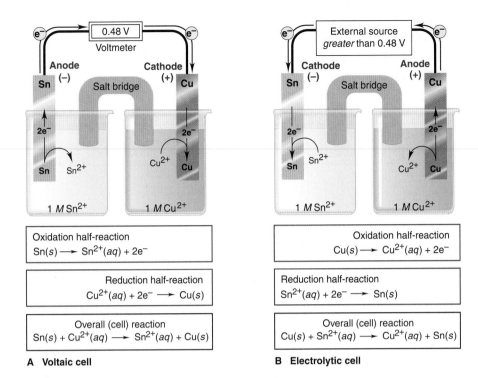

FIGURE 21.23 The tin-copper reaction as the basis of a voltaic and an electrolytic cell. A, At standard conditions, the spontaneous reaction between Sn and Cu^{2+} generates 0.48 V in a voltaic cell. **B,** If more than 0.48 V is supplied, the same apparatus and components become an electrolytic cell, and the nonspontaneous reaction between Cu and Sn^{2+} occurs. Note the changes in electrode charges and direction of electron flow.

be reduced and plate out on the Cu cathode because the cell reaction is spontaneous in that direction:

For the voltaic cell

$$Sn(s) \longrightarrow Sn^{2+}(aq) + 2e^- \qquad \text{[anode; oxidation]}$$
$$\underline{Cu^{2+}(aq) + 2e^- \longrightarrow Cu(s) \qquad \text{[cathode; reduction]}}$$
$$Sn(s) + Cu^{2+}(aq) \longrightarrow Sn^{2+}(aq) + Cu(s) \qquad E^\circ_{cell} = 0.48 \text{ V and } \Delta G^\circ = -93 \text{ kJ}$$

Therefore, the *reverse* cell reaction is *non*spontaneous and never happens of its own accord, as the negative E°_{cell} and positive ΔG° indicate:

$$Cu(s) + Sn^{2+}(aq) \longrightarrow Cu^{2+}(aq) + Sn(s) \qquad E^\circ_{cell} = -0.48 \text{ V and } \Delta G^\circ = 93 \text{ kJ}$$

However, we can make this process happen by supplying from an external source an electric potential *greater than* E°_{cell}. In effect, we have converted the voltaic cell into an electrolytic cell and changed the nature of the electrodes—anode is now cathode, and cathode is now anode (Figure 21.23B):

For the electrolytic cell

$$Cu(s) \longrightarrow Cu^{2+}(aq) + 2e^- \qquad \text{[anode; oxidation]}$$
$$\underline{Sn^{2+}(aq) + 2e^- \longrightarrow Sn(s) \qquad \text{[cathode; reduction]}}$$
$$Cu(s) + Sn^{2+}(aq) \longrightarrow Cu^{2+}(aq) + Sn(s) \qquad \text{[overall (cell) reaction]}$$

Note that in an electrolytic cell, as in a voltaic cell, *oxidation takes place at the anode and reduction takes place at the cathode, but the direction of electron flow and the signs of the electrodes are reversed.*

To understand these changes, keep in mind the *cause* of the electron flow:

- In a voltaic cell, electrons are generated at the anode, so it is negative, and electrons are consumed at the cathode, so it is positive.
- In an electrolytic cell, the electrons come from the external power source, which *supplies* them *to* the cathode, so it is negative, and *removes* them *from* the anode, so it is positive.

Table 21.3 on the next page summarizes the processes and signs in the two types of electrochemical cells.

Table 21.3 **Comparison of Voltaic and Electrolytic Cells**

| Cell Type | ΔG | E_{cell} | Electrode | | |
			Name	Process	Sign
Voltaic	<0	>0	Anode	Oxidation	−
Voltaic	<0	>0	Cathode	Reduction	+
Electrolytic	>0	<0	Anode	Oxidation	+
Electrolytic	>0	<0	Cathode	Reduction	−

Predicting the Products of Electrolysis

Electrolysis, the splitting (lysing) of a substance by the input of electrical energy, is often used to decompose a compound into its elements. Electrolytic cells are involved in key industrial production steps for some of the most commercially important elements, including chlorine, copper, and aluminum. The first laboratory electrolysis of H_2O to H_2 and O_2 was performed in 1800, and the process is still used to produce these gases in ultrahigh purity. The electrolyte in an electrolytic cell can be the pure compound (such as H_2O or a molten salt), a mixture of molten salts, or an aqueous solution of a salt. The products obtained depend on atomic properties and several other factors, so let's examine some actual cases.

Electrolysis of Molten Salts and the Industrial Production of Sodium Many electrolytic applications involve isolating a metal or nonmetal from a molten salt. Predicting the product at each electrode is simple if the salt is pure because *the cation will be reduced and the anion oxidized.* The electrolyte is the molten salt itself, and the ions move through the cell because they are attracted by the oppositely charged electrodes.

Consider the electrolysis of molten (fused) calcium chloride. The two species present are Ca^{2+} and Cl^-, so Ca^{2+} ion is reduced and Cl^- ion is oxidized:

$$2Cl^-(l) \longrightarrow Cl_2(g) + 2e^- \qquad \text{[anode; oxidation]}$$
$$\underline{Ca^{2+}(l) + 2e^- \longrightarrow Ca(s) \qquad \text{[cathode; reduction]}}$$
$$Ca^{2+}(l) + 2Cl^-(l) \longrightarrow Ca(s) + Cl_2(g) \qquad \text{[overall]}$$

Metallic calcium is prepared industrially this way, as are several other active metals as well as the halogens Cl_2 and Br_2.

Another important application is the industrial production of sodium, which involves electrolysis of molten NaCl. The sodium ore is *halite* (largely NaCl), which is obtained either by evaporation of concentrated salt solutions (brines) or by mining vast salt deposits formed from the evaporation of prehistoric seas.

The dry solid is crushed and fused (melted) in an electrolytic apparatus called the **Downs cell** (Figure 21.24). To reduce heating costs, the NaCl (mp = 801°C) is mixed in a 2/3 ratio with $CaCl_2$ to form a mixture that melts at only 580°C. Reduction of the metal ions to Na and Ca takes place at a cylindrical steel cathode, with the molten metals floating on the denser molten salt mixture. As they rise through a short collecting pipe, the liquid Na is siphoned off, while a higher melting Na/Ca alloy solidifies and falls back into the molten electrolyte. Chloride ions are oxidized to Cl_2 gas at a large anode within an inverted cone-shaped chamber. The cell design separates the metals from the Cl_2 to prevent their explosive recombination. The Cl_2 gas is collected, purified, and sold as a valuable byproduct.

Electrolysis of Water and Nonstandard Half-Cell Potentials Before we can analyze the electrolysis products of aqueous salt solutions, we must examine the electrolysis of water itself. Extremely pure water is difficult to electrolyze because

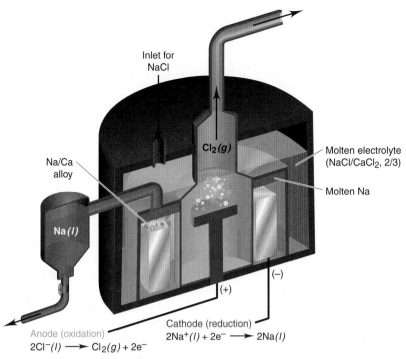

Inlet for
NaCl

$Cl_2(g)$

Na/Ca
alloy

Molten electrolyte
(NaCl/CaCl$_2$, 2/3)

Molten Na

Na(*l*)

(−)

(+)

Anode (oxidation)
$2Cl^-(l) \longrightarrow Cl_2(g) + 2e^-$

Cathode (reduction)
$2Na^+(l) + 2e^- \longrightarrow 2Na(l)$

FIGURE 21.24 The Downs cell for production of sodium. The mixture of solid NaCl and CaCl$_2$ forms the molten electrolyte. Sodium and calcium are formed at the cathode and float, but an Na/Ca alloy solidifies and falls back into the bath while liquid Na is separated. Chlorine gas forms at the anode.

very few ions are present to conduct a current. If we add a small amount of a salt that cannot be electrolyzed in water (such as Na$_2$SO$_4$), however, electrolysis proceeds rapidly. A glass electrolytic cell with separated gas compartments is used to keep the H$_2$ and O$_2$ gases from mixing (Figure 21.25). At the anode, water is oxidized as the O.N. of O changes from −2 to 0:

$$2H_2O(l) \longrightarrow O_2(g) + 4H^+(aq) + 4e^- \qquad E = 0.82\ \text{V} \qquad \text{[anode; oxidation]}$$

At the cathode, water is reduced as the O.N. of H changes from +1 to 0:

$$2H_2O(l) + 2e^- \longrightarrow H_2(g) + 2OH^-(aq) \qquad E = -0.42\ \text{V} \qquad \text{[cathode; reduction]}$$

Adding the half-reactions (which involves combining the H$^+$ and OH$^-$ into H$_2$O and canceling e$^-$ and excess H$_2$O), and calculating E_{cell}, the overall reaction is

$$2H_2O(l) \longrightarrow 2H_2(g) + O_2(g) \qquad E_{cell} = -0.42\ \text{V} - 0.82\ \text{V} = -1.24\ \text{V} \quad \text{[overall]}$$

Notice that these electrode potentials are not written with a degree sign because they are *not* standard electrode potentials. The [H$^+$] and [OH$^-$] are $1.0\times10^{-7}\ M$ rather than the standard-state value of 1 M. These E values are obtained by applying the Nernst equation. For example, the calculation for the anode potential (with $n = 4$) is

$$E_{cell} = E^\circ_{cell} - \frac{0.0592\ \text{V}}{4} \log\left(P_{O_2} \times [H^+]^4\right)$$

The standard potential for the *oxidation* of water is −1.23 V (from Appendix D) and $P_{O_2} \approx 1$ atm in the half-cell, so we have

$$E_{cell} = -1.23\ \text{V} - \left\{\frac{0.0592\ \text{V}}{4} \times [\log 1 + 4 \log (1.0\times10^{-7})]\right\} = -0.82\ \text{V}$$

In aqueous ionic solutions, [H$^+$] and [OH$^-$] are approximately $10^{-7}\ M$ also, so we use these nonstandard E_{cell} values to predict electrode products.

H$_2$ · · · · · · O$_2$

Oxidation half-reaction
$2H_2O(l) \longrightarrow O_2(g) + 4H^+(aq) + 4e^-$

Reduction half-reaction
$2H_2O(l) + 2e^- \longrightarrow H_2(g) + 2OH^-(aq)$

Overall (cell) reaction
$2H_2O(l) \longrightarrow 2H_2(g) + O_2(g)$

FIGURE 21.25 The electrolysis of water. A certain volume of oxygen forms by the oxidation of H$_2$O at the anode *(right)*, and twice that volume of hydrogen forms by the reduction of H$_2$O at the cathode *(left)*.

Electrolysis of Aqueous Salt Solutions; Overvoltage and the Chlor-Alkali Process
Aqueous salt solutions are mixtures of ions *and* water, so we compare electrode potentials to predict the products. When two half-reactions are possible,

- *The reduction with the less negative (more positive) electrode potential occurs.*
- *The oxidation with the less positive (more negative) electrode potential occurs.*

What happens, for instance, when a solution of KI is electrolyzed? The possible oxidizing agents are K^+ and H_2O, and their reduction half-reactions are

$$K^+(aq) + e^- \longrightarrow K(s) \qquad\qquad E° = -2.93 \text{ V}$$
$$2H_2O(l) + 2e^- \longrightarrow H_2(g) + 2OH^-(aq) \qquad E = -0.42 \text{ V} \qquad \text{[reduction]}$$

The less *negative* electrode potential for water means that it is much easier to reduce than K^+, so H_2 forms at the cathode. The possible reducing agents are I^- and H_2O, and their oxidation half-reactions are

$$2I^-(aq) \longrightarrow I_2(s) + 2e^- \qquad\qquad E° = 0.53 \text{ V} \qquad \text{[oxidation]}$$
$$2H_2O(l) \longrightarrow O_2(g) + 4H^+(aq) + 4e^- \qquad E = 0.82 \text{ V}$$

The less *positive* electrode potential for I^- means that a lower potential is needed to oxidize it than to oxidize H_2O, and so I_2 forms at the anode.

Unfortunately, the products predicted from electrode potentials are not always the products that form. For gases such as $H_2(g)$ and $O_2(g)$ to form at metal electrodes, an additional voltage is required. This increment above the expected required voltage is called the **overvoltage.** The phenomenon of overvoltage has major practical significance in the **chlor-alkali process** for the industrial production of chlorine and several other chemicals, which is based on the *electrolytic oxidation of Cl⁻ ion from concentrated aqueous NaCl solutions.* Chlorine ranks among the top 10 chemicals produced in the United States.

Because of overvoltage, electrolysis of NaCl solutions does not yield both of the component elements. Water is easier to reduce than Na^+, so H_2 forms at the cathode, even *with* an overvoltage of 0.6 V:

$$Na^+(aq) + e^- \longrightarrow Na(s) \qquad\qquad E° = -2.71 \text{ V}$$
$$2H_2O(l) + 2e^- \longrightarrow H_2(g) + 2OH^-(aq) \qquad E = -0.42 \text{ V} \ (\approx -1 \text{ V with overvoltage})$$
$$\text{[reduction]}$$

But Cl_2 *does* form at the anode, even though a comparison of electrode potentials would lead us to predict that O_2 should form:

$$2H_2O(l) \longrightarrow O_2(g) + 4H^+(aq) + 4e^- \qquad E = 0.82 \text{ V} \ (\sim 1.4 \text{ V with overvoltage})$$
$$2Cl^-(aq) \longrightarrow Cl_2(g) + 2e^- \qquad\qquad E° = 1.36 \text{ V} \qquad \text{[oxidation]}$$

An overvoltage of $\sim$0.6 V makes the potential for forming O_2 slightly above that for Cl_2. Therefore, the half-reactions for electrolysis of aqueous NaCl are

$$2Cl^-(aq) \longrightarrow Cl_2(g) + 2e^- \qquad\qquad\qquad E° = 1.36 \text{ V} \quad \text{[anode; oxidation]}$$
$$\underline{2H_2O(l) + 2e^- \longrightarrow 2OH^-(aq) + H_2(g) \qquad\qquad\qquad E = -1.0 \text{ V} \ \text{[cathode; reduction]}}$$
$$2Cl^-(aq) + 2H_2O(l) \longrightarrow 2OH^-(aq) + H_2(g) + Cl_2(g) \quad E_{cell} = -1.0 \text{ V} - 1.36 \text{ V} = -2.4 \text{ V}$$

To obtain commercial amounts of Cl_2, a voltage almost twice this value and a current in excess of 3×10^4 A are used.

When we include the spectator ion Na^+, the total ionic equation shows another important product:

$$2Na^+(aq) + 2Cl^-(aq) + 2H_2O(l) \longrightarrow 2Na^+(aq) + 2OH^-(aq) + H_2(g) + Cl_2(g)$$

As Figure 21.26 shows, the sodium salts in the cathode compartment exist as an aqueous mixture of NaCl and NaOH; the NaCl is removed by fractional crystallization, which separates the compounds by differences in solubility. Thus, in this version of the chlor-alkali process, which uses an *asbestos diaphragm* to separate the anode and cathode compartments, the products are Cl_2, H_2, and industrial-grade NaOH, an important base.

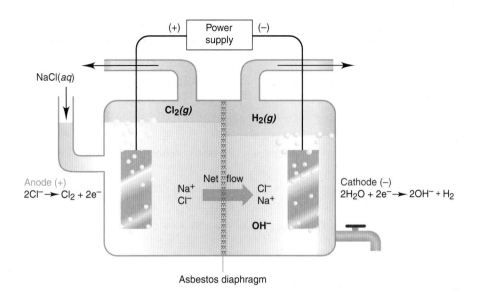

FIGURE 21.26 A diaphragm cell for the chlor-alkali process. This process uses concentrated aqueous NaCl to make NaOH, Cl₂, and H₂ in an electrolytic cell. The difference in liquid level between compartments keeps a net movement of solution into the cathode compartment, which prevents reaction between OH⁻ and Cl₂. The cathode electrolyte is concentrated and fractionally crystallized to give industrial-grade NaOH.

Like other reactive products, H_2 and Cl_2 are kept apart to prevent explosive recombination. Note the higher liquid level in the anode compartment. This slight hydrostatic pressure difference minimizes backflow of NaOH, which prevents the disproportionation (self–oxidation-reduction) reactions of Cl_2 that occur in the presence of OH^-, such as

$$Cl_2(g) + 2OH^-(aq) \longrightarrow Cl^-(aq) + ClO^-(aq) + H_2O(l)$$

A newer chlor-alkali *membrane-cell process,* in which the diaphragm is replaced by a polymeric membrane to separate the cell compartments, has been adopted in much of the industrialized world. The membrane allows only cations to move through it and only from anode to cathode compartments. Thus, as Cl^- ions are removed at the anode through oxidation to Cl_2, Na^+ ions in the anode compartment move through the membrane to the cathode compartment and form an NaOH solution. In addition to forming purer NaOH than the older diaphragm-cell method, the membrane-cell process uses less electricity.

Based on many studies, we can determine which elements can be prepared electrolytically from aqueous solutions of their salts:

1. Cations of less active metals *are* reduced to the metal, including gold, silver, copper, chromium, platinum, and cadmium.
2. Cations of more active metals *are not* reduced, including those in Groups 1A(1) and 2A(2), and Al from 3A(13). Water is reduced to H_2 and OH^- instead.
3. Anions that *are* oxidized, because of overvoltage from O_2 formation, include the halides ($[Cl^-]$ must be high), except for F^-.
4. Anions that *are not* oxidized include F^- and common oxoanions, such as SO_4^{2-}, CO_3^{2-}, NO_3^-, and PO_4^{3-}, because the central nonmetal in these oxoanions is already in its highest oxidation state. Water is oxidized to O_2 and H^+ instead.

SAMPLE PROBLEM 21.8 | Predicting the Electrolysis Products of Aqueous Ionic Solutions

Problem What products form during electrolysis of aqueous solutions of the following salts: **(a)** KBr; **(b)** AgNO₃; **(c)** MgSO₄?
Plan We identify the reacting ions and compare their electrode potentials with those of water, taking the 0.4 to 0.6 V overvoltage into consideration. The reduction half-reaction with the less negative electrode potential occurs at the cathode, and the oxidation half-reaction with the less positive electrode potential occurs at the anode.

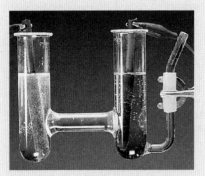

Electrolysis of aqueous KBr.

Solution

(a)
$$K^+(aq) + e^- \longrightarrow K(s) \qquad E° = -2.93 \text{ V}$$
$$2H_2O(l) + 2e^- \longrightarrow H_2(g) + 2OH^-(aq) \qquad E = -0.42 \text{ V}$$

Despite the overvoltage, which makes E for the reduction of water between -0.8 and -1.0 V, H_2O is still easier to reduce than K^+, so $H_2(g)$ forms at the cathode.

$$2Br^-(aq) \longrightarrow Br_2(l) + 2e^- \qquad E° = 1.07 \text{ V}$$
$$2H_2O(l) \longrightarrow O_2(g) + 4H^+(aq) + 4e^- \qquad E = 0.82 \text{ V}$$

Because of the overvoltage, which makes E for the oxidation of water between 1.2 and 1.4 V, Br^- is easier to oxidize than water, so $Br_2(l)$ forms at the anode (see photo).

(b)
$$Ag^+(aq) + e^- \longrightarrow Ag(s) \qquad E° = 0.80 \text{ V}$$
$$2H_2O(l) + 2e^- \longrightarrow H_2(g) + 2OH^-(aq) \qquad E = -0.42 \text{ V}$$

As the cation of an inactive metal, Ag^+ is a better oxidizing agent than H_2O, so Ag forms at the cathode. NO_3^- cannot be oxidized, because N is already in its highest ($+5$) oxidation state. Thus, O_2 forms at the anode:

$$2H_2O(l) \longrightarrow O_2(g) + 4H^+(aq) + 4e^-$$

(c)
$$Mg^{2+}(aq) + 2e^- \longrightarrow Mg(s) \qquad E° = -2.37 \text{ V}$$

Like K^+ in part (a), Mg^{2+} cannot be reduced in the presence of water, so H_2 forms at the cathode. The SO_4^{2-} ion cannot be oxidized because S is in its highest ($+6$) oxidation state. Thus, H_2O is oxidized, and O_2 forms at the anode:

$$2H_2O(l) \longrightarrow O_2(g) + 4H^+(aq) + 4e^-$$

FOLLOW-UP PROBLEM 21.8 Write half-reactions showing the products you predict will form in the electrolysis of aqueous $AuBr_3$.

Industrial Electrochemistry: Purifying Copper and Isolating Aluminum

In addition to the Downs cell for sodium production and the chlor-alkali process for chlorine manufacture, industrial methods based on voltaic and electrolytic cells are used commonly to obtain metals and nonmetals from their ores or to purify them for later use. Here we focus on two key electrochemical processes.

The Electrorefining of Copper The most common copper ore is chalcopyrite, $CuFeS_2$, a mixed sulfide of FeS and CuS. Most remaining deposits contain less than 0.5% Cu by mass. To "win" this small amount of copper from the ore requires several steps, including a final refining to achieve the purity needed for electrical wiring, copper's most important application. More than 2.5 billion pounds of copper is produced in the United States annually.

After removing the iron(II) sulfide and reducing the copper(II) sulfide, the copper obtained is usable for plumbing, but it must be purified for electrical applications by removing unwanted impurities (Fe and Ni) as well as valuable ones (Ag, Au, and Pt). Purification is accomplished by *electrorefining,* which involves the oxidation of Cu to form Cu^{2+} ions in solution, followed by their reduction and the plating out of Cu metal (Figure 21.27). To do this, impure copper is cast into plates to be used as anodes, and cathodes are made from already purified copper. The electrodes are immersed in acidified $CuSO_4$ solution, and a controlled voltage is applied that accomplishes two tasks simultaneously:

1. Copper and the more active impurities (Fe, Ni) are oxidized to their cations, while the less active ones (Ag, Au, Pt) are not. As the anode slabs react, these unoxidized metals fall off as a valuable "anode mud" and are purified separately. Sale of the precious metals in the anode mud nearly offsets the cost of electricity to operate the cell, making Cu wire inexpensive.

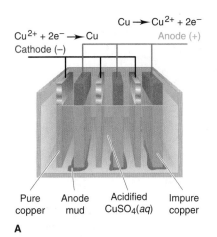

$$Cu \longrightarrow Cu^{2+} + 2e^-$$
Anode (+)

$$Cu^{2+} + 2e^- \longrightarrow Cu$$
Cathode (−)

Pure copper   Anode mud   Acidified $CuSO_4(aq)$ Impure copper

A

B

FIGURE 21.27 The electrorefining of copper. A, Copper is refined electrolytically, using impure slabs of copper as anodes and sheets of pure copper as cathodes. The Cu^{2+} ions released from the anode are reduced to Cu metal and plate out at the cathode. The "anode mud" contains valuable metal byproducts. **B,** A small section of an industrial facility for electrorefining copper.

2. Because Cu is much less active than the Fe and Ni impurities, Cu^{2+} ions are reduced at the cathode, but Fe^{2+} and Ni^{2+} ions remain in solution:

$$Cu^{2+}(aq) + 2e^- \longrightarrow Cu(s) \qquad E° = 0.34 \text{ V}$$
$$Ni^{2+}(aq) + 2e^- \longrightarrow Ni(s) \qquad E° = -0.25 \text{ V}$$
$$Fe^{2+}(aq) + 2e^- \longrightarrow Fe(s) \qquad E° = -0.44 \text{ V}$$

The copper obtained by electrorefining is over 99.99% pure.

The Isolation of Aluminum Aluminum, the most abundant metal in Earth's crust by mass, is found in numerous aluminosilicate minerals. Through eons of weathering, certain of these became *bauxite,* a mixed oxide-hydroxide that is the major ore of aluminum. In general terms, the isolation of aluminum is a two-step process that combines several physical and chemical separations. In the first, the mineral oxide, Al_2O_3, is separated from bauxite; in the second, which we focus on here, the oxide is converted to the metal.

Aluminum is much too strong a reducing agent to be formed at the cathode from aqueous solution, so the oxide itself must be electrolyzed. However, the melting point of Al_2O_3 is very high (2030°C), so major energy (and cost) savings are realized by dissolving the oxide in molten *cryolite* (Na_3AlF_6) to give a mixture that is electrolyzed at ~1000°C. The electrolytic step, called the *Hall-Heroult process,* takes place in a graphite-lined furnace, with the lining itself acting as the cathode. Anodes of graphite dip into the molten Al_2O_3-Na_3AlF_6 mixture (Figure 21.28). The cell typically operates at a moderate voltage of 4.5 V, but with an enormous current flow of 1.0×10^5 to 2.5×10^5 A.

Because the process is complex and still not entirely known, the following reactions are chosen from among several other possibilities. Molten cryolite contains several ions (including AlF_6^{3-}, AlF_4^-, and F^-), which react with Al_2O_3 to form fluoro-oxy ions (including $AlOF_3^{2-}$, $Al_2OF_6^{2-}$, and $Al_2O_2F_4^{2-}$) that dissolve in the mixture. For example,

$$2Al_2O_3(s) + 2AlF_6^{3-}(l) \longrightarrow 3Al_2O_2F_4^{2-}(l)$$

Al forms at the cathode (reduction), shown here with AlF_6^{3-} as reactant:

$$AlF_6^{3-}(l) + 3e^- \longrightarrow Al(l) + 6F^-(l) \qquad \text{[cathode; reduction]}$$

The graphite anodes are oxidized and form carbon dioxide gas. Using one of the fluoro-oxy species as an example, the anode reaction is

$$Al_2O_2F_4^{2-}(l) + 8F^-(l) + C(graphite) \longrightarrow 2AlF_6^{3-}(l) + CO_2(g) + 4e^-$$

[anode; oxidation]

The anodes are consumed in this half-reaction and must be replaced frequently.

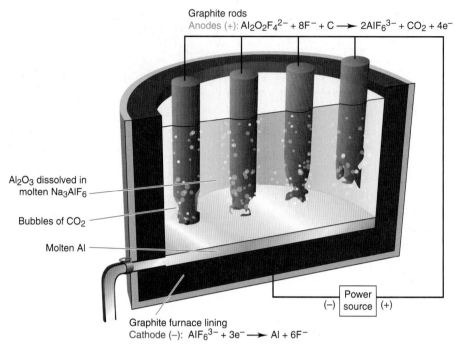

Graphite rods
Anodes (+): $Al_2O_2F_4^{2-} + 8F^- + C \longrightarrow 2AlF_6^{3-} + CO_2 + 4e^-$

Al$_2$O$_3$ dissolved in
molten Na$_3$AlF$_6$

Bubbles of CO$_2$

Molten Al

Power
(−) source (+)

Graphite furnace lining
Cathode (−): $AlF_6^{3-} + 3e^- \longrightarrow Al + 6F^-$

FIGURE 21.28 The electrolytic cell in aluminum manufacture. Purified Al$_2$O$_3$ is mixed with cryolite (Na$_3$AlF$_6$) and melted. Reduction at the graphite furnace lining (cathode) gives molten Al. Oxidation at the graphite rods (anodes) slowly converts them to CO$_2$, so they must be replaced periodically.

Combining the three previous equations gives the overall reaction:

$$2Al_2O_3(\text{in } Na_3AlF_6) + 3C(\text{graphite}) \longrightarrow 4Al(l) + 3CO_2(g) \qquad \text{[overall (cell) reaction]}$$

Aluminum production accounts for more than 5% of total U.S. electrical usage! Estimates for the entire manufacturing process (including mining, maintaining operating conditions, and so forth) show that aluminum recycling requires less than 1% as much energy as manufacturing it from the ore, which explains why recycling has become so widespread.

The Stoichiometry of Electrolysis: The Relation Between Amounts of Charge and Product

As you've seen, the charge flowing through an electrolytic cell yields products at the electrodes. In the electrolysis of molten NaCl, for example, the power source supplies electrons to the cathode, where Na$^+$ ions migrate to pick them up and become Na metal. At the same time, the power source pulls from the anode the electrons that Cl$^-$ ions release as they become Cl$_2$ gas. It follows that the more electrons picked up by Na$^+$ ions and released by Cl$^-$ ions, the greater the amounts of Na and Cl$_2$ that form. This relationship was first determined experimentally by Michael Faraday and is referred to as *Faraday's law of electrolysis: the amount of substance produced at each electrode is directly proportional to the quantity of charge flowing through the cell.*

Each balanced half-reaction shows the amounts (mol) of reactant, electrons, and product involved in the change, so it contains the information we need to answer such questions as "How much material will form as a result of a given

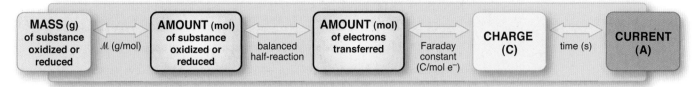

FIGURE 21.29 A summary diagram for the stoichiometry of electrolysis.

quantity of charge?" or, conversely, "How much charge is needed to produce a given amount of material?" To apply Faraday's law,

1. Balance the half-reaction to find the number of moles of electrons needed per mole of product.
2. Use the Faraday constant ($F = 9.65 \times 10^4$ C/mol e$^-$) to find the corresponding charge.
3. Use the molar mass to find the charge needed for a given mass of product.

In practice, to supply the correct amount of electricity, we need some means of finding the charge flowing through the cell. We cannot measure charge directly, but we *can* measure current, the charge flowing per unit time. The SI unit of current is the **ampere (A),** which is defined as a charge of 1 coulomb flowing through a conductor in 1 second:

$$1 \text{ ampere} = 1 \text{ coulomb/second} \quad \text{or} \quad 1 \text{ A} = 1 \text{ C/s} \qquad (21.11)$$

Thus, the current multiplied by the time gives the charge:

$$\text{Current} \times \text{time} = \text{charge} \quad \text{or} \quad A \times s = \frac{C}{s} \times s = C$$

Therefore, we find the charge by measuring the current *and* the time during which the current flows. This, in turn, relates to the amount of product formed. Figure 21.29 summarizes these relationships.

Problems based on Faraday's law often ask you to calculate current, mass of material, or time. The electrode half-reaction provides the key to solving these problems because it is related to the mass for a certain quantity of charge.

As an example, let's consider a typical problem in practical electrolysis: how long does it take to produce 3.0 g of $Cl_2(g)$ by electrolysis of aqueous NaCl using a power supply with a current of 12 A? The problem asks for the time needed to produce a certain mass, so let's first relate mass to number of moles of electrons to find the charge needed. Then, we'll relate the charge to the current to find the time.

We know the mass of Cl_2 produced, so we can find the amount (mol) of Cl_2. The half-reaction tells us that the loss of 2 mol of electrons produces 1 mol of chlorine gas:

$$2Cl^-(aq) \longrightarrow Cl_2(g) + 2e^-$$

We use this relationship as a conversion factor, and multiplying by the Faraday constant gives us the total charge:

$$\text{Charge (C)} = 3.0 \text{ g } Cl_2 \times \frac{1 \text{ mol } Cl_2}{70.90 \text{ g } Cl_2} \times \frac{2 \text{ mol e}^-}{1 \text{ mol } Cl_2} \times \frac{9.65 \times 10^4 \text{ C}}{1 \text{ mol e}^-} = 8.2 \times 10^3 \text{ C}$$

Now we use the relationship between charge and current to find the time needed:

$$\text{Time (s)} = \frac{\text{charge (C)}}{\text{current (A, or C/s)}} = 8.2 \times 10^3 \text{ C} \times \frac{1 \text{ s}}{12 \text{ C}} = 6.8 \times 10^2 \text{ s } (\sim 11 \text{ min})$$

Note that the entire calculation follows Figure 21.29 until the last step:

$$\text{grams of } Cl_2 \Rightarrow \text{moles of } Cl_2 \Rightarrow \text{moles of } e^- \Rightarrow \text{coulombs} \Rightarrow \text{seconds}$$

Sample Problem 21.9 demonstrates the steps as they appear in Figure 21.29.

SAMPLE PROBLEM 21.9   Applying the Relationship Among Current, Time, and Amount of Substance

Problem A technician is plating a faucet with 0.86 g of chromium from an electrolytic bath containing aqueous $Cr_2(SO_4)_3$. If 12.5 min is allowed for the plating, what current is needed?

Plan To find the current, we divide the charge by the time; therefore, we need to find the charge. First we write the half-reaction for Cr^{3+} reduction. From it, we know the number of moles of e^- required per mole of Cr. As the roadmap shows, to find the charge, we convert the mass of Cr needed (0.86 g) to amount (mol) of Cr. The balanced half-reaction gives the amount (mol) of e^- transferred. Then, we use the Faraday constant (9.65×10^4 C/mol e^-) to find the charge and divide by the time (12.5 min, converted to seconds) to obtain the current.

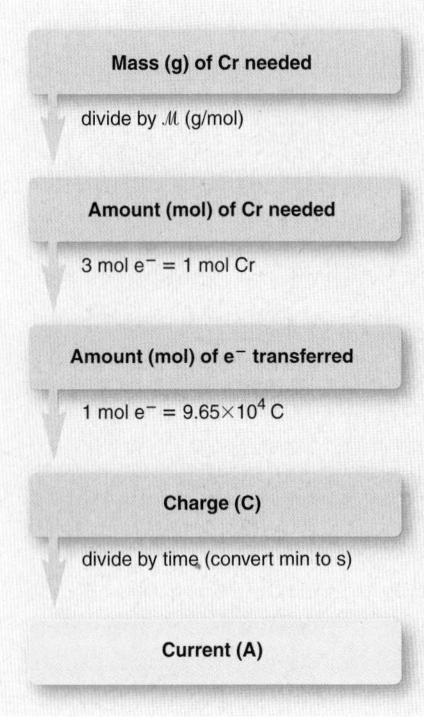

Solution Writing the balanced half-reaction:

$$Cr^{3+}(aq) + 3e^- \longrightarrow Cr(s)$$

Combining steps to find amount (mol) of e^- transferred for mass of Cr needed:

$$\text{Moles of } e^- \text{ transferred} = 0.86 \text{ g Cr} \times \frac{1 \text{ mol Cr}}{52.00 \text{ g Cr}} \times \frac{3 \text{ mol } e^-}{1 \text{ mol Cr}} = 0.050 \text{ mol } e^-$$

Calculating the charge:

$$\text{Charge (C)} = 0.050 \text{ mol } e^- \times \frac{9.65 \times 10^4 \text{ C}}{1 \text{ mol } e^-} = 4.8 \times 10^3 \text{ C}$$

Calculating the current:

$$\text{Current (A)} = \frac{\text{charge (C)}}{\text{time (s)}} = \frac{4.8 \times 10^3 \text{ C}}{12.5 \text{ min}} \times \frac{1 \text{ min}}{60 \text{ s}} = 6.4 \text{ C/s} = 6.4 \text{ A}$$

Check Rounding gives

$$(\sim 0.9 \text{ g})(1 \text{ mol Cr}/50 \text{ g})(3 \text{ mol } e^-/1 \text{ mol Cr}) = 5 \times 10^{-2} \text{ mol } e^-$$

then

$$(5 \times 10^{-2} \text{ mol } e^-)(\sim 1 \times 10^5 \text{ C/mol } e^-) = 5 \times 10^3 \text{ C}$$

and

$$(5 \times 10^3 \text{ C}/12 \text{ min})(1 \text{ min}/60 \text{ s}) = 7 \text{ A}$$

Comment For the sake of introducing Faraday's law, the details of the electroplating process have been simplified here. Actually, electroplating chromium is only 30% to 40% efficient and must be run at a particular temperature range for the plate to appear bright. Nearly 10,000 metric tons (2×10^8 mol) of chromium is used annually for electroplating.

FOLLOW-UP PROBLEM 21.9 Using a current of 4.75 A, how many minutes does it take to plate onto a sculpture 1.50 g of Cu from a $CuSO_4$ solution?

Roadmap (margin):

Mass (g) of Cr needed

divide by $\mathcal{M}$ (g/mol)

Amount (mol) of Cr needed

3 mol e^- = 1 mol Cr

Amount (mol) of e^- transferred

1 mol e^- = 9.65×10^4 C

Charge (C)

divide by time (convert min to s)

Current (A)

SECTION 21.7 SUMMARY

An electrolytic cell uses electrical energy to drive a nonspontaneous reaction. • Oxidation occurs at the anode and reduction at the cathode, but the direction of electron flow and the charges of the electrodes are opposite those in voltaic cells. • When two products can form at each electrode, the more easily oxidized substance reacts at the anode and the more easily reduced at the cathode. • The reduction or oxidation of water takes place at nonstandard conditions. • Overvoltage causes the actual voltage to be unexpectedly high and can affect the electrode product that forms. • The industrial production of many elements, such as sodium, chlorine, copper, and aluminum, utilizes electrolytic cells. • The amount of product that forms depends on the quantity of charge flowing through the cell, which is related to the magnitude of the current and the time it flows.

CHAPTER REVIEW GUIDE

The following sections provide many aids to help you study this chapter. (Numbers in parentheses refer to pages, unless noted otherwise.)

• LEARNING OBJECTIVES *These are concepts and skills to review after studying this chapter.*

Related section (§), sample problem (SP), and end-of-chapter problem (EP) numbers are listed in parentheses.

1. Understand the meanings of *oxidation, reduction, oxidizing agent,* and *reducing agent;* balance redox reactions by the half-reaction method; distinguish between voltaic and electrolytic cells in terms of the sign of ΔG (§ 21.1) (SP 21.1) (EPs 21.1–21.12)
2. Describe the physical makeup of a voltaic cell, and explain the direction of electron flow; draw a diagram and write the notation for a voltaic cell (§ 21.2) (SP 21.2) (EPs 21.13–21.23)
3. Describe how standard electrode potentials ($E^{\circ}_{\text{half-cell}}$ values) are combined to give E°_{cell} and how the standard reference electrode is used to find an unknown $E^{\circ}_{\text{half-cell}}$; explain how the reactivity of a metal is related to its $E^{\circ}_{\text{half-cell}}$; write spontaneous redox reactions using an emf series like that in Appendix D (§ 21.3) (SPs 21.3, 21.4) (EPs 21.24–21.40)
4. Understand how E_{cell} is related to ΔG and the charge flowing through the cell; use the interrelationship of ΔG°, E°_{cell}, and K to calculate any one of these variables; explain how E_{cell} changes as

the cell operates (Q changes), and use the Nernst equation to find E_{cell}; describe how a concentration cell works and calculate its E_{cell} (§ 21.4) (SPs 21.5–21.7) (EPs 21.41–21.56)
5. Understand how a battery operates, and describe the components of primary and secondary batteries and fuel cells (§ 21.5) (EPs 21.57–21.59)
6. Explain how corrosion occurs and is prevented (§ 21.6) (EPs 21.60–21.62)
7. Understand the basis of an electrolytic cell; describe the Downs cell for the production of Na, the chlor-alkali process and the importance of overvoltage for the production of Cl_2, the electrorefining of Cu, and the use of cryolite in the production of Al; know how water influences the products at the electrodes during electrolysis of aqueous salt solutions (§ 21.7) (SP 21.8) (EPs 21.63–21.75, 21.82)
8. Understand the relationship between charge and amount of product, and calculate the current (or time) needed to produce a given amount of product or vice versa (§ 21.7) (SP 21.9) (EPs 21.76–21.81, 21.83, 21.84)

• KEY TERMS *These important terms appear in boldface in the chapter and are defined again in the Glossary.*

electrochemistry (705)
electrochemical cell (705)

Section 21.1
half-reaction method (706)
voltaic (galvanic) cell (709)
electrolytic cell (709)
electrode (709)
electrolyte (709)
anode (709)
cathode (709)

Section 21.2
half-cell (711)
salt bridge (713)

Section 21.3
cell potential (E_{cell}) (715)
voltage (715)
electromotive force (emf) (715)
volt (V) (715)
coulomb (C) (715)

standard cell potential (E°_{cell}) (716)
standard electrode (half-cell) potential ($E^{\circ}_{\text{half-cell}}$) (716)
standard reference half-cell (standard hydrogen electrode) (717)

Section 21.4
Faraday constant (F) (724)
Nernst equation (726)
concentration cell (729)

Section 21.5
battery (732)
fuel cell (735)

Section 21.6
corrosion (736)

Section 21.7
electrolysis (740)
Downs cell (740)
overvoltage (742)
chlor-alkali process (742)
ampere (A) (747)

• KEY EQUATIONS AND RELATIONSHIPS *Numbered and screened concepts are listed for you to refer to or memorize.*

21.1 Relating a spontaneous process to the sign of the cell potential (715):
$$E_{\text{cell}} > 0 \text{ for a spontaneous process}$$

21.2 Relating electric potential to energy and charge in SI units (715):
$$\text{Potential} = \text{energy/charge} \quad \text{or} \quad 1 \text{ V} = 1 \text{ J/C}$$

21.3 Relating standard cell potential to standard electrode potentials in a voltaic cell (716):
$$E^{\circ}_{\text{cell}} = E^{\circ}_{\text{cathode (reduction)}} - E^{\circ}_{\text{anode (oxidation)}}$$

21.4 Defining the Faraday constant (724):
$$F = 9.65 \times 10^4 \frac{\text{J}}{\text{V·mol e}^-} \quad (3 \text{ sf})$$

21.5 Relating the free energy change to the cell potential (724):
$$\Delta G = -nFE_{\text{cell}}$$

21.6 Finding the standard free energy change from the standard cell potential (724):
$$\Delta G^{\circ} = -nFE^{\circ}_{\text{cell}}$$

21.7 Finding the equilibrium constant from the standard cell potential (724):
$$E^{\circ}_{\text{cell}} = \frac{RT}{nF} \ln K$$

21.8 Substituting known values of R, F, and T into Equation 21.7 and converting to common logarithms (725):
$$E^{\circ}_{\text{cell}} = \frac{0.0592 \text{ V}}{n} \log K \quad \text{or} \quad \log K = \frac{nE^{\circ}_{\text{cell}}}{0.0592 \text{ V}} \quad (\text{at } 298.15 \text{ K})$$

21.9 Calculating the nonstandard cell potential (Nernst equation) (726):
$$E_{\text{cell}} = E^{\circ}_{\text{cell}} - \frac{RT}{nF} \ln Q$$

21.10 Substituting known values of R, F, and T into the Nernst equation and converting to common logarithms (727):
$$E_{\text{cell}} = E^{\circ}_{\text{cell}} - \frac{0.0592 \text{ V}}{n} \log Q \quad (\text{at } 298.15 \text{ K})$$

21.11 Relating current to charge and time (747):
$$\text{Current} = \text{charge/time} \quad \text{or} \quad 1 \text{ A} = 1 \text{ C/s}$$

• BRIEF SOLUTIONS TO *FOLLOW-UP PROBLEMS* Compare your own solutions to these calculation steps and answers.

21.1 $6KMnO_4(aq) + 6KOH(aq) + KI(aq) \longrightarrow$
$$6K_2MnO_4(aq) + KIO_3(aq) + 3H_2O(l)$$

21.2
$$Sn(s) \longrightarrow Sn^{2+}(aq) + 2e^-$$
[anode; oxidation]
$$6e^- + 14H^+(aq) + Cr_2O_7^{2-}(aq) \longrightarrow 2Cr^{3+}(aq) + 7H_2O(l)$$
[cathode; reduction]

$3Sn(s) + Cr_2O_7^{2-}(aq) + 14H^+(aq) \longrightarrow$
$$3Sn^{2+}(aq) + 2Cr^{3+}(aq) + 7H_2O(l) \quad \text{[overall]}$$

Cell notation:
$Sn(s) \mid Sn^{2+}(aq) \parallel H^+(aq), Cr_2O_7^{2-}(aq), Cr^{3+}(aq) \mid$ graphite

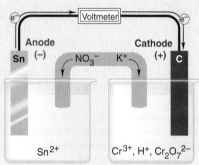

21.3 $Br_2(aq) + 2e^- \longrightarrow 2Br^-(aq) \qquad E^\circ_{bromine} = 1.07$ V
[cathode]
$2V^{3+}(aq) + 2H_2O(l) \longrightarrow 2VO^{2+}(aq) + 4H^+(aq) + 2e^-$
$$E^\circ_{vanadium} = ? \quad \text{[anode]}$$
$E^\circ_{vanadium} = E^\circ_{bromine} - E^\circ_{cell} = 1.07$ V $- 1.39$ V $= -0.32$ V

21.4 $Fe^{2+}(aq) + 2e^- \longrightarrow Fe(s) \qquad\qquad E^\circ = -0.44$ V
$\underline{2[Fe^{2+}(aq) \longrightarrow Fe^{3+}(aq) + e^-] \qquad E^\circ = 0.77 \text{ V}}$
$3Fe^{2+}(aq) \longrightarrow 2Fe^{3+}(aq) + Fe(s)$
$E^\circ_{cell} = -0.44$ V $- 0.77$ V $= -1.21$ V
The reaction is nonspontaneous. The spontaneous reaction is
$2Fe^{3+}(aq) + Fe(s) \longrightarrow 3Fe^{2+}(aq) \qquad E^\circ_{cell} = 1.21$ V
$Fe > Fe^{2+} > Fe^{3+}$

21.5 $Cd(s) + Cu^{2+}(aq) \longrightarrow Cd^{2+}(aq) + Cu(s)$
$\Delta G^\circ = -RT \ln K = -8.314$ J/mol·K $\times 298$ K $\times \ln K$
$$= -143 \text{ kJ}; K = 1.2 \times 10^{25}$$
$E^\circ_{cell} = \dfrac{0.0592 \text{ V}}{2} \log (1.2 \times 10^{25}) = 0.742$ V

21.6 $Fe(s) \longrightarrow Fe^{2+}(aq) + 2e^- \qquad E^\circ = -0.44$ V
$\underline{Cu^{2+}(aq) + 2e^- \longrightarrow Cu(s) \qquad\qquad E^\circ = 0.34 \text{ V}}$
$Fe(s) + Cu^{2+}(aq) \longrightarrow Fe^{2+}(aq) + Cu(s) \quad E^\circ_{cell} = 0.78$ V
So $E_{cell} = 0.78$ V $+ 0.25$ V $= 1.03$ V
$$1.03 \text{ V} = 0.78 \text{ V} - \dfrac{0.0592 \text{ V}}{2} \log \dfrac{[Fe^{2+}]}{[Cu^{2+}]}$$
$$\dfrac{[Fe^{2+}]}{[Cu^{2+}]} = 3.6 \times 10^{-9}$$
$[Fe^{2+}] = 3.6 \times 10^{-9} \times 0.30 \ M = 1.1 \times 10^{-9} \ M$

21.7 $Au^{3+}(aq; 2.5 \times 10^{-2} \ M)$ [B] $\longrightarrow$
$$Au^{3+}(aq; 7.0 \times 10^{-4} \ M) \text{ [A]}$$
$E_{cell} = 0 \text{ V} - \left(\dfrac{0.0592 \text{ V}}{3} \times \log \dfrac{7.0 \times 10^{-4}}{2.5 \times 10^{-2}} \right) = 0.0306$ V
The electrode in A is negative, so it is the anode.

21.8 The reduction with the more positive electrode potential is
$Au^{3+}(aq) + 3e^- \longrightarrow Au(s); E^\circ = 1.50$ V
[cathode; reduction]
Because of overvoltage, O_2 will not form at the anode, so Br_2 will form:
$2Br^-(aq) \longrightarrow Br_2(l) + 2e^-; E^\circ = 1.07$ V
[anode; oxidation]

21.9 $Cu^{2+}(aq) + 2e^- \longrightarrow Cu(s)$; therefore,
2 mol e^-/1 mol Cu = 2 mol e^-/63.55 g Cu
Time (min) = 1.50 g Cu $\times \dfrac{2 \text{ mol } e^-}{63.55 \text{ g Cu}}$
$\times \dfrac{9.65 \times 10^4 \text{ C}}{1 \text{ mol } e^-} \times \dfrac{1 \text{ s}}{4.75 \text{ C}} \times \dfrac{1 \text{ min}}{60 \text{ s}} = 16.0$ min

PROBLEMS

Problems with **colored** numbers are answered in Appendix E. Sections match the text and provide the numbers of relevant sample problems. Bracketed problems are grouped in pairs (indicated by a short rule) that cover the same concept. Comprehensive Problems are based on material from any section or previous chapter.

Note: Unless stated otherwise, all problems refer to systems at 298.15 K (25°C).

Redox Reactions and Electrochemical Cells
(Sample Problem 21.1)

21.1 Define *oxidation* and *reduction* in terms of electron transfer and change in oxidation number.

21.2 Can one half-reaction in a redox process take place independently of the other? Explain.

21.3 Which type of electrochemical cell has $\Delta G_{sys} < 0$? Which type shows an increase in free energy?

21.4 Which statements are true? Correct any that are false.
(a) In a voltaic cell, the anode is negative relative to the cathode.
(b) Oxidation occurs at the anode of a voltaic or an electrolytic cell.
(c) Electrons flow into the cathode of an electrolytic cell.
(d) In a voltaic cell, the surroundings do work on the system.
(e) A metal that plates out of an electrolytic cell appears on the cathode.
(f) The cell electrolyte provides a solution of mobile electrons.

21.5 Consider the following balanced redox reaction:

$$16H^+(aq) + 2MnO_4^-(aq) + 10Cl^-(aq) \longrightarrow 2Mn^{2+}(aq) + 5Cl_2(g) + 8H_2O(l)$$

(a) Which species is being oxidized?
(b) Which species is being reduced?
(c) Which species is the oxidizing agent?
(d) Which species is the reducing agent?
(e) From which species to which does electron transfer occur?
(f) Write the balanced molecular equation, with K^+ and SO_4^{2-} as the spectator ions.

21.6 Consider the following balanced redox reaction:

$$2CrO_2^-(aq) + 2H_2O(l) + 6ClO^-(aq) \longrightarrow 2CrO_4^{2-}(aq) + 3Cl_2(g) + 4OH^-(aq)$$

(a) Which species is being oxidized?
(b) Which species is being reduced?
(c) Which species is the oxidizing agent?
(d) Which species is the reducing agent?
(e) From which species to which does electron transfer occur?
(f) Write the balanced molecular equation, with Na^+ as the spectator ion.

21.7 Balance the following skeleton reactions and identify the oxidizing and reducing agents:
(a) $ClO_3^-(aq) + I^-(aq) \longrightarrow I_2(s) + Cl^-(aq)$ [acidic]
(b) $MnO_4^-(aq) + SO_3^{2-}(aq) \longrightarrow$
$$MnO_2(s) + SO_4^{2-}(aq) \text{ [basic]}$$
(c) $MnO_4^-(aq) + H_2O_2(aq) \longrightarrow Mn^{2+}(aq) + O_2(g)$ [acidic]

21.8 Balance the following skeleton reactions and identify the oxidizing and reducing agents:
(a) $O_2(g) + NO(g) \longrightarrow NO_3^-(aq)$ [acidic]
(b) $CrO_4^{2-}(aq) + Cu(s) \longrightarrow$
$$Cr(OH)_3(s) + Cu(OH)_2(s) \text{ [basic]}$$
(c) $AsO_4^{3-}(aq) + NO_2^-(aq) \longrightarrow$
$$AsO_2^-(aq) + NO_3^-(aq) \text{ [basic]}$$

21.9 Balance the following skeleton reactions and identify the oxidizing and reducing agents:
(a) $BH_4^-(aq) + ClO_3^-(aq) \longrightarrow$
$$H_2BO_3^-(aq) + Cl^-(aq) \text{ [basic]}$$
(b) $CrO_4^{2-}(aq) + N_2O(g) \longrightarrow Cr^{3+}(aq) + NO(g)$ [acidic]
(c) $Br_2(l) \longrightarrow BrO_3^-(aq) + Br^-(aq)$ [basic]

21.10 Balance the following skeleton reactions and identify the oxidizing and reducing agents:
(a) $Sb(s) + NO_3^-(aq) \longrightarrow Sb_4O_6(s) + NO(g)$ [acidic]
(b) $Mn^{2+}(aq) + BiO_3^-(aq) \longrightarrow$
$$MnO_4^-(aq) + Bi^{3+}(aq) \text{ [acidic]}$$
(c) $Fe(OH)_2(s) + Pb(OH)_3^-(aq) \longrightarrow$
$$Fe(OH)_3(s) + Pb(s) \text{ [basic]}$$

21.11 In many residential water systems, the aqueous Fe^{3+} concentration is high enough to stain sinks and turn drinking water light brown. The iron content is analyzed by first reducing the Fe^{3+} to Fe^{2+} and then titrating with MnO_4^- in acidic solution. Balance the skeleton reaction of the titration step:

$$Fe^{2+}(aq) + MnO_4^-(aq) \longrightarrow Mn^{2+}(aq) + Fe^{3+}(aq)$$

21.12 *Aqua regia*, a mixture of concentrated HNO_3 and HCl, was developed by alchemists as a means to "dissolve" gold. The process is actually a redox reaction with the following simplified skeleton reaction:

$$Au(s) + NO_3^-(aq) + Cl^-(aq) \longrightarrow AuCl_4^-(aq) + NO_2(g)$$

(a) Balance the reaction by the half-reaction method.
(b) What are the oxidizing and reducing agents?
(c) What is the function of HCl in aqua regia?

Voltaic Cells: Using Spontaneous Reactions to Generate Electrical Energy
(Sample Problem 21.2)

21.13 Consider the following general voltaic cell:

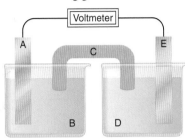

Identify the (a) anode, (b) cathode, (c) salt bridge, (d) electrode at which e^- leave the cell, (e) electrode with a positive charge, and (f) electrode that gains mass as the cell operates (assuming that a metal plates out).

21.14 Why does a voltaic cell not operate unless the two compartments are connected through an external circuit?

21.15 What purpose does the salt bridge serve in a voltaic cell, and how does it accomplish this purpose?

21.16 What is the difference between an active and an inactive electrode? Why are inactive electrodes used? Name two substances commonly used for inactive electrodes.

21.17 When a piece of metal A is placed in a solution containing ions of metal B, metal B plates out on the piece of A.
(a) Which metal is being oxidized?
(b) Which metal is being displaced?
(c) Which metal would you use as the anode in a voltaic cell incorporating these two metals?
(d) If bubbles of H_2 form when B is placed in acid, will they form if A is placed in acid? Explain.

21.18 A voltaic cell is constructed with an Sn/Sn^{2+} half-cell and a Zn/Zn^{2+} half-cell. The zinc electrode is negative.
(a) Write balanced half-reactions and the overall reaction.
(b) Draw a diagram of the cell, labeling electrodes with their charges and showing the directions of electron flow in the circuit and of cation and anion flow in the salt bridge.

21.19 A voltaic cell is constructed with an Ag/Ag^+ half-cell and a Pb/Pb^{2+} half-cell. The silver electrode is positive.
(a) Write balanced half-reactions and the overall reaction.
(b) Draw a diagram of the cell, labeling electrodes with their charges and showing the directions of electron flow in the circuit and of cation and anion flow in the salt bridge.

21.20 Consider the following voltaic cell:

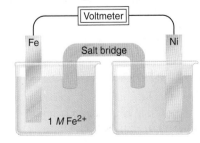

(a) In which direction do electrons flow in the external circuit?
(b) In which half-cell does oxidation occur?
(c) In which half-cell do electrons enter the cell?
(d) At which electrode are electrons consumed?
(e) Which electrode is negatively charged?
(f) Which electrode decreases in mass during cell operation?
(g) Suggest a solution for the cathode electrolyte.
(h) Suggest a pair of ions for the salt bridge.
(i) For which electrode could you use an inactive material?
(j) In which direction do anions within the salt bridge move to maintain charge neutrality?
(k) Write balanced half-reactions and an overall cell reaction.

21.21 Consider the following voltaic cell:

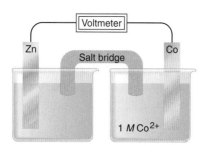

(a) In which direction do electrons flow in the external circuit?
(b) In which half-cell does reduction occur?
(c) In which half-cell do electrons leave the cell?
(d) At which electrode are electrons generated?
(e) Which electrode is positively charged?
(f) Which electrode increases in mass during cell operation?
(g) Suggest a solution for the anode electrolyte.
(h) Suggest a pair of ions for the salt bridge.
(i) For which electrode could you use an inactive material?
(j) In which direction do cations within the salt bridge move to maintain charge neutrality?
(k) Write balanced half-reactions and an overall cell reaction.

21.22 Write the cell notation for the voltaic cell that incorporates each of the following redox reactions:
(a) $Al(s) + Cr^{3+}(aq) \longrightarrow Al^{3+}(aq) + Cr(s)$
(b) $Cu^{2+}(aq) + SO_2(g) + 2H_2O(l) \longrightarrow$
$$Cu(s) + SO_4^{2-}(aq) + 4H^+(aq)$$

21.23 Write a balanced equation from each cell notation:
(a) $Mn(s) \mid Mn^{2+}(aq) \parallel Cd^{2+}(aq) \mid Cd(s)$
(b) $Fe(s) \mid Fe^{2+}(aq) \parallel NO_3^-(aq) \mid NO(g) \mid Pt(s)$

Cell Potential: Output of a Voltaic Cell
(Sample Problems 21.3 and 21.4)

21.24 How is a standard reference electrode used to determine unknown $E^\circ_{half-cell}$ values?

21.25 What does a negative E°_{cell} indicate about a redox reaction? What does a negative E°_{cell} indicate about the reverse reaction?

21.26 The standard cell potential is a thermodynamic state function. How are E° values treated similarly to ΔH°, ΔG°, and S° values? How are they treated differently?

21.27 In basic solution, Se^{2-} and SO_3^{2-} ions react spontaneously:
$2Se^{2-}(aq) + 2SO_3^{2-}(aq) + 3H_2O(l) \longrightarrow$
$$2Se(s) + 6OH^-(aq) + S_2O_3^{2-}(aq) \qquad E^\circ_{cell} = 0.35 \text{ V}$$

(a) Write balanced half-reactions for the process.
(b) If $E^\circ_{sulfite}$ is -0.57 V, calculate $E^\circ_{selenium}$.

21.28 In acidic solution, O_3 and Mn^{2+} ion react spontaneously:
$O_3(g) + Mn^{2+}(aq) + H_2O(l) \longrightarrow$
$$O_2(g) + MnO_2(s) + 2H^+(aq) \qquad E^\circ_{cell} = 0.84 \text{ V}$$

(a) Write the balanced half-reactions.
(b) Using Appendix D to find E°_{ozone}, calculate $E^\circ_{manganese}$.

21.29 Use the emf series (Appendix D) to arrange the species.
(a) In order of *decreasing* strength as *oxidizing* agents: Fe^{3+}, Br_2, Cu^{2+}
(b) In order of *increasing* strength as *oxidizing* agents: Ca^{2+}, $Cr_2O_7^{2-}$, Ag^+

21.30 Use the emf series (Appendix D) to arrange the species.
(a) In order of *decreasing* strength as *reducing* agents: SO_2, $PbSO_4$, MnO_2
(b) In order of *increasing* strength as *reducing* agents: Hg, Fe, Sn

21.31 Balance each skeleton reaction, calculate E°_{cell}, and state whether the reaction is spontaneous:
(a) $Co(s) + H^+(aq) \longrightarrow Co^{2+}(aq) + H_2(g)$
(b) $Mn^{2+}(aq) + Br_2(l) \longrightarrow MnO_4^-(aq) + Br^-(aq)$ [acidic]
(c) $Hg_2^{2+}(aq) \longrightarrow Hg^{2+}(aq) + Hg(l)$

21.32 Balance each skeleton reaction, calculate E°_{cell}, and state whether the reaction is spontaneous:
(a) $Cl_2(g) + Fe^{2+}(aq) \longrightarrow Cl^-(aq) + Fe^{3+}(aq)$
(b) $Mn^{2+}(aq) + Co^{3+}(aq) \longrightarrow MnO_2(s) + Co^{2+}(aq)$ [acidic]
(c) $AgCl(s) + NO(g) \longrightarrow$
$$Ag(s) + Cl^-(aq) + NO_3^-(aq)$$ [acidic]

21.33 Balance each skeleton reaction, calculate E°_{cell}, and state whether the reaction is spontaneous:
(a) $Ag(s) + Cu^{2+}(aq) \longrightarrow Ag^+(aq) + Cu(s)$
(b) $Cd(s) + Cr_2O_7^{2-}(aq) \longrightarrow Cd^{2+}(aq) + Cr^{3+}(aq)$
(c) $Ni^{2+}(aq) + Pb(s) \longrightarrow Ni(s) + Pb^{2+}(aq)$

21.34 Balance each skeleton reaction, calculate E°_{cell}, and state whether the reaction is spontaneous:
(a) $Cu^+(aq) + PbO_2(s) + SO_4^{2-}(aq) \longrightarrow$
$$PbSO_4(s) + Cu^{2+}(aq)$$ [acidic]
(b) $H_2O_2(aq) + Ni^{2+}(aq) \longrightarrow O_2(g) + Ni(s)$ [acidic]
(c) $MnO_2(s) + Ag^+(aq) \longrightarrow MnO_4^-(aq) + Ag(s)$ [basic]

21.35 Use the following half-reactions to write three spontaneous reactions and calculate E°_{cell} for each reaction:
(1) $Al^{3+}(aq) + 3e^- \longrightarrow Al(s)$ $\qquad E^\circ = -1.66 \text{ V}$
(2) $N_2O_4(g) + 2e^- \longrightarrow 2NO_2^-(aq)$ $\qquad E^\circ = 0.867 \text{ V}$
(3) $SO_4^{2-}(aq) + H_2O(l) + 2e^- \longrightarrow SO_3^{2-}(aq) + 2OH^-(aq)$
$$E^\circ = 0.93 \text{ V}$$

21.36 Use the following half-reactions to write three spontaneous reactions and calculate E°_{cell} for each reaction:
(1) $Au^+(aq) + e^- \longrightarrow Au(s)$ $\qquad E^\circ = 1.69 \text{ V}$
(2) $N_2O(g) + 2H^+(aq) + 2e^- \longrightarrow N_2(g) + H_2O(l)$
$$E^\circ = 1.77 \text{ V}$$
(3) $Cr^{3+}(aq) + 3e^- \longrightarrow Cr(s)$ $\qquad E^\circ = -0.74 \text{ V}$

21.37 Use the following half-reactions to write three spontaneous reactions and calculate E°_{cell} for each reaction:
(1) $2HClO(aq) + 2H^+(aq) + 2e^- \longrightarrow Cl_2(g) + 2H_2O(l)$
$$E^\circ = 1.63 \text{ V}$$
(2) $Pt^{2+}(aq) + 2e^- \longrightarrow Pt(s)$ $\qquad E^\circ = 1.20 \text{ V}$
(3) $PbSO_4(s) + 2e^- \longrightarrow Pb(s) + SO_4^{2-}(aq)$ $\qquad E^\circ = -0.31 \text{ V}$

21.38 Use the following half-reactions to write three spontaneous reactions and calculate $E°_{cell}$ for each reaction:
(1) $I_2(s) + 2e^- \longrightarrow 2I^-(aq) \qquad E° = 0.53$ V
(2) $S_2O_8^{2-}(aq) + 2e^- \longrightarrow 2SO_4^{2-}(aq) \qquad E° = 2.01$ V
(3) $Cr_2O_7^{2-}(aq) + 14H^+(aq) + 6e^- \longrightarrow$
$\qquad\qquad 2Cr^{3+}(aq) + 7H_2O(l) \qquad E° = 1.33$ V

21.39 When metal A is placed in a solution of a salt of metal B, the surface of metal A changes color. When metal B is placed in acid solution, gas bubbles form on the surface of the metal. When metal A is placed in a solution of a salt of metal C, no change is observed in the solution or on the metal A surface. Will metal C cause formation of H_2 when placed in acid solution? Rank metals A, B, and C in order of *decreasing* reducing strength.

21.40 When a clean iron nail is placed in an aqueous solution of copper(II) sulfate, the nail becomes coated with a brownish black material.
(a) What is the material coating the iron?
(b) What are the oxidizing and reducing agents?
(c) Can this reaction be made into a voltaic cell?
(d) Write the balanced equation for the reaction.
(e) Calculate $E°_{cell}$ for the process.

Free Energy and Electrical Work
(Sample Problems 21.5 to 21.7)

21.41 (a) How do the relative magnitudes of Q and K relate to the signs of ΔG and E_{cell}? Explain.
(b) Can a cell do work when $Q/K > 1$ or $Q/K < 1$? Explain.

21.42 A voltaic cell consists of a metal A/A^+ electrode and a metal B/B^+ electrode, with the A/A^+ electrode negative. The initial $[A^+]/[B^+]$ is such that $E_{cell} > E°_{cell}$.
(a) How do $[A^+]$ and $[B^+]$ change as the cell operates?
(b) How does E_{cell} change as the cell operates?
(c) What is $[A^+]/[B^+]$ when $E_{cell} = E°_{cell}$? Explain.
(d) Is it possible for E_{cell} to be less than $E°_{cell}$? Explain.

21.43 Explain whether E_{cell} of a voltaic cell will increase or decrease with each of the following changes:
(a) Decrease in cell temperature
(b) Increase in [active ion] in the anode compartment
(c) Increase in [active ion] in the cathode compartment
(d) Increase in pressure of a gaseous reactant in the cathode compartment

21.44 In a concentration cell, is the more concentrated electrolyte in the cathode or the anode compartment? Explain.

21.45 What is the value of the equilibrium constant for the reaction between each pair at 25°C?
(a) $Ni(s)$ and $Ag^+(aq)$ (b) $Fe(s)$ and $Cr^{3+}(aq)$

21.46 What is the value of the equilibrium constant for the reaction between each pair at 25°C?
(a) $Al(s)$ and $Cd^{2+}(aq)$ (b) $I_2(s)$ and $Br^-(aq)$

21.47 Calculate $\Delta G°$ for each of the reactions in Problem 21.45.
21.48 Calculate $\Delta G°$ for each of the reactions in Problem 21.46.

21.49 What are $E°_{cell}$ and $\Delta G°$ of a redox reaction at 25°C for which $n = 1$ and $K = 5.0\times10^4$?
21.50 What are $E°_{cell}$ and $\Delta G°$ of a redox reaction at 25°C for which $n = 2$ and $K = 0.075$?

21.51 A voltaic cell consists of a standard hydrogen electrode in one half-cell and a Cu/Cu^{2+} half-cell. Calculate $[Cu^{2+}]$ when E_{cell} is 0.22 V.
21.52 A voltaic cell consists of an Mn/Mn^{2+} half-cell and a Pb/Pb^{2+} half-cell. Calculate $[Pb^{2+}]$ when $[Mn^{2+}]$ is 1.4 M and E_{cell} is 0.44 V.

21.53 A voltaic cell with Ni/Ni^{2+} and Co/Co^{2+} half-cells has the following initial concentrations: $[Ni^{2+}] = 0.80$ M; $[Co^{2+}] = 0.20$ M.
(a) What is the initial E_{cell}?
(b) What is $[Ni^{2+}]$ when E_{cell} reaches 0.03 V?
(c) What are the equilibrium concentrations of the ions?
21.54 A voltaic cell with Mn/Mn^{2+} and Cd/Cd^{2+} half-cells has the following initial concentrations: $[Mn^{2+}] = 0.090$ M; $[Cd^{2+}] = 0.060$ M.
(a) What is the initial E_{cell}?
(b) What is E_{cell} when $[Cd^{2+}]$ reaches 0.050 M?
(c) What is $[Mn^{2+}]$ when E_{cell} reaches 0.055 V?
(d) What are the equilibrium concentrations of the ions?

21.55 A concentration cell consists of two H_2/H^+ half-cells. Half-cell A has H_2 at 0.90 atm bubbling into 0.10 M HCl. Half-cell B has H_2 at 0.50 atm bubbling into 2.0 M HCl. Which half-cell houses the anode? What is the voltage of the cell?
21.56 A concentration cell consists of two Sn/Sn^{2+} half-cells. The electrolyte in compartment A is 0.13 M $Sn(NO_3)_2$. The electrolyte in B is 0.87 M $Sn(NO_3)_2$. Which half-cell houses the cathode? What is the voltage of the cell?

Electrochemical Processes in Batteries

21.57 What is the direction of electron flow with respect to the anode and the cathode in a battery? Explain.
21.58 Both a D-sized and an AAA-sized alkaline battery have an output of 1.5 V. What property of the cell potential allows this to occur? What is different about these two batteries?
21.59 Many common electrical devices require the use of more than one battery.
(a) How many alkaline batteries must be placed in series to light a flashlight with a 6.0-V bulb?
(b) What is the voltage requirement of a camera that uses six silver batteries?
(c) How many volts can a car battery deliver if two of its anode/cathode cells are shorted?

Corrosion: A Case of Environmental Electrochemistry

21.60 During reconstruction of the Statue of Liberty, Teflon spacers were placed between the iron skeleton and the copper plates that cover the statue. What purpose do these spacers serve?
21.61 Why do steel bridge-supports rust at the waterline but not above or below it?
21.62 Which of the following metals are suitable for use as sacrificial anodes to protect against corrosion of underground iron pipes? If any are not suitable, explain why:
(a) Aluminum (b) Magnesium
(c) Sodium (d) Lead
(e) Nickel (f) Zinc
(g) Chromium

Electrolytic Cells: Using Electrical Energy to Drive Nonspontaneous Reactions
(Sample Problems 21.8 and 21.9)

Note: Unless stated otherwise, assume that the electrolytic cells in the following problems operate at 100% efficiency.

21.63 Consider the following general electrolytic cell:

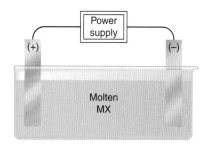

(a) At which electrode does oxidation occur?
(b) At which electrode does elemental M form?
(c) At which electrode are electrons being released by ions?
(d) At which electrode are electrons entering the cell?

21.64 A voltaic cell consists of Cr/Cr^{3+} and Cd/Cd^{2+} half-cells with all components in their standard states. After 10 minutes of operation, a thin coating of cadmium metal has plated out on the cathode. Describe what will happen if you attach the negative terminal of a dry cell (1.5 V) to the cell cathode and the positive terminal to the cell anode.

21.65 Why are $E_{half\text{-}cell}$ values for the oxidation and reduction of water different from $E^{\circ}_{half\text{-}cell}$ values for the same processes?

21.66 In an aqueous electrolytic cell, nitrate ions never react at the anode, but nitrite ions do. Explain.

21.67 How does overvoltage influence the products in the electrolysis of aqueous salts?

21.68 What property allows copper to be purified in the presence of iron and nickel impurities? Explain.

21.69 What is the practical reason for using cryolite in the electrolysis of aluminum oxide?

21.70 In the electrolysis of molten NaBr,
(a) What product forms at the anode?
(b) What product forms at the cathode?

21.71 In the electrolysis of molten BaI_2,
(a) What product forms at the negative electrode?
(b) What product forms at the positive electrode?

21.72 Identify those elements that can be prepared by electrolysis of their aqueous salts: copper, barium, aluminum, bromine.

21.73 Identify those elements that can be prepared by electrolysis of their aqueous salts: strontium, gold, tin, chlorine.

21.74 What product forms at each electrode in the aqueous electrolysis of the following salts: (a) LiF; (b) $SnSO_4$?

21.75 What product forms at each electrode in the aqueous electrolysis of the following salts: (a) $Cr(NO_3)_3$; (b) $MnCl_2$?

21.76 Electrolysis of molten $MgCl_2$ is the final production step in the isolation of magnesium from seawater. Assuming that 45.6 g of Mg metal forms,
(a) How many moles of electrons are required?
(b) How many coulombs are required?
(c) How many amps will produce this amount in 3.50 h?

21.77 Electrolysis of molten NaCl in a Downs cell is the major isolation step in the production of sodium metal. Assuming that 215 g of Na metal forms,
(a) How many moles of electrons are required?
(b) How many coulombs are required?
(c) How many amps will produce this amount in 9.50 h?

21.78 How many grams of radium can form by passing 235 C through an electrolytic cell containing a molten radium salt?

21.79 How many grams of aluminum can form by passing 305 C through an electrolytic cell containing a molten aluminum salt?

21.80 How many seconds does it take to deposit 65.5 g of Zn on a steel gate when 21.0 A is passed through a $ZnSO_4$ solution?

21.81 How many seconds does it take to deposit 1.63 g of Ni on a decorative drawer handle when 13.7 A is passed through a $Ni(NO_3)_2$ solution?

21.82 A professor adds Na_2SO_4 to water to facilitate its electrolysis in a lecture demonstration. (a) What is the purpose of the Na_2SO_4? (b) Why is the water electrolyzed instead of the salt?

21.83 A Downs cell operating at 75.0 A produces 30.0 kg of Na.
(a) What volume of $Cl_2(g)$ is produced at 1.0 atm and 580.°C?
(b) How many coulombs were passed through the cell?
(c) How long did the cell operate?

21.84 Zinc plating (galvanizing) is an important means of corrosion protection. Although the process is done customarily by dipping the object into molten zinc, the metal can also be electroplated from aqueous solutions. How many grams of zinc can be deposited on a steel tank from a $ZnSO_4$ solution when a 0.855-A current flows for 2.50 days?

Comprehensive Problems
Problems with an asterisk (*) are more challenging.

21.85 The MnO_2 used in alkaline batteries can be produced by an electrochemical process of which one half-reaction is
$$Mn^{2+}(aq) + 2H_2O(l) \longrightarrow MnO_2(s) + 4H^+(aq) + 2e^-$$
If a current of 25.0 A is used, how many hours are needed to produce 1.00 kg of MnO_2? At which electrode is the MnO_2 formed?

21.86 The overall cell reaction occurring in an alkaline battery is
$$Zn(s) + MnO_2(s) + H_2O(l) \longrightarrow ZnO(s) + Mn(OH)_2(s)$$
(a) How many moles of electrons flow per mole of reaction?
(b) If 4.50 g of zinc is oxidized, how many grams of manganese dioxide and of water are consumed?
(c) What is the total mass of reactants consumed in part (b)?
(d) How many coulombs are produced in part (b)?
(e) In practice, voltaic cells of a given capacity (coulombs) are heavier than the calculation in part (c) indicates. Explain.

* **21.87** Brass, an alloy of copper and zinc, can be produced by simultaneously electroplating the two metals from a solution containing their 2+ ions. If exactly 65.0% of the total current is used to plate copper, while 35.0% goes to plating zinc, what is the mass percent of copper in the brass?

21.88 Compare and contrast a voltaic cell and an electrolytic cell with respect to each of the following:
(a) Sign of the free energy change
(b) Nature of the half-reaction at the anode
(c) Nature of the half-reaction at the cathode
(d) Charge on the electrode labeled "anode"
(e) Electrode from which electrons leave the cell

* **21.89** A thin circular-disk earring 4.00 cm in diameter is plated with a coating of gold 0.25 mm thick from an Au^{3+} bath.
(a) How many days does it take to deposit the gold on one side of this earring if the current is 0.013 A (d of gold = 19.3 g/cm³)?
(b) How many days does it take to deposit the gold on both sides of a pair of these earrings?
(c) If the price of gold is about \$920 per troy ounce (31.10 g), what is the total cost of the gold plating?

21.90 (a) How many minutes does it take to form 10.0 L of O_2 measured at 99.8 kPa and 28°C from water if a current of 1.3 A passes through the electrolytic cell? (b) What mass of H_2 forms?

21.91 A silver button battery used in a watch contains 0.75 g of zinc and can run until 80% of the zinc is consumed. (a) How many days can the battery run at a current of 0.85 microamps?
(b) When the battery dies, 95% of the Ag_2O has been consumed. How many grams of Ag was used to make the battery? (c) If Ag costs \$13.00 per troy ounce (31.10 g), what is the cost of the Ag consumed each day the watch runs?

21.92 If a chlor-alkali cell used a current of 3×10^4 A, how many pounds of Cl_2 would be produced in a typical 8-h operating day?

21.93 To improve conductivity in the electroplating of automobile bumpers, a thin coating of copper separates the steel from a heavy coating of chromium.
(a) What mass of Cu is deposited on an automobile trim piece if plating continues for 1.25 h at a current of 5.0 A?
(b) If the area of the trim piece is 50.0 cm², what is the thickness of the Cu coating (d of Cu = 8.95 g/cm³)?

21.94 Commercial electrolytic cells for producing aluminum operate at 5.0 V and 100,000 A.
(a) How long does it take to produce exactly 1 metric ton (1000 kg) of aluminum?
(b) How much electrical power (in kilowatt-hours, kW·h) is used [1 W = 1 J/s; 1 kW·h = 3.6×10^3 kJ]?
(c) If electricity costs 0.90¢ per kW·h and cell efficiency is 90.%, what is the cost of producing exactly 1 lb of aluminum?

21.95 Magnesium bars are connected electrically to underground iron pipes to serve as sacrificial anodes.
(a) Do electrons flow from the bar to the pipe or the reverse?
(b) A 12-kg Mg bar is attached to an iron pipe, and it takes 8.5 yr for the Mg to be consumed. What is the average current flowing between the Mg and the Fe during this period?

21.96 Bubbles of H_2 form when metal D is placed in hot H_2O. No reaction occurs when D is placed in a solution of a salt of metal E, but D is discolored and coated immediately when placed in a solution of a salt of metal F. What happens if E is placed in a solution of a salt of metal F? Rank metals D, E, and F in order of *increasing* reducing strength.

* **21.97** The following reactions are used in batteries:

I $2H_2(g) + O_2(g) \longrightarrow 2H_2O(l)$ $E_{cell} = 1.23$ V

II $Pb(s) + PbO_2(s) + 2H_2SO_4(aq) \longrightarrow$
                    $2PbSO_4(s) + 2H_2O(l)$ $E_{cell} = 2.04$ V

III $2Na(l) + FeCl_2(s) \longrightarrow 2NaCl(s) + Fe(s)$
                                    $E_{cell} = 2.35$ V

Reaction I is used in fuel cells, II in the automobile lead-acid battery, and III in an experimental high-temperature battery for powering electric vehicles. The aim is to obtain as much work as possible from a cell, while keeping its weight to a minimum.
(a) In each cell, find the moles of electrons transferred and ΔG.

(b) Calculate the ratio, in kJ/g, of w_{max} to mass of reactants for each of the cells. Which has the highest ratio, which the lowest, and why? (*Note:* For simplicity, ignore the masses of cell components that do not appear in the cell as reactants, including electrode materials, electrolytes, separators, cell casing, wiring, etc.)

21.98 From the skeleton reactions below, create a list of balanced half-reactions in which the strongest oxidizing agent is on top and the weakest is on the bottom:

$$U^{3+}(aq) + Cr^{3+}(aq) \longrightarrow Cr^{2+}(aq) + U^{4+}(aq)$$
$$Fe(s) + Sn^{2+}(aq) \longrightarrow Sn(s) + Fe^{2+}(aq)$$
$$Fe(s) + U^{4+}(aq) \longrightarrow \text{no reaction}$$
$$Cr^{3+}(aq) + Fe(s) \longrightarrow Cr^{2+}(aq) + Fe^{2+}(aq)$$
$$Cr^{2+}(aq) + Sn^{2+}(aq) \longrightarrow Sn(s) + Cr^{3+}(aq)$$

21.99 Use Appendix D to calculate the K_{sp} of AgCl.

21.100 Calculate the K_f of $Ag(NH_3)_2^+$ from

$$Ag^+(aq) + e^- \rightleftharpoons Ag(s) \qquad E° = 0.80 \text{ V}$$
$$Ag(NH_3)_2^+(aq) + e^- \rightleftharpoons Ag(s) + 2NH_3(aq) \qquad E° = 0.37 \text{ V}$$

21.101 Use Appendix D to create an activity series of Mn, Fe, Ag, Sn, Cr, Cu, Ba, Al, Na, Hg, Ni, Li, Au, Zn, and Pb. Rank these metals in order of decreasing reducing strength, and divide them into three groups: those that displace H_2 from water, those that displace H_2 from acid, and those that cannot displace H_2.

21.102 The overall cell reaction for aluminum production is

$$2Al_2O_3(\text{in } Na_3AlF_6) + 3C(\text{graphite}) \longrightarrow 4Al(l) + 3CO_2(g)$$

(a) Assuming 100% efficiency, how many metric tons (t) of Al_2O_3 are consumed per metric ton of Al produced?
(b) Assuming 100% efficiency, how many metric tons of the graphite anode are consumed per metric ton of Al produced?
(c) Actual conditions in an aluminum plant require 1.89 t of Al_2O_3 and 0.45 t of graphite per metric ton of Al. What is the percent yield of Al with respect to Al_2O_3?
(d) What is the percent yield of Al with respect to graphite?
(e) What volume of CO_2 (in m³) is produced per metric ton of Al at operating conditions of 960.°C and exactly 1 atm?

* **21.103** Two concentration cells are prepared, both with 90.0 mL of $0.0100 M$ $Cu(NO_3)_2$ and a Cu bar in each half-cell.
(a) In the first concentration cell, 10.0 mL of 0.500 M NH_3 is added to one half-cell; the complex ion $Cu(NH_3)_4^{2+}$ forms, and E_{cell} is 0.129 V. Calculate K_f for the formation of the complex ion.
(b) Calculate E_{cell} when an additional 10.0 mL of 0.500 M NH_3 is added.
(c) In the second concentration cell, 10.0 mL of 0.500 M NaOH is added to one half-cell; the precipitate $Cu(OH)_2$ forms ($K_{sp} = 2.2 \times 10^{-20}$). Calculate $E°_{cell}$.
(d) What would the molarity of NaOH have to be for the addition of 10.0 mL to result in an $E°_{cell}$ of 0.340 V?

21.104 A voltaic cell has one half-cell with a Cu bar in a 1.00 M Cu^{2+} salt solution, and the other half-cell with a Cd bar in the same volume of a 1.00 M Cd^{2+} salt solution.
(a) Find $E°_{cell}$, $\Delta G°$, and K.
(b) As the cell operates, $[Cd^{2+}]$ increases; find E_{cell} and ΔG when $[Cd^{2+}]$ is 1.95 M.
(c) Find E_{cell}, ΔG, and $[Cu^{2+}]$ at equilibrium.

21.105 If the E_{cell} of the following cell is 0.915 V, what is the pH in the anode compartment?

$$Pt(s) \mid H_2(1.00 \text{ atm}) \mid H^+(aq) \parallel Ag^+(0.100 M) \mid Ag(s)$$

The Main-Group Elements: Applying Principles of Bonding and Structure

Key Principles
to focus on while studying this chapter

- *Hydrogen does not fit into any particular family (group)* because its tiny size and simple structure give it unique properties *(Section 14.1)*.

- Within a family of elements, *similar behavior* results from a *similar outer electron configuration.*

- Because the Period 2 elements have a small atomic size and only four outer-level orbitals, they exhibit some behavior that is *anomalous* within their groups.

- In Period 4 and higher, Group 3A and 4A elements deviate from expected trends because their nuclei attract outer *s* and *p* electrons very strongly due to poor shielding by their inner *d* and *f* electrons.

- Because atoms get larger down a group, *metallic behavior* (such as ability to form cations and basicity of oxides) increases, and this trend becomes especially apparent in Groups 3A to 6A.

- In Groups 3A to 6A, nearly every element exhibits *more than one oxidation state,* and the lower state becomes more common going down the group.

- Many elements occur in different forms *(allotropes),* each with its own properties.

- Group 1A and 7A elements are very reactive because each is one electron away from having a filled outer level; Group 8A elements have a filled outer level and thus are very unreactive.

Recurring Patterns *From the beat of a human heart to the swirls of this Broccoli romanesco, recurring patterns appear throughout nature. In this chapter, you'll discover the recurring patterns of element behavior.*

Outline

In your study of chemistry so far, you've learned how to name compounds, balance equations, and calculate reaction yields. You've seen how heat is related to chemical and physical change, how electron configuration influences atomic properties, how elements bond to form compounds, and how the arrangement of bonding and lone pairs accounts for molecular shapes. You've learned modern theories of bonding and, most recently, seen how atomic and molecular properties give rise to the macroscopic properties of gases, liquids, solids, and solutions.

The purpose of this knowledge, of course, is to make sense of the magnificent diversity of chemical and physical behavior around you. The periodic table, which organizes much of this diversity, was derived from chemical facts observed in countless hours of 18th- and 19th-century research. One of the greatest achievements in science is 20th-century quantum theory, which provides a theoretical basis for the periodic table's arrangement. In this chapter, we apply general ideas of bonding and structure from earlier chapters to the main-group elements to see how their behavior correlates with their position in the periodic table. Don't be concerned, however, if our theories cannot account for all the facts; after all, our models are simple and nature is complex.

14.1 HYDROGEN, THE SIMPLEST ATOM

A hydrogen (H) atom consists of a nucleus with a single proton, surrounded by a single electron. About 90% of all the atoms in the universe are H atoms, making it the most abundant element by far. On Earth, only tiny amounts of the free element (H_2) occur naturally because the molecules are so light that they escape Earth's gravity. However, hydrogen is abundant in combination with oxygen in water. Hydrogen's physical behavior results from its simple structure and low molar mass. Nonpolar gaseous H_2 is colorless and odorless, and its extremely weak dispersion forces result in very low melting ($-259°C$) and boiling points ($-253°C$).

Hydrogen's tiny size, low nuclear charge, and simple electron configuration make it difficult to place in the periodic table. We might think it belongs in Group 1A(1) because it has one valence electron. However, unlike the alkali metals, hydrogen *shares* its electron with nonmetals, and it has a much higher ionization energy and electronegativity than lithium, the highest of the alkali metals. Another possible placement might be with the halogens in Group 7A(17), because hydrogen occurs as a diatomic nonmetal that fills its outer shell either by sharing or by forming a monatomic anion (H^-). But hydrogen lacks the halogens' three valence electron pairs, and the H^- ion is rare and reactive, whereas halide ions (F^-, Cl^-, etc.) are common and stable. Based on several atomic properties, a third possibility might be in the carbon family [Group 4A(14)] because hydrogen has a half-filled valence level and ionization energy, electron affinity, electronegativity, and bond energy values close to those of Group 4A elements; but it shows little physical or chemical behavior similar to members of this family. In this text, hydrogen will appear in either Group 1A(1) or 7A(17), depending on the property being considered.

Highlights of Hydrogen Chemistry

Beyond the enormous impact of hydrogen bonding on physical properties that we already discussed in Chapters 12 and 13, elemental hydrogen is very reactive, combining with nearly every other element to form ionic or covalent hydrides.

Ionic (Saltlike) Hydrides With very reactive metals, such as those in Group 1A(1) and the larger members of Group 2A(2) (Ca, Sr, and Ba), hydrogen forms *saltlike hydrides*—white, crystalline solids composed of the metal cation and the hydride ion:

$$2Li(s) + H_2(g) \longrightarrow 2LiH(s)$$
$$Ca(s) + H_2(g) \longrightarrow CaH_2(s)$$

In water, H^- reacts as a strong base to form H_2 and OH^-:

$$NaH(s) + H_2O(l) \longrightarrow Na^+(aq) + OH^-(aq) + H_2(g)$$

The H^- ion is also a strong reducing agent, as in this example:

$$TiCl_4(l) + 4LiH(s) \longrightarrow Ti(s) + 4LiCl(s) + 2H_2(g)$$

Covalent (Molecular) Hydrides Hydrogen reacts with nonmetals to form many *covalent hydrides*. In most of them, hydrogen has an oxidation number of +1 because the other nonmetal has a higher electronegativity.

Conditions for preparing covalent hydrides depend on the reactivity of the other nonmetal. For example, with stable, triple-bonded N_2, the reaction needs high temperatures (~400°C), high pressures (~250 atm), and a catalyst:

$$N_2(g) + 3H_2(g) \xrightarrow{\text{catalyst}} 2NH_3(g) \quad \Delta H^\circ_{rxn} = -91.8 \text{ kJ}$$

Industrial facilities throughout the world use this reaction to produce millions of tons of ammonia each year for fertilizers, explosives, and synthetic fibers. On the other hand, hydrogen combines rapidly with reactive, single-bonded F_2, even at extremely low temperatures (−196°C):

$$F_2(g) + H_2(g) \longrightarrow 2HF(g) \quad \Delta H^\circ_{rxn} = -546 \text{ kJ}$$

14.2 GROUP 1A(1): THE ALKALI METALS

The first group of elements is named for the alkaline (basic) nature of their oxides and for the basic solutions the elements form in water. Group 1A(1) provides the best example of regular trends with no significant exceptions. All the elements in the group—lithium (Li), sodium (Na), potassium (K), rubidium (Rb), cesium (Cs), and rare, radioactive francium (Fr)—are very reactive metals. The Family Portrait of Group 1A(1) on p. 436 is the first in a series that provides an overview of each of the main groups, summarizing key atomic, physical, and chemical properties.

The Unusual Physical Properties of the Alkali Metals

The alkali metals are softer and have lower melting and boiling points and lower densities than nearly any other metals. This unusual physical behavior can be traced to their atomic size, the largest in their respective periods, and to the ns^1 valence electron configuration. Because the single valence electron is relatively far from the nucleus, there is only weak metallic bonding, which results in a soft consistency (K can be squeezed like clay) and low melting point. And their low densities result from the lowest molar masses and largest atomic radii in their periods.

The High Reactivity of the Alkali Metals

The alkali metals are extremely reactive elements, acting as *powerful reducing agents*. Therefore, they always occur in nature as 1+ cations rather than as free metals. (As we discuss in Section 21.7, highly endothermic reduction processes are needed to prepare the free metals industrially from their molten salts.)

Key Atomic Properties, Physical Properties, and Reactions

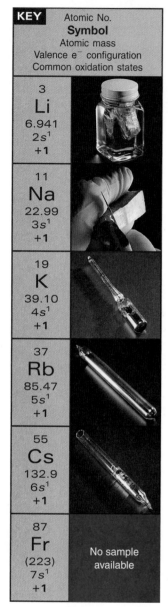

KEY
Atomic No.
Symbol
Atomic mass
Valence e⁻ configuration
Common oxidation states

3 **Li** 6.941 $2s^1$ +1	
11 **Na** 22.99 $3s^1$ +1	
19 **K** 39.10 $4s^1$ +1	
37 **Rb** 85.47 $5s^1$ +1	
55 **Cs** 132.9 $6s^1$ +1	
87 **Fr** (223) $7s^1$ +1	No sample available

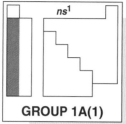

ns^1

GROUP 1A(1)

Atomic radius (pm)		Ionic radius (pm)
Li 152	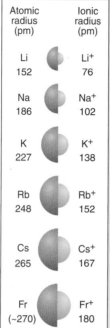	Li⁺ 76
Na 186		Na⁺ 102
K 227		K⁺ 138
Rb 248		Rb⁺ 152
Cs 265		Cs⁺ 167
Fr (~270)		Fr⁺ 180

Atomic Properties

Group electron configuration is ns^1. All members have the +1 oxidation state and form an E^+ ion. Atoms have the largest size and lowest IE and EN in their periods. Down the group, atomic and ionic size increase, while IE and EN decrease.

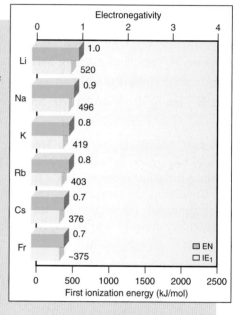

Electronegativity / First ionization energy (kJ/mol)

	EN	IE₁
Li	1.0	520
Na	0.9	496
K	0.8	419
Rb	0.8	403
Cs	0.7	376
Fr	0.7	~375

Physical Properties

Metallic bonding is relatively weak because there is only one valence electron. Therefore, these metals are soft with relatively low melting and boiling points. These values decrease down the group because larger atom cores attract delocalized electrons less strongly. Large atomic size and low atomic mass result in low density; thus density generally increases down the group because mass increases more than size.

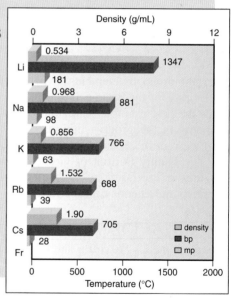

Density (g/mL) / Temperature (°C)

	density	bp	mp
Li	0.534	1347	181
Na	0.968	881	98
K	0.856	766	63
Rb	1.532	688	39
Cs	1.90	705	28
Fr			

Reactions

1. The alkali metals reduce H in H_2O from the +1 to the 0 oxidation state:

$$2E(s) + 2H_2O(l) \longrightarrow 2E^+(aq) + 2OH^-(aq) + H_2(g)$$

The reaction becomes more vigorous down the group.

2. The alkali metals reduce oxygen, but the product depends on the metal. Li forms the oxide, Li_2O; Na forms the peroxide, Na_2O_2; K, Rb, and Cs form the superoxide, EO_2:

$$4Li(s) + O_2(g) \longrightarrow 2Li_2O(s)$$
$$K(s) + O_2(g) \longrightarrow KO_2(s)$$

In emergency breathing units, KO_2 reacts with H_2O and CO_2 in exhaled air to release O_2.

3. The alkali metals reduce hydrogen to form ionic (saltlike) hydrides:

$$2E(s) + H_2(g) \longrightarrow 2EH(s)$$

NaH is an industrial base and reducing agent that is used to prepare other reducing agents, such as $NaBH_4$.

4. The alkali metals reduce halogens to form ionic halides:

$$2E(s) + X_2 \longrightarrow 2EX(s) \qquad (X = F, Cl, Br, I)$$

The ns^1 configuration, which is the basis for their physical properties, is also the reason these metals form salts so readily. Their low ionization energies give rise to small cations, which allow them to lie close to anions, resulting in high lattice energies. Some examples of this reactivity occur with halogens, water, oxygen, and hydrogen. The alkali metals (E) reduce halogens to form ionic solids in highly exothermic reactions:

$$2E(s) + X_2 \longrightarrow 2EX(s) \quad (X = F, Cl, Br, I)$$

They reduce the hydrogen in water, reacting vigorously (Rb and Cs explosively) to form H_2 and a metal hydroxide solution:

$$2E(s) + 2H_2O(l) \longrightarrow 2E^+(aq) + 2OH^-(aq) + H_2(g)$$

They reduce O_2, but the product depends on the metal. Li forms the oxide, Li_2O; Na the peroxide (O.N. of O = -1), Na_2O_2; and K, Rb, and Cs the superoxide (O.N. of O = $-\frac{1}{2}$), EO_2:

$$4Li(s) + O_2(g) \longrightarrow 2Li_2O(s)$$
$$2Na(s) + O_2(g) \longrightarrow Na_2O_2(s)$$
$$K(s) + O_2(g) \longrightarrow KO_2(s)$$

Thus, in air, the metals tarnish rapidly, so Na and K are usually kept under mineral oil (an unreactive liquid) in the laboratory, and Rb and Cs are handled with gloves under an inert argon atmosphere. And, finally, the Group 1A(1) elements reduce molecular hydrogen to form ionic (saltlike) hydrides:

$$2E(s) + H_2(g) \longrightarrow 2EH(s)$$

For a given anion, the trend in lattice energy is the inverse of the trend in cation size: *as the cation becomes larger, the lattice energy becomes smaller.* Figure 14.1 shows this steady decrease in lattice energy within the Group 1A(1) and 2A(2) chlorides. Despite these strong ionic attractions in the solid, *nearly all Group 1A salts are water soluble* because the ions attract water molecules to create a highly exothermic heat of hydration (ΔH_{hydr}).

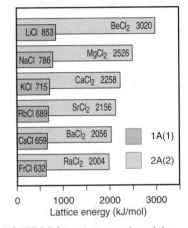

FIGURE 14.1 Lattice energies of the Group 1A(1) and 2A(2) chlorides. The lattice energy decreases regularly in both groups of metal chlorides as the cations become larger. Lattice energies for the 2A chlorides are greater because the 2A cations have higher charge and smaller size.

The Anomalous Behavior of Period 2 Members

A consistent feature within the main groups is that, as a result of their *small atomic size* and *small number of outer-level orbitals,* all the Period 2 members display some anomalous (unrepresentative) behavior within their groups.

In Group 1A(1), Li is the only member that forms a simple oxide and nitride, Li_2O and Li_3N, with O_2 and N_2 in air, and only Li forms molecular compounds with organic halides:

$$2Li(s) + CH_3CH_2Cl(g) \longrightarrow CH_3CH_2Li(s) + LiCl(s)$$

Because of the high charge density of Li^+, many lithium salts have significant covalent character. Thus, halides of Li are more soluble in polar organic solvents than the halides of Na and K.

In Group 2A(2), beryllium displays even more anomalous behavior than Li. Because of the extremely high charge density of Be^{2+}, the discrete ion does not exist, and all Be compounds exhibit covalent bonding. In Group 3A(13), boron is the only member to form a complex family of compounds with metals and covalent compounds with hydrogen (boranes). Carbon, in Group 4A(14), shows extremely unusual behavior: it bonds to itself (and a small number of other elements) so extensively and diversely that it gives rise to countless organic compounds. In Group 5A(15), triple-bonded, gaseous nitrogen is dramatically different from its reactive, solid family members. Oxygen, the only gas in Group 6A(16), is much more reactive than sulfur and the other members. In Group 7A(17), fluorine is so electronegative that it reacts violently with water, and it is the only member that forms a weak hydrohalic acid, HF. And, finally, helium, in Group 8A(18), has the lowest melting and boiling points and the smallest heats of phase change of any noble gas, indeed of any element.

14.3 GROUP 2A(2): THE ALKALINE EARTH METALS

The Group 2A(2) elements are called *alkaline earth metals* because their oxides give basic (alkaline) solutions and melt at such high temperatures that they remained as solids ("earths") in the alchemists' fires. The group includes rare beryllium (Be), common magnesium (Mg) and calcium (Ca), less familiar strontium (Sr) and barium (Ba), and radioactive radium (Ra). The Group 2A(2) Family Portrait presents an overview of these elements.

How Do the Physical Properties of the Alkaline Earth and Alkali Metals Compare?

In general, the elements in Groups 1A(1) and 2A(2) behave as close cousins. Whatever differences occur are due to an additional *s* electron: ns^2 vs. ns^1. Two valence electrons and a nucleus with one additional positive charge make for much stronger metallic bonding. Consequently, Group 2A melting and boiling points are much higher than those of the corresponding 1A metals. Compared with transition metals, such as iron and chromium, the alkaline earths are soft and lightweight, but they are much harder and more dense than the alkali metals. Magnesium is a particularly versatile member. Because it forms a tough oxide layer that prevents further reaction in air, it is alloyed with aluminum for camera bodies and luggage and with the lanthanides for auto engine blocks and missile parts.

How Do the Chemical Properties of the Alkaline Earth and Alkali Metals Compare?

The alkaline earth metals display a wider range of chemical behavior than the alkali metals, largely because of the unrepresentative covalent bonding of beryllium. The second valence electron lies in the same sublevel as the first, so it is poorly shielded and Z_{eff} is greater. Therefore, Group 2A(2) elements have smaller atomic radii and higher ionization energies than Group 1A(1) elements. Yet, despite the higher second IEs required to form the 2+ cations, *all the alkaline earths (except Be) form ionic compounds* because the resulting high lattice energies more than compensate for the large total IEs.

Like the alkali metals, the alkaline earth metals are *strong reducing agents*. They reduce O_2 in air. Except for Be and Mg, which form oxide coatings that adhere tightly to the sample's surface, they reduce H_2O at room temperature to form H_2. With a few exceptions for Be, they reduce halogens, H_2, and N_2 to form the corresponding ionic halides, hydrides, and nitrides (see the Family Portrait).

The Group 2A oxides are very basic (except for amphoteric BeO) and react with acidic oxides to form salts, such as sulfites and carbonates; for example,

$$SrO(s) + CO_2(g) \longrightarrow SrCO_3(s)$$

The natural carbonates limestone and marble are major structural materials and the commercial sources for most 2A compounds.

One of the main differences between the two groups is the lower solubility of 2A salts. With such high lattice energies, most 2A fluorides, carbonates, phosphates, and sulfates are insoluble, unlike the corresponding 1A compounds.

Diagonal Relationships

Diagonal relationships are *similarities between a Period 2 element and one diagonally down and to the right in Period 3*. Three such relationships are of interest to us here (Figure 14.2). The first occurs between Li and Mg. Both form nitrides with N_2, hydroxides and carbonates that decompose easily with heat, organic compounds with a polar covalent metal-carbon bond, and salts with similar

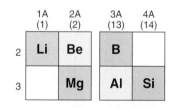

FIGURE 14.2 Three diagonal relationships in the periodic table. Certain Period 2 elements exhibit behaviors that are very similar to those of the Period 3 elements immediately below and to the right. Three such diagonal relationships exist: Li and Mg, Be and Al, and B and Si.

Key Atomic Properties, Physical Properties, and Reactions

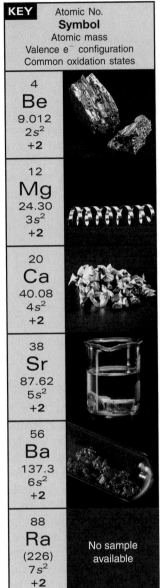

KEY
Atomic No.
Symbol
Atomic mass
Valence e⁻ configuration
Common oxidation states

4	Be	9.012	$2s^2$	+2
12	Mg	24.30	$3s^2$	+2
20	Ca	40.08	$4s^2$	+2
38	Sr	87.62	$5s^2$	+2
56	Ba	137.3	$6s^2$	+2
88	Ra	(226)	$7s^2$	+2

No sample available

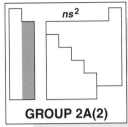

ns^2

GROUP 2A(2)

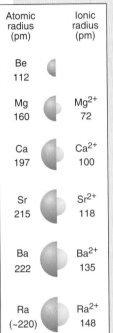

	Atomic radius (pm)	Ionic radius (pm)
Be	112	
Mg	160	Mg^{2+} 72
Ca	197	Ca^{2+} 100
Sr	215	Sr^{2+} 118
Ba	222	Ba^{2+} 135
Ra	(~220)	Ra^{2+} 148

Atomic Properties

Group electron configuration is ns^2 (filled ns sublevel). All members have the +2 oxidation state and, except for Be, form compounds with an E^{2+} ion. Atomic and ionic sizes increase down the group but are smaller than for the corresponding 1A(1) elements. IE and EN decrease down the group but are higher than for the corresponding 1A(1) elements.

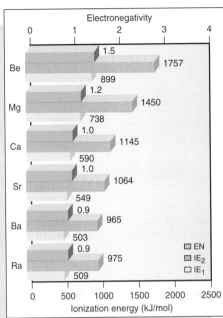

Physical Properties

Metallic bonding involves two valence electrons. These metals are still relatively soft but are much harder than the 1A(1) metals. Melting and boiling points generally decrease, and densities generally increase down the group. These values are much higher than for 1A(1) elements, and the trend is not as regular.

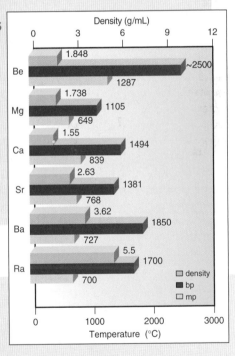

Reactions

1. The metals reduce O_2 to form the oxides:
$$2E(s) + O_2(g) \longrightarrow 2EO(s)$$
Ba also forms the peroxide, BaO_2.

2. The larger metals reduce water to form hydrogen gas:
$$E(s) + 2H_2O(l) \longrightarrow E^{2+}(aq) + 2OH^-(aq) + H_2(g)$$
$$(E = Ca, Sr, Ba)$$
Be and Mg form an oxide coating that allows only slight reaction.

3. The metals reduce halogens to form ionic halides:
$$E(s) + X_2 \longrightarrow EX_2(s) \quad [X = F \text{ (not with Be)}, Cl, Br, I]$$

4. Most of the elements reduce hydrogen to form ionic hydrides:
$$E(s) + H_2(g) \longrightarrow EH_2(s) \quad (E = \text{all except Be})$$

5. The elements reduce nitrogen to form ionic nitrides:
$$3E(s) + N_2(g) \longrightarrow E_3N_2(s)$$

6. Except for amphoteric BeO, the element oxides are basic:
$$EO(s) + H_2O(l) \longrightarrow E^{2+}(aq) + 2OH^-(aq)$$
$Ca(OH)_2$ is a component of cement and mortar.

7. All carbonates undergo thermal decomposition to the oxide:
$$ECO_3(s) \overset{\Delta}{\longrightarrow} EO(s) + CO_2(g)$$
This reaction is used to produce CaO (lime) in huge amounts from naturally occurring limestone.

solubilities. Beryllium in Group 2A(2) and aluminum in Group 3A(13) are another pair. Both metals form oxide coatings, so they don't react with water, and both form amphoteric, extremely hard, high-melting oxides. The third diagonal relationship occurs between the metalloids boron in Group 3A(13) and silicon in Group 4A(14). Both behave electrically as semiconductors and both form weakly acidic, solid oxoacids and flammable, low-melting, strongly reducing, covalent hydrides.

Looking Backward and Forward: Groups 1A(1), 2A(2), and 3A(13)

Throughout this chapter, comparing the previous, current, and upcoming groups (Figure 14.3) will help you keep horizontal trends in mind while examining vertical groups. Little changes from Group 1A to 2A, and all the elements behave as metals. With smaller atomic sizes and stronger metallic bonding, 2A elements are harder, higher melting, and denser than those in 1A. Nearly all 1A and most 2A compounds are ionic. The higher ionic charge in Group 2A (2+ vs. 1+) leads to higher lattice energies and less soluble salts. The range of behavior in 2A is wider than that in 1A because of Be, and the range widens much further in Group 3A, from metalloid boron to metallic thallium.

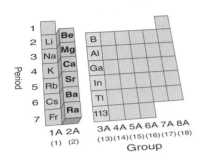

FIGURE 14.3 Standing in Group 2A(2), looking backward to 1A(1) and forward to 3A(13).

14.4 GROUP 3A(13): THE BORON FAMILY

Boron (B) heads the third family of main-group elements, but its properties are not representative, as the Group 3A(13) Family Portrait shows. Metallic aluminum (Al) is more typical of the group, but its great abundance and importance contrast with the rareness of gallium (Ga), indium (In), and thallium (Tl).

How Do Transition Elements Influence Group 3A(13) Properties?

Group 3A(13) is the first in the p block of the periodic table. In Periods 2 and 3, its members lie just one element away from those in Group 2A(2), but in Period 4 and higher, a large gap separates the two groups, with 10 transition elements (d block) each in Periods 4, 5, and 6 and an additional 14 inner transition elements (f block) in Period 6. Because d and f electrons spend very little time near the nucleus, they shield the outer (s and p) electrons in Ga, In, and Tl very little from the stronger nuclear attraction (greater Z_{eff}) (Sections 7.4 and 8.5). As a result, these elements deviate from the usual trends down a group, having smaller atomic radii and larger ionization energies and electronegativities than expected.

With respect to their physical properties, boron is a black, hard, very high-melting, network covalent metalloid, but the other 3A members are shiny, relatively soft, low-melting metals. Aluminum's low density and three valence electrons make it an exceptional conductor: for a given mass, it conducts a current twice as effectively as copper. Gallium has the largest liquid temperature range of any element: it melts in your hand but does not boil until 2403°C.

What New Features Appear in the Chemical Properties of Group 3A(13)?

Looking down Group 3A(13), we see a wide range of chemical behavior. Boron, the first metalloid we've encountered, is very different from the other members of this group. It is much less reactive at room temperature and forms covalent bonds exclusively. Recall from Chapter 8 that the boron atom has three valence electrons, so it has only six electrons around it in several compounds. In boron's smaller compounds, the central B atom attains an octet by bonding with an electron-rich atom, one with a lone pair, as in the reaction of BF_3 and NH_3:

$$BF_3(g) + :NH_3(g) \longrightarrow F_3B-NH_3(g)$$

Key Atomic Properties, Physical Properties, and Reactions

ns^2np^1

GROUP 3A(13)

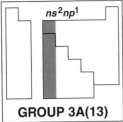

	5
	B
	10.81
	$2s^22p^1$
	+3

	13
	Al
	26.98
	$3s^23p^1$
	+3

	31
	Ga
	69.72
	$4s^24p^1$
	+3, +1

	49
	In
	114.8
	$5s^25p^1$
	+3, +1

	81
	Tl
	204.4
	$6s^26p^1$
	+1

113	Observed in experiments at Dubna, Russia, in 2003
(284)	
$7s^27p^1$	

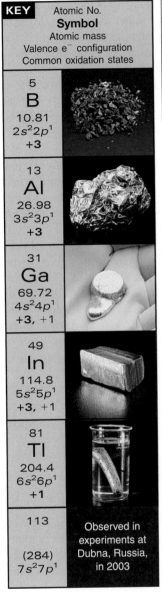

Atomic radius (pm)		Ionic radius (pm)
B 85		
Al 143		Al^{3+} 54
Ga 135		Ga^{3+} 62
In 167		In^{3+} 80
Tl 170		Tl^+ 150

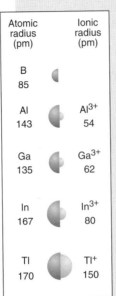

Atomic Properties

Group electron configuration is ns^2np^1. All except Tl commonly display the +3 oxidation state. The +1 state becomes more common down the group. Atomic size is smaller and EN is higher than for 2A(2) elements; IE is lower, however, because it is easier to remove an electron from the higher energy p sublevel. Atomic size, IE, and EN do not change as expected down the group because there are intervening transition and inner transition elements.

Physical Properties

Bonding changes from network covalent in B to metallic in the rest of the group. Thus, B has a much higher melting point than the others, but there is no overall trend. Boiling points decrease down the group. Densities increase down the group.

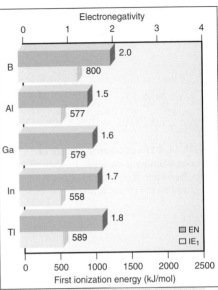

Electronegativity / First ionization energy (kJ/mol)

	EN	IE₁
B	2.0	800
Al	1.5	577
Ga	1.6	579
In	1.7	558
Tl	1.8	589

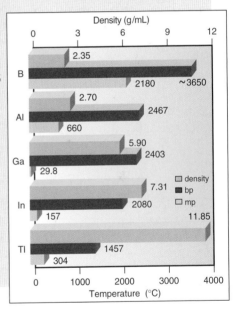

Density (g/mL) / Temperature (°C)

	density	bp	mp
B	2.35	~3650	2180
Al	2.70	2467	660
Ga	5.90	2403	29.8
In	7.31	2080	157
Tl	11.85	1457	304

Reactions

1. The elements react sluggishly, if at all, with water:

$$2Ga(s) + 6H_2O(hot) \longrightarrow 2Ga^{3+}(aq) + 6OH^-(aq) + 3H_2(g)$$

$$2Tl(s) + 2H_2O(steam) \longrightarrow 2Tl^+(aq) + 2OH^-(aq) + H_2(g)$$

Al becomes covered with a layer of Al_2O_3 that prevents further reaction.

2. When strongly heated in pure O_2, all members form oxides:

$$4E(s) + 3O_2(g) \xrightarrow{\Delta} 2E_2O_3(s) \quad (E = B, Al, Ga, In)$$

$$4Tl(s) + O_2(g) \xrightarrow{\Delta} 2Tl_2O(s)$$

Oxide acidity decreases down the group: B_2O_3 (weakly acidic) > Al_2O_3 > Ga_2O_3 > In_2O_3 > Tl_2O (strongly basic), and the +1 oxide is more basic than the +3 oxide.

3. All members reduce halogens (X_2):

$$2E(s) + 3X_2 \longrightarrow 2EX_3 \quad (E = B, Al, Ga, In)$$

$$2Tl(s) + X_2 \longrightarrow 2TlX(s)$$

The BX_3 compounds are volatile and covalent. Trihalides of Al, Ga, and In are (mostly) ionic solids.

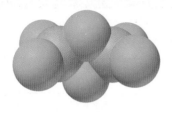

FIGURE 14.4 The dimeric structure of gaseous aluminum chloride. Despite its name, aluminum trichloride exists in the gas phase as the dimer, Al_2Cl_6.

And in its elemental form and many large compounds, boron uses multiple bonds and other types of bonds to attain an octet of electrons around each B atom.

Although aluminum acts physically like a metal, its halides exist in the gas phase as covalent *dimers*—molecules formed by joining two identical smaller molecules (Figure 14.4)—and its oxide is amphoteric rather than basic. Most of the other 3A compounds are ionic, but with more covalent character than similar 2A compounds because the 3A cations can polarize nearby electron clouds more effectively.

Three features are common to the elements of Groups 3A(13) to 6A(16):

1. *Presence of multiple oxidation states.* Many of the larger elements in these groups also have an important oxidation state *two lower than the A-group number.* The lower state occurs when the atoms lose their *np* electrons but not their two *ns* electrons. This phenomenon is often called the *inert-pair effect* (Section 8.5).

2. *Increasing prominence of the lower oxidation state.* When a group exhibits more than one oxidation state, the lower state becomes more prominent going down the group. In Group 3A(13), for instance, all members exhibit the +3 state, but the +1 state first appears with some compounds of gallium and becomes the only important state of thallium.

3. *Relative basicity of oxides.* In general, oxides with the element in a lower oxidation state are more basic than oxides with the element in a higher oxidation state. For example, in Group 3A, In_2O is more basic than In_2O_3. The lower charge of In^+ does not polarize the O^{2-} ion as much as the higher charge of In^{3+} does, so the O^{2-} ion is more available to act as a base. In general, when an element has more than one oxidation state, *it acts more like a metal in its lower state.*

14.5 GROUP 4A(14): THE CARBON FAMILY

All three categories of elements occur within Group 4A(14), from the nonmetal carbon (C) through the metalloids silicon (Si) and germanium (Ge) and down to the metals tin (Sn) and lead (Pb) [Group 4A(14) Family Portrait, p. 443].

How Does the Bonding in an Element Affect Physical Properties?

Trends among the elements of Group 4A(14) and their neighbors in Groups 3A(13) and 5A(15) illustrate how physical properties depend on the type of bonding in an element (Table 14.1). Within Group 4A, the large decrease in melting point between the network covalent solids C and Si is due to longer, weaker bonds in the Si structure; the large decrease between Ge and Sn is due to the

Table 14.1 Bond Type and the Melting Process in Groups 3A(13) to 5A(15)

Period	Group 3A(13)				Group 4A(14)				Group 5A(15)				Key:	
	Element	Bond Type	Melting Point (°C)	ΔH_{fus} (kJ/mol)	Element	Bond Type	Melting Point (°C)	ΔH_{fus} (kJ/mol)	Element	Bond Type	Melting Point (°C)	ΔH_{fus} (kJ/mol)		Metallic
2	B		2180	23.6	C		4100	Very high	N		−210	0.7		Covalent network
3	Al		660	10.5	Si		1420	50.6	P		44.1	2.5		Covalent molecule
4	Ga		30	5.6	Ge		945	36.8	As		816	27.7		Metal
5	In		157	3.3	Sn		232	7.1	Sb		631	20.0		Metalloid
6	Tl		304	4.3	Pb		327	4.8	Bi		271	10.5		Nonmetal

Family Portrait of Group 4A(14): The Carbon Family

Key Atomic Properties, Physical Properties, and Reactions

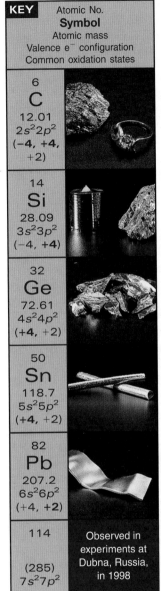

KEY	Atomic No.
	Symbol
	Atomic mass
	Valence e⁻ configuration
	Common oxidation states

6
C
12.01
$2s^2 2p^2$
(**−4, +4, +2**)

14
Si
28.09
$3s^2 3p^2$
(**−4, +4**)

32
Ge
72.61
$4s^2 4p^2$
(**+4, +2**)

50
Sn
118.7
$5s^2 5p^2$
(**+4, +2**)

82
Pb
207.2
$6s^2 6p^2$
(+4, **+2**)

114
Observed in experiments at Dubna, Russia, in 1998
(285)
$7s^2 7p^2$

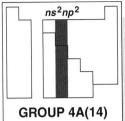

ns^2np^2

GROUP 4A(14)

Atomic radius (pm)	Ionic radius (pm)
C 77	
Si 118	
Ge 122	
Sn 140	Sn²⁺ 118
Pb 146	Pb²⁺ 119

Atomic Properties

Group electron configuration is ns^2np^2. Down the group, the number of oxidation states decreases, and the lower (+2) state becomes more common. Down the group, size increases. Because transition and inner transition elements intervene, IE and EN do not decrease smoothly.

Physical Properties

Trends in properties, such as decreasing hardness and melting point, are due to changes in types of bonding within the solid: covalent network in C, Si, and Ge; metallic in Sn and Pb *(see text)*. Down the group, density increases because of several factors, including differences in crystal packing.

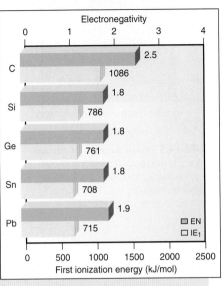

Electronegativity / First ionization energy (kJ/mol)

	EN	IE₁
C	2.5	1086
Si	1.8	786
Ge	1.8	761
Sn	1.8	708
Pb	1.9	715

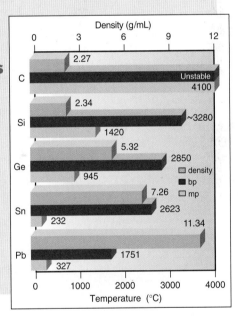

Density (g/mL) / Temperature (°C)

	density	bp	mp
C	2.27	Unstable	4100
Si	2.34	~3280	1420
Ge	5.32	2850	945
Sn	7.26	2623	232
Pb	11.34	1751	327

Reactions

1. The elements are oxidized by halogens:

$$E(s) + 2X_2 \longrightarrow EX_4 \quad (E = C, Si, Ge)$$

The +2 halides are more stable for tin and lead, SnX_2 and PbX_2.

2. The elements are oxidized by O_2:

$$E(s) + O_2(g) \longrightarrow EO_2 \quad (E = C, Si, Ge, Sn)$$

Pb forms the +2 oxide, PbO. Oxides become more basic down the group. The reaction of CO_2 and H_2O provides the weak acidity of natural unpolluted waters:

$$CO_2(g) + H_2O(l) \rightleftharpoons [H_2CO_3(aq)]$$
$$\rightleftharpoons H^+(aq) + HCO_3^-(aq)$$

3. Hydrocarbons react with O_2 to form CO_2 and H_2O. The reaction for methane is adapted to yield heat or electricity:

$$CH_4(g) + 2O_2(g) \longrightarrow CO_2(g) + 2H_2O(g)$$

4. Silica is reduced to form elemental silicon:

$$SiO_2(s) + 2C(s) \longrightarrow Si(s) + 2CO(g)$$

This crude silicon is made ultrapure through zone refining for use in the manufacture of computer chips.

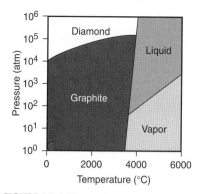

FIGURE 14.5 Phase diagram of carbon. Graphite is the more stable form of carbon at ordinary conditions *(small red circle at extreme lower left)*. Diamond is more stable at very high pressure.

change from network covalent to metallic bonding. Similarly, considering horizontal trends, the large increases in melting point and ΔH_{fus} across a period between Al and Si and between Ga and Ge reflect the change from metallic to network covalent bonding. Note the abrupt rises in these properties from metallic Al, Ga, and Sn to the network covalent metalloids Si, Ge, and Sb, and note the abrupt drops from the covalent networks of C and Si to the individual molecules of N and P.

Allotropism Striking variations in physical properties often appear among **allotropes,** different crystalline or molecular forms of a substance. One allotrope is usually more stable than another at a particular pressure and temperature. Group 4A(14) provides the first of many examples of allotropism. It is difficult to imagine two substances made entirely of the same atom that are more different than graphite and diamond. Graphite is a soft, black electrical conductor, whereas diamond is an extremely hard, colorless electrical insulator. Graphite is the more stable (standard state) form at ordinary temperatures and pressures (Figure 14.5). Fortunately for jewelry owners, diamond changes to graphite at a negligible rate under normal conditions.

In the mid-1980s, a newly discovered allotrope of carbon began generating great interest. Mass spectrometric analysis of soot showed evidence for a soccer ball–shaped molecule of formula C_{60}, dubbed *buckminsterfullerene* (informally called a "buckyball") (Figure 14.6A). Since 1990, when multigram quantities of C_{60} and related fullerenes were prepared, metal atoms have been incorporated into the structure and many different groups (fluorine, hydroxyl, sugars, etc.) have been attached. In 1991, extremely thin (~1 nm in diameter) graphite-like tubes with fullerene ends were prepared (Figure 14.6B). Along their length, such *nanotubes* are stronger than steel and conduct electricity. With potential applications in nanoscale electronics, catalysis, polymers, and medicine, fullerenes and, especially, nanotubes have opened up whole new areas of study for chemists and engineers.

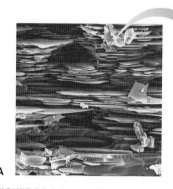

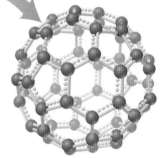

A   **B**

FIGURE 14.6 Buckyballs and nanotubes. A, Crystals of buckminsterfullerene (C_{60}) are shown leading to a ball-and-stick model. The parent of the fullerenes, the "buckyball," is a soccer ball–shaped molecule of 60 carbon atoms. **B,** Nanotubes are single or, as shown in this colorized model, concentric graphite-like tubes (shown here without the usual fullerene ends).

How Does the Type of Bonding Change in Group 4A(14) Compounds?

The Group 4A(14) elements display a wide range of chemical behavior, from the covalent compounds of carbon to the ionic compounds of lead. Carbon's intermediate EN of 2.5 ensures that it virtually always forms covalent bonds, but the larger members of the group form bonds with increasing ionic character. With nonmetals, Si and Ge form strong polar covalent bonds. The most important is the Si—O bond, one of the strongest of any Period 3 element (BE = 368 kJ/mol), which is responsible for the physical and chemical stability of Earth's solid surface.

The pattern of elements having more than one oxidation state also appears here. Thus, compounds of Si(IV) are much more stable than those of Si(II), whereas compounds of Pb(II) are more stable than those of Pb(IV). The 4A elements also behave more like metals in the lower oxidation state. Thus, $SnCl_2$ and $PbCl_2$ are white, relatively high-melting, water-soluble crystals, typical properties of a salt, whereas $SnCl_4$ is a volatile, benzene-soluble liquid, and $PbCl_4$ is a thermally unstable oil. Similarly, SnO and PbO are more basic than SnO_2 and PbO_2.

Highlights of Carbon Chemistry

Carbon is not only an anomaly in its group, but its bonding ability makes it an anomaly throughout the periodic table. As a result of its small size and capacity for four bonds, carbon bonds to itself, a process known as *catenation,* to form chains, branches, and rings that lead to myriad structures. Add a lot of H, some O and N, a bit of S, P, halogens, and a few metals, and you have the whole organic and biological world! Figure 14.7 shows three of the several million known organic compounds. Multiple bonds are common in these structures because the C—C bond is short enough for side-to-side overlap of two half-filled $2p$ orbitals to form π bonds. (We focus on the organic compounds of carbon in Chapter 15.) Because the other 4A members are larger, E—E bonds become longer and weaker down the group, and the presence of empty d orbitals of the larger atoms make their chains much more susceptible to chemical attack. Thus, none form molecules with stable chains.

In contrast to its organic compounds, carbon's inorganic compounds are simple. Metal carbonates in marble, limestone, chalk, and coral occur in enormous deposits throughout the world. Carbonates are used in some antacids because they react with the HCl in stomach acid:

$$CaCO_3(s) + 2HCl(aq) \longrightarrow CaCl_2(aq) + CO_2(g) + H_2O(l)$$

Identical net ionic reactions with sulfuric and nitric acids protect lakes bounded by limestone from the harmful effects of acid rain.

Carbon forms two common gaseous oxides. Carbon dioxide plays a vital role on Earth; through the process of photosynthesis, it is the primary source of carbon in plants, and thus animals as well. In solution, it is the cause of acidity in natural waters. However, its atmospheric buildup from deforestation and excessive use of fossil fuels is severely affecting the global climate. Carbon monoxide is a key component of fuel mixtures and is widely used in the production of methanol, formaldehyde, and other industrial compounds. Its toxicity arises from strong binding to the Fe(II) in hemoglobin, where it prevents the binding of O_2. The cyanide ion (CN^-), which is *isoelectronic* with CO,

$$[:C{\equiv}N:]^- \quad \text{same electronic structure as} \quad :C{\equiv}O:$$

is toxic because it binds to many other essential iron-containing proteins.

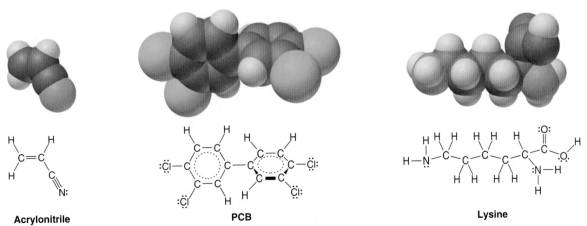

Acrylonitrile   **PCB**   **Lysine**

FIGURE 14.7 Three of the several million known organic compounds. Acrylonitrile is a precursor of acrylic fibers. PCB is an example of a polychlorinated biphenyl. Lysine is one of about 20 amino acids that occur in proteins.

Monocarbon halides (or halomethanes) are tetrahedral molecules. The short, strong bonds in chlorofluorocarbons (CFCs, or Freons) make their long-term persistence in the upper atmosphere a major environmental problem (Chapter 16).

Highlights of Silicon Chemistry

To a great extent, the chemistry of silicon is the chemistry of the *silicon-oxygen bond.* Just as carbon forms unending —C—C— chains, the —Si—O— grouping repeats itself endlessly in **silicates,** the most important minerals on the planet, and in **silicones,** extremely long synthetic molecules that have many applications:

1. *Silicate.* From common sand and clay to semiprecious amethyst and carnelian, silicate minerals dominate the nonliving world. In fact, oxygen and silicon account for four of every five atoms on Earth's surface! The silicate building unit is the *orthosilicate* grouping, —SiO_4—, a tetrahedral arrangement of four oxygens around a central silicon. Several well-known minerals, such as zircon and beryl, the natural source of beryllium, contain SiO_4^{4-} ions or small groups of them linked together (Figure 14.8). In extended structures, one of the O atoms links the next Si—O group to form chains, a second one forms crosslinks to neighboring chains to form sheets, and the third forms more crosslinks to create three-dimensional frameworks. Chains of silicate groups compose the asbestos minerals, sheets give rise to talc and mica, and frameworks occur in quartz and feldspar.

2. *Silicone.* These compounds have two organic groups bonded to each Si atom in a very long Si—O chain, as in *poly(dimethyl siloxane):*

$$\cdots O-\underset{\underset{CH_3}{|}}{\overset{\overset{CH_3}{|}}{Si}}-O-\underset{\underset{CH_3}{|}}{\overset{\overset{CH_3}{|}}{Si}}-O-\underset{\underset{CH_3}{|}}{\overset{\overset{CH_3}{|}}{Si}}-O-\underset{\underset{CH_3}{|}}{\overset{\overset{CH_3}{|}}{Si}}-O-\underset{\underset{CH_3}{|}}{\overset{\overset{CH_3}{|}}{Si}}-O\cdots$$

The organic groups, with their weak intermolecular forces, give silicones flexibility, while the mineral-like —Si—O— backbone gives them thermal stability and inflammability.

Silicone chemists create structures similar to those of the silicates by adding various reactants to create silicone chains, sheets, and frameworks. Chains are oily liquids used as lubricants and as components of car polish and makeup. Sheets are components of gaskets, space suits, and contact lenses. Frameworks find uses as laminates on circuit boards, in nonstick cookware, and in artificial skin and bone.

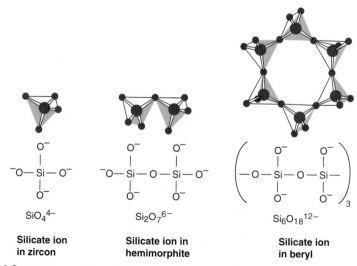

SiO₄⁴⁻ — SiO_4^{4-}

Si₂O₇⁶⁻ — $Si_2O_7^{6-}$

Si₆O₁₈¹²⁻ — $Si_6O_{18}^{12-}$

Silicate ion in zircon

Silicate ion in hemimorphite

Silicate ion in beryl

FIGURE 14.8 Structures of the silicate anions in some minerals.

Looking Backward and Forward: Groups 3A(13), 4A(14), and 5A(15)

Standing in Group 4A(14), we see Group 3A(13) as the transition from the *s* block of metals to the *p* block of mostly metalloids and nonmetals (Figure 14.9). Changes occur in physical behavior, as we move from metals to covalent networks, and in chemical behavior, as cations give way to covalent tetrahedra. Looking ahead to Group 5A(15), we find many compounds with expanded valence shells and the first appearance of monatomic anions.

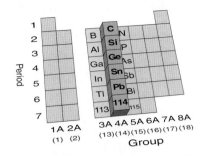

FIGURE 14.9 Standing in Group 4A(14), looking backward to 3A(13) and forward to 5A(15).

14.6 GROUP 5A(15): THE NITROGEN FAMILY

The first two elements of Group 5A(15), gaseous nonmetallic nitrogen (N) and solid nonmetallic phosphorus (P) have great industrial, environmental, and biological significance. Below these nonmetals are two metalloids, arsenic (As) and antimony (Sb), followed by the sole metal, bismuth (Bi), the last nonradioactive element in the periodic table [Group 5A(15) Family Portrait].

The Wide Range of Physical and Chemical Behavior in Group 5A(15)

Group 5A(15) displays the widest range of physical behavior we've seen so far. Nitrogen occurs as a gas consisting of N_2 molecules. Stronger dispersion forces due to heavier, more polarizable P atoms make phosphorus a solid. It has several allotropes. The white form consists of individual tetrahedral molecules (Figure 14.10A), making it low melting and soluble in nonpolar solvents; with a small 60° bond angle and, thus, weak P—P bonds, it is highly reactive (Figure 14.10B). In the red form, the P_4 units exist in chains, which make it much less reactive, high melting, and insoluble (Figure 14.10C). Arsenic consists of extended sheets, and a similar covalent network for Sb gives it a much higher melting point than metallic Bi.

Nearly all Group 5A(15) compounds have *covalent bonds*. A 5A element must *gain* three electrons to form an ion with a noble gas electron configuration. Enormous lattice energy results when 3− anions attract cations, but this occurs for N only with active metals, such as Li_3N and Mg_3N_2 (and perhaps with P in Na_3P).

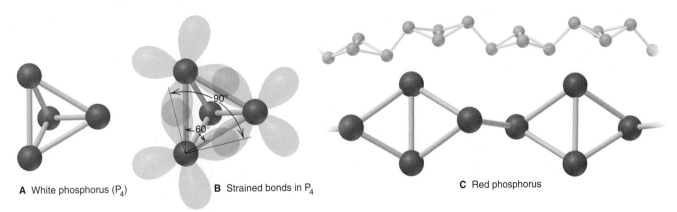

A White phosphorus (P_4)   **B** Strained bonds in P_4 **C** Red phosphorus

FIGURE 14.10 Two allotropes of phosphorus. A, White phosphorus exists as individual P_4 molecules, with the P—P bonds forming the edges of a tetrahedron. **B,** The reactivity of P_4 is due in part to the bond strain that arises from the 60° bond angle. Note how overlap of the 3*p* orbitals is decreased because they do not meet directly end to end (overlap is shown here for only three of the P—P bonds), which makes the bonds easier to break. **C,** In red phosphorus, one of the P—P bonds of the white form has broken and links the P_4 units together into long chains. Lone pairs (not shown) reside in *s* orbitals in both allotropes.

Key Atomic Properties, Physical Properties, and Reactions

KEY
Atomic No.
Symbol
Atomic mass
Valence e⁻ configuration
Common oxidation states

7	
N	
14.01	
$2s^2 2p^3$	
(**−3, +5,** +4, +3, +2, +1)	
15	
P	
30.97	
$3s^2 3p^3$	
(**−3, +5,** +3)	
33	
As	
74.92	
$4s^2 4p^3$	
(−3, +5, +3)	
51	
Sb	
121.8	
$5s^2 5p^3$	
(−3, +5, +3)	
83	
Bi	
209.0	
$6s^2 6p^3$	
(+3)	
115	Observed in experiments at Dubna, Russia, in 2003
(288)	
$7s^2 7p^3$	

$ns^2 np^3$

GROUP 5A(15)

Atomic radius (pm)	Ionic radius (pm)
N 75	N^{3-} 146
P 110	P^{3-} 212
As 120	
Sb 140	
Bi 150	Bi^{3+} 103

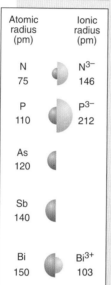

Atomic Properties

Group electron configuration is $ns^2 np^3$. The np sublevel is half-filled, with each p orbital containing one electron. The number of oxidation states decreases down the group, and the lower (+3) state becomes more common. Atomic properties follow generally expected trends. The large (~50%) increase in size from N to P correlates with the much lower IE and EN of P.

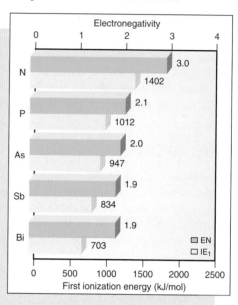

Physical Properties

Physical properties reflect the change from individual molecules (N, P) to network covalent solid (As, Sb) to metal (Bi). Thus, melting points increase and then decrease. Large atomic size and low atomic mass result in low density. Because mass increases more than size down the group, the density of the elements as solids increases. The dramatic increase from P to As is due to the intervening transition elements.

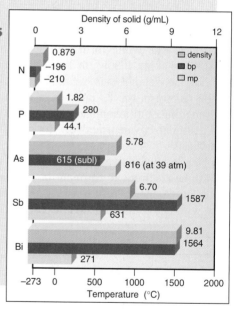

Reactions

1. Nitrogen is "fixed" industrially in the Haber process:

$$N_2(g) + 3H_2(g) \rightleftharpoons 2NH_3(g)$$

Further reactions convert NH_3 to NO, NO_2, and HNO_3 (*Highlights of Nitrogen Chemistry*). Hydrides of some other group members are formed from reaction in water (or with H_3O^+) of a metal phosphide, arsenide, and so forth:

$$Ca_3P_2(s) + 6H_2O(l) \longrightarrow 2PH_3(g) + 3Ca(OH)_2(aq)$$

2. Halides are formed by direct combination of the elements:

$$2E(s) + 3X_2 \longrightarrow 2EX_3 \quad \text{(E = all except N)}$$
$$EX_3 + X_2 \longrightarrow EX_5 \quad \text{(E = all except N and Bi with X = F and Cl, but no } BiCl_5; \text{ E = P for X = Br)}$$

3. Oxoacids are formed from the halides in a reaction with water that is common to many nonmetal halides:

$$EX_3 + 3H_2O(l) \longrightarrow H_3EO_3(aq) + 3HX(aq)$$
$$\text{(E = all except N)}$$
$$EX_5 + 4H_2O(l) \longrightarrow H_3EO_4(aq) + 5HX(aq)$$
$$\text{(E = all except N and Bi)}$$

Note that the oxidation number of E does *not* change.

As in Groups 3A and 4A, as we move down the group there are fewer oxidation states and the lower state becomes more prominent: N exhibits every state possible for a 5A element, from $+5$, as in HNO_3, to -3, as in NH_3; only the $+5$ and $+3$ states are common for P, As, and Sb; and $+3$ is the only common state of Bi. The oxides change from acidic to amphoteric to basic, and the lower oxide is more basic than the higher oxide because the lower oxide's E-to-O bond is more ionic.

Some characteristic reactions appear in the Family Portrait, but we point out some highlights here. All the elements form gaseous hydrides of formula EH_3. Ammonia is made industrially at high pressure and moderately high temperature:

$$N_2(g) + 3H_2(g) \rightleftharpoons 2NH_3(g)$$

The other hydrides are very poisonous and form by reaction in water of a metal phosphide, arsenide, and so forth, which acts as a strong base; for example,

$$Ca_3As_2(s) + 6H_2O(l) \longrightarrow 2AsH_3(g) + 3Ca(OH)_2(aq)$$

Molecular properties of the Group 5A(15) hydrides reveal some interesting patterns that appear again in Group 6A(16):

- Despite a much lower molar mass, NH_3 melts and boils at higher temperatures than the other 5A hydrides as a result of *H bonding*.
- Bond angles decrease from 107.3° for NH_3 to around 90° for the other hydrides, which suggests that the larger atoms use *un*hybridized *p* orbitals.
- E—H bond lengths increase down the group, so bond strength and thermal stability decrease: AsH_3 decomposes at 250°C, SbH_3 at 20°C, and BiH_3 at -45°C.

Through direct combination of the elements, the Group 5A(15) members form all possible trihalides (EX_3) and pentafluorides (EF_5), but few other pentahalides. As with the hydrides, stability of the halides decreases as the E—X bond becomes longer with larger halogens.

In an aqueous reaction pattern *typical of many nonmetal halides,* each 5A halide reacts with water to yield the hydrogen halide and the oxoacid, in which E has the *same* oxidation number as it had in the original halide. For example, PX_5 (O.N. of P = $+5$) produces HX and phosphoric acid (O.N. of P = $+5$):

$$PCl_5(s) + 4H_2O(l) \longrightarrow 5HCl(g) + H_3PO_4(l)$$

Highlights of Nitrogen Chemistry

The most striking highlight of nitrogen chemistry is the *inertness* of N_2. Even though the atmosphere consists of nearly four-fifths N_2 and one-fifth O_2, the searing temperature of a lightning bolt is needed to form significant amounts of nitrogen oxides. Indeed, N_2 reacts at high temperatures with H_2, Li, Group 2A(2) members, B, Al, C, Si, Ge, O_2, and many transition elements. Here we focus on the oxides and the oxoacids and their salts.

Nitrogen Oxides Nitrogen is remarkable for having six stable oxides, each with a *positive* heat of formation because of the great strength of the $N\equiv N$ bond (Table 14.2, next page). Unlike the hydrides and halides of nitrogen, the oxides are planar. Nitrogen displays all its positive oxidation states in these compounds, and in N_2O and N_2O_3, the two N atoms have different states. Of special interest are NO and NO_2.

Nitrogen monoxide (NO; also called nitric oxide) is an odd-electron molecule (see Section 10.1) with recently discovered biochemical functions ranging from neurotransmission to control of blood flow. Its commercial preparation occurs through the oxidation of ammonia during the production of nitric acid:

$$4NH_3(g) + 5O_2(g) \longrightarrow 4NO(g) + 6H_2O(g)$$

Table 14.2 Structures and Properties of the Nitrogen Oxides

Formula	Name	Space-filling Model	Lewis Structure	Oxidation State of N	ΔH_f° (kJ/mol) at 298 K	Comment
N_2O	Dinitrogen monoxide (dinitrogen oxide; nitrous oxide)		$:N{\equiv}N{-}\ddot{O}:$	+1 (0, +2)	82.0	Colorless gas; used as dental anesthetic ("laughing gas") and aerosol propellant
NO	Nitrogen monoxide (nitrogen oxide; nitric oxide)		$:\dot{N}{=}\ddot{O}:$	+2	90.3	Colorless, paramagnetic gas; biochemical messenger; air pollutant
N_2O_3	Dinitrogen trioxide			+3 (+2, +4)	83.7	Reddish brown gas (reversibly dissociates to NO and NO_2)
NO_2	Nitrogen dioxide			+4	33.2	Orange-brown, paramagnetic gas formed during HNO_3 manufacture; poisonous air pollutant
N_2O_4	Dinitrogen tetraoxide			+4	9.16	Colorless to yellow liquid (reversibly dissociates to NO_2)
N_2O_5	Dinitrogen pentaoxide			+5	11.3	Colorless, volatile solid consisting of NO_2^+ and NO_3^-; gas consists of N_2O_5 molecules

It also forms when air is heated to high temperatures in a car engine:

$$N_2(g) + O_2(g) \xrightarrow{\text{high } T} 2NO(g)$$

Heating converts NO to two other oxides:

$$3NO(g) \xrightarrow{\Delta} N_2O(g) + NO_2(g)$$

This redox reaction is called a **disproportionation,** one that involves a substance *acting as both an oxidizing and a reducing agent.* Thus, an atom in the reactant occurs in the products in both lower and higher states: the oxidation state of N in NO (+2) becomes +1 in N_2O and +4 in NO_2.

Nitrogen dioxide (NO_2), a brown poisonous gas, forms to a small extent when NO reacts with additional oxygen:

$$2NO(g) + O_2(g) \rightleftharpoons 2NO_2(g)$$

Like NO, NO_2 is an odd-electron molecule, but the unpaired electron is more localized on the N atom. Thus, NO_2 dimerizes reversibly to dinitrogen tetraoxide:

$$O_2N\cdot(g) + \cdot NO_2(g) \rightleftharpoons O_2N{-}NO_2(g) \quad \text{(or } N_2O_4\text{)}$$

In urban settings, a series of reactions involving sunlight, NO, NO_2, ozone (O_3), unburned gasoline, and various other species form photochemical smog.

Nitrogen Oxoacids and Oxoanions The two common nitrogen oxoacids are nitric acid and nitrous acid. The first two steps in the *Ostwald process* for the production of nitric acid are the oxidations of NH_3 to NO and of NO to NO_2. The final step is a disproportionation, as the oxidation numbers show:

$$3\overset{+4}{NO_2}(g) + H_2O(l) \longrightarrow 2H\overset{+5}{N}O_3(aq) + \overset{+2}{N}O(g)$$

The NO is recycled to make more NO_2.

In nitric acid, as in all oxoacids, *the acidic H is attached to one of the O atoms* (Figure 14.11A). In the laboratory, nitric acid is used as a strong oxidizing acid. The products of its reactions with metals vary with the metal's reactivity and the acid's concentration. In the following examples, notice from the net ionic equations that *the NO_3^- ion is the oxidizing agent*. Nitrate ion that is not reduced is a spectator ion and does not appear in the net ionic equations.

- With an active metal, such as Al, and dilute acid, N is reduced from the +5 state all the way to the −3 state in the ammonium ion, NH_4^+:

$$8Al(s) + 30HNO_3(aq; 1\ M) \longrightarrow 8Al(NO_3)_3(aq) + 3NH_4NO_3(aq) + 9H_2O(l)$$
$$8Al(s) + 30H^+(aq) + 3NO_3^-(aq) \longrightarrow 8Al^{3+}(aq) + 3NH_4^+(aq) + 9H_2O(l)$$

- With a less reactive metal, such as Cu, and more concentrated acid, N is reduced to the +2 state in NO:

$$3Cu(s) + 8HNO_3(aq; 3\ to\ 6\ M) \longrightarrow 3Cu(NO_3)_2(aq) + 4H_2O(l) + 2NO(g)$$
$$3Cu(s) + 8H^+(aq) + 2NO_3^-(aq) \longrightarrow 3Cu^{2+}(aq) + 4H_2O(l) + 2NO(g)$$

- With still more concentrated acid, N is reduced only to the +4 state in NO_2:

$$Cu(s) + 4HNO_3(aq; 12\ M) \longrightarrow Cu(NO_3)_2(aq) + 2H_2O(l) + 2NO_2(g)$$
$$Cu(s) + 4H^+(aq) + 2NO_3^-(aq) \longrightarrow Cu^{2+}(aq) + 2H_2O(l) + 2NO_2(g)$$

Nitrates form when HNO_3 reacts with metals or with their hydroxides, oxides, or carbonates. *All nitrates are soluble in water.*

Nitrous acid, HNO_2 (Figure 14.11B), a much weaker acid than HNO_3, forms when metal nitrites are treated with a strong acid:

$$NaNO_2(aq) + HCl(aq) \longrightarrow HNO_2(aq) + NaCl(aq)$$

These two acids reveal a *general pattern in relative acid strength among oxoacids:* the more O atoms bonded to the central nonmetal, the stronger the acid. We'll discuss the pattern quantitatively in Chapter 18.

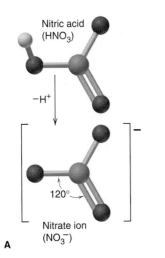

Nitric acid
(HNO₃)

−H⁺

120°

Nitrate ion
(NO₃⁻)

A

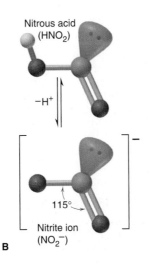

Nitrous acid
(HNO₂)

−H⁺

115°

Nitrite ion
(NO₂⁻)

B

FIGURE 14.11 The structures of nitric and nitrous acids and their oxoanions. A, Nitric acid loses a proton (H^+) to form the trigonal planar nitrate ion (one of three resonance forms is shown). **B,** Nitrous acid, a much weaker acid, forms the planar nitrite ion. Note the effect of nitrogen's lone pair in reducing the ideal 120° bond angle to 115° (one of two resonance forms is shown).

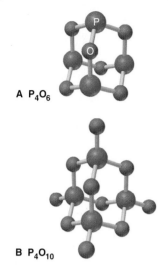

A P_4O_6

B P_4O_{10}

FIGURE 14.12 Important oxides of phosphorus. A, P_4O_6. **B,** P_4O_{10}.

Highlights of Phosphorus Chemistry: Oxides and Oxoacids

Phosphorus forms two important oxides, P_4O_6 and P_4O_{10}. Tetraphosphorus hexaoxide, P_4O_6, forms when white phosphorus, P_4, reacts with limited oxygen:

$$P_4(s) + 3O_2(g) \longrightarrow P_4O_6(s)$$

P_4O_6 has the tetrahedral orientation of the P atoms in P_4, with an O atom between each pair of P atoms (Figure 14.12A). It reacts with water to form phosphor*ous* acid (note the spelling):

$$P_4O_6(s) + 6H_2O(l) \longrightarrow 4H_3PO_3(l)$$

Despite the formula, H_3PO_3 has only two acidic H atoms; the third is bonded to the central P. It is a weak acid in water but reacts completely with strong base:

Salts of phosphorous acid contain the phosphite ion, HPO_3^{2-}.

Commonly known as "phosphorus pentoxide" from the empirical formula (P_2O_5), tetraphosphorus decaoxide, P_4O_{10}, forms when P_4 burns in excess O_2:

$$P_4(s) + 5O_2(g) \longrightarrow P_4O_{10}(s)$$

It has the structure of P_4O_6, but with another O atom bonded to each P atom (Figure 14.12B). P_4O_{10} is a powerful drying agent and, in a vigorous exothermic reaction with water, forms phosphoric acid (H_3PO_4), one of the "top-10" most important compounds in chemical manufacturing:

$$P_4O_{10}(s) + 6H_2O(l) \longrightarrow 4H_3PO_4(l)$$

The presence of many H bonds makes pure H_3PO_4 syrupy, more than 75 times as viscous as water. H_3PO_4 is a weak triprotic acid; in water, it loses one proton:

$$H_3PO_4(l) + H_2O(l) \rightleftharpoons H_2PO_4^-(aq) + H_3O^+(aq)$$

In strong base, however, it dissociates completely to give the three oxoanions:

dihydrogen phosphate ion   hydrogen phosphate ion   phosphate ion

Phosphoric acid has a central role in fertilizer production, and it is also used as a polishing agent for aluminum car trim and as an additive in soft drinks. The various phosphate salts have many essential applications, from paint stripper (Na_3PO_4) to rubber stabilizer (K_3PO_4) to fertilizer [$Ca(H_2PO_4)_2$ and $(NH_4)_2HPO_4$].

Polyphosphates are formed by heating hydrogen phosphates, which lose water as they form P—O—P linkages. This type of reaction, in which an H_2O molecule is lost for every pair of —OH groups that join, is called a **dehydration-condensation**; it occurs in the formation of polyoxoanion chains and other very large molecules, both synthetic and natural, made of repeating units.

14.7 GROUP 6A(16): THE OXYGEN FAMILY

Oxygen (O) and sulfur (S) are among the most important elements in industry, the environment, and organisms. Selenium (Se), tellurium (Te), radioactive polonium (Po), and newly synthesized element 116 lie beneath them in Group 6A(16) [Family Portrait, p. 453].

Family Portrait of Group 6A(16): The Oxygen Family

Key Atomic Properties, Physical Properties, and Reactions

KEY	Atomic No.
	Symbol
	Atomic mass
	Valence e⁻ configuration
	Common oxidation states

8
O
16.00
$2s^2 2p^4$
(−1, **−2**)

16
S
32.07
$3s^2 3p^4$
(**−2**, **+6**, +4, +2)

34
Se
78.96
$4s^2 4p^4$
(−2, **+6**, **+4**, +2)

52
Te
127.6
$5s^2 5p^4$
(−2, **+6**, **+4**, +2)

84
Po
(209)
$6s^2 6p^4$
(**+4**, +2)

116
Observed in experiments at Dubna, Russia, in 2004
(292)
$7s^2 7p^4$

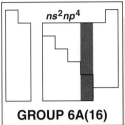

$ns^2 np^4$

GROUP 6A(16)

Atomic radius (pm)		Ionic radius (pm)
O 73		O²⁻ 140
S 103		S²⁻ 184
Se 119		Se²⁻ 198
Te 142		
Po 168		Po⁴⁺ 94

Atomic Properties

Group electron configuration is ns^2np^4. As in Groups 3A(13) and 5A(15), a lower (+4) oxidation state becomes more common down the group. Down the group, atomic and ionic size increase, and IE and EN decrease.

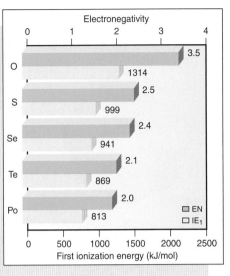

Electronegativity / First ionization energy (kJ/mol):
- O: EN 3.5, IE₁ 1314
- S: EN 2.5, IE₁ 999
- Se: EN 2.4, IE₁ 941
- Te: EN 2.1, IE₁ 869
- Po: EN 2.0, IE₁ 813

Physical Properties

Melting points increase through Te, which has covalent bonding, and then decrease for Po, which has metallic bonding. Densities of the elements as solids increase steadily.

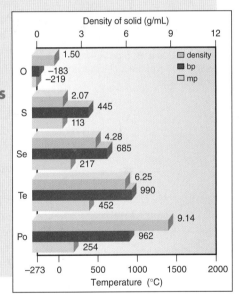

Density of solid (g/mL) / Temperature (°C):
- O: density 1.50, bp −183, mp −219
- S: density 2.07, bp 445, mp 113
- Se: density 4.28, bp 685, mp 217
- Te: density 6.25, bp 990, mp 452
- Po: density 9.14, bp 962, mp 254

Reactions

1. Halides are formed by direct combination:

$$E(s) + X_2(g) \longrightarrow \text{various halides}$$

(E = S, Se, Te; X = F, Cl)

2. The other elements in the group are oxidized by O_2:

$$E(s) + O_2(g) \longrightarrow EO_2 \quad (E = S, Se, Te, Po)$$

SO_2 is oxidized further, and the product is used in the final step of H_2SO_4 manufacture (*Highlights of Sulfur Chemistry*):

$$2SO_2(g) + O_2(g) \longrightarrow 2SO_3(g)$$

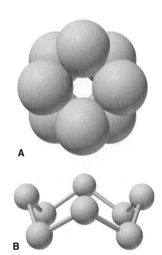

FIGURE 14.13 The cyclo-S_8 molecule. A, Top view of a space-filling model of the cyclo-S_8 molecule. **B,** Side view of a ball-and-stick model of the molecule; note the crownlike shape.

How Do the Oxygen and Nitrogen Families Compare Physically?

Group 6A(16) resembles Group 5A(15) in many respects. Like nitrogen, oxygen occurs as a low-boiling diatomic gas. Like phosphorus, sulfur occurs as a polyatomic molecular solid. Like arsenic, selenium occurs as a gray metalloid. Like antimony, tellurium is slightly more metallic than the preceding member of its group but still displays network covalent bonding. Finally, like bismuth, polonium is a metal. Thus, as in Group 5A, electrical conductivity increases steadily as bonding changes from individual molecules (insulators) to metalloid networks (semiconductors) to a metallic solid (conductor).

Allotropism is common in Group 6A(16). Oxygen has two forms: life-giving dioxygen (O_2) and poisonous triatomic ozone (O_3). O_2 gas is colorless, odorless, paramagnetic, and thermally stable. In contrast, O_3 gas is bluish, has a pungent odor, is diamagnetic, and decomposes in heat and in ultraviolet (UV) light:

$$2O_3(g) \xrightarrow{\text{UV}} 3O_2(g)$$

This ability to absorb high-energy photons makes stratospheric ozone vital to life, and we'll discuss its depletion in Chapter 16.

The S atom's ability to bond to itself over a wide range of bond lengths and angles makes sulfur the allotrope "champion" of the periodic table, with more than 10 forms. The most stable is orthorhombic α-S_8, which consists of crown-shaped molecules of eight atoms, called *cyclo-S_8* (Figure 14.13); all other S allotropes eventually revert to this one. Some selenium allotropes consist of crown-shaped Se_8 molecules. Gray Se consists of layers of helical chains. Its ability to conduct a current when exposed to visible light gave birth to the photocopying industry.

How Do the Oxygen and Nitrogen Families Compare Chemically?

Groups 5A(15) and 6A(16) also have several chemical similarities. Like N and P, O and S bond covalently with almost every other nonmetal, even though they occur as anions much more often. Se and Te form mostly covalent compounds, as do As and Sb, and Po forms many saltlike compounds, as does Bi. In contrast to nitrogen, oxygen has few common oxidation states, but the earlier pattern returns with the other members: among the common positive (+6 and +4) states, the +4 state is seen more often in Te and Po.

Oxygen's high EN (3.5) and great oxidizing strength are second only to those of fluorine. But the other 6A members are much less electronegative, occur as anions much less often, and form hydrides that exhibit no H bonding.

All the elements except O form foul-smelling, poisonous, gaseous hydrides by treatment with acid of the metal sulfide, selenide, and so forth. For example,

$$FeSe(s) + 2HCl(aq) \longrightarrow H_2Se(g) + FeCl_2(aq)$$

In their bonding and stability, Group 6A hydrides are similar to 5A hydrides:

- Only water forms H bonds, so it melts and boils at much higher temperatures than the other hydrides (see Figure 12.13).
- Bond angles drop from 104.5° (nearly tetrahedral) in H_2O to around 90° in hydrides of larger group members, suggesting that the central atom uses *un*hybridized *p* orbitals.
- E—H bond length increases and bond energy decreases down the group. One result is that 6A hydrides are acids in water, as we discuss in Chapter 18.

Except for O, the Group 6A elements form a wide range of halides whose stability depends on *crowding between lone pairs and surrounding halogen (X) atoms.* Therefore, with increasing size of E and X, E—X bond length increases, electron repulsions between lone pairs and X atoms weaken, and a greater number of stable halides form. Thus, S, Se, and Te form hexa-fluorides; Se, Te, and Po form tetrachlorides and tetrabromides; and Te and Po form tetraiodides.

Highlights of Oxygen Chemistry

Oxygen is the most abundant element on Earth's surface, occurring in air as the free element, combined with hydrogen in water, and combined in innumerable oxides, silicates, carbonates, and phosphates. Virtually all O_2 has a biological origin, having been formed for billions of years by photosynthetic algae and multicellular plants in an overall equation that looks simple but involves many steps:

$$nH_2O(l) + nCO_2(g) \xrightarrow{\text{light}} nO_2(g) + (CH_2O)_n \text{ (carbohydrates)}$$

The reverse process occurs during combustion and respiration.

Every element (except He, Ne, and Ar) forms at least one oxide, many by direct combination. For this reason, a useful way to classify elements is by the acid-base properties of their oxides. The oxides of Group 6A(16) exhibit expected trends down the group, with SO_3 the most acidic and PoO_2 the most basic.

Highlights of Sulfur Chemistry: Oxides and Oxoacids

Like phosphorus, sulfur forms two important oxides, sulfur dioxide (SO_2) and sulfur trioxide (SO_3). SO_2 is a colorless, choking gas that forms when S, H_2S, or a metal sulfide burns in air:

$$2H_2S(g) + 3O_2(g) \longrightarrow 2H_2O(g) + 2SO_2(g)$$
$$4FeS_2(s) + 11O_2(g) \longrightarrow 2Fe_2O_3(s) + 8SO_2(g)$$

In water, sulfur dioxide forms sulfurous acid, which exists in equilibrium with hydrated SO_2 rather than as independent H_2SO_3 molecules:

$$SO_2(aq) + H_2O(l) \rightleftharpoons [H_2SO_3(aq)] \rightleftharpoons H^+(aq) + HSO_3^-(aq)$$

(Similarly, carbonic acid occurs in equilibrium with hydrated CO_2 and cannot be isolated as H_2CO_3 molecules.) Sulfurous acid is weak and has two acidic protons, forming the hydrogen sulfite (bisulfite, HSO_3^-) and sulfite (SO_3^{2-}) ions with strong base. S is in the +4 state in SO_3^{2-}, so it can be oxidized easily to the +6 state; thus, sulfites are good reducing agents and are used to preserve foods and wine from air oxidation.

Most SO_2 produced industrially is used to make sulfuric acid. It is first oxidized to SO_3 by heating in O_2 over a catalyst:

$$SO_2(g) + \tfrac{1}{2}O_2(g) \xrightleftharpoons{\text{V}_2\text{O}_5/\text{K}_2\text{O catalyst}} SO_3(g)$$

We discuss catalysts in Chapter 16 and H_2SO_4 production in Chapter 21. These two sulfur oxides also form when sulfur impurities in coal burn and then oxidize further. In contact with rain, they form H_2SO_3 and H_2SO_4 and contribute to a major pollution problem that we discuss in Chapter 19.

Sulfuric acid ranks first among all industrial chemicals in mass produced. The fertilizer, pigment, textile, and detergent industries are just a few that depend on it. The concentrated acid is a viscous, colorless liquid that is 98% H_2SO_4 by mass. It is a strong acid, but only the first proton dissociates completely. The hydrogen sulfate (or bisulfate) ion that results is a weak acid:

hydrogen sulfate ion   sulfate ion

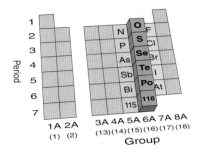

FIGURE 14.14 Standing in Group 6A(16), looking backward to Group 5A(15) and forward to Group 7A(17).

Looking Backward and Forward: Groups 5A(15), 6A(16), and 7A(17)

Groups 5A(15) and 6A(16) are very similar in their physical and chemical trends (Figure 14.14). Their greatest difference is the sluggish behavior of N_2 compared with the striking reactivity of O_2. In both groups, metals appear only as the largest members. From here on, metals and metalloids are left behind: all Group 7A(17) elements are reactive nonmetals. Anion formation, which was rare in 5A and more common in 6A, is a dominant feature of 7A, as is the number of covalent compounds the elements form with oxygen *and* with each other.

14.8 GROUP 7A(17): THE HALOGENS

Our last chance to view very active elements occurs in Group 7A(17). The halogens begin with fluorine (F), the strongest electron "grabber" of all. Chlorine (Cl), bromine (Br), and iodine (I) also form compounds with most elements, and even rare astatine (At) is thought to be reactive [Group 7A(17) Family Portrait, p. 457].

What Accounts for the Regular Changes in the Halogens' Physical Properties?

Like the alkali metals, the halogens display regular trends in physical properties. But they display opposite trends because of differences in bonding. Alkali metal atoms are held together by metallic bonding, which *decreases* in strength down the group. The halogens, on the other hand, exist as diatomic molecules that interact through dispersion forces, which *increase* in strength as the atoms become larger. Thus, at room temperature, F_2 is a very pale yellow gas, Cl_2 a yellow-green gas, Br_2 a brown-orange liquid, and I_2 a purple-black solid.

Why Are the Halogens So Reactive?

The Group 7A(17) elements form many ionic and covalent compounds: metal and nonmetal halides, halogen oxides, and oxoacids. Like the alkali metals, the halogens have an electron configuration one electron away from that of a noble gas: whereas a 1A metal atom must *lose* one electron, a 7A nonmetal atom must *gain* one. It fills its outer level in either of two ways:

1. Gaining an electron from a metal atom, thus forming a negative ion as the metal forms a positive one
2. Sharing an electron pair with a nonmetal atom, thus forming a covalent bond

Down the group, reactivity reflects the decrease in electronegativity, but the exceptional reactivity of elemental F_2 is also related to the weakness of the F—F bond. The F—F bond is short, but F is so small that lone pairs on one atom repel those on the other, which weakens the bond (Figure 14.15). As a result, F_2 reacts with every element (except He, Ne, and Ar), in many cases, explosively.

FIGURE 14.15 Bond energies and bond lengths of the halogens. A, In keeping with the increase in atomic size down the group, bond lengths increase steadily. **B,** The halogens show a general decrease in bond energy as bond length increases. However, F_2 deviates from this trend because its small, close, electron-rich atoms repel each other, thereby lowering its bond energy.

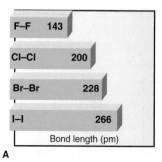

F—F	143
Cl—Cl	200
Br—Br	228
I—I	266
Bond length (pm)	

A

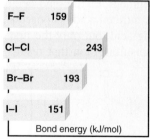

F—F	159
Cl—Cl	243
Br—Br	193
I—I	151
Bond energy (kJ/mol)	

B

Key Atomic Properties, Physical Properties, and Reactions

KEY
Atomic No.
Symbol
Atomic mass
Valence e⁻ configuration
Common oxidation states

| 9 | F | 19.00 | $2s^22p^5$ | (**−1**) |

Photograph not available

| 17 | Cl | 35.45 | $3s^23p^5$ | (**−1**, +7, +5, +3, +1) |

| 35 | Br | 79.90 | $4s^24p^5$ | (**−1**, +7, +5, +3, +1) |

| 53 | I | 126.9 | $5s^25p^5$ | (**−1**, +7, +5, +3, +1) |

| 85 | At | (210) | $6s^26p^5$ | (**−1**) |

Extremely rare, no sample available

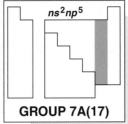

ns^2np^5

GROUP 7A(17)

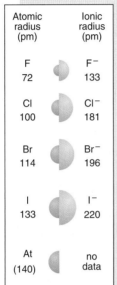

Atomic radius (pm)		Ionic radius (pm)
F 72		F⁻ 133
Cl 100		Cl⁻ 181
Br 114		Br⁻ 196
I 133		I⁻ 220
At (140)		no data

Atomic Properties

Group electron configuration is ns^2np^5; elements lack one electron to complete their outer level. The −1 oxidation state is the most common for all members. Except for F, the halogens exhibit all odd-numbered states (+7 through −1). Down the group, atomic and ionic size increase steadily, as IE and EN decrease.

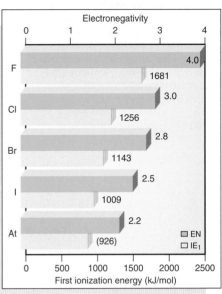

Electronegativity

	EN	IE₁
F	4.0	1681
Cl	3.0	1256
Br	2.8	1143
I	2.5	1009
At	2.2	(926)

First ionization energy (kJ/mol)

Physical Properties

Down the group, melting and boiling points increase smoothly as a result of stronger dispersion forces between larger molecules. The densities of the elements as liquids (at given T) increase steadily with molar mass.

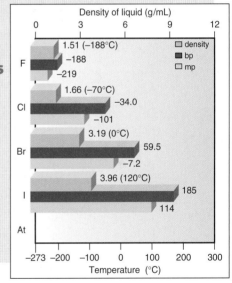

Density of liquid (g/mL)

density ■ bp □ mp

	density	bp	mp
F	1.51 (−188°C)	−188	−219
Cl	1.66 (−70°C)	−34.0	−101
Br	3.19 (0°C)	59.5	−7.2
I	3.96 (120°C)	185	114
At			

Temperature (°C)

Reactions

1. The halogens (X_2) oxidize many metals and nonmetals. The reaction with hydrogen, although not used commercially for HX production (except for high-purity HCl), is characteristic of these strong oxidizing agents:

$$X_2 + H_2(g) \longrightarrow 2HX(g)$$

2. The halogens disproportionate in water:

$$X_2 + H_2O(l) \rightleftharpoons HX(aq) + HXO(aq)$$
$$(X = Cl, Br, I)$$

In aqueous base, the reaction goes to completion to form hypohalites (*see text*) and, at higher temperatures, halates; for example:

$$3Cl_2(g) + 6OH^-(aq) \xrightarrow{\Delta} ClO_3^-(aq) + 5Cl^-(aq) + 3H_2O(l)$$

FIGURE 14.16 The relative oxidizing ability of the halogens. A, Halogen redox behavior is based on atomic properties such as electron affinity, ionic charge density, and electronegativity. A halogen (X_2) higher in the group can oxidize a halide ion (X^-) lower down. **B,** As an example, when aqueous Cl_2 is added to a solution of I^- *(top layer)*, it oxidizes the I^- to I_2, which dissolves in the CCl_4 solvent *(bottom layer)* to give a purple solution.

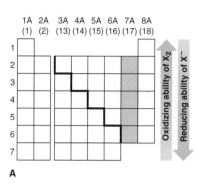

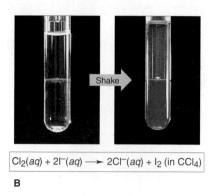

$$Cl_2(aq) + 2I^-(aq) \longrightarrow 2Cl^-(aq) + I_2 \text{ (in } CCl_4)$$

The halogens act as *oxidizing agents* in the majority of their reactions, and halogens higher in the group can oxidize halide ions lower down:

$$F_2(g) + 2X^-(aq) \longrightarrow 2F^-(aq) + X_2(aq) \quad (X = Cl, Br, I)$$

Thus, the oxidizing ability of X_2 *decreases* down the group: the lower the EN, the less strongly each X atom pulls electrons. And the reducing ability of X^- *increases* down the group: the larger the ion, the more easily it gives up its electron (Figure 14.16).

Highlights of Halogen Chemistry

Let's examine the compounds the halogens form with hydrogen and with each other, as well as their oxides, oxoanions, and oxoacids.

The Hydrogen Halides The halogens form gaseous hydrogen halides (HX) through direct combination with H_2 or through the action of a concentrated acid on the metal halide. Commercially, HCl forms as a by-product during the chlorination of hydrocarbons to form useful materials, such as poly(vinyl chloride).

In water, gaseous HX molecules form *hydrohalic acids.* Only HF, with its relatively short, strong bond, forms a weak acid:

$$HF(g) + H_2O(l) \rightleftharpoons H_3O^+(aq) + F^-(aq)$$

The others dissociate completely to form the stoichiometric amount of H_3O^+ ions:

$$HBr(g) + H_2O(l) \longrightarrow H_3O^+(aq) + Br^-(aq)$$

(Recall from Chapter 4 that this type of transfer of a proton from acid to H_2O is considered a type of acid-base reaction; we discuss this idea further in Chapter 18.)

Interhalogen Compounds: The "Halogen Halides" Halogens react exothermically with one another to form many *interhalogen compounds.* The simplest are diatomic molecules, such as ClF or BrCl. Every binary combination of the four common halogens is known. The more electronegative halogen is in the −1 oxidation state, and the less electronegative is in the +1 state; thus, for example, in BrCl, Br is +1 and Cl is −1. Interhalogens of general formula XY_n (n = 3, 5, 7) form when the larger members of the group (X) use d orbitals to expand their valence shells. In every case, the central atom has the *lower electronegativity* and a positive oxidation state; thus, for example, in BrF_3, Br is +3 and F is −1.

Halogen Oxides, Oxoacids, and Oxoanions The Group 7A(17) elements form many oxides that are *powerful oxidizing agents.* Dichlorine monoxide (Cl_2O), chlorine dioxide (ClO_2, with an unpaired electron and Cl in the unusual +4 oxidation state), and dichlorine heptaoxide (Cl_2O_7) are important examples.

The halogen oxoacids and oxoanions are produced by reaction of the halogens and their oxides with water. Most of the oxoacids are stable only in solution. Table 14.3 shows ball-and-stick models of the acids in which each atom has its lowest formal charge; note that H is bonded to O. (We'll discuss factors that determine the relative strengths of the halogen oxoacids in Chapter 18.)

Table 14.3 The Known Halogen Oxoacids*

Central Atom	Hypohalous Acid (HOX)	Halous Acid (HOXO)	Halic Acid (HOXO$_2$)	Perhalic Acid (HOXO$_3$)
	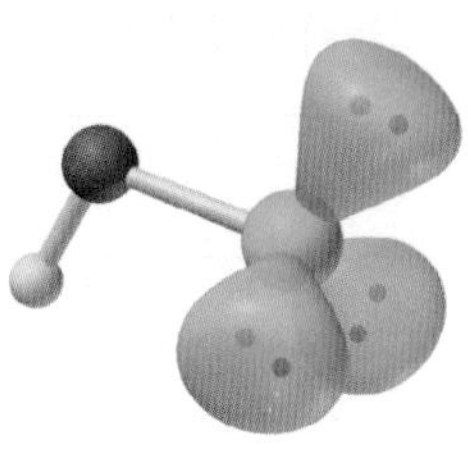	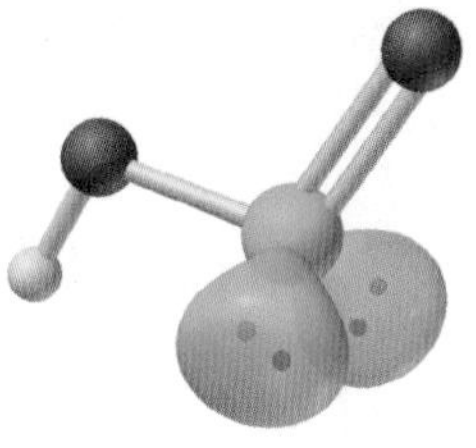	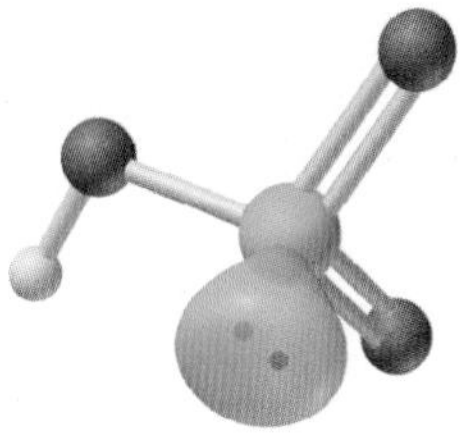	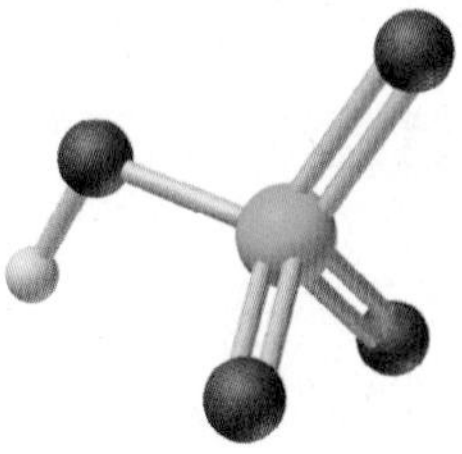
Fluorine	HOF	—	—	—
Chlorine	HOCl	HOClO	HOClO$_2$	HOClO$_3$
Bromine	HOBr	(HOBrO)?	HOBrO$_2$	HOBrO$_3$
Iodine	HOI	—	HOIO$_2$	HOIO$_3$, (HO)$_5$IO
Oxoanion	Hypohalite	Halite	Halate	Perhalate

*Lone pairs are shown only on the halogen atom, and each atom has its lowest formal charge.

The hypohalites (XO$^-$), halites (XO$_2^-$), and halates (XO$_3^-$) are oxidizing agents formed by aqueous disproportionation reactions [see Group 7A(17) Family Portrait]. Potassium chlorate is the oxidizer in "safety" matches. You may have heated it in the lab to form small amounts of O$_2$:

$$2KClO_3(s) \xrightarrow{\Delta} 2KCl(s) + 3O_2(g)$$

Some perhalates are especially strong oxidizing agents. Ammonium perchlorate, prepared from sodium perchlorate, is the oxidizing agent for the aluminum powder in the solid-fuel booster rocket of the space shuttle; each launch uses more than 700 tons of NH$_4$ClO$_4$:

$$10Al(s) + 6NH_4ClO_4(s) \longrightarrow 4Al_2O_3(s) + 12H_2O(g) + 3N_2(g) + 2AlCl_3(g)$$

14.9 GROUP 8A(18): THE NOBLE GASES

The Group 8A(18) elements are helium (He, the second most abundant element in the universe), neon (Ne), argon (Ar, which makes up about 0.93% of Earth's atmosphere), krypton (Kr), xenon (Xe), and radioactive radon (Rn). Only the last three form compounds [Group 8A(18) Family Portrait].

How Can Noble Gases Form Compounds?

Lying at the far right side of the periodic table, the Group 8A(18) elements consist of individual atoms with filled outer levels and the smallest radii in their periods: even Li, the smallest alkali metal (152 pm), is bigger than Rn, the largest noble gas (140 pm). These elements come as close to behaving as ideal gases as any substance. They condense and solidify at very low temperatures; in fact, He requires an increase in pressure to solidify, 25 atm at $-272.2°C$. With only dispersion forces at work, melting and boiling points increase with molar mass.

Ever since their discovery in the late 19th century, these elements were considered, and in fact, were generally referred to as, the "inert" gases. Atomic theory and, more important, all experiments had supported this idea. Then, in 1962, all this changed when the first noble gas compound was prepared.

The discovery of noble gas reactivity is a classic example of clear thinking in the face of an unexpected event. The young inorganic chemist Neil Bartlett was studying platinum fluorides. When he accidentally exposed PtF$_6$ to air, its deep-red color lightened slightly, and analysis showed that the PtF$_6$ had oxidized O$_2$ to form the ionic compound [O$_2$]$^+$[PtF$_6$]$^-$. Knowing that the IE$_1$ of O$_2$ to form

Family Portrait of Group 8A(18): The Noble Gases

Key Atomic Properties, Physical Properties, and Reactions

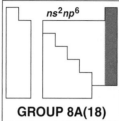

GROUP 8A(18)

ns^2np^6

KEY	Atomic No.
	Symbol
	Atomic mass
	Valence e⁻ configuration
	Common oxidation states

2
He
4.003
$1s^2$
(none)

10
Ne
20.18
$2s^22p^6$
(none)

18
Ar
39.95
$3s^23p^6$
(none)

36
Kr
83.80
$4s^24p^6$
(+2)

54
Xe
131.3
$5s^25p^6$
(+8, +6, +4, +2)

86
Rn
(222)
$6s^26p^6$
(+2)

Mass spectral peak

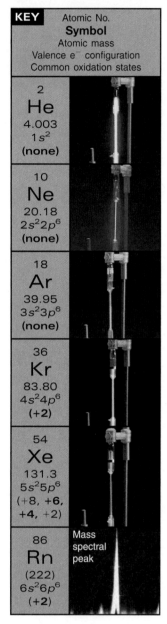

Atomic radius (pm)

He	31
Ne	71
Ar	98
Kr	112
Xe	131
Rn	(140)

Atomic Properties

Group electron configuration is $1s^2$ for He and ns^2np^6 for the others. The valence shell is filled. Only Kr, Xe, and Rn are known to form compounds. The more reactive Xe exhibits all even oxidation states (+2 to +8). This group contains the smallest atoms with the highest IEs in their periods. Down the group, atomic size increases and IE decreases steadily. (EN values are given only for Kr and Xe.)

Physical Properties

Melting and boiling points of these gaseous elements are extremely low but increase down the group because of stronger dispersion forces. Note the extremely small liquid ranges. Densities (at STP) increase steadily, as expected.

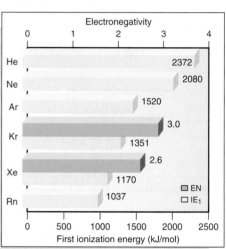

	Electronegativity	First ionization energy (kJ/mol)
He		2372
Ne		2080
Ar		1520
Kr	3.0	1351
Xe	2.6	1170
Rn		1037

EN
IE₁

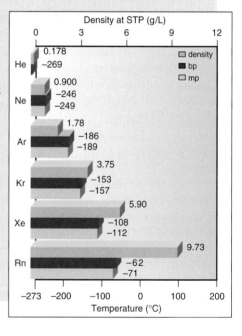

Density at STP (g/L)

	density	bp	mp
He	0.178	−269	
Ne	0.900	−246	−249
Ar	1.78	−186	−189
Kr	3.75	−153	−157
Xe	5.90	−108	−112
Rn	9.73	−62	−71

Temperature (°C)

O_2^+ (1175 kJ/mol) is very close to IE_1 of xenon (1170 kJ/mol), Bartlett reasoned that PtF_6 could oxidize xenon. He prepared $XePtF_6$, an orange-yellow solid, and within a few months, XeF_2 and XeF_4 were also prepared. In addition to its +2 and +4 oxidation states, Xe has the +6 state in several compounds, such as XeF_6 and XeO_3, and the +8 state in the unstable oxide, XeO_4. A few compounds of Kr and Rn have also been made.

Looking Backward and Forward: Groups 7A(17), 8A(18), and 1A(1)

The great reactivity of the Group 7A(17) elements, which form a host of anions, covalent oxides, and oxoanions, lies in stark contrast to the unreactivity of their 8A(18) neighbors. Filled outer levels render the noble gas atoms largely inert, with a limited ability to react directly only with highly electronegative fluorine. The least reactive family stands between the two most reactive: the halogens and the alkali metals (Figure 14.17), and atomic, physical, and chemical properties change dramatically from Group 8A(18) to Group 1A(1).

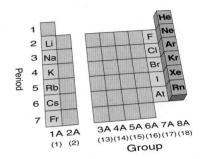

FIGURE 14.17 Standing in Group 8A(18), looking backward at the halogens, Group 7A(17), and ahead to the alkali metals, Group 1A(1).

CHAPTER REVIEW GUIDE

The following sections provide many aids to help you study this chapter. (Numbers in parentheses refer to pages, unless noted otherwise.)

● **LEARNING OBJECTIVES** *These are concepts and skills to review after studying this chapter.*

Related section (§) and end-of-chapter problem (EP) numbers are listed in parentheses.

1. Compare hydrogen with alkali metals and halogens, and distinguish saltlike from covalent hydrides (§ 14.1) (EPs 14.1–14.5)
2. Discuss key features of Group 1A(1), and understand how the ns^1 configuration explains physical and chemical properties (§ 14.2) (EPs 14.7–14.13)
3. Understand the anomalous behaviors of the Period 2 elements (§ 14.2) (EPs 14.6, 14.14, 14.20–14.22)
4. Discuss key features of Group 2A(2), and understand how the ns^2 configuration explains differences between Groups 1A(1) and 2A(2) (§ 14.3) (EPs 14.15, 14.17–14.19)
5. Describe the three main diagonal relationships (§ 14.3) (EPs 14.16, 14.45)
6. Discuss key features of Group 3A(13), especially patterns in oxidation state and oxide acidity; understand how the presence of d and f electrons affects group properties (§ 14.4) (EPs 14.25–14.32)
7. Discuss key features of Group 4A(14), especially patterns in oxidation state and oxide acidity; describe how types of bonding

affect physical behavior of Groups 4A to 6A; give examples of allotropism in these groups; and describe major aspects of carbon and silicon chemistry (§ 14.5) (EPs 14.33–14.45)
8. Discuss key features of Group 5A(15), especially patterns in oxidation state, oxide acidity, and hydride and halide structures; and describe the nitrogen and phosphorus oxides and oxoacids (§ 14.6) (EPs 14.46–14.56)
9. Discuss key features of Group 6A(16); compare the patterns in oxidation state, oxide acidity, and hydride and halide structures with those of Group 5A(15); and describe the sulfur oxides and oxoacids (§ 14.7) (EPs 14.57–14.65)
10. Discuss key features of Group 7A(17), understand how intermolecular forces and the ns^2np^5 configuration account for physical and chemical properties, and describe the halogen oxides and oxoacids (§ 14.8) (EPs 14.66–14.73)
11. Discuss key features of Group 8A(18), understand how intermolecular forces and the ns^2np^6 configuration account for physical and chemical properties, and explain how xenon can form compounds (§ 14.9) (EPs 14.74–14.76)

● **KEY TERMS** *These important terms appear in boldface in the chapter and are defined again in the Glossary.*

Section 14.3	Section 14.5	Section 14.6	
diagonal relationship (438)	allotrope (444)	disproportionation	dehydration-condensation
	silicate (446)	reaction (450)	reaction (452)
	silicone (446)		

PROBLEMS

Problems with colored numbers are answered in Appendix E. Sections match the text and provide the numbers of relevant sample problems. Bracketed problems are grouped in pairs (indicated by a short rule) that cover the same concept. Comprehensive Problems are based on material from any section or previous chapter.

Hydrogen, the Simplest Atom

14.1 Hydrogen has only one proton, but its IE_1 is much greater than that of lithium, which has three protons. Explain.

14.2 Complete and balance the following equations:
(a) An active metal reacting with acid,
$$Al(s) + HCl(aq) \longrightarrow$$
(b) A saltlike (alkali metal) hydride reacting with water,
$$LiH(s) + H_2O(l) \longrightarrow$$

14.3 Complete and balance the following equations:
(a) A saltlike (alkaline earth metal) hydride reacting with water,
$$CaH_2(s) + H_2O(l) \longrightarrow$$
(b) Reduction of a metal halide by hydrogen to form a metal,
$$PdCl_2(aq) + H_2(g) \longrightarrow$$

14.4 Compounds such as $NaBH_4$, $Al(BH_4)_3$, and $LiAlH_4$ are complex hydrides used as reducing agents in many syntheses.
(a) Give the oxidation state of each element in these compounds.
(b) Write a Lewis structure for the polyatomic anion in $NaBH_4$, and predict its shape.

14.5 Unlike the F^- ion, which has an ionic radius close to 133 pm in all alkali metal fluorides, the ionic radius of H^- varies from 137 pm in LiH to 152 pm in CsH. Suggest an explanation for the large variability in the size of H^- but not F^-.

Group 1A(1): The Alkali Metals

14.6 Lithium salts are often much less soluble in water than the corresponding salts of other alkali metals. For example, at 18°C, the concentration of a saturated LiF solution is 1.0×10^{-2} *M*, whereas that of a saturated KF solution is 1.6 *M*. How would you explain this behavior?

14.7 The alkali metals play virtually the same general chemical role in all their reactions. (a) What is this role? (b) How is it based on atomic properties? (c) Using sodium, write two balanced equations that illustrate this role.

14.8 How do atomic properties account for the low densities of the Group 1A(1) elements?

14.9 Each of the following properties shows regular trends in Group 1A(1). Predict whether each increases or decreases *down* the group: (a) density; (b) ionic size; (c) E—E bond energy; (d) IE_1; (e) magnitude of ΔH_{hydr} of E^+ ion.

14.10 Predict whether each of the following properties increases or decreases *up* Group 1A(1): (a) melting point; (b) E—E bond length; (c) hardness; (d) molar volume; (e) lattice energy of EBr.

14.11 Write a balanced equation for the formation from its elements of sodium peroxide, an industrial bleach.

14.12 Write a balanced equation for the formation of rubidium bromide through a reaction of a strong acid and a strong base.

14.13 Although the alkali metal halides can be prepared directly from the elements, the far less expensive industrial route is treatment of the metal carbonate or hydroxide with aqueous hydrohalic acid (HX) followed by recrystallization. Balance the reaction between potassium carbonate and aqueous hydriodic acid.

14.14 Lithium forms several useful organolithium compounds. Calculate the mass percent of Li in the following:
(a) Lithium stearate ($C_{17}H_{35}COOLi$), a water-resistant grease used in cars because it does not harden at cold temperatures
(b) Butyllithium (LiC_4H_9), a reagent in organic syntheses

Group 2A(2): The Alkaline Earth Metals

14.15 How do Groups 1A(1) and 2A(2) compare with respect to reaction of the metals with water?

14.16 Alkaline earth metals are involved in two key diagonal relationships in the periodic table. (a) Give the two pairs of elements in these diagonal relationships. (b) For each pair, cite two similarities that demonstrate the relationship. (c) Why are the members of each pair so similar in behavior?

14.17 The melting points of alkaline earth metals are many times higher than those of the alkali metals. Explain this difference on the basis of atomic properties. Name three other physical properties for which Group 2A(2) metals have higher values than the corresponding 1A(1) metals.

14.18 Write a balanced equation for each reaction:
(a) "Slaking" (treatment with water) of lime, CaO
(b) Combustion of calcium in air

14.19 Write a balanced equation for each reaction:
(a) Thermal decomposition of witherite (barium carbonate)
(b) Neutralization of stomach acid (HCl) by milk of magnesia (magnesium hydroxide)

14.20 In some reactions, Be behaves like a typical alkaline earth metal; in others, it does not. Complete and balance the following equations:
(a) $BeO(s) + H_2O(l) \longrightarrow$
(b) $BeCl_2(l) + Cl^-(l;$ from molten NaCl) $\longrightarrow$
In which reaction does Be behave like the other Group 2A(2) members?

Group 3A(13): The Boron Family

14.21 How does the maximum oxidation number vary across a period in the main groups? Is the pattern in Period 2 different?

14.22 What correlation, if any, exists for the Period 2 elements between group number and the number of covalent bonds the element typically forms? How is the correlation different for elements in Periods 3 to 6?

14.23 How do the transition metals in Period 4 affect the pattern of ionization energies in Group 3A(13)?

14.24 How do the acidities of aqueous solutions of Tl_2O and Tl_2O_3 compare with each other? Explain.

14.25 Despite the expected decrease in atomic size, there is an unexpected drop in the first ionization energy between Groups 2A(2) and 3A(13) in Periods 2 through 4. Explain this pattern in terms of electron configurations and orbital energies.

14.26 Rank the following oxides in order of increasing aqueous *acidity*: Ga_2O_3, Al_2O_3, In_2O_3.

14.27 Rank the following hydroxides in order of increasing aqueous *basicity*: $Al(OH)_3$, $B(OH)_3$, $In(OH)_3$.

14.28 Thallium forms the compound TlI_3. What is the apparent oxidation state of Tl in this compound? Given that the anion is I_3^-, what is the actual oxidation state of Tl? Draw the shape of the anion, giving its VSEPR class and bond angles. Propose a reason why the compound does not exist as $(Tl^{3+})(I^-)_3$.

14.29 Very stable dihalides of the Group 3A(13) metals are known. What is the apparent oxidation state of Ga in $GaCl_2$? Given that $GaCl_2$ consists of a Ga^+ cation and a $GaCl_4^-$ anion, what are the actual oxidation states of Ga? Draw the shape of the anion, giving its VSEPR class and bond angles.

14.30 Give the name and symbol or formula of a Group 3A(13) element or compound that fits each description or use:
(a) Largest temperature range for liquid state of an element
(b) Metal protected from oxidation by adherent oxide coat
(c) Toxic metal that lies between two other toxic metals

14.31 Indium (In) reacts with HCl to form a diamagnetic solid with the formula $InCl_2$.
(a) Write condensed electron configurations for In, In^+, In^{2+}, and In^{3+}.
(b) Which of these species is (are) diamagnetic and which paramagnetic?
(c) What is the apparent oxidation state of In in $InCl_2$?
(d) Given your answers to parts (b) and (c), explain how $InCl_2$ can be diamagnetic.

14.32 Boric acid, $B(OH)_3$ (or H_3BO_3), does not lose a proton in water, but rather bonds to the O atom of an H_2O molecule, which then releases an H^+ ion to form the $B(OH)_4^-$ ion. Use VSEPR theory to draw structures, with ideal bond angles, for boric acid and the anion.

Group 4A(14): The Carbon Family

14.33 How do the physical properties of a network covalent solid and a molecular covalent solid differ? Why?

14.34 How does the basicity of SnO_2 in water compare with that of CO_2? Explain.

14.35 Nearly every compound of silicon has the element in the +4 oxidation state. In contrast, most compounds of lead have the element in the +2 state.
(a) What general observation do these facts illustrate?
(b) Explain in terms of atomic and molecular properties.
(c) Give an analogous example from Group 3A(13).

14.36 The sum of IE_1 through IE_4 for Group 4A(14) elements shows a decrease from C to Si, a slight increase from Si to Ge, a decrease from Ge to Sn, and an increase from Sn to Pb.
(a) What is the expected trend for ionization energy down a group?
(b) Suggest a reason for the deviations from the expected trend.
(c) Which group might show even greater deviations?

14.37 Give explanations for the large drops in melting point from C to Si and from Ge to Sn.

14.38 What is an allotrope? Name a Group 4A(14) element that exhibits allotropism, and name its three allotropes.

14.39 Even though EN values vary relatively little down Group 4A(14), the elements change from nonmetal to metal. Explain.

14.40 How do atomic properties account for the enormous number of carbon compounds? Why don't other Group 4A(14) elements behave similarly?

14.41 Draw a Lewis structure for
(a) The cyclic silicate ion $Si_4O_{12}^{8-}$
(b) A cyclic hydrocarbon with formula C_4H_8

14.42 Draw a Lewis structure for
(a) The cyclic silicate ion $Si_6O_{18}^{12-}$
(b) A cyclic hydrocarbon with formula C_6H_{12}

14.43 Zeolite A, $Na_{12}[(AlO_2)_{12}(SiO_2)_{12}] \cdot 27H_2O$, is used to soften water by replacing Ca^{2+} and Mg^{2+} with Na^+. Hard water from a certain source is 4.5×10^{-3} M Ca^{2+} and 9.2×10^{-4} M Mg^{2+}, and a pipe delivers 25,000 L of this hard water per day. What mass (in kg) of zeolite A is needed to soften a week's supply of the water? (Assume zeolite A loses its capacity to exchange ions when 85 mol % of its Na^+ has been lost.)

14.44 Give the name and symbol or formula of a Group 4A(14) element or compound that fits each description or use:
(a) Hardest known substance
(b) Medicinal antacid
(c) Atmospheric gas implicated in the greenhouse effect
(d) Gas that binds to iron(II) in blood
(e) Toxic metal found in plumbing and paints

14.45 One similarity between B and Si is the explosive combustion of their hydrides in air. Write balanced equations for the combustion of B_2H_6 and of Si_4H_{10}.

Group 5A(15): The Nitrogen Family

14.46 The Group 5A(15) elements form all the trihalides but not pentahalides. Explain.

14.47 As you move down Group 5A(15), the melting points of the elements increase and then decrease. Explain.

14.48 (a) What is the range of oxidation states shown by the elements of Group 5A(15) as you move down the group?
(b) How does this range illustrate the general rule for the range of oxidation states in groups on the right side of the periodic table?

14.49 (a) How does the type of bonding in element oxides correlate with the electronegativity of the elements?
(b) How does the acid-base behavior of element oxides correlate with the electronegativity of the elements?

14.50 (a) How does the metallic character of an element correlate with the *acidity* of its oxide?
(b) What trends, if any, exist in oxide *basicity* across a period and down a group?

14.51 Rank the following oxides in order of increasing acidity in water: Sb_2O_3, Bi_2O_3, P_4O_{10}, Sb_2O_5.

14.52 Complete and balance the following:
(a) $As(s) + \text{excess } O_2(g) \longrightarrow$
(b) $Bi(s) + \text{excess } F_2(g) \longrightarrow$
(c) $Ca_3As_2(s) + H_2O(l) \longrightarrow$

14.53 Complete and balance the following:
(a) $\text{Excess } Sb(s) + Br_2(l) \longrightarrow$
(b) $HNO_3(aq) + MgCO_3(s) \longrightarrow$
(c) $PF_5(g) + H_2O(l) \longrightarrow$

14.54 The pentafluorides of the larger members of Group 5A(15) have been prepared, but N can have only eight electrons. A claim has been made that, at low temperatures, a compound with the empirical formula NF_5 forms. Draw a possible Lewis structure for this compound. (*Hint:* NF_5 is ionic.)

14.55 Give the name and symbol or formula of a Group 5A(15) element or compound that fits each description or use:
(a) Hydride produced at multimillion-ton level
(b) Element(s) essential in plant nutrition
(c) Oxide used as a laboratory drying agent

(d) Odd-electron molecule (two examples)

(e) Element that is an electrical conductor

14.56 Nitrous oxide (N_2O), the "laughing gas" used as an anesthetic by dentists, is made by thermal decomposition of solid NH_4NO_3. Write a balanced equation for this reaction. What are the oxidation states of N in NH_4NO_3 and in N_2O?

Group 6A(16): The Oxygen Family

14.57 Rank the following in order of increasing electrical conductivity, and explain your ranking: Po, S, Se.

14.58 The oxygen and nitrogen families have some obvious similarities and differences.

(a) State two general physical similarities between Group 5A(15) and 6A(16) elements.

(b) State two general chemical similarities between Group 5A(15) and 6A(16) elements.

(c) State two chemical similarities between P and S.

(d) State two physical similarities between N and O.

(e) State two chemical differences between N and O.

14.59 A molecular property of the Group 6A(16) hydrides changes abruptly down the group. This change has been explained in terms of a change in orbital hybridization.

(a) Between what periods does the change occur?

(b) What is the change in the molecular property?

(c) What is the change in hybridization?

(d) What other group displays a similar change?

14.60 Complete and balance the following:

(a) $NaHSO_4(aq) + NaOH(aq) \longrightarrow$

(b) $S_8(s) + \text{excess } F_2(g) \longrightarrow$

(c) $FeS(s) + HCl(aq) \longrightarrow$

14.61 Complete and balance the following:

(a) $H_2S(g) + O_2(g) \longrightarrow$

(b) $SO_3(g) + H_2O(l) \longrightarrow$

(c) $SF_4(g) + H_2O(l) \longrightarrow$

14.62 Is each oxide basic, acidic, or amphoteric in water: (a) SeO_2; (b) N_2O_3; (c) K_2O; (d) BeO; (e) BaO?

14.63 Is each oxide basic, acidic, or amphoteric in water: (a) MgO; (b) N_2O_5; (c) CaO; (d) CO_2; (e) TeO_2?

14.64 Give the name and symbol or formula of a Group 6A(16) element or compound that fits each description or use:

(a) Unstable allotrope of oxygen

(b) Oxide having sulfur in the same oxidation state as in sulfuric acid

(c) Air pollutant produced by burning sulfur-containing coal

14.65 Disulfur decafluoride is intermediate in reactivity between SF_4 and SF_6. It disproportionates at 150°C to these monosulfur fluorides. Write a balanced equation for this reaction, and give the oxidation state of S in each compound.

Group 7A(17): The Halogens

14.66 Iodine monochloride and elemental bromine have nearly the same molar mass and liquid density but very different boiling points.

(a) What molecular property is primarily responsible for this difference in boiling point? What atomic property gives rise to it? Explain.

(b) Which substance has a higher boiling point? Why?

14.67 Explain the change in physical state down Group 7A(17) in terms of molecular properties.

14.68 (a) What are the common oxidation states of the halogens?

(b) Give an explanation based on electron configuration for the range and values of the oxidation states of chlorine.

(c) Why is fluorine an exception to the pattern of oxidation states found for the other group members?

14.69 Select the stronger bond in each pair:

(a) Cl—Cl or Br—Br

(b) Br—Br or I—I

(c) F—F or Cl—Cl. Why doesn't the F—F bond strength follow the group trend?

14.70 A halogen (X_2) disproportionates in base in several steps to X^- and XO_3^-. Write the overall equation for the disproportionation of Br_2 to Br^- and BrO_3^-.

14.71 Complete and balance the following equations. If no reaction occurs, write NR:

(a) $I_2(s) + H_2O(l) \longrightarrow$

(b) $Br_2(l) + I^-(aq) \longrightarrow$

(c) $CaF_2(s) + H_2SO_4(l) \longrightarrow$

14.72 Complete and balance the following equations. If no reaction occurs, write NR:

(a) $Cl_2(g) + I^-(aq) \longrightarrow$

(b) $Br_2(l) + Cl^-(aq) \longrightarrow$

(c) $ClF(g) + F_2(g) \longrightarrow$

14.73 An industrial chemist treats solid NaCl with concentrated H_2SO_4 and obtains gaseous HCl and $NaHSO_4$. When she substitutes solid NaI for NaCl, gaseous H_2S, solid I_2, and S_8 are obtained but no HI.

(a) What type of reaction did the H_2SO_4 undergo with NaI?

(b) Why does NaI, but not NaCl, cause this type of reaction?

(c) To produce HI(g) by the reaction of NaI with an acid, how does the acid have to differ from sulfuric acid?

Group 8A(18): The Noble Gases

14.74 Which noble gas is the most abundant in the universe? In Earth's atmosphere?

14.75 Why do the noble gases have such low boiling points?

14.76 Explain why Xe and, to a limited extent, Kr form compounds, whereas He, Ne, and Ar do not.

Comprehensive Problems

Problems with an asterisk (*) are more challenging.

14.77 The interhalogen IF undergoes the reaction depicted below (I is purple and F is green):

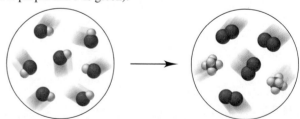

14.78 The main reason alkali metal dihalides (MX_2) do *not* form is the high IE_2 of the metal.

(a) Why is IE_2 so high for alkali metals?

(b) The IE_2 for Cs is 2255 kJ/mol, low enough for CsF_2 to form exothermically ($\Delta H_f^\circ = -125$ kJ/mol). This compound cannot be synthesized, however, because CsF forms with a much greater release of heat ($\Delta H_f^\circ = -530$ kJ/mol). Thus, the breakdown of CsF_2 to CsF happens readily. Write the equation for this breakdown, and calculate the heat of reaction per mole of CsF.

14.79 Xenon tetrafluoride reacts with antimony pentafluoride to form the following ionic complex: $[XeF_3]^+[SbF_6]^-$. (a) Which of the following illustrates the molecular shapes of the reactants and product? (b) How, if at all, does the hybridization of xenon change in the reaction?

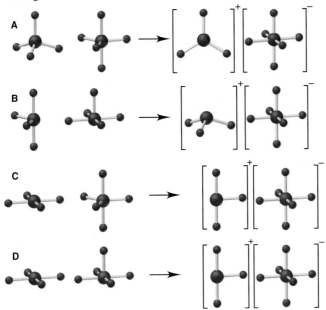

14.80 Semiconductors made from elements in Groups 3A(13) and 5A(15) are typically prepared by direct reaction of the elements at high temperature. An engineer treats 32.5 g of molten gallium with 20.4 L of white phosphorus vapor at 515 K and 195 kPa. If purification losses are 7.2% by mass, how many grams of gallium phosphide will be prepared?

* 14.81 Two substances with empirical formula HNO are hyponitrous acid ($M = 62.04$ g/mol) and nitroxyl ($M = 31.02$ g/mol).
(a) What is the molecular formula of each species?
(b) For each species, draw the Lewis structure having the lowest formal charges. (*Hint:* Hyponitrous acid has an N=N bond.)
(c) Predict the shape around the N atoms of each species.
(d) When hyponitrous acid loses two protons, it forms the hyponitrite ion. Because the double bond restricts rotation (Section 11.2), there are two possible structures for this ion; draw them.

14.82 For the species CO, CN^-, and C_2^{2-},
(a) Draw their Lewis structures.
(b) Draw their MO diagrams (assume $2s$-$2p$ mixing, as in N_2), and give the bond order and electron configuration for each.

* 14.83 The Ostwald process is a series of three reactions used for the industrial production of nitric acid from ammonia.
(a) Write a series of balanced equations for the Ostwald process.
(b) If NO is *not* recycled, how many moles of NH_3 are consumed per mole of HNO_3 produced?
(c) In a typical industrial unit, the process is very efficient, with a 96% yield for the first step. Assuming 100% yields for the subsequent steps, what volume of nitric acid (60.% by mass; $d = 1.37$ g/mL) can be prepared for each cubic meter of a gas mixture that is 90.% air and 10.% NH_3 by volume at the industrial conditions of 5.0 atm and 850.°C?

14.84 What is a disproportionation reaction, and which of the following fit the description?
(a) $I_2(s) + KI(aq) \longrightarrow KI_3(aq)$
(b) $2ClO_2(g) + H_2O(l) \longrightarrow HClO_3(aq) + HClO_2(aq)$

(c) $Cl_2(g) + 2NaOH(aq) \longrightarrow$
$$NaCl(aq) + NaClO(aq) + H_2O(l)$$
(d) $NH_4NO_2(s) \longrightarrow N_2(g) + 2H_2O(g)$
(e) $3MnO_4^{2-}(aq) + 2H_2O(l) \longrightarrow$
$$2MnO_4^-(aq) + MnO_2(s) + 4OH^-(aq)$$
(f) $3AuCl(s) \longrightarrow AuCl_3(s) + 2Au(s)$

14.85 Which group(s) of the periodic table is (are) described by each of the following general statements?
(a) The elements form neutral compounds of VSEPR class AX_3E.
(b) The free elements are strong oxidizing agents and form monatomic ions and oxoanions.
(c) The valence electron configuration allows the atoms to form compounds by combining with two atoms that donate one electron each.
(d) The free elements are strong reducing agents, show only one nonzero oxidation state, and form mainly ionic compounds.
(e) The elements can form stable compounds with only three bonds, but as a central atom, they can accept a pair of electrons from a fourth atom without expanding their valence shell.
(f) Only larger members of the group are chemically active.

14.86 Bromine monofluoride (BrF) disproportionates to bromine gas and bromine tri- and pentafluorides. Use the following to find ΔH_{rxn}° for the decomposition of BrF to its elements:

$3BrF(g) \longrightarrow Br_2(g) + BrF_3(l)$	$\Delta H_{rxn} = -125.3$ kJ
$5BrF(g) \longrightarrow 2Br_2(g) + BrF_5(l)$	$\Delta H_{rxn} = -166.1$ kJ
$BrF_3(l) + F_2(g) \longrightarrow BrF_5(l)$	$\Delta H_{rxn} = -158.0$ kJ

* 14.87 In addition to Al_2Cl_6, aluminum forms other species with bridging halide ions to two aluminum atoms. One such species is the ion $Al_2Cl_7^-$. The ion is symmetrical, with a 180° Al—Cl—Al bond angle.
(a) What orbitals does Al use to bond with the Cl atoms?
(b) What is the shape around each Al?
(c) What is the hybridization of the central Cl?
(d) What do the shape and hybridization suggest about the presence of lone pairs of electrons on the central Cl?

14.88 The bond angles in the nitrite ion, nitrogen dioxide, and the nitronium ion (NO_2^+) are 115°, 134°, and 180°, respectively. Explain these values using Lewis structures and VSEPR theory.

14.89 The triatomic molecular ion H_3^+ was first detected and characterized by J. J. Thomson using mass spectrometry. Use the bond energy of H_2 (432 kJ/mol) and the proton affinity of H_2 ($H_2 + H^+ \longrightarrow H_3^+$; $\Delta H = -337$ kJ/mol) to calculate the heat of reaction for $H + H + H^+ \longrightarrow H_3^+$.

14.90 Element E forms an oxide of general structure A and a chloride of general structure B:

* 14.91 Copper(II) hydrogen arsenite ($CuHAsO_3$) is a green pigment once used in wallpaper; in fact, forensic evidence suggests that Napoleon may have been poisoned by arsenic from his wallpaper. In damp conditions, mold metabolizes this compound to trimethylarsenic [$(CH_3)_3As$], a highly toxic gas.
(a) Calculate the mass percent of As in each compound.
(b) How much $CuHAsO_3$ must react to reach a toxic level in a room that measures 12.35 m × 7.52 m × 2.98 m (arsenic is toxic at 0.50 mg/m³)?

15

Organic Compounds and the Atomic Properties of Carbon

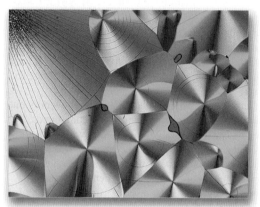

Organic Beauty *A polarized light micrograph of crystals of the amino acid tryptophan reveals a striking pattern. As you'll see in this chapter, organic substances occur throughout every living thing and as countless industrial and medical products.*

Outline

Key Principles
to focus on while studying this chapter

- Carbon's unusual ability to bond to other carbons and to many other nonmetals gives its compounds *structural complexity* and *chemical diversity.* The diversity arises from the presence of *functional groups,* specific combinations of bonded atoms that react in characteristic ways *(Section 15.1).*

- *Hydrocarbons* (compounds containing only C and H) are classified as *alkanes* (all single bonds), *alkenes* (at least one C=C bond), *alkynes* (at least one C≡C bond), and *aromatic* (at least one planar ring with delocalized π electrons). The C=C and C≡C bonds are functional groups *(Section 15.2).*

- Two kinds of *isomers* are important in organic chemistry. *Constitutional (structural) isomers* have different arrangements of atoms. *Stereoisomers* have the same atom arrangement but different spatial orientations. The two types of stereoisomers are either *optical isomers,* mirror images that cannot be superimposed, or *geometric (cis-trans) isomers,* which have different orientations of groups around a C=C bond *(Section 15.2).*

- Three common types of organic reactions are *addition* (two atoms or groups are added and a C=C bond is converted to a C—C bond), *elimination* (two atoms or groups are removed and a C—C bond is converted to a C=C bond), and *substitution* (one atom or group replaces another) *(Section 15.3).*

- *Functional groups* undergo characteristic reactions: groups with only single bonds (*alcohol, amine,* and *alkyl halide*) undergo substitution or elimination; groups with double bonds (*alkene, aldehyde,* and *ketone*) and those with triple bonds (*alkyne* and *nitrile*) undergo addition; and groups with both single and double bonds (*acids, esters,* and *amides*) undergo substitution *(Section 15.4).*

- *Polymers* are made by covalently linking many small repeat units (*monomers*). The monomer can be selected to give *synthetic polymers* desired properties. *Addition polymers* form through a *free-radical chain reaction* involving monomers with a C=C group. *Condensation polymers* consist of monomers with two functional groups that link together by *dehydration-condensation reactions* (Section 15.5).

- *Polysaccharides* (monomer, *sugars*), *proteins* (monomer, *amino acids*), and *nucleic acids* (monomer, *nucleotides*) are *natural polymers.* DNA occurs as a *double helix,* with bases in each strand H-bonded to specific bases in the other. The *base sequence* of an organism's DNA determines the *amino-acid sequences* of its proteins, which determine the protein's structure and function *(Section 15.6).*

Is there any chemical system more remarkable than a living cell? Through delicately controlled mechanisms, it oxidizes food for energy, maintains the concentrations of thousands of aqueous components, interacts continuously with its environment, synthesizes both simple and complex molecules, and even reproduces itself! For all our technological prowess, no human-made system even approaches the cell in its complexity and sheer elegance of function.

This amazing chemical machine consumes, creates, and consists largely of *organic compounds*. Except for a few inorganic salts and ever-present water, nearly everything you put into or on your body—food, medicine, cosmetics, and clothing—consists of organic compounds. Organic fuels warm our homes, cook our meals, and power our society. Major industries are devoted to producing organic compounds, such as polymers, pharmaceuticals, and insecticides.

What *is* an organic compound? Dictionaries define it as "a compound of carbon," but that definition is too general because it includes carbonates, cyanides, carbides, cyanates, and other carbon-containing ionic compounds that most chemists classify as inorganic. Here is a more specific definition: all **organic compounds** contain carbon, nearly always bonded to other carbons and hydrogen, and often to other elements.

In the early 19th century, organic compounds were thought to be fundamentally different from inorganic compounds, to possess a spiritual "vital force," and to be impossible to synthesize. Today, we know that *the same chemical principles govern organic and inorganic systems* because the behavior of a compound arises from the properties of its elements, no matter how marvelous that behavior may be.

15.1 THE SPECIAL NATURE OF CARBON AND THE CHARACTERISTICS OF ORGANIC MOLECULES

Although there is nothing mystical about organic molecules, their indispensable role in biology and industry leads us to ask if carbon has some extraordinary attributes that give it a special chemical "personality." Of course, each element has its own specific properties, and carbon is no more unique than sodium, hafnium, or any other element. But the atomic properties of carbon do give it bonding capabilities beyond those of any other element, which in turn lead to the two obvious characteristics of organic molecules—structural complexity and chemical diversity.

The Structural Complexity of Organic Molecules

Most organic molecules have much more complex structures than most inorganic molecules, and a quick review of carbon's atomic properties and bonding behavior shows why:

1. *Electron configuration, electronegativity, and covalent bonding.* Carbon's ground-state electron configuration of [He] $2s^2 2p^2$—four electrons more than He and four fewer than Ne—means that the formation of carbon ions (C^{4+} and C^{4-}) is energetically impossible under ordinary conditions. Carbon's position in the periodic table (Figure 15.1) and its electronegativity are midway between the most metallic and nonmetallic chemically reactive elements of Period 2: Li = 1.0, C = 2.5, F = 4.0. Therefore, *carbon shares electrons to attain a filled outer (valence) level,* bonding covalently in all its elemental forms and compounds.

2. *Bond properties, catenation, and molecular shape.* The *number* and *strength* of carbon's bonds lead to its outstanding ability to *catenate* (form chains of atoms), which allows it to form a multitude of chemically and thermally stable chain, ring, and branched compounds. Through the process of orbital hybridization (Section 11.1), *carbon forms four bonds in virtually all its compounds,* and they point in as many as four different directions. The small size of carbon allows close approach to another atom and thus greater orbital overlap, meaning that

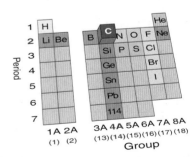

FIGURE 15.1 The position of carbon in the periodic table. Lying at the center of Period 2, carbon has an intermediate electronegativity (EN), and its position at the top of Group 4A(14) means it is relatively small. Other elements common in organic compounds are H, N, O, P, S, and the halogens.

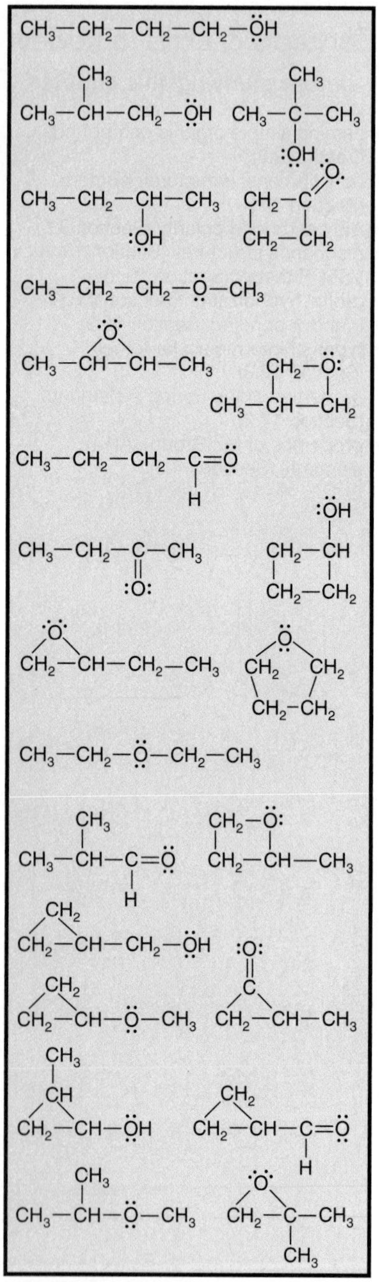

$CH_3-CH_2-CH_2-CH_2-\ddot{O}H$

$CH_3-\overset{\overset{\displaystyle CH_3}{|}}{CH}-CH_2-\ddot{O}H$ $CH_3-\overset{\overset{\displaystyle CH_3}{|}}{\underset{\underset{\displaystyle CH_3}{|}}{C}}-CH_3$

$CH_3-CH_2-\overset{}{\underset{\underset{\displaystyle :\ddot{O}H}{|}}{CH}}-CH_3$ $CH_2-\overset{\ddot{O}}{C}$

$CH_3-CH_2-CH_2-\ddot{O}-CH_3$

$CH_3-\overset{\overset{\displaystyle :\ddot{O}}{|}}{CH}-CH-CH_3$ $CH_2-\ddot{O}$

$CH_3-CH_2-CH_2-C\overset{}{=}\ddot{O}$
$\qquad\qquad\qquad\quad |$
$\qquad\qquad\qquad\quad H$

$CH_3-CH_2-\overset{}{\underset{\underset{\displaystyle :\ddot{O}:}{||}}{C}}-CH_3$ CH_2-CH

$CH_2-CH-CH_2-CH_3$ $CH_2\quad CH_2$

$CH_3-CH_2-\ddot{O}-CH_2-CH_3$

$CH_3-\overset{\overset{\displaystyle CH_3}{|}}{CH}-C\overset{}{=}\ddot{O}$ $CH_2-\ddot{O}$
$\qquad\qquad\quad |$
$\qquad\qquad\quad H$

$CH_2-CH-CH_2-\ddot{O}H$ $:\ddot{O}:$

$CH_2-CH-\ddot{O}-CH_3$ $CH_2-CH-CH_3$

$CH_2-CH-\ddot{O}H$ $CH_2-CH-C\overset{}{=}\ddot{O}$

$CH_3-\overset{\overset{\displaystyle CH_3}{|}}{CH}-\ddot{O}-CH_3$ $CH_2-\overset{\overset{\displaystyle :\ddot{O}:}{||}}{C}-CH_3$

FIGURE 15.2 The chemical diversity of organic compounds. Different arrangements of chains, branches, rings, and heteroatoms give rise to many structures. There are 23 different compounds possible from just four C atoms joined by single bonds, one O atom, and the necessary H atoms.

carbon forms relatively short, strong bonds. The C—C bond is short enough to allow side-to-side overlap of half-filled, unhybridized *p* orbitals and the formation of *multiple bonds,* which restrict rotation of attached groups (see Section 11.2). These features add more possibilities for the molecular shapes of carbon compounds.

3. *Molecular stability.* Although silicon and several other elements also catenate, none can compete with carbon. Atomic and bonding properties confer three crucial differences between C and Si chains that explain why C chains are so stable and, therefore, so common:

- *Atomic size and bond strength.* As atomic size increases down Group 4A(14), bonds between identical atoms become longer and weaker. Thus, a C—C bond (347 kJ/mol) is much stronger than an Si—Si bond (226 kJ/mol).
- *Relative heats of reaction.* A C—C bond (347 kJ/mol) and a C—O bond (358 kJ/mol) have nearly the same energy, so relatively little heat is released when a C chain reacts and one bond replaces the other. In contrast, an Si—O bond (368 kJ/mol) is much stronger than an Si—Si bond (226 kJ/mol), so a large quantity of heat is released when an Si chain reacts.
- *Orbitals available for reaction.* Unlike C, Si has low-energy *d* orbitals that can be attacked (occupied) by the lone pairs of incoming reactants. Thus, for example, ethane (CH_3—CH_3) is stable in water and does not react in air unless sparked, whereas disilane (SiH_3—SiH_3) breaks down in water and ignites spontaneously in air.

The Chemical Diversity of Organic Molecules

In addition to their elaborate geometries, organic compounds are noted for their sheer number and diverse chemical behavior. Several million are known, and thousands more are discovered or synthesized each year. The incredible diversity of organic compounds is also founded on atomic and bonding behavior and is due to three interrelated factors:

1. *Bonding to heteroatoms.* Many organic compounds contain **heteroatoms,** atoms other than C or H. The most common heteroatoms are N and O, but S, P, and the halogens often occur as well. Figure 15.2 shows that 23 different molecular structures are possible from various arrangements of four C atoms singly bonded to each other, the necessary number of H atoms, and just one O atom (either singly or doubly bonded).

2. *Electron density and reactivity.* Most reactions start—that is, a new bond begins to form—*when a region of high electron density on one molecule meets a region of low electron density on another.* These regions may be due to the presence of a multiple bond or to the partial charges that occur in carbon-heteroatom bonds. For example, consider four bonds commonly found in organic molecules:

- *The C—C bond.* When C is singly bonded to another C, as occurs in portions of nearly every organic molecule, the EN values are equal and the bond is nonpolar. Therefore, in general, *C—C bonds are unreactive.*
- *The C—H bond.* This bond, which also occurs in nearly every organic molecule, is very nearly nonpolar because it is short (109 pm) and the EN values of H (2.1) and C (2.5) are close. Thus, *C—H bonds are largely unreactive* as well.
- *The C—O bond.* This bond, which occurs in many types of organic molecules, is highly polar ($\Delta EN = 1.0$), with the O end of the bond electron rich and the C end electron poor. As a result of this imbalance in electron density, *the C—O bond is reactive* and, given appropriate conditions, a reaction will occur there.
- *Bonds to other heteroatoms.* Even when a carbon-heteroatom bond has a small ΔEN, such as that for C—Br ($\Delta EN = 0.3$), or none at all, as for C—S ($\Delta EN = 0$), heteroatoms like these are large, and so their bonds to carbon are long, weak, and thus reactive.

3. *Nature of functional groups.* One of the most important ideas in organic chemistry is that of the **functional group,** a specific combination of bonded atoms that reacts in a *characteristic* way, no matter what molecule it occurs in. In nearly every case, *the reaction of an organic compound takes place at the functional group.* Functional groups vary from carbon-carbon multiple bonds to several combinations of carbon-heteroatom bonds, and each has its own pattern of reactivity. A particular bond may be a functional group itself or *part* of one or more functional groups. For example, the C—O bond occurs in four functional groups. We discuss the reactivity of three of these in this chapter:

alcohol group   carboxylic acid group   ester group

SECTION 15.1 SUMMARY

The structural complexity of organic compounds arises from carbon's small size, intermediate EN, four valence electrons, ability to form multiple bonds, and absence of *d* orbitals in the valence level. These factors lead to chains, branches, and rings of C atoms joined by strong, chemically resistant bonds that point in as many as four directions from each C. • The chemical diversity of organic compounds arises from carbon's ability to bond to many other elements, including O and N, which creates polar bonds and greater reactivity. These factors lead to compounds that contain functional groups, specific portions of molecules that react in characteristic ways.

15.2 THE STRUCTURES AND CLASSES OF HYDROCARBONS

A fanciful, anatomical analogy can be made between an organic molecule and an animal. The carbon-carbon bonds form the skeleton: the longest continual chain is the backbone, and any branches are the limbs. Covering the skeleton is a skin of hydrogen atoms, with functional groups protruding at specific locations, like chemical fingers ready to grab an incoming reactant.

In this section, we "dissect" one group of compounds down to their skeletons and see how to name and draw them. **Hydrocarbons,** the simplest type of organic compound, are a large group of substances containing only H and C atoms. Some common fuels, such as natural gas and gasoline, are hydrocarbon mixtures. Hydrocarbons are also important *feedstocks,* precursor reactants used to make other compounds. Ethylene, acetylene, and benzene, for example, are feedstocks for hundreds of other substances.

Carbon Skeletons and Hydrogen Skins

Let's begin by examining the possible bonding arrangements of C atoms only (we'll leave off the H atoms at first) in simple skeletons without multiple bonds or rings. To distinguish different skeletons, focus on the *arrangement* of C atoms (that is, the successive linkages of one to another) and keep in mind that *groups joined by single (sigma) bonds are relatively free to rotate* (Section 11.2).

Structures with one, two, or three carbons can be arranged in only one way. Whether you draw three C atoms in a line or with a bend, the arrangement is the same. Four C atoms, however, have two possible arrangements—a four-C chain or a three-C chain with a one-C branch at the central C:

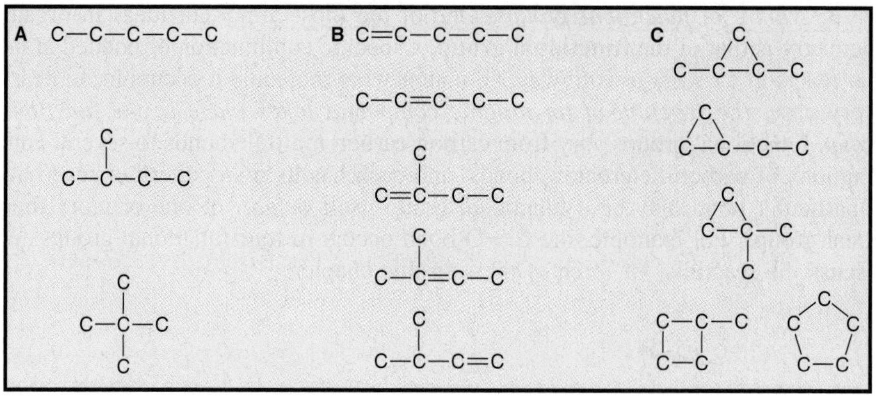

FIGURE 15.3 Some five-carbon skeletons. A, Three five-C skeletons are possible with only single bonds. **B,** Five more skeletons are possible with one C=C bond present. **C,** Five more skeletons are possible with one ring present. Even more would be possible with a ring *and* a double bond.

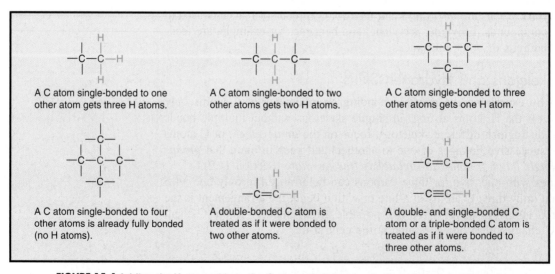

As the total number of C atoms increases, the number of different arrangements increases as well. Five C atoms have 3 possible arrangements; 6 C atoms can be arranged in 5 ways, 7 C atoms in 9 ways, 10 C atoms in 75 ways, and 20 C atoms in more than 300,000 ways! If we include multiple bonds and rings, the number of arrangements increases further. For example, including one C=C bond in the five-C skeletons creates 5 more arrangements, and including one ring creates 5 more (Figure 15.3).

When determining the number of different skeletons for a given number of C atoms, remember that

- Each C atom can form a *maximum* of four single bonds, or two single and one double bond, or one single and one triple bond.
- The *arrangement* of C atoms determines the skeleton, so a straight chain and a bent chain represent the same skeleton.
- Groups joined by single bonds can *rotate,* so a branch pointing down is the same as one pointing up. (Recall that a double bond restricts rotation.)

If we put a hydrogen "skin" on a carbon skeleton, we obtain a hydrocarbon. Figure 15.4 shows that the skeleton has the correct number of H atoms when each C has four bonds. Sample Problem 15.1 provides practice drawing hydrocarbons.

FIGURE 15.4 Adding the H-atom skin to the C-atom skeleton. In a hydrocarbon molecule, each carbon atom bonds to as many hydrogen atoms as needed to give the carbon a total of four bonds.

SAMPLE PROBLEM 15.1 Drawing Hydrocarbons

Problem Draw structures that have different atom arrangements for hydrocarbons with:
(a) Six C atoms, no multiple bonds, and no rings
(b) Four C atoms, one double bond, and no rings
Plan In each case, we draw the longest carbon chain first and then work down to smaller chains with branches at different points along them. The process typically involves trial and error. Then, we add H atoms to give each C a total of four bonds.
Solution (a) Compounds with six C atoms:

6-C chain:
```
        H   H   H   H   H   H
        |   |   |   |   |   |
    H—C—C—C—C—C—C—H
        |   |   |   |   |   |
        H   H   H   H   H   H
```

5-C chains:
```
        H   H   H   H   H                          H
        |   |   |   |   |                        H—C—H
    H—C—C—C—C—C—H              H   H       |    H   H
        |   |   |       |                  H—C—C—C—C—C—H
        H   H   H       H                  |   |   |   |   |
                H—C—H                       H   H   H   H   H
                |
                H
```

4-C chains:
```
            H                               H
          H—C—H                           H—C—H
        H   |   H   H                 H   H   |   H
        |   |   |   |                 |   |   |   |
    H—C—C—C—C—H                   H—C—C—C—C—H
        |   |   |   |                 |   |   |   |
        H   H—C—H   H                 H   H—C—H   H
              |                             |
              H                             H
```

(b) Compounds with four C atoms and one double bond:

4-C chains:
```
        H   H   H   H                     H   H   H   H
        |   |   |   |                     |   |   |   |
    H—C—C=C—C—H               H—C—C—C=C—H
        |       |                         |   |
        H       H                         H   H
```

3-C chain:
```
        H       H
        |       |
    H—C—C=C—H
        |
        H—C—H
        |
        H
```

Check Be sure each skeleton has the correct number of C atoms and multiple bonds and no arrangements are repeated or omitted; remember a double bond counts as two bonds.
Comment Avoid some *common mistakes:*

In (a): C—C—C—C—C is the same skeleton as C—C—C—C—C
        | |
        C   C

        C   C   C
        | | |
    C—C—C—C is the same skeleton as C—C—C—C
        |
        C

In (b): C—C—C=C is the same skeleton as C=C—C—C
The double bond restricts rotation. Thus, in addition to the form shown in part (b), in which the H atoms are on the same side of the C=C bond (called the *cis* form), another possibility is the form in which the H atoms are on opposite sides (called the *trans* form):

```
        H   H       H
        |   |       |
    H—C—C=C—C—H
        |       |   |
        H       H   H
```

(We discuss these forms fully later in this section.)

Also, there are too many bonds to one C in

$$
\begin{array}{c}
\overset{\displaystyle\frown\,5\ bonds}{}\\
H-\underset{\underset{\displaystyle H}{|}}{\overset{\overset{\displaystyle H}{|}}{C}}-\underset{\underset{\displaystyle H-\underset{\underset{\displaystyle H}{|}}{\overset{\overset{\displaystyle |}{}}{C}}-H}{\underset{\displaystyle |}{}}}{\overset{\overset{\displaystyle H}{|}}{C}}=\overset{\overset{\displaystyle H}{|}}{C}-H
\end{array}
$$

FOLLOW-UP PROBLEM 15.1 Draw all hydrocarbons that have five C atoms, one triple bond, and no rings (three arrangements).

Hydrocarbons can be classified into four main groups. In the remainder of this section, we examine the names and some structural features and physical properties of each group. Later, we discuss the chemical behavior of the hydrocarbons.

Alkanes: Hydrocarbons with Only Single Bonds

A hydrocarbon that contains only single bonds is an **alkane** (general formula C_nH_{2n+2}, where n is a positive integer). For example, if $n = 5$, the formula is $C_5H_{[(2\times5)+2]}$, or C_5H_{12}. The alkanes comprise a **homologous series,** one in which each member differs from the next by a $-CH_2-$ (methylene) group. In an alkane, each C is sp^3 hybridized. Because each C is bonded to the *maximum number of other atoms* (C or H), alkanes are referred to as **saturated hydrocarbons.**

Naming Alkanes You learned how to name simple alkanes in Section 2.8. Here we discuss general rules for naming any alkane and, by extension, other organic compounds as well. The key point is that *each chain, branch, or ring has a name based on the **number** of C atoms.* The name of a compound has three portions:

$$\text{PREFIX} + \text{ROOT} + \text{SUFFIX}$$

- *Root:* The root tells the number of C atoms in the longest *continuous* chain in the molecule. The roots for the ten smallest alkanes are shown in Table 15.1. Recall that there are special roots for compounds of one to four C atoms; roots of longer chains are based on Greek numbers.
- *Suffix:* The suffix tells the *type of organic compound* the molecule represents; that is, it identifies the key functional group the molecule possesses. The suffix is placed *after* the root.
- *Prefix:* Each prefix identifies a *group attached to the main chain* and the number of the carbon to which it is attached. Prefixes identifying hydrocarbon branches are the same as root names (Table 15.1) but have *-yl* as their ending. Each prefix is placed *before* the root.

For example, in the name 2-methylbutane, *-but-* is the root (the main chain has four C atoms), *-ane* is the suffix (the compound is an alkane), and *2-methyl-* is the prefix (a one-carbon branch is attached to C-2 of the main chain).
   To obtain the systematic name of a compound,

1. Name the longest chain (root).
2. Add the compound type (suffix).
3. Name any branches (prefix).

Table 15.2 presents the rules for naming any organic compound and applies them to an alkane component of gasoline. Other organic compounds are named with a variety of other prefixes and suffixes (see Table 15.5). In addition to these *systematic* names, we'll also note important *common* names still in use.

Table 15.1 Numerical Roots for Carbon Chains and Branches	
Roots	**Number of C Atoms**
meth-	1
eth-	2
prop-	3
but-	4
pent-	5
hex-	6
hept-	7
oct-	8
non-	9
dec-	10

Table 15.2   Rules for Naming an Organic Compound

1. Naming the longest chain (root)
   (a) Find the longest *continuous* chain of C atoms.
   (b) Select the root that corresponds to the number of C atoms in this chain.

$$CH_3-\overset{\displaystyle CH_3}{\underset{\displaystyle CH_2-CH_3}{CH}}-CH-CH_2-CH_2-CH_3$$

6 carbons $\Longrightarrow$ hex-

2. Naming the compound type (suffix)
   (a) For alkanes, add the suffix *-ane* to the chain root. (Other suffixes appear in Table 15.5 with their functional group and compound type.)
   (b) If the chain forms a ring, the name is preceded by *cyclo-*.

hex- + -ane $\Longrightarrow$ hexane

3. Naming the branches (prefixes) (If the compound has no branches, the name consists of the root and suffix.)
   (a) Each branch name consists of a subroot (number of C atoms) and the ending *-yl* to signify that it is not part of the main chain.
   (b) Branch names precede the chain name. When two or more branches are present, their names appear in *alphabetical* order.
   (c) To specify where the branch occurs along the chain, number the main-chain C atoms consecutively, starting at the end *closer* to a branch, to achieve the *lowest* numbers for the branches. Precede each branch name with the number of the main-chain C to which that branch is attached.

$$CH_3-\overset{\displaystyle CH_3 \text{ methyl}}{\underset{\displaystyle CH_2-CH_3 \text{ ethyl}}{CH}}-CH-CH_2-CH_2-CH_3$$

ethylmethylhexane

$$\overset{1}{CH_3}-\overset{2}{\underset{\displaystyle \underset{\displaystyle CH_2-CH_3}{CH_3}}{CH}}-\overset{3}{CH}-\overset{4}{CH_2}-\overset{5}{CH_2}-\overset{6}{CH_3}$$

3-ethyl-2-methylhexane

Depicting Alkanes with Formulas and Models Chemists have several ways to depict organic compounds. Expanded, condensed, and carbon-skeleton formulas are easy to draw; ball-and-stick and space-filling models show the actual shapes.

The *expanded formula* shows each atom and bond. One type of *condensed formula* groups each C atom with its H atoms. *Carbon-skeleton formulas* show only carbon-carbon bonds and appear as zig-zag lines, often with branches. *Each end or bend of a zig-zag line or branch represents a C atom attached to the number of H atoms that gives it a total of four bonds*:

propane $CH_3-CH_2-CH_3$

2,3-dimethylbutane $CH_3-\overset{\displaystyle CH_3}{\underset{}{CH}}-\overset{\displaystyle CH_3}{\underset{}{CH}}-CH_3$

Figure 15.5 shows these types of formulas, together with ball-and-stick and space-filling models, of the compound named in Table 15.2.

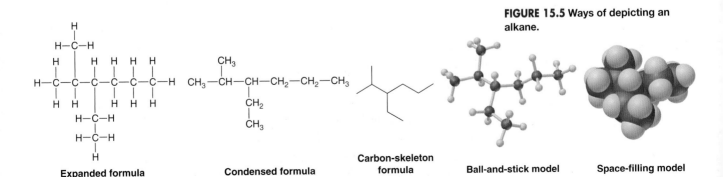

FIGURE 15.5 Ways of depicting an alkane.

Expanded formula   Condensed formula   Carbon-skeleton formula   Ball-and-stick model   Space-filling model

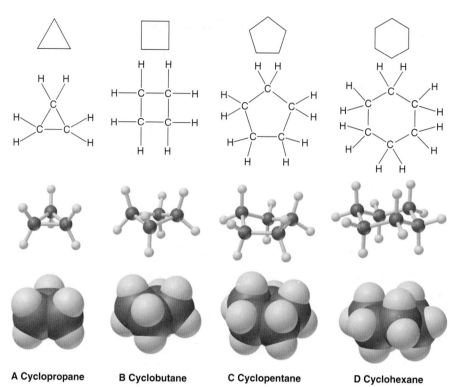

A Cyclopropane   **B Cyclobutane**   **C Cyclopentane**   **D Cyclohexane**

FIGURE 15.6 Depicting cycloalkanes. Cycloalkanes are usually drawn as regular polygons. Each side is a C—C bond, and each corner represents a C atom with its required number of H atoms. The expanded formulas show each bond in the molecule. The ball-and-stick and space-filling models show that, except for cyclopropane, the rings are not planar. These conformations minimize electron repulsions between adjacent H atoms. Cyclohexane **(D)** is shown in its more stable chair conformation.

Cyclic Hydrocarbons A **cyclic hydrocarbon** contains one or more rings in its structure. When a straight-chain alkane (C_nH_{2n+2}) forms a ring, two H atoms are lost as the C—C bond forms to join the two ends of the chain. Thus, *cycloalkanes* have the general formula C_nH_{2n}. Cyclic hydrocarbons are often drawn with carbon-skeleton formulas, as shown at the top of Figure 15.6. Except for three-carbon rings, *cycloalkanes are nonplanar.* This structural feature arises from the tetrahedral shape around each C atom and the need to minimize electron repulsions between adjacent H atoms. As a result, orbital overlap of adjacent C atoms is maximized. The most stable form of cyclohexane, called the *chair conformation,* is shown in Figure 15.6D.

Constitutional Isomerism and the Physical Properties of Alkanes

Recall from Section 3.2 that two or more compounds with the same molecular formula but different properties are called *isomers*. Isomers with *different arrangements of bonded atoms* are **constitutional (or structural) isomers;** alkanes with the same number of C atoms but different skeletons are examples. The smallest alkane to exhibit constitutional isomerism has four C atoms: two different compounds have the formula C_4H_{10}, as shown in Table 15.3. The unbranched one is butane (common name, *n*-butane; *n*- stands for "normal," or having a straight chain), and the other isomer is 2-methylpropane (common name, *iso*butane).

Table 15.3 The Constitutional Isomers of C_4H_{10} and C_5H_{12}

Systematic Name (Common Name)	Expanded Formula	Condensed and Skeleton Formulas	Space-filling Model	Density (g/mL)	Boiling Point (°C)
Butane (*n*-butane)	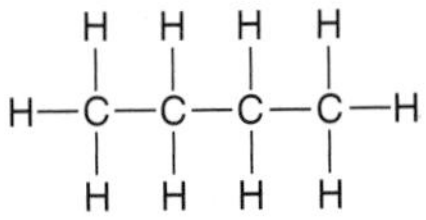 H H H H / H—C—C—C—C—H / H H H H	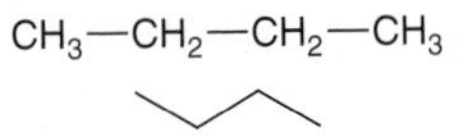 CH_3—CH_2—CH_2—CH_3	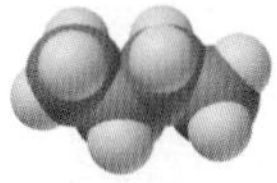	0.579	−0.5
2-Methylpropane (isobutane)	H H H / H—C—C—C—H / H | H / H—C—H / H	CH_3—CH—CH_3 / CH_3		0.549	−11.6
Pentane (*n*-pentane)	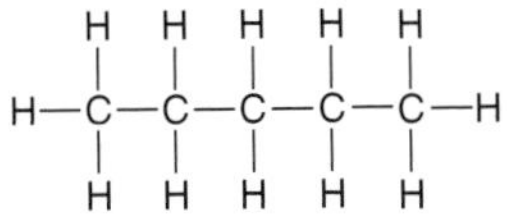 H H H H H / H—C—C—C—C—C—H / H H H H H	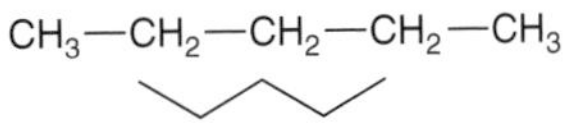 CH_3—CH_2—CH_2—CH_2—CH_3		0.626	36.1
2-Methylbutane (isopentane)	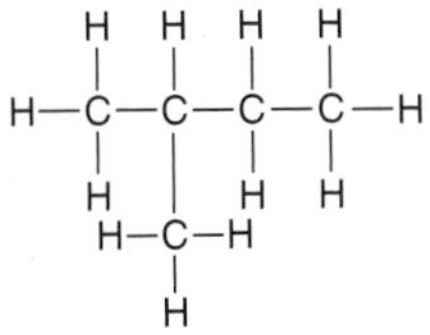 H H H H / H—C—C—C—C—H / H H H H / H—C—H / H	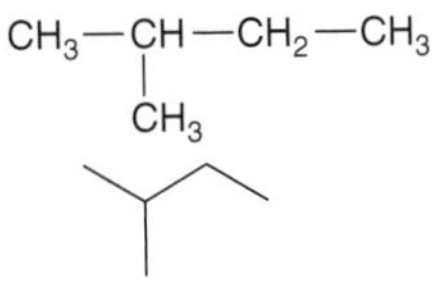 CH_3—CH—CH_2—CH_3 / CH_3	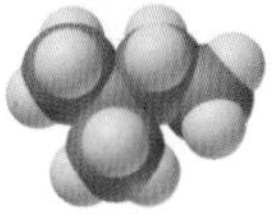	0.620	27.8
2,2-Dimethylpropane (neopentane)	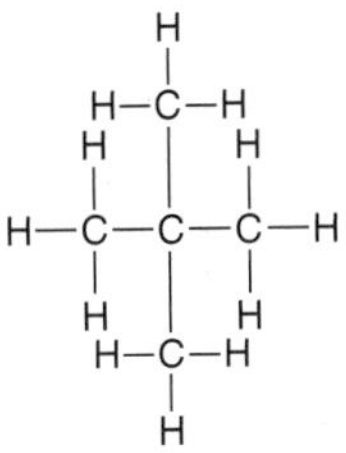 H / H—C—H / H H H / H—C—C—C—H / H H / H—C—H / H	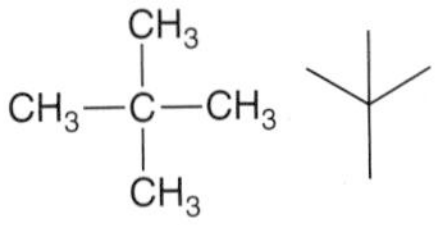 CH_3 / CH_3—C—CH_3 / CH_3	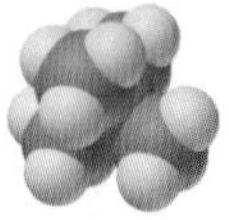	0.614	9.5

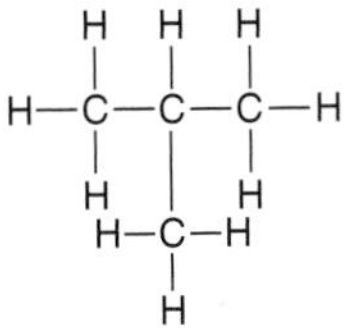

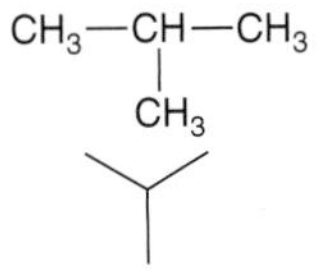

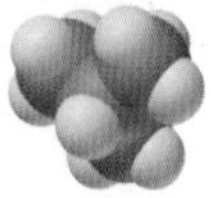

Similarly, three compounds have the formula C_5H_{12} (shown in Table 15.3). The unbranched isomer is pentane (common name, *n*-pentane); the one with a methyl group at C-2 of a four-C chain is 2-methylbutane (common name, *iso*pentane). The third isomer has two methyl branches on C-2 of a three-C chain, so its name is 2,2-dimethylpropane (common name, *neo*pentane).

Because alkanes are nearly nonpolar, their physical properties are determined by dispersion forces, as the boiling points in Table 15.3 show. The four-C alkanes boil lower than the five-C compounds. Moreover, within each group of isomers, the more spherical member (isobutane or neopentane) boils lower than the more elongated one (*n*-butane or *n*-pentane). As you saw in Chapter 12, this trend occurs because a spherical shape leads to less intermolecular contact, and thus lower total dispersion forces, than does an elongated shape.

A particularly clear example of the effect of dispersion forces on physical properties occurs among the unbranched alkanes (*n*-alkanes). Among these compounds, the longer the chain, the greater the intermolecular contact, the stronger the dispersion forces, and the higher the boiling point (Figure 15.7, next page). The solubility of alkanes, and of all hydrocarbons, is easy to predict from the like-dissolves-like rule (Section 13.1). Alkanes are miscible in each other and in other nonpolar solvents, such as benzene, but are nearly insoluble in water. The solubility of pentane in water, for example, is only 0.36 g/L at room temperature.

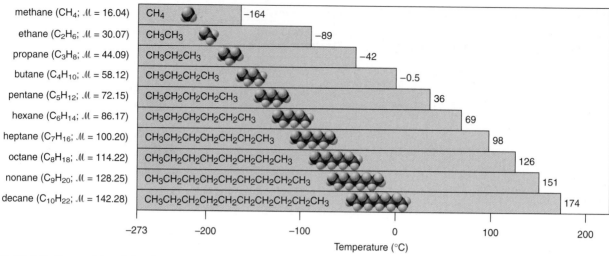

methane (CH$_4$; $\mathcal{M}$ = 16.04)
ethane (C$_2$H$_6$; $\mathcal{M}$ = 30.07)
propane (C$_3$H$_8$; $\mathcal{M}$ = 44.09)
butane (C$_4$H$_{10}$; $\mathcal{M}$ = 58.12)
pentane (C$_5$H$_{12}$; $\mathcal{M}$ = 72.15)
hexane (C$_6$H$_{14}$; $\mathcal{M}$ = 86.17)
heptane (C$_7$H$_{16}$; $\mathcal{M}$ = 100.20)
octane (C$_8$H$_{18}$; $\mathcal{M}$ = 114.22)
nonane (C$_9$H$_{20}$; $\mathcal{M}$ = 128.25)
decane (C$_{10}$H$_{22}$; $\mathcal{M}$ = 142.28)

FIGURE 15.7 Boiling points of the first 10 unbranched alkanes. Boiling point increases smoothly with chain length because dispersion forces increase. Each entry includes the name, molecular formula, molar mass ($\mathcal{M}$, in g/mol), condensed formula, space-filling model, and boiling point at 1 atm pressure.

Chiral Molecules and Optical Isomerism

Another type of isomerism exhibited by some alkanes and many other organic (as well as some inorganic) compounds is called *stereoisomerism*. **Stereoisomers** are molecules with the same arrangement of atoms *but different orientations of groups in space.* Optical isomerism is one type of stereoisomerism: *when two objects are mirror images of each other and cannot be superimposed, they are* **optical isomers,** also called *enantiomers.* To use a familiar example, your right hand is an optical isomer of your left. Look at your right hand in a mirror, and you will see that the *image* is identical to your left hand (Figure 15.8). No matter how you twist your arms around, however, your hands cannot lie on top of each other with all parts superimposed. They are not superimposable because each is *asymmetric:* there is no plane of symmetry that divides your hand into two identical parts.

An asymmetric molecule is called **chiral** (Greek *cheir,* "hand"). Typically, an organic molecule *is chiral if it contains a carbon atom that is bonded to four* **different** *groups.* This C atom is called a *chiral center* or an asymmetric carbon. In 3-methylhexane, for example, C-3 is a chiral center because it is bonded to four different groups: H—, CH$_3$—, CH$_3$—CH$_2$—, and CH$_3$—CH$_2$—CH$_2$— (Figure 15.9A). Like your two hands, the two forms are mirror images and cannot be superimposed on each other: when two of the groups are superimposed, the other two are opposite each other. Thus, the two forms are optical isomers. The central C atom in the amino acid alanine is also a chiral center (Figure 15.9B).

FIGURE 15.8 An analogy for optical isomers. The reflection of your right hand looks like your left hand. Each hand is asymmetric, so you cannot superimpose them with your palms facing in the same direction.

FIGURE 15.9 Two chiral molecules. A, 3-Methylhexane is chiral because C-3 is bonded to four different groups. These two models are optical isomers (enantiomers). **B,** The central C in the amino acid alanine is also bonded to four different groups.

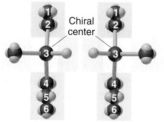

A Optical isomers of 3-methylhexane

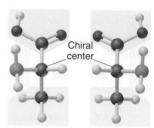

B Optical isomers of alanine

Unlike constitutional isomers, optical isomers are identical in all but two respects:

1. In their physical properties, *optical isomers differ only in the direction that each isomer rotates the plane of polarized light.* A *polarimeter* is used to measure the angle that the plane is rotated. A beam of light consists of waves that oscillate in all planes. A polarizing filter blocks all waves except those in one plane, so the light emerging through the filter is *plane-polarized.* An optical isomer is **optically active** because it rotates the plane of this polarized light. The *dextrorotatory* isomer (designated *d* or +) rotates the plane of the light clockwise; the *levorotatory* isomer (designated *l* or −) is the mirror image of the *d* isomer and rotates the plane counterclockwise. An equimolar mixture of the two isomers does not rotate the plane at all because the opposing rotations cancel.
2. In their chemical properties, *optical isomers differ only in a chiral (asymmetric) chemical environment,* one that distinguishes "right-handed" from "left-handed" molecules. As an analogy, your right hand fits well in your right glove but not in your left glove.

Optical isomerism plays a vital role in living cells. Nearly all carbohydrates and amino acids are optically active, but only one of the isomers is biologically usable. For example, *d*-glucose is metabolized for energy, but *l*-glucose is excreted unused. Similarly, *l*-alanine is incorporated naturally into proteins, but *d*-alanine is not. Many drugs are chiral molecules of which one optical isomer is biologically active and the other has either a different type of activity or none at all.

Alkenes: Hydrocarbons with Double Bonds

A hydrocarbon that contains at least one $C=C$ bond is called an **alkene.** With two H atoms removed to make the double bond, alkenes have the general formula C_nH_{2n}. The double-bonded C atoms are sp^2 hybridized. Because their carbon atoms are bonded to fewer than the maximum of four atoms each, alkenes are considered **unsaturated hydrocarbons.**

Alkene names differ from those of alkanes in two respects:

1. The main chain (root) *must* contain both C atoms of the double bond, even if it is not the longest chain. The chain is numbered from the end *closer* to the $C=C$ bond, and the position of the bond is indicated by the number of the *first* C atom in it.
2. The suffix for alkenes is *-ene.*

For example, there are three four-C alkenes (C_4H_8), two unbranched and one branched (see Sample Problem 15.1b). The branched isomer is 2-methylpropene; the unbranched isomer with the $C=C$ bond between C-1 and C-2 is 1-butene; the unbranched isomer with the $C=C$ bond between C-2 and C-3 is 2-butene. As you'll see next, there are two isomers of 2-butene, but they are of a different sort.

The $C=C$ Bond and Geometric (cis-trans) Isomerism There are two major structural differences between alkenes and alkanes. First, alkanes have a *tetrahedral* geometry (bond angles of ~109.5°) around each C atom, whereas the double-bonded C atoms in alkenes are *trigonal planar* (~120°). Second, the C—C bond *allows* rotation of bonded groups, so the atoms in an alkane continually change their relative positions. In contrast, the π bond of the $C=C$ bond *restricts* rotation, which fixes the relative positions of the atoms bonded to it.

This rotational restriction leads to another type of stereoisomerism. **Geometric isomers** (also called *cis-trans* isomers) have different orientations of

Table 15.4	The Geometric Isomers of 2-Butene			
Systematic Name	Condensed and Skeleton Formulas	Space-filling Model	Density (g/mL)	Boiling Point (°C)
cis-2-Butene	CH_3 CH_3 $\backslash$ $/$ $C=C$ $/$ $\backslash$ H H		0.621	3.7
trans-2-Butene	CH_3 H $\backslash$ $/$ $C=C$ $/$ $\backslash$ H CH_3		0.604	0.9

groups around a double bond (or similar structural feature). Table 15.4 shows the two geometric isomers of 2-butene (also see Comment, Sample Problem 15.1), *cis*-2-butene and *trans*-2-butene. In general, the *cis* isomer has the larger portions of the main chain (in this case, two CH_3 groups) *on the same side* of the double bond, and the *trans* isomer has them on *opposite sides*. For a molecule to have geometric isomers, *each C atom in the C=C bond must be bonded to two different groups*. Like other isomers, geometric isomers have different properties. Note in Table 15.4 that the two 2-butenes differ in molecular shape *and* physical properties. The *cis* isomer has a bend in the chain that the *trans* isomer lacks.

Geometric Isomers and the Chemistry of Vision

The first step in the remarkable sequence of events that allows us to see relies on the different shapes of a pair of geometric isomers. The molecule responsible for receiving the light energy is *retinal,* a 20-C compound with five C=C bonds in its structure. There are two biologically occurring isomers, which have very different shapes: the all-*trans* isomer is elongated, and the 11-*cis* isomer is sharply bent around the double bond between C-11 and C-12.

Certain cells of the retina are packed with rhodopsin, a large protein covalently bonded to 11-*cis*-retinal. The energies of photons of visible light have a range (165–293 kJ/mol) that includes the energy needed to break a C=C π bond (about 250 kJ/mol). Within a few millionths of a second after rhodopsin absorbs a photon, the 11-*cis* π bond breaks, the intact σ bond between C-11 and C-12 rotates, and the π bond re-forms to produce all-*trans* retinal.

This rapid and significant change in shape causes the attached protein to change its shape as well, which triggers a flow of ions into the retina's cells. This ion influx initiates electrical impulses to the optic nerve and brain. Because of the speed and efficiency with which light causes such a large structural change in retinal, natural selection has made it the photon absorber in organisms as different as purple bacteria, mollusks, insects, and vertebrates.

Alkynes: Hydrocarbons with Triple Bonds

Hydrocarbons that contain at least one C≡C bond are called **alkynes.** Their general formula is C_nH_{2n-2} because they have two fewer H atoms than do alkenes with the same number of C atoms. Because a carbon in a C≡C bond can bond to only one other atom, the geometry around each C atom is linear (180°): each C is *sp* hybridized. Alkynes are named in the same way as alkenes, except that the suffix is -*yne*. Because of their localized π electrons, C=C and C≡C bonds are electron rich and act as functional groups. Thus, alkenes and alkynes are much more reactive than alkanes, as we'll discuss in Section 15.4.

SAMPLE PROBLEM 15.2 | Naming Alkanes, Alkenes, and Alkynes

Problem Give the systematic name for each of the following, indicate the chiral center in part (d), and draw two geometric isomers for part (e):

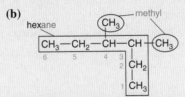

(a)

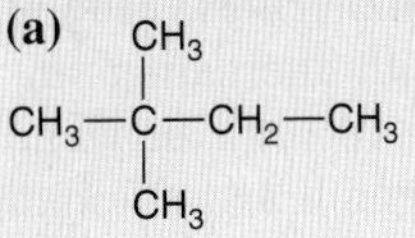

$$CH_3-\overset{\overset{\displaystyle CH_3}{|}}{\underset{\underset{\displaystyle CH_3}{|}}{C}}-CH_2-CH_3$$

(b)

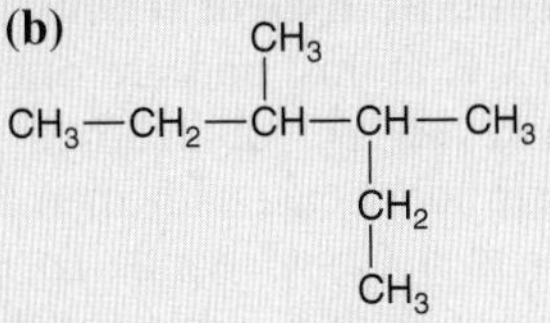

$$CH_3-CH_2-CH-\overset{\overset{\displaystyle CH_3}{|}}{CH}-CH_3$$
$$\underset{\underset{\displaystyle CH_3}{|}}{CH_2}$$

(c)

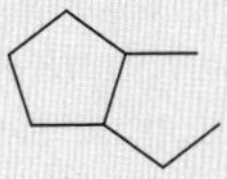

(d)

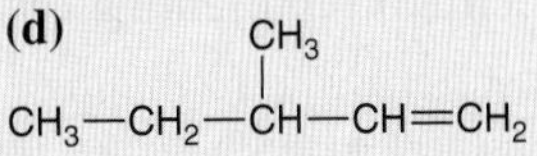

$$CH_3-CH_2-\overset{\overset{\displaystyle CH_3}{|}}{CH}-CH=CH_2$$

(e)

$$CH_3-CH_2-CH=\overset{\overset{\displaystyle CH_3}{|}}{C}-\underset{\underset{\displaystyle CH_3}{|}}{CH}-CH_3$$

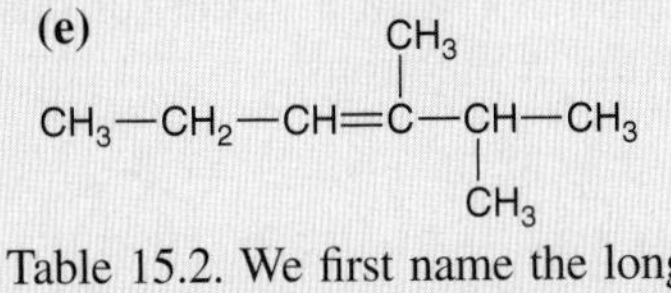

Plan For (a) to (c), we refer to Table 15.2. We first name the longest chain (-*root-* + -*ane*). Then we find the *lowest* branch numbers by counting C atoms from the end *closer* to a branch. Finally, we name each branch (-*root-* + -*yl*) and put the names alphabetically before the chain name. For (d) and (e), the longest chain that *includes* the multiple bond is numbered from the end closer to it. For (d), the chiral center is the C atom bonded to four different groups. In (e), the *cis* isomer has larger groups on the same side of the double bond, and the *trans* isomer has them on opposite sides.

Solution

(a)

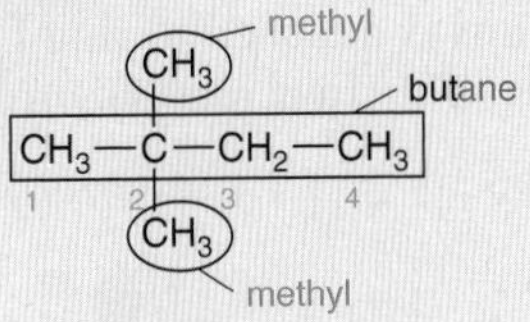

2,2-dimethylbutane

When a type of branch appears more than once, we group the chain numbers and indicate the number of branches with a numerical prefix, such as 2,2-*di*methyl.

(b)

3,4-dimethylhexane

In this case, we can number the chain from either end because the branches are the same and are attached to the two central C atoms.

(c)

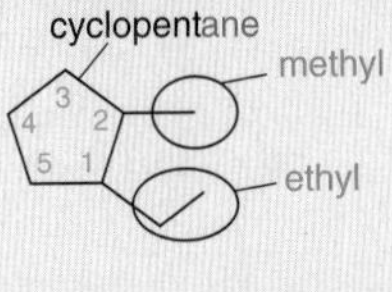

1-ethyl-2-methylcyclopentane

We number the ring C atoms so that a branch is attached to C-1.

(d)

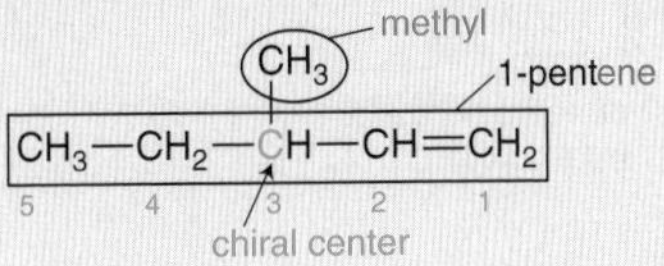

3-methyl-1-pentene

(e)

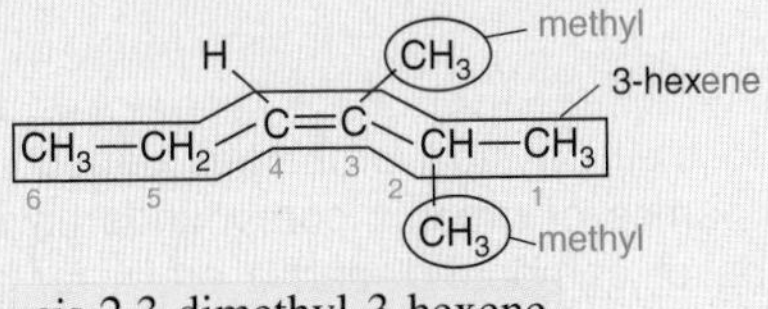

cis-2,3-dimethyl-3-hexene 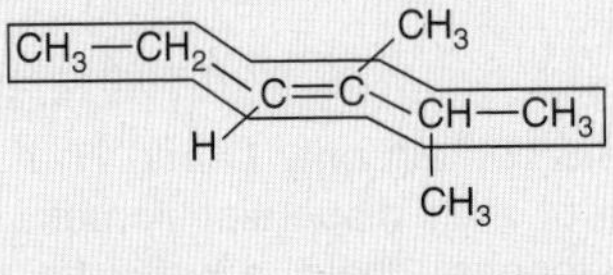   *trans*-2,3-dimethyl-3-hexene

Check A good check (and excellent practice) is to reverse the process by drawing structures for the names to see if you come up with the structures given in the problem.

Comment In part (b), C-3 and C-4 are chiral centers, as are C-1 and C-2 in part (c). However, in (b) the molecule is not chiral: it has a plane of symmetry between C-3 and C-4, so the molecule as a whole does not rotate the plane of polarized light. Avoid these common mistakes: In (b), 2-ethyl-3-methylpentane is wrong: the longest chain is *hexane*. In (c), 1-methyl-2-ethylcyclopentane is wrong: the branch names appear *alphabetically*.

FOLLOW-UP PROBLEM 15.2 Draw condensed formulas for the following compounds: (a) 3-ethyl-3-methyloctane; (b) 1-ethyl-3-propylcyclohexane (also draw a carbon-skeleton formula for this compound); (c) 3,3-diethyl-1-hexyne; (d) *trans*-3-methyl-3-heptene.

Aromatic Hydrocarbons: Cyclic Molecules with Delocalized π Electrons

Unlike the cycloalkanes, **aromatic hydrocarbons** are planar molecules, usually with one or more rings of six C atoms, and are often drawn with alternating single and double bonds. However, as you learned in Section 10.1, in benzene (C_6H_6), all the ring bonds are identical, with their values of length and strength *between* those of a C—C and a C=C bond. To indicate this, benzene is also shown as a resonance hybrid or with a circle (or dashed circle) representing the delocalized character of the π electrons:

The systematic naming of simple aromatic compounds is quite straightforward. Usually, benzene is the parent compound, and attached groups, or *substituents,* are named as prefixes. For example, benzene with one methyl group attached is systematically named *methylbenzene.* With only one substituent present, we do not number the ring C atoms; when two or more groups are attached, however, we number in such a way that one of the groups is attached to ring C-1. Thus, methylbenzene and the three structural isomers with two methyl groups attached are

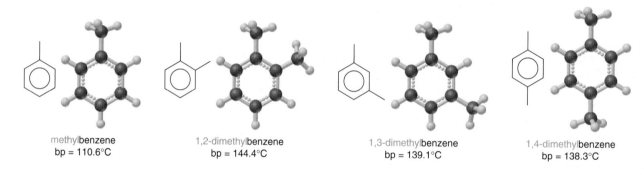

methylbenzene
bp = 110.6°C

1,2-dimethylbenzene
bp = 144.4°C

1,3-dimethylbenzene
bp = 139.1°C

1,4-dimethylbenzene
bp = 138.3°C

The dimethylbenzenes are important solvents and feedstocks for making polyester fibers and dyes. Benzene and many other aromatic hydrocarbons have carcinogenic (cancer-causing) properties.

SECTION 15.2 SUMMARY

Hydrocarbons contain only C and H atoms, so their physical properties depend on the strength of their dispersion forces. • The names of organic compounds have a root for the longest chain, a suffix for the type of compound, and a prefix for any attached group. • Alkanes (C_nH_{2n+2}) have only single bonds. Cycloalkanes (C_nH_{2n}) have ring structures that are typically nonplanar. Alkenes (C_nH_{2n}) have at least one C=C bond. Alkynes (C_nH_{2n-2}) have at least one C≡C bond. Aromatic hydrocarbons have at least one planar ring with delocalized π electrons. • Constitutional (structural) isomers have different atom arrangements. • Stereoisomers (optical and geometric) have the same arrangement of atoms, but their atoms are oriented differently in space. • Optical isomers cannot be superimposed on each other because they are asymmetric, with four different groups bonded to the C that is the chiral center. They have identical physical and chemical properties except in their rotation of plane-polarized light. • Geometric *(cis-trans)* isomers have groups oriented differently around a C=C bond, which restricts rotation. • Light converts a *cis* isomer of retinal to the all-*trans* form, which initiates the visual response.

15.3 SOME IMPORTANT CLASSES OF ORGANIC REACTIONS

Organic reactions are classified according to the chemical process involved. Three important classes are *addition, elimination,* and *substitution* reactions.

From here on, we use the notation of an uppercase R with a single bond, R—, to signify a general organic group attached to one of the atoms shown; you can usually picture R— as an **alkyl group,** a saturated hydrocarbon chain with one bond available to link to another atom. Thus, R—CH_2—Br has an alkyl group attached to a CH_2 group bearing a Br atom; R—CH=CH_2 is an alkene with an alkyl group attached to one of the carbons in the double bond; and so forth. (Often, when more than one R group is present, we write R, R′, R″, and so forth, to indicate that these groups may be different.)

The three classes of organic reactions we discuss here can be identified by comparing the *number of bonds to C* in reactants and products:

1. An **addition reaction** occurs when an unsaturated reactant becomes a saturated product:

$$R-CH=CH-R \ + \ X-Y \ \longrightarrow \ R-\overset{\overset{\textstyle X}{|}}{C}H-\overset{\overset{\textstyle Y}{|}}{C}H-R$$

Note the C atoms are bonded to *more* atoms in the product than in the reactant.

The C=C and C≡C bonds and the C=O bond commonly undergo addition reactions. In each case, the π bond breaks, leaving the σ bond intact. In the product, the two C atoms (or C and O) form two additional σ bonds. In the following addition reaction, H and Cl from HCl add to the double bond in ethylene:

$$CH_2=CH_2 \ + \ H-Cl \ \longrightarrow \ H-CH_2-CH_2-Cl$$

2. **Elimination reactions** are the opposite of addition reactions. They occur when a saturated reactant becomes an unsaturated product:

$$R-\overset{\overset{\textstyle Y}{|}}{C}H-\overset{\overset{\textstyle X}{|}}{C}H_2 \ \longrightarrow \ R-CH=CH_2 \ + \ X-Y$$

Note that the C atoms are bonded to *fewer* atoms in the product than in the reactant. A pair of halogen atoms, an H atom and a halogen atom, or an H atom and an —OH group are typically eliminated, but C atoms are not:

$$CH_3-\overset{\overset{\textstyle OH}{|}}{C}H-\overset{\overset{\textstyle H}{|}}{C}H_2 \ \xrightarrow{H_2SO_4} \ CH_3-CH=CH_2 \ + \ H-OH$$

3. A **substitution reaction** occurs when an atom (or group) from an added reagent substitutes for one in the organic reactant:

$$R-\overset{|}{\underset{|}{C}}-X \ + \ :Y \ \longrightarrow \ R-\overset{|}{\underset{|}{C}}-Y \ + \ :X$$

Note that the C atom is bonded to the *same number* of atoms in the product as in the reactant. The C atom may be saturated or unsaturated, and X and Y can be many different atoms, but generally *not* C. The main flavor ingredient in banana oil, for instance, forms through a substitution reaction; note that the O substitutes for the Cl:

$$CH_3-\overset{\overset{\textstyle O}{||}}{C}-Cl \ + \ HO-CH_2-CH_2-\overset{\overset{\textstyle CH_3}{|}}{C}H-CH_3 \ \longrightarrow$$

$$CH_3-\overset{\overset{\textstyle O}{||}}{C}-O-CH_2-CH_2-\overset{\overset{\textstyle CH_3}{|}}{C}H-CH_3 \ + \ H-Cl$$

SAMPLE PROBLEM 15.3 Recognizing the Type of Organic Reaction

Problem State whether each reaction is an addition, elimination, or substitution:

(a) $CH_3-CH_2-CH_2-Br \longrightarrow CH_3-CH=CH_2 + HBr$

(b) [pentene structure] $+ H_2 \longrightarrow$ [pentane structure]

(c) $CH_3\overset{O}{\overset{\|}{C}}-Br + CH_3CH_2OH \longrightarrow CH_3\overset{O}{\overset{\|}{C}}-OCH_2CH_3 + HBr$

Plan We determine the type of reaction by looking for any change in the number of atoms bonded to C:
• More atoms bonded to C is an *addition*.
• Fewer atoms bonded to C is an *elimination*.
• Same number of atoms bonded to C is a *substitution*.

Solution
(a) Elimination: two bonds in the reactant, C—H and C—Br, are absent in the product, so fewer atoms are bonded to C.
(b) Addition: two more C—H bonds have formed in the product, so more atoms are bonded to C.
(c) Substitution: the reactant C—Br bond becomes a C—O bond in the product, so the same number of atoms are bonded to C.

FOLLOW-UP PROBLEM 15.3 Write a balanced equation for each of the following:
(a) An addition reaction between 2-butene and Cl_2
(b) A substitution reaction between $CH_3-CH_2-CH_2-Br$ and OH^-
(c) The elimination of H_2O from $(CH_3)_3C-OH$

SECTION 15.3 SUMMARY

In an addition reaction, a π bond breaks and the two C atoms bond to more atoms. •
In an elimination reaction, a π bond forms and the two C atoms bond to fewer atoms. • In a substitution reaction, one atom replaces another atom, but the total number of atoms bonded to C does not change.

15.4 PROPERTIES AND REACTIVITIES OF COMMON FUNCTIONAL GROUPS

The central organizing principle of organic reaction chemistry is the *functional group*. To predict how an organic compound might react, we narrow our focus to such groups because *the distribution of electron density in a functional group affects the reactivity*. The electron density can be high, as in the C=C and C≡C bonds, or it can be low at one end of a bond and high at the other, as in the C—Cl and C—O bonds. Such bond sites attract reactants that are charged or polar and begin a sequence of bond-forming and bond-breaking steps that lead to product(s). Table 15.5 lists some of the important functional groups in organic compounds.

When we classify functional groups by bond order (single, double, and so forth), they tend to follow certain patterns of reactivity:

• Functional groups with only single bonds undergo substitution or elimination.
• Functional groups with double or triple bonds undergo addition.
• Functional groups with both single and double bonds undergo substitution.

Table 15.5 Important Functional Groups in Organic Compounds

Functional Group	Compound Type	Prefix or Suffix of Name	Example Lewis Structure	Ball-and-Stick Model	Systematic Name (Common Name)
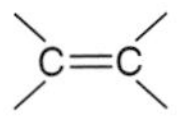 >C=C<	alkene	-ene	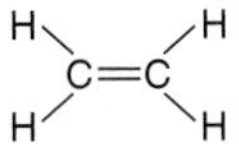 (ethene structure)	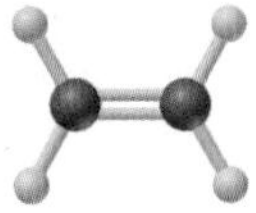	ethene (ethylene)
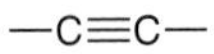 —C≡C—	alkyne	-yne	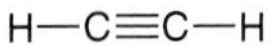 H—C≡C—H		ethyne (acetylene)
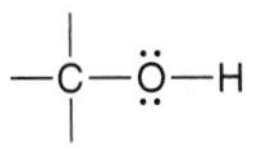 —C—Ö—H	alcohol	-ol	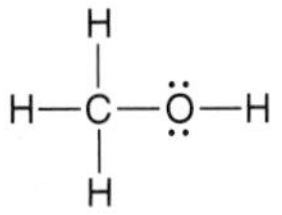 H—C—Ö—H	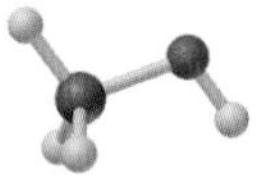	methanol (methyl alcohol)
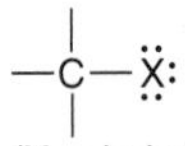 —C—Ẍ: (X = halogen)	haloalkane	halo-	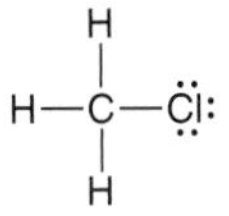 H—C—C̈l:	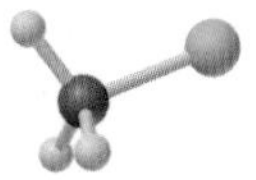	chloromethane (methyl chloride)
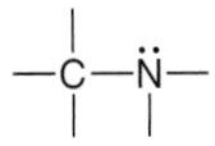 —C—N̈—	amine	-amine	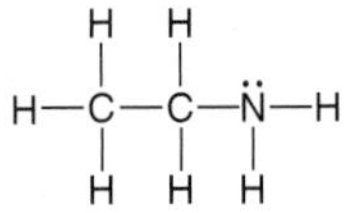 H—C—C—N̈—H	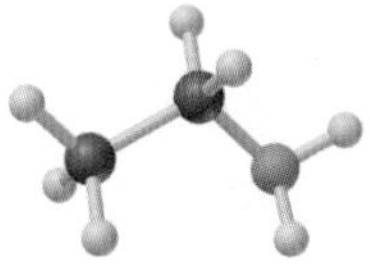	ethanamine (ethylamine)
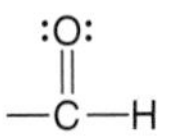 —C—H (with :O: double bond)	aldehyde	-al	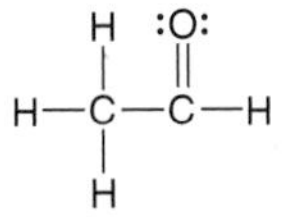 H—C—C—H (with :O:)	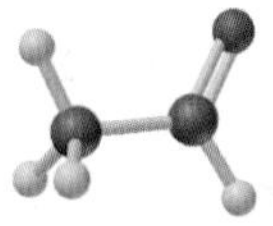	ethanal (acetaldehyde)
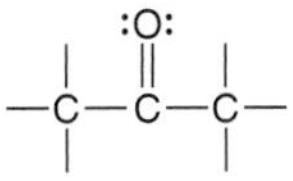 —C—C—C— (with :O: double bond on center C)	ketone	-one	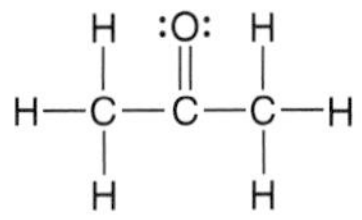 H—C—C—C—H (with :O:)	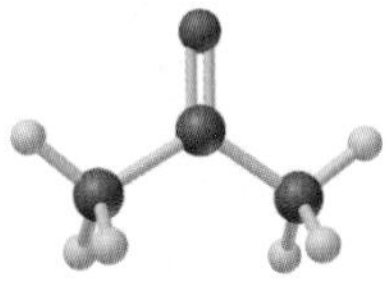	2-propanone (acetone)
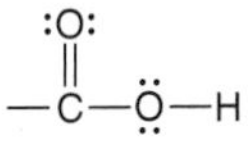 —C—Ö—H (with :O: double bond)	carboxylic acid	-oic acid	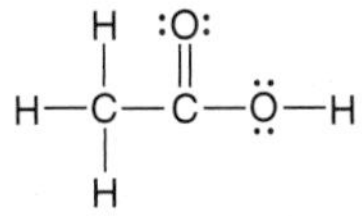 H—C—C—Ö—H (with :O:)	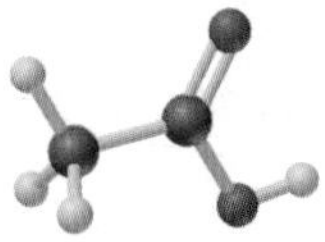	ethanoic acid (acetic acid)
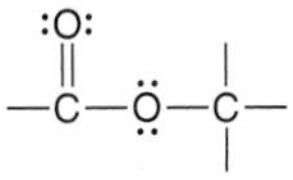 —C—Ö—C— (with :O: double bond)	ester	-oate	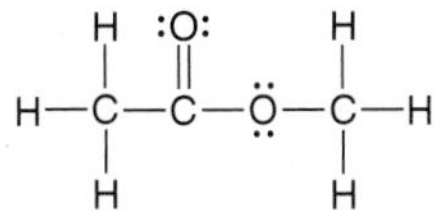 H—C—C—Ö—C—H (with :O:)	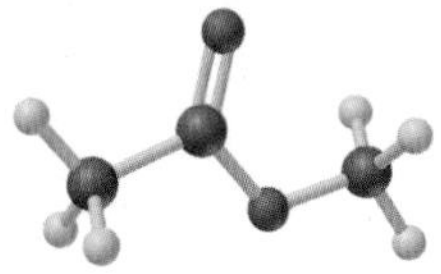	methyl ethanoate (methyl acetate)
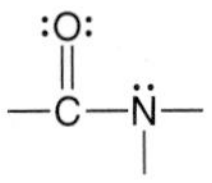 —C—N̈— (with :O: double bond)	amide	-amide	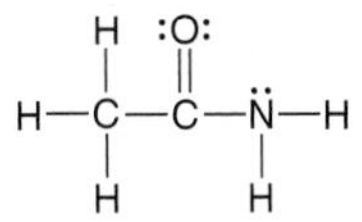 H—C—C—N̈—H (with :O:)	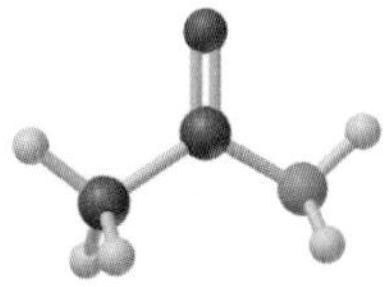	ethanamide (acetamide)
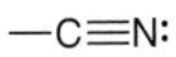 —C≡N:	nitrile	-nitrile	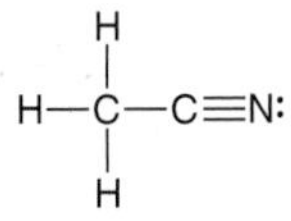 H—C—C≡N:	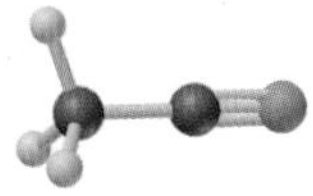	ethanenitrile (acetonitrile, methyl cyanide)

$H_3C—\overset{..}{\underset{..}{O}}H$

Methanol (methyl alcohol)
Byproduct in coal gasification;
de-icing agent; gasoline substitute;
precursor of organic compounds

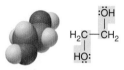

$\overset{\displaystyle :\overset{..}{O}H}{\underset{\displaystyle H\overset{..}{O}:}{\overset{|}{H_2C—CH_2}}}$

1,2-Ethanediol (ethylene glycol)
Main component of auto antifreeze

$\overset{\displaystyle H\overset{..}{O}—CH_2}{\underset{\displaystyle H\overset{..}{O}—\overset{C}{\overset{\|}{\overset{..}{O}:}}}{\overset{|}{H_2\overset{..}{N}—CH}}}$

Serine
Amino acid found in most proteins

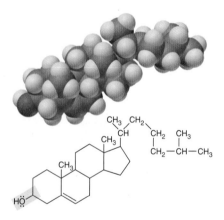

Cholesterol
Major sterol in animals; essential for cell
membranes; precursor of steroid hormones

**FIGURE 15.10 Some molecules with the
alcohol functional group.**

Functional Groups with Only Single Bonds

The most common functional groups with only single bonds are alcohols, haloalkanes, and amines.

Alcohols The **alcohol** functional group consists of carbon bonded to an —OH group, $—\overset{|}{\underset{|}{C}}—\overset{..}{O}—H$, and the general formula of an alcohol is R—OH. Alcohols are named by dropping the final *-e* from the parent hydrocarbon name and adding the suffix *-ol*. Thus, the two-carbon alcohol is ethanol (ethan- + -ol). The common name is the hydrocarbon *root- + -yl,* followed by "alcohol"; thus, the common name of ethanol is ethyl alcohol. (This substance has been consumed as an intoxicant since ancient times; today, it is recognized as the most abused drug in the world.) Alcohols are important laboratory reagents, and the functional group occurs in many biomolecules, including carbohydrates, sterols, and some amino acids. Figure 15.10 shows the names, structures, and uses of some important compounds that contain the alcohol group.

Alcohols undergo elimination and substitution reactions. Dehydration, the elimination of H and OH, requires acid and forms alkenes:

cyclohexanol → cyclohexene + H_2O

Elimination of two H atoms requires inorganic oxidizing agents, such as $K_2Cr_2O_7$ in aqueous H_2SO_4. The reaction oxidizes the HC—OH group to the C=O group (shown with condensed and carbon-skeleton formulas):

$$CH_3—CH_2—\overset{\displaystyle OH}{\overset{|}{CH}}—CH_3 \xrightarrow[H_2SO_4]{K_2Cr_2O_7} CH_3—CH_2—\overset{\displaystyle O}{\overset{\|}{C}}—CH_3$$

2-butanol → 2-butanone

For alcohols with an OH group at the end of the chain (R—CH$_2$—OH), another oxidation occurs. Wine turns sour, for example, when the ethanol in contact with air is oxidized to acetic acid (vinegar):

$$CH_3—\overset{\displaystyle OH}{\overset{|}{CH_2}} \xrightarrow[-H_2O]{\frac{1}{2}O_2} CH_3—\overset{\displaystyle O}{\overset{\|}{CH}} \xrightarrow{\frac{1}{2}O_2} CH_3—\overset{\displaystyle O}{\overset{\|}{C}}—OH$$

Substitution yields products with other single-bonded functional groups. With hydrohalic acids, many alcohols give haloalkanes:

$$R_2CH—OH + HBr \longrightarrow R_2CH—Br + HOH$$

As you'll see below, *the C atom undergoing the change in a substitution is bonded to a more electronegative element,* which makes it partially positive and, thus, a target for a negatively charged or electron-rich group of an incoming reactant.

Haloalkanes A *halogen* atom (X) bonded to C gives the **haloalkane** functional group, $—\overset{|}{\underset{|}{C}}—\overset{..}{\underset{..}{X}}:$, and compounds with the general formula R—X. Haloalkanes (common name, **alkyl halides**) are named by adding the halogen as a prefix to the hydrocarbon name and numbering the C atom to which the halogen is attached, as in bromomethane, 2-chloropropane, or 1,3-diiodohexane.

Just as many alcohols undergo substitution to alkyl halides when treated with halide ions in acid, many alkyl halides undergo substitution to alcohols in base. For example, OH^- attacks the positive C end of the C—X bond and displaces X^-:

$$CH_3-CH_2-CH_2-CH_2-Br + OH^- \longrightarrow CH_3-CH_2-CH_2-CH_2-OH + Br^-$$

1-bromobutane   1-butanol

Substitution by groups such as —CN, —SH, —OR, and $-NH_2$ allows chemists to convert alkyl halides to a host of other compounds.

Just as addition of HX *to* an alkene produces haloalkanes, elimination of HX *from* a haloalkane by reaction with a strong base, such as potassium ethoxide, produces an alkene:

$$CH_3-\overset{\overset{\displaystyle CH_3}{|}}{\underset{\underset{\displaystyle Cl}{|}}{C}}-CH_3 + CH_3-CH_2-OK \longrightarrow CH_3-\overset{\overset{\displaystyle CH_3}{|}}{C}=CH_2 + KCl + CH_3-CH_2-OH$$

2-chloro-2-methylpropane   potassium ethoxide   2-methylpropene

Haloalkanes have many important uses, but many are carcinogenic in mammals, have severe neurological effects in humans, and, to make matters worse, are very stable and accumulate in the environment.

Amines The **amine** functional group is $-\overset{|}{\underset{|}{C}}-\overset{|}{\underset{|}{N}}:$. Chemists classify amines as derivatives of ammonia, with R groups in place of one or more H atoms. *Primary* (1°) amines are RNH_2, *secondary* (2°) amines are R_2NH, and *tertiary* (3°) amines are R_3N. Like ammonia, amines have trigonal pyramidal shapes and a lone pair of electrons on a partially negative N atom (Figure 15.11). Systematic names drop the final *-e* of the alkane and add the suffix *-amine,* as in ethanamine. However, there is still wide usage of common names, in which the suffix *-amine* follows the name of the alkyl group; thus, methylamine has one methyl group attached to N, diethylamine has two ethyl groups attached, and so forth. Figure 15.12 shows that the amine functional group occurs in many biomolecules.

Amines undergo substitution reactions in which the lone pair of N attacks the partially positive C in an alkyl halide to displace X^- and form a larger amine:

$$2CH_3-CH_2-\overset{..}{N}H_2 + CH_3-CH_2-Cl \longrightarrow CH_3-CH_2-\underset{\underset{\displaystyle CH_3-CH_2}{|}}{\overset{..}{N}H} + CH_3-CH_2-\overset{+}{N}H_3Cl^-$$

ethylamine   chloroethane   diethylamine   ethylammonium chloride

(One molecule of ethylamine participates in the substitution, while the other binds the released H^+ and prevents it from remaining on the diethylamine product.)

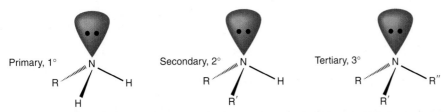

Primary, 1°   Secondary, 2°   Tertiary, 3°

FIGURE 15.11 General structures of amines. Amines have a trigonal pyramidal shape and are classified by the number of R groups bonded to N. The lone pair of the nitrogen atom is the key to amine reactivity.

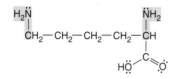

Lysine (primary amine)
Amino acid found in
most proteins

Adenine (primary amine)
Component of nucleic
acids

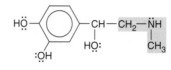

**Epinephrine (adrenaline;
secondary amine)**
Neurotransmitter in brain;
hormone released
during stress

Cocaine (tertiary amine)
Brain stimulant; widely
abused drug

FIGURE 15.12 Some biomolecules with the amine functional group.

SAMPLE PROBLEM 15.4 Predicting the Reactions of Alcohols, Alkyl Halides, and Amines

Problem Determine the reaction type and predict the product(s) for each of the following reactions:
(a) $CH_3—CH_2—CH_2—I + NaOH \longrightarrow$
(b) $CH_3—CH_2—Br + 2CH_3—CH_2—CH_2—NH_2 \longrightarrow$

(c) $CH_3—\underset{\underset{OH}{|}}{CH}—CH_3 \xrightarrow[H_2SO_4]{Cr_2O_7{}^{2-}}$

Plan We first determine the functional group(s) of the reactant(s) and then examine any inorganic reagent(s) to decide on the possible reaction type, keeping in mind that, in general, these functional groups undergo substitution or elimination. (a) The reactant is an alkyl halide, so the OH⁻ of the inorganic reagent substitutes for the —I. (b) The reactants are an amine and an alkyl halide, so the N: of the amine substitutes for the —Br. (c) The reactant is an alcohol, the inorganic reagents form a strong oxidizing agent, and the alcohol undergoes elimination to a carbonyl compound.

Solution (a) Substitution: The products are $CH_3—CH_2—CH_2—OH + NaI$

(b) Substitution: The products are $CH_3—CH_2—CH_2—\underset{\underset{CH_2—CH_3}{|}}{NH} + CH_3—CH_2—CH_2—\overset{+}{N}H_3Br^-$

(c) Elimination: (oxidation): The product is $CH_3—\underset{\underset{O}{\|}}{C}—CH_3$

Check The only changes should be at the functional group.

FOLLOW-UP PROBLEM 15.4 Fill in the blank in each of the following reactions. (*Hint:* Examine any inorganic compounds and the organic product to determine the organic reactant.)

(a) _____ $+ CH_3—ONa \longrightarrow CH_3—CH=\underset{\underset{CH_3}{|}}{C}—CH_3 + NaCl + CH_3—OH$

(b) _____ $\xrightarrow[H_2SO_4]{Cr_2O_7{}^{2-}} CH_3—CH_2—\underset{\underset{O}{\|}}{C}—OH$

Functional Groups with Double Bonds

The most important functional groups with double bonds are the C=C of alkenes and the C=O of aldehydes and ketones. Both appear in many organic and biological molecules. *Their most common reaction type is addition.*

Alkenes Although the $\diagdown$C=C$\diagup$ functional group in an alkene can be converted to the —C≡C— group of an alkyne, *alkenes typically undergo addition.* The electron-rich double bond is readily attracted to the partially positive H atoms of hydronium ions and hydrohalic acids, yielding alcohols and alkyl halides, respectively:

$$CH_3-\underset{\underset{CH_3}{|}}{C}=CH_2 \; + \; H_3O^+ \longrightarrow CH_3-\underset{\underset{OH}{|}}{\overset{\overset{CH_3}{|}}{C}}-CH_3 \; + \; H^+$$

2-methylpropene   2-methyl-2-propanol

$$CH_3-CH=CH_2 \; + \; HCl \longrightarrow CH_3-\underset{\underset{Cl}{|}}{\overset{\overset{Cl}{|}}{C}H}-CH_3$$

propene   2-chloropropane

Aldehydes and Ketones The C=O bond, or **carbonyl group,** is one of the most chemically versatile. In the **aldehyde** functional group, the carbonyl C is bonded to H (and often to another C), so it occurs *at the end of a chain,* $R-\underset{}{\overset{\overset{H}{|}}{C}}=O$. Aldehyde names drop the final *-e* from the alkane name and add *-al*. For example, the three-C aldehyde is propanal. In the **ketone** functional group, the carbonyl C is bonded to two other C atoms, $-\underset{}{\overset{}{C}}-\overset{\overset{:O:}{||}}{C}-\underset{}{\overset{}{C}}-$, so it occurs *within the chain.*

Ketones, $R-\overset{\overset{O}{||}}{C}-R'$, are named by numbering the carbonyl C, dropping the final *-e* from the alkane name, and adding *-one*. For example, the unbranched, five-C ketone with the carbonyl C as C-2 in the chain is named 2-pentanone. Figure 15.13 shows some common carbonyl compounds.

FIGURE 15.13 Some common aldehydes and ketones.

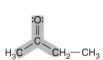

Methanal (formaldehyde)
Used to make resins in plywood, dishware, countertops; biological preservative

Ethanal (acetaldehyde)
Narcotic product of ethanol metabolism; used to make perfumes, flavors, plastics, other chemicals

Benzaldehyde
Artificial almond flavoring

2-Propanone (acetone)
Solvent for fat, rubber, plastic, varnish, lacquer; chemical feedstock

2-Butanone (methyl ethyl ketone)
Important solvent

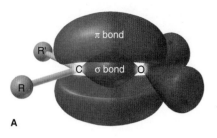

A

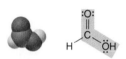

B

FIGURE 15.14 The carbonyl group.
A, The σ and π bonds that make up the
C=O bond of the carbonyl group. **B,** The
charged resonance form shows that the
C=O bond is polar (ΔEN = 1.0).

Like the C=C bond, the C=O bond is *electron rich;* unlike the C=C bond, it is *highly polar* (ΔEN = 1.0). Figure 15.14 shows the bond types of the carbonyl group and emphasizes its polarity with a charged resonance form. Aldehydes and ketones are formed by the oxidation of alcohols:

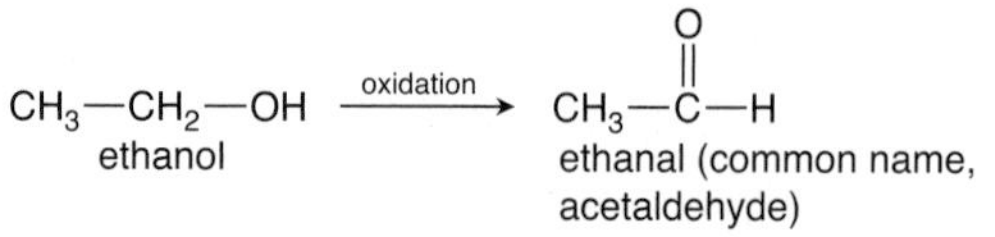

$$CH_3-CH_2-OH \xrightarrow{\text{oxidation}} CH_3-\overset{\displaystyle O}{\overset{\|}{C}}-H$$

ethanol   ethanal (common name, acetaldehyde)

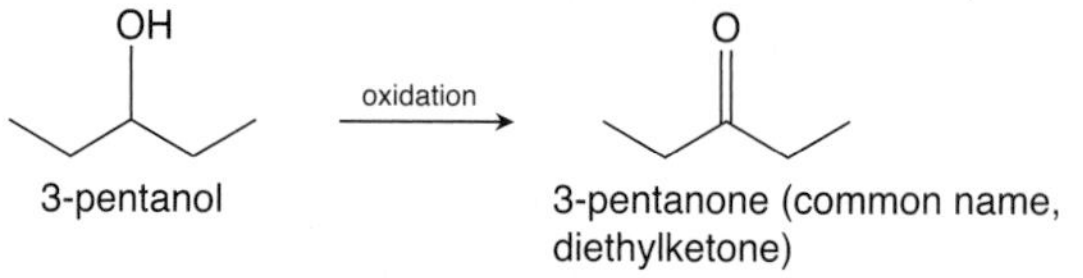

3-pentanol $\xrightarrow{\text{oxidation}}$ 3-pentanone (common name, diethylketone)

Conversely, as a result of their unsaturation, carbonyl compounds can undergo *addition* and be reduced to alcohols:

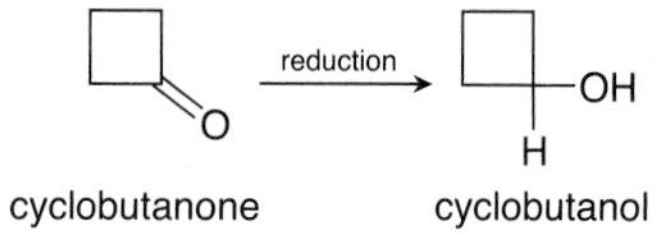

cyclobutanone $\xrightarrow{\text{reduction}}$ cyclobutanol

Functional Groups with Both Single and Double Bonds

A family of three functional groups contains a C double bonded to O (a carbonyl group) *and* single bonded to O or N. The parent of the family is the **carboxylic acid** group, $-\overset{\displaystyle :O:}{\overset{\|}{C}}-\ddot{O}H$, also called the *carboxyl group* and written —COOH. *The most important reaction type of this family is substitution from one member to another.* Substitution for the —OH by the —OR of an alcohol gives the **ester** group, $-\overset{\displaystyle :O:}{\overset{\|}{C}}-\ddot{O}-R$; substitution by the $-\ddot{N}-$ of an amine gives the **amide** group, $-\overset{\displaystyle :O:}{\overset{\|}{C}}-\overset{\displaystyle |}{\underset{\displaystyle \cdots}{N}}-$.

Carboxylic Acids Carboxylic acids, $R-\overset{\displaystyle O}{\overset{\|}{C}}-OH$, are named by dropping the *-e* from the alkane name and adding *-oic acid;* however, many common names are used. For example, the four-C acid is butanoic acid (the carboxyl C is counted when choosing the root); its common name is butyric acid. Figure 15.15 shows some important carboxylic acids. The carboxyl C already has three bonds, so it forms only one other. In formic acid (methanoic acid), the carboxyl C bonds to an H, but in all other carboxylic acids it bonds to a chain or ring.

Carboxylic acids are weak acids in water:

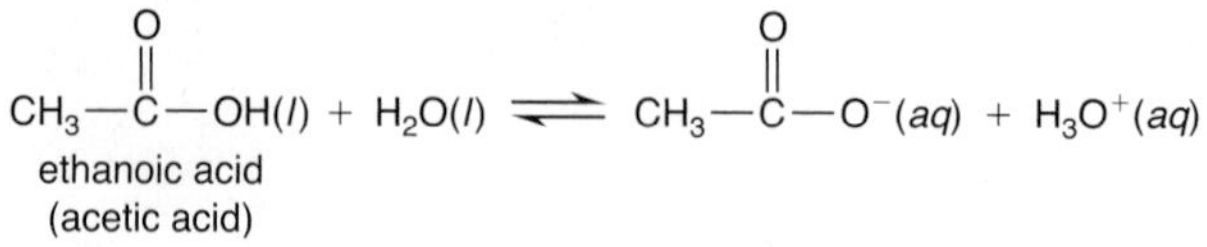

$$CH_3-\overset{\displaystyle O}{\overset{\|}{C}}-OH(l) + H_2O(l) \rightleftharpoons CH_3-\overset{\displaystyle O}{\overset{\|}{C}}-O^-(aq) + H_3O^+(aq)$$

ethanoic acid
(acetic acid)

At equilibrium in acid solutions of typical concentration, more than 99% of the acid molecules are undissociated at any given moment. In strong base, however, they react completely to form a salt and water:

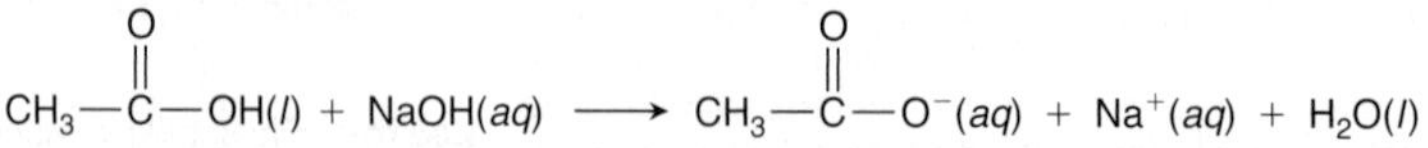

$$CH_3-\overset{\displaystyle O}{\overset{\|}{C}}-OH(l) + NaOH(aq) \longrightarrow CH_3-\overset{\displaystyle O}{\overset{\|}{C}}-O^-(aq) + Na^+(aq) + H_2O(l)$$

The anion is the *carboxylate ion,* named by dropping *-oic acid* and adding *-oate;* the sodium salt of butanoic acid, for instance, is sodium butanoate.

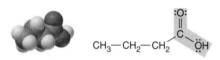

Methanoic acid (formic acid)
An irritating component
of ant and bee stings

$$CH_3-CH_2-CH_2-\overset{\displaystyle :O:}{\overset{\|}{C}}-\ddot{O}H$$

Butanoic acid (butyric acid)
Odor of rancid butter;
suspected component of
monkey sex attractant

Benzoic acid
Calorimetric standard;
used in preserving food,
dyeing fabric, curing tobacco

$$CH_3(CH_2)_{16}-\overset{\displaystyle :O:}{\overset{\|}{C}}-\ddot{O}H$$

Octadecanoic acid (stearic acid)
Found in animal fats; used in
making candles and soaps

FIGURE 15.15 Some molecules with the carboxylic acid functional group.

Carboxylic acids with long hydrocarbon chains are **fatty acids,** an essential group of compounds found in all cells. Animal fatty acids have saturated chains (see stearic acid, Figure 15.15, *bottom*), whereas many from vegetable sources are unsaturated. Fatty acid salts are soaps, with their cations usually from Group 1A(1) or 2A(2). When clothes with greasy spots are immersed in soapy water, the nonpolar "tails" of the soap molecules interact with the grease, while the ionic "heads" interact with the water. Agitation of the water rinses the grease away.

Substitution of carboxylic acids occurs through a two-step sequence: *addition plus elimination equals substitution.* Addition to the trigonal planar shape of the carbonyl group gives an unstable tetrahedral species, which immediately undergoes elimination to revert to a trigonal planar product:

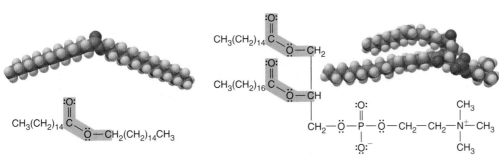

Strong heating of carboxylic acids forms an **acid anhydride** through a type of substitution called a *dehydration-condensation reaction* (Section 14.6), in which two molecules condense into one with loss of water:

Esters *An alcohol and a carboxylic acid form an ester.* The first part of an ester name designates the alcohol portion and the second the acid portion (named in the same way as the carboxylate ion). For example, the ester formed between ethanol and ethanoic acid is ethyl ethanoate (common name, ethyl acetate), a solvent for nail polish and model glue.

The ester group occurs commonly in **lipids,** a large group of fatty biological substances. Most dietary fats are *triglycerides,* esters that are composed of three fatty acids linked to the alcohol 1,2,3-trihydroxypropane (common name, glycerol) and that function as energy stores. Some important lipids are shown in Figure 15.16; lecithin is one of several phospholipids that make up the lipid bilayer in all cell membranes.

Esters, like acid anhydrides, form through a dehydration-condensation reaction; in this case, it is called an *esterification:*

Note that the esterification reaction is reversible. The opposite of dehydration-condensation is called **hydrolysis,** in which the O atom of water is attracted to the partially positive C atom of the ester, cleaving (lysing) the molecule into two parts. One part receives water's —OH, and the other part receives water's other H.

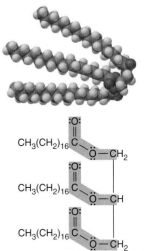

Cetyl palmitate The most common lipid in whale blubber

Lecithin Phospholipid found in all cell membranes

Tristearin Typical dietary fat used as an energy store in animals

FIGURE 15.16 Some lipid molecules with the ester functional group.

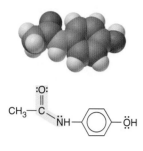

:O:
$CH_3-\overset{\displaystyle \overset{\| }{C}}{}-\overset{\displaystyle \ddot{N}H}{}-\!\!\!\!\!\!\diagdown\!\!\!\!\!\!\diagup\!\!\!\!\!\!-\ddot{O}H$

Acetaminophen
Active ingredient in nonaspirin
pain relievers; used to make dyes
and photographic chemicals

:O:
$H-\overset{\displaystyle \overset{\| }{C}}{}-\overset{\displaystyle \underset{CH_3}{\ddot{N}}}{}-CH_3$

**N,N-Dimethylmethanamide
(dimethylformamide)**
Major organic solvent; used in
production of synthetic fibers

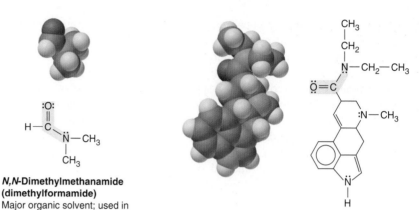

Lysergic acid diethylamide (LSD-25) A potent hallucinogen

FIGURE 15.17 Some molecules with the amide functional group.

Amides The product of a substitution between an amine (or NH_3) and an ester is an amide. The partially negative N of the amine is attracted to the partially positive C of the ester, an alcohol (ROH) is lost, and an amide forms:

$$CH_3-\overset{\displaystyle \overset{O}{\| }}{C}-O-CH_3 \;+\; H\overset{\displaystyle \underset{H}{\ddot{N}}}{}-CH_2-CH_3 \longrightarrow CH_3-\overset{\displaystyle \overset{O}{\| }}{C}-\overset{\displaystyle \overset{H}{N}}{}-CH_2-CH_3 \;+\; CH_3-OH$$

methyl ethanoate   ethanamine   N-ethylethanamide   methanol
(methyl acetate)   (ethylamine)   (N-ethylacetamide)

Amides are named by denoting the amine portion with *N*- and replacing *-oic acid* from the parent carboxylic acid with *-amide*. In the amide from the previous reaction, the ethyl group comes from the amine, and the acid portion comes from ethanoic acid (acetic acid). Some amides are shown in Figure 15.17.

Amides are hydrolyzed in hot water (or base) to a carboxylic acid (or carboxylate ion) and an amine. Thus, even though amides are not normally formed in the following way, they can be viewed as the result of a reversible dehydration-condensation:

$$R-\overset{\displaystyle \overset{O}{\| }}{C}\boxed{-OH + H}-\overset{\displaystyle \overset{H}{N}}{}-R' \rightleftharpoons R-\overset{\displaystyle \overset{O}{\| }}{C}-\overset{\displaystyle \overset{H}{N}}{}-R' + HOH$$

The most important example of the amide group is the *peptide bond* (discussed in Section 15.6), which links amino acids in a protein.

SAMPLE PROBLEM 15.5 | Predicting Reactions of the Carboxylic Acid Family

Problem Predict the product(s) of the following reactions:

(a) $CH_3-CH_2-CH_2-\overset{\displaystyle \overset{O}{\| }}{C}-OH \;+\; CH_3-\overset{\displaystyle \overset{OH}{| }}{CH}-CH_3 \overset{H^+}{\rightleftharpoons}$

(b) $CH_3-\overset{\displaystyle \underset{CH_3}{| }}{CH}-CH_2-CH_2-\overset{\displaystyle \overset{O}{\| }}{C}-NH-CH_2-CH_3 \overset{NaOH}{\underset{H_2O}{\longrightarrow}}$

Plan We discussed substitution reactions (including addition-elimination and dehydration-condensation) and hydrolysis. (a) A carboxylic acid and an alcohol react, so the reaction must be a substitution to form an ester and water. (b) An amide reacts with OH^-, so it is hydrolyzed to an amine and a sodium carboxylate.

Solution (a) Formation of an ester:

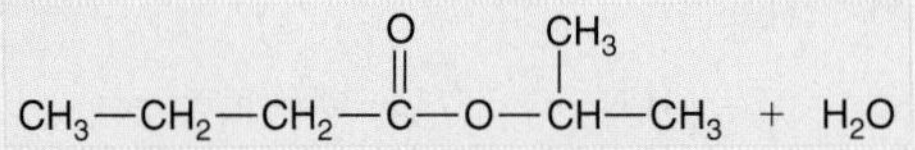

$$CH_3-CH_2-CH_2-\overset{\overset{\displaystyle O}{\|}}{C}-O-\overset{\overset{\displaystyle CH_3}{|}}{CH}-CH_3 \ + \ H_2O$$

(b) Basic hydrolysis of an amide:

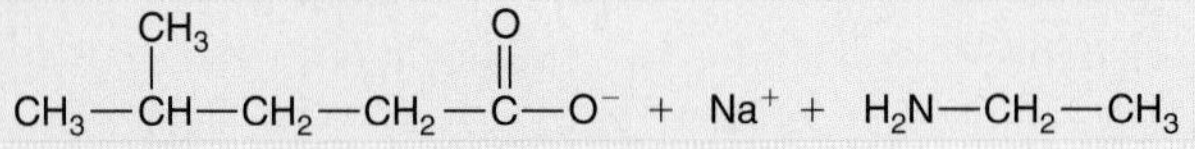

$$\overset{\overset{\displaystyle CH_3}{|}}{CH_3-CH}-CH_2-CH_2-\overset{\overset{\displaystyle O}{\|}}{C}-O^- \ + \ Na^+ \ + \ H_2N-CH_2-CH_3$$

Check Note that in part (b), the carboxylate ion forms, rather than the acid, because the aqueous NaOH that is present reacts with the carboxylic acid.

FOLLOW-UP PROBLEM 15.5 Fill in the blanks in the following reactions:

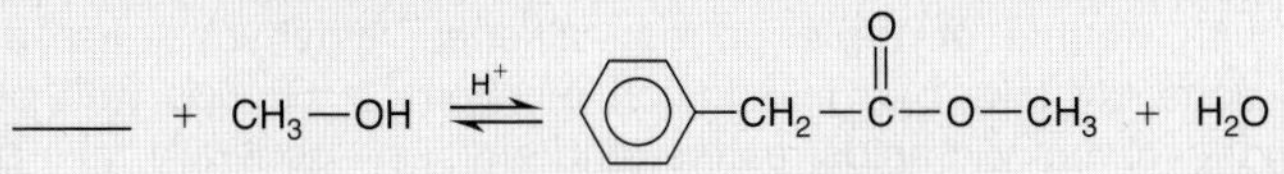

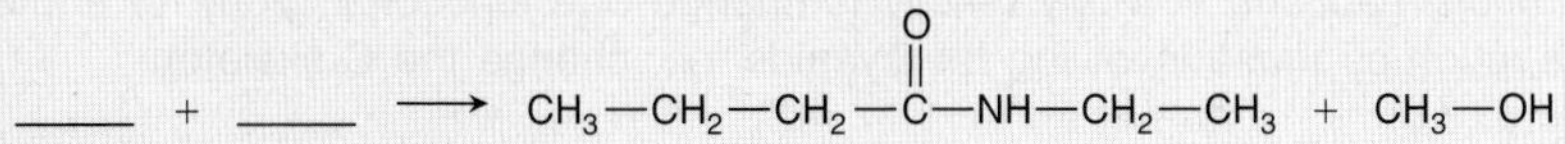

(a) _____ + CH$_3$—OH $\overset{H^+}{\rightleftharpoons}$ (○)—CH$_2$—$\overset{\overset{\displaystyle O}{\|}}{C}$—O—CH$_3$ + H$_2$O

(b) _____ + _____ $\longrightarrow$ CH$_3$—CH$_2$—CH$_2$—$\overset{\overset{\displaystyle O}{\|}}{C}$—NH—CH$_2$—CH$_3$ + CH$_3$—OH

Functional Groups with Triple Bonds

There are only two important functional groups with triple bonds. *Alkynes*, with their electron-rich —C≡C— group, undergo addition (by H$_2$O, H$_2$, HX, X$_2$, and so forth) to form double-bonded or saturated compounds:

$$\underset{\text{propyne}}{CH_3-C\equiv CH} \ \overset{H_2}{\longrightarrow} \ \underset{\text{propene}}{CH_3-CH=CH_2} \ \overset{H_2}{\longrightarrow} \ \underset{\text{propane}}{CH_3-CH_2-CH_3}$$

Nitriles (R—C≡N) contain the **nitrile** group (—C≡N:) and are made by substituting a CN$^-$ (cyanide) ion for X$^-$ in a reaction with an alkyl halide:

$$CH_3-CH_2-Cl \ + \ NaCN \ \longrightarrow \ CH_3-CH_2-C\equiv N \ + \ NaCl$$

This reaction is useful because it *increases the hydrocarbon chain by one C atom.* Nitriles are versatile because once they are formed, they can be reduced to amines or hydrolyzed to carboxylic acids:

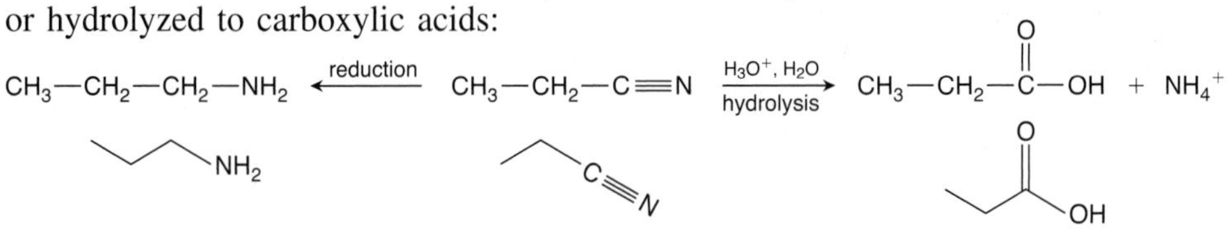

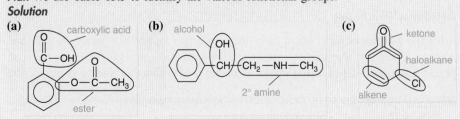

SAMPLE PROBLEM 15.6   Recognizing Functional Groups

Problem Circle and name the functional groups in the following molecules:

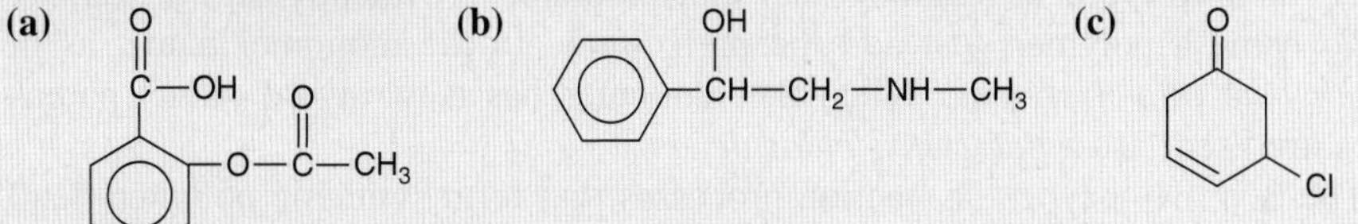

(a)

(b)

(c)

Plan We use Table 15.5 to identify the various functional groups.

Solution

(a)
carboxylic acid
ester

(b)
alcohol
2° amine

(c)
ketone
haloalkane
alkene

FOLLOW-UP PROBLEM 15.6 Circle and name the functional groups:

(a)

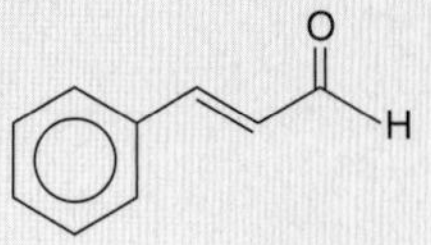

(b) $H_2N-\overset{\overset{\displaystyle O}{\|}}{C}-CH_2-\underset{\underset{\displaystyle Br}{|}}{CH}-CH_3$

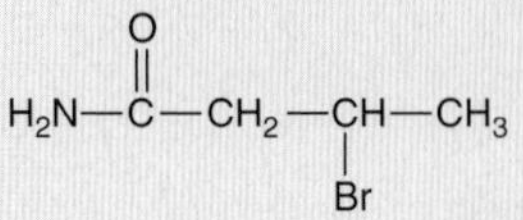

SECTION 15.4 SUMMARY

Organic reactions are initiated when regions of high and low electron density of different reactant molecules attract each other. • Groups containing only single bonds—alcohols, amines, and alkyl halides—take part in substitution and elimination reactions. • Groups with double or triple bonds—alkenes, aldehydes, ketones, alkynes, and nitriles—generally take part in addition reactions. • Groups with both double and single bonds—carboxylic acids, esters, and amides—generally take part in substitution reactions. • Many reactions change one functional group to another, but some, such as those involving the cyanide ion, change the C skeleton.

15.5 THE MONOMER-POLYMER THEME I: SYNTHETIC MACROMOLECULES

In its simplest form, a **polymer** (Greek, "many parts") is an extremely large molecule, or **macromolecule,** consisting of a covalently linked chain of smaller molecules, called **monomers** (Greek, "one part"). The monomer is the *repeat unit* of the polymer, and a typical polymer may have from hundreds to hundreds of thousands of repeat units. There are many types of monomers, and their chemical structures allow for the complete repertoire of intermolecular forces. *Synthetic* polymers are created by chemical reactions in the laboratory; *natural* polymers (or *biopolymers*) are created by chemical reactions within organisms, and we'll discuss them in the next section.

Virtually every home, car, electronic device, and processed food contains synthetic polymers in its structure or packaging. You interact with dozens of these materials each day—from paints to floor coverings to clothing to the paper coating and adhesives in this textbook. Some of these materials, like those used in food containers, do not break down in the environment and have created a serious waste-disposal problem. Others are being actively recycled into numerous useful products, such as garbage bags, outdoor furniture, roofing tiles, and even marine pilings and roadside curbs. Still others, such as artificial skin, heart valve components, and hip joints, are designed to have a very long life (see silicones in Section 14.5). In this section, we'll see how synthetic polymers are named and discuss the two types of reactions that link monomers covalently into a chain.

To name a polymer, just add the prefix *poly-* to the monomer name, as in *polyethylene* or *polystyrene*. When the monomer has a two-word name, parentheses are used, as in *poly(vinyl chloride)*.

The two major types of reaction processes that form synthetic polymers lend their names to the resulting polymer classes—addition and condensation.

Addition Polymers

Addition polymers form when monomers undergo an addition reaction with one another. These are also called *chain-reaction* (or *chain-growth*) *polymers* because as each monomer adds to the chain, it forms a new reactive site to continue the process. The monomers of most addition polymers have the $\overset{\diagdown}{\underset{\diagup}{C}}=\overset{\diagup}{\underset{\diagdown}{C}}$ grouping.

Table 15.6 Some Major Addition Polymers

Monomer	Polymer	Applications
$H_2C=CH_2$ (all H)	polyethylene	Plastic bags; bottles; toys
$F_2C=CF_2$ (all F)	polytetrafluoroethylene	Cooking utensils (e.g., Teflon)
$H_2C=CH(CH_3)$	polypropylene	Carpeting (indoor-outdoor); bottles
$H_2C=CH(Cl)$	poly(vinyl chloride)	Plastic wrap; garden hose; indoor plumbing
$H_2C=CH(C_6H_5)$	polystyrene	Insulation; furniture; packing materials
$H_2C=CH(CN)$	polyacrylonitrile	Yarns, fabrics, and wigs (e.g., Orlon, Acrilan)
$H_2C=CH(O-CO-CH_3)$	poly(vinyl acetate)	Adhesives; paints; textile coatings; computer disks
$H_2C=C(Cl)_2$	poly(vinylidene chloride)	Food wrap (e.g., Saran)
$H_2C=C(CH_3)(CO-O-CH_3)$	poly(methyl methacrylate)	Glass substitute (e.g., Lucite, Plexiglas); bowling balls; paint

As you can see from Table 15.6, the essential differences between an acrylic sweater, a plastic grocery bag, and a bowling ball are due to the different groups that are attached to the double-bonded C atoms of the monomer.

The *free-radical polymerization* of ethene (ethylene, $CH_2=CH_2$) to polyethylene is a simple example of the addition process. In Figure 15.18 (on the next page), the monomer reacts to form a *free radical,* a species with an unpaired electron, that seeks an electron from another monomer to form a covalent bond. The process begins when an *initiator,* usually a peroxide, generates a free radical that attacks the π bond of an ethylene unit, forming a σ bond with one of the electrons and leaving the other unpaired. This new free radical then attacks the π bond of another ethylene, joining it to the chain end, and the backbone of the polymer grows one unit longer. This process continues until two free radicals form a covalent bond or a very stable free radical is formed by addition of an *inhibitor* molecule.

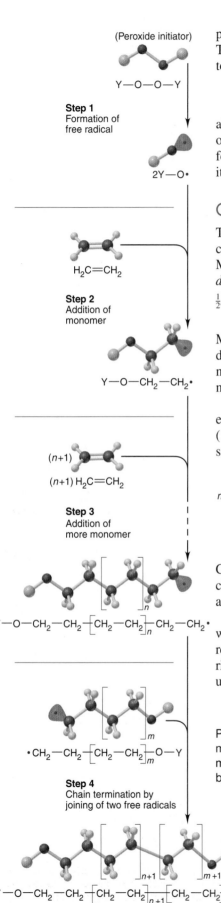

(Peroxide initiator)

Y—O—O—Y

Step 1
Formation of
free radical

2Y—O•

H₂C=CH₂

Step 2
Addition of
monomer

Y—O—CH₂—CH₂•

(n+1)

(n+1) H₂C=CH₂

Step 3
Addition of
more monomer

Y—O—CH₂—CH₂—[CH₂—CH₂]ₙ—CH₂—CH₂•

•CH₂—CH₂—[CH₂—CH₂]ₘ—O—Y

Step 4
Chain termination by
joining of two free radicals

Y—O—CH₂—CH₂—[CH₂—CH₂]ₙ₊₁[CH₂—CH₂]ₘ₊₁—O—Y

The most important polymerization reactions are *stereoselective* to create polymers whose repeat units have groups spatially oriented in particular ways. Through the use of these reactions, polyethylene chains with molar masses of 10^4 to 10^5 g/mol are made by varying conditions and reagents.

Similar methods are used to make polypropylenes, $+CH_2-CH+_n$, that have

$$CH_3$$

all the CH_3 groups of the repeat units oriented either on one side of the chain or on alternating sides. The different orientations lead to chains that pack differently, which leads to differences in such physical properties as density, rigidity, and elasticity.

Condensation Polymers

The monomers of **condensation polymers** must have *two functional groups;* we can designate such a monomer as A—**R**—B (where **R** is the rest of the molecule). Most commonly, the monomers link when an A group on one undergoes a *dehydration-condensation reaction* with a B group on another:

$$\tfrac{1}{2}n\text{H}-\text{A}-\text{R}-\text{B}-\text{OH} + \tfrac{1}{2}n\text{H}-\text{A}-\text{R}-\text{B}-\text{OH} \xrightarrow{-(n-1)\text{HOH}}$$

$$\text{H}+\text{A}-\text{R}-\text{B}+_n\text{OH}$$

Many condensation polymers are *copolymers,* those consisting of two or more different repeat units. For example, condensation of carboxylic acid and amine monomers forms *polyamides (nylons),* whereas carboxylic acid and alcohol monomers form *polyesters.*

One of the most common polyamides is *nylon-66,* manufactured by mixing equimolar amounts of a six-C diamine (1,6-diaminohexane) and a six-C diacid (1,6-hexanedioic acid). The basic amine reacts with the acid to form a "nylon salt." Heating drives off water and forms the amide bonds:

$$n\text{HO}-\overset{\overset{\text{O}}{\|}}{\text{C}}-(\text{CH}_2)_4-\overset{\overset{\text{O}}{\|}}{\text{C}}-\text{OH} + n\text{H}_2\text{N}-(\text{CH}_2)_6-\text{NH}_2 \xrightarrow[-(2n-1)\text{H}_2\text{O}]{\Delta}$$

$$\text{HO}\left[\overset{\overset{\text{O}}{\|}}{\text{C}}-(\text{CH}_2)_4-\overset{\overset{\text{O}}{\|}}{\text{C}}-\text{NH}-(\text{CH}_2)_6-\text{NH}\right]_n\text{H}$$

Covalent bonds within the chains give nylons great strength, and H bonds between chains give them great flexibility. About half of all nylons are made to reinforce automobile tires; the others are used for rugs, clothing, fishing line, and so forth.

Dacron, a popular polyester fiber, is woven from polymer strands formed when equimolar amounts of 1,4-benzenedicarboxylic acid and 1,2-ethanediol react. Blending these polyester fibers with various amounts of cotton gives fabrics that are durable, easily dyed, and crease resistant. Extremely thin Mylar films, used for recording tape and food packaging, are also made from this polymer.

SECTION 15.5 SUMMARY

Polymers are extremely large molecules that are made of repeat units called monomers. • Addition polymers are formed from unsaturated monomers that commonly link through free-radical reactions. • Most condensation polymers are formed by linking two types of monomer through a dehydration-condensation reaction.

FIGURE 15.18 Steps in the free-radical polymerization of ethylene. In this polymerization method, free radicals initiate, propagate, and terminate the formation of an addition polymer. An initiator (Y—O—O—Y) is split to form two molecules of a free radical (Y—O·). The free radical attacks the π bond of a monomer and creates another free radical (Y—O—CH₂—CH₂·). The process continues, and the chain grows (propagates) until an inhibitor is added (not shown) or two free radicals combine.

15.6 THE MONOMER-POLYMER THEME II: BIOLOGICAL MACROMOLECULES

The monomer-polymer theme was being played out in nature eons before humans employed it to such great advantage. Biological macromolecules are nothing more than condensation polymers created by nature's reaction chemistry and improved through evolution. These remarkable molecules are the greatest proof of the versatility of carbon and its handful of atomic partners.

Natural polymers are the "stuff of life"—polysaccharides, proteins, and nucleic acids. Some have structures that make wood strong, hair curly, fingernails hard, and wool flexible. Others speed up the myriad reactions that occur in every cell or defend the body against infection. Still others possess the genetic information organisms need to forge other biomolecules. Remarkable as these giant molecules are, the functional groups of their monomers and the reactions that link them are identical to those for other, smaller organic molecules, and the same intermolecular forces that dissolve smaller molecules stabilize these giant molecules in the aqueous medium of the cell.

Sugars and Polysaccharides

In essence, the same chemical change occurs when you burn a piece of wood or eat a piece of bread. Wood and bread are mixtures of *carbohydrates,* substances that provide energy through oxidation.

Monomer Structure and Linkage   Glucose and other simple sugars are called **monosaccharides** and consist of carbon chains with attached hydroxyl and carbonyl groups. In addition to their roles as individual molecules engaged in energy metabolism, they serve as the monomer units of **polysaccharides.** Most natural polysaccharides are formed from five- and six-C units. In aqueous solution, *an alcohol group and the aldehyde (or ketone) group of a given monosaccharide react with each other to form a cyclic molecule with either a five- or six-membered ring* (Figure 15.19A). When two monosaccharides undergo a dehydration-condensation reaction, a **disaccharide** forms. For example, sucrose (table sugar) is a disaccharide of glucose and fructose (Figure 15.19B).

A polysaccharide consists of *many* monosaccharide units linked covalently. The three major natural polysaccharides consist entirely of glucose units, but they differ in the details of how they are linked. *Cellulose* is the most abundant organic chemical on Earth. More than 50% of the carbon in plants occurs in the cellulose of stems and leaves; wood is largely cellulose, and cotton is more than 90% cellulose. It consists of long chains of glucose H-bonded to one another to form planes that H bond to planes above and below. Thus, the great strength of wood is due largely to H bonds. *Starch* serves as the energy storage molecule in plants. It occurs as a helical molecule of several thousand glucose units mixed with a highly

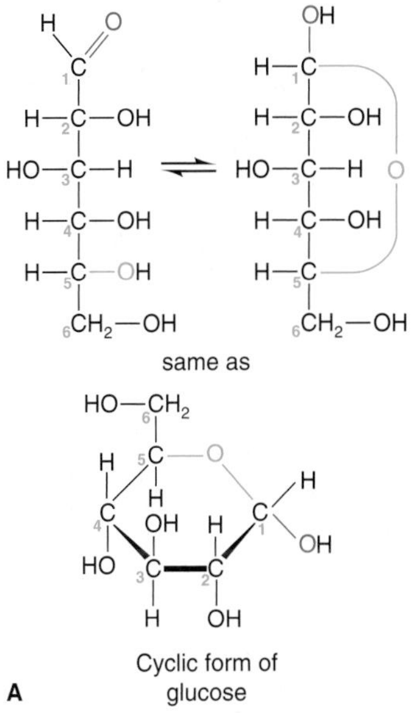

A Cyclic form of glucose

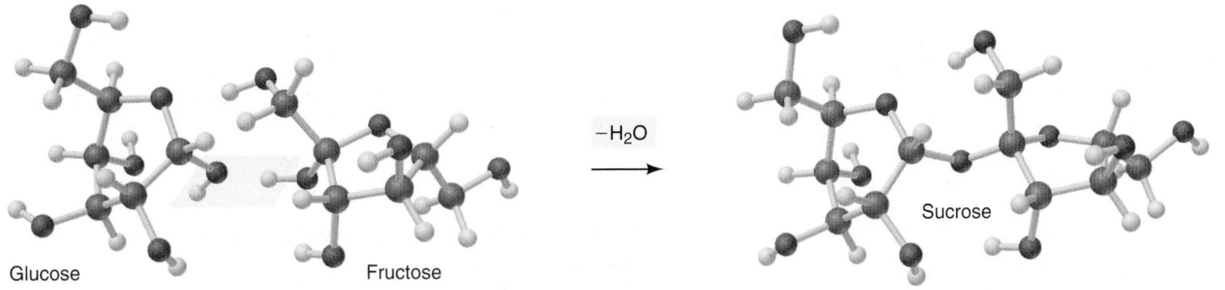

B Glucose   Fructose   Sucrose

−H₂O

FIGURE 15.19 The structure of glucose in aqueous solution and the formation of a disaccharide. A, A molecule of glucose undergoes an internal addition reaction between the aldehyde group of C-1 and the alcohol group of C-5 to form a cyclic monosaccharide. **B,** In a dehydration-condensation reaction, the monosaccharides glucose and fructose form the disaccharide sucrose (table sugar) and a water molecule.

branched, bushlike molecule of up to a million glucose units. *Glycogen* functions as the energy store in animals. It occurs in liver and muscle cells as insoluble granules consisting of even more highly branched molecules made from 1000 to more than 500,000 glucose units. The bonds between glucose units in these polymers differ in their chirality. Humans lack the enzyme to break the particular link in cellulose, so we cannot digest it (unfortunately!), but we can break the links in starch and glycogen.

Amino Acids and Proteins

As you saw in Section 15.5, synthetic polyamides (such as nylon-66) are formed from two monomers, one with a carboxyl group at each end and the other with an amine group at each end. **Proteins,** the polyamides of nature, are unbranched polymers formed from monomers called **amino acids,** *each of which has a carboxyl group and an amine group.*

Monomer Structure and Linkage An amino acid has both its carboxyl and amine groups attached to the α-*carbon,* the second C atom in the chain. Proteins are made up of about 20 different types of amino acids, each with its own particular R group (Figure 15.20).

FIGURE 15.20 The common amino acids. About 20 different amino acids occur in proteins. The R groups are screened gray, and the α-carbons *(boldface),* with carboxyl and amino groups, are screened yellow. Here the amino acids are shown with the charges they have under physiological conditions. They are grouped by polarity, acid-base character, and presence of an aromatic ring. The R groups play a major role in the shape and function of the protein.

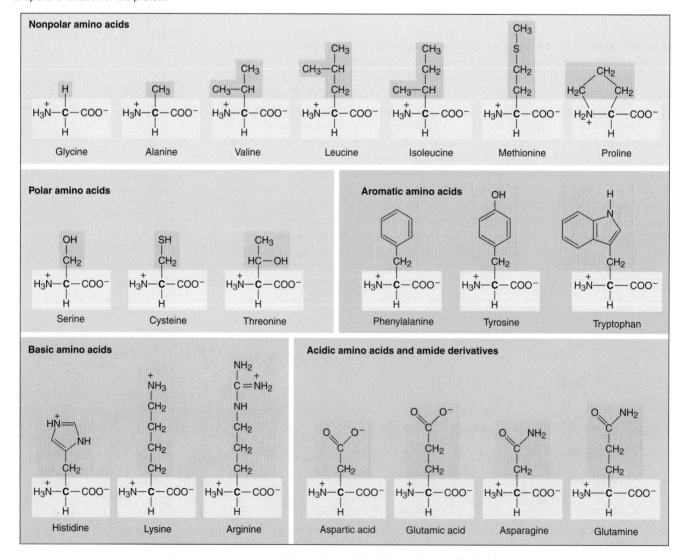

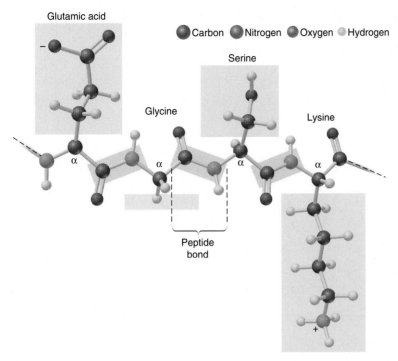

FIGURE 15.21 A portion of a polypeptide chain. The peptide bond holds monomers together in a protein. Three peptide bonds *(orange screens)* join four amino acids in this portion of a polypeptide chain. Note the repeating pattern of the chain: peptide bond—α-carbon—peptide bond—α-carbon— and so on. Also note that the side chains *(gray screens)* dangle off the main chain.

In the aqueous cell fluid, the NH_2 and COOH groups of amino acids are charged because the carboxyl group transfers an H^+ ion to H_2O to form H_3O^+, which transfers the H^+ to the amine group. The overall process is, in effect, an intramolecular acid-base reaction:

An H atom is the third group bonded to the α-carbon, and the fourth is the R group (also called the *side chain*).

Each amino acid is linked to the next one through a *peptide (amide) bond* formed by a dehydration-condensation reaction in which the carboxyl group of one monomer reacts with the amine group of the next. Therefore, the polypeptide chain—the backbone of the protein—has a repeating sequence that consists of an *α-carbon bonded to an amide group bonded to the next α-carbon bonded to the next amide group,* and so forth (Figure 15.21). The various R groups dangle from the α-carbons on alternate sides of the chain.

The Hierarchy of Protein Structure *Each type of protein has its own amino acid composition,* a specific number and proportion of the various amino acids. However, it is not the composition that defines the protein's role in the cell; rather, *the sequence of amino acids determines the protein's shape and function.* Proteins range from about 50 to several thousand amino acids, yet even a small protein of 100 amino acids has an enormous number of possible sequences of the 20 types of amino acids ($20^{100} \approx 10^{130}$). In fact, though, only a tiny fraction of these possibilities occur in actual proteins. For example, even in an organism as complex as a human being, there are only about 10^5 different types of protein.

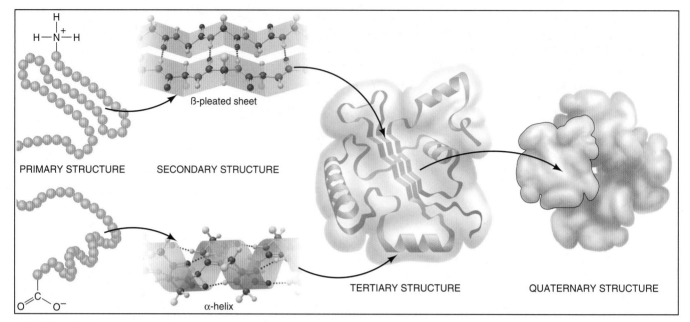

PRIMARY STRUCTURE   SECONDARY STRUCTURE   β-pleated sheet   α-helix   TERTIARY STRUCTURE   QUATERNARY STRUCTURE

FIGURE 15.22 The structural hierarchy of proteins. A typical protein's structure can be viewed at different levels. Primary structure (shown as a long string of balls leaving and returning to the picture frame) is the sequence of amino acids. Secondary structure consists of highly ordered regions that occur as an α-helix or a β-pleated sheet. Tertiary structure combines these ordered regions with random coil sections. In many proteins, several tertiary units interact to give the quaternary structure.

A protein folds into its *native shape* as it is being synthesized in the cell. Biochemists define a hierarchy for the overall structure of a protein (Figure 15.22):

1. *Primary (1°) structure,* the most basic level, refers to the sequence of covalently bonded amino acids in the polypeptide chain.
2. *Secondary (2°) structure* refers to sections of the chain that, as a result of H bonding between nearby peptide groupings, adopt shapes called α-helices and β-pleated sheets.
3. *Tertiary (3°) structure* refers to the three-dimensional folding of the whole polypeptide chain, which results from many forces. The —SH ends of two cysteine side chains form a covalent *disulfide* bridge (—S—S—) that brings together distant parts of the chain. Polar and ionic side chains interact with surrounding water through ion-dipole forces and H bonds. And nonpolar side chains interact through dispersion forces within the nonaqueous protein interior. Thus, *soluble proteins have polar-ionic exteriors and nonpolar interiors.*
4. *Quaternary (4°) structure,* the most complex level, occurs in proteins made up of several polypeptide chains (subunits) and refers to the way the chains assemble into the overall protein.

Note that *only the 1° structure involves covalent bonds; the 2°, 3°, and 4° structures rely primarily on intermolecular forces.*

The Relation Between Structure and Function Two broad classes of proteins differ in the complexity of their amino acid compositions and sequences and, therefore, in their structure and function:

1. *Fibrous proteins* are key components of materials that require strength and flexibility. They have simple amino acid compositions and repetitive structures. Consider collagen, the most common animal protein, which makes up as much as 40% of human body weight. More than 30% of its amino acids are glycine, and another 20% are proline. It exists as long, triple-helical cable in which the peptide C=O groups in one chain form H bonds to the peptide N—H groups in another. As the main component of tendons, skin, and blood vessels, collagen has a high tensile strength; in fact, a 1-mm thick strand can support a 10-kg weight!

2. *Globular proteins* have complex compositions, often containing all 20 common amino acids in varying proportions. They are typically compact, with a wide variety of shapes and functions—as antibodies, hormones, and enzymes, to name a few. The locations of particular amino-acid R groups are crucial to a globular protein's function. In enzymes, for example, these groups bring the reactants together through intermolecular forces and stretch their bonds to speed their reaction to products. Experiment shows that a slight change in a critical R group decreases function dramatically. This fact supports the essential idea that *the protein's amino acid sequence determines its structure, which in turn determines its function:*

SEQUENCE $\Longrightarrow$ STRUCTURE $\Longrightarrow$ FUNCTION

Nucleotides and Nucleic Acids

An organism's nucleic acids construct its proteins. And, given that the proteins determine how the organism looks and behaves, no job could be more essential.

Monomer Structure and Linkage **Nucleic acids** are *polynucleotides,* unbranched polymers that consist of **mononucleotides,** each of which consists of an N-containing base, a sugar, and a phosphate group. The two types of nucleic acid, *ribonucleic acid* (RNA) and *deoxyribonucleic acid* (DNA), differ in the sugar portions of their mononucleotides: RNA contains *ribose,* and DNA contains *deoxyribose,* in which —H substitutes for —OH on the second C of ribose.

The cellular precursors that form a nucleic acid are *nucleoside triphosphates* (Figure 15.23A). Dehydration-condensation reactions between them create a chain

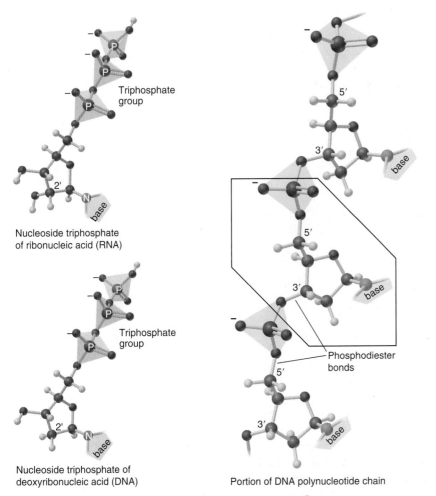

A

Nucleoside triphosphate of ribonucleic acid (RNA)

Triphosphate group

Nucleoside triphosphate of deoxyribonucleic acid (DNA)

Triphosphate group

B

Portion of DNA polynucleotide chain

Phosphodiester bonds

FIGURE 15.23 Nucleic acid precursors and their linkage. A, In the cell, nucleic acids are constructed from nucleoside triphosphates, precursors of the mononucleotide units. Each one consists of an N-containing base (structure not shown), a sugar, and a triphosphate group. In RNA *(top),* the sugar is ribose; in DNA, it is 2′-deoxyribose (C atoms of the sugar are denoted by a number primed, e.g., 2′; note the absence of an —OH group on C-2 of the ring). **B,** A tiny segment of the polynucleotide chain of DNA shows the phosphodiester bonds that link the 5′-OH group of one sugar to the 3′-OH group of the next and are formed through dehydration-condensation reactions (which also release diphosphate ion). The bases dangle off the chain.

with the repeating pattern —*sugar—phosphate—sugar—phosphate—,* and so on (Figure 15.23B). Attached to each sugar is one of four N-containing bases—thymine (T), cytosine (C), guanine (G), and adenine (A). In RNA, uracil (U) substitutes for thymine. The bases dangle off the sugar-phosphate chain, much as R groups dangle off the polypeptide chain of a protein.

DNA Structure and Base Pairing In the cell nucleus, the many millions of nucleotides in DNA occur as two chains wrapped around each other in a **double helix** (Figure 15.24). Intermolecular forces play a central role in stabilizing this structure. On the exterior, negatively charged sugar-phosphate chains form ion-dipole and H bonds with the aqueous surroundings. In the interior, the flat, nitrogen-containing bases stack above each other, which allows extensive interaction through dispersion forces.

Most important, *each base in one chain "pairs" with a specific base in the other through H bonding.* The essential feature of these **base pairs,** which is crucial to the structure and function of DNA, is that *each type of base is always paired with the same partner:* A with T and G with C. Thus, *the base sequence of one chain is the complement of the sequence of the other.* For example, the sequence A—C—T on one chain is *always* paired with T—G—A on the other: A with T, C with G, and T with A.

Each DNA molecule is folded into a tangled mass that forms one of the cell's *chromosomes.* The DNA molecule is amazingly long and thin: if the largest human chromosome were stretched out, it would be 4 cm long; in the cell nucleus, however, it is wound into a rounded structure only 5 nm wide—8 million times shorter!

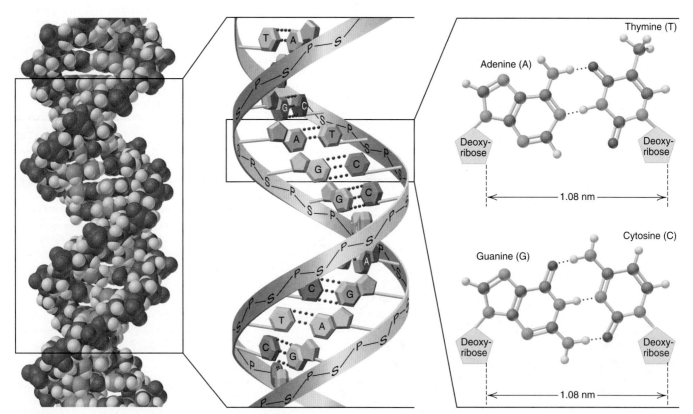

FIGURE 15.24 The double helix of DNA. A segment of DNA is shown as a space-filling model *(left).* The boxed area is expanded *(center)* to show how the polar sugar(S)-phosphate(P) backbone faces the watery outside, and the nonpolar bases form H bonds to each other in the DNA core. The boxed area is expanded *(right)* to show how a pyrimidine and a purine always form H-bonded base pairs to maintain the double helix width. The members of the pairs are always the same: A pairs with T, and G pairs with C.

From DNA to Protein Segments of the DNA chains are the *genes* that contain the chemical information for synthesizing the organism's proteins. In the **genetic code,** each base acts as a "letter," each three-base sequence as a "word," and *each word codes for a specific amino acid.* For example, the sequence C—A—C codes for the amino acid histidine, A—A—G codes for lysine, and so on. Through a complex process that occurs largely through *H bonding between base pairs,* the DNA message of three-base words is transcribed into an RNA message of three-base words, which is then translated into a sequence of amino acids that are linked to make a protein:

DNA BASE SEQUENCE $\Longrightarrow$ RNA BASE SEQUENCE $\Longrightarrow$ PROTEIN AMINO-ACID SEQUENCE

The biopolymers provide striking evidence that the same atomic properties that give rise to covalent bonds, molecular shape, and intermolecular forces provide the means for all life forms to flourish.

SECTION 15.6 SUMMARY

Polysaccharides, proteins, and nucleic acids are formed by dehydration-condensation reactions. • Polysaccharides are formed from cyclic monosaccharides, such as glucose. Cellulose, starch, and glycogen have structural or energy-storage roles. • Proteins are polyamides formed from as many as 20 different types of amino acids. Fibrous proteins have extended shapes and play structural roles. Globular proteins have compact shapes and play metabolic, immunologic, and hormonal roles. The amino acid sequence of a protein determines its shape and function. • Nucleic acids (DNA and RNA) are polynucleotides consisting of four different mononucleotides. The base sequence of DNA determines the amino-acid sequences of an organism's proteins. Hydrogen bonding between specific base pairs is the key to DNA structure as well as protein synthesis and DNA replication.

CHAPTER REVIEW GUIDE

The following sections provide many aids to help you study this chapter. (Numbers in parentheses refer to pages, unless noted otherwise.)

• LEARNING OBJECTIVES *These are concepts and skills to know after studying this chapter.*

Related section (§), sample problem (SP), and end-of-chapter problem (EP) numbers are listed in parentheses.

1. Explain why carbon's atomic properties lead to formation of four strong bonds, multiple bonds, chains, and functional groups (§ 15.1) (EPs 15.1–15.4)
2. Name and draw alkanes, alkenes, and alkynes with expanded, condensed, and carbon-skeleton formulas (§ 15.2) (SPs 15.1, 15.2a–c) (EPs 15.5, 15.9–15.18, 15.29)
3. Distinguish among constitutional, optical, and geometric isomers (§ 15.2) (SP 15.2d, e) (EPs 15.6–15.8, 15.19–15.28, 15.30, 15.31)

4. Describe three types of organic reactions (addition, elimination, and substitution) and identify each type from reactants and products (§ 15.3) (SP 15.3) (EPs 15.32–15.36)
5. Understand the properties and reaction types of the various functional groups (§ 15.4) (SPs 15.4–15.6) (EPs 15.37–15.58)
6. Discuss the formation of addition and condensation polymers and draw abbreviated polymer structures (§ 15.5) (EPs 15.59–15.67)
7. Describe the three types of natural polymers, explain how amino-acid sequence determines protein shape, and thus function, draw small peptides, and use the sequence of one DNA strand to predict the sequence of the other (§ 15.6) (EPs 15.68–15.79)

• KEY TERMS *These important terms appear in boldface in the chapter and are defined again in the Glossary.*

organic compound (467)

Section 15.1
heteroatom (468)
functional group (469)

Section 15.2
hydrocarbon (469)
alkane (C_nH_{2n+2}) (472)
homologous series (472)

saturated hydrocarbon (472)
cyclic hydrocarbon (474)
constitutional (structural) isomers (474)
stereoisomers (476)
optical isomers (476)
chiral molecule (476)
optically active (477)

alkene (C_nH_{2n}) (477)
unsaturated hydrocarbon (477)
geometric *(cis-trans)* isomers (477–478)
alkyne (C_nH_{2n-2}) (478)
aromatic hydrocarbon (480)

Section 15.3
alkyl group (481)

addition reaction (481)
elimination reaction (481)
substitution reaction (481)

Section 15.4
alcohol (484)
haloalkane (alkyl halide) (484)
amine (485)
carbonyl group (487)

● KEY TERMS *continued*

aldehyde (487)	lipid (489)	addition polymer (492)	amino acid (496)
ketone (487)	hydrolysis (489)	condensation polymer (494)	nucleic acid (499)
carboxylic acid (488)	nitrile (491)		mononucleotide (499)
ester (488)	**Section 15.5**	**Section 15.6**	double helix (500)
amide (488)	polymer (492)	monosaccharide (495)	base pair (500)
fatty acid (489)	macromolecule (492)	polysaccharide (495)	genetic code (501)
acid anhydride (489)	monomer (492)	disaccharide (495)	
		protein (496)	

● BRIEF SOLUTIONS TO **FOLLOW-UP PROBLEMS** *Compare your own solutions to these calculation steps and answers.*

PROBLEMS

Problems with colored numbers are answered in Appendix E. Sections match the text and provide the numbers of relevant sample problems. Bracketed problems are grouped in pairs (indicated by a short rule) that cover the same concept. Comprehensive Problems are based on material from any section or previous chapter.

The Special Nature of Carbon and the Characteristics of Organic Molecules

15.1 Explain each of the following statements in terms of atomic properties:
(a) Carbon engages in covalent rather than ionic bonding.

(b) Carbon has four bonds in all its organic compounds.
(c) Carbon forms neither stable cations, like many metals, nor stable anions, like many nonmetals.
(d) Carbon bonds to itself more extensively than does any other element.
(e) Carbon forms stable multiple bonds.

15.2 Carbon bonds to many elements other than itself.
(a) Name six elements that commonly bond to carbon in organic compounds.
(b) Which of these elements are heteroatoms?
(c) Which of these elements are more electronegative than carbon? Less electronegative?

(d) How does bonding of carbon to heteroatoms increase the number of organic compounds?

15.3 Silicon lies just below carbon in Group 4A(14) and also forms four covalent bonds. Why aren't there as many silicon compounds as carbon compounds?

15.4 Which of these bonds to carbon would you expect to be relatively reactive: C—H, C—C, C—I, C=O, C—Li? Explain.

The Structures and Classes of Hydrocarbons
(Sample Problems 15.1 and 15.2)

15.5 (a) What structural feature is associated with each type of hydrocarbon: an alkane; a cycloalkane; an alkene; an alkyne?
(b) Give the general formula for each.
(c) Which hydrocarbons are considered saturated?

15.6 Define each type of isomer: (a) constitutional; (b) geometric; (c) optical. Which types of isomers are stereoisomers?

15.7 Among alkenes, alkynes, and aromatic hydrocarbons, only alkenes exhibit *cis-trans* isomerism. Why don't the others?

15.8 Which objects are asymmetric (have no plane of symmetry): (a) a circular clock face; (b) a football; (c) a dime; (d) a brick; (e) a hammer; (f) a spring?

15.9 Draw all possible skeletons for a 7-C compound with
(a) A 6-C chain and 1 double bond
(b) A 5-C chain and 1 double bond
(c) A 5-C ring and no double bonds

15.10 Draw all possible skeletons for a 6-C compound with
(a) A 5-C chain and 2 double bonds
(b) A 5-C chain and 1 triple bond
(c) A 4-C ring and no double bonds

15.11 Add the correct number of hydrogens to each of the skeletons in Problem 15.9.

15.12 Add the correct number of hydrogens to each of the skeletons in Problem 15.10.

15.13 Draw correct structures, by making a single change, for any that are incorrect:

(a) CH_3—$\overset{\overset{\displaystyle CH_3}{|}}{CH}$—$CH_2$—$CH_3$ (b) CH_3=CH—CH_2—CH_3

(c) CH≡C—$\underset{\underset{\displaystyle CH_3}{|}}{\underset{\underset{\displaystyle CH_2}{|}}{C}}$—$CH_2$—$CH_3$ (d) CH_3—⟨benzene ring⟩—CH_3

15.14 Draw correct structures, by making a single change, for any that are incorrect:

(a) CH_3—CH=CH—CH_2—CH_3 (b) [cyclopentadiene with two CH₃ groups]

(c) CH_3—C≡CH—CH_2—CH_3 (d) CH_3—CH_2—$\overset{\overset{\displaystyle CH_3}{|}}{C}$—$CH_2$—$CH_2$—$CH_3$

15.15 Draw the structure or give the name of each compound:
(a) 2,3-dimethyloctane
(b) 1-ethyl-3-methylcyclohexane

(c) CH_3—CH_2—$\overset{\overset{\displaystyle CH_3}{|}}{CH}$—$\underset{\underset{\displaystyle CH_2-CH_3}{|}}{CH}$—$CH_2$ (d) [branched structure]

15.16 Draw the structure or give the name of each compound:

(a) [branched structure]   (b)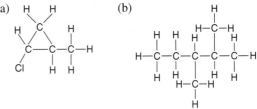

(c) 1,2-diethylcyclopentane   (d) 2,4,5-trimethylnonane

15.17 Each of the following names is wrong. Draw structures based on them, and correct the names:
(a) 4-methylhexane   (b) 2-ethylpentane
(c) 2-methylcyclohexane   (d) 3,3-methyl-4-ethyloctane

15.18 Each of the following names is wrong. Draw structures based on them, and correct the names:
(a) 3,3-dimethylbutane   (b) 1,1,1-trimethylheptane
(c) 1,4-diethylcyclopentane   (d) 1-propylcyclohexane

15.19 Each of the following compounds can exhibit optical activity. Circle the chiral center(s) in each:

(a) [structure with Cl]   (b) [structure]

15.20 Each of the following compounds can exhibit optical activity. Circle the chiral center(s) in each:

(a) 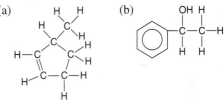   (b) [structure with OH and benzene ring]

15.21 Draw structures from the following names, and determine which compounds are optically active:
(a) 3-bromohexane
(b) 3-chloro-3-methylpentane
(c) 1,2-dibromo-2-methylbutane

15.22 Draw structures from the following names, and determine which compounds are optically active:
(a) 1,3-dichloropentane
(b) 3-chloro-2,2,5-trimethylhexane
(c) 1-bromo-1-chlorobutane

15.23 Which of the following structures exhibit geometric isomerism? Draw and name the two isomers in each case:
(a) CH_3—CH_2—CH=CH—CH_3 (b) [cyclohexane with CH=CH group]

(c) CH_3—$\overset{\overset{\displaystyle CH_3}{|}}{C}$=CH—$\overset{\overset{\displaystyle CH_3}{|}}{CH}$—$CH_2$—$CH_3$

15.24 Which of the following structures exhibit geometric isomerism? Draw and name the two isomers in each case:

(a) CH_3—$\overset{\overset{\displaystyle CH_3}{|}}{\underset{\underset{\displaystyle CH_3}{|}}{C}}$—CH=CH—$CH_3$ (b) [branched structure]

(c) Cl—CH_2—CH=$\overset{\overset{\displaystyle CH_3}{|}}{C}$—$CH_2$—$CH_2$—$CH_2$—$CH_3$

15.25 Which compounds exhibit geometric isomerism? Draw and name the two isomers in each case:
(a) propene   (b) 3-hexene
(c) 1,1-dichloroethene   (d) 1,2-dichloroethene

15.26 Which compounds exhibit geometric isomerism? Draw and name the two isomers in each case:
(a) 1-pentene   (b) 2-pentene
(c) 1-chloropropene   (d) 2-chloropropene

15.27 Draw and name all the constitutional isomers of dichlorobenzene.

15.28 Draw and name all the constitutional isomers of trimethylbenzene.

15.29 Butylated hydroxytoluene (BHT) is a common preservative added to cereals and other dry foods. Its systematic name is 1-hydroxy-2,6-di-*tert*-butyl-4-methylbenzene (where "*tert*-butyl" is 1,1-dimethylethyl). Draw the structure of BHT.

15.30 There are two compounds with the name 2-methyl-3-hexene, but only one with the name 2-methyl-2-hexene. Explain with structures.

15.31 Any tetrahedral atom with four different groups attached can be a chiral center. Which of these compounds is optically active?
(a) CHClBrF   (b) $NBrCl_2H^+$ (c) $PFClBrI^+$ (d) SeFClBrH

Some Important Classes of Organic Reactions
(Sample Problem 15.3)

15.32 Determine the type of each of the following reactions:

(a) $CH_3—CH_2—\overset{\overset{\displaystyle Br}{|}}{C}H—CH_3 \xrightarrow[\Delta]{NaOH}$
$CH_3—CH=CH—CH_3 + NaBr + H_2O$

(b) $CH_3—CH=CH—CH_2—CH_3 + H_2 \xrightarrow{Pt}$
$CH_3—CH_2—CH_2—CH_2—CH_3$

15.33 Determine the type of each of the following reactions:

(a) $CH_3—\overset{\overset{\displaystyle O}{||}}{C}H + HCN \longrightarrow CH_3—\overset{\overset{\displaystyle OH}{|}}{C}H—CN$

(b) $CH_3—\overset{\overset{\displaystyle O}{||}}{C}—O—CH_3 + CH_3—NH_2 \xrightarrow{H^+}$
$CH_3—\overset{\overset{\displaystyle O}{||}}{C}—NH—CH_3 + CH_3—OH$

15.34 Write equations for the following:
(a) An addition reaction between H_2O and 3-hexene (H^+ speeds the reaction but is not consumed)
(b) An elimination reaction between 2-bromopropane and hot potassium ethoxide, $CH_3—CH_2—OK$ (KBr and ethanol are also products)
(c) A light-induced substitution reaction between Cl_2 and ethane to form 1,1-dichloroethane

15.35 Write equations for the following:
(a) A substitution reaction between 2-bromopropane and KI
(b) An addition reaction between cyclohexene and Cl_2
(c) An addition reaction between 2-propanone and H_2 (the reaction occurs on an Ni metal surface)

15.36 Phenylethylamine is a natural substance that is structurally similar to amphetamine. It is found in sources as diverse as almond oil and human urine, where it occurs at elevated concentrations as a result of stress and certain forms of schizophrenia. One method of synthesizing the compound for pharmacological and psychiatric studies involves two steps:

phenylethylamine

Classify each step as an addition, elimination, or substitution.

Properties and Reactivities of Common Functional Groups
(Sample Problems 15.4 to 15.6)

15.37 Compounds with nearly identical molar masses often have very different physical properties. Choose the compound with the higher value for each of the following properties, and explain your choice.
(a) Solubility in water: chloroethane or methylethylamine
(b) Melting point: diethyl ether or 1-butanol
(c) Boiling point: trimethylamine or propylamine

15.38 Fill in each blank with a general formula for the type of compound formed:

15.39 Why does the C=O group react differently from the C=C group? Show an example of the difference.

15.40 Many substitution reactions involve an initial electrostatic attraction between reactants. Show where this attraction arises in the formation of an amide from an amine and an ester.

15.41 What reaction type is common to the formation of esters and acid anhydrides? What is the other product?

15.42 Both alcohols and carboxylic acids undergo substitution, but the processes are very different. Explain.

15.43 Name the type of organic compound from the following description of its functional group:
(a) Polar group that has only single bonds and does not include O or N
(b) Group that is polar and has a triple bond
(c) Group that has single and double bonds and is acidic in water
(d) Group that has a double bond and must be at the end of a C chain

15.44 Name the type of organic compound from the following description of its functional group:
(a) N-containing group with single and double bonds
(b) Group that is not polar and has a double bond
(c) Polar group that has a double bond and cannot be at the end of a C chain
(d) Group that has only single bonds and is basic in water

15.45 Circle and name the functional group(s) in each compound:

(a) $CH_3—CH=CH—CH_2—OH$ (b) $Cl—CH_2—\overset{}{\underset{}{\bigcirc}}—\overset{\overset{\displaystyle O}{||}}{C}—OH$

(c) [structure: cyclohexene with C(=O)—N—CH₃]   (d) $N\equiv C-CH_2-\overset{O}{\underset{\|}{C}}-CH_3$

(e) [structure: cyclopropane—C(=O)—O—CH₂—CH₃]

15.46 Circle and name the functional group(s) in each compound:

(a) [HO—C(=O)—CH₂—C(=O)—H]

(b) $I-CH_2-CH_2-C\equiv CH$

(c) $CH_2=CH-CH_2-\overset{O}{\underset{\|}{C}}-O-CH_3$

(d) $CH_3-NH-\overset{O}{\underset{\|}{C}}-\overset{O}{\underset{\|}{C}}-O-CH_3$

(e) $CH_3-\overset{Br}{\underset{|}{CH}}-CH=CH-CH_2-NH-CH_3$

15.47 Draw all possible alcohols with the formula $C_5H_{12}O$.
15.48 Draw all possible aldehydes and ketones with the formula $C_5H_{10}O$.
15.49 Draw all possible amines with the formula $C_4H_{11}N$.
15.50 Draw all possible carboxylic acids with the formula $C_5H_{10}O_2$.

15.51 Draw the organic product formed when the following compounds undergo a substitution reaction:
(a) Acetic acid and methylamine
(b) Butanoic acid and 2-propanol
(c) Formic acid and 2-methyl-1-propanol
15.52 Draw the organic product formed when the following compounds undergo a substitution reaction:
(a) Acetic acid and 1-hexanol
(b) Propanoic acid and dimethylamine
(c) Ethanoic acid and diethylamine

15.53 Draw condensed formulas for the carboxylic acid and alcohol portions of the following esters:

(a) [structure: pentanoate ethyl ester]

(b) [structure: benzene—C(=O)—O—CH₂—CH₂—CH₃]

(c) $CH_3-CH_2-O-\overset{O}{\underset{\|}{C}}-CH_2-CH_2-$ [benzene ring]

15.54 Draw condensed formulas for the carboxylic acid and amine portions of the following amides:

(a) H_3C-[benzene]$-CH_2-\overset{O}{\underset{\|}{C}}-NH_2$

(b) [structure: isopropyl—C(=O)—N—CH₂CH₃]   (c) $H\overset{O}{\underset{\|}{C}}-NH-$[benzene]

15.55 Fill in the expected organic substances:

(a) $CH_3-CH_2-Br \xrightarrow{OH^-}$ ____ $\xrightarrow[H^+]{CH_3-CH_2-\overset{O}{\underset{\|}{C}}-OH}$ ____

(b) $CH_3-CH_2-\overset{Br}{\underset{|}{CH}}-CH_3 \xrightarrow{CN^-}$ ____ $\xrightarrow{H_3O^+,\ H_2O}$ ____
15.56 Fill in the expected organic substances:

(a) $CH_3-CH_2-CH=CH_2 \xrightarrow{H^+,\ H_2O}$ ____ $\xrightarrow{Cr_2O_7^{2-},\ H^+}$ ____

(b) $CH_3-CH_2-OH\ +$ ____ $\xrightarrow{H_3O^+,\ H_2O}$

$CH_3-CH_2-O-\overset{O}{\underset{\|}{C}}-CH_2-CH_3$

15.57 (a) Draw the four isomers of $C_5H_{12}O$ that can be oxidized to an aldehyde. (b) Draw the three isomers of $C_5H_{12}O$ that can be oxidized to a ketone. (c) Draw the isomers of $C_5H_{12}O$ that cannot be easily oxidized to an aldehyde or ketone. (d) Name any isomer that is an alcohol.

15.58 Ethyl formate ($H\overset{O}{\underset{\|}{C}}-O-CH_2-CH_3$) is added to foods to give them the flavor of rum. How would you synthesize ethyl formate from ethanol, methanol, and any inorganic reagents?

The Monomer-Polymer Theme I: Synthetic Macromolecules

15.59 Name the reaction processes that lead to the two types of synthetic polymers.
15.60 Which functional group is common to the monomers that make up addition polymers? What makes these polymers different from one another?
15.61 Which intermolecular force is primarily responsible for the different types of polyethylene? Explain.
15.62 Which of the two types of synthetic polymer is more similar chemically to biopolymers? Explain.
15.63 Which two functional groups react to form nylons? Polyesters?
15.64 Draw an abbreviated structure for the following polymers, with brackets around the repeat unit:

(a) Poly(vinyl chloride) (PVC) from [structure: CH₂=CHCl]

(b) Polypropylene from [structure: CH₂=CHCH₃]

15.65 Draw an abbreviated structure for the following polymers, with brackets around the repeat unit:
(a) Teflon from   (b) Polystyrene from
[structure: CF₂=CF₂]   [structure: CH₂=CH-phenyl]

15.66 Write a balanced equation for the reaction between 1,4-benzenedicarboxylic acid and 1,2-dihydroxyethane to form the polyester Dacron. Draw an abbreviated structure for the polymer, with brackets around the repeat unit.
15.67 Write a balanced equation for the reaction of the monomer dihydroxydimethylsilane *(below)* to form the condensation polymer known as Silly Putty.

$HO-\overset{\overset{CH_3}{|}}{\underset{\underset{CH_3}{|}}{Si}}-OH$

The Monomer-Polymer Theme II: Biological Macromolecules

15.68 Which type of polymer is formed from each of the following monomers: (a) amino acids; (b) alkenes; (c) simple sugars; (d) mononucleotides?

15.69 What is the key structural difference between fibrous and globular proteins? How is it related, in general, to the proteins' amino acid composition?

15.70 Protein shape, function, and amino acid sequence are interrelated. Which determines which?

15.71 What is base pairing? How does it pertain to DNA structure?

15.72 Draw the R group of (a) alanine; (b) histidine; (c) methionine.
15.73 Draw the R group of (a) glycine; (b) isoleucine; (c) tyrosine.

15.74 Draw the structure of each of the following tripeptides:
(a) Aspartic acid-histidine-tryptophan
(b) Glycine-cysteine-tyrosine with the charges existing in cell fluid

15.75 Draw the structure of each of the following tripeptides:
(a) Lysine-phenylalanine-threonine
(b) Alanine-leucine-valine with the charges that exist in cell fluid

15.76 Write the sequence of the complementary DNA strand that pairs with each of the following DNA base sequences:
(a) TTAGCC   (b) AGACAT

15.77 Write the sequence of the complementary DNA strand that pairs with each of the following DNA base sequences:
(a) GGTTAC   (b) CCCGAA

15.78 Protein shapes are maintained by a variety of forces that arise from interactions between the amino-acid R groups. Name the amino acid that possesses each R group and the force that could arise in each of the following interactions:

(a) —CH₂—SH with HS—CH₂—

(b) —(CH₂)₄—NH₃⁺ with ⁻O—C(=O)—CH₂—

(c) —CH₂—C(=O)—NH₂ with HO—CH₂—

(d) —CH(CH₃)—CH₃ with ⟨◯⟩—CH₂—

15.79 Amino acids have an average molar mass of 100 g/mol. How many bases on a single strand of DNA are needed to code for a protein with a molar mass of 5×10^5 g/mol?

Comprehensive Problems

Problems with an asterisk (*) are more challenging.

15.80 A synthesis of 2-butanol was performed by treating 2-bromobutane with hot sodium hydroxide solution. The yield was 60%, indicating that a significant portion of the reactant was converted into a second product. Predict what this other product might be.

15.81 Pyrethrins, such as jasmolin II (*below*), are a group of natural compounds synthesized by flowers of the genus *Chrysanthemum* (known as pyrethrum flowers) to act as insecticides.
(a) Circle and name the functional groups in jasmolin II.
(b) What is the hybridization of the numbered carbons?
(c) Which, if any, of the numbered carbons are chiral centers?

* **15.82** Compound A is branched and optically active and contains C, H, and O. (a) A 0.500-g sample burns in excess O_2 to yield 1.25 g of CO_2 and 0.613 g of H_2O. Determine the empirical formula. (b) When 0.225 g of compound A vaporizes at 755 torr and 97°C, the vapor occupies 78.0 mL. Determine the molecular formula. (c) Careful oxidation of the compound yields a ketone. Name and draw compound A and circle the chiral center.

15.83 Vanillin (*right*) is a naturally occurring flavoring agent used in many food products. Name each functional group that contains oxygen. Which carbon-oxygen bond is shortest?

15.84 The genetic code consists of a series of three-base words that each code for a given amino acid.
(a) Using the selections from the genetic code shown below, determine the amino acid sequence coded by the following segment of RNA:

UCCACAGCCUAUAUGGCAAACUUGAAG

AUG = methionine	CCU = proline	CAU = histidine
UGG = tryptophan	AAG = lysine	UAU = tyrosine
GCC = alanine	UUG = leucine	CGG = arginine
UGU = cysteine	AAC = asparagine	ACA = threonine
UCC = serine	GCA = alanine	UCA = serine

(b) What is the complementary DNA sequence from which this RNA sequence was made?

* **15.85** Sodium propanoate ($CH_3—CH_2—C(=O)—ONa$) is a common preservative found in breads, cheeses, and pies. How would you synthesize sodium propanoate from 1-propanol and any inorganic reagents?

15.86 Supply the missing organic and/or inorganic substances:

(a) $CH_3—CH(Cl)—CH_3 \xrightarrow{?} CH_3—CH=CH_2 \xrightarrow{?} CH_3—CH(Br)—CH_2(Br)$

(b) $CH_3—CH_2—CH_2—OH \xrightarrow{?} CH_3—CH_2—C(=O)—OH + \underline{\ ?\ } \xrightarrow{?}$

$CH_3—CH_2—C(=O)—O—CH_2—⟨◯⟩$

22

The Transition Elements and Their Coordination Compounds

Exploring the Center of the Table *Many transition elements, like the titanium in this bicycle, are among the most useful metals known. In this chapter, you'll see why transition elements and their compounds differ so markedly from main-group elements.*

Outline

22.1 Properties of the Transition Elements
Electron Configurations
Atomic and Physical Properties
Chemical Properties

22.2 Coordination Compounds
Structures of Complex Ions
Formulas and Names
Isomerism

22.3 Theoretical Basis for the Bonding and Properties of Complexes
Valence Bond Theory
Crystal Field Theory
Complexes in Biological Systems

Key Principles
to focus on while studying this chapter

- In the *transition elements* (*d* block) and *inner transition elements* (*f* block), inner orbitals are being filled, resulting in horizontal and vertical trends in atomic properties that differ markedly from those of the main-group elements (*Section 22.1*).

- Because the outer *ns* electrons are close in energy to the inner $(n − 1)d$ electrons, transition elements can use different numbers of their electrons in bonding. Transition elements have *multiple oxidation states,* and the lower states display more *metallic* behavior (ionic bonding and basic oxides). The compounds of ions with a partially filled *d* sublevel are *colored* and *paramagnetic (Section 22.1).*

- Many transition elements form *coordination compounds,* which consist of a *complex ion* and counter ions. A complex ion has a *central metal cation* and surrounding molecular or anionic *ligands.* The number of ligands bound to the metal determines the *shape* of the complex ion. Different positions and bonding arrangements of ligands lead to various types of *isomerism (Section 22.2).*

- According to *valence bond theory,* the shapes of complex ions arise from *hybridization* of different combinations of *d, s,* and *p* orbitals (*Section 22.3*).

- According to *crystal field theory,* ligands approaching a metal ion *split its d-orbital energies,* creating two sets of orbitals. Each type of ligand causes a characteristic difference (*crystal field splitting energy,* Δ) between the energies of the two sets, which allows us to rank ligands in a *spectrochemical series.* The energy difference between the two sets of *d* orbitals is related to the color of the compound, and the *electron occupancy* of the two sets determines the magnetic behavior of the compound *(Section 22.3).*

Our exploration of the elements to this point is far from complete; in fact, we have skirted the majority of them and some of the most familiar. Whereas most important uses of the main-group elements involve their compounds, the transition elements are remarkably useful in their uncombined form. Figure 22.1 shows that the **transition elements** (transition metals) make up the *d* block (B groups) and *f* block (*inner transition elements*).

In addition to copper, whose importance in plumbing and wiring we noted in Chapter 21, many other transition elements have essential uses: iron in steel, chromium in automobile parts, gold and silver in jewelry, tungsten in lightbulb filaments, platinum in automobile catalytic converters, titanium in bicycle frames and aircraft parts, and zinc in batteries, to mention just a few of the better known elements. You may be less aware of zirconium in nuclear-reactor liners, vanadium in axles and crankshafts, molybdenum in boiler plates, nickel in coins, tantalum in organ-replacement parts, palladium in telephone-relay contacts—the list goes on and on. As ions, many of these elements also play vital roles in living organisms.

In this chapter, we cover the *d*-block elements only. We first discuss some properties of the elements and then focus on the most distinctive feature of their chemistry, the formation of coordination compounds—substances that contain complex ions and offer new insights into chemical bonding.

Concepts & Skills to Review
before studying this chapter

- properties of light (Section 7.1)
- electron shielding of nuclear charge (Section 8.2)
- electron configuration, ionic size, and magnetic behavior (Sections 8.3 to 8.5)
- valence bond theory (Section 11.1)
- constitutional, geometric, and optical isomerism (Section 15.2)
- Lewis acid-base concepts (Section 18.8)
- complex-ion formation (Section 19.4)
- redox behavior and standard electrode potentials (Section 21.3)

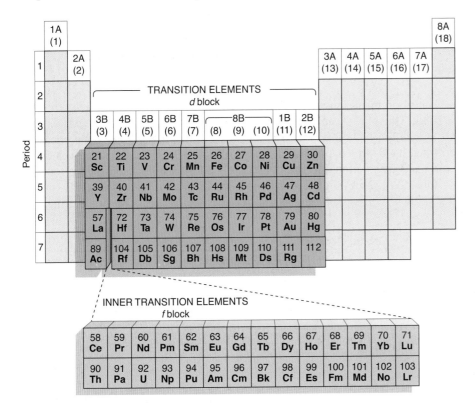

FIGURE 22.1 The transition elements (*d* block) and inner transition elements (*f* block) in the periodic table.

22.1 PROPERTIES OF THE TRANSITION ELEMENTS

The transition elements differ considerably in physical and chemical behavior from the main-group elements. In some ways, they are more uniform: main-group elements in each period change from metal to nonmetal, but *all transition elements are metals*. In other ways, the transition elements are more diverse: most main-group ionic compounds are colorless and diamagnetic, but *many transition metal compounds are highly colored and paramagnetic*. We first discuss electron configurations of the atoms and ions, and then examine certain key properties of transition elements, with an occasional comparison to the main-group elements.

Scandium, Sc; 3B(3)

Titanium, Ti; 4B(4)

Vanadium, V; 5B(5)

Chromium, Cr; 6B(6)

Manganese, Mn; 7B(7)

FIGURE 22.2 The Period 4 transition metals. Samples of all ten elements appear as pure metals, in chunk or powder form, in periodic-table order on this and the facing page.

Electron Configurations of the Transition Metals and Their Ions

The *d*-block (B-group) transition elements occur in four series that lie within Periods 4–7. Each transition series represents the filling of five *d* orbitals and, thus, contains ten elements. The first of these series occurs in Period 4 and consists of scandium (Sc) through zinc (Zn) (Figure 22.2). In 1996 and 1997, elements 110 through 112 were synthesized; thus, all 40 *d*-block elements are known. Lying between the first and second members of the *d*-block transition series in Periods 6 and 7 are the inner transition elements, whose *f* orbitals are being filled.

Even though there are several exceptions, in general, the *condensed* ground-state electron configuration for the elements in each *d*-block series is

$$[\text{noble gas}]\, ns^2(n-1)d^x, \text{ with } n = 4 \text{ to } 7 \text{ and } x = 1 \text{ to } 10$$

In Periods 6 and 7, the condensed configuration includes the *f* sublevel:

$$[\text{noble gas}]\, ns^2(n-2)f^{14}(n-1)d^x, \text{ with } n = 6 \text{ or } 7$$

The *partial* (valence-level) electron configuration for the *d*-block elements excludes the noble gas core and the filled inner *f* sublevel:

$$ns^2(n-1)d^x$$

Transition metal ions form by *the loss of the ns electrons before the (n − 1)d electrons.* Thus, the electron configuration of Ti^{2+} is $[Ar]\,3d^2$, *not* $[Ar]\,4s^2$, and Ti^{2+} is referred to as a d^2 ion. Ions of different metals with the same configuration often have similar properties: both Mn^{2+} and Fe^{3+} (d^5 ions) have pale colors in aqueous solution and form complex ions with similar magnetic properties.

Table 22.1 shows a general pattern in number of unpaired electrons (or half-filled orbitals) across the Period 4 transition series. Note that the number increases

Table 22.1	Orbital Occupancy of the Period 4 Transition Metals		
Element	**Partial Orbital Diagram**		**Unpaired Electrons**
	4s — 3d — 4p		
Sc	[↑↓] [↑][ ][ ][ ][ ] [ ][ ][ ]		1
Ti	[↑↓] [↑][↑][ ][ ][ ] [ ][ ][ ]		2
V	[↑↓] [↑][↑][↑][ ][ ] [ ][ ][ ]		3
Cr	[↑] [↑][↑][↑][↑][↑] [ ][ ][ ]		6
Mn	[↑↓] [↑][↑][↑][↑][↑] [ ][ ][ ]		5
Fe	[↑↓] [↑↓][↑][↑][↑][↑] [ ][ ][ ]		4
Co	[↑↓] [↑↓][↑↓][↑][↑][↑] [ ][ ][ ]		3
Ni	[↑↓] [↑↓][↑↓][↑↓][↑][↑] [ ][ ][ ]		2
Cu	[↑] [↑↓][↑↓][↑↓][↑↓][↑↓] [ ][ ][ ]		1
Zn	[↑↓] [↑↓][↑↓][↑↓][↑↓][↑↓] [ ][ ][ ]		0

Iron, Fe; 8B(8)

Cobalt, Co; 8B(9)

Nickel, Ni; 8B(10)

Copper, Cu; 1B(11)

Zinc, Zn; 2B(12)

in the first half of the series and, when pairing begins, decreases through the second half. As you'll see, it is the electron configuration of the transition metal *atom* that correlates with physical properties of the *element,* such as density and magnetic behavior, whereas it is the electron configuration of the *ion* that determines the properties of the *compounds.*

SAMPLE PROBLEM 22.1 Writing Electron Configurations of Transition Metal Atoms and Ions

Problem Write *condensed* electron configurations for the following:
(a) Zr   **(b)** V^{3+} **(c)** Mo^{3+}
(Assume that elements in higher periods behave like those in Period 4.)
Plan We locate the element in the periodic table and count its position in the respective transition series. These elements are in Periods 4 and 5, so the general configuration is [noble gas] $ns^2(n-1)d^x$. For the ions, we recall that ns electrons are lost first.
Solution (a) Zr is the second element in the $4d$ series: $[Kr]\,5s^24d^2$.
(b) V is the third element in the $3d$ series: $[Ar]\,4s^23d^3$. In forming V^{3+}, three electrons are lost (two $4s$ and one $3d$), so V^{3+} is a d^2 ion: $[Ar]\,3d^2$.
(c) Mo lies below Cr in Group 6B(6), so we expect the same exception as for Cr. Thus, Mo is $[Kr]\,5s^14d^5$. To form the ion, Mo loses the one $5s$ and two of the $4d$ electrons, so Mo^{3+} is a d^3 ion: $[Kr]\,4d^3$.

Check Figure 8.5 shows we're correct for the atoms. Be sure that charge plus number of d electrons in the ion equals the sum of outer s and d electrons in the atom.

FOLLOW-UP PROBLEM 22.1 Write *partial* electron configurations for the following:
(a) Ag^+ **(b)** Cd^{2+} **(c)** Ir^{3+}

Atomic and Physical Properties of the Transition Elements

The atomic properties of the transition elements contrast in several ways with those of a comparable set of main-group elements (Section 8.4).

Trends Across a Period Consider the variations in atomic size, electronegativity, and ionization energy across Period 4:

- *Atomic size.* Atomic size decreases overall across the period (Figure 22.3A, next page). However, there is a smooth, steady decrease across the main groups because the electrons are added to *outer* orbitals, which shield the increasing nuclear charge poorly. This steady decrease is suspended throughout the transition series, where *atomic size decreases at first but then remains fairly constant.* Recall that the d electrons fill *inner* orbitals, so they shield outer electrons from the increasing nuclear charge very efficiently. As a result, the outer $4s$ electrons are not pulled closer.
- *Electronegativity.* Electronegativity generally increases across the period but, once again, the transition elements exhibit a relatively *small change in electronegativity* (Figure 22.3B, next page), consistent with the relatively small change in size. In contrast, the main groups show a steady, much steeper increase between the metal potassium (0.8) and the nonmetal bromine (2.8). The transition elements all have intermediate electronegativity values, much like the metallic members of Groups 3A(13) to 5A(15).

FIGURE 22.3 Horizontal trends in key atomic properties of the Period 4 elements. The atomic radius (**A**), electronegativity (**B**), and first ionization energy (**C**) of the Period 4 elements are shown as posts of different heights, with darker shades for the transition series. The transition elements exhibit smaller, less regular changes for these properties than do the main-group elements.

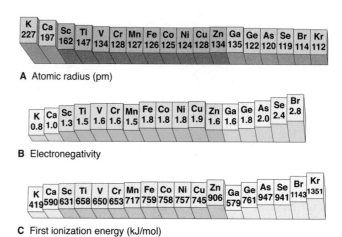

FIGURE 22.3 Horizontal trends in key atomic properties of the Period 4 elements. The atomic radius (**A**), electronegativity (**B**), and first ionization energy (**C**) of the Period 4 elements are shown as posts of different heights, with darker shades for the transition series. The transition elements exhibit smaller, less regular changes for these properties than do the main-group elements.

- *Ionization energy.* The ionization energies of the Period 4 main-group elements rise steeply from left to right, more than tripling from potassium (419 kJ/mol) to krypton (1351 kJ/mol), as electrons become more difficult to remove from the poorly shielded, increasing nuclear charge. In the transition metals, however, the *first ionization energies increase relatively little* because the inner $3d$ electrons shield efficiently (Figure 22.3C); thus, the outer $4s$ electron experiences only a slightly higher effective nuclear charge.

Trends Within a Group Vertical trends for transition elements are also different from those for the main groups.

- *Atomic size.* As expected, atomic size of transition elements increases from Period 4 to 5, as it does for the main-group elements, but there is virtually *no size increase from Period 5 to 6* (Figure 22.4A). The lanthanides ($Z = 58$ to 71), with their buried $4f$ sublevel, appear between the $4d$ (Period 5) and $5d$ (Period 6) series. Therefore, an element in Period 6 is separated from the one above it in Period 5 by 32 elements (ten $4d$, six $5p$, two $6s$, and fourteen $4f$ orbitals) instead of just 18. The extra shrinkage that results from the increase in nuclear charge due to the addition of 14 protons is called the **lanthanide contraction.** By coincidence, this *decrease* is about equal to the normal *increase* between periods, so the Periods 5 and 6 transition elements have about the same atomic sizes.
- *Electronegativity.* The vertical trend in electronegativity seen in most transition groups is opposite the trend in main groups. Here, we see an *increase* in electronegativity from Period 4 to Period 5, but then no further increase in Period 6 (Figure 22.4B). The heavier elements, especially gold (EN = 2.4), become quite electronegative, with values exceeding those of most metalloids and even some nonmetals (e.g., EN of Te and of P = 2.1).
- *Ionization energy.* The relatively small increase in size combined with the relatively large increase in nuclear charge also explains why *the first ionization energy generally increases* down a transition group (Figure 22.4C). This trend also runs counter to the pattern in the main groups, in which heavier members are so much larger that their outer electron is *easier* to remove.
- *Density.* Atomic size, and therefore volume, is inversely related to density. Across a period, densities increase, then level off, and finally dip a bit at the end of a series (Figure 22.4D). Down a transition group, densities increase dramatically because atomic volumes change little from Period 5 to 6, but atomic masses increase significantly. As a result, the Period 6 series contains some of the densest elements: tungsten, rhenium, osmium, iridium, platinum, and gold have densities about 20 times that of water and twice that of lead.

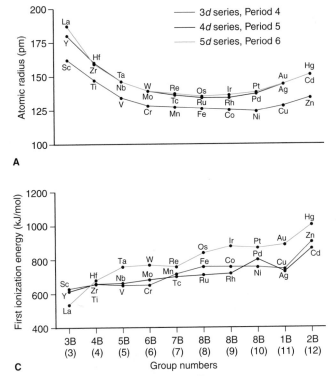

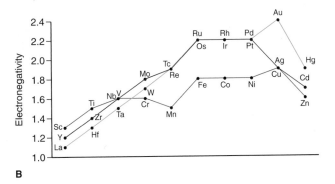

FIGURE 22.4 Vertical trends in key properties within the transition elements. The trends are unlike those for the main-group elements in several ways: **A,** The second and third members of a transition metal group are nearly the same size. **B,** Electronegativity increases down a transition group. **C,** First ionization energies are highest at the bottom of a transition group. **D,** Densities increase down a transition group because mass increases faster than volume.

Chemical Properties of the Transition Metals

Like their atomic and physical properties, the chemical properties of the transition elements are very different from those of the main-group elements. Let's examine the key properties in the Period 4 transition series.

Oxidation States One of the most characteristic chemical properties of the transition metals is the occurrence of *multiple oxidation states*. For example, in their compounds, vanadium exhibits two common positive oxidation states, chromium three, and manganese three (Figure 22.5A), and many other oxidation states are seen less often. The ns and $(n-1)d$ electrons are so close in energy that transition elements can use all or most of these electrons in bonding. This behavior is markedly different from that of the main-group metals, which display one or, at most, two oxidation states in their compounds.

The highest oxidation state of elements in Groups 3B(3) through 7B(7) is equal to the group number (Table 22.2, next page). These oxidation states are seen when the elements combine with highly electronegative oxygen or fluorine. For instance, in the oxoanion solutions shown in Figure 22.5B, vanadium occurs as the vanadate ion (VO_4^{3-}; O.N. of V = +5), chromium occurs as the dichromate ion ($Cr_2O_7^{2-}$; O.N. of Cr = +6), and manganese occurs as the permanganate ion (MnO_4^-; O.N. of Mn = +7). In contrast, elements in Groups 8B(8), 8B(9), and 8B(10) exhibit fewer oxidation states, and the highest state is less common and never equal to the group number. For example, we never encounter iron in the +8 state and only rarely in the +6 state. The +2 and +3 states are the most common ones for iron and cobalt, and the +2 state is most common for nickel, copper, and zinc. *The +2 oxidation state is common because ns^2 electrons are readily lost.*

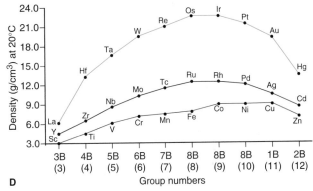

FIGURE 22.5 Aqueous oxoanions of transition elements. A, Often, a given transition element has multiple oxidation states. Here, Mn is shown in the +2 (Mn^{2+}, *left*), the +6 (MnO_4^{2-}, *middle*), and the +7 (MnO_4^-, *right*) states. **B,** The highest possible oxidation state equals the group number in these oxoanions: VO_4^{3-} *(left)*, $Cr_2O_7^{2-}$ *(middle)*, and MnO_4^- *(right)*.

Table 22.2 Oxidation States and d-Orbital Occupancy of the Period 4 Transition Metals*

Oxidation State	3B (3) Sc	4B (4) Ti	5B (5) V	6B (6) Cr	7B (7) Mn	8B (8) Fe	8B (9) Co	8B (10) Ni	1B (11) Cu	2B (12) Zn
0	d^1	d^2	d^3	d^5	d^5	d^6	d^7	d^8	d^{10}	d^{10}
+1			d^3	d^5	d^5	d^6	d^7	d^8	d^{10}	
+2		d^2	d^3	d^4	d^5	d^6	d^7	d^8	d^9	d^{10}
+3	d^0	d^1	d^2	d^3	d^4	d^5	d^6	d^7	d^8	
+4		d^0	d^1	d^2	d^3	d^4	d^5	d^6		
+5			d^0	d^1	d^2		d^4			
+6				d^0	d^1	d^2				
+7					d^0					

*The most important orbital occupancies are in color.

Table 22.3 Standard Electrode Potentials of Period 4 M^{2+} Ions

Half-Reaction	$E°$ (V)
$Ti^{2+}(aq) + 2e^- \rightleftharpoons Ti(s)$	−1.63
$V^{2+}(aq) + 2e^- \rightleftharpoons V(s)$	−1.19
$Cr^{2+}(aq) + 2e^- \rightleftharpoons Cr(s)$	−0.91
$Mn^{2+}(aq) + 2e^- \rightleftharpoons Mn(s)$	−1.18
$Fe^{2+}(aq) + 2e^- \rightleftharpoons Fe(s)$	−0.44
$Co^{2+}(aq) + 2e^- \rightleftharpoons Co(s)$	−0.28
$Ni^{2+}(aq) + 2e^- \rightleftharpoons Ni(s)$	−0.25
$Cu^{2+}(aq) + 2e^- \rightleftharpoons Cu(s)$	0.34
$Zn^{2+}(aq) + 2e^- \rightleftharpoons Zn(s)$	−0.76

Metallic Behavior and Reducing Strength Atomic size and oxidation state have a major effect on the nature of bonding in transition metal compounds. Like the metals in Groups 3A(13), 4A(14), and 5A(15), the transition elements in their *lower* oxidation states behave chemically more like metals. That is, *ionic bonding is more prevalent for the lower oxidation states, and covalent bonding is more prevalent for the higher states.* For example, at room temperature, $TiCl_2$ is an ionic solid, whereas $TiCl_4$ is a molecular liquid. In the higher oxidation states, the atoms have higher charge densities, so they polarize the electron clouds of the nonmetal ions more strongly and the bonding becomes more covalent. For the same reason, the oxides become less basic as the oxidation state increases: TiO is weakly basic in water, whereas TiO_2 is amphoteric (reacts with both acid and base).

Table 22.3 shows the standard electrode potentials of the Period 4 transition metals in their +2 oxidation state in acid solution. Note that, in general, reducing strength decreases across the series. All the Period 4 transition metals, except copper, are active enough to reduce H^+ from aqueous acid to form hydrogen gas. In contrast to the rapid reaction at room temperature of the Group 1A(1) and 2A(2) metals with water, however, the transition metals have an oxide coating that allows rapid reaction only with hot water or steam.

Color and Magnetism of Compounds *Most main-group ionic compounds are colorless* because the metal ion has a filled outer level (noble gas electron configuration). With only much higher energy orbitals available to receive an excited electron, the ion does not absorb visible light. In contrast, electrons in a partially filled *d* sublevel can absorb visible wavelengths and move to slightly higher energy *d* orbitals. As a result, *many transition metal compounds have striking colors.* Exceptions are the compounds of scandium, titanium(IV), and zinc, which are colorless because their metal ions have either an empty *d* sublevel (Sc^{3+} or Ti^{4+}: [Ar] $3d^0$) or a filled one (Zn^{2+}: [Ar] $3d^{10}$) (Figure 22.6).

FIGURE 22.6 Colors of representative compounds of the Period 4 transition metals. Staggered from left to right, the compounds are scandium oxide *(white)*, titanium(IV) oxide *(white)*, vanadyl sulfate dihydrate *(light blue)*, sodium chromate *(yellow)*, manganese(II) chloride tetrahydrate *(light pink)*, potassium ferricyanide *(red-orange)*, cobalt(II) chloride hexahydrate *(violet)*, nickel(II) nitrate hexahydrate *(green)*, copper(II) sulfate pentahydrate *(blue)*, and zinc sulfate heptahydrate *(white)*.

Magnetic properties are also related to sublevel occupancy (Section 8.5). Recall that a *paramagnetic* substance has atoms or ions with unpaired electrons, which cause it to be attracted to an external magnetic field. A *diamagnetic* substance has only paired electrons, so it is unaffected (or slightly repelled) by a magnetic field. *Most main-group metal ions are diamagnetic* for the same reason they are colorless: all their electrons are paired. In contrast, *many transition metal compounds are paramagnetic because of their unpaired d electrons*. For example, $MnSO_4$ is paramagnetic, but $CaSO_4$ is diamagnetic. The Ca^{2+} ion has the electron configuration of argon, whereas Mn^{2+} has a d^5 configuration. Transition metal ions with a d^0 or d^{10} configuration are diamagnetic and colorless.

SECTION 22.1 SUMMARY

All transition elements are metals. • Atoms of *d*-block elements have $(n - 1)d$ orbitals being filled, and their ions have an empty *ns* orbital. • Unlike the trends in the main-group elements, atomic size, electronegativity, and first ionization energy change relatively little across a transition series. Because of the lanthanide contraction, atomic size changes little from Period 5 to 6 in a transition metal group; thus, electronegativity, first ionization energy, and density *increase* down a group. • Transition metals typically have several oxidation states, with the +2 state most common. The elements exhibit more metallic behavior in their lower states. • Most Period 4 transition metals are active enough to reduce hydrogen ion from acid solution. • Many transition metal compounds are colored and paramagnetic because the metal ion has unpaired *d* electrons.

22.2 COORDINATION COMPOUNDS

The most distinctive aspect of transition metal chemistry is the formation of **coordination compounds** (also called *complexes*). These are substances that contain at least one **complex ion,** a species consisting of *a central metal cation (either a transition metal or a main-group metal) that is bonded to molecules and/or anions called **ligands.*** In order to maintain charge neutrality in the coordination compound, the complex ion is typically associated with other ions, called **counter ions.**

A typical coordination compound appears in Figure 22.7A: the coordination compound is $[Co(NH_3)_6]Cl_3$, the complex ion (always enclosed in square brackets) is $[Co(NH_3)_6]^{3+}$, the six NH_3 molecules bonded to the central Co^{3+} are ligands, and the three Cl^- ions are counter ions. *A coordination compound behaves like*

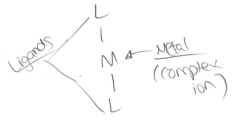

FIGURE 22.7 Components of a coordination compound. Coordination compounds, shown here as models *(top)*, perspective drawings *(middle)*, and chemical formulas *(bottom)*, typically consist of a complex ion and counter ions to neutralize the charge. The complex ion has a central metal ion surrounded by ligands. **A,** When solid $[Co(NH_3)_6]Cl_3$ dissolves, the complex ion and the counter ions separate, but the ligands remain bound to the metal ion. Six ligands around the metal ion give the complex ion an octahedral geometry. **B,** Complex ions with a central d^8 metal ion have four ligands and a square planar geometry.

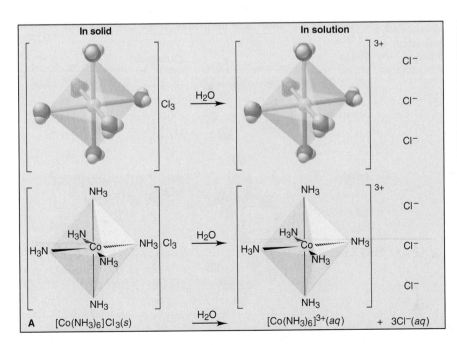

A $[Co(NH_3)_6]Cl_3(s)$ $\xrightarrow{H_2O}$ $[Co(NH_3)_6]^{3+}(aq)$ $+ \ 3Cl^-(aq)$

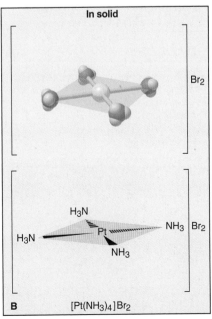

B $[Pt(NH_3)_4]Br_2$

an electrolyte in water: the complex ion and counter ions separate from each other. But the complex ion behaves like a polyatomic ion: *the ligands and central metal ion remain attached.* Thus, as Figure 22.7A shows, 1 mol of $[Co(NH_3)_6]Cl_3$ yields 1 mol of $[Co(NH_3)_6]^{3+}$ ions and 3 mol of Cl^- ions.

We discussed the Lewis acid-base properties of hydrated metal ions, which are a type of complex ion, in Section 18.8, and we examined complex-ion equilibria in Section 19.4. In this section, we consider the bonding, structure, and properties of complex ions.

Complex Ions: Coordination Numbers, Geometries, and Ligands

A complex ion is described by the metal ion and the number and types of ligands attached to it. Its structure has three key characteristics—coordination number, geometry, and number of donor atoms per ligand:

- *Coordination number.* The **coordination number** is the *number of ligand atoms* that are bonded directly to the central metal ion and is *specific* for a given metal ion in a particular oxidation state and compound. In general, *the most common coordination number in complex ions is 6,* but 2 and 4 are often seen, and some higher ones are also known.
- *Geometry.* The geometry (shape) of a complex ion depends on the coordination number and nature of the metal ion. Table 22.4 shows the geometries associated with the coordination numbers 2, 4, and 6, with some examples of each. A complex ion whose metal ion has a coordination number of 2 is *linear.* The coordination number 4 gives rise to either of two geometries—square planar or tetrahedral. Most d^8 metal ions form *square planar* complex ions (Figure 22.7B). The d^{10} ions are among those that form *tetrahedral* complex ions. A coordination number of 6 results in an *octahedral* geometry, as shown by $[Co(NH_3)_6]^{3+}$ in Figure 22.7A. Note the similarity with some of the molecular shapes in VSEPR theory (Section 10.2).
- *Donor atoms per ligand.* The ligands of complex ions are *molecules or anions* with one or more **donor atoms** that each *donate a lone pair of electrons* to the metal ion to form a covalent bond. Because they have at least one lone pair, donor atoms often come from Group 5A(15), 6A(16), or 7A(17).

Table 22.4	**Coordination Numbers and Shapes of Some Complex Ions**		
Coordination Number	**Shape**		**Examples**
2	Linear		$[CuCl_2]^-$, $[Ag(NH_3)_2]^+$, $[AuCl_2]^-$
4	Square planar		$[Ni(CN)_4]^{2-}$, $[PdCl_4]^{2-}$, $[Pt(NH_3)_4]^{2+}$, $[Cu(NH_3)_4]^{2+}$
4	Tetrahedral	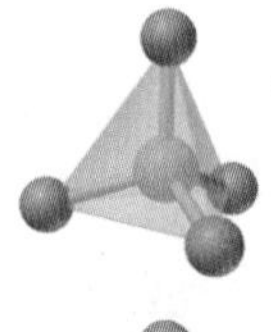	$[Cu(CN)_4]^{3-}$, $[Zn(NH_3)_4]^{2+}$, $[CdCl_4]^{2-}$, $[MnCl_4]^{2-}$
6	Octahedral	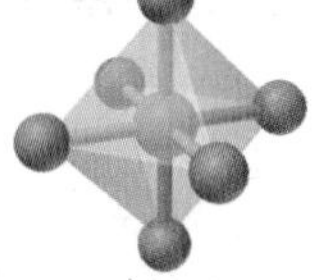	$[Ti(H_2O)_6]^{3+}$, $[V(CN)_6]^{4-}$, $[Cr(NH_3)_4Cl_2]^+$, $[Mn(H_2O)_6]^{2+}$, $[FeCl_6]^{3-}$, $[Co(en)_3]^{3+}$

Table 22.5 Some Common Ligands in Coordination Compounds

Ligand Type	Examples

Monodentate

$H_2\overset{..}{O}$: water   :$\overset{..}{\underset{..}{F}}$:$^-$ fluoride ion   [:C≡N:]$^-$ cyanide ion   [:$\overset{..}{\underset{..}{O}}$—H]$^-$ hydroxide ion

:NH_3 ammonia   :$\overset{..}{\underset{..}{Cl}}$:$^-$ chloride ion   [:$\overset{..}{\underset{..}{S}}$=C=$\overset{..}{N}$:]$^-$ thiocyanate ion   [:$\overset{..}{\underset{..}{O}}$—N=$\overset{..}{O}$:]$^-$ nitrite ion
       or   or

Bidentate

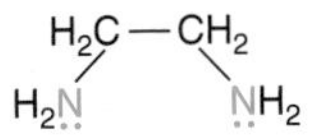

ethylenediamine (en)   oxalate ion

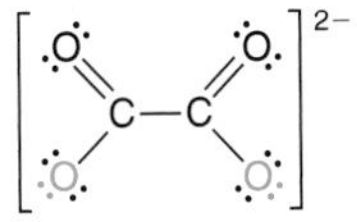

HON C

Polydentate

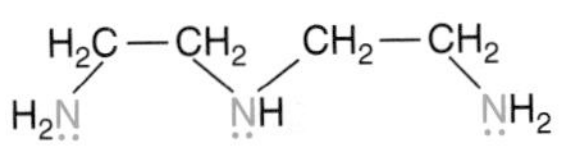

diethylenetriamine   triphosphate ion   ethylenediaminetetraacetate ion (EDTA^{4-})

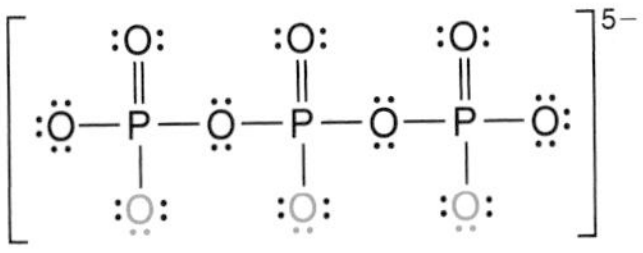

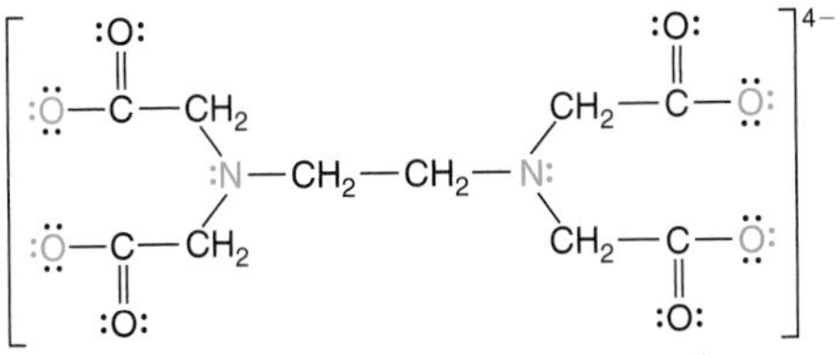

Ligands are classified in terms of the number of donor atoms, or "teeth," that each uses to bond to the central metal ion. *Monodentate* (Latin, "one-toothed") ligands, such as Cl$^-$ and NH_3, use a single donor atom. *Bidentate* ligands have two donor atoms, each of which bonds to the metal ion. *Polydentate* ligands have more than two donor atoms. Table 22.5 shows some common ligands in coordination compounds (with each donor atom and its lone pair in color). Bidentate and polydentate ligands give rise to *rings* in the complex ion. For instance, ethylenediamine (abbreviated *en* in formulas) has a chain of four atoms (:N—C—C—N:), so it forms a five-membered ring, with the two electron-donating N atoms bonded to the metal atom. Such ligands seem to grab the metal ion like claws, so a complex ion that contains them is also called a **chelate** (pronounced "KEY-late"; Greek *chela*, "crab's claw").

Formulas and Names of Coordination Compounds

There are three important rules for writing the formulas of coordination compounds, with the first two matching those for writing formulas of any ionic compounds:

1. *The cation is written before the anion.*
2. *The charge of the cation(s) is balanced by the charge of the anion(s).*
3. *For the complex ion, neutral ligands are written before anionic ligands, and the formula for the whole ion is placed in brackets.*

Let's apply these rules as we examine the combinations of ions in several coordination compounds. *The whole complex ion may be a cation or an anion.* A complex cation has anionic counter ions, and a complex anion has cationic counter ions. It's easy to find the charge of the central metal ion. For example, in $K_2[Co(NH_3)_2Cl_4]$, two K$^+$ counter ions balance the charge of the complex anion $[Co(NH_3)_2Cl_4]^{2-}$, which contains two NH_3 molecules and four Cl$^-$ ions as ligands. The two NH_3 are neutral, the four Cl$^-$ have a total charge of 4$-$, and the entire complex ion has a charge of 2$-$, so the central metal ion must be Co^{2+}:

Charge of complex ion = Charge of metal ion + total charge of ligands

$$2- = \text{Charge of metal ion} + [(2 \times 0) + (4 \times 1-)]$$

So,   Charge of metal ion = (2$-$) $-$ (4$-$) = 2$+$

In the compound $[Co(NH_3)_4Cl_2]Cl$, the complex ion is $[Co(NH_3)_4Cl_2]^+$ and one Cl^- is the counter ion. The four NH_3 ligands are neutral, the two Cl^- ligands have a total charge of $2-$, and the complex cation has a charge of $1+$, so the central metal ion must be Co^{3+} [that is, $1+ = (3+) + (2-)$]. Some coordination compounds have a complex cation *and* a complex anion, as in $[Co(NH_3)_5Br]_2[Fe(CN)_6]$. In this compound, the complex cation is $[Co(NH_3)_5Br]^{2+}$, with Co^{3+}, and the complex anion is $[Fe(CN)_6]^{4-}$, with Fe^{2+}.

Coordination compounds were originally named after the person who first prepared them or from their color, and some of these common names are still used, but most coordination compounds are named systematically through a set of rules:

1. *The cation is named before the anion.* In naming $[Co(NH_3)_4Cl_2]Cl$, for example, we name the $[Co(NH_3)_4Cl_2]^+$ ion before the Cl^- ion. Thus, the name is

    tetraamminedichlorocobalt(III) chloride

    The only space in the name appears between the cation and the anion.

2. *Within the complex ion, the ligands are named, in alphabetical order,* **before** *the metal ion.* Note that in the $[Co(NH_3)_4Cl_2]^+$ ion of the compound named in rule 1, the four NH_3 and two Cl^- are named before the Co^{3+}.

3. *Neutral ligands generally have the molecule name,* but there are a few exceptions (Table 22.6). *Anionic ligands drop the -ide and add -o after the root name;* thus, the name *fluoride* for the F^- ion becomes the ligand name *fluoro*. The two ligands in $[Co(NH_3)_4Cl_2]^+$ are *ammine* (NH_3) and *chloro* (Cl^-) with *ammine* coming before *chloro* alphabetically.

Table 22.6 Names of Some Neutral and Anionic Ligands

Neutral		Anionic	
Name	**Formula**	**Name**	**Formula**
Aqua	H_2O	Fluoro	F^-
Ammine	NH_3	Chloro	Cl^-
Carbonyl	CO	Bromo	Br^-
Nitrosyl	NO	Iodo	I^-
		Hydroxo	OH^-
		Cyano	CN^-

4. *A numerical prefix indicates the number of ligands of a particular type.* For example, *tetra*ammine denotes *four* NH_3, and *di*chloro denotes *two* Cl^-. Other prefixes are *tri-, penta-,* and *hexa-*. These prefixes do *not* affect the alphabetical order; thus, *tetraammine* comes before *dichloro*. Because some ligand names already contain a numerical prefix (such as ethylene*di*amine), we use *bis* (2), *tris* (3), or *tetrakis* (4) to indicate the number of such ligands, followed by the ligand name in parentheses. For example, a complex ion that has two ethylenediamine ligands has *bis(ethylenediamine)* in its name.

5. *The oxidation state of the central metal ion is given by a Roman numeral (in parentheses) only* if the metal ion can have more than one state, as in the compound named in rule 1.

6. *If the complex ion is an anion, we drop the ending of the metal name and add -ate.* Thus, the name for $K[Pt(NH_3)Cl_5]$ is

    potassium amminepentachloroplatinate(IV)

(Note that there is one K^+ counter ion, so the complex anion has a charge of $1-$. The five Cl^- ligands have a total charge of $5-$, so Pt must be in the $+4$ oxidation state.) For some metals, we use the Latin root with the *-ate* ending, as shown in Table 22.7. For example, the name for $Na_4[FeBr_6]$ is

    sodium hexabromoferrate(II)

Table 22.7 Names of Some Metal Ions in Complex Anions

Metal	Name in Anion
Iron	Ferrate
Copper	Cuprate
Lead	Plumbate
Silver	Argentate
Gold	Aurate
Tin	Stannate

SAMPLE PROBLEM 22.2 Writing Names and Formulas of Coordination Compounds

Problem (a) What is the systematic name of $Na_3[AlF_6]$?
(b) What is the systematic name of $[Co(en)_2Cl_2]NO_3$?
(c) What is the formula of tetraamminebromochloroplatinum(IV) chloride?
(d) What is the formula of hexaamminecobalt(III) tetrachloroferrate(III)?
Plan We use the rules that were presented above and refer to Tables 22.6 and 22.7.
Solution **(a)** The complex ion is $[AlF_6]^{3-}$. There are six *(hexa-)* F^- ions *(fluoro)* as ligands, so we have *hexafluoro*. The complex ion is an anion, so the ending of the metal ion (aluminum) must be changed to *-ate*: hexafluoroaluminate. Aluminum has only the $+3$ oxidation state, so we do *not* use a Roman numeral. The positive counter ion is named first and separated from the anion by a space: sodium hexafluoroaluminate.

(b) Listed alphabetically, there are two Cl^- *(dichloro)* and two en *[bis(ethylenediamine)]* as ligands. The complex ion is a cation, so the metal name is unchanged, but we specify its oxidation state because cobalt can have several. One NO_3^- balances the $1+$ cation charge: with $2-$ for two Cl^- and 0 for two en, the metal must be *cobalt(III)*. The word *nitrate* follows a space: dichlorobis(ethylenediamine)cobalt(III) nitrate.

(c) The central metal ion is written first, followed by the neutral ligands and then (in alphabetical order) by the negative ligands. *Tetraammine* is four NH_3, *bromo* is one Br^-, *chloro* is one Cl^-, and *platinate(IV)* is Pt^{4+}, so the complex ion is $[Pt(NH_3)_4BrCl]^{2+}$. Its $2+$ charge is the sum of $4+$ for Pt^{4+}, 0 for four NH_3, $1-$ for one Br^-, and $1-$ for one Cl^-. To balance the $2+$ charge, we need two Cl^- counter ions: $[Pt(NH_3)_4BrCl]Cl_2$.

(d) This compound consists of two different complex ions. In the cation, *hexaammine* is six NH_3 and *cobalt(III)* is Co^{3+}, so the cation is $[Co(NH_3)_6]^{3+}$. The $3+$ charge is the sum of $3+$ for Co^{3+} and 0 for six NH_3. In the anion, *tetrachloro* is four Cl^-, and *ferrate(III)* is Fe^{3+}, so the anion is $[FeCl_4]^-$. The $1-$ charge is the sum of $3+$ for Fe^{3+} and $4-$ for four Cl^-. In the neutral compound, one $3+$ cation is balanced by three $1-$ anions: $[Co(NH_3)_6][FeCl_4]_3$.

Check Reverse the process to be sure you obtain the name or formula asked for in the problem.

FOLLOW-UP PROBLEM 22.2 **(a)** What is the name of $[Cr(H_2O)_5Br]Cl_2$?
(b) What is the formula of barium hexacyanocobaltate(III)?

Isomerism in Coordination Compounds

Isomers are compounds with the same chemical formula but different properties. We discussed many aspects of isomerism in the context of organic compounds in Section 15.2; it may be helpful to review that section now. Figure 22.8 presents an overview of the most common types of isomerism in coordination compounds.

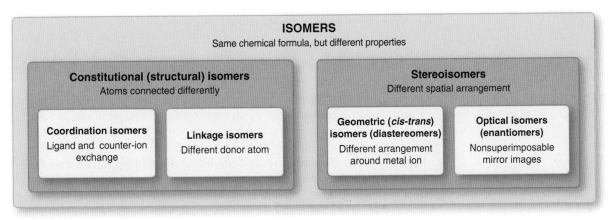

FIGURE 22.8 Important types of isomerism in coordination compounds.

Constitutional Isomers: Same Atoms Connected Differently Two compounds with the same formula, but with the atoms connected differently, are called **constitutional (structural) isomers.** Coordination compounds exhibit two types of constitutional isomers: one involves a difference in the composition of the complex ion, the other in the donor atom of the ligand.

1. **Coordination isomers** occur when the composition of the complex ion changes but not that of the compound. One way this type of isomerism occurs is when ligand and counter ion exchange positions, as in $[Pt(NH_3)_4Cl_2](NO_2)_2$ and $[Pt(NH_3)_4(NO_2)_2]Cl_2$. In the first compound, the Cl^- ions are the ligands, and the NO_2^- ions are counter ions; in the second, the roles are reversed. Another way that this type of isomerism occurs is in compounds of two complex ions in which the two sets of ligands in one compound are reversed in the other, as in $[Cr(NH_3)_6][Co(CN)_6]$ and $[Co(NH_3)_6][Cr(CN)_6]$; note that NH_3 is a ligand of Cr^{3+} in one compound and of Co^{3+} in the other.

2. **Linkage isomers** occur when the composition of the complex ion remains the same but the attachment of the ligand donor atom changes. Some ligands can bind to the metal ion through *either of two donor atoms.* For example, the nitrite ion can bind through a lone pair on either the N atom (*nitro,* O_2N:) or one of the O atoms (*nitrito,* ONO:) to give linkage isomers, as in the orange compound pentaammine*nitro*cobalt(III) chloride $[Co(NH_3)_5(NO_2)]Cl_2$ (Figure 22.9A) and its reddish linkage isomer pentaammine*nitrito*cobalt(III) chloride $[Co(NH_3)_5(ONO)]Cl_2$ (Figure 22.9B). Another example of a ligand with two different donor atoms is the cyanate ion, which can attach via a lone pair on the O atom (*cyanato,* NCO:) or the N atom (*isocyanato,* OCN:); the thiocyanate ion behaves similarly, attaching via the S atom or the N atom:

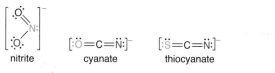

nitrite   cyanate   thiocyanate

FIGURE 22.9 Linkage isomers of a complex ion.

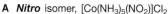

A *Nitro* isomer, $[Co(NH_3)_5(NO_2)]Cl_2$ **B** *Nitrito* isomer, $[Co(NH_3)_5(ONO)]Cl_2$

Stereoisomers: Different Spatial Arrangements of Atoms **Stereoisomers** are compounds that have the same atomic connections but different spatial arrangements. The two types we discussed for organic compounds, called *geometric* and *optical* isomers, are seen with coordination compounds as well:

1. **Geometric isomers** (also called *cis-trans* isomers or *diastereomers*) occur when atoms or groups of atoms are arranged differently in space relative to the central metal ion. For example, the square planar $[Pt(NH_3)_2Cl_2]$ has two arrangements, giving rise to two compounds (Figure 22.10A). The isomer with identical ligands *next* to each other is *cis*-diamminedichloroplatinum(II), and the one with identical ligands *across* from each other is *trans*-diamminedichloroplatinum(II); the *cis* isomer has striking antitumor activity, but the *trans* isomer has none! Octahedral complexes also exhibit *cis-trans* isomerism (Figure 22.10B). The *cis* isomer of the $[Co(NH_3)_4Cl_2]^+$ ion has the two Cl^- ligands next to each other and is violet; the *trans* isomer has these two ligands across from each other and is green.

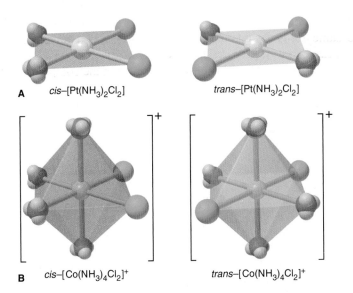

A *cis*–[Pt(NH₃)₂Cl₂]   *trans*–[Pt(NH₃)₂Cl₂]

B *cis*–[Co(NH₃)₄Cl₂]⁺   *trans*–[Co(NH₃)₄Cl₂]⁺

FIGURE 22.10 Geometric *(cis-trans)* isomerism. A, The *cis* and *trans* isomers of the square planar coordination compound [Pt(NH₃)₂Cl₂]. **B,** The *cis* and *trans* isomers of the octahedral complex ion [Co(NH₃)₄Cl₂]⁺. The colored shapes represent the actual colors of the species.

2. **Optical isomers** (also called *enantiomers*) occur when a molecule and its mirror image cannot be superimposed (see Figures 15.8 and 15.9). Octahedral complex ions show many examples of optical isomerism, which we can observe by rotating one isomer and seeing if it is superimposable on the other isomer (its mirror image). For example, as you can see in Figure 22.11A, the two structures (I and II) of [Co(en)₂Cl₂]⁺, the *cis*-dichlorobis(ethylenediamine)cobalt(III) ion, are mirror images of each other. Rotate structure I 180° around a vertical axis, and you obtain III. The Cl⁻ ligands of III match those of II, but the en ligands do not: II and III (rotated I) are not superimposable; therefore, they are optical isomers. Unlike other types of isomers, which have distinct physical properties, optical isomers are physically identical in all ways but one: *the direction in which they rotate the plane of polarized light.* One isomer is designated *d*-[Co(en)₂Cl₂]⁺ and the other is *l*-[Co(en)₂Cl₂]⁺, depending on whether it rotates

FIGURE 22.11 Optical isomerism in an octahedral complex ion. A, Structure I and its mirror image, structure II, are optical isomers of *cis*-[Co(en)₂Cl₂]⁺. Rotating structure I gives structure III, which is *not* the same as structure II. (The curved wedges represent the bidentate ligand ethylenediamine, H₂N—CH₂—CH₂—NH₂.) **B,** The *trans* isomer does *not* have optical isomers. Rotating structure I gives III, which is *identical* to II, the mirror image of I.

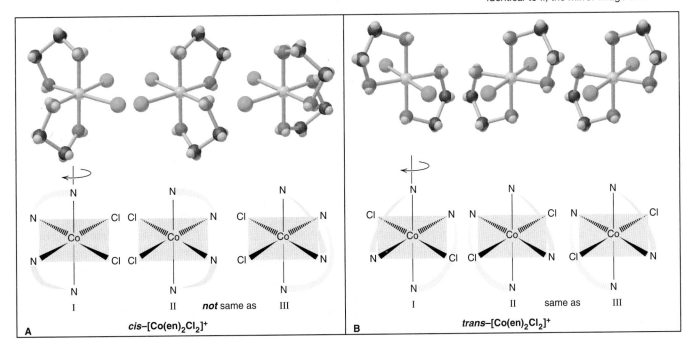

A   I   II   *not* same as   III   *cis*-[Co(en)₂Cl₂]⁺

B   I   II   same as   III   *trans*-[Co(en)₂Cl₂]⁺

the plane of polarized light to the right (*d-* for "dextro-") or to the left (*l-* for "levo-"). (The *d-* or *l-* designation can only be determined experimentally, *not* by examination of the structure.) In contrast, as shown in Figure 22.11B, the two structures of the *trans*-dichlorobis(ethylenediamine)cobalt(III) ion are *not* optical isomers: rotate I 90° around a vertical axis and you obtain III, which *is* super-imposable on II.

(a)   *trans*   *cis*

Mirror

not the same as

Rotate

(b)

SAMPLE PROBLEM 22.3 Determining the Type of Stereoisomerism

Problem Draw all stereoisomers for each of the following and state the type of isomerism:
(a) [Pt(NH₃)₂Br₂] (square planar)   **(b)** [Cr(en)₃]³⁺ (en = H₂N̈CH₂CH₂N̈H₂)
Plan We first determine the geometry around each metal ion and the nature of the ligands. If there are two different ligands that can be placed in different positions relative to each other, geometric *(cis-trans)* isomerism occurs. Then, we see whether the mirror image of an isomer is superimposable on the original. If it is *not,* optical isomerism occurs.
Solution (a) The Pt(II) complex is square planar, and there are two different monodentate ligands. Each pair of ligands can lie next to or across from each other (see structures in margin). Thus, geometric isomerism occurs. Each isomer *is* superimposable on its mirror image, so there is no optical isomerism.
(b) Ethylenediamine (en) is a bidentate ligand. Cr^{3+} has a coordination number of 6 and an octahedral geometry, like Co^{3+}. The three bidentate ligands are identical, so there is no geometric isomerism. However, the complex ion has a nonsuperimposable mirror image (see structures in margin). Thus, optical isomerism occurs.

FOLLOW-UP PROBLEM 22.3 What stereoisomers, if any, are possible for the [Co(NH₃)₂(en)Cl₂]⁺ ion?

SECTION 22.2 SUMMARY

Coordination compounds consist of a complex ion and charge-balancing counter ions. The complex ion has a central metal ion bonded to neutral and/or anionic ligands, which have one or more donor atoms that each provide a lone pair of electrons. • The most common geometry is octahedral (six ligand atoms bonding). • Formulas and names of coordination compounds follow systematic rules. • These compounds can exhibit constitutional isomerism (coordination and linkage) and stereoisomerism (geometric and optical).

22.3 THEORETICAL BASIS FOR THE BONDING AND PROPERTIES OF COMPLEXES

In this section, we consider two models that address, in different ways, several key features of complexes: how metal-ligand bonds form, why certain geometries are preferred, and why these complexes are brightly colored and often paramagnetic.

Application of Valence Bond Theory to Complex Ions

Valence bond (VB) theory, which helped explain bonding and structure in main-group compounds (Section 11.1), is also used to describe bonding in complex ions. In the formation of a complex ion, the filled ligand orbital overlaps the empty metal-ion orbital. *The ligand (Lewis base) donates the electron pair, and the metal ion (Lewis acid) accepts it to form one of the covalent bonds of the complex ion (Lewis adduct)* (Section 18.8). Such a bond, in which one atom in the bond contributes both electrons, is called a **coordinate covalent bond,** although, once formed, it is identical to any covalent single bond. Recall that the VB concept of hybridization proposes the mixing of particular combinations of *s,* *p,* and *d* orbitals to give sets of hybrid orbitals, which have specific geometries. Similarly, for coordination compounds, the model proposes that *the number and type of metal-ion hybrid orbitals occupied by ligand lone pairs determine the* *geometry of the complex ion.* Let's discuss the orbital combinations that lead to octahedral, square planar, and tetrahedral geometries.

Octahedral Complexes The hexaamminechromium(III) ion, $[Cr(NH_3)_6]^{3+}$, illustrates the application of VB theory to an *octahedral complex* (Figure 22.12). The six lowest energy empty orbitals of the Cr^{3+} ion—two 3d, one 4s, and three 4p—mix and become six equivalent d^2sp^3 hybrid orbitals that point toward the corners of an octahedron.* Six NH_3 molecules donate lone pairs from their nitrogens to form six metal-ligand bonds. The three unpaired 3d electrons of the central Cr^{3+} ion ([Ar] $3d^3$), which make the complex ion paramagnetic, remain in unhybridized orbitals.

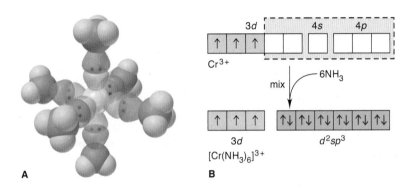

A   **B**

FIGURE 22.12 Hybrid orbitals and bonding in the octahedral [Cr(NH₃)₆]³⁺ ion. **A,** VB depiction of the Cr(NH₃)₆³⁺ ion. **B,** The partial orbital diagrams depict the mixing of two 3d, one 4s, and three 4p orbitals in Cr³⁺ to form six d^2sp^3 hybrid orbitals, which are filled with six NH₃ lone pairs *(red)*.

Square Planar Complexes Metal ions with a d^8 configuration usually form *square planar complexes* (Figure 22.13). In the $[Ni(CN)_4]^{2-}$ ion, for example, the model proposes that one 3d, one 4s, and two 4p orbitals of Ni^{2+} mix and form four dsp^2 hybrid orbitals, which point to the corners of a square and accept one electron pair from each of four CN^- ligands.

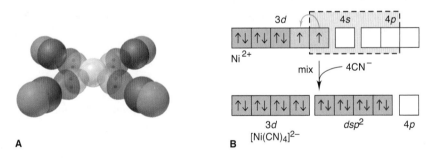

A   **B**

FIGURE 22.13 Hybrid orbitals and bonding in the square planar [Ni(CN)₄]²⁻ ion. **A,** VB depiction of [Ni(CN)₄]²⁻. **B,** Two lone 3d electrons pair up and free one 3d orbital for hybridization with the 4s and two of the 4p orbitals to form four dsp^2 orbitals, which become occupied with lone pairs *(red)* from four CN⁻ ligands.

A look at the ground-state electron configuration of the Ni^{2+} ion, however, raises a key question: how can the Ni^{2+} ion ([Ar] $3d^8$) offer an empty 3d orbital for accepting a lone pair, if its eight 3d electrons lie in three filled and two half-filled orbitals? Apparently, in the d^8 configuration of Ni^{2+}, electrons in the half-filled orbitals pair up and leave one 3d orbital empty. This explanation is consistent with the fact that the complex is diamagnetic (no unpaired electrons). Moreover, it requires that the energy *gained* by using a 3d orbital for bonding in the hybrid orbital is greater than the energy *required* to overcome repulsions from pairing the 3d electrons.

---

*Note the distinction between the hybrid-orbital designation here and that for octahedral molecules like SF₆. The designation gives the orbitals in energy order within a given n value. In the $[Cr(NH_3)_6]^{3+}$ complex ion, the d orbitals have a *lower n* value than the s and p orbitals, so the hybrid orbitals are d^2sp^3. For the orbitals in SF₆, the d orbitals have the *same n* value as the s and p, so the hybrid orbitals are sp^3d^2.

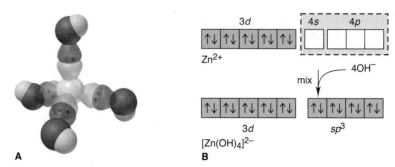

A

B

FIGURE 22.14 Hybrid orbitals and bonding in the tetrahedral [Zn(OH)$_4$]$^{2-}$ ion. A, VB depiction of [Zn(OH)$_4$]$^{2-}$. **B,** Mixing one 4s and three 4p orbitals gives four sp^3 hybrid orbitals available for accepting lone pairs *(red)* from OH$^-$ ligands.

Tetrahedral Complexes Metal ions that have a filled *d* sublevel, such as Zn^{2+} ([Ar] 3d^{10}), often form *tetrahedral complexes* (Figure 22.14). For the complex ion [Zn(OH)$_4$]$^{2-}$, for example, VB theory proposes that the lowest available Zn^{2+} orbitals—one 4s and three 4p—mix to become four sp^3 hybrid orbitals that point to the corners of a tetrahedron and are occupied by four lone pairs, one from each of four OH$^-$ ligands.

Crystal Field Theory

The VB model is easy to picture and rationalizes bonding and shape, but it treats the orbitals as little more than empty "slots" for accepting electron pairs. Consequently, it gives no insight into the colors of coordination compounds and sometimes predicts their magnetic properties incorrectly. In contrast to the VB approach, **crystal field theory** provides little insight about metal-ligand bonding but explains color and magnetism clearly. To do so, it highlights the *effects on the d-orbital energies of the metal ion as the ligands approach.* Before we discuss this theory, let's consider what causes a substance to be colored.

What Is Color? White light is electromagnetic radiation consisting of all wavelengths (λ) in the visible range (Section 7.1). It can be dispersed into a spectrum of colors, each of which has a narrower range of wavelengths. Objects appear colored in white light because they absorb certain wavelengths and reflect or transmit others: an opaque object *reflects* light, whereas a clear one *transmits* it. The reflected or transmitted light enters the eye and the brain perceives a color. If an object *absorbs* all visible wavelengths, it appears black; if it *reflects* all, it appears white.

Each color has a *complementary* color. For example, green and red are complementary colors. A mixture of complementary colors absorbs all visible wavelengths and appears black. Figure 22.15 shows these relationships on an artist's color wheel, where complementary colors appear as wedges opposite each other.

An object has a particular color for one of two reasons:

- It reflects (or transmits) light of *that* color. Thus, if an object absorbs all wavelengths *except* green, the reflected (or transmitted) light enters our eyes and is interpreted as green.
- It absorbs light of the *complementary* color. Thus, if the object absorbs only red, the *complement* of green, the remaining mixture of reflected (or transmitted) wavelengths enters our eyes and is interpreted as green also.

Table 22.8 lists the color absorbed and the resulting color perceived.

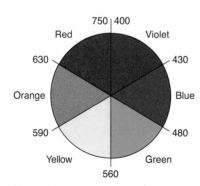

FIGURE 22.15 An artist's wheel. Colors, with approximate wavelength ranges (in nm), are shown as wedges. Complementary colors, such as red and green, lie opposite each other.

Table 22.8	Relation Between Absorbed and Observed Colors			
Absorbed Color	**λ (nm)**	**Observed Color**	**λ (nm)**
Violet	400	Green-yellow	560
Blue	450	Yellow	600
Blue-green	490	Red	620
Yellow-green	570	Violet	410
Yellow	580	Dark blue	430
Orange	600	Blue	450
Red	650	Green	520

Splitting of _d_ Orbitals in an Octahedral Field of Ligands The crystal field model explains that the properties of complexes result from the splitting of _d_-orbital energies, which arises from electrostatic interactions between metal ion and ligands. The model assumes that a complex ion forms as a result of _electrostatic attractions between the metal cation and the negative charge of the ligands._ This negative charge is either partial, as in a polar neutral ligand like NH_3, or full, as in an anionic ligand like Cl^-. The ligands approach the metal ion along the mutually perpendicular _x_, _y_, and _z_ axes, which minimizes the overall energy of the system.

Picture what happens as the ligands approach. Figure 22.16A shows six ligands moving toward a metal ion to form an octahedral complex. Let's see how the various _d_ orbitals of the metal ion are affected as the complex forms. As the ligands approach, their electron pairs repel electrons in the five _d_ orbitals. In the isolated metal ion, the _d_ orbitals have equal energies despite their different orientations. In the electrostatic field of ligands, however, the _d_ electrons are _repelled unequally because their orbitals have different orientations._ Because the ligands move along the _x_, _y_, and _z_ axes, they approach _directly toward_ the lobes of the $d_{x^2-y^2}$ and d_{z^2} orbitals (Figure 22.16B and C) but _between_ the lobes of the d_{xy}, d_{xz}, and d_{yz} orbitals (Figure 22.16D to F). Thus, electrons in the $d_{x^2-y^2}$ and d_{z^2} orbitals experience _stronger_ repulsions than those in the d_{xy}, d_{xz}, and d_{yz} orbitals.

An energy diagram of the orbitals shows that all five _d_ orbitals are higher in energy in the forming complex than in the free metal ion because of repulsions

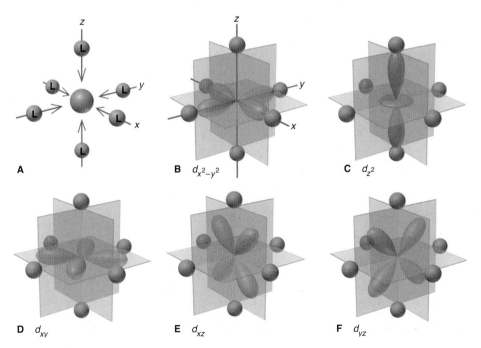

A

B $d_{x^2-y^2}$

C d_{z^2}

D d_{xy}

E d_{xz}

F d_{yz}

FIGURE 22.16 The five _d_ orbitals in an octahedral field of ligands. The direction of ligand approach influences the strength of repulsions of electrons in the five metal _d_ orbitals. **A,** We assume that ligands approach a metal ion along the three linear axes in an octahedral orientation. **B** and **C,** Lobes of the $d_{x^2-y^2}$ and d_{z^2} orbitals lie _directly in line_ with the approaching ligands, so repulsions are stronger. **D** to **F,** Lobes of the d_{xy}, d_{xz}, and d_{yz} orbitals lie _between_ the approaching ligands, so repulsions are weaker.

FIGURE 22.17 Splitting of *d*-orbital energies by an octahedral field of ligands. Electrons in the *d* orbitals of the free metal ion experience an *average* net repulsion in the negative ligand field that increases all *d*-orbital energies. Electrons in the t_{2g} set are repelled less than those in the e_g set. The energy difference between these two sets is the crystal field splitting energy, Δ.

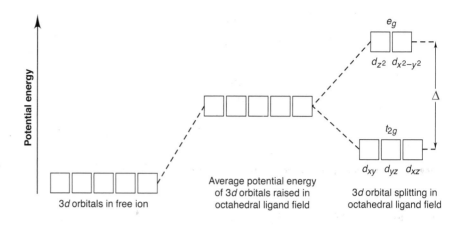

3*d* orbitals in free ion

Average potential energy of 3*d* orbitals raised in octahedral ligand field

3*d* orbital splitting in octahedral ligand field

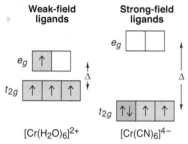

FIGURE 22.18 The effect of the ligand on splitting energy. Ligands interacting strongly with metal-ion *d* orbitals, such as CN^-, produce a larger Δ than those interacting weakly, such as H_2O.

from the approaching ligands, but *the orbital energies split, with two d orbitals higher in energy than the other three* (Figure 22.17). The two higher energy orbitals are called e_g **orbitals,** and the three lower energy ones are t_{2g} **orbitals.** (These designations refer to features of the orbitals that need not concern us here.)

The splitting of orbital energies is called the *crystal field effect,* and the difference in energy between the e_g and t_{2g} sets of orbitals is the **crystal field splitting energy (Δ).** Different ligands create crystal fields of different strengths and, thus, cause the *d*-orbital energies to split to different extents. **Strong-field ligands** lead to a *larger* splitting energy (larger Δ); **weak-field ligands** lead to a *smaller* splitting energy (smaller Δ). For instance, H_2O is a weak-field ligand, and CN^- is a strong-field ligand (Figure 22.18). The magnitude of Δ relates directly to the color and magnetic properties of a complex.

Explaining the Colors of Transition Metal Compounds The remarkably diverse colors of coordination compounds are determined by the energy difference (Δ) between the t_{2g} and e_g orbital sets in their complex ions. When the ion absorbs light in the visible range, electrons are excited ("jump") from the lower energy t_{2g} level to the higher e_g level. In Chapter 7, you saw that the *difference* between two electronic energy levels in the ion is equal to the energy (and inversely related to the wavelength) of the absorbed photon:

$$\Delta E_{\text{electron}} = E_{\text{photon}} = h\nu = hc/\lambda$$

The substance has a color because only certain wavelengths of the incoming white light are absorbed.

Consider the $[Ti(H_2O)_6]^{3+}$ ion, which appears purple in aqueous solution (Figure 22.19). Hydrated Ti^{3+} is a d^1 ion, with the *d* electron in one of the three

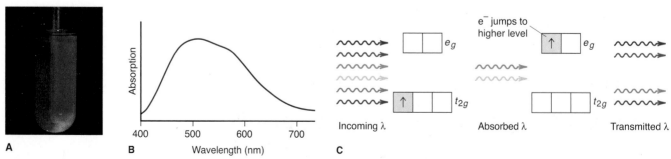

FIGURE 22.19 The color of $[Ti(H_2O)_6]^{3+}$. A, The hydrated Ti^{3+} ion is purple in aqueous solution. **B,** An absorption spectrum shows that incoming wavelengths corresponding to green and yellow light are absorbed, whereas other wavelengths are transmitted. **C,** A partial orbital diagram depicts the colors absorbed in the excitation of the *d* electron to the higher level.

lower energy t_{2g} orbitals. The energy difference (Δ) between the t_{2g} and e_g orbitals in this ion corresponds to the energy of photons spanning the green and yellow range. When white light shines on the solution, these colors of light are absorbed, and the electron jumps to one of the e_g orbitals. Red, blue, and violet light are transmitted, so the solution appears purple.

Absorption spectra show the wavelengths absorbed by a given metal ion with different ligands and by different metal ions with the same ligand. From such data, we relate the energy of the absorbed light to the Δ values, and two important observations emerge:

1. *For a given ligand, the color depends on the oxidation state of the metal ion.* For example, as shown in Figure 22.20A, a solution of $[V(H_2O)_6]^{2+}$ ion is violet, and a solution of $[V(H_2O)_6]^{3+}$ ion is yellow.
2. *For a given metal ion, the color depends on the ligand.* Even a single ligand substitution can have a major effect on the wavelengths absorbed and, thus, the color, as you can see for the two Cr^{3+} complex ions that are shown in Figure 22.20B.

The second observation allows us to rank ligands into a **spectrochemical series** with regard to their ability to split *d*-orbital energies. An abbreviated series, moving from weak-field ligands (small splitting, small Δ) to strong-field ligands (large splitting, large Δ), is shown in Figure 22.21.

Using this series, we can predict the *relative* size of Δ for a series of octahedral complexes of the same metal ion. Although it is difficult to predict the actual color of a given complex, we can determine whether a complex will absorb longer or shorter wavelengths than other complexes in the series.

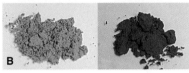

FIGURE 22.20 Effects of the metal oxidation state and of ligand identity on color. A, Solutions of $[V(H_2O)_6]^{2+}$ *(left)* and $[V(H_2O)_6]^{3+}$ *(right)* ions have different colors. **B,** A change in even a single ligand can influence the color. The $[Cr(NH_3)_6]^{3+}$ ion is yellow-orange *(left);* the $[Cr(NH_3)_5Cl]^{2+}$ ion is purple *(right).*

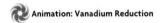 Animation: Vanadium Reduction

---

SAMPLE PROBLEM 22.4 Ranking Crystal Field Splitting Energies for Complex Ions of a Given Metal

Problem Rank the ions $[Ti(H_2O)_6]^{3+}$, $[Ti(NH_3)_6]^{3+}$, and $[Ti(CN)_6]^{3-}$ in terms of the relative value of Δ and of the energy of visible light absorbed.

Plan The formulas show that titanium's oxidation state is $+3$ in the three ions. From the information given in Figure 22.21, we rank the ligands in terms of crystal field strength: the stronger the ligand, the greater the splitting, and the higher the energy of light absorbed.

Solution The ligand field strength is in the order $CN^- > NH_3 > H_2O$, so the relative size of Δ and energy of light absorbed is

$$[Ti(CN)_6]^{3-} > [Ti(NH_3)_6]^{3+} > [Ti(H_2O)_6]^{3+}$$

FOLLOW-UP PROBLEM 22.4 Which complex ion absorbs visible light of higher energy, $[V(H_2O)_6]^{3+}$ or $[V(NH_3)_6]^{3+}$?

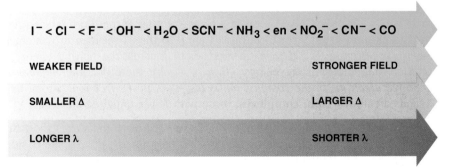

$I^- < Cl^- < F^- < OH^- < H_2O < SCN^- < NH_3 < en < NO_2^- < CN^- < CO$

WEAKER FIELD	STRONGER FIELD
SMALLER Δ	LARGER Δ
LONGER λ	SHORTER λ

FIGURE 22.21 The spectrochemical series. As the crystal field strength of the ligand increases, the splitting energy (Δ) increases, so shorter wavelengths (λ) of light must be absorbed to excite electrons. Water is usually a weak-field ligand.

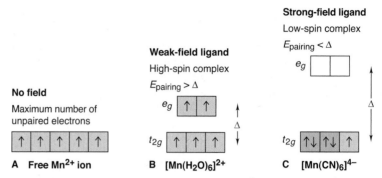

FIGURE 22.22 High-spin and low-spin complex ions of Mn²⁺. A, The free Mn^{2+} ion has five unpaired electrons. **B,** Bonded to weak-field ligands (smaller Δ), Mn^{2+} still has five unpaired electrons (high-spin complex). **C,** Bonded to strong-field ligands (larger Δ), Mn^{2+} has only one unpaired electron (low-spin complex).

Explaining the Magnetic Properties of Transition Metal Complexes The splitting of energy levels influences magnetic properties by affecting the number of *unpaired* electrons in the metal ion's d orbitals. Based on Hund's rule (Section 8.3), electrons occupy orbitals one at a time as long as orbitals of equal energy are available. When all lower energy orbitals are half-filled, the next electron can

- enter a half-filled orbital and pair up by overcoming a repulsive *pairing energy* ($E_{pairing}$), or
- enter an empty, higher energy orbital by overcoming the crystal field splitting energy (Δ).

Thus, *the relative sizes of $E_{pairing}$ and Δ determine the occupancy of the d orbitals.* The orbital occupancy pattern, in turn, determines the number of unpaired electrons and, thus, the paramagnetic behavior of the ion.

As an example, the isolated Mn^{2+} ion ([Ar] $3d^5$) has five unpaired electrons in $3d$ orbitals of equal energy (Figure 22.22A). In an octahedral field of ligands, the orbital energies split. The orbital occupancy is affected by the ligand in one of two ways:

1. *Weak-field ligands and high-spin complexes.* Weak-field ligands, such as H_2O in $[Mn(H_2O)_6]^{2+}$, cause a *small* splitting energy, so it takes *less* energy for d electrons to jump to the e_g set than to pair up in the t_{2g} set. As a result, the d electrons remain unpaired (Figure 22.22B). With weak-field ligands, the pairing energy is *greater* than the splitting energy ($E_{pairing} > \Delta$); therefore, *the number of unpaired electrons in the complex ion is the **same** as in the free ion.* Weak-field ligands create **high-spin complexes,** those with the *maximum* number of unpaired electrons.

2. *Strong-field ligands and low-spin complexes.* In contrast, strong-field ligands, such as CN^- in $[Mn(CN)_6]^{4-}$, cause a *large* splitting of the d-orbital energies, so it takes *more* energy for electrons to jump to the e_g set than to pair up in the t_{2g} set (Figure 22.22C). With strong-field ligands, the pairing energy is *smaller* than the splitting energy ($E_{pairing} < \Delta$); therefore, *the number of unpaired electrons in the complex ion is **less** than in the free ion.* Strong-field ligands create **low-spin complexes,** those with *fewer* unpaired electrons.

Orbital diagrams for the d^1 through d^9 ions in octahedral complexes show that both high-spin and low-spin options are possible only for d^4, d^5, d^6, and d^7 ions (Figure 22.23). With three lower energy t_{2g} orbitals available, the d^1, d^2, and d^3 ions always form high-spin complexes because there is no need to pair up. Similarly, d^8 and d^9 ions always form high-spin complexes: because the t_{2g} set is filled with six electrons, the two e_g orbitals *must* have either two (d^8) or one (d^9) unpaired electron.

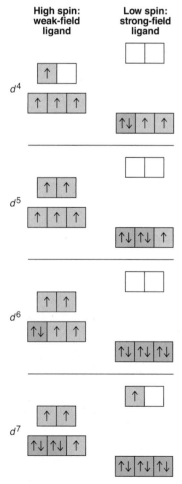

FIGURE 22.23 Orbital occupancy for high-spin and low-spin complexes of d^4 through d^7 metal ions.

SAMPLE PROBLEM 22.5 Identifying Complex Ions as High Spin or Low Spin

Problem Iron(II) forms an essential complex in hemoglobin. For each of the two octahedral complex ions $[Fe(H_2O)_6]^{2+}$ and $[Fe(CN)_6]^{4-}$, draw an orbital splitting diagram, predict the number of unpaired electrons, and identify the ion as low spin or high spin.

Plan The Fe^{2+} electron configuration gives us the number of d electrons, and the spectrochemical series in Figure 22.21 shows the relative strengths of the two ligands. We draw the diagrams, separating the t_{2g} and e_g sets by a greater distance for the strong-field ligand. Then we add electrons, noting that a weak-field ligand gives the *maximum* number of unpaired electrons and a high-spin complex, whereas a strong-field ligand leads to electron pairing and a low-spin complex.

Solution Fe^{2+} has the [Ar] $3d^6$ configuration. According to Figure 22.21, H_2O produces smaller splitting than CN^-. The diagrams are shown in the margin. The $[Fe(H_2O)_6]^{2+}$ ion has four unpaired electrons (high spin), and the $[Fe(CN)_6]^{4-}$ ion has no unpaired electrons (low spin).

Comments 1. H_2O is a weak-field ligand, so it almost always forms high-spin complexes.
2. These results are correct, but we cannot confidently predict the spin of a complex without having actual values for Δ and $E_{pairing}$.
3. Cyanide ions and carbon monoxide are highly toxic because they interact with the iron cations in essential proteins.

FOLLOW-UP PROBLEM 22.5 How many unpaired electrons do you expect for $[Mn(CN)_6]^{3-}$? Is this ion a high-spin or low-spin complex?

Crystal Field Splitting in Tetrahedral and Square Planar Complexes

Four ligands around a metal ion also cause d-orbital splitting, but the magnitude and pattern of the splitting depend on whether the ligands are in a tetrahedral or a square planar arrangement.

- *Tetrahedral complexes.* With the ligands approaching from the corners of a tetrahedron, none of the five d orbitals is directly in their paths (Figure 22.24). Thus, splitting of d-orbital energies is *less* in a tetrahedral complex than in an octahedral complex having the same ligands:

$$\Delta_{tetrahedral} < \Delta_{octahedral}$$

Minimal repulsions arise if the ligands approach the d_{xy}, d_{yz}, and d_{xz} orbitals closer than they approach the d_{z^2} and $d_{x^2-y^2}$ orbitals. This situation is the *opposite of the octahedral case*, and the relative d-orbital energies are reversed: the d_{xy}, d_{yz}, and d_{xz} orbitals become *higher* in energy than the d_{z^2} and $d_{x^2-y^2}$ orbitals. *Only high-spin tetrahedral complexes are known* because the magnitude of Δ is so small.

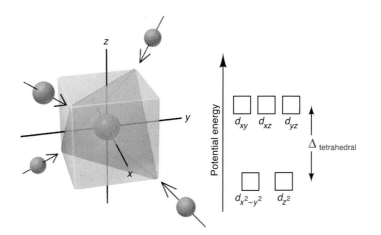

FIGURE 22.24 Splitting of d-orbital energies by a tetrahedral field of ligands. Electrons in d_{xy}, d_{yz}, and d_{xz} orbitals experience greater repulsions than those in $d_{x^2-y^2}$ and d_{z^2}, so the tetrahedral splitting pattern is the opposite of the octahedral pattern.

• *Square planar complexes.* The effects of the ligand field in the square planar case are easier to picture if we imagine starting with an octahedral geometry and then remove the two ligands along the *z*-axis, as depicted in Figure 22.25. With no *z*-axis interactions present, the d_{z^2} orbital energy decreases greatly, and the energies of the other orbitals with a *z*-axis component, the d_{xz} and d_{yz}, also decrease. As a result, the two *d* orbitals in the *xy* plane interact most strongly with the ligands, and because the $d_{x^2-y^2}$ orbital has its lobes *on* the axes, its energy is highest. As a consequence of this splitting pattern, square planar complexes with d^8 metal ions, such as $[PdCl_4]^{2-}$, are diamagnetic, with four pairs of *d* electrons filling the four lowest energy orbitals. Thus, as a general rule, *square planar complexes are low spin.*

FIGURE 22.25 Splitting of *d*-orbital energies by a square planar field of ligands. In a square planar field, the energies of d_{xz}, d_{yz}, and especially d_{z^2} orbitals decrease relative to the octahedral pattern.

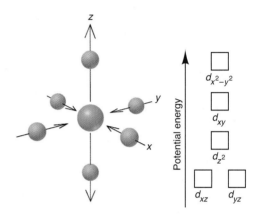

At this point, a final word about bonding theories may be helpful. As you have seen, the VB approach offers a simple picture of bond formation but does not explain color. The crystal field model predicts color and magnetic behavior but offers no insight about the covalent nature of metal-ligand bonding. Chemists now rely on *ligand field–molecular orbital theory,* which combines aspects of the previous two models with MO theory (Section 11.3). It yields information on bond properties that result from orbital overlap and on the spectral and magnetic properties that result from the splitting of a metal ion's *d* orbitals.

Transition Metal Complexes in Biological Systems

In addition to four *building-block elements* (C, O, H, and N) and seven elements known as *macronutrients* (Na, Mg, P, S, Cl, K, and Ca), organisms contain a large number of *trace elements,* most of which are transition metals. With the exception of Sc, Ti, and Ni (in most species), the Period 4 transition elements are essential to many organisms (Table 22.9), and plants require Mo (from Period 5) as well. The principles of bonding and *d*-orbital splitting are the same in complex biomolecules containing transition metals as in simple inorganic systems. We focus here on an iron-containing complex.

Iron plays a crucial role in oxygen transport in all vertebrates. The O_2-transporting protein hemoglobin (Figure 22.26A) consists of four folded chains, each cradling the Fe-containing complex *heme*. Heme consists of iron(II) bonded to four N lone pairs of a tetradentate ring ligand known as a *porphyrin* to give a square planar complex. (Porphyrins are common biological ligands that are also found in chlorophyll, with Mg^{2+} at the center, and in vitamin B_{12}, with Co^{3+} at the center.) In hemoglobin (Figure 22.26B), the complex is *octahedral,* with the

Table 22.9	Essential Transition Metals in Humans
Element	**Function**
Vanadium	Fat metabolism
Chromium	Glucose utilization
Manganese	Cell respiration
Iron	Oxygen transport; ATP formation
Cobalt	Component of vitamin B_{12}; development of red blood cells
Copper	Hemoglobin synthesis; ATP formation
Zinc	Elimination of CO_2; protein digestion

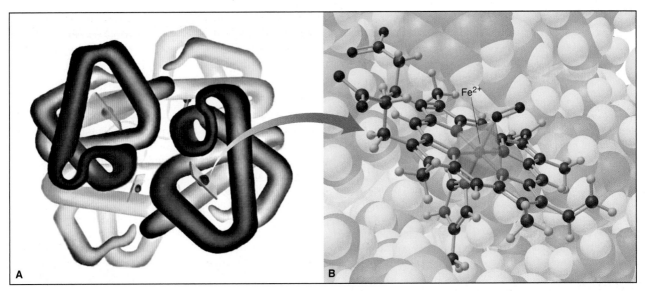

FIGURE 22.26 Hemoglobin and the octahedral complex in heme. **A,** Hemoglobin consists of four protein chains, each with a bound heme complex. (Illustration by Irving Geis. Rights owned by Howard Hughes Medical Institute. Not to be used without permission.) **B,** In the oxygenated form of hemoglobin, the octahedral complex in heme has iron(II) at the center surrounded by the four N atoms of the porphyrin ring, a fifth N from histidine *(below)*, and an O_2 molecule *(above)*.

fifth ligand of iron(II) being an N atom from a nearby amino acid (histidine), and the sixth an O atom from either an O_2 (shown) or an H_2O molecule.

Hemoglobin exists in two forms. In the arteries and lungs, the Fe^{2+} ion in heme binds to O_2; in the veins and tissues, O_2 is replaced by H_2O. Because H_2O is a weak-field ligand, the d^6 Fe^{2+} ion is part of a high-spin complex, and the relatively small d-orbital splitting makes venous blood absorb light at the red (low-energy) end of the spectrum and look purplish blue. On the other hand, O_2 is a strong-field ligand, so it increases the splitting energy and gives a low-spin complex. Thus, arterial blood absorbs at the blue (high-energy) end of the spectrum, which accounts for its bright red color.

Carbon monoxide is toxic because it binds to Fe^{2+} ion in heme about 200 times more strongly than O_2, which prevents the heme group from functioning:

$$\text{heme}-\text{CO} + O_2 \rightleftharpoons \text{heme}-O_2 + \text{CO}$$

Like O_2, CO is a strong-field ligand, which results in a bright red color of the blood. Because the binding is an equilibrium process, breathing extremely high concentrations of O_2 displaces CO from the heme and reverses CO poisoning.

SECTION 22.3 SUMMARY

Valence bond theory pictures bonding in complex ions as arising from coordinate covalent bonding between Lewis bases (ligands) and Lewis acids (metal ions). Ligand lone pairs occupy hybridized metal-ion orbitals to form complex ions with characteristic shapes. • Crystal field theory explains the color and magnetism of complexes. • As the result of a surrounding field of ligands, the d-orbital energies of the metal ion split. The magnitude of this crystal field splitting energy (Δ) depends on the charge of the metal ion and the crystal field strength of the ligand. • The size of Δ influences the energy of the photon absorbed (color) and the number of unpaired d electrons (paramagnetism). Strong-field ligands create a large Δ and produce low-spin complexes that absorb light of higher energy (shorter λ); the reverse is true of weak-field ligands. • Several transition metals form complexes within proteins and are therefore important in living systems.

CHAPTER REVIEW GUIDE

The following sections provide many aids to help you study this chapter. (Numbers in parentheses refer to pages, unless noted otherwise.)

● LEARNING OBJECTIVES *These are concepts and skills to review after studying this chapter.*

Related section (§), sample problem (SP), and end-of-chapter problem (EP) numbers are listed in parentheses.

1. Write electron configurations of transition metal atoms and ions; compare periodic trends in atomic properties of transition elements with those of main-group elements; explain why transition elements have multiple oxidation states, how their metallic behavior (type of bonding and oxide acidity) changes with oxidation state, and why many of their compounds are colored and paramagnetic (§ 22.1) (SP 22.1) (EPs 22.1–22.17)
2. Be familiar with the coordination numbers, geometries, and ligands of complex ions; name and write formulas for coordination compounds; describe the types of constitutional and stereo-isomerism they exhibit (§ 22.2) (SPs 22.2, 22.3) (EPs 22.18–22.39)
3. Correlate the shape of a complex ion with the number and type of hybrid orbitals of the central metal ion (§ 22.3) (EPs 22.40, 22.41, 22.47, 22.48)
4. Describe how approaching ligands cause d-orbital energies to split and give rise to octahedral, tetrahedral, and square-planar complexes; explain crystal field splitting energy (Δ) and how it accounts for the colors of complexes; explain how the relative magnitudes of pairing energy and Δ determine the magnetic properties of complexes; use a spectrochemical series to rank complex ions in terms of Δ, and determine if a complex is high spin or low spin (§ 22.3) (SPs 22.4, 22.5) (EPs 22.42–22.46, 22.49–22.57)

● KEY TERMS *These important terms appear in boldface in the chapter and are defined again in the Glossary.*

transition elements (757)

Section 22.1
lanthanide contraction (760)

Section 22.2
coordination compound (763)
complex ion (763)
ligand (763)
counter ion (763)
coordination number (764)

donor atom (764)
chelate (765
isomer (767)
constitutional (structural)
  isomers (768)
coordination isomers (768)
linkage isomers (768)
stereoisomers (768)

geometric *(cis-trans)*
  isomers (768)
optical isomers (769)

Section 22.3
coordinate covalent
  bond (770)
crystal field theory (772)
e_g orbital (774)

t_{2g} orbital (774)
crystal field splitting energy
  (Δ) (774)
strong-field ligand (774)
weak-field ligand (774)
spectrochemical series (775)
high-spin complex (776)
low-spin complex (776)

● BRIEF SOLUTIONS TO *FOLLOW-UP PROBLEMS* *Compare your own solutions to these calculations steps and answers.*

22.1 (a) Ag^+: $4d^{10}$
(b) Cd^{2+}: $4d^{10}$
(c) Ir^{3+}: $5d^6$
22.2 (a) Pentaaquabromochromium(III) chloride
(b) $Ba_3[Co(CN)_6]_2$
22.3 Two sets of *cis-trans* isomers, and the two *cis* isomers are optical isomers.

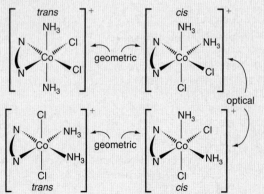

22.4 Both metal ions are V^{3+}; in terms of ligand field energy, $NH_3 > H_2O$, so $[V(NH_3)_6]^{3+}$ absorbs light of higher energy.
22.5 The metal ion is Mn^{3+}: [Ar] $3d^4$.

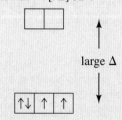

large Δ

Two unpaired d electrons; low-spin complex

PROBLEMS

*Problems with **colored** numbers are answered in Appendix E. Sections match the text and provide the numbers of relevant sample problems. Bracketed problems are grouped in pairs (indicated by a short rule) that cover the same concept. Comprehensive Problems are based on material from any section or previous chapter.*

Note: In these problems, the term *electron configuration* refers to the condensed, ground-state electron configuration.

Properties of the Transition Elements
(Sample Problem 22.1)

22.1 (a) Write the general electron configuration of a transition element in Period 5.
(b) Write the general electron configuration of a transition element in Period 6.

22.2 What is the general rule concerning the order in which electrons are removed from a transition metal atom to form an ion? Give an example from Group 5B(5). Name two types of measurements used to study electron configurations of ions.

22.3 How does the variation in atomic size across a transition series contrast with the change across the main-group elements of the same period? Why?

22.4 (a) What is the lanthanide contraction?
(b) How does it affect atomic size down a group of transition elements?
(c) How does it influence the densities of the Period 6 transition elements?

22.5 (a) What is the range in electronegativity values across the first ($3d$) transition series?
(b) What is the range across Period 4 of main-group elements?
(c) Explain the difference between the two ranges.

22.6 (a) Explain the major difference between the number of oxidation states of most transition elements and that of most main-group elements.
(b) Why is the $+2$ oxidation state so common among transition elements?

22.7 (a) What difference in behavior distinguishes a paramagnetic substance from a diamagnetic one?
(b) Why are paramagnetic ions common among the transition elements but not the main-group elements?
(c) Why are colored solutions of metal ions common among the transition elements but not the main-group elements?

22.8 Using the periodic table to locate each element, write the electron configuration of (a) V; (b) Y; (c) Hg.

22.9 Using the periodic table to locate each element, write the electron configuration of (a) Ru; (b) Cu; (c) Ni.

22.10 Give the electron configuration and the number of unpaired electrons for each of the following ions: (a) Sc^{3+}; (b) Cu^{2+}; (c) Fe^{3+}; (d) Nb^{3+}.

22.11 Give the electron configuration and the number of unpaired electrons for each of the following ions: (a) Cr^{3+}; (b) Ti^{4+}; (c) Co^{3+}; (d) Ta^{2+}.

22.12 Which transition metals have a maximum oxidation state of $+6$?

22.13 Which transition metals have a maximum oxidation state of $+4$?

22.14 In which compound does Cr exhibit greater metallic behavior, CrF_2 or CrF_6? Explain.

22.15 VF_5 is a liquid that boils at $48°C$, whereas VF_3 is a solid that melts above $800°C$. Explain this difference in properties.

22.16 Which oxide, CrO_3 or CrO, forms a more acidic aqueous solution? Explain.

22.17 Which oxide, Mn_2O_3 or Mn_2O_7, displays more basic behavior? Explain.

Coordination Compounds
(Sample Problems 22.2 and 22.3)

22.18 Describe the makeup of a complex ion, including the nature of the ligands and their interaction with the central metal ion. Explain how a complex ion can be positive or negative and how it occurs as part of a neutral coordination compound.

22.19 What is the coordination number of a metal ion in a complex ion? How does it differ from oxidation number?

22.20 What structural feature is characteristic of a complex described as a chelate?

22.21 What geometries are associated with the coordination numbers 2, 4, and 6?

22.22 In what sense is a complex ion the adduct of a Lewis acid-base reaction?

22.23 Is a linkage isomer a type of constitutional isomer or stereoisomer? Explain.

22.24 Give systematic names for the following formulas:
(a) $[Ni(H_2O)_6]Cl_2$ (b) $[Cr(en)_3](ClO_4)_3$ (c) $K_4[Mn(CN)_6]$

22.25 Give systematic names for the following formulas:
(a) $[Co(NH_3)_4(NO_2)_2]Cl$ (b) $[Cr(NH_3)_6][Cr(CN)_6]$
(c) $K_2[CuCl_4]$

22.26 What are the charge and coordination number of the central metal ion(s) in each compound of Problem 22.24?

22.27 What are the charge and coordination number of the central metal ion(s) in each compound of Problem 22.25?

22.28 Give systematic names for the following formulas:
(a) $K[Ag(CN)_2]$ (b) $Na_2[CdCl_4]$ (c) $[Co(NH_3)_4(H_2O)Br]Br_2$

22.29 Give systematic names for the following formulas:
(a) $K[Pt(NH_3)Cl_5]$ (b) $[Cu(en)(NH_3)_2][Co(en)Cl_4]$
(c) $[Pt(en)_2Br_2](ClO_4)_2$

22.30 Give formulas corresponding to the following names:
(a) Tetraamminezinc sulfate
(b) Pentaamminechlorochromium(III) chloride
(c) Sodium bis(thiosulfato)argentate(I)

22.31 Give formulas corresponding to the following names:
(a) Dibromobis(ethylenediamine)cobalt(III) sulfate
(b) Hexaamminechromium(III) tetrachlorocuprate(II)
(c) Potassium hexacyanoferrate(II)

22.32 What is the coordination number of the metal ion and the number of individual ions per formula unit in each of the compounds in Problem 22.30?

22.33 What is the coordination number of the metal ion and the number of individual ions per formula unit in each of the compounds in Problem 22.31?

22.34 Which of these ligands can give rise to linkage isomerism: (a) NO_2^-; (b) SO_2; (c) NO_3^-? Explain with Lewis structures.

22.35 Which of these ligands can give rise to linkage isomerism: (a) SCN^-; (b) $S_2O_3^{2-}$ (thiosulfate); (c) HS^-? Explain with Lewis structures.

22.36 For any of the following that can exist as isomers, state the type of isomerism and draw the structures:
(a) $[Pt(CH_3NH_2)_2Br_2]$ (b) $[Pt(NH_3)_2FCl]$
(c) $[Pt(H_2O)(NH_3)FCl]$

22.37 For any of the following that can exist as isomers, state the type of isomerism and draw the structures:
(a) $[Zn(en)F_2]$ (b) $[Zn(H_2O)(NH_3)FCl]$
(c) $[Pd(CN)_2(OH)_2]^{2-}$

22.38 For any of the following that can exist as isomers, state the type of isomerism and draw the structures:
(a) $[PtCl_2Br_2]^{2-}$ (b) $[Cr(NH_3)_5(NO_2)]^{2+}$
(c) $[Pt(NH_3)_4I_2]^{2+}$

22.39 For any of the following that can exist as isomers, state the type of isomerism and draw the structures:
(a) $[Co(NH_3)_5Cl]Br_2$ (b) $[Pt(CH_3NH_2)_3Cl]Br$
(c) $[Fe(H_2O)_4(NH_3)_2]^{2+}$

Theoretical Basis for the Bonding and Properties of Complexes
(Sample Problems 22.4 and 22.5)

22.40 According to valence bond theory, what set of orbitals is used by a Period 4 metal ion in forming (a) a square planar complex; (b) a tetrahedral complex?

22.41 A metal ion is described as using a d^2sp^3 set of orbitals when forming a complex. What is the coordination number of the metal ion and the shape of the complex?

22.42 A complex in solution absorbs green light. What is the color of the solution?

22.43 (a) What is the crystal field splitting energy (Δ)?
(b) How does it arise for an octahedral field of ligands?
(c) How is it different for a tetrahedral field of ligands?

22.44 What is the distinction between a weak-field ligand and a strong-field ligand? Give an example of each.

22.45 How do the relative magnitudes of $E_{pairing}$ and Δ affect the paramagnetism of a complex?

22.46 Why are there both high-spin and low-spin octahedral complexes but only high-spin tetrahedral complexes?

22.47 Give the number of d electrons (n of d^n) for the central metal ion in each of these species: (a) $[TiCl_6]^{2-}$; (b) $K[AuCl_4]$; (c) $[RhCl_6]^{3-}$.

22.48 Give the number of d electrons (n of d^n) for the central metal ion in each of these species: (a) $[Cr(H_2O)_6](ClO_3)_2$; (b) $[Mn(CN)_6]^{2-}$; (c) $[Ru(NO)(en)_2Cl]Br$.

22.49 Which of these ions *cannot* form both high- and low-spin octahedral complexes: (a) Ti^{3+}; (b) Co^{2+}; (c) Fe^{2+}; (d) Cu^{2+}?

22.50 Which of these ions *cannot* form both high- and low-spin octahedral complexes: (a) Mn^{3+}; (b) Nb^{3+}; (c) Ru^{3+}; (d) Ni^{2+}?

22.51 Draw orbital-energy splitting diagrams and use the spectrochemical series to show the orbital occupancy for each of the following (assuming that H_2O is a weak-field ligand):
(a) $[Cr(H_2O)_6]^{3+}$ (b) $[Cu(H_2O)_4]^{2+}$ (c) $[FeF_6]^{3-}$

22.52 Draw orbital-energy splitting diagrams and use the spectrochemical series to show the orbital occupancy for each of the following:
(a) $[Cr(CN)_6]^{3-}$ (b) $[Rh(CO)_6]^{3+}$ (c) $[Co(OH)_6]^{4-}$

22.53 Rank the following complex ions in order of *increasing* Δ and energy of visible light absorbed: $[Cr(NH_3)_6]^{3+}$, $[Cr(H_2O)_6]^{3+}$, $[Cr(NO_2)_6]^{3-}$.

22.54 Rank the following complex ions in order of *decreasing* Δ and energy of visible light absorbed: $[Cr(en)_3]^{3+}$, $[Cr(CN)_6]^{3-}$, $[CrCl_6]^{3-}$.

22.55 A complex, ML_6^{2+}, is violet. The same metal forms a complex with another ligand, Q, that creates a weaker field. What color might MQ_6^{2+} be expected to show? Explain.

22.56 $[Cr(H_2O)_6]^{2+}$ is violet. Another CrL_6 complex is green. Can ligand L be CN^-? Can it be Cl^-? Explain.

22.57 Three of the complex ions that are formed by Co^{3+} are $[Co(H_2O)_6]^{3+}$, $[Co(NH_3)_6]^{3+}$, and $[CoF_6]^{3-}$. These ions have the observed colors (listed in arbitrary order) yellow-orange, green, and blue. Match each complex with its color. Explain.

Comprehensive Problems
Problems with an asterisk (*) are more challenging.

* 22.58 How many different formulas are there for octahedral complexes with a metal M and four ligands A, B, C, and D? Give the number of isomers for each formula and describe the isomers.

22.59 Correct each name that has an error:
(a) $Na[FeBr_4]$, sodium tetrabromoferrate(II)
(b) $[Ni(NH_3)_6]^{2+}$, nickel hexaammine ion
(c) $[Co(NH_3)_3I_3]$, triamminetriiodocobalt(III)
(d) $[V(CN)_6]^{3-}$, hexacyanovanadium(III) ion
(e) $K[FeCl_4]$, potassium tetrachloroiron(III)

* 22.60 For the compound $[Co(en)_2Cl_2]Cl$, give:
(a) The coordination number of the metal ion
(b) The oxidation number of the central metal ion
(c) The number of individual ions per formula unit
(d) The moles of AgCl that precipitate immediately when 1 mol of compound is dissolved in water and treated with $AgNO_3$

22.61 Consider the square planar complex shown at right. Which of the structures below are geometric isomers of it?

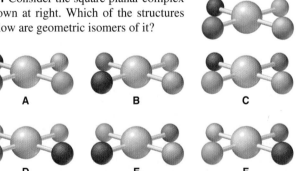

A   B   C

D   E   F

22.62 Hexafluorocobaltate(III) ion is a high-spin complex. Draw the orbital-energy splitting diagram for its d orbitals.

22.63 A salt of each of the ions in Table 22.3 is dissolved in water. A Pt electrode is immersed in each solution and connected to a 0.38-V battery. All of the electrolytic cells are run for the same amount of time with the same current.

(a) In which cell(s) will a metal plate out? Explain.

(b) Which cell will plate out the least mass of metal? Explain.

22.64 In many species, a transition metal has an unusually high or low oxidation state. Write balanced equations for the following and find the oxidation state of the transition metal in the product:

(a) Iron(III) ion reacts with hypochlorite ion in basic solution to form ferrate ion (FeO_4^{2-}), Cl^-, and water.

(b) Heating sodium superoxide, NaO_2, with Co_3O_4 produces Na_4CoO_4 and O_2 gas.

(c) Heating cesium tetrafluorocuprate(II) with F_2 gas under pressure gives Cs_2CuF_6.

(d) Potassium tetracyanonickelate(II) reacts with hydrazine (N_2H_4) in basic solution to form $K_4[Ni_2(CN)_6]$ and N_2 gas.

22.65 An octahedral complex with three different ligands (A, B, and C) can have formulas with three different ratios of the ligands:

$[MA_4BC]^{n+}$, such as $[Co(NH_3)_4(H_2O)Cl]^{2+}$

$[MA_3B_2C]^{n+}$, such as $[Cr(H_2O)_3Br_2Cl]$

$[MA_2B_2C_2]^{n+}$, such as $[Cr(NH_3)_2(H_2O)_2Br_2]^+$

For each example, give the name, state the type(s) of isomerism present, and draw all isomers.

22.66 In $[Cr(NH_3)_6]Cl_3$, the $[Cr(NH_3)_6]^{3+}$ ion absorbs visible light in the blue-violet range, and the compound is yellow-orange. In $[Cr(H_2O)_6]Br_3$, the $[Cr(H_2O)_6]^{3+}$ ion absorbs visible light in the red range, and the compound is blue-gray. Explain these differences in light absorbed and colors of the compounds.

22.67 The orbital occupancies for the d orbitals of several complex ions are diagrammed below.

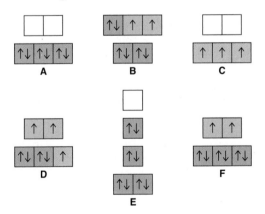

(a) Which diagram corresponds to the orbital occupancy of the cobalt ion in $[Co(CN)_6]^{3-}$?

(b) If diagram D depicts the orbital occupancy of the cobalt ion in $[CoF_6]^n$, what is the value of n?

(c) $[NiCl_4]^{2-}$ is paramagnetic and $[Ni(CN)_4]^{2-}$ is diamagnetic. Which diagrams correspond to the orbital occupancies of the nickel ions in these species?

(d) Diagram C shows the orbital occupancy of V^{2+} in the octahedral complex VL_6. Can you determine whether L is a strong- or weak-field ligand? Explain.

22.68 Ionic liquids have many applications in engineering and materials science. The dissolution of the metavanadate ion in chloroaluminate ionic liquids has been studied:

$$VO_3^- + AlCl_4^- \longrightarrow VO_2Cl_2^- + AlOCl_2^-$$

(a) What is the oxidation number of V and Al in each ion?

(b) In reactions with V_2O_5, acid concentration affects the product. At low acid concentration, $VO_2Cl_2^-$ and VO_3^- form:

$$V_2O_5 + HCl \longrightarrow VO_2Cl_2^- + VO_3^- + H^+$$

At high acid concentration, $VOCl_3$ forms:

$$V_2O_5 + HCl \longrightarrow VOCl_3 + H_2O$$

Balance each equation, and state which, if either, involves a redox process.

(c) What mass of $VO_2Cl_2^-$ or $VOCl_3$ can form from 12.5 g of V_2O_5 and the appropriate concentration of acid?

22.69 Several coordination isomers, with both Co and Cr as 3+ ions, have the molecular formula $CoCrC_6H_{18}N_{12}$.

(a) Give the name and formula of the isomer in which the Co complex ion has six NH_3 groups.

(b) Give the name and formula of the isomer in which the Co complex ion has one CN and five NH_3 groups.

* 22.70 The enzyme carbonic anhydrase has zinc in a tetrahedral complex at its active site. Suggest a structural reason why carbonic anhydrase synthesized with Ni^{2+}, Fe^{2+}, or Mn^{2+} in place of Zn^{2+} gives an enzyme with less catalytic efficiency.

* 22.71 The effect of entropy on reactions is evident in the stabilities of certain complexes.

(a) Using the criterion of number of product particles, predict which of the following will be favored in terms of ΔS_{rxn}°:

$[Cu(NH_3)_4]^{2+}(aq) + 4H_2O(l) \longrightarrow$
$$[Cu(H_2O)_4]^{2+}(aq) + 4NH_3(aq)$$

$[Cu(H_2NCH_2CH_2NH_2)_2]^{2+}(aq) + 4H_2O(l) \longrightarrow$
$$[Cu(H_2O)_4]^{2+}(aq) + 2en(aq)$$

(b) Given that the Cu—N bond strength is approximately the same in both complexes, which complex will be more stable in water (less likely to exchange their ligands for H_2O molecules)? Explain.

22.72 The extent of crystal field splitting is often determined from spectra.

(a) Given the wavelength (λ) of maximum absorption, find the crystal field splitting energy (Δ), in kJ/mol, for each of the following complex ions:

Ion	λ (nm)	Ion	λ (nm)
$[Cr(H_2O)_6]^{3+}$	562	$[Fe(H_2O)_6]^{2+}$	966
$[Cr(CN)_6]^{3-}$	381	$[Fe(H_2O)_6]^{3+}$	730
$[CrCl_6]^{3-}$	735	$[Co(NH_3)_6]^{3+}$	405
$[Cr(NH_3)_6]^{3+}$	462	$[Rh(NH_3)_6]^{3+}$	295
$[Ir(NH_3)_6]^{3+}$	244		

(b) Construct a spectrochemical series for the ligands in the Cr complexes.

(c) Use the Fe data to state how oxidation state affects Δ.

(d) Use the Co, Rh, and Ir data to state how period number affects Δ.

23

Nuclear Reactions and Their Applications

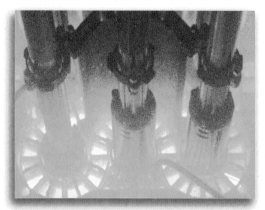

Producing with Nuclear Power In addition to supplying energy, many nuclear reactors, like this one in Idaho, produce medical and industrial isotopes.

Outline

Key Principles
to focus on while studying this chapter

- *Nuclear reactions* differ markedly from chemical reactions in several ways: (1) Element identity typically *does* change in a nuclear reaction. (2) Nuclear particles and, much less often, electrons participate. (3) Nuclear reactions release so much energy that the mass *does* change. (4) Rates of nuclear reactions are *not* affected by temperature, catalysts, or, except rarely, the compound in which the element occurs *(Introduction)*.

- In a balanced nuclear reaction, the total mass number (A) and total charge (Z) of the reactants must equal those of the products. Protons and neutrons are called *nucleons;* a plot of number of neutrons (N) versus number of protons (Z) for all nuclei shows a narrow *band of stability.* Unstable nuclei undergo various types of radioactive decay. The type can often be predicted by taking into account a nuclide's mass relative to the atomic mass and N/Z ratio. Nuclear stability is associated with filled *nucleon levels.* Certain heavy nuclei undergo a *decay series* to reach stability *(Section 23.1)*.

- Radioactive decay is a *first-order process,* so the decay rate *(activity)* depends *only* on the number of nuclei. The *half-life,* or time required for half the nuclei present to decay, does *not* depend on the number of nuclei. In *radiocarbon dating,* the age of an object is determined by comparing its ^{14}C activity with that of living things *(Section 23.2)*.

- *Particle accelerators* change one element into another *(nuclear transmutation)* by bombarding nuclei with high-energy particles *(Section 23.3)*.

- *Ionizing radiation* causes chemical changes in matter. The harm caused in living matter depends on the ionizing ability and penetrating power of the radiation. Cosmic rays and decay of radioactive minerals give rise to a natural *background radiation (Section 23.4)*.

- *Isotopes* of an element have nearly identical chemical properties. A small amount of a radioactive isotope of an element mixed with a large amount of the stable isotope can act as a *tracer* for studying reaction pathways, physical movements of substances, and medical problems *(Section 23.5)*.

- The mass of a nucleus is *less* than the sum of its nucleon masses, and Einstein's equation gives the energy equivalent to this *mass difference,* which is the *nuclear binding energy.* The *binding energy per nucleon* is a measure of nuclide stability. Heavy nuclides split *(fission)* and light nuclides join *(fusion)* to release energy, thus increasing the binding energy per nucleon *(Section 23.6)*.

- Nuclear power plants employ a fission *chain reaction* to create steam that generates electricity. Safety concerns center on leaks and long-term disposal of waste. Commercial energy from fusion is still in early development *(Section 23.7)*.

F ar below the outer fringes of its cloud of electrons lies the atom's tiny, dense core. For nearly the entire text, we have focused on an atom's electrons, treating the nucleus as their electrostatic anchor, examining the effect of its positive charge on atomic properties and, ultimately, chemical behavior. But, for the scientists probing the structure and behavior of the nucleus itself, *there* is the scene of real action, one that holds enormous potential benefit and great mystery and wonder.

Society is ambivalent about the applications of nuclear research, however. The promise of abundant energy and treatments for disease comes hand-in-hand with the threat of nuclear waste contamination, reactor accidents, and unimaginable destruction from nuclear war or terrorism. Can the power of the nucleus be harnessed for our benefit, or are the risks too great? In this chapter, we discuss the principles that can help you consider this vital question knowledgeably.

The changes that occur in atomic nuclei are strikingly different from chemical changes. In chemical reactions, electrons are shared or transferred to form *compounds*, while nuclei sit by passively, never changing their identities. In nuclear reactions, the roles are reversed, as electrons in their orbitals take part much less often, while the nuclei undergo changes that, in nearly every case, form different *elements*. Nuclear reactions are often accompanied by energy changes a million times greater than those in chemical reactions, energy changes so great that changes in mass *are* detectable. Moreover, nuclear reaction yields and rates are *not* subject to the effects of pressure, temperature, and catalysis. Table 23.1 summarizes these general differences.

Concepts & Skills to Review
before studying this chapter

- discovery of the atomic nucleus (Section 2.4)
- protons, neutrons, mass number, and the $^A_Z X$ notation (Section 2.5)
- half-life and first-order reaction rate (Section 16.4)

Table 23.1 Comparison of Chemical and Nuclear Reactions

Chemical Reactions	Nuclear Reactions
1. One substance is converted into another, but atoms never change identity.	1. Atoms of one element typically are converted into atoms of another element.
2. Orbital electrons are involved as bonds break and form; nuclear particles do not take part.	2. Protons, neutrons, and other particles are involved; orbital electrons take part much less often.
3. Reactions are accompanied by relatively small changes in energy and no measurable changes in mass.	3. Reactions are accompanied by relatively large changes in energy and measurable changes in mass.
4. Reaction rates are influenced by temperature, concentration, catalysts, and the compound in which an element occurs.	4. Reaction rates depend on number of nuclei, but are not affected by temperature, catalysts, or, except on rare occasions, the compound in which an element occurs.

23.1 RADIOACTIVE DECAY AND NUCLEAR STABILITY

A stable nucleus remains intact indefinitely, but *the great majority of nuclei are unstable.* An unstable nucleus exhibits **radioactivity:** it spontaneously disintegrates, or *decays,* by emitting radiation. In Section 23.2, you'll see that each type of unstable nucleus has its own characteristic *rate* of radioactive decay, which can range from less than a billionth of a second to billions of years. In this section, we consider important terms and notation for nuclei, discuss some of the key events in the discovery of radioactivity, and describe the various types of radioactive decay and how to predict which type occurs for a given nucleus.

The Components of the Nucleus: Terms and Notation

Recall from Chapter 2 that the nucleus contains essentially all the atom's mass but is only about 10^{-5} times its radius (or 10^{-15} times its volume). Obviously, the nucleus is incredibly dense: about 10^{14} g/mL. *Protons* and *neutrons,* the elementary particles that make up the nucleus, are called **nucleons.** The term **nuclide** refers to a nucleus with a particular composition, that is, with specific numbers of the two types of nucleons. Most elements occur in nature as a mixture of **isotopes,** atoms with the characteristic number of protons of the element but different numbers of neutrons. Therefore, each isotope of an element is a particular nuclide that we identify by its numbers of protons and neutrons. For example, oxygen has three naturally occurring isotopes—the most abundant contains eight protons and eight neutrons, whereas the least abundant contains eight protons and nine neutrons.

The relative mass and charge of a particle—a nucleon, another elementary particle, or a nucleus—is described by the notation $_{Z}^{A}X$, where X is the *symbol* for the particle, A is the *mass number,* or the total number of nucleons, and Z is the *charge* of the particle; for nuclei, A is the *sum of protons and neutrons* and Z is the *number of protons* (atomic number). In this notation, the three subatomic elementary particles are

$$_{-1}^{0}e \text{ (electron), } _{1}^{1}p \text{ (proton), and } _{0}^{1}n \text{ (neutron)}$$

(A proton is also sometimes represented as $_{1}^{1}H^{+}$.) The number of neutrons (N) in a nucleus is the mass number (A) minus the atomic number (Z): $N = A - Z$. The two naturally occurring stable isotopes of chlorine, for example, have 17 protons ($Z = 17$), but one has 18 neutrons ($_{17}^{35}Cl$, also written ^{35}Cl) and the other has 20 ($_{17}^{37}Cl$, or ^{37}Cl). Nuclides can also be designated with the element name followed by the mass number, for example, chlorine-35 and chlorine-37. In naturally occurring samples of an element or its compounds, *the isotopes of the element are present in specific proportions* that can vary only very slightly. Thus, in a sample of sodium chloride (or any Cl-containing substance), 75.77% of the Cl atoms are chlorine-35 and the remaining 24.23% are chlorine-37.

To understand this chapter, it's very important that you are comfortable with nuclear notations, so please take a moment to review Sample Problem 2.4 (p. 43) and Problems 2.24 to 2.31 (pp. 65 and 66).

Types of Radioactive Decay; Balancing Nuclear Equations

When a nuclide of an element decays, it emits radiation and, under most circumstances, changes into a nuclide of a different element. The three natural types of radioactive emission are

- **Alpha particles** (symbolized α, $_{2}^{4}\alpha$, or $_{2}^{4}He^{2+}$) are identical to helium-4 nuclei.
- **Beta particles** (symbolized β, β^{-}, or sometimes $_{-1}^{0}\beta$) are high-speed electrons. (The emission of electrons from the nucleus may seem strange, but as you'll see shortly, they result from a nuclear reaction.)
- **Gamma rays** (symbolized γ, or sometimes $_{0}^{0}\gamma$) are very high-energy photons.

Figure 23.1 illustrates the behavior of these emissions in an electric field: α particles curve to a small extent toward the negative plate, β particles curve to a greater extent toward the positive plate, and γ rays are not affected by the electric field.

When a nuclide decays, it forms a nuclide of lower energy, and the excess energy is carried off by the emitted radiation and the recoiling nucleus. The decaying, or reactant, nuclide is called the *parent;* the product nuclide is called the *daughter.* Nuclides can decay in several ways. As each of the major types of decay is introduced (summarized in Table 23.2), we'll show examples of that type and apply the key principle used to balance nuclear reactions: *the total Z (charge, number of protons) and the total A (sum of protons and neutrons) of the reactants equal those of the products:*

$$\text{Total } _{\text{Total } Z}^{\text{Total } A} \text{ Reactants } = \text{Total } _{\text{Total } Z}^{\text{Total } A} \text{ Products} \qquad (23.1)$$

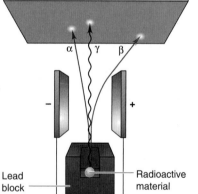

ZnS-coated screen
(or photographic plate)

Lead block

Radioactive material

Voltage source

FIGURE 23.1 Three types of radioactive emissions in an electric field. Positively charged α particles curve toward the negative plate; negatively charged β particles curve toward the positive plate. (Later, we'll give these the symbol β^{-}.) The curvature is greater for β particles because they have much lower mass. The γ rays, uncharged high-energy photons, are unaffected by the field.

| Table 23.2 | **Modes of Radioactive Decay*** | | | | |

Mode	Emission	Decay Process	Change in		
			A	**Z**	**N**
α Decay	α ($_2^4He^{2+}$)	α expelled	-4	-2	-2
β^- Decay[†]	β^- ($_{-1}^{0}\beta$)	nucleus with xp^+ and yn^0 → nucleus with $(x+1)p^+$ and $(y-1)n^0$ + $_{-1}^{0}\beta$ β^- expelled	0	$+1$	-1
		Net: $_0^1n$ in nucleus → $_1^1p$ in nucleus + $_{-1}^{0}\beta$ β^- expelled			
Positron (β^+) emission[†]	β^+ ($_1^0\beta$)	nucleus with xp^+ and yn^0 → nucleus with $(x-1)p^+$ and $(y+1)n^0$ + $_1^0\beta$ β^+ expelled	0	-1	$+1$
		Net: $_1^1p$ in nucleus → $_0^1n$ in nucleus + $_1^0\beta$ β^+ expelled			
Electron (e^-) capture (EC)[†]	x-ray	low-energy orbital → nucleus with xp^+ and yn^0 → nucleus with $(x-1)p^+$ and $(y+1)n^0$	0	-1	$+1$
		Net: $_{-1}^0e$ absorbed from low-energy orbital + $_1^1p$ in nucleus → $_0^1n$ in nucleus			
Gamma (γ) emission	γ	excited nucleus → stable nucleus + γ γ photon radiated	0	0	0

*Nuclear chemists consider β^- decay, positron emission, and electron capture to be three decay modes of the more general process known as beta decay (see text).

[†]Neutrinos (ν) or antineutrinos ($\bar{\nu}$) are also formed during the three types of beta decay. Although we will not include them in other equations in the chapter, keep in mind that antineutrinos are always expelled during β^- decay, and neutrinos are expelled during β^+ emission and e^- capture.

1. **Alpha (α) decay** involves the loss of an α particle from a nucleus. For each α particle emitted by the parent, *A decreases by 4 and Z decreases by 2* in the daughter. Every element beyond bismuth (Bi; $Z = 83$) is radioactive and exhibits α decay. Thus, α *decay is the most common means for a heavy, unstable nucleus to become more stable.* For example, radium undergoes α decay to yield radon (Rn; $Z = 86$):

$$^{226}_{88}\text{Ra} \longrightarrow {}^{222}_{86}\text{Rn} + {}^{4}_{2}\alpha$$

Note that the *A* value for Ra equals the sum of the *A* values for Rn and α ($226 = 222 + 4$), and that the *Z* value for Ra equals the sum of the *Z* values for Rn and α ($88 = 86 + 2$).

2. **Beta (β) decay** is a more general class of radioactive decay that includes three types: β^- decay, β^+ emission, and electron capture.

- **β^- decay** (or *negatron emission*) involves the ejection of a β^- particle from the nucleus. This change does not involve expulsion of a β^- particle that was in the nucleus; rather, *a neutron is converted into a proton, which remains in the nucleus, and a β^- particle, which is expelled immediately:*

$$^{1}_{0}\text{n} \longrightarrow {}^{1}_{1}\text{p} + {}^{0}_{-1}\beta$$

As always, the totals of the *A* and the *Z* values for reactant and products are equal. Radioactive nickel-63 becomes stable copper-63 through β^- decay:

$$^{63}_{28}\text{Ni} \longrightarrow {}^{63}_{29}\text{Cu} + {}^{0}_{-1}\beta$$

Another example is the β^- decay of carbon-14, used in radiocarbon dating:

$$^{14}_{6}\text{C} \longrightarrow {}^{14}_{7}\text{N} + {}^{0}_{-1}\beta$$

Note that *β^- decay results in a product nuclide with A the same but with Z one higher (one more proton) than in the reactant nuclide.* In other words, an atom of the element with the next *higher* atomic number is formed.

- **Positron (β^+) emission** involves the emission of a β^+ particle from the nucleus. A key idea of modern physics is that most fundamental particles have corresponding *antiparticles* with the same mass but opposite charge. (The neutrino and antineutrino are an example.) The **positron** is the antiparticle of the electron. Positron emission occurs through a process in which *a proton in the nucleus is converted into a neutron, and a positron is expelled.* In terms of the effect on *A* and *Z*, *positron emission has the opposite effect of β^- decay: the daughter has the same A but Z is one lower (one fewer proton) than the parent.* Thus, an atom of the element with the next *lower* atomic number forms. Carbon-11, a synthetic radioisotope, decays to a stable boron isotope through β^+ emission:

$$^{11}_{6}\text{C} \longrightarrow {}^{11}_{5}\text{B} + {}^{0}_{1}\beta$$

- **Electron (e$^-$) capture (EC)** occurs when the nucleus interacts with an electron in an orbital from a low atomic energy level. The net effect is that *a proton is transformed into a neutron:*

$$^{1}_{1}\text{p} + {}^{0}_{-1}\text{e} \longrightarrow {}^{1}_{0}\text{n}$$

(We use the symbol "e" to distinguish an orbital electron from a beta particle, β.) The orbital vacancy is quickly filled by an electron that moves down from a higher energy level, and that process continues through still higher energy levels, with x-ray photons and neutrinos carrying off the energy difference in each step. Radioactive iron forms stable manganese through electron capture:

$$^{55}_{26}\text{Fe} + {}^{0}_{-1}\text{e} \longrightarrow {}^{55}_{25}\text{Mn} + h\nu \text{ (x-rays and neutrinos)}$$

Even though the processes are different, *electron capture has the same net effect as positron emission: Z lower by 1, A unchanged.*

3. **Gamma (γ) emission** involves the radiation of high-energy γ photons from an excited nucleus. Just as an atom in an excited *electronic* state reduces its energy by emitting photons, usually in the UV and visible ranges (see Section 7.2), a nucleus in an excited state lowers its energy by emitting γ photons, which are of much higher energy (much shorter wavelength) than UV photons. Many nuclear processes leave the nucleus in an excited state, so γ *emission accompanies many other (but mostly β) types of decay*. Several γ photons (also called γ rays) of different energies can be emitted from an excited nucleus as it returns to the ground state, as in this case:

$$^{215}_{84}\text{Po} \longrightarrow {}^{211}_{82}\text{Pb} + {}^{4}_{2}\alpha \text{ (several } \gamma \text{ emitted)}$$

Gamma emission is common subsequent to β^- decay, as in the following:

$$^{99}_{43}\text{Tc} \longrightarrow {}^{99}_{43}\text{Ru} + {}^{0}_{-1}\beta \text{ (several } \gamma \text{ emitted)}$$

Because γ rays have no mass or charge, *γ emission does not change A or Z*. Two gamma rays are emitted when a particle and an antiparticle annihilate each other. In the medical technique *positron-emission tomography* (Section 23.5), a positron and an electron annihilate each other (with all A and Z values shown):

$$^{0}_{1}\beta + {}^{0}_{-1}\text{e} \longrightarrow 2{}^{0}_{0}\gamma$$

SAMPLE PROBLEM 23.1 | Writing Equations for Nuclear Reactions

Problem Write balanced equations for the following nuclear reactions:
(a) Naturally occurring thorium-232 undergoes α decay.
(b) Zirconium-86 undergoes electron capture.
Plan We first write a skeleton equation that includes the mass numbers, atomic numbers, and symbols of all the particles on the correct sides of the equation, showing the unknown product particle as ${}^{A}_{Z}\text{X}$. Then, because the total of mass numbers and the total of charges on the left side and the right side must be equal, we solve for A and Z, and use Z to determine X from the periodic table.
Solution (a) Writing the skeleton equation, with the α particle as a product:

$$^{232}_{90}\text{Th} \longrightarrow {}^{A}_{Z}\text{X} + {}^{4}_{2}\alpha$$

Solving for A and Z and balancing the equation: For A, $232 = A + 4$, so $A = 228$. For Z, $90 = Z + 2$, so $Z = 88$. From the periodic table, we see that the element with $Z = 88$ is radium (Ra). Thus, the balanced equation is

$$^{232}_{90}\text{Th} \longrightarrow {}^{228}_{88}\text{Ra} + {}^{4}_{2}\alpha$$

(b) Writing the skeleton equation, with the captured electron as a reactant:

$$^{86}_{40}\text{Zr} + {}^{0}_{-1}\text{e} \longrightarrow {}^{A}_{Z}\text{X}$$

Solving for A and Z and balancing the equation: For A, $86 + 0 = A$, so $A = 86$. For Z, $40 + (-1) = Z$, so $Z = 39$. The element with $Z = 39$ is yttrium (Y), so we have

$$^{86}_{40}\text{Zr} + {}^{0}_{-1}\text{e} \longrightarrow {}^{86}_{39}\text{Y}$$

Check Always read across superscripts and then across subscripts, with the yield arrow as an equal sign, to check your arithmetic. In part (a), for example, $232 = 228 + 4$, and $90 = 88 + 2$.

FOLLOW-UP PROBLEM 23.1 Write a balanced equation for the reaction in which a nuclide undergoes β^- decay and produces cesium-133.

Nuclear Stability and the Mode of Decay

There are several ways that an unstable nuclide might decay, but can we predict how it will decay? Indeed, can we predict whether a given nuclide will decay at all? Our knowledge of the nucleus is much less complete than that of the whole atom, but some patterns emerge by observing the naturally occurring nuclides.

The Band of Stability Two key factors determine the stability of a nuclide. The first is the number of neutrons (N), the number of protons (Z), and their ratio (N/Z), which we calculate from $(A - Z)/Z$. This factor relates primarily to nuclides that undergo one of the three modes of β decay. The second factor affecting stability is the total mass of the nuclide, which mostly relates to nuclides that undergo α decay.

Figure 23.2A is a plot of number of neutrons vs. number of protons for all stable nuclides. Note the following:

- The points form a narrow **band of stability** that gradually curves above the line for $N = Z$ ($N/Z = 1$).
- Very few stable nuclides exist with $N/Z < 1$; the only two are ^1_1H and ^3_2He.
- Many lighter nuclides with $N = Z$ are stable, such as ^4_2He, $^{12}_6C$, $^{16}_8O$, and $^{20}_{10}Ne$; the heaviest of these is $^{40}_{20}Ca$. Thus, for lighter nuclides, one neutron for each proton ($N = Z$) is enough to provide stability.
- The N/Z ratio of stable nuclides gradually increases as Z increases. A few examples are noted on the figure: for $^{56}_{26}Fe$, $N/Z = 1.15$; for $^{107}_{47}Ag$, $N/Z = 1.28$; for $^{184}_{74}W$, $N/Z = 1.49$, and, finally, for $^{209}_{83}Bi$, $N/Z = 1.52$. Thus, for heavier stable nuclides, $N > Z$ ($N/Z > 1$), and N increases faster than Z. As we discuss below, if N/Z of a nuclide is either too high (above the band) or not high enough (below the band), the nuclide is unstable and undergoes one of the three modes of beta decay.
- All nuclides with $Z > 83$ are unstable. Thus, the largest members of main groups 1A(1) through 8A(18), actinium and the actinides ($Z = 89$–103), and the other elements of the fourth (6d) transition series ($Z = 104$–112), are radioactive and (as discussed below) undergo α decay.

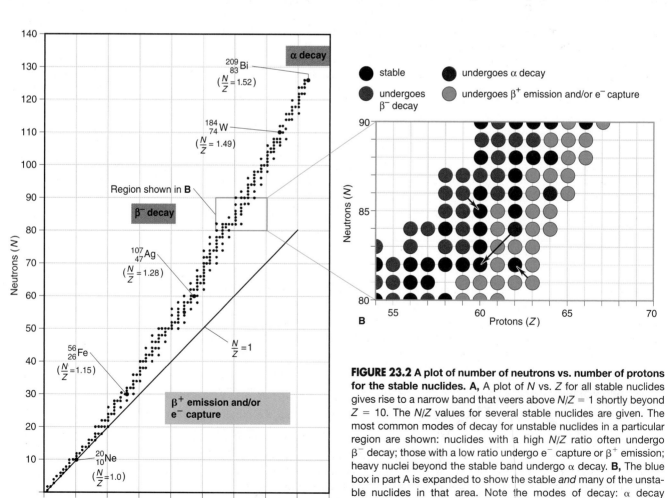

FIGURE 23.2 A plot of number of neutrons vs. number of protons for the stable nuclides. A, A plot of N vs. Z for all stable nuclides gives rise to a narrow band that veers above $N/Z = 1$ shortly beyond $Z = 10$. The N/Z values for several stable nuclides are given. The most common modes of decay for unstable nuclides in a particular region are shown: nuclides with a high N/Z ratio often undergo β⁻ decay; those with a low ratio undergo e⁻ capture or β⁺ emission; heavy nuclei beyond the stable band undergo α decay. **B,** The blue box in part A is expanded to show the stable *and* many of the unstable nuclides in that area. Note the modes of decay: α decay decreases both N and Z by 2; β⁻ decay decreases N and increases Z by 1; β⁺ emission and e⁻ capture increase N and decrease Z by 1.

Stability and Nuclear Structure The oddness or evenness of N and Z values is related to some important patterns of nuclear stability. Two interesting points become apparent when we classify the known stable nuclides:

- Elements with an even Z (number of protons) usually have a larger number of stable nuclides than elements with an odd Z. Table 23.3 demonstrates this point for cadmium ($Z = 48$) through xenon ($Z = 54$).
- Well over half the stable nuclides have *both* even N and even Z. Only four nuclides with odd N and odd Z are stable: ^2_1H, ^6_3Li, $^{10}_5B$, and $^{14}_7N$.

To explain the stability from even values of N and Z, one model of nuclear structure postulates that protons and neutrons lie in *nucleon energy levels*, and that greater stability results from the *pairing of spins* of like nucleons. (Note the analogy to electron energy levels and the stability from pairing of electron spins.)

Just as noble gases—with 2, 10, 18, 36, 54, and 86 electrons—are exceptionally stable because they have filled *electron* levels, nuclides with N or Z values of 2, 8, 20, 28, 50, 82 (and $N = 126$) are exceptionally stable. These so-called *magic numbers* are thought to correspond to the numbers of protons or neutrons in filled *nucleon* levels. A few examples are $^{50}_{22}Ti$ ($N = 28$), $^{88}_{38}Sr$ ($N = 50$), and the ten stable nuclides of tin ($Z = 50$). Some extremely stable nuclides have doubly magic numbers: ^4_2He, $^{16}_8O$, $^{40}_{20}Ca$, and $^{208}_{82}Pb$ ($N = 126$).

Table 23.3 **Number of Stable Nuclides for Elements 48 to 54***

Element	Atomic No. (Z)	No. of Nuclides
Cd	**48**	8
In	49	2
Sn	**50**	10
Sb	51	2
Te	**52**	8
I	53	1
Xe	**54**	9

*Even Z shown in boldface.

SAMPLE PROBLEM 23.2   **Predicting Nuclear Stability**

Problem Which of the following nuclides would you predict to be stable and which radioactive: **(a)** $^{18}_{10}Ne$; **(b)** $^{32}_{16}S$; **(c)** $^{236}_{90}Th$; **(d)** $^{123}_{56}Ba$? Explain.

Plan In order to evaluate the stability of each nuclide, we determine the N and Z values, the N/Z ratio from $(A - Z)/Z$, the value of Z, stable N/Z ratios (from Figure 23.2), and whether Z and N are even or odd.

Solution (a) Radioactive. This nuclide has $N = 8$ ($18 - 10$) and $Z = 10$, so $N/Z = \dfrac{18 - 10}{10} = 0.8$. Except for hydrogen-1 and helium-3, no nuclides with $N < Z$ are stable; despite even N and Z, this nuclide has too few neutrons to be stable.

(b) Stable. This nuclide has $N = Z = 16$, so $N/Z = 1.0$. With $Z < 20$ and even N and Z, this nuclide is most likely stable.

(c) Radioactive. This nuclide has $Z = 90$, and every nuclide with $Z > 83$ is radioactive.

(d) Radioactive. This nuclide has $N = 67$ and $Z = 56$, so $N/Z = 1.20$. For Z values of 55 to 60, Figure 23.2A shows $N/Z \geq 1.3$, so this nuclide has too few neutrons to be stable.

Check By consulting a table of isotopes, such as the one in the *CRC Handbook of Chemistry and Physics*, we find that our predictions are correct.

FOLLOW-UP PROBLEM 23.2 Why is $^{31}_{15}P$ stable but $^{30}_{15}P$ unstable?

Predicting the Mode of Decay An unstable nuclide generally decays in a mode that shifts its N/Z ratio toward the band of stability. This fact is illustrated in Figure 23.2B, which expands a small region of Figure 23.2A to show the stable *and* many of the unstable nuclides in that region, as well as their modes of decay.

Note the following points:

1. *Neutron-rich nuclides.* Nuclides with too many neutrons for stability (a high N/Z) lie above the band of stability. They undergo β^- *decay*, which converts a neutron into a proton, thus reducing the value of N/Z.

2. *Proton-rich nuclides.* Nuclides with too many protons for stability (a low N/Z) lie below the band. They undergo β^+ *emission* and/or e^- *capture*, both of which convert a proton into a neutron, thus increasing the value of N/Z. (The rate of e^- capture increases with Z, so β^+ emission is more common among lighter elements and e^- capture more common among heavier elements.)

3. *Heavy nuclides.* Nuclides with $Z > 83$ are too heavy to be stable and undergo α *decay*, which reduces their Z and N values by two units per emission.

If we have the information in Figure 23.2, predicting the mode of decay of an unstable nuclide is just a matter of comparing its N/Z ratio with those in the nearby region of the band of stability. But, even when Figure 23.2 is not available, we can often make an educated guess at the mode of decay. The atomic mass of an element represents the weighted average of its naturally occurring isotopes, so we would expect the mass number A of a *stable* nuclide to be relatively close to the atomic mass. If an *unstable* nuclide of the element (given Z) has an A value higher than the atomic mass, it is neutron rich and will probably decay by β^- emission. If, on the other hand, the unstable nuclide has an A value lower than the atomic mass, it is proton rich and will probably decay by β^+ emission and/or e^- capture. In the next sample problem, we compare the mass number with the atomic mass to help us predict the mode of decay of an unstable nuclide and then check the prediction with the N/Z values in Figure 23.2.

SAMPLE PROBLEM 23.3   Predicting the Mode of Nuclear Decay

Problem Use the atomic mass of the element to predict the mode(s) of decay of the following radioactive nuclides: **(a)** $^{12}_{5}\text{B}$; **(b)** $^{234}_{92}\text{U}$; **(c)** $^{81}_{33}\text{As}$; **(d)** $^{127}_{57}\text{La}$.

Plan If the nuclide is too heavy to be stable ($Z > 83$), it undergoes α decay. For other cases, we use the Z value to locate the element in the periodic table and obtain its atomic mass. If the mass number of the nuclide is higher than the atomic mass, the nuclide has too many neutrons: N too high $\Rightarrow \beta^-$ decay. If the mass number is lower than the atomic mass, the nuclide has too many protons: Z too high $\Rightarrow \beta^+$ emission and/or e^- capture.

Solution **(a)** This nuclide has $Z = 5$, which is boron (B), and the atomic mass is 10.81. The nuclide's A value of 12 is higher than its atomic mass, so this nuclide is neutron rich. It will probably undergo β^- decay lowering N to 6 and raising Z to 6 to form the stable $^{12}_{6}\text{C}$.

(b) This nuclide has $Z = 92$, so it will undergo α decay and decrease its total mass.

(c) This nuclide has $Z = 33$, which is arsenic (As), and the atomic mass is 74.92. The A value of 81 is higher, so this nuclide is neutron rich and will probably undergo β^- decay.

(d) This nuclide has $Z = 57$, which is lanthanum (La), and the atomic mass is 138.9. The A value of 127 is lower, so this nuclide is proton rich and will probably undergo β^+ emission and/or e^- capture.

Check To confirm our predictions in (a), (c), and (d), let's compare each nuclide's N/Z ratio to those in the band of stability. **(a)** This nuclide has $N = 7$ and $Z = 5$, so $N/Z = 1.40$, which is too high for this region of the band; it will undergo β^- decay. **(c)** This nuclide has $N = 48$ and $Z = 33$, so $N/Z = 1.45$, which is too high for this region of the band; it undergoes β^- decay. **(d)** This nuclide has $N = 70$ and $Z = 57$, so $N/Z = 1.23$, which is too low for this region of the band; it undergoes β^+ emission and/or e^- capture. Our predictions based on N/Z *values* were the same as those based on atomic mass.

Comment Both possible modes of decay are observed for the nuclide in part (d).

FOLLOW-UP PROBLEM 23.3 Use the A value for the nuclide and the atomic mass in the periodic table to predict the mode of decay of **(a)** $^{61}_{26}\text{Fe}$; **(b)** $^{241}_{95}\text{Am}$.

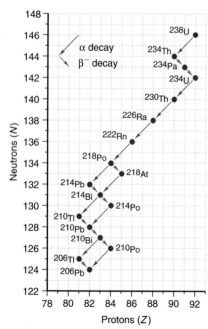

FIGURE 23.3 The ^{238}U decay series.
Uranium-238 *(top right)* undergoes a series of 14 steps involving α or β^- decay until lead-206 forms *(bottom left)*.

Decay Series A parent nuclide may undergo a series of decay steps before a stable daughter nuclide forms. The succession of steps is called a **decay series,** or **disintegration series,** and is typically depicted on a gridlike display. Figure 23.3 shows the decay series from uranium-238 to lead-206. Numbers of neutrons (N) are plotted against numbers of protons (Z) to form the grid, which displays a series of α and β^- decays. The typical zigzag pattern arises because $N > Z$, which means that α decay, which reduces both N and Z by two units, decreases Z by a slightly greater percentage than it does N. Therefore, α decays result in neutron-rich daughters, which undergo β^- decay to gain more stability. Note that a given nuclide can undergo both types of decay. (Gamma emission accompanies many of these steps but does not affect the type of nuclide.) This series is one of three that occur in nature. All end with isotopes of lead whose nuclides all have one

($Z = 82$) or two ($N = 126$, $Z = 82$) magic numbers. A second series begins with uranium-235 and ends with lead-207, and a third begins with thorium-232 and ends with lead-208. (Neptunium-237 began a fourth series, but its half-life is so much less than the age of Earth that only traces of it remain today.)

SECTION 23.1 SUMMARY

Nuclear reactions are normally not affected by reaction conditions or chemical composition and release much more energy than chemical reactions. • To become more stable, a radioactive nuclide may emit α particles ($^4_2$He nuclei), β particles (β^- or $_{-1}^{0}\beta$; high-speed electrons), positrons (β^+ or $_{1}^{0}\beta$), or γ rays (high-energy photons) or may capture an orbital electron ($_{-1}^{0}$e). • A narrow band of neutron-to-proton ratios (N/Z) includes those of all the stable nuclides. • Certain "magic numbers" of neutrons and protons are associated with very stable nuclides. • By comparing a nuclide's mass number with the atomic mass and its N/Z ratio with those in the band of stability, we can predict that, in general, neutron-rich nuclides undergo β^- decay and proton-rich nuclides undergo β^+ emission and/or e$^-$ capture. Heavy nuclides ($Z > 83$) undergo α decay. • Three naturally occurring decay series all end in isotopes of lead.

23.2 THE KINETICS OF RADIOACTIVE DECAY

Chemical and nuclear systems both tend toward maximum stability. Just as the concentrations in a chemical system change in a predictable direction to give a stable equilibrium ratio, the type and number of nucleons in an unstable nucleus change in a predictable direction to give a stable N/Z ratio. As you know, however, the tendency of a chemical system to become more stable tells nothing about how long that process will take, and the same holds true for nuclear systems. In this section, we examine the kinetics of nuclear change; later, we'll examine the energetics of nuclear change.

The Rate of Radioactive Decay

 **Animation: Radioactive Decay**

Radioactive nuclei decay at a characteristic rate, regardless of the chemical substance in which they occur. The *decay rate,* or **activity ($\mathscr{A}$),** of a radioactive sample is the change in number of nuclei ($\mathscr{N}$) divided by the change in time (t). As we saw with chemical reaction rates, because the number of nuclei is *decreasing,* a minus sign precedes the expression for the decay rate:

$$\text{Decay rate } (\mathscr{A}) = -\frac{\Delta \mathscr{N}}{\Delta t}$$

The SI unit of radioactivity is the **becquerel (Bq);** it is defined as one disintegration per second (d/s): 1 Bq = 1 d/s. A much larger and more common unit of radioactivity is the **curie (Ci).** Originally, the curie was defined as the number of disintegrations per second in 1 g of radium-226, but it is now a fixed quantity:

$$1 \text{ Ci} = 3.70 \times 10^{10} \text{ d/s} \tag{23.2}$$

Because the curie is so large, the millicurie (mCi) and microcurie (μCi) are commonly used. We often express the radioactivity of a sample in terms of *specific activity,* the decay rate per gram.

An activity is meaningful only when we consider the large number of nuclei in a macroscopic sample. Suppose there are 1×10^{15} radioactive nuclei of a particular type in a sample and they decay at a rate of 10% per hour. Although any particular nucleus in the sample might decay in a microsecond or in a million hours, the *average* of all decays results in 10% of the entire collection of nuclei disintegrating each hour. During the first hour, 10% of the *original* number, or 1×10^{14} nuclei, will decay. During the next hour, 10% of the remaining 9×10^{14} nuclei, or 9×10^{13} nuclei, will decay. During the next hour, 10% of those remaining will decay, and so forth. Thus, for a large collection of radioactive nuclei, *the number decaying per unit time is proportional to the number present:*

$$\text{Decay rate } (\mathcal{A}) \propto \mathcal{N} \qquad \text{or} \qquad \mathcal{A} = k\mathcal{N}$$

where k is called the **decay constant** and is characteristic of each type of nuclide. The larger the value of k, the higher is the decay rate: larger $k \Rightarrow$ higher $\mathcal{A}$.

Combining the two rate expressions just given, we obtain

$$\mathcal{A} = -\frac{\Delta \mathcal{N}}{\Delta t} = k\mathcal{N} \tag{23.3}$$

Note that the activity depends only on $\mathcal{N}$ raised to the first power (and on the constant value of k). Therefore, *radioactive decay is a first-order process* (see Section 16.3). The only difference in the case of nuclear decay is that we consider the *number* of nuclei rather than their concentration.

Half-Life of Radioactive Decay Decay rates are also commonly expressed in terms of the fraction of nuclei that decay over a given time interval. The **half-life ($t_{1/2}$)** of a nuclide is the time it takes for half the nuclei present in a sample to decay. *The number of nuclei remaining is halved after each half-life.* Thus, half-life has the same meaning for a nuclear change as for a chemical change (Section 16.4). Figure 23.4 shows the decay of carbon-14, which has a half-life of 5730 years, in terms of number of ^{14}C nuclei remaining:

$$^{14}_{6}C \longrightarrow {}^{14}_{7}N + {}^{0}_{-1}\beta$$

We can also consider the half-life in terms of mass of substance. As ^{14}C decays, the mass of ^{14}C decreases while the mass of ^{14}N increases. If we start with 1.0 g of ^{14}C, half that mass of ^{14}C (0.50 g) will be left after 5730 years, half of that mass (0.25 g) after another 5730 years, and so on. The activity depends on the number of nuclei, so the activity is halved after each succeeding half-life as well.

We determine the half-life of a nuclear reaction from its rate constant. Rearranging Equation 23.3 and integrating over time gives an expression for finding the number of nuclei remaining after a given time t, $\mathcal{N}_t$:

$$\ln \frac{\mathcal{N}_t}{\mathcal{N}_0} = -kt \qquad \text{or} \qquad \mathcal{N}_t = \mathcal{N}_0 e^{-kt} \qquad \text{and} \qquad \ln \frac{\mathcal{N}_0}{\mathcal{N}_t} = kt \tag{23.4}$$

where $\mathcal{N}_0$ is the number of nuclei at $t = 0$. (Note the similarity to Equation 16.4, p. 521.) To calculate the half-life ($t_{1/2}$), we set $\mathcal{N}_t$ equal to $\frac{1}{2}\mathcal{N}_0$ and solve for $t_{1/2}$:

$$\ln \frac{\mathcal{N}_0}{\frac{1}{2}\mathcal{N}_0} = kt_{1/2} \qquad \text{so} \qquad t_{1/2} = \frac{\ln 2}{k} \tag{23.5}$$

Animation: Half-Life

FIGURE 23.4 Decrease in number of ^{14}C nuclei over time. A plot of number of ^{14}C nuclei vs. time gives a downward-sloping curve. In each half-life (5730 years), half the ^{14}C nuclei present undergo decay. A plot of mass of ^{14}C (or any other variable proportional to number of nuclei) vs. time has the same shape.

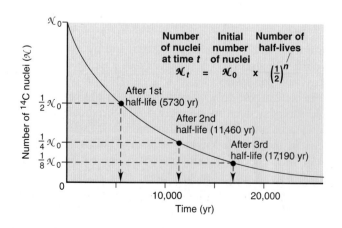

Exactly analogous to the half-life of a first-order chemical change, *this half-life is **not** dependent on the number of nuclei and is inversely related to the decay constant:*

$$\text{large } k \Rightarrow \text{short } t_{1/2} \quad \text{and} \quad \text{small } k \Rightarrow \text{long } t_{1/2}$$

The decay constants and half-lives of radioactive nuclides vary over a very wide range, even for the nuclides of a given element (Table 23.4).

Table 23.4	**Decay Constants (k) and Half-Lives ($t_{1/2}$) of Beryllium Isotopes**	
Nuclide	**k**	**$t_{1/2}$**
$^{7}_{4}\text{Be}$	1.30×10^{-2}/day	53.3 days
$^{8}_{4}\text{Be}$	1.0×10^{16}/s	6.7×10^{-17} s
$^{9}_{4}\text{Be}$	Stable	
$^{10}_{4}\text{Be}$	4.3×10^{-7}/yr	1.6×10^{6} yr
$^{11}_{4}\text{Be}$	5.02×10^{-2}/s	13.8 s

SAMPLE PROBLEM 23.4   Finding the Number of Radioactive Nuclei

Problem Strontium-90 is a radioactive byproduct of nuclear reactors that behaves biologically like calcium, the element above it in Group 2A(2). When ^{90}Sr is ingested by mammals, it is found in their milk and eventually in the bones of those drinking the milk. If a sample of ^{90}Sr has an activity of 1.2×10^{12} d/s, what are the activity and the fraction of nuclei that have decayed after 59 yr ($t_{1/2}$ of ^{90}Sr = 29 yr)?

Plan The fraction of nuclei that have decayed is the change in number of nuclei, expressed as a fraction of the starting number. The activity of the sample ($\mathcal{A}$) is proportional to the number of nuclei ($\mathcal{N}$), so we know that

$$\text{Fraction decayed} = \frac{\mathcal{N}_0 - \mathcal{N}_t}{\mathcal{N}_0} = \frac{\mathcal{A}_0 - \mathcal{A}_t}{\mathcal{A}_0}$$

We are given $\mathcal{A}_0$ (1.2×10^{12} d/s), so we find $\mathcal{A}_t$ from the integrated form of the first-order rate equation (Equation 23.4), in which t is 59 yr. To solve that equation, we first need k, which we can calculate from the given $t_{1/2}$ (29 yr).

Solution Calculating the decay constant k:

$$t_{1/2} = \frac{\ln 2}{k} \quad \text{so} \quad k = \frac{\ln 2}{t_{1/2}} = \frac{0.693}{29 \text{ yr}} = 0.024 \text{ yr}^{-1}$$

Applying Equation 23.4 to calculate $\mathcal{A}_t$, the activity remaining at time t:

$$\ln \frac{\mathcal{N}_0}{\mathcal{N}_t} = \ln \frac{\mathcal{A}_0}{\mathcal{A}_t} = kt \quad \text{or} \quad \ln \mathcal{A}_0 - \ln \mathcal{A}_t = kt$$

So,
$$\ln \mathcal{A}_t = -kt + \ln \mathcal{A}_0 = -(0.024 \text{ yr}^{-1} \times 59 \text{ yr}) + \ln (1.2 \times 10^{12} \text{ d/s})$$
$$\ln \mathcal{A}_t = -1.4 + 27.81 = 26.4$$
$$\mathcal{A}_t = 2.9 \times 10^{11} \text{ d/s}$$

(All the data contain two significant figures, so we retained two in the answer.) Calculating the fraction decayed:

$$\text{Fraction decayed} = \frac{\mathcal{A}_0 - \mathcal{A}_t}{\mathcal{A}_0} = \frac{1.2 \times 10^{12} \text{ d/s} - 2.9 \times 10^{11} \text{ d/s}}{1.2 \times 10^{12} \text{ d/s}} = 0.76$$

Check The answer is reasonable: t is about 2 half-lives, so $\mathcal{A}_t$ should be about $\frac{1}{4}\mathcal{A}_0$, or about 0.3×10^{12}; therefore, the activity should have decreased by about $\frac{3}{4}$.

Comment 1. A useful substitution of Equation 23.4 for finding $\mathcal{A}_t$, the activity at time t, is $\mathcal{A}_t = \mathcal{A}_0 e^{-kt}$.

2. Another way to find the fraction of activity (or nuclei) remaining incorporates the number of half-lives ($t/t_{1/2}$). By combining Equations 23.4 and 23.5 and substituting $(\ln 2)/t_{1/2}$ for k, we obtain

$$\ln \frac{\mathcal{N}_0}{\mathcal{N}_t} = \left(\frac{\ln 2}{t_{1/2}}\right) t = \frac{t}{t_{1/2}} \ln 2 = \ln 2^{t/t_{1/2}}$$

Inverting the ratio gives
$$\ln \frac{\mathcal{N}_t}{\mathcal{N}_0} = \ln \left(\frac{1}{2}\right)^{t/t_{1/2}}$$

Taking the antilog gives

$$\text{Fraction remaining} = \frac{\mathcal{N}_t}{\mathcal{N}_0} = \left(\frac{1}{2}\right)^{t/t_{1/2}} = \left(\frac{1}{2}\right)^{59/29} = 0.24$$

So,
$$\text{Fraction decayed} = 1.00 - 0.24 = 0.76$$

FOLLOW-UP PROBLEM 23.4 Sodium-24 ($t_{1/2}$ = 15 h) is used to study blood circulation. If a patient is injected with an aqueous solution of $^{24}\text{NaCl}$ whose activity is 2.5×10^9 d/s, how much activity is in the patient's body and excreted fluids after 4.0 days?

Radioisotopic Dating

The historical record fades rapidly with time and virtually disappears for events of more than a few thousand years ago. Much of our understanding of prehistory comes from a technique called **radioisotopic dating,** which uses **radioisotopes** to determine the age of an object. The method supplies data in fields as diverse as art history, archeology, geology, and paleontology.

The technique of *radiocarbon dating,* for which the American chemist Willard F. Libby won the Nobel Prize in chemistry in 1960, is based on measuring the amounts of ^{14}C and ^{12}C in materials of biological origin. The accuracy of the method falls off after about six half-lives of ^{14}C ($t_{1/2} = 5730$ yr), so it is used to date objects up to about 36,000 years old.

Here is how the method works. High-energy cosmic rays, consisting mainly of protons, enter the atmosphere from outer space and initiate a cascade of nuclear reactions; some produce neutrons that bombard ordinary ^{14}N atoms to form ^{14}C:

$$^{14}_{7}N + ^{1}_{0}n \longrightarrow ^{14}_{6}C + ^{1}_{1}p$$

Through the competing processes of formation and radioactive decay, the amount of ^{14}C in the atmosphere has remained nearly constant.

The ^{14}C atoms combine with O_2, diffuse throughout the lower atmosphere, and enter the total carbon pool as gaseous $^{14}CO_2$ and aqueous $H^{14}CO_3^-$. They mix with ordinary $^{12}CO_2$ and $H^{12}CO_3^-$, reaching a constant $^{12}C/^{14}C$ ratio of about $10^{12}/1$. Carbon atoms in the CO_2 are taken up by plants during photosynthesis, and then taken up and excreted by animals that eat the plants. Thus, the $^{12}C/^{14}C$ ratio of a living organism is the same as the ratio in the environment. When an organism dies, however, it no longer absorbs or releases CO_2, so the $^{12}C/^{14}C$ ratio steadily increases because *the amount of ^{14}C decreases as it decays:*

$$^{14}_{6}C \longrightarrow ^{14}_{7}N + ^{0}_{-1}\beta$$

The difference between the $^{12}C/^{14}C$ ratio in a dead organism and the ratio in living organisms reflects the time elapsed since the organism died.

As you saw in Sample Problem 23.4, the first-order rate equation can be expressed in terms of a ratio of activities:

$$\ln \frac{\mathcal{N}_0}{\mathcal{N}_t} = \ln \frac{\mathcal{A}_0}{\mathcal{A}_t} = kt$$

We use this expression in radiocarbon dating, where $\mathcal{A}_0$ is the activity in a living organism and $\mathcal{A}_t$ is the activity in the object whose age is unknown. Solving for t gives the age of the object:

$$t = \frac{1}{k} \ln \frac{\mathcal{A}_0}{\mathcal{A}_t} \qquad (23.6)$$

To determine the ages of more ancient objects or of objects that do not contain carbon, different radioisotopes are measured. For example, by comparing the ratio of ^{238}U ($t_{1/2} = 4.5 \times 10^9$ yr) to its final decay product, ^{206}Pb, geochemists found that the oldest known surface rocks on Earth—granite in western Greenland—are about 3.7 billion years old. The ratio $^{238}U/^{206}Pb$ in samples from meteorites gives 4.65 billion years for the age of the Solar System, and thus Earth.

SAMPLE PROBLEM 23.5   Applying Radiocarbon Dating

Problem The charred bones of a sloth in a cave in Chile represent the earliest evidence of human presence at the southern tip of South America. A sample of the bone has a specific activity of 5.22 disintegrations per minute per gram of carbon (d/min·g). If the $^{12}C/^{14}C$ ratio for living organisms results in a specific activity of 15.3 d/min·g, how old are the bones ($t_{1/2}$ of $^{14}C = 5730$ yr)?

Plan We first calculate k from the given $t_{1/2}$ (5730 yr). Then we apply Equation 23.6 to find the age (t) of the bones, using the given activities of the bones ($\mathcal{A}_t = 5.22$ d/min·g) and of a living organism ($\mathcal{A}_0 = 15.3$ d/min·g).

Solution Calculating k for ^{14}C decay:

$$k = \frac{\ln 2}{t_{1/2}} = \frac{0.693}{5730 \text{ yr}} = 1.21 \times 10^{-4} \text{ yr}^{-1}$$

Calculating the age (t) of the bones:

$$t = \frac{1}{k} \ln \frac{\mathcal{A}_0}{\mathcal{A}_t} = \frac{1}{1.21 \times 10^{-4} \text{ yr}^{-1}} \ln \left(\frac{15.3 \text{ d/min·g}}{5.22 \text{ d/min·g}}\right) = 8.89 \times 10^3 \text{ yr}$$

The bones are about 8900 years old.

Check The activity of the bones is between $\frac{1}{2}$ and $\frac{1}{4}$ the activity of a living organism, so the age should be between one and two half-lives (5730 to 11,460 yr).

FOLLOW-UP PROBLEM 23.5 A sample of wood from an Egyptian mummy case has a specific activity of 9.41 d/min·g. How old is the case?

SECTION 23.2 SUMMARY

The decay rate (activity) of a sample is proportional to the number of radioactive nuclei. Nuclear decay is a first-order process, so the half-life is a constant for each nuclide. • Radioisotopic methods, such as ^{14}C dating, determine the ages of objects by measuring the ratio of specific isotopes in the sample.

23.3 NUCLEAR TRANSMUTATION: INDUCED CHANGES IN NUCLEI

The alchemists' dream of changing base metals into gold was never realized, but in the early 20th century, nuclear physicists found that they *could* change one element into another. Research into **nuclear transmutation,** the *induced* conversion of one nucleus into another, was closely linked with research into atomic structure and led to the discovery of the neutron and to the production of artificial radioisotopes. Later, high-energy bombardment of nuclei in particle accelerators began a scientific endeavor, which continues to this day, of creating many new nuclides and a growing number of new elements.

During the 1930s and 1940s, researchers probing the nucleus bombarded elements with neutrons, α particles, protons, and **deuterons** (nuclei of the stable hydrogen isotope deuterium, ^2H). Neutrons are especially useful as projectiles because they have no charge and thus are not repelled as they approach a target nucleus. The other particles are all positive, so early researchers found it difficult to give them enough energy to overcome their repulsion by the target nuclei. Beginning in the 1930s, however, **particle accelerators** were invented to impart high kinetic energies to particles by placing them in an electric field, usually in combination with a magnetic field.

A major advance was the *linear accelerator,* a series of separated tubes of increasing length that, through a source of alternating voltage, change their charge from positive to negative in synchrony with the movement of the particle through them (Figure 23.5). A proton, for example, exits the first tube just when that tube becomes positive and the next tube negative. Repelled by the first tube and

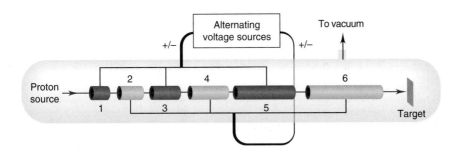

FIGURE 23.5 Schematic of a linear accelerator. The voltage of each tubular section is alternated, so that the positively charged particle (a proton here) is repelled from the section it is leaving and attracted to the section it is entering. As a result, the particle's speed is continually increased.

FIGURE 23.6 Schematic of a cyclotron accelerator. The magnets lie within an evacuated chamber above and below two "dees," open, D-shaped electrodes that act like the tubes in the linear design. The particle is accelerated as it passes from one dee, which is momentarily positive, to the other, which is momentarily negative. Its speed and radius increase until it is deflected toward the target nucleus.

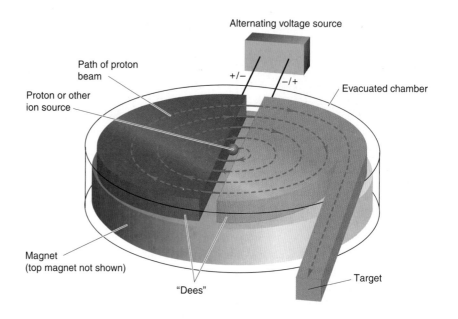

attracted by the second, the proton accelerates across the gap between them. The process is performed in stages to achieve high particle energies without having to apply a single high voltage. A 40-ft linear accelerator with 46 tubes, built in California after World War II, accelerated protons to speeds several million times faster than earlier accelerators. The *cyclotron* (Figure 23.6), invented by E. O. Lawrence in 1930, applies the principle of the linear accelerator but uses electromagnets to give the particle a spiral path, thus saving space.

Scientists use accelerators for many applications, from producing radioisotopes used in medical applications to studying the fundamental nature of matter. Perhaps the most specific application for chemists is the synthesis of **transuranium elements,** those with atomic numbers higher than uranium, the heaviest naturally occurring element. Some reactions that were used to form several of these elements appear in Table 23.5.

SECTION 23.3 SUMMARY

One nucleus can be transmuted to another through bombardment with high-energy particles. • Accelerators increase the kinetic energy of particles. They are used to produce transuranium elements and radioisotopes for medical use.

Table 23.5	**Formation of Some Transuranium Nuclides***				
Reaction					**Half-life of Product**
$^{239}_{94}\text{Pu}$	$+$ 2^{1}_{0}n	$\longrightarrow$	$^{241}_{95}\text{Am}$	$+$ $^{0}_{-1}\beta$	432 yr
$^{239}_{94}\text{Pu}$	$+$ $^{4}_{2}\alpha$	$\longrightarrow$	$^{242}_{96}\text{Cm}$	$+$ $^{1}_{0}\text{n}$	163 days
$^{241}_{95}\text{Am}$	$+$ $^{4}_{2}\alpha$	$\longrightarrow$	$^{243}_{97}\text{Bk}$	$+$ 2^{1}_{0}n	4.5 h
$^{242}_{96}\text{Cm}$	$+$ $^{4}_{2}\alpha$	$\longrightarrow$	$^{245}_{98}\text{Cf}$	$+$ $^{1}_{0}\text{n}$	45 min
$^{253}_{99}\text{Es}$	$+$ $^{4}_{2}\alpha$	$\longrightarrow$	$^{256}_{101}\text{Md}$	$+$ $^{1}_{0}\text{n}$	76 min
$^{243}_{95}\text{Am}$	$+$ $^{18}_{8}\text{O}$	$\longrightarrow$	$^{256}_{103}\text{Lr}$	$+$ 5^{1}_{0}n	28 s

*Like chemical reactions, nuclear reactions may occur in several steps. For example, the first reaction here is actually an overall process that occurs in three steps:

(1) $^{239}_{94}\text{Pu} + ^{1}_{0}\text{n} \longrightarrow ^{240}_{94}\text{Pu}$ (2) $^{240}_{94}\text{Pu} + ^{1}_{0}\text{n} \longrightarrow ^{241}_{94}\text{Pu}$ (3) $^{241}_{94}\text{Pu} \longrightarrow ^{241}_{95}\text{Am} + ^{0}_{-1}\beta$

23.4 THE EFFECTS OF NUCLEAR RADIATION ON MATTER

In 1986, an accident at the Chernobyl nuclear facility in the former Soviet Union released radioactivity that, according to the World Health Organization, will cause thousands of cancer deaths. In the same year, isotopes used in medical treatment emitted radioactivity that prevented thousands of cancer deaths. In this section and Section 23.5, we examine radioactivity's harmful and beneficial effects.

The key to both of these effects is that *nuclear changes cause chemical changes in surrounding matter.* In other words, even though the nucleus of an atom may undergo a reaction with little or no involvement of the atom's electrons, the emissions from that reaction *do* affect the electrons of nearby atoms.

Virtually all radioactivity causes **ionization** in surrounding matter, as the emissions collide with atoms and dislodge electrons:

$$\text{Atom} \xrightarrow{\text{ionizing radiation}} \text{ion}^+ + e^-$$

From each ionization event, a cation and a free electron result, and the number of such *cation-electron pairs* produced is directly related to the energy of the incoming **ionizing radiation.**

Effects of Ionizing Radiation on Living Matter

Ionizing radiation has a destructive effect on living tissue, and if the ionized atom is part of a key biological macromolecule or cell membrane, the results can be devastating to the cell and perhaps the organism.

Units of Radiation Dose and Its Effects To measure the effects of ionizing radiation, we need a unit for radiation dose. Units of radioactive decay, such as the becquerel and curie, measure the number of decay events in a given time but not their energy or absorption by matter. The number of cation-electron pairs produced in a given amount of living tissue is a measure of the energy absorbed by the tissue. The SI unit is the **gray (Gy),** equal to 1 joule of energy absorbed per kilogram of body tissue: 1 Gy = 1 J/kg. A more widely used unit is the **rad (radiation-absorbed dose),** which is equal to 0.01 Gy:

$$1 \text{ rad} = 0.01 \text{ J/kg} = 0.01 \text{ Gy}$$

To measure actual tissue damage, we must account for differences in the strength of the radiation, the exposure time, and the type of tissue. To do this, we multiply the number of rads by a *relative biological effectiveness* (RBE) factor, which depends on the effect of a given type of radiation on a given tissue or body part. The product is the **rem (roentgen equivalent for man),** the unit of radiation dosage equivalent to a given amount of tissue damage in a human:

$$\text{no. of rems} = \text{no. of rads} \times \text{RBE}$$

Doses are often expressed in millirems (10^{-3} rem). The SI unit for dosage equivalent is the **sievert (Sv).** It is defined in the same way as the rem but with absorbed dose in grays; thus, 1 rem = 0.01 Sv.

Penetrating Power of Emissions The effect on living tissue of a radiation dose depends on the penetrating power *and* ionizing ability of the radiation. Figure 23.7 depicts the differences in penetrating power of the three common emissions. Note, in general, that *penetrating power is inversely related to the mass, charge, and energy of the emission.* In other words, if a particle interacts strongly with matter, it penetrates only slightly, and vice versa:

- *α Particles.* Alpha particles are massive and highly charged, which means that they interact with matter most strongly of the three common types of emissions. As a result, they penetrate so little that a piece of paper, light clothing, or the outer layer of skin can stop α radiation from an external source. Internally, however, such as from ingestion, an α emitter can cause grave localized damage through extensive ionization.

α (~0.03 mm)

β (~2 mm)

γ (~10 cm)

FIGURE 23.7 Penetrating power of radioactive emissions. Penetrating power is often measured in terms of the depth of water that stops 50% of the incoming radiation. (Water is the main component of living tissue.) Alpha particles, with the highest mass and charge, have the lowest penetrating power, and γ rays have the highest. (Average values of actual penetrating distances are shown.)

- *Beta Particles and Positrons.* Beta particles (β^-) and positrons (β^+) have less charge and much less mass than α particles, so they interact less strongly with matter. Even though a given particle has less chance of causing ionization, a β^- (or β^+) emitter is a more destructive external source because the particles penetrate deeper. Specialized heavy clothing or a thick (0.5 cm) piece of metal is required to stop these particles.
- *γ Rays.* Neutral, massless γ rays interact least with matter and, thus, penetrate most. A block of lead several inches thick is needed to stop them. Therefore, an external γ ray source is the most dangerous because the energy can ionize many layers of living tissue.

Sources of Ionizing Radiation

We are continuously exposed to ionizing radiation from natural and artificial sources (Table 23.6). Indeed, life evolved in the presence of natural ionizing radiation, called **background radiation.** The same radiation that alters bonds in DNA and causes harmful mutations also causes beneficial mutations that, over evolutionary time, allow species to change.

Background radiation has several sources. One source is *cosmic radiation,* which increases with altitude because of decreased absorption by the atmosphere. Thus, people in Denver absorb twice as much cosmic radiation as people in Los Angeles; even a jet flight involves measurable absorption. The sources of most background radiation are thorium and uranium minerals present in rocks and soil.

Table 23.6 Typical Radiation Doses from Natural and Artificial Sources	
Source of Radiation	**Average Adult Exposure**
Natural	
Cosmic radiation	30−50 mrem/yr
Radiation from the ground	
From clay soil and rocks	~25−170 mrem/yr
In wooden houses	10−20 mrem/yr
In brick houses	60−70 mrem/yr
In concrete (cinder block) houses	60−160 mrem/yr
Radiation from the air (mainly radon)	
Outdoors, average value	20 mrem/yr
In wooden houses	70 mrem/yr
In brick houses	130 mrem/yr
In concrete (cinder block) houses	260 mrem/yr
Internal radiation from minerals in tap water and daily intake of food (^{40}K, ^{14}C, Ra)	~40 mrem/yr
Artificial	
Diagnostic x-ray methods	
Lung (local)	0.04−0.2 rad/film
Kidney (local)	1.5−3 rad/film
Dental (dose to the skin)	≤1 rad/film
Therapeutic radiation treatment	Locally ≤ 10,000 rad
Other sources	
Jet flight (4 h)	~1 mrem
Nuclear testing	<4 mrem/yr
Nuclear power industry	<1 mrem/yr
Total average value	100−200 mrem/yr

Radon, the heaviest noble gas [Group 8A(18)], is a radioactive product of uranium and thorium decay. Its concentration in the air we breathe is associated with certain common building materials and types of local soil and rocks. Its decay products cause most of the damage. About 150 g of K^+ ions is dissolved in the water in the tissues of an average adult, and 0.0118% of these ions are radioactive ^{40}K. The presence of these substances and of atmospheric $^{14}CO_2$ makes all food, water, clothing, and building materials slightly radioactive.

The largest artificial source of radiation, and the easiest to control, is medical diagnostic procedures, especially x-rays. The radiation dosage from nuclear testing and radioactive waste disposal is miniscule for most people, but exposures for those living near test sites or disposal areas may be much higher.

SECTION 23.4 SUMMARY

All radioactive emissions cause ionization. • The effect of ionizing radiation on living matter depends on the quantity of energy absorbed and its penetrating power, and the extent of ionization in a given type of tissue. Radiation dose for the human body is measured in rem. • All organisms are exposed to varying quantities of natural ionizing radiation.

23.5 APPLICATIONS OF RADIOISOTOPES

Our ability to detect minute amounts of radioisotopes makes them powerful tools for studying processes in biochemistry, medicine, materials science, environmental studies, and many other scientific and industrial fields. Such uses depend on the fact that *isotopes of an element exhibit **very** similar chemical and physical behavior.* In other words, except for having a less stable nucleus, a radioisotope has nearly the same chemical properties as a nonradioactive isotope of that element. For example, the fact that $^{14}CO_2$ is utilized by a plant in the same way as $^{12}CO_2$ forms the basis of radiocarbon dating.

Radioactive Tracers

A tiny amount of a radioisotope mixed with a large amount of the stable isotope can act as a **tracer,** a chemical "beacon" emitting radiation that signals the presence of the substance.

Reaction Pathways Tracers help us choose from among possible reaction pathways. One well-studied example is the reaction between periodate and iodide ions:

$$IO_4^-(aq) + 2I^-(aq) + H_2O(l) \longrightarrow I_2(s) + IO_3^-(aq) + 2OH^-(aq)$$

Is IO_3^- the result of IO_4^- reduction or I^- oxidation? When we add "cold" (nonradioactive) IO_4^- to a solution of I^- that contains some "hot" (radioactive, indicated in red) $^{131}I^-$, we find that the I_2 is radioactive, not the IO_3^-:

$$IO_4^-(aq) + 2\,^{131}I^-(aq) + H_2O(l) \longrightarrow {}^{131}I_2(s) + IO_3^-(aq) + 2OH^-(aq)$$

These results show that IO_3^- forms through the reduction of IO_4^-, and that I_2 forms through the oxidation of I^-. To confirm this pathway, we add IO_4^- containing some $^{131}IO_4^-$ to a solution of I^-. As we expected, the IO_3^- is radioactive, not the I_2:

$$^{131}IO_4^-(aq) + 2I^-(aq) + H_2O(l) \longrightarrow I_2(s) + {}^{131}IO_3^-(aq) + 2OH^-(aq)$$

Thus, tracers act like "handles" we can "hold" to follow the changing reactants.

Far more complex pathways can be followed with tracers as well. The photosynthetic pathway, the most essential and widespread metabolic process on Earth, in which energy from sunlight is used to form the chemical bonds of glucose, has an overall reaction that looks quite simple:

$$6CO_2(g) + 6H_2O(l) \xrightarrow[\text{chlorophyll}]{\text{light}} C_6H_{12}O_6(s) + 6O_2(g)$$

However, the actual process is extremely complex: 13 enzyme-catalyzed steps are required to incorporate each C atom from CO_2, so the six CO_2 molecules incorporated to form a molecule of $C_6H_{12}O_6$ require six repetitions of the pathway. Melvin Calvin and his coworkers took seven years to determine the pathway. He won the Nobel Prize in chemistry in 1961 for this remarkable achievement.

Material Flow Tracers are used in studies of solid surfaces and the flow of materials. Metal atoms hundreds of layers deep within a solid have been shown to exchange with metal ions from the surrounding solution within a matter of minutes. Chemists and engineers use tracers to study material movement in semiconductor chips, paint, and metal plating, in detergent action, and in the process of corrosion, to mention just a few of many applications.

Hydrologic engineers use tracers to study the volume and flow of large bodies of water. By following radionuclides that formed during atmospheric nuclear bomb tests (^3H in H_2O, $^{90}Sr^{2+}$, and $^{137}Cs^+$), scientists have mapped the flow of water from land to lakes and streams to oceans. They also use tracers to study the surface and deep ocean currents that circulate around the globe, as well as the mechanisms of hurricane formation and the mixing of the troposphere and stratosphere. Industries employ tracers to study material flow during the manufacturing process, such as the flow of ore pellets in smelting kilns, the paths of wood chips and bleach in paper mills, the diffusion of fungicide into lumber, and in a particularly important application, the porosity and leakage of oil and gas wells in geological formations.

Activation Analysis Another use of tracers is in *neutron activation analysis* (NAA). In this method, neutrons bombard a nonradioactive sample, converting a small fraction of its atoms to radioisotopes, which exhibit characteristic decay patterns, such as γ-ray spectra, that reveal the elements present. Unlike chemical analysis, NAA leaves the sample virtually intact, so the method can be used to determine the composition of a valuable object or a very small sample. For example, a painting thought to be a 16th-century Dutch masterpiece was shown through NAA to be a 20th-century forgery, because a microgram-sized sample of its pigment contained much less silver and antimony than the pigments used by the Dutch masters. Forensic chemists use NAA to detect traces of ammunition on a suspect's hand or traces of arsenic in the hair of a victim of poisoning.

Medical Diagnosis The largest use of radioisotopes is in medical science. In fact, over 25% of U.S. hospital admissions are for diagnoses based on data from radioisotopes. Tracers with half-lives of a few minutes to a few days are employed to observe specific organs and body parts. For example, a healthy thyroid gland incorporates dietary I^- into iodine-containing hormones at a known rate. To assess thyroid function, the patient drinks a solution containing a trace amount of $Na^{131}I$, and a scanning monitor follows the uptake of $^{131}I^-$ into the thyroid (Figure 23.8).

Tracers are also used to measure physiological processes, such as blood flow. The rate at which the heart pumps blood, for example, can be observed by injecting ^{59}Fe, which becomes incorporated into the hemoglobin of blood cells. Several radioisotopes used in medical diagnosis are listed in Table 23.7.

Positron-emission tomography (PET) is a powerful imaging method for observing brain structure and function. A biological substance is synthesized with one of its atoms replaced by an isotope that emits positrons. The substance is injected into a patient's bloodstream, from which it is taken up into the brain. The isotope emits positrons, each of which annihilates a nearby electron. In this process, two γ photons are emitted simultaneously 180° from each other:

$$^0_1\beta + ^{\ \ 0}_{-1}e \longrightarrow 2^0_0\gamma$$

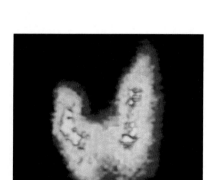

FIGURE 23.8 The use of radioisotopes to image the thyroid gland. Thyroid scanning is used to assess nutritional deficiencies, inflammation, tumor growth, and other thyroid-related ailments. In ^{131}I scanning, the thyroid gland absorbs $^{131}I^-$ ions, which undergo β⁻ decay that exposes a photographic film. The asymmetric image indicates disease.

Table 23.7	**Some Radioisotopes Used as Medical Tracers**
Isotope	**Body Part or Process**
^{11}C, ^{18}F, ^{13}N, ^{15}O	PET studies of brain, heart
^{60}Co, ^{192}Ir	Cancer therapy
^{64}Cu	Metabolism of copper
^{59}Fe	Blood flow, spleen
^{67}Ga	Tumor imaging
^{123}I, ^{131}I	Thyroid
^{111}In	Brain, colon
^{42}K	Blood flow
^{81m}Kr	Lung
^{99m}Tc	Heart, thyroid, liver, lung, bone
^{201}Tl	Heart muscle
^{90}Y	Cancer, arthritis

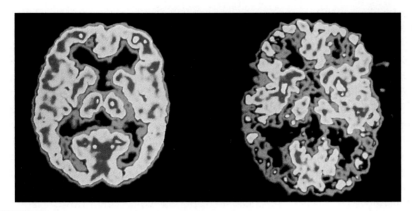

Animation: Nuclear Medicine

FIGURE 23.9 PET and brain activity. These PET scans show brain activity in a normal person *(left)* and in a patient with Alzheimer's disease *(right)*. Red and yellow indicate relatively high activity within a region.

An array of detectors around the patient's head pinpoints the sites of γ emission, and the image is analyzed by computer. Two of the isotopes used are ^{15}O, injected as $H_2{}^{15}$O to measure blood flow, and ^{18}F bonded to a glucose analog to measure glucose uptake, which is an indicator of energy metabolism. Among many fascinating PET findings are those that show how changes in blood flow and glucose uptake accompany normal or abnormal brain activity (Figure 23.9). In a recent nonmedical development, substances incorporating ^{11}C and ^{15}O are being investigated using PET to learn how molecules interact with and move along the surface of a catalyst.

Additional Applications of Ionizing Radiation

To be used as a tracer, a radioisotope need only emit radiation that can be detected. Many other uses of radioisotopes depend on ionizing radiation of higher energy.

Cancer cells divide more rapidly than normal cells, so radioisotopes that interfere with cell division kill more cancer cells than normal ones. Implants of ^{198}Au or of ^{90}Sr, which decays to the γ-emitting ^{90}Y, have been used to destroy pituitary and breast tumor cells, and γ rays from ^{60}Co have been used to destroy tumors of the brain and other body parts.

Irradiation of food increases shelf life by killing microorganisms that cause rotting or spoilage (Figure 23.10), but the practice is quite controversial. Advocates point to the benefits of preserving fresh foods, grains, and seeds for long periods, whereas opponents suggest that irradiation might lower the food's nutritional content or produce harmful byproducts. Irradiation also provides a way to destroy newer, more resistant bacterial strains that survive the increasing use of the more common antibiotics in animal feed. The United Nations has approved irradiation for potatoes, wheat, chicken, and strawberries, and, in 2003, the U.S. Food and Drug Administration approved it as well.

Ionizing radiation has been used to control harmful insects. Captured males are sterilized by radiation and released to mate, thereby reducing the number of offspring. This method has been used to control the Mediterranean fruit fly in California and disease-causing insects, such as the tsetse fly and malarial mosquito, in other parts of the world.

Nonirradiated   Irradiated

FIGURE 23.10 The increased shelf life of irradiated food.

SECTION 23.5 SUMMARY

Radioisotopic tracers have been used to study reaction mechanisms, material flow, elemental composition, and medical conditions. • Ionizing radiation has been used in devices that destroy cancer tissue, kill organisms that spoil food, and control insect populations.

23.6 THE INTERCONVERSION OF MASS AND ENERGY

Most of the nuclear processes we've considered so far have involved radioactive decay, in which a nucleus emits one or a few small particles or photons to become a more stable, slightly lighter nucleus. Two other nuclear processes cause much greater mass changes. In nuclear **fission,** a heavy nucleus splits into two much lighter nuclei, emitting several small particles at the same time. In nuclear **fusion,** the opposite process occurs: two lighter nuclei combine to form a heavier one. Both fission and fusion release enormous quantities of energy. Let's take a look at the origins of this energy by first examining the change in mass that accompanies the breakup of a nucleus into its nucleons and then considering the energy that is equivalent to this mass change.

The Mass Difference Between a Nucleus and Its Nucleons

For almost a century, we have known that mass and energy are interconvertible. Thus, the separate mass and energy conservation laws are combined to state that *the total quantity of mass-energy in the universe is constant.* Therefore, when *any* reacting system releases or absorbs energy, it also loses or gains mass.

This relation between mass and energy is not important for chemical reactions because the energy changes involved in breaking or forming chemical bonds are so small that the mass changes are negligible. For example, when 1 mol of water breaks up into its atoms, heat is absorbed and we have:

$$H_2O(g) \longrightarrow 2H(g) + O(g) \qquad \Delta H°_{rxn} = 2 \times BE \text{ of } O—H = 934 \text{ kJ}$$

We find the mass that is equivalent to this energy from *Einstein's equation:*

$$E = mc^2 \qquad \text{or} \qquad \Delta E = \Delta mc^2 \qquad \text{so} \qquad \Delta m = \frac{\Delta E}{c^2} \qquad (23.7)$$

where Δm is the mass difference between reactants and products:

$$\Delta m = m_{products} - m_{reactants}$$

Substituting the heat of reaction (in J/mol) for ΔE and the numerical value for c $(2.9979 \times 10^8 \text{ m/s})$, we obtain

$$\Delta m = \frac{9.34 \times 10^5 \text{ J/mol}}{(2.9979 \times 10^8 \text{ m/s})^2} = 1.04 \times 10^{-11} \text{ kg/mol} = 1.04 \times 10^{-8} \text{ g/mol}$$

(Units of kg/mol are obtained because the joule includes the kilogram: 1 J = 1 kg·m^2/s^2.) The mass of 1 mol of H_2O molecules (reactant) is about 10 ng *less* than the combined masses of 2 mol of H atoms and 1 mol of O atoms (products), a change difficult to measure with even the most sophisticated balance. Such minute mass changes when bonds break or form allow us to assume that, for all practical purposes, mass is conserved in *chemical* reactions.

The much larger mass change that accompanies a *nuclear* process is related to the enormous energy required to bind the nucleus together from its parts. In an analogy with the calculation above involving the water molecule, consider the change in mass that occurs when one ^{12}C nucleus breaks apart into its nucleons— six protons and six neutrons:

$$^{12}C \longrightarrow 6^1_1p + 6^1_0n$$

We calculate this mass difference in a special way. By combining the mass of six H *atoms* and six neutrons and then subtracting the mass of one ^{12}C *atom,* the masses of the electrons cancel: six e$^-$ (in six ^1H atoms) cancel six e$^-$ (in one ^{12}C atom). The mass of one ^1H atom is 1.007825 amu, and the mass of one neutron is 1.008665 amu, so

$$\text{Mass of six }^1H \text{ atoms} = 6 \times 1.007825 \text{ amu} = 6.046950 \text{ amu}$$
$$\underline{\text{Mass of six neutrons} = 6 \times 1.008665 \text{ amu} = 6.051990 \text{ amu}}$$
$$\text{Total mass} = 12.098940 \text{ amu}$$

The mass of the reactant, one ^{12}C atom, is 12 amu (exactly). The mass difference (Δm) we obtain is the total mass of the nucleons minus the mass of the nucleus:

$$\Delta m = 12.098940 \text{ amu} - 12.000000 \text{ amu}$$
$$= 0.098940 \text{ amu}/^{12}\text{C} = 0.098940 \text{ g/mol } ^{12}\text{C}$$

First, and most important, note that *the mass of the nucleus is **less** than the combined masses of its nucleons:* there is *always* a mass decrease when nucleons form a nucleus. Second, note that the mass change of this nuclear process (9.89×10^{-2} g/mol) is nearly 10 million times that of the chemical process (10.4×10^{-9} g/mol) we saw earlier and easily observed on any laboratory balance.

Nuclear Binding Energy and the Binding Energy per Nucleon

Once again, Einstein's equation for the relation between mass and energy allows us to find the energy equivalent of the mass change. For ^{12}C, after converting grams to kilograms, we have

$$\Delta E = \Delta mc^2 = (9.8940 \times 10^{-5} \text{ kg/mol})(2.9979 \times 10^8 \text{ m/s})^2$$
$$= 8.8921 \times 10^{12} \text{ J/mol} = 8.8921 \times 10^9 \text{ kJ/mol}$$

This quantity of energy is called the **nuclear binding energy** for carbon-12. The nuclear binding energy is the energy required to break *1 mol of nuclei into their individual nucleons:*

$$\text{Nucleus} + \text{nuclear binding energy} \longrightarrow \text{nucleons}$$

Thus, the nuclear binding energy is qualitatively analogous to the sum of bond energies of a covalent compound or the lattice energy of an ionic compound. But, quantitatively, nuclear binding energies are typically several million times greater.

We use joules to express the binding energy per mole of nuclei, but the joule is much too large a unit to express the binding energy of a single nucleus. Instead, nuclear scientists use the **electron volt (eV)**, the energy an electron acquires when it moves through a potential difference of 1 volt:

$$1 \text{ eV} = 1.602 \times 10^{-19} \text{ J}$$

Binding energies are commonly expressed in millions of electron volts, that is, in *mega–electron volts* (MeV):

$$1 \text{ MeV} = 10^6 \text{ eV} = 1.602 \times 10^{-13} \text{ J}$$

A particularly useful factor converts the atomic mass unit to its energy equivalent in electron volts:

$$1 \text{ amu} = 931.5 \times 10^6 \text{ eV} = 931.5 \text{ MeV} \qquad (23.8)$$

Earlier we found the mass change when ^{12}C breaks apart into its nucleons to be 0.098940 amu. The binding energy per ^{12}C nucleus, expressed in MeV, is

$$\frac{\text{Binding energy}}{^{12}\text{C nucleus}} = 0.098940 \text{ amu} \times \frac{931.5 \text{ MeV}}{1 \text{ amu}} = 92.16 \text{ MeV}$$

We can compare the stability of nuclides of different elements by determining the *binding energy per nucleon.* For ^{12}C, we have

$$\text{Binding energy per nucleon} = \frac{\text{binding energy}}{\text{no. of nucleons}} = \frac{92.16 \text{ MeV}}{12 \text{ nucleons}} = 7.680 \text{ MeV/nucleon}$$

SAMPLE PROBLEM 23.6 Calculating the Binding Energy per Nucleon

Problem Iron-56 is an extremely stable nuclide. Compute the binding energy per nucleon for ^{56}Fe and compare it with that for ^{12}C (mass of ^{56}Fe atom = 55.934939 amu; mass of ^{1}H atom = 1.007825 amu; mass of neutron = 1.008665 amu).

Plan Iron-56 has 26 protons and 30 neutrons. We calculate the mass difference, Δm, when the nucleus forms by subtracting the given mass of one ^{56}Fe atom from the sum of the masses of 26 ^{1}H atoms and 30 neutrons. To find the binding energy per nucleon, we multiply Δm by the equivalent in MeV (931.5 MeV/amu) and divide by the number of nucleons (56).

Solution Calculating the mass difference, Δm:

Mass difference = $[(26 \times \text{mass } ^1\text{H atom}) + (30 \times \text{mass neutron})] - \text{mass } ^{56}\text{Fe atom}$
$= [(26)(1.007825 \text{ amu}) + (30)(1.008665 \text{ amu})] - 55.934939 \text{ amu}$
$= 0.52846 \text{ amu}$

Calculating the binding energy per nucleon:

$$\text{Binding energy per nucleon} = \frac{0.52846 \text{ amu} \times 931.5 \text{ MeV/amu}}{56 \text{ nucleons}} = 8.790 \text{ MeV/nucleon}$$

An ^{56}Fe nucleus would require more energy per nucleon to break up into its nucleons than would ^{12}C (7.680 MeV/nucleon), so ^{56}Fe is more stable than ^{12}C.

Check The answer is consistent with the great stability of ^{56}Fe. Given the number of decimal places in the values, rounding to check the math is useful only to find a *major* error. The number of nucleons (56) is an exact number, so we retain four significant figures.

FOLLOW-UP PROBLEM 23.6 Uranium-235 is an essential component of the fuel in nuclear power plants. Calculate the binding energy per nucleon for ^{235}U. Is this nuclide more or less stable than ^{12}C (mass of ^{235}U atom = 235.043924 amu)?

Fission or Fusion: Means of Increasing the Binding Energy Per Nucleon Calculations similar to those in Sample Problem 23.6 for other nuclides show that the binding energy per nucleon varies considerably. The essential point is that *the greater the binding energy per nucleon, the more stable the nuclide.*

Figure 23.11 shows a plot of the binding energy per nucleon vs. mass number. It provides information about nuclide stability and the two possible processes nuclides can undergo to form more stable nuclides. Most nuclides with fewer than 10 nucleons have a relatively small binding energy per nucleon. The ^{4}He nucleus is an exception—it is stable enough to be emitted intact as an α particle. Above $A = 12$, the binding energy per nucleon varies from about 7.6 to 8.8 MeV.

FIGURE 23.11 The variation in binding energy per nucleon. A plot of the binding energy per nucleon vs. mass number shows that nuclear stability is greatest in the region near ^{56}Fe. Lighter nuclei may undergo fusion to become more stable; heavier ones may undergo fission. Note the exceptional stability of ^{4}He among extremely light nuclei.

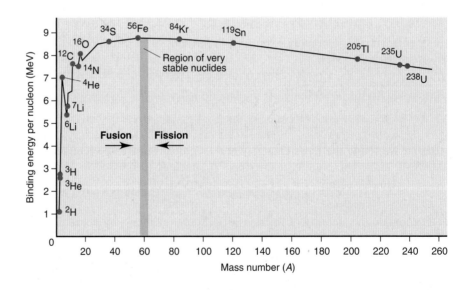

The most important observation is that *the binding energy per nucleon peaks at elements with $A \approx 60$.* In other words, nuclides become more stable with increasing mass number up to around 60 nucleons and then become less stable with higher numbers of nucleons. The existence of a peak of stability suggests that there are two ways nuclides can increase their binding energy per nucleon:

- *Fission.* A heavier nucleus can *split into lighter ones (closer to $A \approx 60$)* by undergoing fission. The product nuclei have greater binding energy per nucleon (are more stable) than the reactant nucleus, and the difference in *energy is released.* Nuclear power plants generate energy through fission, as do atomic bombs.

- *Fusion.* Lighter nuclei, on the other hand, can *combine to form a heavier one (closer to A ≈ 60)* by undergoing fusion. Once again, the product is more stable than the reactants, and *energy is released.* The Sun and other stars generate energy through fusion, as do thermonuclear (hydrogen) bombs. In these examples and in all current research efforts for developing fusion as a useful energy source, hydrogen nuclei fuse to form the very stable helium-4 nucleus.

In Section 23.7, we examine fission and fusion and the industrial energy facilities designed to utilize them.

> ### SECTION 23.6 SUMMARY
> The mass of a nucleus is less than the sum of the masses of its nucleons. The energy equivalent to this mass difference is the nuclear binding energy, often expressed in units of MeV. • The binding energy per nucleon is a measure of nuclide stability and varies with the number of nucleons. Nuclides with $A ≈ 60$ are most stable. • Lighter nuclides join (fusion) or heavier nuclides split (fission) to create more stable products.

23.7 APPLICATIONS OF FISSION AND FUSION

Of the many beneficial applications of nuclear reactions, the greatest is the potential for almost limitless amounts of energy. Our experience with nuclear energy from power plants, however, has shown that we must improve ways to tap this energy source safely and economically and deal with the waste generated. In this section, we discuss how fission and fusion occur and how we are applying them.

The Process of Nuclear Fission

During the mid-1930s, scientists bombarded uranium ($Z = 92$) with neutrons in an attempt to synthesize transuranium elements. Many of the unstable nuclides produced were tentatively identified as having $Z > 92$, but four years later, one of these was shown to be an isotope of barium ($Z = 56$). The Austrian physicist Lise Meitner and her nephew, Otto Frisch, proposed that barium resulted from the *splitting* of the uranium nucleus into *smaller* nuclei, a process that they called *fission* as an analogy to cell division in biology.

The ^{235}U nucleus can split in many different ways, giving rise to various daughter nuclei, but all routes have the same general features. Figure 23.12 depicts one of these fission patterns. Neutron bombardment results in a highly excited ^{236}U nucleus, which splits apart in 10^{-14} s. The products are two nuclei of unequal

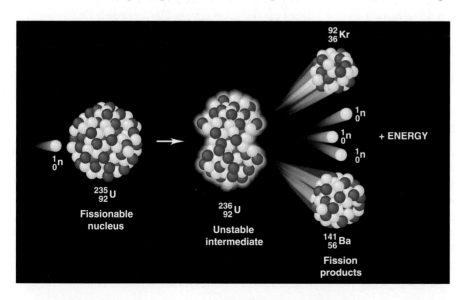

FIGURE 23.12 Induced fission of ^{235}U. A neutron bombarding a ^{235}U nucleus results in an extremely unstable ^{236}U nucleus, which becomes distorted in the act of splitting. In this case, which shows one of many possible splitting patterns, the products are ^{92}Kr and ^{141}Ba. Three neutrons and a great deal of energy are also released.

FIGURE 23.13 A chain reaction of ^{235}U.
If a sample exceeds the critical mass, neutrons produced by the first fission event collide with other nuclei, causing their fission and the production of more neutrons to continue the process. Note that various product nuclei form. The vertical dashed lines identify succeeding "generations" of neutrons.

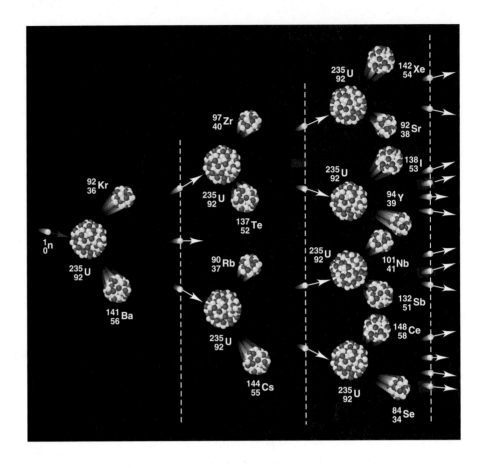

mass, two or three neutrons (average of 2.4), and a large quantity of energy. A single ^{235}U nucleus releases 3.5×10^{-11} J when it splits; 1 mol of ^{235}U (about $\frac{1}{2}$ lb) releases 2.1×10^{13} J—a billion times as much energy as burning $\frac{1}{2}$ lb of coal (about 2×10^4 J)!

We harness the energy of nuclear fission, much of which eventually appears as heat, by means of a **chain reaction,** illustrated in Figure 23.13: the two to three neutrons that are released by the fission of one nucleus collide with other fissionable nuclei and cause them to split, releasing more neutrons, which then collide with other nuclei, and so on, in a self-sustaining process. In this manner, the energy released increases rapidly because each fission event in a chain reaction releases two to three times as much energy as the preceding one.

Whether a chain reaction occurs depends on the mass (and thus the volume) of the fissionable sample. If the piece of uranium is large enough, the product neutrons strike another fissionable nucleus *before* flying out of the sample, and a chain reaction takes place. The mass required to achieve a chain reaction is called the **critical mass.** If the sample has less than the critical mass (a *subcritical mass*), too many product neutrons leave the sample before they collide with and cause the fission of another ^{235}U nucleus, and thus a chain reaction does not occur.

Nuclear Energy Reactors Like a coal-fired power plant, *a nuclear power plant generates heat to produce steam, which turns a turbine attached to an electric generator.* But a nuclear plant has the potential to produce electric power much more cleanly than can the combustion of coal.

Heat generation takes place in the **reactor core** of a nuclear plant (Figure 23.14). The core contains the *fuel rods,* which consist of fuel enclosed in tubes of a corrosion-resistant zirconium alloy. The fuel is uranium(IV) oxide (UO$_2$) that has been *enriched* from 0.7% ^{235}U, the natural abundance of this fissionable isotope, to the 3% to 4% ^{235}U required to sustain a chain reaction in a practical volume.

FIGURE 23.14 A light-water nuclear reactor. A, Photo of a facility showing the concrete containment shell and nearby water source. **B,** Schematic of a light-water reactor.

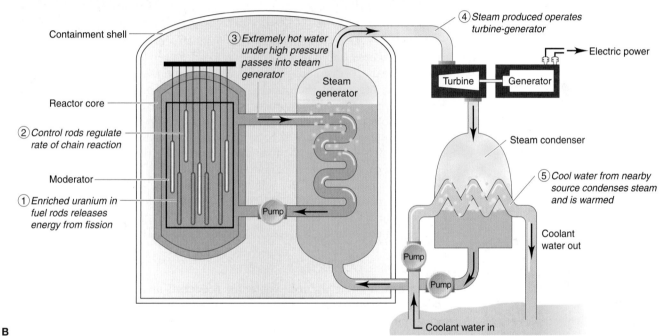

B

Sandwiched between the fuel rods are movable *control rods* made of cadmium or boron (or, in nuclear submarines, hafnium), substances that absorb neutrons very efficiently. When the control rods are moved between the fuel rods, the chain reaction slows because fewer neutrons are available to bombard uranium atoms; when they are removed, the chain reaction speeds up. Neutrons that leave the fuel-rod assembly collide with a *reflector,* usually made of a beryllium alloy, which absorbs very few neutrons. Reflecting the neutrons back to the fuel rods speeds the chain reaction.

Flowing around the fuel and control rods in the reactor core is the *moderator,* a substance that slows the neutrons, making them much better at causing fission than the fast ones emerging directly from the fission event. In most modern reactors, the moderator also acts as the *coolant,* the fluid that transfers the released heat to the steam-producing region. *Light-water reactors* use H_2O as the moderator because ^1H absorbs neutrons to some extent. Heavy-water reactors use D_2O because it absorbs very few neutrons, leaving more available for fission. Thus, heavy-water reactors can use uranium that has been *less enriched.* As the coolant flows around the encased fuel, pumps circulate it through coils that transfer its heat to the water reservoir. Steam formed in the reservoir turns the turbine that runs the generator. The steam is then condensed in large cooling towers, using water from a lake or river to absorb heat, and returned to the water reservoir.

Some major accidents at nuclear plants have caused decidedly negative public reactions. In 1979, malfunctions of coolant pumps and valves at the Three-Mile Island facility in Pennsylvania led to melting of some of the fuel and damage to the reactor core, but the release of only a very small amount (about 1 Ci) of radioactive gases into the atmosphere. In 1986, a million times as much radioactivity (1 MCi) was released when a cooling system failure at the Chernobyl plant in Ukraine caused a much greater melting of fuel and an uncontrolled reaction. High-pressure steam and ignited graphite moderator rods caused the reactor building to explode and expel radioactive debris. Carried by prevailing winds, the radioactive particles contaminated vegetables and milk in much of Europe.

Despite potential safety problems, nuclear power remains an important source of electricity. Since the late 1990s, nearly every European country has employed nuclear power, and it is the major power source in some countries—50% of the electricity in Sweden and almost 80% in France. Currently, the United States obtains about 20% of its electricity from nuclear power, and Canada slightly less.

However, even a smoothly operating plant has certain inherent problems. The problem of *thermal pollution* is common to all power plants. Water used to condense the steam is several degrees warmer when returned to its source, which can harm aquatic organisms (Section 13.3). A more serious problem is *nuclear waste disposal*. Many of the fission products formed in nuclear reactors have long half-lives, and no satisfactory plan for their permanent disposal has yet been devised. Proposals to place the waste in containers and bury them in deep bedrock cannot possibly be field-tested for the thousands of years the material will remain harmful. Leakage of radioactive material into groundwater is a danger, and earthquakes can occur even in geologically stable regions. Despite studies indicating that the proposed disposal site at Yucca Mountain, Nevada, is too geologically active, the U.S. government approved the site. It remains to be seen whether we can operate fission reactors *and* dispose of the waste safely and economically.

The Promise of Nuclear Fusion

Nuclear fusion is the ultimate source of nearly all the energy on Earth because almost all other sources depend, directly or indirectly, on the energy produced by nuclear fusion in the Sun. But the Sun and other stars generate more than energy; in fact, *all the elements larger than hydrogen were formed in fusion and decay processes within stars.*

Much research is being devoted to making nuclear fusion a practical, direct source of energy on Earth. To understand the advantages of fusion, let's consider one of the most discussed fusion reactions, in which deuterium and tritium react:

$$^2_1H + {}^3_1H \longrightarrow {}^4_2He + {}^1_0n$$

This reaction produces 1.7×10^9 kJ/mol, an enormous quantity of energy with no radioactive byproducts. Moreover, the reactant nuclei are relatively easy to come by. Thus, in principle, fusion seems very promising and may represent an ideal source of power. However, some extremely difficult technical problems remain. Fusion requires enormous energy in the form of heat to give the positively charged nuclei enough kinetic energy to force themselves together. The fusion of deuterium and tritium, for example, occurs at practical rates at about 10^8 K, a temperature hotter than the Sun's core! How can such conditions be achieved?

Two research approaches hold promise. In one, atoms are stripped of their electrons at high temperatures, resulting in a gaseous *plasma*, a neutral mixture of positive nuclei and electrons. Because extreme temperatures are needed for fusion, no *material* can contain the plasma. The most successful approach to date has been to enclose the plasma within a magnetic field. Figure 23.15 shows the

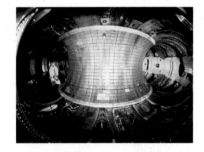

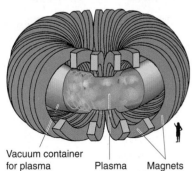

Vacuum container
for plasma   Plasma   Magnets

FIGURE 23.15 The tokamak design for magnetic containment of a fusion plasma. The donut-shaped chamber of the tokamak (photo, *top;* schematic, *bottom*) contains the plasma within a helical magnetic field.

tokamak design: a donut-shaped container in which a helical magnetic field confines the plasma and prevents it from contacting the walls. Scientists at the Princeton University Plasma Physics facility have achieved some success in generating energy from fusion this way. In another approach, the high temperature is reached by using many focused lasers to compress and heat the fusion reactants. In any event, one or more major breakthroughs are needed before fusion will be realized as a practical, everyday source of energy.

SECTION 23.7 SUMMARY

In nuclear fission, neutron bombardment causes a nucleus to split into two smaller nuclei and release neutrons that split other nuclei, giving rise to a chain reaction. • A nuclear power plant controls the rate of the chain reaction to produce heat that creates steam, which is used to generate electricity. • Potential hazards, such as radiation leaks, thermal pollution, and disposal of nuclear waste, remain current concerns. • Nuclear fusion holds great promise as a source of clean abundant energy, but it requires extremely high temperatures and is not yet practical.

CHAPTER REVIEW GUIDE

The following sections provide many aids to help you study this chapter. (Numbers in parentheses refer to pages, unless noted otherwise.)

● **LEARNING OBJECTIVES** *These are concepts and skills to review after studying this chapter.*

Related section (§), sample problem (SP), and end-of-chapter problem (EP) numbers are listed in parentheses.

1. Describe the differences between nuclear and chemical changes; identify the three types of radioactive emissions and the types of radioactive decay, and know how each changes A and Z; explain how a decay series leads to a stable nuclide; write and balance nuclear equations; use the N/Z ratio to predict nuclear stability and the type of decay a nuclide undergoes (§ 23.1) (SPs 23.1–23.3) (EPs 23.1–23.16)
2. Understand why radioactive decay is a first-order process and the meaning of half-life; convert among units of radioactivity, and calculate specific activity, decay constant, half-life, and number of nuclei; estimate the age of an object from its specific activity (§ 23.2) (SPs 23.4, 23.5) (EPs 23.17–23.30)
3. Describe how particle accelerators are used to synthesize new nuclides and write balanced equations for nuclear transmutations (§ 23.3) (EPs 23.31–23.35)

4. Distinguish between excitation and ionization, and describe their effects on matter; convert among units of radiation dose, and understand the penetrating power of emissions and how ionizing radiation is used beneficially (§ 23.4) (EPs 23.36–23.42)
5. Describe how radioisotopes are used in research, elemental analysis, and diagnosis (§ 23.5) (EPs 23.43–23.45)
6. Explain the mass difference and how it is related to nuclear binding energy; understand how nuclear stability is related to binding energy per nucleon and why unstable nuclides undergo either fission or fusion; use Einstein's equation to find mass-energy equivalence in J and eV; compare nuclide stability from binding energy per nucleon (§ 23.6) (SP 23.6) (EPs 23.46–23.52)
7. Discuss the pros and cons of power generation by nuclear fission, and evaluate the potential of nuclear fusion (§ 23.7) (EPs 23.53–23.59)

● **KEY TERMS** *These important terms appear in boldface in the chapter and are defined again in the Glossary.*

Section 23.1
radioactivity (785)
nucleon (786)
nuclide (786)
isotope (786)
alpha (α) particle (786)
beta (β) particle (786)
gamma (γ) ray (786)
alpha (α) decay (788)
beta (β) decay (788)
β⁻ decay (788)
positron (β⁺) emission (788)
positron (788)

electron (e⁻) capture (EC) (788)
gamma (γ) emission (789)
band of stability (790)
decay (disintegration)
  series (792)

Section 23.2
activity ($\mathcal{A}$) (793)
becquerel (Bq) (793)
curie (Ci) (793)
decay constant (794)
half-life ($t_{1/2}$) (794)
radioisotopic dating (796)
radioisotope (796)

Section 23.3
nuclear transmutation (797)
deuteron (797)
particle accelerator (797)
transuranium element (798)

Section 23.4
ionization (799)
ionizing radiation (799)
gray (Gy) (799)
rad (*radiation-absorbed dose*) (799)
rem (*roentgen equivalent for man*) (799)

sievert (Sv) (799)
background radiation (800)

Section 23.5
tracer (801)

Section 23.6
fission (804)
fusion (804)
nuclear binding energy (805)
electron volt (eV) (805)

Section 23.7
chain reaction (808)
critical mass (808)
reactor core (808)

• KEY EQUATIONS AND RELATIONSHIPS *Numbered and screened concepts are listed for you to refer to or memorize.*

23.1 Balancing a nuclear equation (786):

$$\text{Total } A\text{ Reactants} = \text{Total } A\text{ Products}$$
$$\text{Total } Z\text{ Reactants} = \text{Total } Z\text{ Products}$$

23.2 Defining the unit of radioactivity (curie, Ci) (793):

$$1 \text{ Ci} = 3.70 \times 10^{10} \text{ disintegrations per second (d/s)}$$

23.3 Expressing the decay rate (activity) for radioactive nuclei (794):

$$\text{Decay rate } (\mathscr{A}) = -\frac{\Delta \mathscr{N}}{\Delta t} = k\mathscr{N}$$

23.4 Finding the number of nuclei remaining after a given time, $\mathscr{N}_t$ (794):

$$\mathscr{N}_t = \mathscr{N}_0 e^{-kt} \quad \text{and} \quad \ln\frac{\mathscr{N}_0}{\mathscr{N}_t} = kt$$

23.5 Finding the half-life of a radioactive nuclide (794):

$$t_{1/2} = \frac{\ln 2}{k}$$

23.6 Calculating the time to reach a given specific activity (age of an object in radioisotopic dating) (796):

$$t = \frac{1}{k} \ln\frac{\mathscr{A}_0}{\mathscr{A}_t}$$

23.7 Adapting Einstein's equation to calculate mass difference and/or nuclear binding energy (804):

$$\Delta m = \frac{\Delta E}{c^2} \quad \text{or} \quad \Delta E = \Delta mc^2$$

23.8 Relating the atomic mass unit to its energy equivalent in MeV (805):

$$1 \text{ amu} = 931.5 \times 10^6 \text{ eV} = 931.5 \text{ MeV}$$

• BRIEF SOLUTIONS TO **FOLLOW-UP PROBLEMS** *Compare your own solutions to these calculation steps and answers.*

23.1 $^{133}_{54}\text{Xe} \longrightarrow {}^{133}_{55}\text{Cs} + {}^{0}_{-1}\beta$

23.2 Phosphorus-31 has a slightly higher N/Z ratio and an even N (16).

23.3 (a) $N/Z = 1.35$; too high for this region of band: β decay
(b) Mass too high for stability: α decay

23.4 $\ln \mathscr{A}_t = -kt + \ln \mathscr{A}_0$

$$= -\left(\frac{\ln 2}{15 \text{ h}} \times 4.0 \text{ days} \times \frac{24 \text{ h}}{1 \text{ day}}\right) + \ln(2.5\times10^9)$$
$$= 17.20$$
$$\mathscr{A}_t = 3.0\times10^7 \text{ d/s}$$

23.5 $t = \frac{1}{k} \ln\frac{\mathscr{A}_0}{\mathscr{A}_t} = \frac{5730 \text{ yr}}{\ln 2} \ln\left(\frac{15.3 \text{ d/min·g}}{9.41 \text{ d/min·g}}\right) = 4.02\times10^3 \text{ yr}$

The mummy case is about 4000 years old.

23.6 ^{235}U has 92 $^{1}_{1}\text{p}$ and 143 $^{1}_{0}\text{n}$.

$\Delta m = [(92 \times 1.007825 \text{ amu}) + (143 \times 1.008665 \text{ amu})]$
$\qquad\qquad - 235.043924 \text{ amu} = 1.9151 \text{ amu}$

$$\frac{\text{Binding energy}}{\text{nucleon}} = \frac{1.9151 \text{ amu} \times \dfrac{931.5 \text{ MeV}}{1 \text{ amu}}}{235 \text{ nucleons}}$$

$$= 7.591 \text{ MeV/nucleon}$$

Therefore, ^{235}U is less stable than ^{12}C.

PROBLEMS

Problems with colored numbers are answered in Appendix E. Sections match the text and provide the numbers of relevant sample problems. Bracketed problems are grouped in pairs (indicated by a short rule) that cover the same concept. Comprehensive Problems are based on material from any section or previous chapter.

Radioactive Decay and Nuclear Stability
(Sample Problems 23.1 to 23.3)

23.1 How do chemical and nuclear reactions differ in
(a) Magnitude of the energy change?
(b) Effect on rate of increasing temperature?
(c) Effect on rate of higher reactant concentration?
(d) Effect on yield of higher reactant concentration?

23.2 Which of the following types of radioactive decay produce an atom of a *different* element: (a) alpha; (b) beta; (c) gamma; (d) positron; (e) electron capture? Show how Z and N change, if at all, with each type.

23.3 Why is $^{3}_{2}\text{He}$ stable but $^{2}_{2}\text{He}$ so unstable that it has never been detected?

23.4 How do the modes of decay differ for a neutron-rich nuclide and a proton-rich nuclide?

23.5 Why can't you use the position of a nuclide's N/Z ratio relative to the band of stability to predict whether it is more likely to decay by positron emission or by electron capture?

23.6 Write balanced nuclear equations for the following:
(a) Alpha decay of $^{234}_{92}\text{U}$
(b) Electron capture by neptunium-232
(c) Positron emission by $^{12}_{7}\text{N}$

23.7 Write balanced nuclear equations for the following:
(a) β^- decay of sodium-26
(b) β^- decay of francium-223
(c) α decay of $^{212}_{83}\text{Bi}$

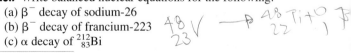

23.8 Write balanced nuclear equations for the following:
(a) Formation of $^{48}_{22}\text{Ti}$ through positron emission
(b) Formation of silver-107 through electron capture
(c) Formation of polonium-206 through alpha decay

23.9 Write balanced nuclear equations for the following:
(a) Production of $^{241}_{95}$Am through β^- decay
(b) Formation of $^{228}_{89}$Ac through β^- decay
(c) Formation of $^{203}_{83}$Bi through α decay

23.10 Which nuclide(s) would you predict to be stable? Why?
(a) $^{20}_{8}$O   (b) $^{59}_{27}$Co   (c) $^{9}_{3}$Li

23.11 Which nuclide(s) would you predict to be stable? Why?
(a) $^{146}_{60}$Nd   (b) $^{114}_{48}$Cd   (c) $^{88}_{42}$Mo

23.12 What is the most likely mode of decay for each?
(a) $^{238}_{92}$U   (b) $^{48}_{24}$Cr   (c) $^{50}_{25}$Mn

23.13 What is the most likely mode of decay for each?
(a) $^{61}_{26}$Fe   (b) $^{41}_{17}$Cl   (c) $^{110}_{44}$Ru

23.14 Why is $^{52}_{24}$Cr the most stable isotope of chromium?

23.15 Why is $^{40}_{20}$Ca the most stable isotope of calcium?

23.16 Neptunium-237 is the parent nuclide of a decay series that starts with α emission, followed by β^- emission, and then two more α emissions. Write a balanced nuclear equation for each step.

The Kinetics of Radioactive Decay
(Sample Problems 23.4 and 23.5)

23.17 What is the reaction order of radioactive decay? Explain.

23.18 After 1 minute, half the radioactive nuclei remain from an original sample of six nuclei. Is it valid to conclude that $t_{1/2}$ equals 1 minute? Would this conclusion be valid if the original sample contained 6×10^{12} nuclei? Explain.

23.19 Radioisotopic dating depends on the constant rate of decay and formation of various nuclides in a sample. How is the proportion of ^{14}C kept relatively constant in living organisms?

23.20 What is the specific activity (in Ci/g) if 1.55 mg of an isotope emits 1.66×10^{6} α particles per second?

23.21 What is the specific activity (in Bq/g) if 8.58 μg of an isotope emits 7.4×10^{4} α particles per minute?

23.22 If 1.00×10^{-12} mol of ^{135}Cs emits 1.39×10^{5} β particles in 1.00 yr, what is the decay constant?

23.23 If 6.40×10^{-9} mol of ^{176}W emits 1.07×10^{15} positrons in 1.00 h, what is the decay constant?

23.24 The isotope $^{212}_{83}$Bi has a half-life of 1.01 yr. What mass (in mg) of a 2.00-mg sample will not have decayed after 3.75×10^{3} h?

23.25 The half-life of radium-226 is 1.60×10^{3} yr. How many hours will it take for a 2.50-g sample to decay to the point where 0.185 g of the isotope remains?

23.26 A rock contains 270 μmol of ^{238}U ($t_{1/2} = 4.5\times10^{9}$ yr) and 110 μmol of ^{206}Pb. Assuming that all the ^{206}Pb comes from decay of the ^{238}U, estimate the rock's age.

23.27 A fabric remnant from a burial site has a ^{14}C/^{12}C ratio of 0.735 of the original value. How old is the fabric?

23.28 Due to decay of ^{40}K, cow's milk has a specific activity of about 6×10^{-11} mCi per milliliter. How many disintegrations of ^{40}K nuclei are there per minute in 1.0 qt of milk?

23.29 Plutonium-239 ($t_{1/2} = 2.41\times10^{4}$ yr) represents a serious nuclear waste disposal problem. If seven half-lives are required to reach a tolerable level of radioactivity, how long must ^{239}Pu be stored?

23.30 A volcanic eruption melts a large area of rock, and all gases are expelled. After cooling, $^{40}_{18}$Ar accumulates from the ongoing decay of $^{40}_{19}$K in the rock ($t_{1/2} = 1.25\times10^{9}$ yr). When a piece of rock is analyzed, it is found to contain 1.38 mmol of ^{40}K and 1.14 mmol of ^{40}Ar. How long ago did the rock cool?

Nuclear Transmutation: Induced Changes in Nuclei

23.31 Why must the electrical polarity of the tubes in a linear accelerator be reversed at very short time intervals?

23.32 Why does bombardment with protons usually require higher energies than bombardment with neutrons?

23.33 Name the unidentified species in each transmutation, and write a full nuclear equation:
(a) Bombardment of ^{10}B with an α particle yields a neutron and a nuclide.
(b) Bombardment of ^{28}Si with ^{2}H yields ^{29}P and another particle.
(c) Bombardment of a nuclide with an α particle yields two neutrons and ^{244}Cf.

23.34 Name the unidentified species in each transmutation, and write a full nuclear equation:
(a) Bombardment of a nuclide with a γ photon yields a proton, a neutron, and ^{29}Si.
(b) Bombardment of ^{252}Cf with ^{10}B yields five neutrons and a nuclide.
(c) Bombardment of ^{238}U with a particle yields three neutrons and ^{239}Pu.

23.35 Elements 104, 105, and 106 have been named rutherfordium (Rf), dubnium (Db), and seaborgium (Sg), respectively. These elements are synthesized from californium-249 by bombardment with carbon-12, nitrogen-15, and oxygen-18 nuclei, respectively. Four neutrons are formed in each reaction as well. Write balanced nuclear equations for the formation of these elements.

The Effects of Nuclear Radiation on Matter

23.36 The effects on matter of γ rays and α particles differ. Explain.

23.37 Why is ionizing radiation more dangerous to children than to adults?

23.38 A 135-lb person absorbs 3.3×10^{-7} J of energy from radioactive emissions. (a) How many rads does she receive? (b) How many grays (Gy) does she receive?

23.39 A 3.6-kg laboratory animal receives a single dose of 8.92×10^{-4} Gy. (a) How many rads did the animal receive? (b) How many joules did the animal absorb?

23.40 A 70.-kg person exposed to ^{90}Sr absorbs 6.0×10^{5} β^- particles, each with an energy of 8.74×10^{-14} J. (a) How many grays does the person receive? (b) If the RBE is 1.0, how many millirems is this? (c) What is the equivalent dose in sieverts (Sv)?

23.41 A laboratory rat weighs 265 g and absorbs 1.77×10^{10} β^- particles, each with an energy of 2.20×10^{-13} J. (a) How many rads does the animal receive? (b) What is this dose in Gy? (c) If the RBE is 0.75, what is the equivalent dose in Sv?

23.42 A small region of a cancer patient's brain is exposed for 24.0 min to 475 Bq of radioactivity from ^{60}Co for treatment of a tumor. If the brain mass exposed is 1.858 g and each β^- particle emitted has an energy of 5.05×10^{-14} J, what is the dose in rads?

Applications of Radioisotopes

23.43 Describe two ways that radioactive tracers are used in organisms.

23.44 Why is neutron activation analysis (NAA) useful to art historians and criminologists?

23.45 The oxidation of methanol to formaldehyde can be accomplished by reaction with chromic acid:

$$6H^+(aq) + 3CH_3OH(aq) + 2H_2CrO_4(aq) \longrightarrow$$
$$3CH_2O(aq) + 2Cr^{3+}(aq) + 8H_2O(l)$$

The reaction can be studied with the stable isotope tracer ^{18}O and mass spectrometry. When a small amount of $CH_3^{18}OH$ is present in the alcohol reactant, $CH_2^{18}O$ forms. When a small amount of $H_2Cr^{18}O_4$ is present, $H_2^{18}O$ forms. Does chromic acid or methanol supply the O atom to the aldehyde? Explain.

The Interconversion of Mass and Energy
(Sample Problem 23.6)

Note: Use the following data to solve the problems in this section: mass of ^1H atom = 1.007825 amu; mass of neutron = 1.008665 amu.

23.46 What is a mass difference, and how does it arise?

23.47 What is the binding energy per nucleon? Why is the binding energy per nucleon, rather than per nuclide, used to compare nuclide stability?

23.48 A ^3H nucleus decays with an energy of 0.01861 MeV. Convert this energy into (a) electron volts; (b) joules.

23.49 Arsenic-84 decays with an energy of 1.57×10^{-15} kJ per nucleus. Convert this energy into (a) eV; (b) MeV.

23.50 Cobalt-59 is the only stable isotope of this transition metal. One ^{59}Co atom has a mass of 58.933198 amu. Calculate the binding energy (a) per nucleon in MeV; (b) per atom in MeV; (c) per mole in kJ.

23.51 Iodine-131 is one of the most important isotopes used in the diagnosis of thyroid cancer. One atom has a mass of 130.906114 amu. Calculate the binding energy (a) per nucleon in MeV; (b) per atom in MeV; (c) per mole in kJ.

23.52 The ^{80}Br nuclide decays by either β^- decay or e^- capture. (a) What is the product of each process? (b) Which process releases more energy? (Masses of atoms: ^{80}Br = 79.918528 amu; ^{80}Kr = 79.916380 amu; ^{80}Se = 79.916520 amu; neglect the mass of the electron involved.)

Applications of Fission and Fusion

23.53 In what main way is fission different from radioactive decay? Are all fission events in a chain reaction identical? Explain.

23.54 What is the purpose of enrichment in the preparation of fuel rods?

23.55 Describe the nature and purpose of these components of a nuclear reactor: (a) control rods; (b) moderator.

23.56 State an advantage and a disadvantage of heavy-water reactors compared to light-water reactors.

23.57 What are the expected advantages of fusion reactors over fission reactors?

23.58 The reaction that will probably power the first commercial fusion reactor is $^3_1H + ^2_1H \longrightarrow ^4_2He + ^1_0n$. How much energy would be produced per mole of reaction? (Masses of atoms: ^3_1H = 3.01605 amu; ^2_1H = 2.0140 amu; ^4_2He = 4.00260 amu; mass of ^1_0n = 1.008665 amu.)

23.59 Write balanced nuclear equations for the following:
(a) β^- decay of sodium-26
(b) β^- decay of francium-223
(c) α decay of $^{212}_{83}Bi$

Comprehensive Problems
Problems with an asterisk (*) are more challenging.

23.60 Some $^{243}_{95}Am$ was present when Earth formed, but it all decayed in the next billion years. The first three steps in this decay series are emission of an α particle, a β^- particle, and another α particle. What other isotopes were present on the young Earth in a rock that contained some $^{243}_{95}Am$?

23.61 The scene below depicts a neutron bombarding ^{235}U:

$$^1_0 \bigcirc + ^{235}_{92} \bigcirc \longrightarrow ^{144}_{55} \bullet + \bullet_? + 2\, ^1_0 \bigcirc$$

(a) Is this an example of fission or of fusion? (b) Identify the other nuclide formed. (c) What is the most likely mode of decay of the nuclide with $Z = 55$?

23.62 Curium-243 undergoes α decay to plutonium-239:

$$^{243}Cm \longrightarrow ^{239}Pu + ^4He$$

(a) Calculate the change in mass, Δm (in kg). (Masses: ^{243}Cm = 243.0614 amu; ^{239}Pu = 239.0522 amu; ^4He = 4.0026 amu; 1 amu = 1.661×10^{-24} g.)
(b) Calculate the energy released in joules.
(c) Calculate the energy released in kJ/mol of reaction, and comment on the difference between this value and a typical heat of reaction for a chemical change of a few hundred kJ/mol.

23.63 Plutonium "triggers" for nuclear weapons were manufactured at the Rocky Flats plant in Colorado. An 85-kg worker inhaled a dust particle containing 1.00 µg of $^{239}_{94}Pu$, which resided in his body for 16 h ($t_{1/2}$ of ^{239}Pu = 2.41×10^4 yr; each disintegration released 5.15 MeV). (a) How many rads did he receive? (b) How many grays?

23.64 Archeologists removed some charcoal from a Native American campfire, burned it in O_2, and bubbled the CO_2 formed into $Ca(OH)_2$ solution (limewater). The $CaCO_3$ that precipitated was filtered and dried. If 4.58 g of the $CaCO_3$ had a radioactivity of 3.2 d/min, how long ago was the campfire?

23.65 ^{238}U ($t_{1/2}$ = 4.5×10^9 yr) begins a decay series that ultimately forms ^{206}Pb. The scene below depicts the relative number of ^{238}U atoms (red) and ^{206}Pb atoms (green) in a mineral. If all the Pb comes from ^{238}U, calculate the age of the sample.

23.66 A 5.4-µg sample of $^{226}RaCl_2$ has a radioactivity of 1.5×10^5 Bq. Calculate $t_{1/2}$ of ^{226}Ra.

23.67 The major reaction taking place during hydrogen fusion in a young star is $4\,^1_1H \longrightarrow ^4_2He + 2\,^0_1\beta + 2\,^0_0\gamma + $ energy. How much energy (in MeV) is released per He nucleus formed? Per mole of He? (Masses: $_1^1H$ atom = 1.007825 amu; $_2^4He$ atom = 4.00260 amu; positron = 5.48580×10^{-4} amu.)

23.68 A sample of AgCl emits 175 nCi/g. A saturated solution prepared from the solid emits 1.25×10^{-2} Bq/mL due to radioactive Ag^+ ions. What is the molar solubility of AgCl?

23.69 In the 1950s, radioactive material was spread over the land from aboveground nuclear tests. A woman drinks some contaminated milk and ingests 0.0500 g of ^{90}Sr, which is taken up by bones and teeth and not eliminated. (a) How much ^{90}Sr ($t_{1/2}$ = 29 yr) is present in her body after 10 yr? (b) How long will it take for 99.9% of the ^{90}Sr to decay?

* **23.70** Technetium-99m is a metastable nuclide used in numerous cancer diagnostic and treatment programs. It is prepared just before use because it decays rapidly through γ emission:

$$^{99m}Tc \longrightarrow {}^{99}Tc + \gamma$$

Use the data below to determine (a) the half-life of ^{99m}Tc, and (b) the percentage of the isotope that is lost if it takes 2.0 h to prepare and administer the dose.

Time (h)	γ Emission (photons/s)
0	5000.
4	3150.
8	2000.
12	1250.
16	788 ·
20	495

* **23.71** What volume of radon will be produced per hour at STP from 1.000 g of ^{226}Ra ($t_{1/2}$ = 1599 yr; 1 yr = 8766 h; mass of one ^{226}Ra atom = 226.025402 amu)?

23.72 Which isotope in each pair would you predict to be more stable? Why?
(a) $^{140}_{55}Cs$ or $^{133}_{55}Cs$ (b) $^{79}_{35}Br$ or $^{78}_{35}Br$
(c) $^{28}_{12}Mg$ or $^{24}_{12}Mg$ (d) $^{14}_7N$ or $^{18}_7N$

23.73 The scene below represents a reaction (with neutrons gray and protons purple) that occurs during the lifetime of a star. (a) Write a balanced nuclear equation for the reaction. (b) If the mass difference is 7.7×10^{-2} amu, find the energy (kJ) released.

23.74 The 23rd-century starship *Enterprise* uses a substance called "dilithium crystals" as its fuel.
(a) Assuming this material is the result of fusion, what is the product of the fusion of two ^6Li nuclei?
(b) How much energy is released per kilogram of dilithium formed? (Mass of one ^6Li atom is 6.015121 amu.)
(c) When four ^1H atoms fuse to form ^4He, how many positrons are released?
(d) To determine the energy potential of the fusion processes in parts (b) and (c), compare the changes in mass per kilogram of dilithium and of ^4He.
(e) Compare the change in mass per kilogram in part (b) to that for the formation of ^4He by the method used in current fusion reactors (Section 23.7). (For masses, see Problem 23.58.)

(f) Using early 21st-century fusion technology, how much tritium can be produced per kilogram of ^6Li in the following reaction: $^6_3Li + {}^1_0n \longrightarrow {}^4_2He + {}^3_1H$? When this amount of tritium is fused with deuterium, what is the change in mass? How does this quantity compare with that for dilithium in part (b)?

23.75 Nuclear disarmament could be accomplished if weapons were not "replenished." The tritium in warheads decays to helium with a half-life of 12.26 yr and must be replaced or the weapon is useless. What fraction of the tritium is lost in 5.50 yr?

23.76 Gadolinium-146 undergoes electron capture. Identify the product, and use Figure 23.2 to find the modes of decay and the other two nuclides in the series below:

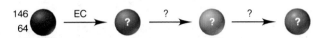

23.77 A decay series starts with the synthetic isotope $^{239}_{92}U$. The first four steps are emissions of a β^- particle, another β^-, an α particle, and another α. Write a balanced nuclear equation for each step. Which natural series could be started by this sequence?

23.78 The approximate date of a San Francisco earthquake is to be found by measuring the ^{14}C activity ($t_{1/2}$ = 5730 yr) of parts of a tree uprooted during the event. The tree parts have an activity of 12.9 d/min·g C, and a living tree has an activity of 15.3 d/min·g C. How long ago did the earthquake occur?

23.79 Carbon from the most recent remains of an extinct Australian marsupial, called *Diprotodon,* has a specific activity of 0.61 pCi/g. Modern carbon has a specific activity of 6.89 pCi/g. How long ago did the *Diprotodon* apparently become extinct?

* **23.80** With our early 21st-century technology, hydrogen fusion requires temperatures around 10^8 K, but lower temperatures can be used if the hydrogen is compressed. In the late 24th century, the starship *Leinad* uses such methods to fuse hydrogen at 10^6 K.
(a) What is the kinetic energy of an H atom at 1.00×10^6 K?
(b) How many H atoms are heated to 1.00×10^6 K from the energy of one H and one anti-H atom annihilating each other?
(c) If these H atoms fuse into ^4He atoms (with the loss of two positrons per ^4He formed), how much energy (in J) is generated?
(d) How much more energy is generated by the fusion in (c) than by the hydrogen-antihydrogen collision in (b)?
(e) Should the captain of the *Leinad* change the technology and produce ^3He (mass = 3.01603 amu) instead of ^4He?

23.81 Seaborgium-263 (Sg; Z = 106) was the first isotope of this element synthesized. It was made, together with four neutrons, by bombarding californium-249 with oxygen-18. The nuclide then decayed by three α emissions. Write balanced equations for the synthesis and three decay steps of ^{263}Sg.

23.82 Representations of three nuclei (with neutrons gray and protons purple) are shown below. Nucleus 1 is stable, but 2 and 3 are not. (a) Write the symbol for each isotope. (b) What is (are) the most likely mode(s) of decay for 2 and 3?

1   2   3

Appendix B

STANDARD THERMODYNAMIC VALUES FOR SELECTED SUBSTANCES*

Substance or Ion	ΔH_f° (kJ/mol)	ΔG_f° (kJ/mol)	S° (J/mol·K)	Substance or Ion	ΔH_f° (kJ/mol)	ΔG_f° (kJ/mol)	S° (J/mol·K)
$e^-(g)$	0	0	20.87	$CaCO_3(s)$	−1206.9	−1128.8	92.9
Aluminum				$CaO(s)$	−635.1	−603.5	38.2
$Al(s)$	0	0	28.3	$Ca(OH)_2(s)$	−986.09	−898.56	83.39
$Al^{3+}(aq)$	−524.7	−481.2	−313	$Ca_3(PO_4)_2(s)$	−4138	−3899	263
$AlCl_3(s)$	−704.2	−628.9	110.7	$CaSO_4(s)$	−1432.7	−1320.3	107
$Al_2O_3(s)$	−1676	−1582	50.94	Carbon			
Barium				$C(graphite)$	0	0	5.686
$Ba(s)$	0	0	62.5	$C(diamond)$	1.896	2.866	2.439
$Ba(g)$	175.6	144.8	170.28	$C(g)$	715.0	669.6	158.0
$Ba^{2+}(g)$	1649.9	—	—	$CO(g)$	−110.5	−137.2	197.5
$Ba^{2+}(aq)$	−538.36	−560.7	13	$CO_2(g)$	−393.5	−394.4	213.7
$BaCl_2(s)$	−806.06	−810.9	126	$CO_2(aq)$	−412.9	−386.2	121
$BaCO_3(s)$	−1219	−1139	112	$CO_3^{2-}(aq)$	−676.26	−528.10	−53.1
$BaO(s)$	−548.1	−520.4	72.07	$HCO_3^-(aq)$	−691.11	587.06	95.0
$BaSO_4(s)$	−1465	−1353	132	$H_2CO_3(aq)$	−698.7	−623.42	191
Boron				$CH_4(g)$	−74.87	−50.81	186.1
$B(\beta$-rhombo-hedral)	0	0	5.87	$C_2H_2(g)$	227	209	200.85
				$C_2H_4(g)$	52.47	68.36	219.22
$BF_3(g)$	−1137.0	−1120.3	254.0	$C_2H_6(g)$	−84.667	−32.89	229.5
$BCl_3(g)$	−403.8	−388.7	290.0	$C_3H_8(g)$	−105	−24.5	269.9
$B_2H_6(g)$	35	86.6	232.0	$C_4H_{10}(g)$	−126	−16.7	310
$B_2O_3(s)$	−1272	−1193	53.8	$C_6H_6(l)$	49.0	124.5	172.8
$H_3BO_3(s)$	−1094.3	−969.01	88.83	$CH_3OH(g)$	−201.2	−161.9	238
Bromine				$CH_3OH(l)$	−238.6	−166.2	127
$Br_2(l)$	0	0	152.23	$HCHO(g)$	−116	−110	219
$Br_2(g)$	30.91	3.13	245.38	$HCOO^-(aq)$	−410	−335	91.6
$Br(g)$	111.9	82.40	174.90	$HCOOH(l)$	−409	−346	129.0
$Br^-(g)$	−218.9	—	—	$HCOOH(aq)$	−410	−356	164
$Br^-(aq)$	−120.9	−102.82	80.71	$C_2H_5OH(g)$	−235.1	−168.6	282.6
$HBr(g)$	−36.3	−53.5	198.59	$C_2H_5OH(l)$	−277.63	−174.8	161
Cadmium				$CH_3CHO(g)$	−166	−133.7	266
$Cd(s)$	0	0	51.5	$CH_3COOH(l)$	−487.0	−392	160
$Cd(g)$	112.8	78.20	167.64	$C_6H_{12}O_6(s)$	−1273.3	−910.56	212.1
$Cd^{2+}(aq)$	−72.38	−77.74	−61.1	$C_{12}H_{22}O_{11}(s)$	−2221.7	−1544.3	360.24
$CdS(s)$	−144	−141	71	$CN^-(aq)$	151	166	118
Calcium				$HCN(g)$	135	125	201.7
$Ca(s)$	0	0	41.6	$HCN(l)$	105	121	112.8
$Ca(g)$	192.6	158.9	154.78	$HCN(aq)$	105	112	129
$Ca^{2+}(g)$	1934.1	—	—	$CS_2(g)$	117	66.9	237.79
$Ca^{2+}(aq)$	−542.96	−553.04	−55.2	$CS_2(l)$	87.9	63.6	151.0
$CaF_2(s)$	−1215	−1162	68.87	$CH_3Cl(g)$	−83.7	−60.2	234
$CaCl_2(s)$	−795.0	−750.2	114	$CH_2Cl_2(l)$	−117	−63.2	179

*All values at 298 K.

(*Continued*)

Substance or Ion	ΔH_f° (kJ/mol)	ΔG_f° (kJ/mol)	S° (J/mol·K)	Substance or Ion	ΔH_f° (kJ/mol)	ΔG_f° (kJ/mol)	S° (J/mol·K)
$CHCl_3(l)$	−132	−71.5	203	$Fe^{2+}(aq)$	−87.9	−84.94	−113
$CCl_4(g)$	−96.0	−53.7	309.7	$FeCl_2(s)$	−341.8	−302.3	117.9
$CCl_4(l)$	−139	−68.6	214.4	$FeCl_3(s)$	−399.5	−334.1	142
$COCl_2(g)$	−220	−206	283.74	$FeO(s)$	−272.0	−251.4	60.75
Cesium				$Fe_2O_3(s)$	−825.5	−743.6	87.400
$Cs(s)$	0	0	85.15	$Fe_3O_4(s)$	−1121	−1018	145.3
$Cs(g)$	76.7	49.7	175.5	Lead			
$Cs^+(g)$	458.5	427.1	169.72	$Pb(s)$	0	0	64.785
$Cs^+(aq)$	−248	−282.0	133	$Pb^{2+}(aq)$	1.6	−24.3	21
$CsF(s)$	−554.7	−525.4	88	$PbCl_2(s)$	−359	−314	136
$CsCl(s)$	−442.8	−414	101.18	$PbO(s)$	−218	−198	68.70
$CsBr(s)$	−395	−383	121	$PbO_2(s)$	−276.6	−219.0	76.6
$CsI(s)$	−337	−333	130	$PbS(s)$	−98.3	−96.7	91.3
Chlorine				$PbSO_4(s)$	−918.39	−811.24	147
$Cl_2(g)$	0	0	223.0	Lithium			
$Cl(g)$	121.0	105.0	165.1	$Li(s)$	0	0	29.10
$Cl^-(g)$	−234	−240	153.25	$Li(g)$	161	128	138.67
$Cl^-(aq)$	−167.46	−131.17	55.10	$Li^+(g)$	687.163	649.989	132.91
$HCl(g)$	−92.31	−95.30	186.79	$Li^+(aq)$	−278.46	−293.8	14
$HCl(aq)$	−167.46	−131.17	55.06	$LiF(s)$	−616.9	−588.7	35.66
$ClO_2(g)$	102	120	256.7	$LiCl(s)$	−408	−384	59.30
$Cl_2O(g)$	80.3	97.9	266.1	$LiBr(s)$	−351	−342	74.1
Chromium				$LiI(s)$	−270	−270	85.8
$Cr(s)$	0	0	23.8	Magnesium			
$Cr^{3+}(aq)$	−1971	—	—	$Mg(s)$	0	0	32.69
$CrO_4^{2-}(aq)$	−863.2	−706.3	38	$Mg(g)$	150	115	148.55
$Cr_2O_7^{2-}(aq)$	−1461	−1257	214	$Mg^{2+}(g)$	2351	—	—
Copper				$Mg^{2+}(aq)$	−461.96	−456.01	−118
$Cu(s)$	0	0	33.1	$MgCl_2(s)$	−641.6	−592.1	89.630
$Cu(g)$	341.1	301.4	166.29	$MgCO_3(s)$	−1112	−1028	65.86
$Cu^+(aq)$	51.9	50.2	−26	$MgO(s)$	−601.2	−569.0	26.9
$Cu^{2+}(aq)$	64.39	64.98	−98.7	$Mg_3N_2(s)$	−461	−401	88
$Cu_2O(s)$	−168.6	−146.0	93.1	Manganese			
$CuO(s)$	−157.3	−130	42.63	$Mn(s, \alpha)$	0	0	31.8
$Cu_2S(s)$	−79.5	−86.2	120.9	$Mn^{2+}(aq)$	−219	−223	−84
$CuS(s)$	−53.1	−53.6	66.5	$MnO_2(s)$	−520.9	−466.1	53.1
Fluorine				$MnO_4^-(aq)$	−518.4	−425.1	190
$F_2(g)$	0	0	202.7	Mercury			
$F(g)$	78.9	61.8	158.64	$Hg(l)$	0	0	76.027
$F^-(g)$	−255.6	−262.5	145.47	$Hg(g)$	61.30	31.8	174.87
$F^-(aq)$	−329.1	−276.5	−9.6	$Hg^{2+}(aq)$	171	164.4	−32
$HF(g)$	−273	−275	173.67	$Hg_2^{2+}(aq)$	172	153.6	84.5
Hydrogen				$HgCl_2(s)$	−230	−184	144
$H_2(g)$	0	0	130.6	$Hg_2Cl_2(s)$	−264.9	−210.66	196
$H(g)$	218.0	203.30	114.60	$HgO(s)$	−90.79	−58.50	70.27
$H^+(aq)$	0	0	0	Nitrogen			
$H^+(g)$	1536.3	1517.1	108.83	$N_2(g)$	0	0	191.5
Iodine				$N(g)$	473	456	153.2
$I_2(s)$	0	0	116.14	$N_2O(g)$	82.05	104.2	219.7
$I_2(g)$	62.442	19.38	260.58	$NO(g)$	90.29	86.60	210.65
$I(g)$	106.8	70.21	180.67	$NO_2(g)$	33.2	51	239.9
$I^-(g)$	−194.7	—	—	$N_2O_4(g)$	9.16	97.7	304.3
$I^-(aq)$	−55.94	−51.67	109.4	$N_2O_5(g)$	11	118	346
$HI(g)$	25.9	1.3	206.33	$N_2O_5(s)$	−43.1	114	178
Iron				$NH_3(g)$	−45.9	−16	193
$Fe(s)$	0	0	27.3	$NH_3(aq)$	−80.83	26.7	110
$Fe^{3+}(aq)$	−47.7	−10.5	−293	$N_2H_4(l)$	50.63	149.2	121.2

(*Continued*)

Substance or Ion	ΔH_f° (kJ/mol)	ΔG_f° (kJ/mol)	S° (J/mol·K)	Substance or Ion	ΔH_f° (kJ/mol)	ΔG_f° (kJ/mol)	S° (J/mol·K)
$NO_3^-(aq)$	−206.57	−110.5	146	$Ag(g)$	289.2	250.4	172.892
$HNO_3(l)$	−173.23	−79.914	155.6	$Ag^+(aq)$	105.9	77.111	73.93
$HNO_3(aq)$	−206.57	−110.5	146	$AgF(s)$	−203	−185	84
$NF_3(g)$	−125	−83.3	260.6	$AgCl(s)$	−127.03	−109.72	96.11
$NOCl(g)$	51.71	66.07	261.6	$AgBr(s)$	−99.51	−95.939	107.1
$NH_4Cl(s)$	−314.4	−203.0	94.6	$AgI(s)$	−62.38	−66.32	114
Oxygen				$AgNO_3(s)$	−45.06	19.1	128.2
$O_2(g)$	0	0	205.0	$Ag_2S(s)$	−31.8	−40.3	146
$O(g)$	249.2	231.7	160.95	Sodium			
$O_3(g)$	143	163	238.82	$Na(s)$	0	0	51.446
$OH^-(aq)$	−229.94	−157.30	−10.54	$Na(g)$	107.76	77.299	153.61
$H_2O(g)$	−241.826	−228.60	188.72	$Na^+(g)$	609.839	574.877	147.85
$H_2O(l)$	−285.840	−237.192	69.940	$Na^+(aq)$	−239.66	−261.87	60.2
$H_2O_2(l)$	−187.8	−120.4	110	$NaF(s)$	−575.4	−545.1	51.21
$H_2O_2(aq)$	−191.2	−134.1	144	$NaCl(s)$	−411.1	−384.0	72.12
Phosphorus				$NaBr(s)$	−361	−349	86.82
$P_4(s, \text{white})$	0	0	41.1	$NaOH(s)$	−425.609	−379.53	64.454
$P(g)$	314.6	278.3	163.1	$Na_2CO_3(s)$	−1130.8	−1048.1	139
$P(s, \text{red})$	−17.6	−12.1	22.8	$NaHCO_3(s)$	−947.7	−851.9	102
$P_2(g)$	144	104	218	$NaI(s)$	−288	−285	98.5
$P_4(g)$	58.9	24.5	280	Strontium			
$PCl_3(g)$	−287	−268	312	$Sr(s)$	0	0	54.4
$PCl_3(l)$	−320	−272	217	$Sr(g)$	164	110	164.54
$PCl_5(g)$	−402	−323	353	$Sr^{2+}(g)$	1784	—	—
$PCl_5(s)$	−443.5	—	—	$Sr^{2+}(aq)$	−545.51	−557.3	−39
$P_4O_{10}(s)$	−2984	−2698	229	$SrCl_2(s)$	−828.4	−781.2	117
$PO_4^{3-}(aq)$	−1266	−1013	−218	$SrCO_3(s)$	−1218	−1138	97.1
$HPO_4^{2-}(aq)$	−1281	−1082	−36	$SrO(s)$	−592.0	−562.4	55.5
$H_2PO_4^-(aq)$	−1285	−1135	89.1	$SrSO_4(s)$	−1445	−1334	122
$H_3PO_4(aq)$	−1277	−1019	228	Sulfur			
Potassium				$S(\text{rhombic})$	0	0	31.9
$K(s)$	0	0	64.672	$S(\text{monoclinic})$	0.3	0.096	32.6
$K(g)$	89.2	60.7	160.23	$S(g)$	279	239	168
$K^+(g)$	514.197	481.202	154.47	$S_2(g)$	129	80.1	228.1
$K^+(aq)$	−251.2	−282.28	103	$S_8(g)$	101	49.1	430.211
$KF(s)$	−568.6	−538.9	66.55	$S^{2-}(aq)$	41.8	83.7	22
$KCl(s)$	−436.7	−409.2	82.59	$HS^-(aq)$	−17.7	12.6	61.1
$KBr(s)$	−394	−380	95.94	$H_2S(g)$	−20.2	−33	205.6
$KI(s)$	−328	−323	106.39	$H_2S(aq)$	−39	−27.4	122
$KOH(s)$	−424.8	−379.1	78.87	$SO_2(g)$	−296.8	−300.2	248.1
$KClO_3(s)$	−397.7	−296.3	143.1	$SO_3(g)$	−396	−371	256.66
$KClO_4(s)$	−432.75	−303.2	151.0	$SO_4^{2-}(aq)$	−907.51	−741.99	17
Rubidium				$HSO_4^-(aq)$	−885.75	−752.87	126.9
$Rb(s)$	0	0	69.5	$H_2SO_4(l)$	−813.989	−690.059	156.90
$Rb(g)$	85.81	55.86	169.99	$H_2SO_4(aq)$	−907.51	−741.99	17
$Rb^+(g)$	495.04	—	—	Tin			
$Rb^+(aq)$	−246	−282.2	124	$Sn(\text{white})$	0	0	51.5
$RbF(s)$	−549.28	—	—	$Sn(\text{gray})$	3	4.6	44.8
$RbCl(s)$	−435.35	−407.8	95.90	$SnCl_4(l)$	−545.2	−474.0	259
$RbBr(s)$	−389.2	−378.1	108.3	$SnO_2(s)$	−580.7	−519.7	52.3
$RbI(s)$	−328	−326	118.0	Zinc			
Silicon				$Zn(s)$	0	0	41.6
$Si(s)$	0	0	18.0	$Zn(g)$	130.5	94.93	160.9
$SiF_4(g)$	−1614.9	−1572.7	282.4	$Zn^{2+}(aq)$	−152.4	−147.21	−106.5
$SiO_2(s)$	−910.9	−856.5	41.5	$ZnO(s)$	−348.0	−318.2	43.9
Silver				$ZnS(s, \text{zinc}$	−203	−198	57.7
$Ag(s)$	0	0	42.702	blende$)$			

EQUILIBRIUM CONSTANTS FOR SELECTED SUBSTANCES*

Dissociation (Ionization) Constants (K_a) of Selected Acids

Name and Formula	Lewis Structure[†]	K_{a1}	K_{a2}	K_{a3}
Acetic acid CH_3COOH	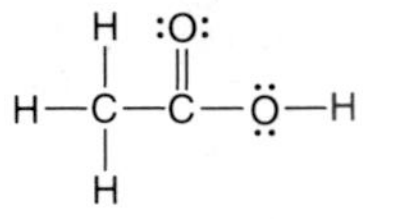	1.8×10^{-5}		
Acetylsalicylic acid[††] $CH_3COOC_6H_4COOH$	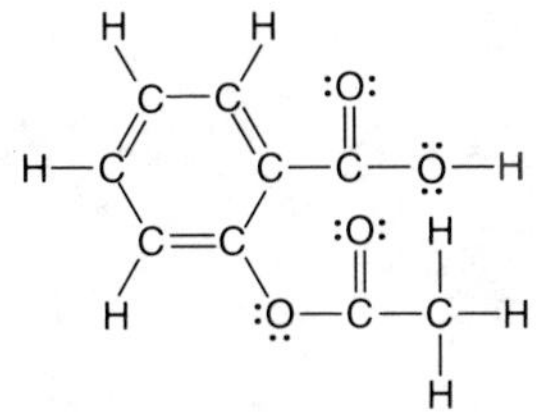	3.6×10^{-4}		
Adipic acid $HOOC(CH_2)_4COOH$	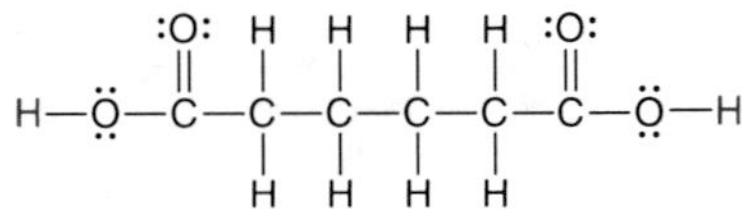	3.8×10^{-5}	3.8×10^{-6}	
Arsenic acid H_3AsO_4	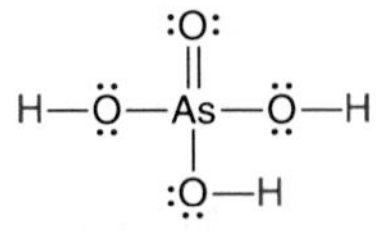	6×10^{-3}	1.1×10^{-7}	3×10^{-12}
Ascorbic acid $H_2C_6H_6O_6$	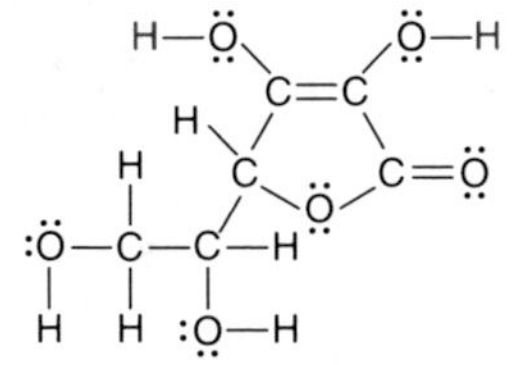	1.0×10^{-5}	5×10^{-12}	
Benzoic acid C_6H_5COOH	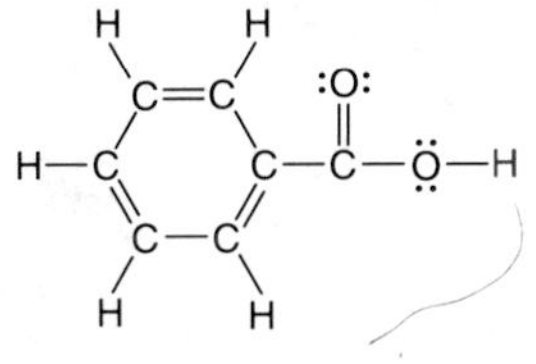	6.3×10^{-5}		
Carbonic acid H_2CO_3	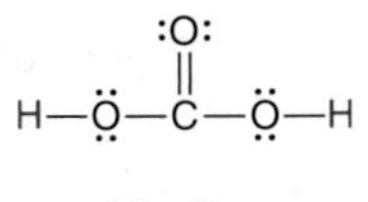	4.5×10^{-7}	4.7×10^{-11}	
Chloroacetic acid $ClCH_2COOH$	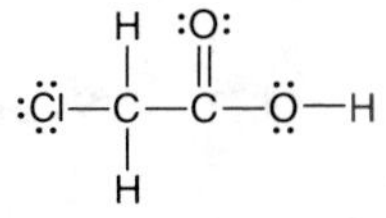	1.4×10^{-3}		
Chlorous acid $HClO_2$	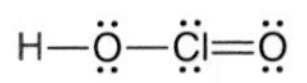	1.1×10^{-2}		

*All values at 298 K, except for acetylsalicylic acid.
[†]Acidic (ionizable) proton(s) shown in red. Structures shown have lowest formal charges.
[††]At 37°C in 0.15 M NaCl.

(Continued)

Dissociation (Ionization) Constants (K_a) of Selected Acids

Name and Formula	Lewis Structure[†]	K_{a1}	K_{a2}	K_{a3}
Citric acid $HOOCCH_2C(OH)(COOH)CH_2COOH$		7.4×10^{-4}	1.7×10^{-5}	4.0×10^{-7}
Formic acid $HCOOH$		1.8×10^{-4}		
Glyceric acid $HOCH_2CH(OH)COOH$		2.9×10^{-4}		
Glycolic acid $HOCH_2COOH$		1.5×10^{-4}		
Glyoxylic acid $HC(O)COOH$		3.5×10^{-4}		
Hydrocyanic acid HCN		6.2×10^{-10}		
Hydrofluoric acid HF		6.8×10^{-4}		
Hydrosulfuric acid H_2S		9×10^{-8}	1×10^{-17}	
Hypobromous acid $HBrO$		2.3×10^{-9}		
Hypochlorous acid $HClO$		2.9×10^{-8}		
Hypoiodous acid HIO		2.3×10^{-11}		
Iodic acid HIO_3		1.6×10^{-1}		
Lactic acid $CH_3CH(OH)COOH$		1.4×10^{-4}		
Maleic acid $HOOCCH{=}CHCOOH$		1.2×10^{-2}	4.7×10^{-7}	

(Continued)

Dissociation (Ionization) Constants (K_a) of Selected Acids (*continued*)

Name and Formula	Lewis Structure†	K_{a1}	K_{a2}	K_{a3}
Malonic acid HOOCCH$_2$COOH		1.4×10^{-3}	2.0×10^{-6}	
Nitrous acid HNO$_2$		7.1×10^{-4}		
Oxalic acid HOOCCOOH		5.6×10^{-2}	5.4×10^{-5}	
Phenol C$_6$H$_5$OH		1.0×10^{-10}		
Phenylacetic acid C$_6$H$_5$CH$_2$COOH		4.9×10^{-5}		
Phosphoric acid H$_3$PO$_4$		7.2×10^{-3}	6.3×10^{-8}	4.2×10^{-13}
Phosphorous acid HPO(OH)$_2$		3×10^{-2}	1.7×10^{-7}	
Propanoic acid CH$_3$CH$_2$COOH		1.3×10^{-5}		
Pyruvic acid CH$_3$C(O)COOH		2.8×10^{-3}		
Succinic acid HOOCCH$_2$CH$_2$COOH		6.2×10^{-5}	2.3×10^{-6}	
Sulfuric acid H$_2$SO$_4$		Very large	1.0×10^{-2}	
Sulfurous acid H$_2$SO$_3$		1.4×10^{-2}	6.5×10^{-8}	

Dissociation (Ionization) Constants (K_b) of Selected Amine Bases

Name and Formula	Lewis Structure*	K_{b1}	K_{b2}
Ammonia NH_3		1.76×10^{-5}	
Aniline $C_6H_5NH_2$		4.0×10^{-10}	
Diethylamine $(CH_3CH_2)_2NH$		8.6×10^{-4}	
Dimethylamine $(CH_3)_2NH$		5.9×10^{-4}	
Ethanolamine $HOCH_2CH_2NH_2$		3.2×10^{-5}	
Ethylamine $CH_3CH_2NH_2$		4.3×10^{-4}	
Ethylenediamine $H_2NCH_2CH_2NH_2$		8.5×10^{-5}	7.1×10^{-8}
Methylamine CH_3NH_2		4.4×10^{-4}	
tert-Butylamine $(CH_3)_3CNH_2$		4.8×10^{-4}	
Piperidine $C_5H_{10}NH$		1.3×10^{-3}	
n-Propylamine $CH_3CH_2CH_2NH_2$		3.5×10^{-4}	

*Blue type indicates the basic nitrogen and its lone pair.   (*Continued*)

Dissociation (Ionization) Constants (K_b) of Selected Amine Bases (*continued*)

Name and Formula	Lewis Structure*	K_{b1}	K_{b2}
Isopropylamine $(CH_3)_2CHNH_2$		4.7×10^{-4}	
Propylenediamine $H_2NCH_2CH_2CH_2NH_2$		3.1×10^{-4}	3.0×10^{-6}
Pyridine C_5H_5N		1.7×10^{-9}	
Triethylamine $(CH_3CH_2)_3N$		5.2×10^{-4}	
Trimethylamine $(CH_3)_3N$		6.3×10^{-5}	

Dissociation (Ionization) Constants (K_a) of Some Hydrated Metal Ions

Free Ion	Hydrated Ion	K_a
Fe^{3+}	$Fe(H_2O)_6^{3+}(aq)$	6×10^{-3}
Sn^{2+}	$Sn(H_2O)_6^{2+}(aq)$	4×10^{-4}
Cr^{3+}	$Cr(H_2O)_6^{3+}(aq)$	1×10^{-4}
Al^{3+}	$Al(H_2O)_6^{3+}(aq)$	1×10^{-5}
Cu^{2+}	$Cu(H_2O)_6^{2+}(aq)$	3×10^{-8}
Pb^{2+}	$Pb(H_2O)_6^{2+}(aq)$	3×10^{-8}
Zn^{2+}	$Zn(H_2O)_6^{2+}(aq)$	1×10^{-9}
Co^{2+}	$Co(H_2O)_6^{2+}(aq)$	2×10^{-10}
Ni^{2+}	$Ni(H_2O)_6^{2+}(aq)$	1×10^{-10}

Formation Constants (K_f) of Some Complex Ions

Complex Ion	K_f
$Ag(CN)_2^-$	3.0×10^{20}
$Ag(NH_3)_2^+$	1.7×10^7
$Ag(S_2O_3)_2^{3-}$	4.7×10^{13}
AlF_6^{3-}	4×10^{19}
$Al(OH)_4^-$	3×10^{33}
$Be(OH)_4^{2-}$	4×10^{18}
CdI_4^{2-}	1×10^6
$Co(OH)_4^{2-}$	5×10^9
$Cr(OH)_4^-$	8.0×10^{29}
$Cu(NH_3)_4^{2+}$	5.6×10^{11}
$Fe(CN)_6^{4-}$	3×10^{35}
$Fe(CN)_6^{3-}$	4.0×10^{43}
$Hg(CN)_4^{2-}$	9.3×10^{38}
$Ni(NH_3)_6^{2+}$	2.0×10^8
$Pb(OH)_3^-$	8×10^{13}
$Sn(OH)_3^-$	3×10^{25}
$Zn(CN)_4^{2-}$	4.2×10^{19}
$Zn(NH_3)_4^{2+}$	7.8×10^8
$Zn(OH)_4^{2-}$	3×10^{15}

Solubility-Product Constants (K_{sp}) of Slightly Soluble Ionic Compounds

Name, Formula	K_{sp}	Name, Formula	K_{sp}
Carbonates		Cobalt(II) hydroxide, $Co(OH)_2$	1.3×10^{-15}
Barium carbonate, $BaCO_3$	2.0×10^{-9}	Copper(II) hydroxide, $Cu(OH)_2$	2.2×10^{-20}
Cadmium carbonate, $CdCO_3$	1.8×10^{-14}	Iron(II) hydroxide, $Fe(OH)_2$	4.1×10^{-15}
Calcium carbonate, $CaCO_3$	3.3×10^{-9}	Iron(III) hydroxide, $Fe(OH)_3$	1.6×10^{-39}
Cobalt(II) carbonate, $CoCO_3$	1.0×10^{-10}	Magnesium hydroxide, $Mg(OH)_2$	6.3×10^{-10}
Copper(II) carbonate, $CuCO_3$	3×10^{-12}	Manganese(II) hydroxide, $Mn(OH)_2$	1.6×10^{-13}
Lead(II) carbonate, $PbCO_3$	7.4×10^{-14}	Nickel(II) hydroxide, $Ni(OH)_2$	6×10^{-16}
Magnesium carbonate, $MgCO_3$	3.5×10^{-8}	Zinc hydroxide, $Zn(OH)_2$	3×10^{-16}
Mercury(I) carbonate, Hg_2CO_3	8.9×10^{-17}	**Iodates**	
Nickel(II) carbonate, $NiCO_3$	1.3×10^{-7}	Barium iodate, $Ba(IO_3)_2$	1.5×10^{-9}
Strontium carbonate, $SrCO_3$	5.4×10^{-10}	Calcium iodate, $Ca(IO_3)_2$	7.1×10^{-7}
Zinc carbonate, $ZnCO_3$	1.0×10^{-10}	Lead(II) iodate, $Pb(IO_3)_2$	2.5×10^{-13}
Chromates		Silver iodate, $AgIO_3$	3.1×10^{-8}
Barium chromate, $BaCrO_4$	2.1×10^{-10}	Strontium iodate, $Sr(IO_3)_2$	3.3×10^{-7}
Calcium chromate, $CaCrO_4$	1×10^{-8}	Zinc iodate, $Zn(IO_3)_2$	3.9×10^{-6}
Lead(II) chromate, $PbCrO_4$	2.3×10^{-13}	**Oxalates**	
Silver chromate, Ag_2CrO_4	2.6×10^{-12}	Barium oxalate dihydrate, $BaC_2O_4 \cdot 2H_2O$	1.1×10^{-7}
Cyanides		Calcium oxalate monohydrate, $CaC_2O_4 \cdot H_2O$	2.3×10^{-9}
Mercury(I) cyanide, $Hg_2(CN)_2$	5×10^{-40}	Strontium oxalate monohydrate,	
Silver cyanide, $AgCN$	2.2×10^{-16}	$SrC_2O_4 \cdot H_2O$	5.6×10^{-8}
Halides		**Phosphates**	
Fluorides		Calcium phosphate, $Ca_3(PO_4)_2$	1.2×10^{-29}
Barium fluoride, BaF_2	1.5×10^{-6}	Magnesium phosphate, $Mg_3(PO_4)_2$	5.2×10^{-24}
Calcium fluoride, CaF_2	3.2×10^{-11}	Silver phosphate, Ag_3PO_4	2.6×10^{-18}
Lead(II) fluoride, PbF_2	3.6×10^{-8}	**Sulfates**	
Magnesium fluoride, MgF_2	7.4×10^{-9}	Barium sulfate, $BaSO_4$	1.1×10^{-10}
Strontium fluoride, SrF_2	2.6×10^{-9}	Calcium sulfate, $CaSO_4$	2.4×10^{-5}
Chlorides		Lead(II) sulfate, $PbSO_4$	1.6×10^{-8}
Copper(I) chloride, $CuCl$	1.9×10^{-7}	Radium sulfate, $RaSO_4$	2×10^{-11}
Lead(II) chloride, $PbCl_2$	1.7×10^{-5}	Silver sulfate, Ag_2SO_4	1.5×10^{-5}
Silver chloride, $AgCl$	1.8×10^{-10}	Strontium sulfate, $SrSO_4$	3.2×10^{-7}
Bromides		**Sulfides**	
Copper(I) bromide, $CuBr$	5×10^{-9}	Cadmium sulfide, CdS	1.0×10^{-24}
Silver bromide, $AgBr$	5.0×10^{-13}	Copper(II) sulfide, CuS	8×10^{-34}
Iodides		Iron(II) sulfide, FeS	8×10^{-16}
Copper(I) iodide, CuI	1×10^{-12}	Lead(II) sulfide, PbS	3×10^{-25}
Lead(II) iodide, PbI_2	7.9×10^{-9}	Manganese(II) sulfide, MnS	3×10^{-11}
Mercury(I) iodide, Hg_2I_2	4.7×10^{-29}	Mercury(II) sulfide, HgS	2×10^{-50}
Silver iodide, AgI	8.3×10^{-17}	Nickel(II) sulfide, NiS	3×10^{-16}
Hydroxides		Silver sulfide, Ag_2S	8×10^{-48}
Aluminum hydroxide, $Al(OH)_3$	3×10^{-34}	Tin(II) sulfide, SnS	1.3×10^{-23}
Cadmium hydroxide, $Cd(OH)_2$	7.2×10^{-15}	Zinc sulfide, ZnS	2.0×10^{-22}
Calcium hydroxide, $Ca(OH)_2$	6.5×10^{-6}		

STANDARD ELECTRODE (HALF-CELL) POTENTIALS*

Half-Reaction	$E°$ (V)
$F_2(g) + 2e^- \rightleftharpoons 2F^-(aq)$	+2.87
$O_3(g) + 2H^+(aq) + 2e^- \rightleftharpoons O_2(g) + H_2O(l)$	+2.07
$Co^{3+}(aq) + e^- \rightleftharpoons Co^{2+}(aq)$	+1.82
$H_2O_2(aq) + 2H^+(aq) + 2e^- \rightleftharpoons 2H_2O(l)$	+1.77
$PbO_2(s) + 3H^+(aq) + HSO_4^-(aq) + 2e^- \rightleftharpoons PbSO_4(s) + 2H_2O(l)$	+1.70
$Ce^{4+}(aq) + e^- \rightleftharpoons Ce^{3+}(aq)$	+1.61
$MnO_4^-(aq) + 8H^+(aq) + 5e^- \rightleftharpoons Mn^{2+}(aq) + 4H_2O(l)$	+1.51
$Au^{3+}(aq) + 3e^- \rightleftharpoons Au(s)$	+1.50
$Cl_2(g) + 2e^- \rightleftharpoons 2Cl^-(aq)$	+1.36
$Cr_2O_7^{2-}(aq) + 14H^+(aq) + 6e^- \rightleftharpoons 2Cr^{3+}(aq) + 7H_2O(l)$	+1.33
$MnO_2(s) + 4H^+(aq) + 2e^- \rightleftharpoons Mn^{2+}(aq) + 2H_2O(l)$	+1.23
$O_2(g) + 4H^+(aq) + 4e^- \rightleftharpoons 2H_2O(l)$	+1.23
$Br_2(l) + 2e^- \rightleftharpoons 2Br^-(aq)$	+1.07
$NO_3^-(aq) + 4H^+(aq) + 3e^- \rightleftharpoons NO(g) + 2H_2O(l)$	+0.96
$2Hg^{2+}(aq) + 2e^- \rightleftharpoons Hg_2^{2+}(aq)$	+0.92
$Hg_2^{2+}(aq) + 2e^- \rightleftharpoons 2Hg(l)$	+0.85
$Ag^+(aq) + e^- \rightleftharpoons Ag(s)$	+0.80
$Fe^{3+}(aq) + e^- \rightleftharpoons Fe^{2+}(aq)$	+0.77
$O_2(g) + 2H^+(aq) + 2e^- \rightleftharpoons H_2O_2(aq)$	+0.68
$MnO_4^-(aq) + 2H_2O(l) + 3e^- \rightleftharpoons MnO_2(s) + 4OH^-(aq)$	+0.59
$I_2(s) + 2e^- \rightleftharpoons 2I^-(aq)$	+0.53
$O_2(g) + 2H_2O(l) + 4e^- \rightleftharpoons 4OH^-(aq)$	+0.40
$Cu^{2+}(aq) + 2e^- \rightleftharpoons Cu(s)$	+0.34
$AgCl(s) + e^- \rightleftharpoons Ag(s) + Cl^-(aq)$	+0.22
$SO_4^{2-}(aq) + 4H^+(aq) + 2e^- \rightleftharpoons SO_2(g) + 2H_2O(l)$	+0.20
$Cu^{2+}(aq) + e^- \rightleftharpoons Cu^+(aq)$	+0.15
$Sn^{4+}(aq) + 2e^- \rightleftharpoons Sn^{2+}(aq)$	+0.13
$2H^+(aq) + 2e^- \rightleftharpoons H_2(g)$	0.00
$Pb^{2+}(aq) + 2e^- \rightleftharpoons Pb(s)$	−0.13
$Sn^{2+}(aq) + 2e^- \rightleftharpoons Sn(s)$	−0.14
$N_2(g) + 5H^+(aq) + 4e^- \rightleftharpoons N_2H_5^+(aq)$	−0.23
$Ni^{2+}(aq) + 2e^- \rightleftharpoons Ni(s)$	−0.25
$Co^{2+}(aq) + 2e^- \rightleftharpoons Co(s)$	−0.28
$PbSO_4(s) + H^+(aq) + 2e^- \rightleftharpoons Pb(s) + HSO_4^-(aq)$	−0.31
$Cd^{2+}(aq) + 2e^- \rightleftharpoons Cd(s)$	−0.40
$Fe^{2+}(aq) + 2e^- \rightleftharpoons Fe(s)$	−0.44
$Cr^{3+}(aq) + 3e^- \rightleftharpoons Cr(s)$	−0.74
$Zn^{2+}(aq) + 2e^- \rightleftharpoons Zn(s)$	−0.76
$2H_2O(l) + 2e^- \rightleftharpoons H_2(g) + 2OH^-(aq)$	−0.83
$Mn^{2+}(aq) + 2e^- \rightleftharpoons Mn(s)$	−1.18
$Al^{3+}(aq) + 3e^- \rightleftharpoons Al(s)$	−1.66
$Mg^{2+}(aq) + 2e^- \rightleftharpoons Mg(s)$	−2.37
$Na^+(aq) + e^- \rightleftharpoons Na(s)$	−2.71
$Ca^{2+}(aq) + 2e^- \rightleftharpoons Ca(s)$	−2.87
$Sr^{2+}(aq) + 2e^- \rightleftharpoons Sr(s)$	−2.89
$Ba^{2+}(aq) + 2e^- \rightleftharpoons Ba(s)$	−2.90
$K^+(aq) + e^- \rightleftharpoons K(s)$	−2.93
$Li^+(aq) + e^- \rightleftharpoons Li(s)$	−3.05

*All values at 298 K. Written as reductions; $E°$ value refers to all components in their standard states: 1 M for dissolved species; 1 atm pressure for the gas behaving ideally; the pure substance for solids and liquids.

Appendix E

ANSWERS TO SELECTED PROBLEMS

Chapter 16

16.2 Reaction rate is proportional to concentration. An increase in pressure will increase the concentration, resulting in an increased reaction rate. **16.3** The addition of water will dilute the concentrations of all dissolved solutes, and the rate of the reaction will decrease. **16.5** An increase in temperature affects the rate of a reaction by increasing the number of collisions between particles, but more importantly, the energy of collisions increases. Both these factors increase the rate of reaction. **16.8**(a) The slope of the line joining any two points on a graph of concentration versus time gives the average rate between the two points. The closer the points, the closer the average rate will be to the instantaneous rate. (b) The initial rate is the instantaneous rate at the point on the graph where time = 0, that is, when reactants are mixed.

16.10

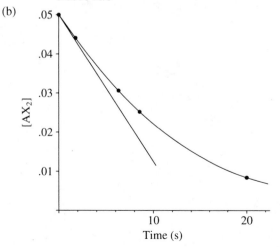

16.12(a) $\text{rate} = -\left(\dfrac{1}{2}\right)\dfrac{\Delta[AX_2]}{\Delta t}$

$= -\left(\dfrac{1}{2}\right)\dfrac{(0.0088\ M - 0.0500\ M)}{(20.0\ s - 0\ s)}$

$= 0.0010\ M/s$

The initial rate is higher than the average rate because the rate will decrease as reactant concentration decreases.

16.14 $\text{rate} = -\dfrac{\Delta[A]}{\Delta t} = -\dfrac{1}{2}\dfrac{\Delta[B]}{\Delta t} = \dfrac{\Delta[C]}{\Delta t}$; 0.2 mol/L·s

16.16 $2N_2O_5(g) \longrightarrow 4NO_2(g) + O_2(g)$

16.19(a) $\text{rate} = -\dfrac{1}{3}\dfrac{\Delta[O_2]}{\Delta t} = \dfrac{1}{2}\dfrac{\Delta[O_3]}{\Delta t}$ (b) 1.45×10^{-5} mol/L·s

16.20(a) k is the rate constant, the proportionality constant in the rate law; it is reaction and temperature specific. (b) m represents the order of the reaction with respect to [A], and n represents the order of the reaction with respect to [B]. The order of a reactant does not necessarily equal its stoichiometric coefficient in the balanced equation. (c) L^2/mol^2·min **16.21**(a) Rate doubles. (b) Rate decreases by a factor of four. (c) Rate increases by a factor of nine. **16.22** first order in BrO_3^-; first order in Br^-; second order in H^+; fourth order overall **16.24**(a) Rate doubles. (b) Rate is halved. (c) The rate increases by a factor of 16. **16.26**(a) second order in A; first order in B (b) $\text{rate} = k[A]^2[B]$ (c) $5.00\times10^3\ L^2/mol^2$·min **16.29**(a) first order (b) second order (c) zero order **16.31** 7 s **16.33**(a) $k = 0.0660\ \text{min}^{-1}$ (b) 21.0 min

16.36 Measure the rate constant at a series of temperatures and plot $\ln k$ versus $1/T$. The slope of the line equals $-E_a/R$. **16.38** $0.033\ s^{-1}$ **16.42** No, other factors that affect the fraction of collisions that lead to reaction are the energy and orientation of the collisions. **16.45** At the same temperature, both reaction mixtures have the same average kinetic energy, but not the same velocity. The trimethylamine molecule has greater mass than the ammonia molecule, so trimethylamine molecules will collide less often with HCl. Moreover, the bulky groups bonded to nitrogen in trimethylamine mean that collisions with HCl having the correct orientation occur less frequently. Therefore, the rate of the first reaction is greater. **16.46** 12 unique collisions **16.48** 2.96×10^{-18} **16.50**(a)

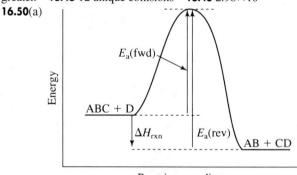

(b) 2.70×10^2 kJ/mol (c)

16.52(a) Because the enthalpy change is positive, the reaction is endothermic.

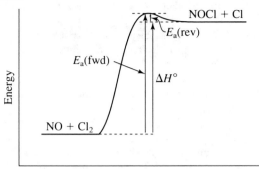

(b) 3 kJ   (c) :Cl⋯⋯Cl⋯N≋O:

16.53 The rate of an overall reaction depends on the rate of the slowest step. The rate of the overall reaction will be slower than the average of the individual rates because the average includes faster rates as well.   **16.57** The probability of three particles colliding with one another with the proper energy and orientation is much less than the probability for two particles.   **16.58** No, the overall rate law must contain only reactants (no intermediates), and the overall rate is determined by the slow step.
16.59(a) $CO_2(aq) + 2OH^-(aq) \longrightarrow CO_3^{2-}(aq) + H_2O(l)$
   (b) $HCO_3^-(aq)$
   (c) (1) molecularity = 2; $rate_1 = k_1[CO_2][OH^-]$
      (2) molecularity = 2; $rate_2 = k_2[HCO_3^-][OH^-]$
   (d) Yes
16.60(a) $Cl_2(g) + 2NO_2(g) \longrightarrow 2NO_2Cl(g)$ (b) $Cl(g)$
   (c) (1) molecularity = 2; $rate_1 = k_1[Cl_2][NO_2]$
      (2) molecularity = 2; $rate_2 = k_2[Cl][NO_2]$ (d) Yes
16.61(a) $A(g) + B(g) + C(g) \longrightarrow D(g)$
   (b) X and Y are intermediates.

Step	Molecularity	Rate Law
$A(g) + B(g) \rightleftharpoons X(g)$	bimolecular	$rate_1 = k_1[A][B]$
$X(g) + C(g) \longrightarrow Y(g)$	bimolecular	$rate_2 = k_2[X][C]$
$Y(g) \longrightarrow D(g)$	unimolecular	$rate_3 = k_3[Y]$

(d) yes   (e) yes   **16.63** The proposed mechanism is valid because the individual steps are chemically reasonable and add to give the overall equation, and the rate law for the mechanism matches the observed rate law.   **16.66** No. A catalyst changes the mechanism of a reaction to one with lower activation energy. Lower activation energy means a faster reaction. An increase in temperature does not influence the activation energy, but increases the fraction of collisions with sufficient energy to equal or exceed the activation energy.   **16.69** 4.61×10^4 J/mol   **16.72**(a) Rate increases 2.5 times.   (b) Rate is halved.   (c) Rate decreases by a factor of 0.01.   (d) Rate does not change.   **16.76** 57 yr
16.78(a) 0.21 h^{-1}; 3.3 h   (b) 6.6 h   (c) If the concentration of sucrose is relatively low, the concentration of water remains nearly constant even with small changes in the amount of water. This gives an apparent zero-order reaction with respect to water. Thus, the reaction is first order overall because the rate does not change with changes in the amount of water.

16.83 7.3×10^3 J/mol   **16.84**(a) 2.4×10^{-15} M
(b) 2.4×10^{-11} mol/L·s

Chapter 20

20.2 A spontaneous process occurs by itself, whereas a nonspontaneous process requires a continuous input of energy to make it happen. It is possible to cause a nonspontaneous process to occur, but the process stops once the energy source is removed. A reaction that is nonspontaneous under one set of conditions may be spontaneous under a different set of conditions.   **20.5** The transition from liquid to gas involves a greater increase in dispersal of energy and freedom of motion than does the transition from solid to liquid.   **20.6** In an exothermic reaction, $\Delta S_{surr} > 0$. In an endothermic reaction, $\Delta S_{surr} < 0$. A chemical cold pack for injuries is an example of an application using a spontaneous endothermic process.   **20.8**(a), (b), and (c)   **20.10**(a) positive (b) negative   (c) negative   **20.12**(a) negative   (b) negative (c) positive   **20.14**(a) positive   (b) negative   (c) positive **20.16**(a) positive   (b) negative   (c) positive   **20.18**(a) Butane. The double bond in 2-butene restricts freedom of rotation. (b) $Xe(g)$ because it has the greater molar mass.   (c) $CH_4(g)$. Gases have greater entropy than liquids.   **20.20**(a) diamond < graphite < charcoal. Freedom of motion is least in the network solid; more freedom between graphite sheets; most freedom in amorphous solid.   (b) ice < liquid water < water vapor. Entropy increases as a substance changes from solid to liquid to gas.   (c) O atoms < O_2 < O_3. Entropy increases with molecular complexity.   **20.22**(a) $ClO_4^-(aq) > ClO_3^-(aq) > ClO_2^-(aq)$; decreasing molecular complexity   (b) $NO_2(g) > NO(g) > N_2(g)$. N_2 has lower standard molar entropy because it consists of two of the same atoms; the other species have two different types of atoms. NO_2 is more complex than NO.   (c) $Fe_3O_4(s) > Fe_2O_3(s) > Al_2O_3(s)$. Fe_3O_4 is more complex and has more mass. Fe_2O_3 has more mass than Al_2O_3.   **20.26** For a system at equilibrium, $\Delta S_{univ} = \Delta S_{sys} + \Delta S_{surr} = 0$. For a system moving to equilibrium, $\Delta S_{univ} > 0$.   **20.27** $S°_{Cl_2O(g)} = 2S°_{HClO(g)} - \Delta S°_{rxn}$ **20.28**(a) negative; $\Delta S° = -172.4$ J/K   (b) positive; $\Delta S° = 141.6$ J/K   (c) negative; $\Delta S° = -837$ J/K   **20.30** $\Delta S° = 93.1$ J/K; yes, the positive sign of ΔS is expected because there is a net increase in the number of gas molecules.   **20.32** -75.6 J/K **20.35** -97.2 J/K   **20.37** A spontaneous process has $\Delta S_{univ} > 0$. Since the absolute temperature is always positive, ΔG_{sys} must be negative ($\Delta G_{sys} < 0$) for a spontaneous process.   **20.39** ΔH_{rxn} is positive and $\Delta S°_{sys}$ is positive. Melting is an example.
20.40(a) -1138.0 kJ   (b) -1379.4 kJ   (c) -224 kJ
20.42(a) -1138 kJ   (b) -1379 kJ   (c) -226 kJ   **20.44**(a) Entropy decreases ($\Delta S°$ is negative) because the number of moles of gas decreases. The combustion of CO releases energy ($\Delta H°$ is negative).   (b) -257.2 kJ or -257.3 kJ, depending on the method **20.46**(a) $\Delta H°_{rxn} = 90.7$ kJ; $\Delta S°_{rxn} = 221$ J/K   (b) at 28°C, $\Delta G° = 24.3$ kJ; at 128°C, $\Delta G° = 2.2$ kJ; at 228°C, $\Delta G° = -19.9$ kJ

(c) For the substances in their standard states, the reaction is nonspontaneous at 28°C, near equilibrium at 128°C, and spontaneous at 228°C.   **20.48** $\Delta H° = 30910$ J, $\Delta S° = 93.15$ J/K, $T = 331.8$ K   **20.50**(a) $\Delta H°_{rxn} = -241.826$ kJ, $\Delta S°_{rxn} = -44.4$ J/K, $\Delta G°_{rxn} = -228.60$ kJ   (b) Yes. The reaction will become nonspontaneous at higher temperatures.   (c) The reaction is spontaneous below 5.45×10^3 K.   **20.52**(a) $\Delta G°$ is a relatively large positive value.   (b) $K \gg 1$. Q depends on initial conditions, not equilibrium conditions.   **20.55** The standard free energy change, $\Delta G°$, applies when all components of the system are in their standard states; $\Delta G° = \Delta G$ when all concentrations equal 1 M and all partial pressures equal 1 atm.   **20.56**(a) 1.7×10^6 (b) 3.89×10^{-34} (c) 1.26×10^{48} **20.58** 4.89×10^{-51} **20.60** 3.36×10^5 **20.62** 2.7×10^4 J/mol; no **20.64**(a) 2.9×10^4 J/mol   (b) The reverse direction, formation of reactants, is spontaneous so the reaction proceeds to the left. (c) 7.0×10^3 J/mol; the reaction proceeds to the left to reach equilibrium.   **20.66**(a) no T (b) 163 kJ   (c) 1×10^2 kJ/mol **20.69**(a) spontaneous   (b) +   (c) +   (d) −   (e) −, not spontaneous   (f) −   **20.71**(a) 2.3×10^2 (b) Administer oxygen-rich air to counteract the CO poisoning. **20.75**(a) $2N_2O_5(g) + 6F_2(g) \longrightarrow 4NF_3(g) + 5O_2(g)$ (b) $\Delta G°_{rxn} = -569$ kJ   (c) $\Delta G°_{rxn} = -5.60\times10^2$ kJ/mol **20.78**(a) $\Delta H°_{rxn} = 470.5$ kJ; $\Delta S°_{rxn} = 558.4$ J/K   (b) The reaction will be spontaneous at high T, because the $-T\Delta S$ term will be larger in magnitude than ΔH.   (c) no   (d) 842.5 K   **20.80**(a) yes, negative Gibbs free energy   (b) Yes. It becomes spontaneous at 270.8 K.   (c) 234 K. The temperature is different because the ΔH and ΔS values for N_2O_5 vary with physical state. **20.84**(a) 465 K   (b) 6.59×10^{-4} (c) The reaction rate is higher at the higher temperature. The shorter time required (kinetics) overshadows the lower yield (thermodynamics).

Chapter 21

21.1 Oxidation is the loss of electrons and results in a higher oxidation number; reduction is the gain of electrons and results in a lower oxidation number.   **21.2** No, one half-reaction cannot take place independently because there is a transfer of electrons from one substance to another. If one substance loses electrons, another substance must gain them.   **21.3** Spontaneous reactions, $\Delta G_{sys} < 0$, take place in voltaic cells (also called galvanic cells). Nonspontaneous reactions, $\Delta G_{sys} > 0$, take place in electrolytic cells.   **21.5**(a) Cl^- (b) MnO_4^- (c) MnO_4^- (d) Cl^- (e) from Cl^- to MnO_4^- (f) $8H_2SO_4(aq) + 2KMnO_4(aq) + 10KCl(aq) \longrightarrow$
$$2MnSO_4(aq) + 5Cl_2(g) + 8H_2O(l) + 6K_2SO_4(aq)$$
21.7(a) $ClO_3^-(aq) + 6H^+(aq) + 6I^-(aq) \longrightarrow$
$$Cl^-(aq) + 3H_2O(l) + 3I_2(s)$$
Oxidizing agent is ClO_3^- and reducing agent is I^-.
(b) $2MnO_4^-(aq) + H_2O(l) + 3SO_3^{2-}(aq) \longrightarrow$
$$2MnO_2(s) + 3SO_4^{2-}(aq) + 2OH^-(aq)$$
Oxidizing agent is MnO_4^- and reducing agent is SO_3^{2-}.
(c) $2MnO_4^-(aq) + 6H^+(aq) + 5H_2O_2(aq) \longrightarrow$
$$2Mn^{2+}(aq) + 8H_2O(l) + 5O_2(g)$$
Oxidizing agent is MnO_4^- and reducing agent is H_2O_2

21.10(a) $4NO_3^-(aq) + 4H^+(aq) + 4Sb(s) \longrightarrow$
$$4NO(g) + 2H_2O(l) + Sb_4O_6(s)$$
Oxidizing agent is NO_3^- and reducing agent is Sb.
(b) $5BiO_3^-(aq) + 14H^+(aq) + 2Mn^{2+}(aq) \longrightarrow$
$$5Bi^{3+}(aq) + 7H_2O(l) + 2MnO_4^-(aq)$$
Oxidizing agent BiO_3^- and reducing agent is Mn^{2+}.
(c) $Pb(OH)_3^-(aq) + 2Fe(OH)_2(s) \longrightarrow$
$$Pb(s) + 2Fe(OH)_3(s) + OH^-(aq)$$
Oxidizing agent is $Pb(OH)_3^-$ and reducing agent is $Fe(OH)_2$.
21.12(a) $Au(s) + 3NO_3^-(aq) + 4Cl^-(aq) + 6H^+(aq) \longrightarrow$ $AuCl_4^-(aq) + 3NO_2(g) + 3H_2O(l)$ (b) Oxidizing agent is NO_3^- and reducing agent is Au.   (c) HCl provides chloride ions that combine with the gold(III) ion to form the stable $AuCl_4^-$ ion.   **21.13**(a) A   (b) E   (c) C   (d) A   (e) E   (f) E   **21.16** An active electrode is a reactant or product in the cell reaction. An inactive electrode does not take part in the reaction and is present only to conduct a current. Platinum and graphite are commonly used as inactive electrodes.   **21.17**(a) A   (b) B   (c) A (d) Hydrogen bubbles will form when metal A is placed in acid. Metal A is a better reducing agent than metal B, so if metal B reduces H^+ in acid, then metal A will also.   **21.18**(a) Oxidation: $Zn(s) \longrightarrow Zn^{2+}(aq) + 2e^-$
Reduction: $Sn^{2+}(aq) + 2e^- \longrightarrow Sn(s)$
Overall: $Zn(s) + Sn^{2+}(aq) \longrightarrow Zn^{2+}(aq) + Sn(s)$

(b)

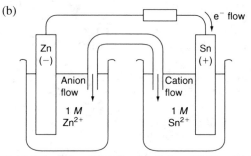

21.20(a) left to right   (b) left   (c) right   (d) Ni   (e) Fe   (f) Fe (g) 1 M $NiSO_4$ (h) K^+ and NO_3^- (i) neither   (j) from right to left   (k) Oxidation: $Fe(s) \longrightarrow Fe^{2+}(aq) + 2e^-$
Reduction: $Ni^{2+}(aq) + 2e^- \longrightarrow Ni(s)$
Overall: $Fe(s) + Ni^{2+}(aq) \longrightarrow Fe^{2+}(aq) + Ni(s)$
21.22(a) $Al(s) \mid Al^{3+}(aq) \parallel Cr^{3+}(aq) \mid Cr(s)$
(b) $Pt(s) \mid SO_2(g) \mid SO_4^{2-}(aq), H^+(aq) \parallel Cu^{2+}(aq) \mid Cu(s)$
21.25 A negative $E°_{cell}$ indicates that the redox reaction is not spontaneous, that is, $\Delta G° > 0$. The reverse reaction is spontaneous with $E°_{cell} > 0$.   **21.26** Similar to other state functions, $E°$ changes sign when a reaction is reversed. Unlike $\Delta G°$, $\Delta H°$, and $S°$, $E°$ (the ratio of energy to charge) is an intensive property. When the coefficients in a reaction are multiplied by a factor, the values of $\Delta G°$, $\Delta H°$, and $S°$ are multiplied by that factor. However, $E°$ does not change because both the energy and charge are multiplied by the factor and thus their ratio remains unchanged.
21.27(a) Oxidation: $Se^{2-}(aq) \longrightarrow Se(s) + 2e^-$
Reduction: $2SO_3^{2-}(aq) + 3H_2O(l) + 4e^- \longrightarrow$
$$S_2O_3^{2-}(aq) + 6OH^-(aq)$$
(b) $E°_{anode} = E°_{cathode} - E°_{cell} = -0.57$ V $- 0.35$ V $= -0.92$ V

21.29(a) $Br_2 > Fe^{3+} > Cu^{2+}$ (b) $Ca^{2+} < Ag^+ < Cr_2O_7^{2-}$
21.31(a) $Co(s) + 2H^+(aq) \longrightarrow Co^{2+}(aq) + H_2(g)$
  $E°_{cell} = 0.28$ V; spontaneous
 (b) $2Mn^{2+}(aq) + 5Br_2(l) + 8H_2O(l) \longrightarrow$
    $2MnO_4^-(aq) + 10Br^-(aq) + 16H^+(aq)$
  $E°_{cell} = -0.44$ V; not spontaneous
 (c) $Hg_2^{2+}(aq) \longrightarrow Hg^{2+}(aq) + Hg(l)$
  $E°_{cell} = -0.07$ V; not spontaneous
21.33(a) $2Ag(s) + Cu^{2+}(aq) \longrightarrow 2Ag^+(aq) + Cu(s)$
  $E°_{cell} = -0.46$ V; not spontaneous
 (b) $Cr_2O_7^{2-}(aq) + 3Cd(s) + 14H^+(aq) \longrightarrow$
    $2Cr^{3+}(aq) + 3Cd^{2+}(aq) + 7H_2O(l)$
  $E°_{cell} = 1.73$ V; spontaneous
 (c) $Pb(s) + Ni^{2+}(aq) \longrightarrow Pb^{2+}(aq) + Ni(s)$
  $E°_{cell} = -0.12$ V; not spontaneous
21.35 $3N_2O_4(g) + 2Al(s) \longrightarrow 6NO_2^-(aq) + 2Al^{3+}(aq)$
  $E°_{cell} = 0.867$ V $- (-1.66$ V$) = 2.53$ V
  $2Al(s) + 3SO_4^{2-}(aq) + 3H_2O(l) \longrightarrow$
    $2Al^{3+}(aq) + 3SO_3^{2-}(aq) + 6OH^-(aq)$
  $E°_{cell} = 2.59$ V
  $SO_4^{2-}(aq) + 2NO_2^-(aq) + H_2O(l) \longrightarrow$
    $SO_3^{2-}(aq) + N_2O_4(g) + 2OH^-(aq)$
  $E°_{cell} = 0.06$ V
21.37 $2HClO(aq) + Pt(s) + 2H^+(aq) \longrightarrow$
    $Cl_2(g) + Pt^{2+}(aq) + 2H_2O(l)$
  $E°_{cell} = 0.43$ V
  $2HClO(aq) + Pb(s) + SO_4^{2-}(aq) + 2H^+(aq) \longrightarrow$
    $Cl_2(g) + PbSO_4(s) + 2H_2O(l)$
  $E°_{cell} = 1.94$ V
  $Pt^{2+}(aq) + Pb(s) + SO_4^{2-}(aq) \longrightarrow Pt(s) + PbSO_4(s)$
  $E°_{cell} = 1.51$ V
21.39 Yes; C > A > B   **21.42** $A(s) + B^+(aq) \longrightarrow A^+(aq) +$
$B(s)$ with $Q = [A^+]/[B^+]$.   (a) $[A^+]$ increases and $[B^+]$ decreases.   (b) E_{cell} decreases.
(c) $E_{cell} = E°_{cell} - (RT/nF) \ln ([A^+]/[B^+])$
$E_{cell} = E°_{cell}$ when $(RT/nF) \ln ([A^+]/[B^+]) = 0$. This occurs
when $\ln ([A^+]/[B^+]) = 0$, that is, $[A^+]$ equals $[B^+]$.
(d) Yes, when $[A^+] > [B^+]$.   **21.44** In a concentration cell,
the overall reaction decreases the concentration of the more
concentrated electrolyte because it is reduced in the cathode com-
partment.   **21.45**(a) 3×10^{35} (b) 4×10^{-31} **21.47**(a) -2.03×10^5 J
(b) 1.73×10^5 J   **21.49** $\Delta G° = -2.7 \times 10^4$ J; $E° = 0.28$ V
21.51 8.8×10^{-5} M **21.53**(a) 0.05 V   (b) 0.50 M (c) $[Co^{2+}] =$
0.91 M; $[Ni^{2+}] = 0.09$ M **21.55** A; 0.085 V   **21.57** Electrons
flow from the anode, where oxidation occurs, to the cathode,
where reduction occurs. The electrons always flow from the anode
to the cathode no matter what type of battery.   **21.58** A D-sized
alkaline battery is much larger than an AAA-sized one, so the
D-sized battery contains greater amounts of the cell components.
The cell potential is an intensive property and does not depend on
the amounts of the cell components. The total charge, however,
depends on the amount of cell components so the D-sized battery
produces more charge than the AAA-sized battery.   **21.60** The

Teflon spacers keep the two metals separated so the copper cannot
conduct electrons that would promote the corrosion (rusting) of the
iron skeleton.   **21.62** Sacrificial anodes are made of metals with
$E°$ less than that of iron, -0.44 V, so they are more easily oxidized
than iron. Only (b), (f), and (g) will work for iron. (a) will form an
oxide coating that prevents further oxidation. (c) would react with
groundwater quickly.   **21.64** To reverse the reaction requires
0.34 V with the cell in its standard state. A 1.5 V cell supplies
more than enough potential, so the cadmium metal is oxidized to
Cd^{2+} and chromium plates out.   **21.66** The oxidation number of
N in NO_3^- is $+5$, the maximum O.N. for N. In the nitrite ion,
NO_2^-, the O.N. of N is $+3$, so nitrogen can be further oxidized.
21.68 Iron and nickel are more easily oxidized and less easily reduced than copper. They are separated from copper in the roasting
step and converted to slag. In the electrorefining process, all three
metals are in solution, but only Cu^{2+} ions are reduced at the
cathode to form $Cu(s)$.   **21.70**(a) Br_2 (b) Na   **21.72** copper and
bromine
21.74(a) Anode: $2H_2O(l) \longrightarrow O_2(g) + 4H^+(aq) + 4e^-$
    Cathode: $2H_2O(l) + 2e^- \longrightarrow H_2(g) + 2OH^-(aq)$
 (b) Anode: $2H_2O(l) \longrightarrow O_2(g) + 4H^+(aq) + 4e^-$
    Cathode: $Sn^{2+}(aq) + 2e^- \longrightarrow Sn(s)$
21.76(a) 3.75 mol e^- (b) 3.62×10^5 C   (c) 28.7 A
21.78 0.275 g Ra   **21.80** 9.20×10^3 s   **21.82**(a) The sodium and
sulfate ions make the water conductive so the current will flow
through the water, facilitating electrolysis. Pure water, which
contains very low (10^{-7} M) concentrations of H^+ and OH^-, conducts electricity very poorly.   (b) The reduction of H_2O has a
more positive half-potential than does the reduction of Na^+; the
oxidation of H_2O is the only reaction possible because SO_4^{2-}
cannot be oxidized. Thus, it is easier to reduce H_2O than Na^+
and easier to oxidize H_2O than SO_4^{2-}.   **21.83**(a) 4.6×10^4 L
(b) 1.26×10^8 C   (c) 1.68×10^6 s   **21.84** 62.6 g Zn
21.87 64.3 mass % Cu   **21.89**(a) 8 days   (b) 32 days   (c) $717
21.91(a) 2.4×10^4 days   (b) 2.1 g   (c) 3.4×10^{-5} dollars
21.92 7×10^2 lb Cl_2 **21.94**(a) 1.073×10^5 s   (b) 1.5×10^4 kW·h
(c) 6.8¢   **21.96** F < D < E. If metal E and a salt of metal F are
mixed, the salt is reduced, producing metal F because E has the
greatest reducing strength of the three metals.
21.97(a) Cell I: 4 mol electrons; $\Delta G = -4.75 \times 10^5$ J
    Cell II: 2 mol electrons; $\Delta G = -3.94 \times 10^5$ J
    Cell III: 2 mol electrons; $\Delta G = -4.53 \times 10^5$ J
 (b) Cell I: -13.2 kJ/g
    Cell II: -0.613 kJ/g
    Cell III: -2.62 kJ/g
Cell I has the highest ratio (most energy released per
gram) because the reactants have very low mass, while
Cell II has the lowest ratio because the reactants have
large masses.

21.98 $Sn^{2+}(aq) + 2e^- \longrightarrow Sn(s)$
$Cr^{3+}(aq) + e^- \longrightarrow Cr^{2+}(aq)$
$Fe^{2+}(aq) + 2e^- \longrightarrow Fe(s)$
$U^{4+}(aq) + e^- \longrightarrow U^{3+}(aq)$

21.101 Li > Ba > Na > Al > Mn > Zn > Cr > Fe > Ni > Sn > Pb > Cu > Ag > Hg > Au. Metals with potentials lower than that of water (-0.83 V) can displace H_2 from water: Li, Ba, Na, Al, and Mn. Metals with potentials lower than that of hydrogen (0.00 V) can displace H_2 from acid: Li, Ba, Na, Al, Mn, Zn, Cr, Fe, Ni, Sn, and Pb. Metals with potentials greater than that of hydrogen (0.00 V) cannot displace H_2: Cu, Ag, Hg, and Au.

21.102(a) 1.890 t Al_2O_3 (b) 0.3339 t C (c) 100% (d) 74% (e) 2.813×10^3 m^3 **21.103**(a) 5.3×10^{-11} (b) 0.20 V (c) 0.43 V (d) 8.2×10^{-4} M NaOH **21.105** 2.94

Chapter 14

14.1 The outermost electron is attracted by a smaller effective nuclear charge in Li because of shielding by the inner electrons, and it is farther from the nucleus in Li. Both of these factors lead to a lower ionization energy.

14.2(a) $2Al(s) + 6HCl(aq) \longrightarrow 2AlCl_3(aq) + 3H_2(g)$
(b) $LiH(s) + H_2O(l) \longrightarrow LiOH(aq) + H_2(g)$

14.4(a) $NaBH_4$: +1 for Na, +3 for B, −1 for H
$Al(BH_4)_3$: +3 for Al, +3 for B, −1 for H
$LiAlH_4$: +1 for Li, +3 for Al, −1 for H
(b) tetrahedral

$$\left[\begin{array}{c} H \\ | \\ H-B-H \\ | \\ H \end{array} \right]^-$$

14.7(a) reducing agent (b) Alkali metals have relatively low ionization energies, which means they easily lose the outermost electron.
(c) $2Na(s) + 2H_2O(l) \longrightarrow 2Na^+(aq) + 2OH^-(aq) + H_2(g)$
$2Na(s) + Cl_2(g) \longrightarrow 2NaCl(s)$

14.9 Density and ionic size increase down a group; the other three properties decrease down a group.

14.11 $2Na(s) + O_2(g) \longrightarrow Na_2O_2(s)$

14.13 $K_2CO_3(s) + 2HI(aq) \longrightarrow 2KI(aq) + H_2O(l) + CO_2(g)$

14.17 Group 2A(2) metals have an additional bonding electron to increase the strength of metallic bonding, which leads to higher melting points, higher boiling points, greater hardness, and greater density.

14.18(a) $CaO(s) + H_2O(l) \longrightarrow Ca(OH)_2(s)$
(b) $2Ca(s) + O_2(g) \longrightarrow 2CaO(s)$

14.20(a) $BeO(s) + H_2O(l) \longrightarrow$ no reaction
(b) $BeCl_2(l) + 2Cl^-$(solvated) $\longrightarrow BeCl_4^{2-}$(solvated).
This behaves like other Group 2A(2) elements.

14.22 For Groups 1A(1) to 4A(14), the number of covalent bonds equals the (old) group number. For Groups 5A(15) to 7A(17), it equals 8 minus the (old) group number. There are exceptions in Period 3 to Period 6 because it is possible for the 3A(13) to 7A(17) elements to use d orbitals and form more bonds. **14.25** The electron removed from Group 2A(2) atoms occupies the outer s orbital, whereas in Group 3A(13) atoms, the electron occupies the outer p orbital. For example, the electron configuration for

Be is $1s^2 2s^2$ and for B it is $1s^2 2s^2 2p^1$. It is easier to remove the p electron of B than an s electron of Be, because the energy of a p orbital is higher than that of the s orbital of the same level. Even though atomic size decreases because of increasing Z_{eff}, IE decreases from 2A(2) to 3A(13).

14.26 $In_2O_3 < Ga_2O_3 < Al_2O_3$ **14.28** Apparent O.N., +3; actual O.N., +1. The anion I_3^- has the general formula AX_2E_3 and bond angles of 180°. $(Tl^{3+})(I^-)_3$ does not exist because of the low strength of the Tl—I bond. $\left[:\ddot{I}—\ddot{I}—\ddot{I}: \right]^-$

14.33 In general, network solids have very high melting and boiling points and are very hard, while molecular solids have low melting and boiling points and are soft. The properties of network solids reflect the necessity of breaking covalent bonds throughout the substances, whereas the properties of molecular solids reflect the weaker intermolecular forces between individual molecules.

14.34 Basicity in water is greater for the oxide of a metal. Tin(IV) oxide is more basic in water than carbon dioxide because tin has more metallic character than carbon. **14.36**(a) Ionization energy generally decreases down a group. (b) The deviations (increases) from the expected trend are due to the presence of the first transition series between Si and Ge and of the lanthanides between Sn and Pb. (c) Group 3A(13) **14.39** Atomic size increases down a group. As atomic size increases, ionization energy decreases and so it is easier to form a positive ion. An atom that is easier to ionize exhibits greater metallic character.

14.41(a)

$$\left[\begin{array}{c} :\ddot{O}: \quad :\ddot{O}: \\ | \quad\quad | \\ :\ddot{O}—Si—\ddot{O}—Si—\ddot{O}: \\ | \quad\quad | \\ :\ddot{O}: \quad :\ddot{O}: \\ | \quad\quad | \\ :\ddot{O}—Si—\ddot{O}—Si—\ddot{O}: \\ | \quad\quad | \\ :\ddot{O}: \quad :\ddot{O}: \end{array} \right]^{8-}$$

(b)

$$\begin{array}{c} H \quad H \\ | \quad\; | \\ H—C—C—H \\ | \quad\; | \\ H—C—C—H \\ | \quad\; | \\ H \quad H \end{array}$$

14.44(a) diamond, C (b) calcium carbonate, $CaCO_3$ (c) carbon dioxide, CO_2 (d) carbon monoxide, CO (e) lead, Pb

14.48(a) -3 to $+5$ (b) For a group of nonmetals, the oxidation states range from the lowest, group number -8, or $5-8 = -3$ for Group 5A, to the highest, equal to the group number, or $+5$ for Group 5A. **14.49**(a) The greater the electronegativity of the element, the more covalent the bonding is in its oxide. (b) The more electronegative the element, the more acidic the oxide is.

14.52(a) $4As(s) + 5O_2(g) \longrightarrow 2As_2O_5(s)$
(b) $2Bi(s) + 3F_2(g) \longrightarrow 2BiF_3(s)$
(c) $Ca_3As_2(s) + 6H_2O(l) \longrightarrow 3Ca(OH)_2(s) + 2AsH_3(g)$

14.58(a) Boiling point and conductivity vary in similar ways down both groups. (b) Degree of metallic character and types of bonding vary in similar ways down both groups. (c) Both P and S have allotropes, and both bond covalently with almost every other nonmetal. (d) Both N and O are diatomic gases at normal temperatures and pressures. (e) O_2 is a reactive gas, whereas N_2 is not. Nitrogen can have any of six oxidation states, whereas oxygen has two.

4.60(a) $NaHSO_4(aq) + NaOH(aq) \longrightarrow Na_2SO_4(aq) + H_2O(l)$
(b) $S_8(s) + 24F_2(g) \longrightarrow 8SF_6(g)$
(c) $FeS(s) + 2HCl(aq) \longrightarrow H_2S(g) + FeCl_2(aq)$
4.62(a) acidic   (b) acidic   (c) basic   (d) amphoteric
(?) basic   **14.64**(a) O_3, ozone   (b) SO_3, sulfur trioxide
(?) SO_2, sulfur dioxide   **14.65** $S_2F_{10}(g) \longrightarrow SF_4(g) + SF_6(g)$;
.N. of S in S_2F_{10} is +5; O.N. of S in SF_4 is +4; O.N. of S in
F_6 is +6.   **14.66**(a) Polarity is the molecular property that is
-sponsible for the difference in boiling points between iodine
monochloride (polar) and bromine (nonpolar). It arises from dif-
-rent EN values of the bonded atoms.   (b) The boiling point of
olar ICl is higher than the boiling point of Br_2.   **14.68**(a) -1,
1, +3, +5, +7   (b) The electron configuration for Cl is [Ne]
$s^2 3p^5$. By gaining one electron, Cl achieves an octet. By form-
ng covalent bonds, Cl completes or expands its valence level by
maintaining electron pairs in bonds or as lone pairs.   (c) Fluo-
ine has only the -1 oxidation state because its small size and
osence of d orbitals prevent it from forming more than one
ovalent bond.   **14.69**(a) Cl—Cl bond is stronger than Br—Br
ond.   (b) Br—Br bond is stronger than I—I bond.
:) Cl—Cl bond is stronger than F—F bond. The fluorine atoms
-e so small that electron-electron repulsion of the lone pairs de-
-eases the strength of the bond.
4.70(a) $3Br_2(l) + 6OH^-(aq) \longrightarrow$
$$5Br^-(aq) + BrO_3^-(aq) + 3H_2O(l)$$
4.71(a) $I_2(s) + H_2O(l) \longrightarrow HI(aq) + HIO(aq)$
(b) $Br_2(l) + 2I^-(aq) \longrightarrow I_2(s) + 2Br^-(aq)$
(c) $CaF_2(s) + H_2SO_4(l) \longrightarrow CaSO_4(s) + 2HF(g)$
4.74 helium; argon   **14.75** Only dispersion forces hold atoms of
oble gases together.   **14.78** (a) Second ionization energies for
kali metals are so high because the electron being removed is
om the next lower energy level and these are very tightly held
y the nucleus.
) $2CsF_2(s) \longrightarrow 2CsF(s) + F_2(g)$; -405 kJ/mol.
4.81(a) hyponitrous acid, $H_2N_2O_2$; nitroxyl, HNO
(b) H—Ö—N̈=N̈—Ö—H   H—N̈=Ö:
(c) In both species the shape is bent about the N atoms.
(d)

$$\begin{bmatrix} \ddot{N}{=}\ddot{N} \\ \diagup \quad \diagdown \\ :\ddot{O}: \qquad :\ddot{O}: \end{bmatrix}^{2-} \qquad \begin{bmatrix} :\ddot{O}: \\ \diagup \\ \ddot{N}{=}\ddot{N} \\ \diagup \\ :\ddot{O}: \end{bmatrix}^{2-}$$

4.84 In a disproportionation reaction, a substance acts as both a
-ducing agent and an oxidizing agent because atoms of an ele-
ent within the substance attain both higher and lower oxidation
-ates in the products. The disproportionation reactions are b, c,
, e, and f.   **14.85**(a) Group 5A(15)   (b) Group 7A(17)
) Group 6A(16)   (d) Group 1A(1)   (e) Group 3A(13)
) Group 8A(18)   **14.86** 117.2 kJ
4.87

$$\begin{bmatrix} \quad :\ddot{C}l: \qquad :\ddot{C}l: \\ \qquad | \qquad\qquad | \\ :\ddot{C}l{-}Al{-}\ddot{C}l{-}Al{-}\ddot{C}l: \\ \qquad | \qquad\qquad | \\ \quad :\ddot{C}l: \qquad :\ddot{C}l: \end{bmatrix}^-$$

(a) sp^3 orbitals   (b) tetrahedral   (c) Since the ion is linear, the
central Cl atom must be sp hybridized.   (d) The sp hybridization
means there are no lone pairs on the central Cl atom. Instead, the
extra four electrons interact with the empty d orbitals on the
Al atoms to form double bonds between the chlorine and each
aluminum atom.
14.88 $\left[\ddot{O}{=}\ddot{N}{-}\ddot{O}: \right]^- \longleftrightarrow \left[:\ddot{O}{-}\ddot{N}{=}\ddot{O} \right]^-$

$$\ddot{O}{=}\dot{N}{-}\ddot{O}: \longleftrightarrow :\ddot{O}{-}\dot{N}{=}\ddot{O}$$

$$\left[\ddot{O}{=}N{=}\ddot{O} \right]^+$$

The nitronium ion (NO_2^+) has a linear shape because the
central N atom has two surrounding electron groups, which
achieve maximum repulsion at 180°. The nitrite ion (NO_2^-)
bond angle is more compressed than the nitrogen dioxide
(NO_2) bond angle because the lone pair of electrons takes up
more space than the lone electron.   **14.91**(a) 39.96 mass %
in $CuHAsO_3$; As, 62.42 mass % in $(CH_3)_3As$
(b) 0.35 g $CuHAsO_3$

Chapter 15

15.1(a) Carbon's electronegativity is midway between the most
metallic and nonmetallic elements of Period 2. To attain a filled
outer level, carbon forms covalent bonds to other atoms in molecules, network covalent solids, and polyatomic ions.
(b) Since carbon has four valence shell electrons, it forms four
covalent bonds to attain an octet.   (c) To reach the He electron
configuration, a carbon atom must lose four electrons, requiring
too much energy to form the C^{4+} cation. To reach the Ne electron configuration, the carbon atom must gain four electrons, also
requiring too much energy to form the C^{4-} anion.   (d) Carbon
is able to bond to itself extensively because its small size allows
for close approach and great orbital overlap. The extensive orbital overlap results in a strong, stable bond.   (e) The C—C
bond is short enough to allow sideways overlap of unhybridized
p orbitals of neighboring C atoms. The sideways overlap of p orbitals results in the π bonds that are part of double and triple
bonds.   **15.2**(a) C, H, O, N, P, S, and halogens   (b) Heteroatoms
are atoms of any element other than carbon and hydrogen.
(c) More electronegative than C: N, O, F, Cl, and Br; less electronegative than C: H and P. Sulfur and iodine have the same
electronegativity as carbon.   (d) Since carbon can bond to a
wide variety of heteroatoms and to carbon atoms, it can form
many different compounds.   **15.4** The C—H and C—C bonds
are unreactive because electron density is shared equally between
the two atoms. The C—I bond is somewhat reactive because it is
long and weak. The C=O bond is reactive because oxygen is

more electronegative than carbon and the electron-rich π bond makes it attract electron-poor atoms. The C—Li bond is also reactive because the bond polarity results in an electron-rich region around carbon and an electron-poor region around lithium.

15.5(a) An alkane and a cycloalkane are organic compounds that consist of carbon and hydrogen and have only single bonds. A cycloalkane has a ring of carbon atoms. An alkene is a hydrocarbon with at least one double bond. An alkyne is a hydrocarbon with at least one triple bond. (b) alkane = C_nH_{2n+2}, cycloalkane = C_nH_{2n}, alkene = C_nH_{2n}, alkyne = C_nH_{2n-2} (c) Alkanes and cycloalkanes are saturated hydrocarbons.

15.8(a), (c), and (f)

15.9(a)

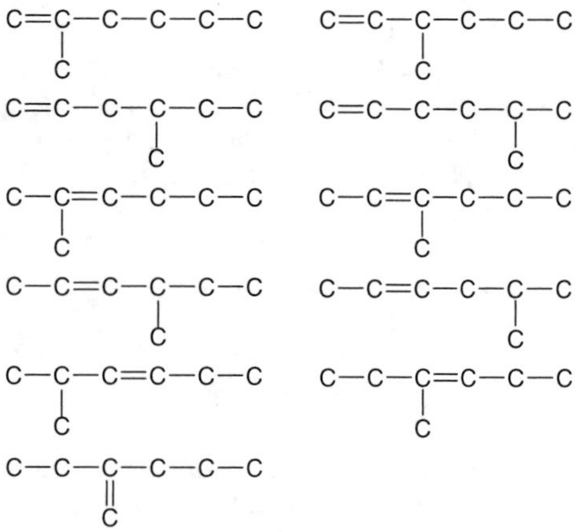

$$C{=}C{-}C{-}C{-}C{-}C \text{ with } C \text{ branch}$$

(b)

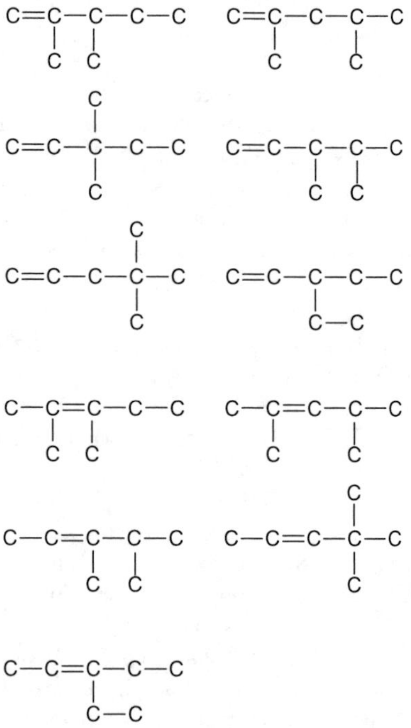

(c)

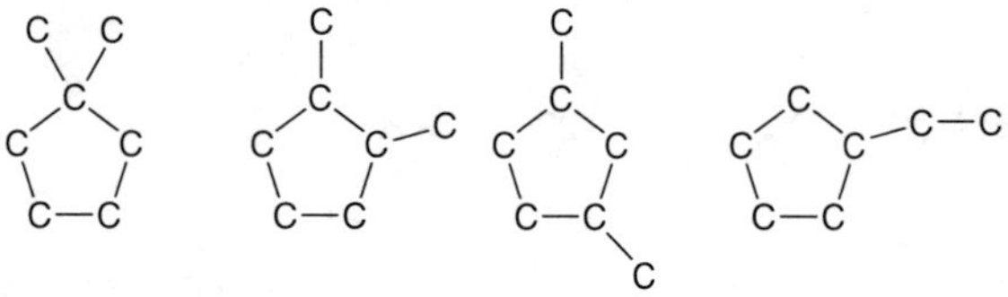

15.11(a)

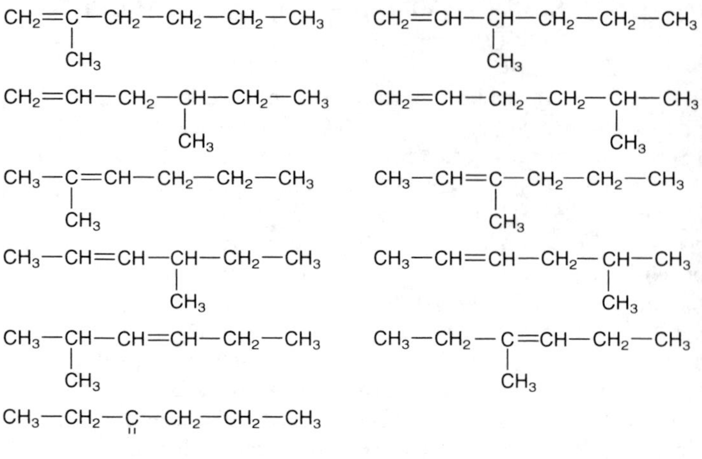

$CH_2{=}C{-}CH_2{-}CH_2{-}CH_2{-}CH_3$ with CH_3 branch

$CH_2{=}CH{-}CH{-}CH_2{-}CH_2{-}CH_3$ with CH_3 branch

$CH_2{=}CH{-}CH_2{-}CH{-}CH_2{-}CH_3$ with CH_3 branch

$CH_2{=}CH{-}CH_2{-}CH_2{-}CH{-}CH_3$ with CH_3 branch

$CH_3{-}C{=}CH{-}CH_2{-}CH_2{-}CH_3$ with CH_3 branch

$CH_3{-}CH{=}C{-}CH_2{-}CH_2{-}CH_3$ with CH_3 branch

$CH_3{-}CH{=}CH{-}CH{-}CH_2{-}CH_3$ with CH_3 branch

$CH_3{-}CH{=}CH{-}CH_2{-}CH{-}CH_3$ with CH_3 branch

$CH_3{-}CH{-}CH{=}CH{-}CH_2{-}CH_3$ with CH_3 branch

$CH_3{-}CH_2{-}C{=}CH{-}CH_2{-}CH_3$ with CH_3 branch

$CH_3{-}CH_2{-}C{-}CH_2{-}CH_2{-}CH_3$ with CH_3 branch

(b)

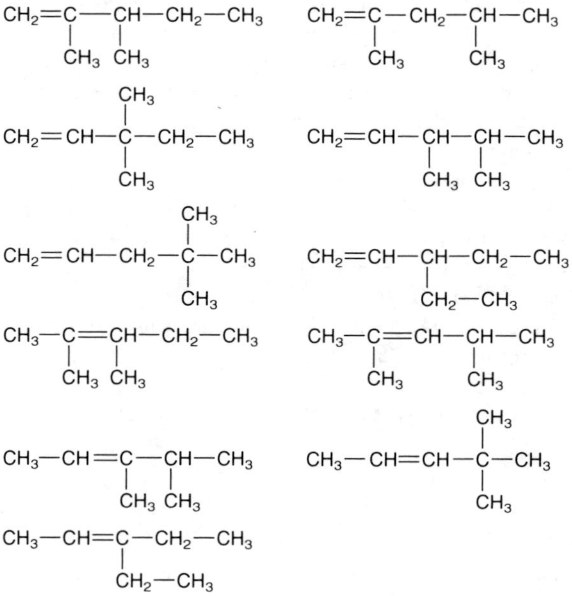

$CH_2{=}C{-}CH{-}CH_2{-}CH_3$ with CH_3 CH_3 branches

$CH_2{=}C{-}CH_2{-}CH{-}CH_3$ with CH_3 CH_3 branches

$CH_2{=}CH{-}C{-}CH_2{-}CH_3$ with CH_3 CH_3 branches

$CH_2{=}CH{-}CH{-}CH{-}CH_3$ with CH_3 CH_3 branches

$CH_2{=}CH{-}CH_2{-}C{-}CH_3$ with CH_3 CH_3 branches

$CH_2{=}CH{-}CH{-}CH_2{-}CH_3$ with $CH_2{-}CH_3$ branch

$CH_3{-}C{=}CH{-}CH_2{-}CH_3$ with CH_3 CH_3 branches

$CH_3{-}C{=}CH{-}CH{-}CH_3$ with CH_3 CH_3 branches

$CH_3{-}CH{=}C{-}CH{-}CH_3$ with CH_3 CH_3 branches

$CH_3{-}CH{=}CH{-}C{-}CH_3$ with CH_3 CH_3 branches

$CH_3{-}CH{=}C{-}CH_2{-}CH_3$ with $CH_2{-}CH_3$ branch

(c)

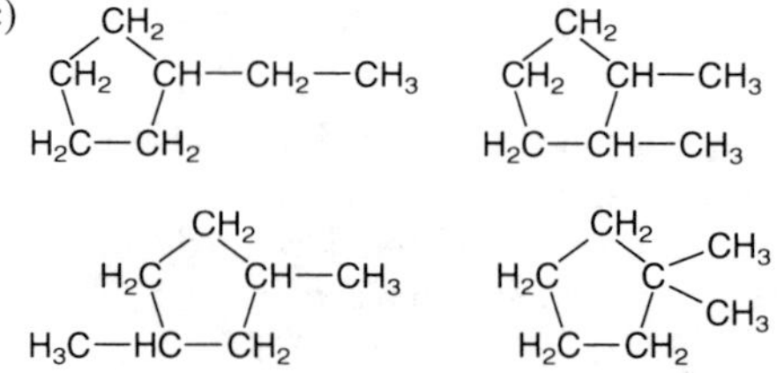

15.13(a) $CH_3{-}C{-}CH_2{-}CH_3$ with CH_3 above and CH_3 below

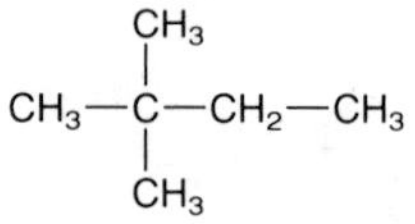

(b) $H_2C{=}CH{-}CH_2{-}CH_3$

(c) $HC{\equiv}C{-}CH{-}CH_3$ with $CH_2{-}CH_3$ branch

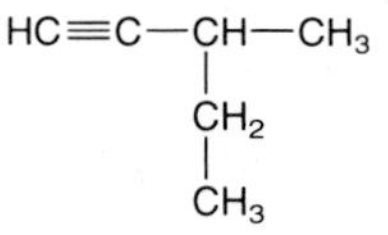

(d) Structure is correct.

15.15(a)

CH₃—CH—CH—CH₂—CH₂—CH₂—CH₂—CH₃ (with CH₃ above second C and CH₃ below third C)

(b) (cyclohexane ring with CH₂—CH₃ at position 1 and CH₃ at position 3; ring numbered 1–6)

(c) 3,4-dimethylheptane   (d) 2,2-dimethylbutane

15.17(a)

CH₃—CH₂—CH₂—CH—CH₂—CH₃ (with CH₃ above the fourth C)

Correct name is 3-methylhexane.

(b)

CH₃—CH₂—CH₂—CH—CH₃ (with CH₂—CH₃ above the fourth C)

Correct name is 3-methylhexane.

(c) (cyclohexane ring with CH₃ substituent)

Correct name is methylcyclohexane.

(d)

CH₃—CH₂—C—CH—CH₂—CH₂—CH₂—CH₃ (with CH₃ above the third C, and CH₃ and CH₂—CH₃ below the third and fourth C)

Correct name is 4-ethyl-3,3-dimethyloctane.

15.19(a) (cyclopropane ring with H,H on top C; left C bearing Cl and H; right C bearing CH₃)

(b)

CH₃—CH₂—Ⓒ—C—CH₃ (with H and CH₃ above, CH₃ and H below)

15.21(a) 3-Bromohexane is optically active.

CH₃—CH₂—ⒸH—CH₂—CH₂—CH₃ (with Br below)

(b) 3-Chloro-3-methylpentane is not optically active.

CH₃—CH₂—C—CH₂—CH₃ (with CH₃ above and Cl below)

(c) 1,2-Dibromo-2-methylbutane is optically active.

CH₂—Ⓒ—CH₂—CH₃ (with CH₃ above; Br below first C and Br below second C)

15.23(a)

(cis-2-pentene: H,H on top, CH₃CH₂ and CH₃ on bottom) (trans-2-pentene: H and CH₃ on top, CH₃CH₂ and H on bottom)

cis-2-pentene   *trans*-2-pentene

(b) (cis-1-cyclohexylpropene: H,H on top; cyclohexyl and CH₃ on bottom) (trans-1-cyclohexylpropene: H and CH₃ on top; cyclohexyl and H on bottom)

cis-1-cyclohexylpropene   *trans*-1-cyclohexylpropene

(c) no geometric isomers

15.25(a) no geometric isomers

(b) CH₃—CH₂ and CH₂—CH₃ (cis-3-hexene, both on top, H,H on bottom) CH₃—CH₂ and H (trans-3-hexene, H and CH₂—CH₃ on bottom)

cis-3-hexene   *trans*-3-hexene

(c) no geometric isomers

(d) (cis-1,2-dichloroethene: Cl,Cl on top, H,H on bottom) (trans-1,2-dichloroethene: Cl and H on top, H and Cl on bottom)

cis-1,2-dichloroethene   *trans*-1,2-dichloroethene

15.27

(benzene ring with two Cl at 1,2 positions) (benzene ring with two Cl at 1,3 positions) (benzene ring with two Cl at 1,4 positions)

1,2-dichlorobenzene   1,3-dichlorobenzene   1,4-dichlorobenzene
(*o*-dichlorobenzene)   (*m*-dichlorobenzene)   (*p*-dichlorobenzene)

15.29 (benzene ring with OH at top, C(CH₃)₃ groups at positions 2 and 6, and CH₃ at position 4)

15.30

(cis-2-methyl-3-hexene: CH₃—CH(CH₃) and CH₂—CH₃ with H,H on bottom) (trans-2-methyl-3-hexene: CH₃—CH(CH₃) and H on top, H and CH₂—CH₃ on bottom)

cis-2-methyl-3-hexene   *trans*-2-methyl-3-hexene

The compound 2-methyl-2-hexene does not have *cis-trans* isomers.   **15.32**(a) elimination   (b) addition

15.34(a) CH₃CH₂CH=CHCH₂CH₃ + H₂O $\xrightarrow{H^+}$

     CH₃CH₂CH₂CH(OH)CH₂CH₃

(b) CH₃CHBrCH₃ + CH₃CH₂OK ⟶

     CH₃CH=CH₂ + CH₃CH₂OH + KBr

(c) CH₃CH₃ + 2Cl₂ $\xrightarrow{h\nu}$ CHCl₂CH₃ + 2HCl

15.37(a) Methylethylamine is more soluble because it has the ability to form H bonds with water molecules.   (b) 1-Butanol has a higher melting point because it can form intermolecular H bonds.   (c) Propylamine has a higher boiling point because it contains N—H bonds that allow H bonding, and trimethylamine cannot form H bonds.   **15.39** Both groups react by addition to the π bond. The very polar C=O bond attracts the electron-rich O of water to the partially positive C. There is no such polarity in the alkene, so either C atom can be attacked.

$$CH_3-CH_2-\overset{\overset{\displaystyle O}{\|}}{C}-CH_2-CH_3 + H_2O \xrightarrow{H^+}$$

$$CH_3-CH_2-\overset{\overset{\displaystyle OH}{|}}{\underset{\underset{\displaystyle OH}{|}}{C}}-CH_2-CH_3$$

$$CH_3-CH_2-CH=CH-CH_3 + H_2O \xrightarrow{H^+}$$

$$CH_3-CH_2-\overset{\overset{}{}}{\underset{\underset{\displaystyle OH}{|}}{CH}}-CH_2-CH_3 + CH_3-CH_2-CH_2-\overset{}{\underset{\underset{\displaystyle OH}{|}}{CH}}-CH_3$$

15.41 Esters and acid anhydrides form through dehydration-condensation reactions, and water is the other product.
15.43(a) alkyl halide   (b) nitrile   (c) carboxylic acid   (d) aldehyde
15.45(a) CH_3-(CH=CH)$-$(CH$_2$$-$OH)
          alkene   alcohol

(b)
(Cl$-$CH$_2$)$-$⬡$-$(C(=O)$-$OH)
haloalkane   carboxylic acid

(c) amide, alkene
(d) (N≡C)$-$(CH$_2$$-$C(=O)$-CH_3$)
     nitrile   ketone

(e) ▱$-$C(=O)$-$O$-$(CH$_2$)$-$CH$_3$
         ester

15.47 $H_3C-CH_2-CH_2-CH_2-CH_2-OH$
$H_3C-CH_2-CH_2-\underset{\underset{\displaystyle OH}{|}}{CH}-CH_3$

$H_3C-\underset{\underset{\displaystyle CH_3}{|}}{CH}-\underset{\underset{\displaystyle OH}{|}}{CH}-CH_3$ $H_3C-\underset{\underset{\displaystyle CH_3}{|}}{\overset{\overset{\displaystyle OH}{|}}{C}}-CH_2-CH_3$

$H_3C-CH_2-\underset{\underset{\displaystyle OH}{|}}{CH}-CH_2-CH_3$ $H_3C-\underset{\underset{\displaystyle CH_3}{|}}{CH}-CH_2-CH_2-OH$

$H_3C-CH_2-\underset{\underset{\displaystyle CH_3}{|}}{CH}-CH_2-OH$ $H_3C-\underset{\underset{\displaystyle CH_3}{|}}{\overset{\overset{\displaystyle CH_3}{|}}{C}}-CH_2-OH$

15.49 $H_3C-CH_2-CH_2-CH_2-NH_2$ $H_3C-CH_2-\underset{\underset{\displaystyle NH_2}{|}}{CH}-CH_3$

$H_3C-\underset{\underset{\displaystyle CH_3}{|}}{CH}-CH_2-NH_2$ $H_3C-\underset{\underset{\displaystyle CH_3}{|}}{\overset{\overset{\displaystyle CH_3}{|}}{C}}-NH_2$

$H_3C-CH_2-\underset{\underset{\displaystyle H}{|}}{N}-CH_2-CH_3$ $H_3C-CH_2-CH_2-\underset{\underset{\displaystyle H}{|}}{N}-CH_3$

$H_3C-CH_2-\underset{\underset{\displaystyle CH_3}{|}}{N}-CH_3$ $H_3C-\underset{\underset{\displaystyle CH_3}{|}}{CH}-\underset{\underset{\displaystyle H}{|}}{N}-CH_3$

15.51(a)
$$CH_3-\overset{\overset{\displaystyle O}{\|}}{C}-\underset{\underset{\displaystyle H}{|}}{N}-CH_3$$

(b)
$$CH_3-CH_2-CH_2-\overset{\overset{\displaystyle O}{\|}}{C}-O-\underset{\underset{\displaystyle CH_3}{}}{\overset{\overset{\displaystyle CH_3}{|}}{CH}}-CH_3$$

(c)
$$H-\overset{\overset{\displaystyle O}{\|}}{C}-O-CH_2-\underset{\underset{\displaystyle CH_3}{}}{\overset{\overset{\displaystyle CH_3}{|}}{CH}}-CH_3$$

15.53(a)
$$CH_3-(CH_2)_4-\overset{\overset{\displaystyle O}{\|}}{C}-OH \quad \text{and} \quad HO-CH_2-CH_3$$

(b)
⬡$-$C(=O)$-$OH   and $HO-CH_2-CH_2-CH_3$

(c)
$$CH_3-CH_2-OH \quad \text{and} \quad HO-\overset{\overset{\displaystyle O}{\|}}{C}-CH_2-CH_2-⬡$$

15.55(a) CH_3-CH_2-OH

$$CH_3-CH_2-\overset{\overset{\displaystyle O}{\|}}{C}-O-CH_2-CH_3$$

(b)
$$CH_3-CH_2-\underset{\underset{\displaystyle C\equiv N}{}}{\overset{\overset{\displaystyle C\equiv N}{|}}{CH}}-CH_3$$

$$CH_3-CH_2-\underset{\underset{\displaystyle C=O}{|}}{\overset{\overset{\displaystyle OH}{|}}{CH}}-CH_3$$

15.59 addition reactions and condensation reactions   **15.61** Dispersion forces strongly attract the long, unbranched chains of high-density polyethylene (HDPE). Low-density polyethylene (LDPE) has branching in the chains that prevents packing and weakens the attractions.   **15.63** An amine and a carboxylic acid react to form nylon; a carboxylic acid and an alcohol form a polyester.
15.64(a)
$$\left[\begin{array}{c} \overset{\displaystyle H}{|} \ \overset{\displaystyle H}{|} \\ -C-C- \\ \underset{\displaystyle H}{|} \ \underset{\displaystyle Cl}{|} \end{array}\right]_n$$
(b)
$$\left[\begin{array}{c} \overset{\displaystyle H}{|} \ \overset{\displaystyle H}{|} \\ -C-C- \\ \underset{\displaystyle H}{|} \ \underset{\displaystyle CH_3}{|} \end{array}\right]_n$$

15.66
$$nHO-\overset{\overset{\displaystyle O}{\|}}{C}-⬡-\overset{\overset{\displaystyle O}{\|}}{C}-OH + nHO-CH_2-CH_2-OH \longrightarrow$$

$$HO\left[\overset{\overset{\displaystyle O}{\|}}{C}-⬡-\overset{\overset{\displaystyle O}{\|}}{C}-O-CH_2-CH_2-O\right]_n H + 2n-1\ H_2O$$

15.68(a) condensation   (b) addition   (c) condensation
(d) condensation   **15.70** The amino acid sequence in a protein determines its shape and structure, which determine its function.
15.72(a) CH_3 (b) imidazole ring with =$\overset{+}{N}H$, HN, CH_2 (c) CH_3, S, CH_2, CH_2

15.74(a)

(b)

15.76(a) AATCGG   (b) TCTGTA   **15.78**(a) Both R groups are from cysteine, which can form a disulfide bond (covalent bond). (b) Lysine and aspartic acid give a salt link.   (c) Asparagine and serine will hydrogen bond.   (d) Valine and phenylalanine interact through dispersion forces.   **15.80** $CH_3-CH=CH-CH_3$

15.81(a)

(b) Carbon 1 is sp^2 hybridized.   Carbon 2 is sp^3 hybridized. Carbon 3 is sp^3 hybridized.   Carbon 4 is sp^2 hybridized. Carbon 5 is sp^3 hybridized.   Carbons 6 and 7 are sp^2 hybridized.

(c) Carbons 2, 3, and 5 are chiral centers, as they are each bonded to four different groups.

15.83

The shortest carbon-oxygen bond is the double bond in the aldehyde group.

Chapter 22

22.1(a) $1s^22s^22p^63s^23p^64s^23d^{10}4p^65s^24d^x$
(b) $1s^22s^22p^63s^23p^64s^23d^{10}4p^65s^24d^{10}5p^66s^24f^{14}5d^x$
22.4(a) The elements should increase in size as they increase in mass from Period 5 to Period 6. Because 14 additional elements lie between Periods 5 and 6, the effective nuclear charge increases significantly; so the atomic size decreases, or "contracts." This effect is significant enough that Zr^{4+} and Hf^{4+} are almost the same size but differ greatly in atomic mass.   (b) The atomic size increases from Period 4 to Period 5, but stays fairly constant from Period 5 to Period 6.   (c) Atomic mass increases signifi-

cantly from Period 5 to Period 6, but atomic radius (and thus volume) increases slightly, so Period 6 elements are very dense. **22.7**(a) A paramagnetic substance is attracted to a magnetic field, while a diamagnetic substance is slightly repelled by one. (b) Ions of transition elements often have half-filled d orbitals whose unpaired electrons make the ions paramagnetic. Ions of main-group elements usually have a noble gas configuration with no partially filled levels.   (c) Some d orbitals in the transition element ions are empty, which allows an electron from one d orbital to move to a slightly higher energy one. The energy required for this transition is small and falls in the visible wavelength range. All orbitals are filled in ions of main-group elements, so enough energy would have to be added to move an electron to the next principal energy level, not just another orbital within the same energy level. This amount of energy is very large and much greater than the visible range of wavelengths.
22.8(a) $1s^22s^22p^63s^23p^64s^23d^3$
(b) $1s^22s^22p^63s^23p^64s^23d^{10}4p^65s^24d^1$ (c) [Xe] $6s^24f^{14}5d^{10}$
22.10(a) [Ar], no unpaired electrons   (b) [Ar] $3d^9$, one unpaired electron   (c) [Ar] $3d^5$, five unpaired electrons   (d) [Kr] $4d^2$, two unpaired electrons   **22.12** Cr, Mo, and W   **22.14** In CrF_2, because the chromium is in a lower oxidation state.
22.16 CrO_3, with Cr in a higher oxidation state, yields a more acidic aqueous solution.   **22.19** The coordination number indicates the number of ligand atoms bonded to the metal ion. The oxidation number represents the number of electrons lost to form the ion. The coordination number is unrelated to the oxidation number.   **22.21** 2, linear; 4, tetrahedral or square planar; 6, octahedral   **22.24**(a) hexaaquanickel(II) chloride (b) tris(ethylenediamine)chromium(III) perchlorate   (c) potassium hexacyanomanganate(II)   **22.26**(a) 2+, 6   (b) 3+, 6 (c) 2+, 6   **22.28**(a) potassium dicyanoargentate(I)   (b) sodium tetrachlorocadmate(II)   (c) tetraammineaquabromocobalt(III) bromide   **22.30**(a) $[Zn(NH_3)_4]SO_4$ (b) $[Cr(NH_3)_5Cl]Cl_2$ (c) $Na_3[Ag(S_2O_3)_2]$ **22.32**(a) 4, two ions   (b) 6, three ions (c) 2, four ions   **22.34**(a) The nitrite ion forms linkage isomers because it can bind to the metal ion through either the nitrogen or one of the oxygen atoms—both have a lone pair of electrons.

(b) Sulfur dioxide molecules form linkage isomers because both the sulfur and the oxygen atoms can bind the central metal ion.

(c) Nitrate ions have three oxygen atoms, all with a lone pair that can bond to the metal ion, but all of the oxygen atoms are equivalent, so there are no linkage isomers.

$$\left[:\overset{..}{\text{O}}\!-\!\text{N}\!=\!\overset{..}{\text{O}} \atop :\overset{..}{\text{O}}: \right]^{-}$$

22.36(a) geometric isomerism

Br   Br   Br   NH$_2$CH$_3$
    Pt   and   Pt
CH$_3$NH$_2$ NH$_2$CH$_3$ CH$_3$NH$_2$ Br
    cis   *trans*

(b) geometric isomerism

H$_3$N   NH$_3$ H$_3$N   F
    Pt   and   Pt
Cl   F   Cl   NH$_3$
    cis   *trans*

(c) geometric isomerism

H$_2$O   NH$_3$ H$_2$O   NH$_3$ H$_2$O   F
    Pt   and   Pt   and   Pt
Cl   F   F   Cl   Cl   NH

22.38(a) geometric isomerism

$$\left[\text{Cl} \atop \text{Br} \overset{\text{Cl}}{\underset{\text{Br}}{\text{Pt}}} \right]^{2-} \text{and} \left[\text{Cl} \atop \text{Br} \overset{\text{Br}}{\underset{\text{Cl}}{\text{Pt}}} \right]^{2-}$$
    cis   *trans*

(b) linkage isomerism

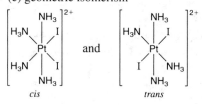

(c) geometric isomerism

$$\left[\begin{array}{c} \text{NH}_3 \\ \text{H}_3\text{N} \;|\; \text{I} \\ \text{Pt} \\ \text{H}_3\text{N} \;|\; \text{I} \\ \text{NH}_3 \end{array} \right]^{2+} \text{and} \left[\begin{array}{c} \text{NH}_3 \\ \text{H}_3\text{N} \;|\; \text{I} \\ \text{Pt} \\ \text{I} \;|\; \text{NH}_3 \\ \text{NH}_3 \end{array} \right]^{2+}$$
    cis   *trans*

22.40(a) dsp^2 (b) sp^3 **22.43**(a) The crystal field splitting energy (Δ) is the energy difference between the two sets of d orbitals that result from the bonding of ligands to a central transition metal atom. (b) In an octahedral field of ligands, the ligands approach along the x-, y-, and z-axes. The $d_{x^2-y^2}$ and d_{z^2} orbitals are located *along* the x-, y-, and z-axes, so ligand interaction is higher in energy. The other orbital-ligand interactions are lower in energy because the d_{xy}, d_{yz}, and d_{xz} orbitals are located *between* the x-, y-, and z-axes. (c) In a tetrahedral field of ligands, the ligands do not approach along the x-, y-, and z-axes. The ligand interaction is greater for the d_{xy}, d_{yz}, and d_{xz} orbitals and lesser for the $d_{x^2-y^2}$ and d_{z^2} orbitals. Therefore, the crystal field splitting is reversed, and the d_{xy}, d_{yz}, and d_{xz} orbitals are higher in energy than the $d_{x^2-y^2}$ and d_{z^2} orbitals. **22.45** If Δ is greater than E_{pairing}, electrons will pair their spins in the lower energy d orbitals before adding as unpaired electrons to the higher energy d orbitals. If Δ is less than E_{pairing}, electrons will add as unpaired electrons to the higher energy d orbitals before pairing in the lower energy d orbitals. **22.47**(a) no d electrons (b) eight d electrons (c) six d electrons **22.49**(a) and (d)
22.51

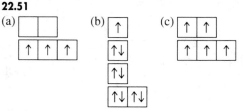

22.53 $[\text{Cr}(\text{H}_2\text{O})_6]^{3+} < [\text{Cr}(\text{NH}_3)_6]^{3+} < [\text{Cr}(\text{NO}_2)_6]^{3-}$
22.55 A violet complex absorbs yellow-green light. The light absorbed by a complex with a weaker field ligand would be at a lower energy and higher wavelength. Light of lower energy than yellow-green light is yellow, orange, or red. The color observed would be blue or green. **22.60**(a) 6 (b) +3 (c) two (d) 1 mol
22.65 $[\text{Co}(\text{NH}_3)_4(\text{H}_2\text{O})\text{Cl}]^{2+}$

tetraammineaquachlorocobalt(III) ion

2 geometric isomers

$$\left[\begin{array}{c} \text{NH}_3 \\ \text{H}_3\text{N} \cdots \text{Cl} \\ \text{Co} \\ \text{H}_3\text{N} \;|\; \text{OH}_2 \\ \text{NH}_3 \end{array} \right]^{2+} \left[\begin{array}{c} \text{NH}_3 \\ \text{H}_3\text{N} \cdots \text{Cl} \\ \text{Co} \\ \text{H}_2\text{O} \;|\; \text{NH}_3 \\ \text{NH}_3 \end{array} \right]^{2+}$$
    cis   *trans*

$[\text{Cr}(\text{H}_2\text{O})_3\text{Br}_2\text{Cl}]$ triaquadibromochlorochromium(III)

3 geometric isomers

$$\left[\begin{array}{c} \text{H}_2\text{O} \\ \text{H}_2\text{O} \cdots \text{Cr} \cdots \text{Br} \\ \text{Br} \;\; \text{H}_2\text{O} \;\; \text{Cl} \end{array} \right] \left[\begin{array}{c} \text{H}_2\text{O} \\ \text{H}_2\text{O} \cdots \text{Cr} \cdots \text{Br} \\ \text{Cl} \;\; \text{H}_2\text{O} \;\; \text{Br} \end{array} \right] \left[\begin{array}{c} \text{Cl} \\ \text{H}_2\text{O} \cdots \text{Cr} \cdots \text{Br} \\ \text{H}_2\text{O} \;\; \text{H}_2\text{O} \;\; \text{Br} \end{array} \right]$$
Br's are *trans*   Br's are *cis*   Br's and H$_2$O's are *cis*
                  H$_2$O's are *cis* and *trans*

$[Cr(NH_3)_2(H_2O)_2Br_2]^+$
diamminediaquadibromochromium(III) ion

6 isomers (5 geometric)

all ligands are *trans*   only NH_3 is *trans*   only Br is *trans*

only H_2O is *trans*   optical isomers
all three ligands are *cis*

22.71(a) The first reaction shows no change in the number of particles. In the second reaction, the number of reactant particles is greater than the number of product particles. A decrease in the number of particles means a decrease in entropy. Based on entropy change only, the first reaction is favored.   (b) The ethylenediamine complex will be more stable with respect to ligand exchange in water because the entropy change for that exchange is unfavorable.

Chapter 23

23.1(a) Chemical reactions are accompanied by relatively small changes in energy; nuclear reactions are accompanied by relatively large changes in energy.   (b) Increasing temperature increases the rate of a chemical reaction but has no effect on a nuclear reaction.   (c) Both chemical and nuclear reaction rates increase with higher reactant concentrations.   (d) If the reactant is limiting in a chemical reaction, then more reactant produces more product and the yield increases. The presence of more radioactive reactant results in more decay product, so a higher reactant concentration increases the yield.   **23.2**(a) Z down by 2, N down by 2   (b) Z up by 1, N down by 1   (c) no change in Z or N (d) Z down by 1, N up by 1;   (e) Z down by 1, N up by 1; A different element is produced in all cases except c.   **23.4** A neutron-rich nuclide decays by beta decay. A neutron-poor nuclide undergoes positron decay or electron capture.

23.6(a) $^{234}_{92}U \longrightarrow {}^{4}_{2}He + {}^{230}_{90}Th$

(b) $^{232}_{93}Np + {}^{0}_{-1}e \longrightarrow {}^{232}_{92}U$

(c) $^{12}_{7}N \longrightarrow {}^{0}_{1}\beta + {}^{12}_{6}C$

23.8(a) $^{48}_{23}V \longrightarrow {}^{48}_{22}Ti + {}^{0}_{1}\beta$

(b) $^{107}_{48}Cd + {}^{0}_{-1}e \longrightarrow {}^{107}_{47}Ag$

(c) $^{210}_{86}Rn \longrightarrow {}^{206}_{84}Po + {}^{4}_{2}He$

23.10(a) Appears stable because its N and Z values are both magic numbers, but its N/Z ratio (1.50) is too high; it is unstable. (b) Appears unstable because its Z value is an odd number, but its N/Z ratio (1.19) is in the band of stability, so it is stable   (c) Unstable because its N/Z ratio is too high.   **23.12**(a) alpha decay (b) positron decay or electron capture   (c) positron decay or electron capture   **23.14** Stability results from a favorable N/Z

ratio, even numbered N and/or Z, and the occurrence of magic numbers. The N/Z ratio of ^{52}Cr is 1.17, which is within the band of stability. The fact that Z is even does not account for the variation in stability because all isotopes of chromium have the same Z. However, ^{52}Cr has 28 neutrons, so N is both an even number and a magic number for this isotope only.   **23.18** No, it is not valid to conclude that $t_{1/2}$ equals 1 min because the number of nuclei is so small. Decay rate is an average rate and is only meaningful when the sample is macroscopic and contains a large number of nuclei. For the sample containing 6×10^{12} nuclei, the conclusion is valid.   **23.20** 2.89×10^{-2} Ci/g   **23.22** 2.31×10^{-7} yr^{-1} **23.24** 1.49 mg   **23.26** 2.2×10^{9} yr   **23.28** 1×10^{2} dpm **23.32** Protons are repelled from the target nuclei due to interaction with like (positive) charges. Higher energy is required to overcome the repulsion.

23.33(a) $^{13}_{7}N$; $^{10}_{5}B + {}^{4}_{2}He \longrightarrow {}^{1}_{0}n + {}^{13}_{7}N$

(b) $^{1}_{0}n$; $^{28}_{14}Si + {}^{2}_{1}H \longrightarrow {}^{29}_{15}P + {}^{1}_{0}n$

(c) $^{242}_{96}Cm$; $^{242}_{96}Cm + {}^{4}_{2}He \longrightarrow 2\,{}^{1}_{0}n + {}^{244}_{98}Cf$

23.37 Ionizing radiation is more dangerous to children because their rapidly dividing cells are more susceptible to radiation than an adult's slowly dividing cells.   **23.38**(a) 5.4×10^{-7} rad (b) 5.4×10^{-9} Gy   **23.40**(a) 7.5×10^{-10} Gy   (b) 7.5×10^{-5} mrem   (c) 7.5×10^{-10} Sv   **23.42** 1.86×10^{-3} rad   **23.44** NAA does not destroy the sample, while chemical analyses do. Neutrons bombard a nonradioactive sample, inducing some atoms within the sample to be radioactive. The radioisotopes decay by emitting radiation characteristic of each isotope.   **23.45** The oxygen isotope in the methanol reactant appears in the formaldehyde product. The oxygen isotope in the chromic acid reactant appears in the water product. The isotope traces the oxygen in methanol to the oxygen in formaldehyde.   **23.48**(a) 1.861×10^{4} eV (b) 2.981×10^{-15} J   **23.50**(a) 8.768 MeV/nucleon (b) 517.3 MeV/atom   (c) 4.99×10^{10} kJ/mol   **23.53** Radioactive decay is a spontaneous process in which unstable nuclei emit radioactive particles and energy. Fission occurs as the result of high-energy bombardment of nuclei with small particles that cause the nuclei to break into smaller nuclides, radioactive particles, and energy. All fission events are not the same. The nuclei split in a number of ways to produce several different products. **23.56** The water serves to slow the neutrons so that they are better able to cause a fission reaction. Heavy water is a better moderator because it does not absorb neutrons as well as light water does, so more neutrons are available to initiate the fission process. However, D_2O does not occur naturally in great abundance, so its production adds to the cost of a heavy-water reactor. **23.62**(a) 1.1×10^{-29} kg   (b) 9.8×10^{-13} J   (c) 5.9×10^{8} kJ/mol. This is approximately 1 million times larger than a typical heat of reaction.   **23.64** 8.0×10^{3} yr   **23.68** 1.35×10^{-5} M **23.70**(a) 5.99 h   (b) 21%   **23.71** 4.904×10^{-9} L/h **23.80**(a) 2.07×10^{-17} J   (b) 1.45×10^{7} H atoms (c) 1.4960×10^{-5} J   (d) 1.4959×10^{-5} J   (e) No, the Captain should continue using the current technology.

Numbers in parentheses refer to the page(s) on which a term is introduced and/or discussed.

A

absolute scale (also *Kelvin scale*)   The preferred temperature scale in scientific work, which has absolute zero (0 K, or $-273.15°C$) as the lowest temperature. (18) [See also *kelvin (K)*.]

absorption spectrum   The spectrum produced when atoms absorb specific wavelengths of incoming light and become excited from lower to higher energy levels. (227)

accuracy   The closeness of a measurement to the actual value. (24)

acid   In common laboratory terms, any species that produces H^+ ions when dissolved in water. (123) (See also *Arrhenius, Brønsted-Lowry,* and *Lewis acid-base definitions.*)

acid anhydride   A compound, sometimes formed by a dehydration-condensation reaction of an oxoacid, that yields two molecules of the acid when it reacts with water. (489)

acid-base buffer (also *buffer*)   A solution that resists changes in pH when a small amount of either strong acid or strong base is added. (632)

acid-base indicator   A species whose color is different in acid and in base, which is used to monitor the equivalence point of a titration or the pH of a solution. (600)

acid-base reaction   Any reaction between an acid and a base. (123) (See also *neutralization reaction.*)

acid-base titration curve   A plot of the pH of a solution of acid (or base) versus the volume of base (or acid) added to the solution. (641)

acid-dissociation (acid-ionization) constant (K_a)   An equilibrium constant for the dissociation of an acid (HA) in H_2O to yield the conjugate base (A^-) and H_3O^+:

$$K_a = \frac{[H_3O^+][A^-]}{[HA]} \qquad (594)$$

actinides   The Period 7 elements that constitute the second inner transition series (5*f* block), which includes thorium (Th; $Z = 90$) through lawrencium (Lr; $Z = 103$). (258)

activated complex   (See *transition state.*)

activation energy (E_a)   The minimum energy with which molecules must collide to react. (527)

active site   The region of an enzyme formed by specific amino acid side chains at which catalysis occurs. (542)

activity ($\mathcal{A}$) (also *decay rate*)   The change in number of nuclei ($\mathcal{N}$) of a radioactive sample divided by the change in time (t). (793)

activity series of the metals   A listing of metals arranged in order of their decreasing strength as reducing agents in aqueous reactions. (136)

actual yield   The amount of product actually obtained in a chemical reaction. (97)

addition polymer (also *chain reaction,* or *chain-growth, polymer*)   A polymer formed when monomers (usually containing C=C) combine through an addition reaction. (492)

addition reaction   A type of organic reaction in which atoms linked by a multiple bond become bonded to more atoms. (481)

adduct   The product of a Lewis acid-base reaction characterized by the formation of a new covalent bond. (621)

adenosine triphosphate (ATP)   A high-energy molecule that serves most commonly as a store and source of energy in organisms. (693)

alcohol   An organic compound (ending, *-ol*) that contains a $-\overset{|}{\underset{|}{C}}-\overset{..}{\underset{..}{O}}-H$ functional group. (484)

aldehyde   An organic compound (ending, *-al*) that contains the carbonyl functional group (C=$\overset{..}{\underset{..}{O}}$) in which the carbonyl C is also bonded to H. (487)

alkane   A hydrocarbon that contains only single bonds (general formula, C_nH_{2n+2}). (472)

alkene   A hydrocarbon that contains at least one C=C bond (general formula, C_nH_{2n}). (477)

alkyl group   A saturated hydrocarbon chain with one bond available. (481)

alkyl halide   (See *haloalkane.*)

alkyne   A hydrocarbon that contains at least one C≡C bond (general formula, C_nH_{2n-2}). (478)

allotrope   One of two or more crystalline or molecular forms of an element. In general, one allotrope is more stable than another at a particular pressure and temperature. (444)

alloy   A mixture with metallic properties that consists of solid phases of two or more pure elements, a solid-solid solution, or distinct intermediate phases. (404)

alpha (α) decay   A radioactive process in which an alpha particle is emitted from a nucleus. (788)

alpha particle (α or $^4_2He^{2+}$)   A positively charged particle, identical to a helium -4 nucleus, that is one of the common types of radioactive emissions. (786)

amide   An organic compound that contains the $-\overset{\overset{:O:}{\|}}{C}-\overset{|}{\underset{|}{N}}-$ functional group. (488)

amine   An organic compound (general formula, $-\overset{|}{\underset{|}{C}}-\overset{|}{\underset{|}{N}}-$) derived structurally by replacing one or more H atoms of ammonia with alkyl groups; a weak organic base. (485)

amino acid   An organic compound [general formula, $H_2N-CH(R)-COOH$] with at least one carboxyl and one amine group on the same molecule; the monomer unit of a protein. (496)

amorphous solid   A solid that occurs in different shapes because it lacks extensive molecular-level ordering of its particles. (379)

ampere (A)   The SI unit of electric current; 1 ampere of current results when 1 coulomb flows through a conductor in 1 second. (747)

amphoteric   Able to act as either an acid or a base. (268)

amplitude   The height of the crest (or depth of the trough) of a wave; related to the intensity of the energy. (216)

angular momentum quantum number (*l*) (or *orbital-shape quantum number*)   An integer from 0 to $n - 1$ that is related to the shape of an atomic orbital. (234)

anion   A negatively charged ion. (49)

anode   The electrode at which oxidation occurs in an electrochemical cell. Electrons are given up by the reducing agent and leave the cell at the anode. (709)

antibonding MO   A molecular orbital formed when wave functions are subtracted from each other, which decreases electron density between the nuclei and leaves a node. Electrons occupying such an orbital destabilize the molecule. (344)

aqueous solution   A solution in which water is the solvent. (61)

aromatic hydrocarbon   A compound of C and H with one or more rings of C atoms (often drawn with alternating C—C and C=C bonds), in which there is extensive delocalization of π electrons. (480)

Arrhenius acid-base definition   A model of acid-base behavior in which an acid is a substance that has H in its formula and produces H^+ in water, and a base is a substance that has OH in its formula and produces OH^- in water. (592)

Arrhenius equation   An equation that expresses the exponential relationship between temperature and the rate constant: $k = Ae^{-E_a/RT}$. (527)

atmosphere   (See *standard atmosphere*.)

atom   The smallest particle of an element that retains the chemical nature of the element. A neutral, spherical entity composed of a positively charged central nucleus surrounded by one or more negatively charged electrons. (37)

atomic mass (also *atomic weight*)   The average of the masses of the naturally occurring isotopes of an element weighted according to their abundances. (45)

atomic mass unit (amu) [also *dalton (Da)*]   A mass exactly equal to $\frac{1}{12}$ the mass of a carbon-12 atom. (44)

atomic number (Z)   The unique number of protons in the nucleus of each atom of an element (equal to the number of electrons in the neutral atom). An integer that expresses the positive charge of a nucleus in multiples of the electronic charge. (43)

atomic orbital (also *wave function*)   A mathematical expression that describes the motion of the electron's matter-wave in terms of time and position in the region of the nucleus. The term is used qualitatively to mean the region of space in which there is a high probability of finding the electron. (232)

atomic size   A term referring to the atomic radius, one-half the distance between nuclei of identical bonded elements. (259) (See also *covalent radius* and *metallic radius*.)

atomic solid   A solid consisting of individual atoms held together by dispersion forces; the frozen noble gases are the only examples. (386)

atomic symbol (or *element symbol*)   A one- or two-letter abbreviation for the English, Latin, or Greek name of an element. (43)

atomic weight   (See *atomic mass*.)

ATP   (See *adenosine triphosphate*.)

aufbau principle (or *building-up principle*)   The conceptual basis of a process of building up atoms by adding one proton (and one or more neutrons) at a time to the nucleus and one electron around it to obtain the ground-state electron configurations of the elements. (250)

autoionization (also *self-ionization*)   A reaction in which two molecules of a substance react to give ions. The most important example is for water:

$$2H_2O(l) \rightleftharpoons H_3O^+(aq) + OH^-(aq) \qquad (586)$$

average rate   The change in concentration of reactants (or products) divided by a finite time period. (511)

Avogadro's law   The gas law stating that, at fixed temperature and pressure, equal volumes of any ideal gas contain equal numbers of particles, and, therefore, the volume of a gas is directly proportional to its amount (mol): $V \propto n$. (154)

Avogadro's number   A number $(6.022 \times 10^{23}$ to four significant figures) equal to the number of atoms in exactly 12 g of carbon-12; the number of atoms, molecules, or formula units in one mole of an element or compound. (72)

axial group   A group (or atom) that lies above or below the trigonal plane of a trigonal bipyramidal molecule, or a similar structural feature in a molecule. (320)

B

background radiation   Natural ionizing radiation, the most important form of which is cosmic radiation. (800)

balancing coefficient (also *stoichiometric coefficient*)   A numerical multiplier of all the atoms in the formula immediately following it in a chemical equation. (85)

band of stability   The narrow band of stable nuclides that appears on a plot of number of neutrons vs. number of protons for all nuclides. (790)

band theory   An extension of molecular orbital (MO) theory that explains many properties of metals, in particular, the differences in electrical conductivity of conductors, semiconductors, and insulators. (389)

barometer   A device used to measure atmospheric pressure. Most commonly, a tube open at one end, which is filled with mercury and inverted into a dish of mercury. (148)

base   In common laboratory terms, any species that produces OH^- ions when dissolved in water. (123) (See also *Brønsted-Lowry, Arrhenius,* and *Lewis acid-base definitions*.)

base-dissociation (base-ionization) constant (K_b)   An equilibrium constant for the reaction of a base (B) with H_2O to yield the conjugate acid (BH^+) and OH^-:

$$K_b = \frac{[BH^+][OH^-]}{[B]} \qquad (610)$$

base pair   Two complementary bases in mononucleotides that are H bonded to each other; guanine (G) always pairs with cytosine (C), and adenine (A) always pairs with thymine (T) (or uracil, U). (500)

base unit (also *fundamental unit*)   A unit that defines the standard for one of the seven physical quantities in the International System of Units (SI). (14)

battery   A self-contained group of voltaic cells arranged in series. (732)

becquerel (Bq)   The SI unit of radioactivity; 1 Bq = 1 d/s (disintegration per second). (793)

bent shape (also *V shape*)   A molecular shape that arises when a central atom is bonded to two other atoms and has one or two lone pairs; occurs as the AX_2E shape class (bond angle $< 120°$) in the trigonal planar arrangement and as the AX_2E_2 shape class (bond angle $< 109.5°$) in the tetrahedral arrangement. (318)

β⁻ decay   A radioactive process in which a beta particle is emitted from a nucleus. (788)

beta (β) decay   A class of radioactive decay that includes β⁻ decay, β⁺ emission, and e⁻ capture. (788)

beta particle (β, β⁻, or $_{-1}^{0}β$)   A negatively charged particle identified as a high-speed electron that is one of the common types of radioactive emissions. (786)

bimolecular reaction An elementary reaction involving the collision of two reactant species. (535)

binary covalent compound A compound that consists of atoms of two elements in which bonding occurs primarily through electron sharing. (57)

binary ionic compound A compound that consists of the oppositely charged ions of two elements. (49)

body-centered cubic unit cell A unit cell in which a particle lies at each corner and in the center of a cube. (380)

boiling point (bp or T_b) The temperature at which the vapor pressure of a gas equals the external (atmospheric) pressure. (365)

boiling point elevation (ΔT_b) The increase in the boiling point of a solvent caused by the presence of dissolved solute. (418)

bond angle The angle formed by the nuclei of two surrounding atoms with the nucleus of the central atom at the vertex. (316)

bond energy (BE) (or *bond strength*) The enthalpy change accompanying the breakage of a given bond in a mole of gaseous molecules. (289)

bond length The distance between the nuclei of two bonded atoms. (289)

bond order The number of electron pairs shared by two bonded atoms. (288)

bonding MO A molecular orbital formed when wave functions are added to each other, which increases electron density between the nuclei. Electrons occupying such an orbital stabilize the molecule. (344)

bonding pair (also *shared pair*) An electron pair shared by two nuclei; the mutual attraction between the nuclei and the electron pair forms a covalent bond. (288)

Boyle's law The gas law stating that, at constant temperature and amount of gas, the volume occupied by a gas is inversely proportional to the applied (external) pressure: $V \propto 1/P$. (150)

Brønsted-Lowry acid-base definition A model of acid-base behavior based on proton transfer, in which an acid and a base are defined, respectively, as species that donate and accept a proton. (600)

buffer (See *acid-base buffer.*)

buffer capacity A measure of the ability of a buffer to resist a change in pH; related to the total concentrations and relative proportions of buffer components. (637)

buffer range The pH range over which a buffer acts effectively; related to the relative component concentrations. (638)

C

calibration The process of correcting for systematic error of a measuring device by comparing it to a known standard. (24)

calorie (cal) A unit of energy defined as exactly 4.184 joules; originally defined as the heat needed to raise the temperature of 1 g of water 1°C (from 14.5°C to 15.5°C). (190)

calorimeter A device used to measure the heat released or absorbed by a physical or chemical process taking place within it. (196)

capillarity (or *capillary action*) A property that results in a liquid rising through a narrow space against the pull of gravity. (376)

carbonyl group The C=O grouping of atoms. (487)

carboxylic acid An organic compound (ending, *-oic acid*)

$$:O:$$
$$\|$$

that contains the $-C-\ddot{O}H$ group. (488)

catalyst A substance that increases the rate of a reaction without being used up in the process. (540)

cathode The electrode at which reduction occurs in an electrochemical cell. Electrons enter the cell and are acquired by the oxidizing agent at the cathode. (709)

cathode ray The ray of light emitted by the cathode (negative electrode) in a gas discharge tube; travels in straight lines, unless deflected by magnetic or electric fields. (39)

cation A positively charged ion. (49)

cell potential (E_{cell}) (also *electromotive force,* or *emf; cell voltage*) The potential difference between the electrodes of an electrochemical cell when no current flows. (715)

Celsius scale (formerly *centigrade scale*) A temperature scale in which the freezing and boiling points of water are defined as 0°C and 100°C, respectively. (18)

chain reaction In nuclear fission, a self-sustaining process in which neutrons released by splitting of one nucleus cause other nuclei to split, which releases more neutrons, and so on. (808)

change in enthalpy (ΔH) The change in internal energy plus the product of the constant pressure and the change in volume: $\Delta H = \Delta E + P\Delta V$; the heat lost or gained at constant pressure: $\Delta H = q_P$. (193)

charge density The ratio of the charge of an ion to its volume. (406)

Charles's law The gas law stating that at constant pressure, the volume occupied by a fixed amount of gas is directly proportional to its absolute temperature: $V \propto T$. (152)

chelate A complex ion in which the metal ion is bonded to a bidentate or polydentate ligand. (765)

chemical bond The force that holds two atoms together in a molecule (or formula unit). (48)

chemical change (also *chemical reaction*) A change in which a substance is converted into a substance with different composition and properties. (3)

chemical equation A statement that uses chemical formulas to express the identities and quantities of the substances involved in a chemical or physical change. (85)

chemical formula A notation of atomic symbols and numerical subscripts that shows the type and number of each atom in a molecule or formula unit of a substance. (52)

chemical kinetics The study of the rates and mechanisms of reactions. (508)

chemical property A characteristic of a substance that appears as it interacts with, or transforms into, other substances. (3)

chemical reaction (See *chemical change.*)

chemistry The scientific study of matter and the changes it undergoes. (2)

chiral molecule One that is not superimposable on its mirror image; an optically active molecule. In organic compounds, a chiral molecule typically contains a C atom bonded to four different groups (asymmetric C). (476)

chlor-alkali process An industrial method that electrolyzes concentrated aqueous NaCl and produces Cl_2, H_2, and NaOH. (742)

cis-trans isomers (See *geometric isomers.*)

Clausius-Clapeyron equation An equation that expresses the relationship between vapor pressure P of a liquid and temperature T:

$$\ln P = \frac{-\Delta H_{vap}}{R}\left(\frac{1}{T}\right) + C, \text{ where } C \text{ is a constant} \quad (365)$$

colligative property A property of a solution that depends on the number, not the identity, of solute particles. (416) (See also *boiling point elevation, freezing point depression, osmotic pressure,* and *vapor pressure lowering.*)

collision theory   A model that explains reaction rate as the result of particles colliding with a certain minimum energy. (529)

combustion analysis   A method for determining the formula of a compound from the amounts of its combustion products; used commonly for organic compounds. (82)

common-ion effect   The shift in the position of an ionic equilibrium away from formation of an ion that is caused by the addition (or presence) of that ion. (633)

complex   (See *coordination compound.*)

complex ion   An ion consisting of a central metal ion bonded covalently to molecules and/or anions called ligands. (659, 763)

composition   The types and amounts of simpler substances that make up a sample of matter. (2)

compound   A substance composed of two or more elements that are chemically combined in fixed proportions. (32)

concentration   A measure of the quantity of solute dissolved in a given quantity of solution. (99)

concentration cell   A voltaic cell in which both compartments contain the same components but at different concentrations. (729)

condensation   The process of a gas changing into a liquid. (358)

condensation polymer   A polymer formed by monomers with two functional groups that are linked together in a dehydration-condensation reaction. (494)

conduction band   In band theory, the empty, higher energy portion of the band of molecular orbitals into which electrons move when conducting heat and electricity. (390)

conductor   A substance (usually a metal) that conducts an electric current well. (390)

conjugate acid-base pair   Two species related to each other through the gain or loss of a proton; the acid has one more proton than its conjugate base. (601)

constitutional isomers (also *structural isomers*)   Compounds with the same molecular formula but different arrangements of atoms. (474, 768)

controlled experiment   An experiment that measures the effect of one variable at a time by keeping other variables constant. (8)

conversion factor   A ratio of equivalent quantities that is equal to 1 and used to convert the units of a quantity. (10)

coordinate covalent bond   A covalent bond formed when one atom donates both electrons to give the shared pair; once formed, it is identical to any covalent single bond. (770)

coordination compound (also *complex*)   A substance containing at least one complex ion. (763)

coordination isomers   Two or more coordination compounds with the same composition in which the complex ions have different ligand arrangements. (768)

coordination number   In a crystal, the number of nearest neighbors surrounding a particle. (380) In a complex, the number of ligand atoms bonded to the central metal ion. (764)

core electrons   (See *inner electrons.*)

corrosion   The natural redox process that results in unwanted oxidation of a metal. (736)

coulomb (C)   The SI unit of electric charge. One coulomb is the charge of 6.242×10^{18} electrons; one electron possesses a charge of 1.602×10^{-19} C. (715)

Coulomb's law   A law stating that the electrostatic force associated with two charges A and B is directly proportional to the product

of their magnitudes and inversely proportional to the square of the distance between them:

$$\text{electrostatic force} \propto \frac{\text{charge A} \times \text{charge B}}{(\text{distance})^2} \qquad (284)$$

counter ion   A simple ion associated with a complex ion in a coordination compound. (763)

coupling of reactions   The pairing of reactions of which one releases enough free energy for the other to occur. (692)

covalent bond   A type of bond in which atoms are bonded through the sharing of two electrons; the mutual attraction of the nuclei and an electron pair that holds atoms together in a molecule. (50, 287)

covalent bonding   The idealized bonding type that is based on localized electron-pair sharing between two atoms with little difference in their tendencies to lose or gain electrons (most commonly nonmetals). (280)

covalent compound   A compound that consists of atoms bonded together by shared electron pairs. (48)

covalent radius   One-half the distance between nuclei of identical covalently bonded atoms. (260)

critical mass   The minimum mass needed to achieve a chain reaction. (808)

critical point   The point on a phase diagram above which the vapor cannot be condensed to a liquid; the end of the liquid-gas curve. (367)

crystal field splitting energy (Δ)   The difference in energy between two sets of metal-ion d orbitals that results from electrostatic interactions with the surrounding ligands. (774)

crystal field theory   A model that explains the color and magnetism of coordination compounds based on the effects of ligands on metal-ion d-orbital energies. (772)

crystalline solid   Solid with a well-defined shape because of the orderly arrangement of the atoms, molecules, or ions. (379)

cubic closest packing   A crystal structure based on the face-centered cubic unit cell in which the layers have an *abcabc . . .* pattern. (382)

cubic meter (m^3)   The SI derived unit of volume. (15)

curie (Ci)   The most common unit of radioactivity, defined as the number of nuclei disintegrating each second in 1 g of radium-226; $1 \text{ Ci} = 3.70 \times 10^{10}$ d/s (disintegrations per second). (793)

cyclic hydrocarbon   A hydrocarbon with one or more rings in its structure. (474)

D

d orbital   An atomic orbital with $l = 2$. (238)

dalton (Da)   A unit of mass identical to *atomic mass unit.* (44)

Dalton's law of partial pressures   A gas law stating that, in a mixture of unreacting gases, the total pressure is the sum of the partial pressures of the individual gases: $P_{\text{total}} = P_1 + P_2 + P_3 + \cdots$ (162)

data   Pieces of quantitative information obtained by observation. (8)

de Broglie wavelength   The wavelength of a moving particle obtained from the de Broglie equation: $\lambda = h/mu.$ (229)

decay constant   The rate constant k for radioactive decay. (794)

decay rate   (See *activity.*)

decay series (also *disintegration series*)   The succession of steps a parent nucleus undergoes as it decays into a stable daughter nucleus. (792)

dehydration-condensation reaction A reaction in which H and OH groups on two molecules react to form water as one of the products. (452)

delocalization (See *electron-pair delocalization.*)

density (*d*) An intensive physical property of a substance at a given temperature and pressure, defined as the ratio of the mass to the volume: $d = m/V$. (17)

deposition The process of changing directly from gas to solid. (359)

derived unit Any of various combinations of the seven SI base units. (14)

deuterons Nuclei of the stable hydrogen isotope deuterium, ^{2}H. (797)

diagonal relationship Physical and chemical similarities between a Period 2 element and one located diagonally down and to the right in Period 3. (438)

diamagnetism The tendency of a species not to be attracted (or to be slightly repelled) by a magnetic field as a result of its electrons being paired. (271)

diastereomers (See *geometric isomers.*)

diffraction The phenomenon in which a wave striking the edge of an object bends around it. A wave passing through a slit as wide as its wavelength forms a semicircular wave. (217)

diffusion The movement of one fluid through another. (173)

dimensional analysis (also *factor-label method*) A calculation method in which arithmetic steps are accompanied by the appropriate canceling of units. (11)

dipole-dipole force The intermolecular attraction between oppositely charged poles of nearby polar molecules. (370)

dipole–induced dipole force The intermolecular attraction between a polar molecule and the oppositely charged pole it induces in a nearby molecule. (401)

dipole moment (μ) A measure of molecular polarity; the magnitude of the partial charges on the ends of a molecule (in coulombs) times the distance between them (in meters). (325)

disaccharide An organic compound formed by a dehydration-condensation reaction between two simple sugars (monosaccharides). (495)

disintegration series (See *decay series.*)

dispersion force (also *London force*) The intermolecular attraction between all particles as a result of instantaneous polarizations of their electron clouds; the intermolecular force primarily responsible for the condensed states of nonpolar substances. (373)

disproportionation reaction A reaction in which a given substance is both oxidized and reduced. (450)

donor atom An atom that donates a lone pair of electrons to form a covalent bond, usually from ligand to metal ion in a complex. (764)

double bond A covalent bond that consists of two bonding pairs; two atoms sharing four electrons in the form of one σ and one π bond. (288)

double-displacement reaction (See *metathesis reaction.*)

double helix The two intertwined polynucleotide strands held together by H bonds that form the structure of DNA (deoxyribonucleic acid). (500)

Downs cell An industrial apparatus that electrolyzes molten NaCl to produce sodium and chlorine. (740)

dynamic equilibrium In a chemical or physical change, the condition at which the forward and reverse processes are taking place at the same rate, so there is no net change in the amounts of reactants or products. (364)

E

e_g orbitals The set of orbitals (composed of $d_{x^2-y^2}$ and d_{z^2}) that results when the energies of the metal-ion d orbitals are split by a ligand field. This set is higher in energy than the other (t_{2g}) set in an octahedral field of ligands and lower in energy in a tetrahedral field. (774)

effective collision A collision in which the particles meet with sufficient energy and an orientation that allows them to react. (530)

effective nuclear charge (Z_{eff}) The nuclear charge an electron actually experiences as a result of shielding effects due to the presence of other electrons. (249)

effusion The process by which a gas escapes from its container through a tiny hole into an evacuated space. (172)

electrochemical cell A system that incorporates a redox reaction to produce or use electrical energy. (705)

electrochemistry The study of the relationship between chemical change and electrical work. (705)

electrode The part of an electrochemical cell that conducts the electricity between the cell and the surroundings. (709)

electrolysis The nonspontaneous lysing (splitting) of a substance, often to its component elements, by supplying electrical energy. (740)

electrolyte A substance that conducts a current when it dissolves in water. (115, 417) A mixture of ions, in which the electrodes of an electrochemical cell are immersed, that conducts a current. (417)

electrolytic cell An electrochemical system that uses electrical energy to drive a nonspontaneous chemical reaction ($\Delta G > 0$). (709)

electromagnetic (EM) radiation (or *electromagnetic energy, radiant energy*) Oscillating, perpendicular electric and magnetic fields moving simultaneously through space as waves and manifested as visible light, x-rays, microwaves, radio waves, and so on. (215)

electromagnetic spectrum The continuum of wavelengths of radiant energy. (216)

electromotive force (emf) (See *cell potential.*) (715)

electron (e⁻) A subatomic particle that possesses a unit negative charge (1.60218×10^{-19} C) and occupies the space around the atomic nucleus. (42)

electron affinity (EA) The energy change (in kJ) accompanying the addition of one mole of electrons to one mole of gaseous atoms or ions. (265)

electron (e⁻) capture (EC) A type of radioactive decay in which a nucleus draws in an orbital electron, usually one from the lowest energy level, and releases energy. (788)

electron cloud An imaginary representation of an electron's rapidly changing position around the nucleus over time. (232)

electron configuration The distribution of electrons within the orbitals of the atoms of an element; also the notation for such a distribution. (246)

electron deficient Referring to a bonded atom, such as Be or B, that has fewer than eight valence electrons. (313)

electron density diagram (or *electron probability density diagram*) The pictorial representation for a given energy sublevel of the quantity ψ^2 (the probability density of the electron lying within a particular tiny volume) as a function of r (distance from the nucleus). (232)

electron volt (eV) The energy (in joules, J) that an electron acquires when it moves through a potential difference of 1 volt; $1 \text{ eV} = 1.602 \times 10^{-19}$ J. (805)

electronegativity (EN) The relative ability of a bonded atom to attract shared electrons. (296)

electronegativity difference (ΔEN) The difference in electronegativities between the atoms in a bond. (298)

electron-pair delocalization (also *delocalization*) The process by which electron density is spread over several atoms rather than remaining between two. (310)

electron-sea model A qualitative description of metallic bonding proposing that metal atoms pool their valence electrons into a delocalized "sea" of electrons in which the metal cores (metal ions) are submerged in an orderly array. (388)

element The simplest type of substance with unique physical and chemical properties. An element consists of only one kind of atom, so it cannot be broken down into simpler substances. (32)

elementary reaction (or *elementary step*) A simple reaction that describes a single molecular event in a proposed reaction mechanism. (535)

elimination reaction A type of organic reaction in which C atoms are bonded to fewer atoms in the product than in the reactant, which leads to multiple bonding. (481)

emission spectrum The line spectrum produced when excited atoms return to lower energy levels and emit photons characteristic of the element. (227)

empirical formula A chemical formula that shows the lowest relative numbers of atoms of elements in a compound. (52)

enantiomers (See *optical isomers.*)

end point The point in a titration at which the indicator changes color. (127, 642)

endothermic process One occurring with an absorption of heat from the surroundings and therefore an increase in the enthalpy of the system ($\Delta H > 0$). (194)

energy The capacity to do work, that is, to move matter. (6) [See also *kinetic energy* (E_k) and *potential energy* (E_p).]

enthalpy (H) A thermodynamic quantity that is the sum of the internal energy plus the product of the pressure and volume. (193)

enthalpy diagram A graphic depiction of the enthalpy change of a system. (194)

enthalpy of hydration (ΔH_{hydr}) (See *heat of hydration.*)

enthalpy of solution (ΔH_{soln}) (See *heat of solution.*)

entropy (S) A thermodynamic quantity related to the number of ways the energy of a system can be dispersed through the motions of its particles. (407, 673)

enzyme A biological macromolecule (usually a protein) that acts as a catalyst. (542)

equatorial group A group (or atom) that lies in the trigonal plane of a trigonal bipyramidal molecule, or a similar structural feature in a molecule. (320)

equilibrium (See *dynamic equilibrium.*)

equilibrium constant (K) The value obtained when equilibrium concentrations are substituted into the reaction quotient. (554)

equilibrium vapor pressure (See *vapor pressure.*)

equivalence point The point in a titration when the number of moles of the added species is stoichiometrically equivalent to the original number of moles of the other species. (126, 642)

ester An organic compound that contains the $-\overset{\overset{\textstyle \text{:O:}}{\|}}{C}-\overset{..}{\underset{..}{O}}-\overset{|}{C}-$ group. (488)

exact number A quantity, usually obtained by counting or based on a unit definition, that has no uncertainty associated with it and, therefore, contains as many significant figures as a calculation requires. (23)

excited state Any electron configuration of an atom or molecule other than the lowest energy (ground) state. (223)

exclusion principle A principle developed by Wolfgang Pauli stating that no two electrons in an atom can have the same set of four quantum numbers. The principle arises from the fact that an orbital has a maximum occupancy of two electrons and their spins are paired. (248)

exothermic process One occurring with a release of heat to the surroundings and therefore a decrease in the enthalpy of the system ($\Delta H < 0$). (194)

expanded valence shell A valence level that can accommodate more than 8 electrons by using available d orbitals; occurs only for elements in Period 3 or higher. (314)

experiment A clear set of procedural steps that tests a hypothesis. (8)

extensive property A property, such as mass, that depends on the quantity of substance present. (17)

F

face-centered cubic unit cell A unit cell in which a particle occurs at each corner and in the center of each face of a cube. (380)

factor-label method (See *dimensional analysis.*)

Faraday constant (F) The physical constant representing the charge of 1 mol of electrons: $F = 96,485$ C/mol e$^-$. (724)

fatty acid A carboxylic acid that has a long hydrocarbon chain and is derived from a natural source. (489)

first law of thermodynamics (See *law of conservation of energy.*)

fission The process by which a heavier nucleus splits into lighter nuclei with the release of energy. (804)

formal charge The hypothetical charge on an atom in a molecule or ion, equal to the number of valence electrons minus the sum of all the unshared and half the shared valence electrons. (311)

formation constant (K_f) An equilibrium constant for the formation of a complex ion from the hydrated metal ion and ligands. (660)

formation equation An equation in which 1 mole of a compound forms from its elements. (203)

formula mass The sum (in amu) of the atomic masses of a formula unit of an ionic compound. (58)

formula unit The chemical unit of a compound that contains the number and type of atoms (or ions) expressed in the chemical formula. (53)

fossil fuel Any fuel, including coal, petroleum, and natural gas, derived from the products of the decay of dead organisms. (205)

fraction by mass (also *mass fraction*) The portion of a compound's mass contributed by an element; the mass of an element in a compound divided by the mass of the compound. (35)

free energy (G) A thermodynamic quantity that is the difference between the enthalpy and the product of the absolute temperature and the entropy: $G = H - TS$. (686)

free radical A molecular or atomic species with one or more unpaired electrons, which typically make it very reactive. (313)

freezing The process of cooling a liquid until it solidifies. (358)

freezing point depression (ΔT_f) A lowering of the freezing point of a solvent caused by the presence of dissolved solute particles. (420)

frequency (ν)   The number of cycles a wave undergoes per second, expressed in units of 1/second, or s^{-1} [also called hertz (Hz)]. (215)

frequency factor (A)   The product of the collision frequency Z and an orientation probability factor p that is specific for a reaction. (530)

fuel cell (or *flow battery*)   A battery that is not self-contained and in which electricity is generated by the controlled oxidation of a fuel. (735)

functional group   A specific combination of atoms, typically containing a carbon-carbon multiple bond and/or carbon-heteroatom bond, that reacts in a characteristic way no matter what molecule it occurs in. (469)

fundamental unit   (See *base unit.*)

fusion   (See *melting.*)

fusion (nuclear)   The process by which light nuclei combine to form a heavier nucleus with the release of energy. (804)

G

galvanic cell   (See *voltaic cell.*)

gamma emission   The type of radioactive decay in which gamma rays are emitted from an excited nucleus. (789)

gamma (γ) ray   A very high-energy photon. (786)

gas   One of the three states of matter. A gas fills its container regardless of the shape. (4)

genetic code   The set of three-base sequences that is translated into specific amino acids during the process of protein synthesis. (501)

geometric isomers (also *cis-trans isomers* or *diastereomers*)   Stereoisomers in which the molecules have the same connections between atoms but differ in the spatial arrangements of the atoms. The *cis* isomer has similar groups on the same side of a structural feature; the *trans* isomer has them on opposite sides. (477–78, 768)

Graham's law of effusion   A gas law stating that the rate of effusion of a gas is inversely proportional to the square root of its density (or molar mass):

$$\text{rate} \propto \frac{1}{\sqrt{\mathcal{M}}} \qquad (172)$$

gray (Gy)   The SI unit of absorbed radiation dose; 1 Gy = 1 J/kg tissue. (799)

ground state   The electron configuration of an atom or ion that is lowest in energy. (223)

group   A vertical column in the periodic table. (46)

H

H bond   (See *hydrogen bond.*)

Haber process   An industrial process used to form ammonia from its elements. (582)

half-cell   A portion of an electrochemical cell in which a half-reaction takes place. (711)

half-life ($t_{1/2}$)   In chemical processes, the time required for half the initial reactant concentration to be consumed. (523) In nuclear processes, the time required for half the initial number of nuclei in a sample to decay. (794)

half-reaction method   A method of balancing redox reactions by treating the oxidation and reduction half-reactions separately. (706)

haloalkane (also *alkyl halide*)   A hydrocarbon with one or more halogen atoms (X) in place of H; contains a group. (484)

heat (q)   The energy transferred between objects because of differences in their temperatures only; thermal energy. (18, 188)

heat capacity   The quantity of heat required to change the temperature of an object by 1 K. (195)

heat of fusion (ΔH°_{fus})   The enthalpy change occurring when 1 mol of a solid substance melts. (358)

heat of hydration (ΔH_{hydr}) (also *enthalpy of hydration*)   The enthalpy change occurring when 1 mol of a gaseous species is hydrated. The sum of the enthalpies from separating water molecules and mixing the gaseous species with them. (406)

heat of reaction (ΔH°_{rxn})   The enthalpy change of a reaction. (194)

heat of solution (ΔH_{soln}) (also *enthalpy of solution*)   The enthalpy change occurring when a solution forms from solute and solvent. The sum of the enthalpies from separating solute and solvent molecules and mixing them. (405)

heat of sublimation (ΔH°_{subl})   The enthalpy change occurring when 1 mol of a solid substance changes directly to a gas. The sum of the heats of fusion and vaporization. (359)

heat of vaporization (ΔH°_{vap})   The enthalpy change occurring when 1 mol of a liquid substance vaporizes. (358)

heating-cooling curve   A plot of temperature vs. time for a substance when heat is absorbed or released by the system at a constant rate. (360)

Henderson-Hasselbalch equation   An equation for calculating the pH of a buffer system:

$$\text{pH} = \text{p}K_a + \log\left(\frac{[\text{base}]}{[\text{acid}]}\right) \qquad (637)$$

Henry's law   A law stating that the solubility of a gas in a liquid is directly proportional to the partial pressure of the gas above the liquid: $S_{gas} = k_H \times P_{gas}$. (411)

Hess's law of heat summation   A law stating that the enthalpy change of an overall process is the sum of the enthalpy changes of the individual steps of the process. (201)

heteroatom   Any atom in an organic compound other than C or H. (468)

heterogeneous catalyst   A catalyst that occurs in a different phase from the reactants, usually a solid interacting with gaseous or liquid reactants. (541)

heterogeneous mixture   A mixture that has one or more visible boundaries among its components. (61)

hexagonal closest packing   A crystal structure based on the hexagonal unit cell in which the layers have an *abab . . .* pattern. (382)

high-spin complex   Complex ion that has the same number of unpaired electrons as in the isolated metal ion; contains weak-field ligands. (776)

homogeneous catalyst   A catalyst (gas, liquid, or soluble solid) that exists in the same phase as the reactants. (541)

homogeneous mixture (also *solution*)   A mixture that has no visible boundaries among its components. (61)

homologous series   A series of organic compounds in which each member differs from the next by a —CH_2— (methylene) group. (472)

homonuclear diatomic molecule   A molecule composed of two identical atoms. (346)

Hund's rule   A principle stating that when orbitals of equal energy are available, the electron configuration of lowest energy has the maximum number of unpaired electrons with parallel spins. (252)

hybrid orbital   An atomic orbital postulated to form during bonding by the mathematical mixing of specific combinations of nonequivalent orbitals in a given atom. (334)

hybridization   A postulated process of orbital mixing to form hybrid orbitals. (334)

hydrate   A compound in which a specific number of water molecules are associated with each formula unit. (55)

hydration   Solvation in water. (406)

hydration shell   The oriented cluster of water molecules that surrounds an ion in aqueous solution. (400)

hydrocarbon   An organic compound that contains only H and C atoms. (469)

hydrogen bond (H bond)   A type of dipole-dipole force that arises between molecules that have an H atom bonded to a small, highly electronegative atom with lone pairs, usually N, O, or F. (371)

hydrogenation   The addition of hydrogen to a carbon-carbon multiple bond to form a carbon-carbon single bond. (542)

hydrolysis   Cleaving a molecule by reaction with water, in which one part of the molecule bonds to the water —OH and the other to the water H. (489)

hydronium ion (H_3O^+)   A proton covalently bonded to a water molecule. (591)

hypothesis   A testable proposal made to explain an observation. If inconsistent with experimental results, a hypothesis is revised or discarded. (8)

I

ideal gas   A hypothetical gas that exhibits linear relationships among volume, pressure, temperature, and amount (mol) at all conditions; approximated by simple gases at ordinary conditions. (150)

ideal gas law (or *ideal gas equation*)   An equation that expresses the relationships among volume, pressure, temperature, and amount (mol) of an ideal gas: $PV = nRT$. (155)

ideal solution   A solution whose vapor pressure equals the mole fraction of the solvent times the vapor pressure of the pure solvent; approximated only by very dilute solutions. (417) (See also *Raoult's law.*)

indicator   (See *acid-base indicator.*)

infrared (IR)   Radiation in the region of the electromagnetic spectrum between the microwave and visible regions. (216)

infrared (IR) spectroscopy   An instrumental technique for determining the types of bonds in a covalent molecule by measuring the absorption of IR radiation. (292)

initial rate   The instantaneous rate occurring as soon as the reactants are mixed, that is, at $t = 0$. (512)

inner electrons (also *core electrons*)   Electrons that fill all the energy levels of an atom except the valence level; electrons also present in atoms of the previous noble gas and any completed transition series. (257)

inner transition elements   The elements of the periodic table in which f orbitals are being filled; the lanthanides and actinides. (258)

instantaneous rate   The reaction rate at a particular time, given by the slope of a tangent to a plot of reactant concentration vs. time. (511)

insulator   A substance (usually a nonmetal) that does not conduct an electric current. (390)

integrated rate law   A mathematical expression for reactant concentration as a function of time. (520)

intensive property   A property, such as density, that does not depend on the quantity of substance present. (17)

intermolecular forces (or *interparticle forces*)   The attractive and repulsive forces among the particles—molecules, atoms, or ions—in a sample of matter. (357)

internal energy (E)   The sum of the kinetic and potential energies of all the particles in a system. (187)

ion   A charged particle that forms from an atom (or covalently bonded group of atoms) when it gains or loses one or more electrons. (49)

ion-dipole force   The intermolecular attractive force between an ion and a polar molecule (dipole). (370)

ion–induced dipole force   The intermolecular attractive force between an ion and the dipole it induces in the electron cloud of a nearby particle. (401)

ion pair   A pair of ions that form a gaseous ionic molecule; sometimes formed when a salt boils. (286)

ion-product constant for water (K_w)   The equilibrium constant for the autoionization of water:

$$K_w = [H_3O^+][OH^-] \qquad\qquad (596)$$

ionic atmosphere   A cluster of ions of net opposite charge surrounding a given ion in solution. (424)

ionic bonding   The idealized type of bonding based on the attraction of oppositely charged ions that arise through electron transfer between atoms with large differences in their tendencies to lose or gain electrons (typically metals and nonmetals). (279)

ionic compound   A compound that consists of oppositely charged ions. (48)

ionic radius   The size of an ion as measured by the distance between the centers of adjacent ions in a crystalline ionic compound. (272)

ionic solid   A solid whose unit cell contains cations and anions. (386)

ionization   The process by which a substance absorbs energy from high-energy radioactive particles and loses an electron to become ionized. (799)

ionization energy (IE)   The energy (in kJ) required to remove completely one mole of electrons from one mole of gaseous atoms or ions. (262)

ionizing radiation   The high-energy radiation that forms ions in a substance by causing electron loss. (799)

isoelectronic   Having the same number and configuration of electrons as another species. (269)

isomer   One of two or more compounds with the same molecular formula but different properties, often as a result of different arrangements of atoms. (83, 767)

isotopes   Atoms of a given atomic number (that is, of a specific element) that have different numbers of neutrons and therefore different mass numbers. (43, 786)

isotopic mass   The mass (in amu) of an isotope relative to the mass of the carbon-12 isotope. (45)

J

joule (J)   The SI unit of energy; $1\ J = 1\ kg\cdot m^2/s^2$. (190)

K

kelvin (K)   The SI base unit of temperature. The kelvin is the same size as the Celsius degree. (18)

Kelvin scale   (See *absolute scale.*)

ketone   An organic compound (ending, *-one*) that contains a carbonyl group bonded to two other C atoms, $-\overset{\displaystyle |}{\underset{\displaystyle |}{C}}-\overset{\displaystyle :O:}{\overset{\displaystyle \|}{\underset{\displaystyle |}{C}}}-\overset{\displaystyle |}{\underset{\displaystyle |}{C}}-$. (487)

kilogram (kg)   The SI base unit of mass. (16)

kinetic energy (E_k)   The energy an object has because of its motion. (6)

kinetic-molecular theory   The model that explains gas behavior in terms of particles in random motion whose volumes and interactions are negligible. (167)

L

lanthanide contraction   The additional decrease in atomic and ionic size, beyond the expected trend, caused by the poor shielding of the increasing nuclear charge by *f* electrons in the elements following the lanthanides. (760)

lanthanides (also *rare earths*)   The Period 6 (4*f*) series of inner transition elements, which includes cerium (Ce; *Z* = 58) through lutetium (Lu; *Z* = 71). (258)

lattice   The three-dimensional arrangement of points created by choosing each point to be at the same location within each particle of a crystal; thus, the lattice consists of all points with identical surroundings. (380)

lattice energy ($\Delta H°_{lattice}$)   The enthalpy change (always positive) that occurs when 1 mol of an ionic compound separates into gaseous ions, with all components in their standard states. (284)

law   (See *natural law.*)

law of chemical equilibrium (also *law of mass action*)   The law stating that when a system reaches equilibrium at a given temperature, the ratio of quantities that make up the reaction quotient has a constant numerical value. (556)

law of conservation of energy (also *first law of thermodynamics*)   A basic observation that the total energy of the universe is constant: $\Delta E_{universe} = \Delta E_{system} + \Delta E_{surroundings} = 0$. (190)

law of definite (or constant) composition   A mass law stating that, no matter what its source, a particular compound is composed of the same elements in the same parts (fractions) by mass. (35)

law of mass action   (See *law of chemical equilibrium.*)

law of mass conservation   A mass law stating that the total mass of substances does not change during a chemical reaction. (34)

law of multiple proportions   A mass law stating that if elements A and B react to form two compounds, the different masses of B that combine with a fixed mass of A can be expressed as a ratio of small whole numbers. (36)

Le Châtelier's principle   A principle stating that if a system in a state of equilibrium is disturbed, it will undergo a change that shifts its equilibrium position in a direction that reduces the effect of the disturbance. (573)

level (also *shell*)   A specific energy state of an atom given by the principal quantum number *n*. (235)

Lewis acid-base definition   A model of acid-base behavior in which acids and bases are defined, respectively, as species that accept and donate an electron pair. (621)

Lewis electron-dot symbol   A notation in which the element symbol represents the nucleus and inner electrons, and surrounding dots represent the valence electrons. (281)

Lewis structure (or *Lewis formula*)   A structural formula consisting of electron-dot symbols, with lines as bonding pairs and dots as lone pairs. (306)

ligand   A molecule or anion bonded to a central metal ion in a complex ion. (659, 763)

like-dissolves-like rule   An empirical observation stating that substances having similar kinds of intermolecular forces dissolve in each other. (400)

limiting reactant (or *limiting reagent*)   The reactant that is consumed when a reaction occurs and therefore the one that determines the maximum amount of product that can form. (93)

line spectrum   A series of separated lines of different colors representing photons whose wavelengths are characteristic of an element. (221) (See also *emission spectrum.*)

linear arrangement   The geometric arrangement obtained when two electron groups maximize their separation around a central atom. (317)

linear shape   A molecular shape formed by three atoms lying in a straight line, with a bond angle of 180° (shape class AX_2 or AX_2E_3). (317)

linkage isomers   Coordination compounds with the same composition but with different ligand donor atoms linked to the central metal ion. (768)

lipid   Any of a class of biomolecules, including fats and oils, that are soluble in nonpolar solvents. (489)

liquid   One of the three states of matter. A liquid fills a container to the extent of its own volume and thus forms a surface. (4)

liter (L)   A non-SI unit of volume equivalent to 1 cubic decimeter (0.001 m^3). (15)

London force   (See *dispersion force.*)

lone pair (also *unshared pair*)   An electron pair that is part of an atom's valence shell but not involved in covalent bonding. (288)

low-spin complex   Complex ion that has fewer unpaired electrons than in the free metal ion because of the presence of strong-field ligands. (776)

M

macromolecule   (See *polymer.*)

magnetic quantum number (m_l) (or *orbital-orientation quantum number*)   An integer from $-l$ through 0 to $+l$ that specifies the orientation of an atomic orbital in the three-dimensional space about the nucleus. (234)

mass   The quantity of matter an object contains. Balances are designed to measure mass. (16)

mass fraction   (See *fraction by mass.*)

mass number (A)   The total number of protons and neutrons in the nucleus of an atom. (43)

mass percent (also *mass %* or *percent by mass*)   The fraction by mass expressed as a percentage. A concentration term [% (w/w)] expressed as the mass in grams of solute dissolved per 100. g of solution. (35, 413–14)

mass spectrometry   An instrumental method for measuring the relative masses of particles in a sample by creating charged particles and separating them according to their mass-charge ratio. (44)

matter   Anything that possesses mass and occupies volume. (2)

melting (also *fusion*)   The change of a substance from a solid to a liquid. (358)

melting point (mp or T_f)   The temperature at which the solid and liquid forms of a substance are at equilibrium. (366)

metal   A substance or mixture that is relatively shiny and malleable and is a good conductor of heat and electricity. In reactions, metals tend to transfer electrons to nonmetals and form ionic compounds. (47)

metallic bonding   An idealized type of bonding based on the attraction between metal ions and their delocalized valence electrons. (280) (See also *electron-sea model*.)

metallic radius   One-half the distance between the nuclei of adjacent individual atoms in a crystal of an element. (259)

metallic solid   A solid whose individual atoms are held together by metallic bonding. (387)

metalloid (also *semimetal*)   An element with properties between those of metals and nonmetals. (47)

metathesis reaction (also *double-displacement reaction*)   A reaction in which atoms or ions of two compounds exchange bonding partners. (120)

meter (m)   The SI base unit of length. The distance light travels in a vacuum in 1/299,792,458 second. (15)

milliliter (mL)   A volume (0.001 L) equivalent to 1 cm^3. (15)

millimeter of mercury (mmHg)   A unit of pressure based on the difference in the heights of mercury in a barometer or manometer. Renamed the *torr* in honor of Evangelista Torricelli. (149)

miscible   Soluble in any proportion. (399)

mixture   A group of two or more elements and/or compounds that are physically intermingled. (33)

MO bond order   One-half the difference between the numbers of electrons in bonding and antibonding MOs. (345)

model (also *theory*)   A simplified conceptual picture based on experiment that explains how an aspect of nature occurs. (9)

molality (*m*)   A concentration term expressed as number of moles of solute dissolved in 1000 g (1 kg) of solvent. (413)

molar heat capacity (C)   The quantity of heat required to change the temperature of 1 mol of a substance by 1 K. (196)

molar mass (ℳ) (or *gram-molecular weight*)   The mass of 1 mol of entities (atoms, molecules, or formula units) of a substance, in units of g/mol. (74)

molar solubility   The solubility expressed in terms of amount (mol) of dissolved solute per liter of solution. (651)

molarity (M)   A concentration term expressed as the moles of solute dissolved in 1 L of solution. (99)

mole (mol)   The SI base unit for amount of a substance. The amount that contains a number of objects equal to the number of atoms in exactly 12 g of carbon-12. (72)

mole fraction (X)   A concentration term expressed as the ratio of moles of one component of a mixture to the total moles present. (163, 414)

molecular equation   A chemical equation showing a reaction in solution in which reactants and products appear as intact, undissociated compounds. (118)

molecular formula   A formula that shows the actual number of atoms of each element in a molecule. (52)

molecular mass (or *molecular weight*)   The sum (in amu) of the atomic masses of a formula unit of a compound. (58)

molecular orbital (MO)   An orbital of given energy and shape that extends over a molecule and can be occupied by no more than two electrons. (343)

molecular orbital (MO) diagram   A depiction of the relative energy and number of electrons in each MO, as well as the atomic orbitals from which the MOs form. (345)

molecular orbital (MO) theory   A model that describes a molecule as a collection of nuclei and electrons in which the electrons occupy orbitals that extend over the entire molecule. (343)

molecular polarity   The overall distribution of electronic charge in a molecule, determined by its shape and bond polarities. (324)

molecular shape   The three-dimensional structure defined by the relative positions of the atomic nuclei in a molecule. (316)

molecular solid   A solid held together by intermolecular forces between individual molecules. (386)

molecularity   The number of reactant particles involved in an elementary step. (535)

molecule   A structure consisting of two or more atoms that are chemically bound together and behave as an independent unit. (32)

monatomic ion   An ion derived from a single atom. (49)

monomer   A small molecule, linked covalently to others of the same or similar type to form a polymer, on which the repeat unit of the polymer is based. (492)

mononucleotide   A monomer unit of a nucleic acid, consisting of an N-containing base, a sugar, and a phosphate group. (499)

monosaccharide   A simple sugar; a polyhydroxy ketone or aldehyde with three to nine C atoms. (495)

N

natural law (also *law*)   A summary, often in mathematical form, of a universal observation. (8)

Nernst equation   An equation stating that the voltage of an electrochemical cell under any conditions depends on the standard cell voltage and the concentrations of the cell components:

$$E_{cell} = E_{cell}^{\circ} - \frac{RT}{nF} \ln Q \qquad (726)$$

net ionic equation   A chemical equation of a reaction in solution in which spectator ions have been eliminated to show the actual chemical change. (119)

network covalent solid   A solid in which all the atoms are bonded covalently. (387)

neutralization   In the Arrhenius acid-base definition, the combination of the H^+ ion from the acid and the OH^- ion from the base to form H_2O. (592)

neutralization reaction   An acid-base reaction that yields water and a solution of a salt; when a strong acid reacts with a stoichiometrically equivalent amount of a strong base, the solution is neutral. (123)

neutron (n⁰)   An uncharged subatomic particle found in the nucleus, with a mass slightly greater than that of a proton. (42)

nitrile   An organic compound containing the $-C\equiv N$: group. (491)

node   A region of an orbital where the probability of finding the electron is zero. (237)

nonelectrolyte   A substance whose aqueous solution does not conduct an electric current. (117, 417)

nonmetal   An element that lacks metallic properties. In reactions, nonmetals tend to bond with each other to form covalent compounds or accept electrons from metals to form ionic compounds. (47)

nonpolar covalent bond   A covalent bond between identical atoms that share the bonding pair equally. (298)

nuclear binding energy   The energy required to break 1 mol of nuclei of an element into individual nucleons. (805)

nuclear transmutation   The induced conversion of one nucleus into another by bombardment with a particle. (797)

nucleic acid   An unbranched polymer consisting of mononucleotides that occurs as two types, DNA and RNA (deoxyribonucleic and ribonucleic acids), which differ chemically in the nature of the sugar portion of the mononucleotides. (499)

nucleon   A subatomic particle that makes up a nucleus; a proton or neutron. (786)

nucleus   The tiny central region of the atom that contains all the positive charge and essentially all the mass. (41)

nuclide   A nuclear species with specified numbers of protons and neutrons. (786)

O

observation   A fact obtained with the senses, often with the aid of instruments. Quantitative observations provide data that can be compared objectively. (8)

octahedral arrangement   The geometric arrangement obtained when six electron groups maximize their space around a central atom; when all six groups are bonding groups, the molecular shape is octahedral (AX_6; ideal bond angle = 90°). (321)

octet rule   The observation that when atoms bond, they often lose, gain, or share electrons to attain a filled outer shell of eight electrons. (282)

optical isomers (also *enantiomers*)   A pair of stereoisomers consisting of a molecule and its mirror image that cannot be superimposed on each other. (476, 769)

optically active   Able to rotate the plane of polarized light. (477)

orbital diagram   A depiction of electron number and spin in an atom's orbitals by means of arrows in a series of small boxes, lines, or circles. (251)

organic compound   A compound in which carbon is nearly always bonded to at least one other carbon, to hydrogen, and often to other elements. (467)

osmosis   The process by which solvent flows through a semipermeable membrane from a dilute to a concentrated solution. (421)

osmotic pressure (II)   The pressure that results from the inability of solute particles to cross a semipermeable membrane. The pressure required to prevent the net movement of solvent across the membrane. (421)

outer electrons   Electrons that occupy the highest energy level (highest n value) and are, on average, farthest from the nucleus. (257)

overvoltage   The additional voltage, usually associated with gaseous products, that is required above the standard cell voltage to accomplish electrolysis. (742)

oxidation   The loss of electrons by a species, accompanied by an increase in oxidation number. (130)

oxidation number (O.N.) (also *oxidation state*)   A number equal to the magnitude of the charge an atom would have if its shared electrons were held completely by the atom that attracts them more strongly. (131)

oxidation-reduction reaction (also *redox reaction*)   A process in which there is a net movement of electrons from one reactant (reducing agent) to another (oxidizing agent). (129)

oxidation state   (See *oxidation number.*)

oxidizing agent   The substance that accepts electrons in a redox reaction and undergoes a decrease in oxidation number. (131)

oxoanion   An anion in which an element is bonded to one or more oxygen atoms. (55)

P

p orbital   An atomic orbital with $l = 1$. (238)

packing efficiency   The percentage of the available volume occupied by atoms, ions, or molecules in a unit cell. (382)

paramagnetism   The tendency of a species with unpaired electrons to be attracted by an external magnetic field. (271)

partial ionic character   An estimate of the actual charge separation in a bond (caused by the electronegativity difference of the bonded atoms) relative to complete separation. (298)

partial pressure   The portion of the total pressure contributed by a gas in a mixture of gases. (162)

particle accelerator   A device used to impart high kinetic energies to nuclear particles. (797)

pascal (Pa)   The SI unit of pressure; $1 \text{ Pa} = 1 \text{ N/m}^2$. (148)

penetration   The process by which an outer electron moves through the region occupied by the core electrons to spend part of its time closer to the nucleus; penetration increases the average effective nuclear charge for that electron. (249)

percent by mass (mass %)   (See *mass percent.*)

percent yield (% yield)   The actual yield of a reaction expressed as a percentage of the theoretical yield. (97)

period   A horizontal row of the periodic table. (46)

periodic law   A law stating that when the elements are arranged by atomic number, they exhibit a periodic recurrence of properties. (246)

periodic table of the elements   A table in which the elements are arranged by atomic number into columns (groups) and rows (periods). (46)

pH   The negative common logarithm of $[H_3O^+]$. (597)

phase   A physically distinct portion of a system. (357)

phase change   A physical change from one phase to another, usually referring to a change in physical state. (357)

phase diagram   A diagram used to describe the stable phases and phase changes of a substance as a function of temperature and pressure. (366)

photoelectric effect   The observation that when monochromatic light of sufficient frequency shines on a metal, an electric current is produced. (219)

photon   A quantum of electromagnetic radiation. (220)

physical change   A change in which the physical form (or state) of a substance, but not its composition, is altered. (3)

physical property   A characteristic shown by a substance itself, without interacting with or changing into other substances. (3)

pi (π) bond   A covalent bond formed by sideways overlap of two atomic orbitals that has two regions of electron density, one above and one below the internuclear axis. (341)

pi (π) MO   A molecular orbital formed by combination of two atomic (usually p) orbitals whose orientations are perpendicular to the internuclear axis. (347)

Planck's constant (h)   A proportionality constant relating the energy and the frequency of a photon, equal to 6.626×10^{-34} J·s. (219)

polar covalent bond   A covalent bond in which the electron pair is shared unequally, so the bond has partially negative and partially positive poles. (297)

polar molecule   A molecule with an unequal distribution of charge as a result of its polar covalent bonds and shape. (114)

polarizability   The ease with which a particle's electron cloud can be distorted. (372)

polyatomic ion An ion in which two or more atoms are bonded covalently. (51)

polymer (also *macromolecule*) An extremely large molecule that results from the covalent linking of many simpler molecular units (monomers). (492)

polyprotic acid An acid with more than one ionizable proton. (689)

polysaccharide A macromolecule composed of many simple sugars linked covalently. (495)

positron (β^+ or $^0_1\beta$) The antiparticle of an electron. (788)

positron (β^+) emission A type of radioactive decay in which a positron is emitted from a nucleus. (788)

potential energy (E_p) The energy an object has as a result of its position relative to other objects or because of its composition. (6)

precipitate The insoluble product of a precipitation reaction. (119)

precipitation reaction A reaction in which two soluble ionic compounds form an insoluble product, a precipitate. (119)

precision (also *reproducibility*) The closeness of a measurement to other measurements of the same phenomenon in a series of experiments. (24)

pressure (P) The force exerted per unit of surface area. (147)

pressure-volume work (PV work) A type of work in which a volume change occurs against an external pressure. (189)

principal quantum number (n) A positive integer that specifies the energy and relative size of an atomic orbital. (234)

probability contour A shape that defines the volume around an atomic nucleus within which an electron spends a given percentage of its time. (233)

product A substance formed in a chemical reaction. (85)

property A characteristic that gives a substance its unique identity. (2)

protein A natural, linear polymer composed of any of about 20 types of amino acid monomers linked together by peptide bonds. (496)

proton (p^+) A subatomic particle found in the nucleus that has a unit positive charge (1.60218×10^{-19} C). (42)

proton acceptor A substance that accepts an H^+ ion; a Brønsted-Lowry base. (600)

proton donor A substance that donates an H^+ ion; a Brønsted-Lowry acid. (600)

pseudo–noble gas configuration The $(n-1)d^{10}$ configuration of a *p*-block metal atom that has emptied its outer energy level. (269)

Q

quantum A packet of energy equal to $h\nu$. The smallest quantity of energy that can be emitted or absorbed. (219)

quantum mechanics The branch of physics that examines the wave motion of objects on the atomic scale. (231)

quantum number A number that specifies a property of an orbital or an electron. (219)

R

rad (radiation-absorbed dose) The quantity of radiation that results in 0.01 J of energy being absorbed per kilogram of tissue; 1 rad = 0.01 J/kg tissue = 0.01 Gy. (799)

radial probability distribution plot The graphic depiction of the total probability distribution (sum of ψ^2) of an electron in the region near the nucleus. (232)

radioactivity The emissions resulting from the spontaneous disintegration of an unstable nucleus. (785)

radioisotope An isotope with an unstable nucleus that decays through radioactive emissions. (796)

radioisotopic dating A method for determining the age of an object based on the rate of decay of a particular radioactive nuclide. (796)

random error Human error that occurs in all measurements and results in values *both* higher and lower than the actual value. (24)

Raoult's law A law stating that the vapor pressure of a solution is directly proportional to the mole fraction of solvent: $P_{\text{solvent}} = X_{\text{solvent}} \times P^\circ_{\text{solvent}}$. (417)

rare earths (See *lanthanides*.)

rate constant (k) The proportionality constant that relates the reaction rate to reactant (and product) concentrations. (514)

rate-determining step (or *rate-limiting step*) The slowest step in a reaction mechanism and therefore the step that limits the overall rate. (536)

rate law (or *rate equation*) An equation that expresses the rate of a reaction as a function of reactant (and product) concentrations. (514)

reactant A starting substance in a chemical reaction. (85)

reaction energy diagram A graph that shows the potential energy of a reacting system as it progresses from reactants to products. (532)

reaction intermediate A substance that is formed and used up during the overall reaction and therefore does not appear in the overall equation. (535)

reaction mechanism A series of elementary steps that sum to the overall reaction and is consistent with the rate law. (534)

reaction order The exponent of a reactant concentration in a rate law that shows how the rate is affected by changes in that concentration. (514)

reaction quotient (Q) A ratio of terms for a given reaction consisting of product concentrations multiplied together and divided by reactant concentrations multiplied together, each raised to the power of their balancing coefficient. The value of Q changes until the system reaches equilibrium, at which point it equals K. (556)

reaction rate The change in the concentrations of reactants (or products) with time. (510)

reactor core The part of a nuclear reactor that contains the fuel rods and generates heat from fission. (808)

redox reaction (See *oxidation-reduction reaction*.)

reducing agent The substance that donates electrons in a redox reaction and undergoes an increase in oxidation number. (131)

reduction The gain of electrons by a species, accompanied by a decrease in oxidation number. (130)

refraction A phenomenon in which a wave changes its speed and therefore its direction as it passes through a phase boundary. (217)

rem (roentgen equivalent for man) The unit of radiation dosage for a human based on the product of the number of rads and a factor related to the biological tissue; 1 rem = 0.01 Sv. (799)

reproducibility (See *precision*.)

resonance hybrid The weighted average of the resonance structures of a molecule. (309)

resonance structure (or *resonance form*) One of two or more Lewis structures for a molecule that cannot be adequately depicted by a single structure. Resonance structures differ only in the position of bonding and lone electron pairs. (309)

rms (root-mean-square) speed (u_{rms})   The speed of a molecule having the average kinetic energy; very close to the most probable speed. (171)

round off   The process of removing digits based on a series of rules to obtain an answer with the proper number of significant figures (or decimal places). (22)

S

s orbital   An atomic orbital with $l = 0$. (236)

salt   An ionic compound that results from an Arrhenius acid-base reaction. (125)

salt bridge   An inverted U tube containing a solution of nonreacting electrolyte that connects the compartments of a voltaic cell and maintains neutrality by allowing ions to flow between compartments. (713)

saturated hydrocarbon   A hydrocarbon in which each C is bonded to four other atoms. (472)

saturated solution   A solution that contains the maximum amount of dissolved solute at a given temperature in the presence of undissolved solute. (409)

Schrödinger equation   An equation that describes how the electron matter-wave changes in space around the nucleus. Solutions of the equation provide allowable energy levels of the H atom. (231)

scientific method   A process of creative thinking and testing aimed at objective, verifiable discoveries of the causes of natural events. (8)

second (s)   The SI base unit of time. (20)

second law of thermodynamics   A law stating that a process occurs spontaneously in the direction that increases the entropy of the universe. (676)

seesaw shape   A molecular shape caused by the presence of one equatorial lone pair in a trigonal bipyramidal arrangement (AX_4E). (320)

self-ionization   (See *autoionization.*)

semiconductor   A substance whose electrical conductivity is poor at room temperature but increases significantly with rising temperature. (390)

semimetal   (See *metalloid.*)

semipermeable membrane   A membrane that allows solvent, but not solute, to pass through. (421)

shared pair   (See *bonding pair.*)

shell   (See *level.*)

shielding   The ability of other electrons, especially inner ones, to lessen the nuclear attraction for an outer electron. (249)

SI unit   A unit composed of one or more of the base units of the Système International d'Unités, a revised metric system. (13)

side reaction   An undesired chemical reaction that consumes some of the reactant and reduces the overall yield of the desired product. (97)

sievert (Sv)   The SI unit of human radiation dosage; 1 Sv = 100 rem. (799)

sigma (σ) bond   A type of covalent bond that arises through end-to-end orbital overlap and has most of its electron density along the bond axis. (340)

sigma (σ) MO   A molecular orbital that is cylindrically symmetrical about an imaginary line that runs through the nuclei of the component atoms. (345)

significant figures   The digits obtained in a measurement. The greater the number of significant figures, the greater the certainty of the measurement. (21)

silicate   A type of compound found throughout rocks and soil and consisting of repeating —Si—O groupings and, in most cases, metal cations. (446)

silicone   A type of synthetic polymer containing —Si—O repeat units, with organic groups and crosslinks. (446)

simple cubic unit cell   A unit cell in which a particle occurs at each corner of a cube. (380)

single bond   A bond that consists of one shared electron pair. (288)

solid   One of the three states of matter. A solid has a fixed shape that does not conform to the container shape. (4)

solubility (S)   The maximum amount of solute that dissolves in a fixed quantity of a particular solvent at a specified temperature when excess solute is present. (399)

solubility-product constant (K_{sp})   An equilibrium constant for the dissolving of a slightly soluble ionic compound in water. (650)

solute   The substance that dissolves in the solvent. (98, 399)

solution   (See *homogeneous mixture.*)

solvated   Surrounded closely by solvent molecules. (115)

solvation   The process of surrounding a solute particle with solvent particles. (406)

solvent   The substance in which the solute(s) dissolve. (98, 399)

sp hybrid orbital   An orbital formed by the mixing of one s and one p orbital of a central atom. (334)

sp^2 hybrid orbital   An orbital formed by the mixing of one s and two p orbitals of a central atom. (336)

sp^3 hybrid orbital   An orbital formed by the mixing of one s and three p orbitals of a central atom. (336)

sp^3d hybrid orbital   An orbital formed by the mixing of one s, three p, and one d orbital of a central atom. (337)

sp^3d^2 hybrid orbital   An orbital formed by the mixing of one s, three p, and two d orbitals of a central atom. (338)

specific heat capacity (c)   The quantity of heat required to change the temperature of 1 gram of a substance by 1 K. (196)

spectator ion   An ion that is present as part of a reactant but is not involved in the chemical change. (119)

spectrochemical series   A ranking of ligands in terms of their ability to split d-orbital energies. (775)

spectrophotometry   A group of instrumental techniques that create an electromagnetic spectrum to measure the atomic and molecular energy levels of a substance. (227)

speed of light (c)   A fundamental constant giving the speed at which electromagnetic radiation travels in a vacuum: $c = 2.99792458 \times 10^8$ m/s. (216)

spin quantum number (m_s)   A number, either $+\frac{1}{2}$ or $-\frac{1}{2}$, that indicates the direction of electron spin. (247)

spontaneous change   A change that occurs by itself, that is, without an ongoing input of energy. (670)

square planar shape   A molecular shape (AX_4E_2) caused by the presence of two axial lone pairs in an octahedral arrangement. (321)

square pyramidal shape   A molecular shape (AX_5E) caused by the presence of one lone pair in an octahedral arrangement. (321)

standard atmosphere (atm)   The average atmospheric pressure measured at sea level, defined as 1.01325×10^5 Pa. (148)

standard cell potential (E°_{cell})   The potential of a cell measured with all components in their standard states and no current flowing. (716)

standard electrode potential ($E^\circ_{half-cell}$) (also *standard half-cell potential*)   The standard potential of a half-cell, with the half-reaction written as a reduction. (716)

standard entropy of reaction (ΔS°_{rxn})   The entropy change that occurs when all components are in their standard states. (682)

standard free energy change (ΔG°)   The free energy change that occurs when all components are in their standard states. (687)

standard free energy of formation (ΔG°_f)   The standard free energy change that occurs when 1 mol of a compound is made from its elements. (688)

standard half-cell potential   (See *standard electrode potential*.)

standard heat of formation (ΔH°_f)   The enthalpy change that occurs when 1 mol of a compound forms from its elements, with all substances in their standard states. (203)

standard heat of reaction (ΔH°_{rxn})   The enthalpy change that occurs during a reaction, with all substances in their standard states. (203)

standard hydrogen electrode   (See *standard reference half-cell*.)

standard molar entropy (S°)   The entropy of 1 mol of a substance in its standard state. (677)

standard molar volume   The volume of 1 mol of an ideal gas at standard temperature and pressure: 22.4141 L. (154)

standard reference half-cell (also *standard hydrogen electrode*)   A specially prepared platinum electrode immersed in $1\,M$ $H^+(aq)$ through which H_2 gas at 1 atm is bubbled. $E^\circ_{half\text{-}cell}$ is defined as 0 V. (717)

standard states   A set of specifications used to compare thermodynamic data: 1 atm for gases behaving ideally, $1\,M$ for dissolved species, or the pure substance for liquids and solids. (203)

standard temperature and pressure (STP)   The reference conditions for a gas:

$$0^\circ C\ (273.15\ K)\ \text{and}\ 1\ \text{atm}\ (760\ \text{torr}) \qquad (154)$$

state function   A property of a system determined by its current state, regardless of how it arrived at that state. (191)

state of matter   One of the three physical forms of matter: solid, liquid, or gas. (4)

stationary state   In the Bohr model, one of the allowable energy levels of the atom in which it does not release or absorb energy. (223)

stereoisomers   Molecules with the same connections of atoms but different orientations of groups in space. (476, 768) (See also *geometric isomers* and *optical isomers*.)

stoichiometric coefficient   (See *balancing coefficient*.)

stoichiometry   The study of the mass-mole-number relationships of chemical formulas and reactions. (72)

strong-field ligand   A ligand that causes larger crystal field splitting energy and therefore is part of a low-spin complex. (774)

structural formula   A formula that shows the actual numbers of atoms, their relative placement, and the bonds between them. (52)

structural isomers   (See *constitutional isomers*.)

sublevel (or *subshell*)   An energy substate of an atom within a level. Given by the n and l values, the sublevel designates the size and shape of the atomic orbitals. (235)

sublimation   The process by which a solid changes directly into a gas. (359)

substance   A type of matter, either an element or a compound, that has a fixed composition. (32)

substitution reaction   An organic reaction that occurs when an atom (or group) from one reactant substitutes for one in another reactant. (481)

superconductivity   The ability to conduct a current with no loss of energy to resistive heating. (391)

supersaturated solution   An unstable solution in which more solute is dissolved than in a saturated solution. (409)

surface tension   The energy required to increase the surface area of a liquid by a given amount. (375)

surroundings   All parts of the universe other than the system being considered. (186)

system   The defined part of the universe under study. (186)

systematic error   A type of error producing values that are all either higher or lower than the actual value, often caused by faulty equipment or a consistent fault in technique. (24)

T

t_{2g} orbitals   The set of orbitals (composed of d_{xy}, d_{yz}, and d_{xz}) that results when the energies of the metal-ion d orbitals are split by a ligand field. This set is lower in energy than the other (e_g) set in an octahedral field and higher in energy in a tetrahedral field. (774)

T shape   A molecular shape caused by the presence of two equatorial lone pairs in a trigonal bipyramidal arrangement (AX_3E_2). (320)

temperature (T)   A measure of how hot or cold a substance is relative to another substance. (18)

tetrahedral arrangement   The geometric arrangement formed when four electron groups maximize their separation around a central atom; when all four groups are bonding groups, the molecular shape is tetrahedral (AX_4; ideal bond angle 109.5°). (318)

theoretical yield   The amount of product predicted by the stoichiometrically equivalent molar ratio in the balanced equation. (97)

theory   (See *model*.)

thermochemical equation   A chemical equation that shows the heat of reaction for the amounts of substances specified. (199)

thermochemistry   The branch of thermodynamics that focuses on the heat involved in chemical reactions. (186)

thermodynamics   The study of heat (thermal energy) and its interconversions. (186)

thermometer   A device for measuring temperature that contains a fluid that expands or contracts within a graduated tube. (18)

third law of thermodynamics   A law stating that the entropy of a perfect crystal is zero at 0 K. (676)

titration   A method of determining the concentration of a solution by monitoring its reaction with a solution of known concentration. (126)

torr   A unit of pressure identical to 1 mmHg. (149)

total ionic equation   A chemical equation for an aqueous reaction that shows all the soluble ionic substances dissociated into ions. (118)

tracer   A radioisotope that signals the presence of the species of interest by emitting nonionizing radiation. (801)

transition element (or *transition metal*)   An element that occupies the d block of the periodic table; one whose d orbitals are being filled. (254, 757)

transition state (also *activated complex*)   An unstable species formed in an effective collision of reactants that exists momentarily when the system is highest in energy and that can either form products or re-form reactants. (531)

transition state theory   A model that explains how the energy of reactant collision is used to form a high-energy transitional species that can change to reactant or product. (531)

transuranium element   An element with atomic number higher than that of uranium ($Z = 92$). (798)

trigonal bipyramidal arrangement The geometric arrangement formed when five electron groups maximize their separation around a central atom. When all five groups are bonding groups, the molecular shape is trigonal bipyramidal (AX_5; ideal bond angles, axial-center-equatorial = 90° and equatorial-center-equatorial = 120°). (320)

trigonal planar arrangement The geometric arrangement formed when three electron groups maximize their separation around a central atom. (317)

trigonal planar shape A molecular shape (AX_3) formed when three atoms around a central atom lie at the corners of an equilateral triangle; ideal bond angle = 120°. (317)

trigonal pyramidal shape A molecular shape (AX_3E) caused by the presence of one lone pair in a tetrahedral arrangement. (319)

triple bond A covalent bond that consists of three bonding pairs, two atoms sharing six electrons; one σ and two π bonds. (288)

triple point The pressure and temperature at which three phases of a substance are in equilibrium. In a phase diagram, the point at which three phase-transition curves meet. (367)

U

ultraviolet (UV) Radiation in the region of the electromagnetic spectrum between the visible and the x-ray regions. (216)

uncertainty A characteristic of every measurement that results from the inexactness of the measuring device and the necessity of estimating when taking a reading. (20)

uncertainty principle The principle stated by Werner Heisenberg that it is impossible to know simultaneously the exact position and velocity of a particle; the principle becomes important only for particles of very small mass. (231)

unimolecular reaction An elementary reaction that involves the decomposition or rearrangement of a single particle. (535)

unit cell The smallest portion of a crystal that, if repeated in all three directions, gives the crystal. (380)

universal gas constant (R) A proportionality constant that relates the energy, amount of substance, and temperature of a system; $R = 0.0820578$ atm·L/mol·K = 8.31447 J/mol·K. (155)

unsaturated hydrocarbon A hydrocarbon with at least one carbon-carbon multiple bond; one in which at least two C atoms are bonded to fewer than four atoms. (477)

unsaturated solution A solution in which more solute can be dissolved at a given temperature. (409)

unshared pair (See *lone pair.*)

V

V shape (See *bent shape.*)

valence band In band theory, the lower energy portion of the band of molecular orbitals, which is filled with valence electrons. (390)

valence bond (VB) theory A model that attempts to reconcile the shapes of molecules with those of atomic orbitals through the concepts of orbital overlap and hybridization. (333)

valence electrons The electrons involved in compound formation; in main-group elements, the electrons in the valence (outer) level. (257)

valence-shell electron-pair repulsion (VSEPR) theory A model explaining that the shapes of molecules and ions result from minimizing electron-pair repulsions around a central atom. (316)

van der Waals equation An equation that accounts for the behavior of real gases. (176)

van der Waals radius One-half of the closest distance between the nuclei of identical nonbonded atoms. (369)

vapor pressure (also *equilibrium vapor pressure*) The pressure exerted by a vapor at equilibrium with its liquid in a closed system. (364)

vapor pressure lowering (ΔP) The lowering of the vapor pressure of a solvent caused by the presence of dissolved solute particles. (417)

vaporization The process of changing from a liquid to a gas. (358)

variable A quantity that can have more than a single value. (8) (See also *controlled experiment.*)

viscosity A measure of the resistance of a liquid to flow. (377)

volt (V) The SI unit of electric potential: 1 V = 1 J/C. (715)

voltage (See *cell potential.*)

voltaic cell (also *galvanic cell*) An electrochemical cell that uses a spontaneous reaction to generate electric energy. (709)

volume (V) The space occupied by a sample of matter. (15)

volume percent [% (v/v)] A concentration term defined as the volume of solute in 100. volumes of solution. (414)

W

wave function (See *atomic orbital.*)

wavelength (λ) The distance between any point on a wave and the corresponding point on the next wave, that is, the distance a wave travels during one cycle. (215)

wave-particle duality The principle stating that both matter and energy have wavelike and particle-like properties. (230)

weak-field ligand A ligand that causes smaller crystal field splitting energy and therefore is part of a high-spin complex. (774)

weight The force exerted by a gravitational field on an object. (16)

work (w) The energy transferred when an object is moved by a force. (188)

X

x-ray diffraction analysis An instrumental technique used to determine spatial dimensions of a crystal structure by measuring the diffraction patterns caused by x-rays impinging on the crystal. (384)